Y0-DMB-410

EVLİYA ÇELEBİ IN ALBANIA AND ADJACENT REGIONS (KOSOVO, MONTENEGRO, OHRID)

EVLİYA ÇELEBİ'S BOOK OF TRAVELS

Land and People of the Ottoman Empire in the Seventeenth Century

A CORPUS OF PARTIAL EDITIONS

edited by

KLAUS KREISER

VOLUME V

EVLİYA ÇELEBİ IN ALBANIA AND ADJACENT REGIONS (KOSOVO, MONTENEGRO, OHRID)

EVLİYA ÇELEBİ IN
ALBANIA
AND ADJACENT REGIONS
(KOSOVO, MONTENEGRO, OHRID)

THE RELEVANT SECTIONS OF THE SEYAHATNAME
EDITED WITH TRANSLATION, COMMENTARY AND INTRODUCTION

BY

ROBERT DANKOFF

AND

ROBERT ELSIE

BRILL
LEIDEN · BOSTON · KÖLN
2000

This book is printed on acid-free paper.

Library of Congress Cataloging-in-Publication Data

Dankoff, Robert.
Evliya Çelebi in Albania and adjacent regions : Kosovo, Montenegro, Ohrid / by Robert Dankoff and Robert Elsie.
p. cm. — (Evliya Çelebi's book of travels : land and people of the Ottoman Empire in the seventeenth century ; v. 5)
Includes bibliographical references (p.) and index.
ISBN 9004116249
1. Albania—Description and travel—Early works to 1800. 2. Kosovo (Serbia)—Description and travel—Early works to 1800. 3. Montenegro—Description and travel—Early works to 1800. 4. Ohrid (Macedonia)—Description and travel—Early works to 1800. 5. Evliya Çelebi, 1611 ? -1682?—Journeys—Balkan Peninsula. I. Dankoff, Robert. II. Elsie, Robert, 1950- III. Title.
G460.E952513 vol. 5
[DR916 1999]
914.9604'25—dc21

99-046289

Die Deutsche Bibliothek - CIP-Einheitsaufnahme

Evliya Çelebi's book of travels : land and people of the Ottoman empire in the seventeenth century ; a corpus of partial editions / ed. by Klaus Kreiser. - Leiden ; Boston ; Köln : Brill,
Einheitssacht.: Seyāḥatnāme
Literaturangaben
Vol. 5. Evliya Çelebi : Evliya Çelebi in Albania and adjacent regions (Kosovo, Montenegro, Ohrid). 2000
Evliya Çelebi:
Evliya Çelebi : in Albania and adjacent regions (Kosovo, Montenegro, Ohrid) / by Robert Dankoff and Robert Elsie.- Leiden ; Boston ; Köln : Brill, 2000
(Evliya Çelebi's book of travels ; Vol. 5)
ISBN 90-04-11624-9

ISSN 0922-7768
ISBN 90 04 11624 9

© Copyright 2000 by Koninklijke Brill NV, Leiden, The Netherlands

All rights reserved. No part of this publication may be reproduced, translated, stored in a retrieval system, or transmitted in any form or by any means, electronic, mechanical, photocopying, recording or otherwise, without prior written permission from the publisher.

Authorization to photocopy items for internal or personal use is granted by Brill provided that the appropriate fees are paid directly to The Copyright Clearance Center, 222 Rosewood Drive, Suite 910 Danvers MA 01923, USA. Fees are subject to change.

PRINTED IN THE NETHERLANDS

CONTENTS

Map 1

Introduction 3

Text and Translation 9

Part I: Kosovo, 1660 10

Part II: Northern Albania and Montenegro, 1662 26

Part III: Southern Albania, 1670 58

Bibliography 226

Glossary 228

Index 230

Facsimile of the Manuscript 243

Plates

SERBIA
MONTENEGRO
KOSOVO
ALBANIA
MACEDONIA
GREECE
Zveçan
Mitrovica
Vushtrria
Prishtina
Gjakova
Kaçanik
Skopje
Kotor
Podgorica
Budva
Bar
Ulcinj
Shkodër
Bushat
Spas
Lezha
Mamurras
Tirana
Durrës
Kavaja
Elbasan
Peqin
Bashtova
Struga
Ohrid
Pogradec
Berat
Vlora
Këlcyra
Tepelena
Përmet
Gjirokastër
Delvinaki
Delvina
[KOSOVO] : Journey of 1660
[N. ALBANIA] : Journey of 1662
[S. ALBANIA] : Journey of 1670
0
75 Miles
120.7 Kilometers

INTRODUCTION

The Turkish traveller Evliya Çelebi toured Kosovo in December of 1660, northern Albania and Montenegro in February of 1662, and southern Albania in November of 1670. In the present volume, we have extracted his descriptions of these regions from the very extensive accounts of his peregrinations in the Balkans, covering much of Books V through VIII of his *Seyāḥatnāme* or *Book of Travels*.[1]

The occasion of the first of these journeys was the transfer of Evliya's patron, Melek Ahmed Paşa, from the governorship of Bosnia (residence: Banja Luka) to that of Rumeli (residence: Sofia).[2] In the Paşa's train, Evliya passed through Kosovo stopping at Mitrovica, Vushtrria (Vuçitërna), Kosovo Polje, Prishtina and Kaçanik. His account of this journey, between Novi Pazar and Skopje, is contained in the autograph ms. of Book V, fols. 167a-169a. This comprises Part I of the present volume. This section is edited here for the first time. Translations into Serbo-Croatian, based on the inadequate printed text (Istanbul, vol. 5, 1897, pp. 547-53), are found in Čohadžić 1905 (pp. 25-27) and in Šabanović 1954 (repr. 1979 and 1996, pp. 268-80). There are also Albanian translations in Vuçitërni 1930 and in Kaleshi 1955 (pp. 424-32).

A little over one year later, Melek Paşa had just returned to Belgrade from active engagement with the Ottoman troops in Transylvania when he was summoned to the capital. Short of funds, he sent Evliya to Albania to collect some debts. Evliya stopped in Tirana, Lezha (Alessio), Shkodër (Scutari), Podgorica and Ulcinj, then proceeded to Sofia where he was reunited with Melek Paşa before returning to Istanbul. His account of this journey, between Mileševo and Skopje, is contained in the autograph ms. of Book VI,

---

[1] For general information about Evliya and his magnum opus, see Bruinessen and Boeschoten 1988, Dankoff and Kreiser 1992.

Manuscript references to Books I-X of the *Seyāḥatnāme* are as follows: Bağdat 304 (I and II), Bağdat 305 (III and IV), Bağdat 307 (V), Revan 1457 (VI), Bağdat 308 (VII and VIII), Bağdat 306 (IX), İÜTY 5973 (X). References give Book, folio, and line numbers. Other page numbers (without a or b) refer to the Istanbul printed text, 10 vols., 1886-1938.

[2] For Melek Ahmed Paşa's career, see Dankoff 1991a *Intimate Life*.

fols. 33a-36b. This comprises Part II of the present volume. This section, which until now has only been available in an inadequate printed text[3] (Istanbul, vol. 6, 1900, pp. 106-117), is also edited here for the first time. The earlier Albanian translation in Vuçitërni 1930 was based on the printed Turkish text and also excludes, for instance, the sample of the Albanian language.[4]

Evliya participated in the Candia campaign and the final Ottoman conquest of Crete in 1669. The following year, after the capture of Mania in the Peleponnese, the Ottoman commander 'Ali Paşa sent Evliya on a mission to Albania requesting troops and workmen to help rebuild the fortress of Zarnata, and thus to safeguard Mania against reconquest by the Venetians.[5] Evliya passed through Delvina, Gjirokastër, Tepelena, Përmet, Berat, Vlora, Durrës, Kavaja, Elbasan, Ohrid[6] and Pogradec before continuing on through Macedonia and Bulgaria to the Ottoman court in Edirne. His account of this journey, from Corfu to Macedonia, is contained in the autograph ms. of Book VIII, fols. 352a-372b. This comprises Part III of the present volume. This section has been available in a fairly good edition (Istanbul, vol. 8, 1928, pp. 668-746), and is here re-edited on the basis of

---

[3] In his 1930 article, Franz Babinger wrote (pp. 139-40) that: "die Abschnitte des VI. Bandes wie alles, was in dieser höchst mangelhaften und dürftigen Erstausgabe abgedruckt wurde, vermutlich von Fehlern und Auslassungen nicht frei sind. Man ... kann nur wünschen, dass die sechs ersten Bände so rasch wie möglich in wissenschaftlich brauchbarer Neuausgabe zugänglich gemacht werden." After nearly seventy years we can only echo his wish. Several of Babinger's suspicions have been confirmed; thus he thought (p. 140, n. 2) that Yjan at 106:22 must be an error for Tiran, and that is indeed the case (see 33a1).

[4] Evliya's sample of Albanian language was omitted from the printed text (111:23). It was first mentioned in the scholarly literature in Dankoff 1989, 24, and first published in Dankoff 1991b *Glossary*, 112.

[5] VIII 337b8-13 (609): *'Alī Paşa ḥaqīre der-i devlete gidecek Fetiḥ-nāme-yi Żarnatayı miftāḥlarıyle ve niçe yüz mektūblar verüp Arnavudistān içinde yolumuz üzre olan beş sancaq yerde olan sancaq beglerinñ ve cümle qal'e neferātlarınñ nıṣf 'askerleri ve cümle serdārlarñ elleri altında olan yeñiçeri ve ṭopcı ve cebecileri ve qul oğlanları ve neqadar eli berātlı pādişāh qulı geçinenleri ve sancaq paşası 'askerleri ve her sancaqda neqadar ırġaṭ ve neccār ve bennā ve çerāḥorān re'āyā ve kireççi ve ṭaşcılar var ise qāḍīler ile cümle vilāyet-i Manyaya gelüp muḥāfaẓa édüp Kelafa (?) qal'esin müceddiden binā olunmasıyçün bu ḥaqīre meẕkūr [u] merqūm 'askerlerñ taḥṣīli fermānıyle meẕkūr sancaqlara gönderüp.*

[6] In the present-day Republic of Macedonia.

the autograph ms. There is a rudimentary Albanian translation of this section in Vuçiterni 1930 and a detailed analysis of this journey in Babinger 1930.

The *Seyāḥatnāme* contains a wealth of material on cultural history, folklore and geography from the countries Evliya Çelebi visited. For seventeenth-century Albania, and in particular for the interior of the country, it constitutes a mine of information and is a work of inestimable value. Other sources of Albanian history for this period are rare. The little which has survived from the nebulous annals of early Albanian history has been compiled in Zamputi 1989, 1990. Among such documents are legal and merchant correspondence with Venice and Ragusa (Dubrovnik), ecclesiastical reports to the Propaganda Fide in Rome, and Turkish registers. All these works pale in significance, however, when compared to the relevant sections of the *Seyāḥatnāme* edited here.

Evliya's work offers us detailed itineraries through a virtual *terra incognita*, including, among many other things, surprisingly accurate descriptions of market towns, fortresses, mosques, pilgrimage sites and pleasure-grounds. His writings are of particular interest for our knowledge of the spread of Islam and the dervish orders in Albania. Evliya's descriptions of Albanian towns and villages reveal that these encompassed all the elements of a refined Islamic culture, of which tragically few traces have survived the course of history.[7] The sample of the Albanian language recorded by Evliya is also an unusual and valuable contribution to Albanian cultural and linguistic history.[8]

With the exception of some bandit-ridden roads, the Albania which Evliya depicts is remarkably prosperous and well-governed. Concentrating as he does on urban civilization and religious and administrative institutions, Evliya appears to be oblivious of the Albanian clan structures and rivalries.[9] The Ottoman administrative

---

[7] See Kiel 1990 for a survey of the architectural monuments of Ottoman Albania. Kiel's pioneering work, which makes full use of Evliya's information, is extremely valuable.

[8] See Elsie 1998.

[9] An incident at Tepelena (recounted at VIII 356b27 - 357a1) does illustrate fierce clan loyalties in that region.

system is so firmly entrenched that when, in Part III, Evliya conveys sultanic decrees for the defense of Mania, the military contingents muster without a hitch and march off toward the Peloponnese. If this draconian exaction caused any difficulty or roused any opposition, Evliya is silent about it.

While telling us little or nothing about Albanian tribal structure, Evliya is very informative about the (legendary) origins of the Albanian people. The story told here twice in Part III (VIII 353a and 367b-368a) about Cebel-i Elheme[10] is also found in the Circassian section of the *Seyāḥatnāme* (II 256b) and is adumbrated in several other passages as well (I 197b17, VII 100a [467], 148b [718], IX 179a [392]). The name Cebel-i Elheme (Jabal-i Alhama in the English translation) is a corruption of Jabala ibn al-Ayham, a well-known historical figure "whose personality dominates the scene in the story of Arab-Byzantine relations during the Muslim Conquests."[11] The Circassian Mamluks, who ruled Egypt and Syria from the end of the fourteenth century until the Ottoman conquest in 1517, claimed this Jabala as their ancestor.[12] The legend connecting Jabala to the Circassians was still current among the Mamluks in Evliya's day.[13] Possibly it was Evliya himself who extended it to include the Albanians, and who posited the Qurayshi identity of the hero, perhaps based on the similarity of the Albanian toponym Kurvelesh (Quryeleş in Evliya).

---

[10] The form Cebel al-Himme found in Dankoff and Kreiser 1992, 21, 85, 97, is mistaken and should be corrected. There is a very careful vocalization of Cebel-i Elheme at VII 148b18,20.

[11] Irfan Kawar, "D̲jabala b. al-Ayham," *Encyclopedia of Islam, New Edition*, vol. II (1965), 354. See also Irfan Shahid, "Ghassān *Post* Ghassān," in: C. E. Bosworth et. al., ed., *The Islamic World From Classical to Modern Times [Essays in Honor of Bernard Lewis]* (Princeton: The Darwin Press, 1989), 323-36, esp. 324-28. The correct identification was already made by Babinger 1930, 176.

[12] See D. Ayalon, "Čerkes ii. Mamlūk Period," *Encyclopedia of Islam, New Edition*, vol. II (1965), 24.

[13] See P. M. Holt, "The Exalted Lineage of Riḍwān Bey: Some Observations on a Seventeenth-Century Mamluk Genealogy," *Bulletin of the School of Oriental and African Studies* 22 (1959), 221-30.

The transcription and translation follow the protocols established in the earlier volumes of this series, particularly Dankoff 1990 (but using *q* instead of *ḳ*, and maintaining the modern Turkish spelling of transcribed words in the translation). Where Evliya fails to indicate vowels, a progressive vocalization is assumed (thus *olunur* rather than *olınur*, etc.). Exceptions reflect Evliya's own pointings (thus VIII 360a13 *ṣusızlığı*, 368a12 *olmış*, etc.).

It should be kept in mind that most of the Turkish text edited here is in a very defective state — being (per hypothesis) the earliest stage of Evliya's draft of a fair copy of his work, with only the consonantal skeleton and with few diacritics or pointings. In some folios (VIII 363a-368b, 370a-371b, 373b — see facsimile) the autograph manuscript, used for this edition, has been pointed rather thoroughly, but often mistakenly, by a later hand.

Note the following conventions in the Turkish text:

( )	line markers, editorial notes
[ ]	not in the manuscript, restored to the text
——	illegible
-----	lacuna in the text, blank space
/	blank line
{ }	in the margin or below the line
*	period indicating rhymed prose

The forms of place names chosen for the translation are those in current use among the present inhabitants, except where another form is commonly used in English publications.

The Glossary includes all terms left in italics in the translation.

The Index includes names of persons, places, languages, and ethnic and tribal groups, and the administrative term Voyvada (voyvoda). Items are indexed according to the Turkish form, with cross-reference to the English form if different.

TEXT AND TRANSLATION

Part I: Kosovo, 1660

[V 167a] (21) Andan ----- sā'atde *evṣāf-ı* ----- *ya'nī qal'e-yi bālā Mitroviçse*. Lisān-ı latince ----- demekdir. (22) Bānīsi Ṣırf qırallarından Seleşti Qıral bināsıdır. Fātiḥi bi'z-zāt sene ----- tārīḫinde Ġāzī Ḫüdāvendigār ya'nī Sulṭān Murād-ı evvel ibni (23) Orḫan Ġāzīdir kim bu qal'eyi fetḥ édüp ba'dehu Qoṣ-ova cenginde yedi kerre yüz biñ küffārı dendān-ı tīġden geçirüp (24) piyādece leşleri seyr édüp şühedāları Klāb Nehri kenārında bir yére yıġarken küffār leşleri içinden menkūs Qoblaki[1] (25) nām bir kefere qalqub Sulṭān Murādı şehīd éder. Bir rivāyetde ba'de'l-ceng-ü-cidāl mezkūr kāfir elçilik taqrībiyle dest-būs-ı (26) pādişāhīye gelince dal ḫancer-i zū'l-ficām olup Murād Ḫān Ġāzīyi şehīd édince atına binüp firār éderken buqadar 'asker-i islām buqadar (27) silāḥ üşürürler, aṣlā yıqamazlar, bir fertūte 'avret eydir: "Bire atını ṭırnaġından uruñ, yoḫsa atı bile cümle demir (28) geyim içindedir" deyince bir qolı quvvetli[2] atınıñ ṭırnaġına bir oq urunca at ile kāfir zīr ü zeber olunca ġāzīler üşüp demir geyimiñ (29) yaqasından gücile yol bulup kāfiri boġazlayup depelerler. Ḥālā ol zemāndan berü Āl-i 'Osmāna kāfirden bir elçi gelse (30) pādişāh taḫt üzre qarār-dāde olup pādişāhıñ ḫil'atine müselsel bir uzun yeñi elçiler öperken iki ṭarafdan elçileri (31) berk dutup ibtidā yer öpdirüp ṣoñra sekiz adım uzun yeñi öpdirüp pādişāh yanına qomadıqları Ġāzī Ḫüdāvendigārıñ (32) şehīd olduġı günden qānūn-ı Āl-i 'Osmān qalmışdır.

Anıñiçün bu Mitroviçse qal'esine qal'e-yi menḥūs derler kim bu qal'e-yi bālā (33) Qos-ova ṣaḥrāsınıñ maġribī cānibi nihāyetinde ḥavālesiz yumurṭa-miṣāl şekl-i müdevver seng-ṭırāş bir qal'e-yi ṣavaş

[1] Text: *Qoflaki* (?).
[2] Altered to *qanlı*.

I: JOURNEY THROUGH KOSOVO, 1660

From there [Novi Pazar], in ----- hours, we arrived at *the lofty fortress of Mitrovica*. The name is Latin[1] meaning ----- . It was built by King Seleshti,[2] one of the kings of Serbia. This town was conquered in person by Ghazi Khudavendigar, Sultan Murad I son of Orhan Ghazi, in the year ----- . During the battle of Kosovo Polje, Sultan Murad put 700,000 infidels to the sword. While he was going about the battlefield on foot, and the bodies of his martyred soldiers were being piled up on the bank of the Llap river, an inauspicious infidel named Koblaki[3] rose from among the carcasses of the infidel soldiers and slew him. According to another version the assassination took place after the battle, when the aforementioned infidel, pretending to be an envoy, approached to kiss the hand of the Sultan, but then drew his dagger and slew him. He then mounted his horse and set off in flight. A huge number of Ottoman troops rushed around him with their weapons, yet no one was able to knock the assassin off his horse. An old woman cried out: "Oh warriors, strike his horse on the hoof, for both he and his horse are entirely covered in mail." As soon as she said this, a strong-armed bowman shot at the horse's hoof, and horse and rider both came tumbling down. The soldiers crowded around, broke through his mail collar and slit his throat. Ever since that time, whenever an envoy approaches one of the Ottoman dynasty, the sultan sits on his throne and the envoy kisses a long sleeve attached to the sultan's robe while being held tightly on both sides. The envoy is first made to kiss the ground and then the sleeve, which is eight paces in length, and he is not allowed any nearer. That has been the custom under Ottoman law since the day on which Ghazi Khudavendigar was murdered.

Because of that incident, this lofty fortress of Mitrovica is called The Inauspicious Fortress. Situated at the extreme western point of the Kosovo plain, it is not dominated by any higher ground. It is oval shaped and constructed of chiselled stonework. It is extremely solid

---

[1] In Evliya's usage, "Latin" often means Slavic. See Dankoff 1989, 29.

[2] Cannot be identified with a historical figure.

[3] Elsewhere Evliya gives the name as Viloş Qoblaki (I 176b34), and Vilaşqobla (I 23b34). The assassination is traditionally attributed to Miloš Kobilić or Obilić.

(34) meteris ve lağım qabūl etmez bir ḥıṣn-ı ḥaṣīn ve sedd-i metīndir. Ancaq bir qapusı var. İçinde aṣlā ma'mūrātdan bir eyü binā yoqdur.

[167b] Ammā bu qal'e dibinden ----- cārīdir, Arnavudluqda İpek Dağlarından gelüp Nehr-i Klāb ile bir olup éner, Nehr-i Moravaya (2) maḫlūṭ olur.

Bu qal'eye bu diyārlarda Qos-ova Mitroviçsesi derler, birine daḫi Serem Mitroviçsesi derler, ammā anıñ (3) qal'esi ḫarābdır. -----

(4) Ve bu qal'e-yi Mitroviçseye bir oq menzili ba'īd *ziyāret-i Muṣṭafā Baba*, tekyesinde fuqarā-yı Bektaşiyānı var, ba'żı āyende vü revendegān qonar.

(5) Ve bu tekyeye muttaṣıl *Evṣāf-ı āḫirü'l-ḥudūd-ı qaṣaba-yı İzevçan.* Eyālet-i Bosna bu maḥalde temām olup cümle Rūm-eli a'yānlarınıñ (6) yaqında olanları bu maḥalde paşa efendimize alay-ı 'aẓīm ile istiqbāle çıqup mübārek-bād qurbānları kesilüp fuqarālara bezl olundı. Ve paşa (7) efendimiz İzevçan cāmi'inde iki rik'at namāz qılup fuqarāya teṣadduqlar etdi. Bu rabṭa-yı ma'mūra Qos-ova ṣaḥrāsında üçyüz kiremit (8) ile mestūr ḫāneli ve cāmi' ve ḫān u ḥammāmı ve bir qaç fāḫir (?) dükkānlı ve ḥākim[l]i ve voyvadalı ma'mūr[1] qaṣabadır. Bosna eyāletiniñ bir ucı (9) bu maḥalde ve bir ucı Qara Dağlarda ve bir ṭarafı Podġoriçse ve Kilimente ve qal'e-yi Qoṭurda, bir semti Dobra-venedikde (10) ve bir ucı Burun Qullesinde ve ——de ve bir ucı Pupuşqa ve Pirmojya ve İspilitde ve bir cānib-i ġarbda Şibenik ve Zadrada (11) ve semt-i şimāle Zirin-oğlında ve bir ṭarâfı Cernik sancağında Qanija ile müşādır, ve bir ṭarâfı Pojġa ile müşādır, ve bir (12) semti Budin eyāletiyle ve bir ucı İzvornikde Serem sancağıyle müşādır, ve cānib-i şarqīsi Rūm-eli Alaca Ḥiṣārıyle müşādır, (13) ve bir ucı bu qıble semtinde bu İzevçanda ve Vuçitirin sancağıyle müşā bir sevād-ı mu'aẓẓam eyālet-i kebīrdir kim bunda[n] evlā qal'eler bir diyārda yoqdur.[2]

---

[1] Text: *ve ma'mūr.*

[2] Omitted here is a section on the walled towns (*qal'e*) of Bosnia.

and cannot be undermined with trenches or tunnels. There is a single gate. Inside, there are no memorable buildings.

At the base of the fortress flows the ----- river, which originates in the mountains of Peja[1] in Albania, joins the Llap river, and flows down until it joins the Morava. In these regions, this fortress is called Mitrovica of Kosovo. There is also a fortress called Mitrovica of Srem,[2] but it is in ruins.

At bowshot range from the fortress is the shrine of Mustafa Baba, with a *tekke* inhabited by Bektashi dervishes, where travelers can spend the night.

Near this *tekke* is *the town of Zveçan, at the utmost frontier*. This is where the *eyalet* of Bosnia comes to an end. All the notables from the nearby regions of Rumelia gathered at this place in grand procession to wish our master the Pasha a safe journey. They slaughtered animals and distributed the meat to the poor. Our master the Pasha performed two prostrations at the Zveçan mosque and distributed alms.

This prosperous town on the Kosovo plain consists of 300 houses with tiled roofs. It has a congregational mosque, a *han*, a bathhouse, and several fine shops. It is the seat of a governor (*hakim*) and a *voyvoda*.

This town constitutes one end of the *eyalet* of Bosnia, the other being in Montenegro. The *eyalet* is bordered on one side by Podgorica, Kelmendi, and the fortress of Kotor; on another by Venetian Dubrovnik; on another by Burun Kullesi (Cape Tower) and ——[3]; on another by the towns of Pupuška, Primorje, and Split; to the west by Šibenik and Zadar; to the north by Zrin; on another side by Kanija in the *sancak* of Cernik; on another by Požega; on another by the *eyalet* of Buda; on another by Zvornik in the *sancak* of Srem; to the east by Rumelian Alaca Hisar; and to the south by this Zveçan and the *sancak* of Vushtrria. It is a great and populous *eyalet*, and there are no better fortresses in any other region.[4]

---

[1] Town in western Kosovo, Serbo-Croatian Peć, Turkish İpek.
[2] Serbo-Croatian Sremska Mitrovica.
[3] Illegible.
[4] Omitted here is a section on the walled towns of Bosnia.

[168a] (8) *Rūm-eli eyāleti qurā ve qaṣabātları ve qılā‘ [u] şehirlerin beyān éder.* (9) Evvelā ibtidā Rūm-eli ḥükminde zikr olunan qaṣaba-yı İzevçandan qalqup cānib-i qıbleye Qos-ova ṣaḥrā-yı bī-pāyānı içre 7 sā‘atde (10) *evṣāf-ı ----- ya‘nī livā-yı qadīm qal‘e-yi Vuçitirin.* Lisān-ı latince ----- demekdir. (11) Bānīsi Ṣırf qırallarıdır. Sene 792 tārīḫinde bi’z-zāt Ġāzī Ḫüdāvendigār fetḥidir. Ba‘de’l-fetiḥ bir daḫi küffāra cā-yı emān olmasın içün qal‘esi münhedim (12) olunup ḥālā temelleri ẓāhir ü bāhirdir. Rūm-eli eyāletinde sancaq begi taḫtidir. Beginiñ ṭaraf-ı pādişāhīden ḫāṣṣ-ı hümāyūnı ----- aqçedir. (13) Ve livāsında ----- ze‘āmetdir ve ----- ‘aded tīmārdır. Alay begisi ve çeri başısı ve yüz başısı vardır. Bu ṭā’ifeleriñ qānūn üzre cebe(14)lüleri ile beginiñ ‘askeriyle cümle dörd biñ ‘asker olur. Müftīsi ve naqībi ve yüz elli aqçe pāyesiyle qāḍīsi ve ----- ‘aded nāḥiye (15) qurāları var. Sipāh ketḫüdā yeri ve yeñiçeri serdārı ve muḥtesibi ve bācdārı ve ḫarāc aġası ve a‘yān [u] eşrāfları vardır. -----

(16) Cümle ----- ‘aded maḥallātdır. Evvela Şühedā maḥallesi, Alay-beg-zādē maḥallesi, Eski Maḥalle, Yuqaru Maḥalle, Aşaġı Maḥalle; ma‘lūmum bunlardır.

(17) Ve cümle ----- ‘aded kārgīr-binā taḥtānī vü fevqānī ve serāpā kiremit örtüli iki biñ ma‘mūr ḫāne-yi vāsi‘lerdir. -----

(18) Ve cümle ----- ‘aded miḥrābdır. Evvelā çārsū içre Eski Cāmi‘, Ḫüdāvendigār evqāfıdır; ----- (19) ----- bunlardan mā‘adā mesācidlerdir.

(20) Medrese ve tekyeleri ve mektebleri me müte‘addid ḫānları ve maḥkeme qurbında bir kesīf ḥammāmı var, ammā çārsūsı azdır, bez̠z̠āzistānı (21) ve me’ākil ‘imāreti yoqdur, ammā her ḫānedānlarında āyende vü revendeye ni‘metleri mebzūldur. Cezīre-yi Girid fetḥi açılmazdan muqaddem bu şehr içre (22) yüz elli ḫānedān ṣāḥibi a‘yān-ı kibār sarāyları qapanmışdır, ḥālā anıñiçün bu şehir ḫarāba yüz dutmuşdur, ammā inşā’allāh yine ‘amār olur, zīrā (23) Qos-ova gibi maḥṣūldār zemīn-i vāsi‘atü’l-aqṭāra vāqı‘ olup āb [u]

Now follows a description of the towns and villages of the *eyalet* of Rumeli.

Leaving Zveçan we travelled south for 7 hours across the boundless plain of Kosovo and arrived at the ancient *sancak* (*liva*), *the walled town of Vushtrria.*[1] The name is Latin meaning ----- . It was founded by the kings of Serbia. In 792 (1389) it was conquered in person by Ghazi Khudavendigar. After the conquest, the fortress was razed so that it would never again be a refuge for the infidels. The foundations are still visible. It is the seat of a *sancak-beg* in the *eyalet* of Rumeli, and is an imperial grant to the *beg* with an income of ----- *akçe*. The *sancak* includes ----- *zeamet*s and ----- *timar*s. It has an *alay-beg*, a *çeribaşı*, and a captain. According to statute it must muster 4000 armed men including the armed retainers of these timariots and the soldiers of the *beg*. It has a *müfti*, a *nakibüleşraf* and a *kadi* with a salary level of 150 *akçe*. There are ----- surrounding villages. It also has a steward of the *sipahi*s, a commander of the janissaries, a market inspector, a collector of tolls, a poll-tax official, plus dignitaries and notables.

There are a total of ----- quarters, of which the most famous are the quarter of the Martyrs, the Alay-beg-zade quarter, the Old quarter, the Upper quarter, and the Lower quarter. There are 2000 one- and two-story houses in good condition, made of stone and with tiled roofs.

Altogether there are ----- prayer-niches. First of all, in the bazaar, is the Eski Cami (Old Congregational Mosque), supported by pious foundations established by Khudavendigar (Sultan Murad I). ----- All the rest are neighborhood mosques (*mescid*). There are a *medrese*, *tekke*s, schools, and several *han*s. Near the courthouse is a dingy bathhouse. The bazaar is small, with no *bedestan* or eating establishments, but all the houses in the town show great hospitality to travellers. Before the campaign to conquer Crete began[2], the mansions of 150 dignitaries and notables were closed up and for this reason the town has fallen into decay. God willing, its prosperity will be restored, since it is situated on the broad and fertile Kosovo plain

[1] Formerly known as Vuçitërna, Serbo-Croatian Vučitrn, Turkish Vuçitirin.
[2] In 1055/1645. The campaign ended with the victory at Candia in 1080/1669.

havāsı laṭīfdir, zīrā zemīni Nova Borda dağları dāmeninde (24) bāġ u bāġçeli şehr-i ġarībdir.

Nehr-i Klāb ṣaḥrāsından cerêyān éder. İbtidā ṭulū'ı Arnavudluqdan gelüp mezkūr Mitroviçse qal'esi (25) dibinde Nehr-i ----- maḫlūṭ olup andan Nehr-i Morava ile Nehr-i Ṭunaya munṣabb olur.

Bu şehir ḫalqı cümle Rūm-eli qavmıdır, (26) çoqluq lisān-ı Bosnevī tekellüm etmezler, eks̱eriyyā Arnavud lisānın ve Türk lisānın tekellüm éderler. Cümle çoqa es̱vāblar geyüp serḥadli (27) kürk ve semmūr alçaq tāclı qırmızı qalpaq geyüp qalpağıñ kürkin çevirüp qalpaqları kenārında siyāh dārāyī pervāzları görinüp (28) teybend quşaq ve qortela varsaq bıçaq ṭaşıyup qırmızı ṣıqma gümüş qopçalı çaqşırlar ile qūbādī nāzük babuç (29) geyerler kim eyālet-i Rūm-éli insānı böyle libās-ı fāḫirelerdir.

Bu şehirden qalqup cānib-i qıbleye Qos-ovası ṣaḥrāsı içre Nehr-i Klāb kenārıyle (30) giderken *evṣāf-ı türbe-yi pür-envār, ziyāretgāh-ı sa'īd eş-şehīd Ġāzī Ḫüdāvendigār, ṭābe s̱erāh, qaddesenā 'llāhu bi-sırrihi'l-'azīz.* (31) Nehr-i Klāb kenārında beyābān içre qalmış bir qubbe-yi 'ālī içinde mübārek qalb-i şerīfleri ve cemī'i aḫlāṭ-ı fażalātları bu maḥalde sene 792[1] tārīḫinde (32) ceng-i 'aẓīm olup bālāda taḥrīr olduğı üzre menkūs Qoblaki nām la'īn ü bī-dīn böyle bir pādişāh-ı cem-cenābı[2] şehīd édüp baṭn-ı şerīfin (33) yardıqlarında cemī'i yürek ü böbrek ü ciger ü qalbin bu maḥalle defn édüp ba'dehu bu qubbe-yi 'ulyāyı Yıldırım Bāyezīd Ḫān binā etmişdir.

(34) Devlet-i Āl-i 'Os̱mānda ----- 'aded ceng-i 'aẓīm olmuşdur. Evvelā biri bu Qos-ova cengidir; biri Yıldırım Ḫān cengidir; biri

---

[1] Text: 852.
[2] Altered to *cem-cāhı*.

and is blessed with a delightful climate. It is an isolated town, whose territory, at the foot of the Novobërda mountains, has many vineyards and gardens.[1]

Through this part of the plain flows the Llap river, which has its source in Albania,[2] joins the ----- river at the foot of the aforementioned fortress of Mitrovica, and then joins the Morava which flows into the Danube.

The inhabitants of Vushtrria are Rumelians. Most of them do not speak Bosnian but do speak Albanian and Turkish. They wear broadcloth garments and frontier-style red calpacs with low crests of fur and sable. They turn around (?) the fur of their calpacs, and black silken fringes are visible on the edges. They have *teybend* waistbands, carry knives of the *kortela varsak* variety, and wear red trousers with silver buttons and elegant *kubadi* shoes.[3] Such is the fine dress of the Rumelians.

We set out from this town following the banks of the Llap across the Kosovo plain heading south. *The radiant shrine of the martyr Sultan, Ghazi Khudavendigar, may his earth be sweet, may God hallow his mystery.* We visited the site, situated in a wilderness on the banks of the Llap, where the noble heart and other internal organs of our martyred Sultan Murad I lie buried in a high domed mausoleum. As I indicated above, a great battle took place here in the year 792 (1389) in which the damned and inauspicious Koblaki martyred such a marvelous sultan. The Sultan's belly was slit open and his kidneys, liver, and heart were removed and buried here. Later this lofty mausoleum was constructed by Sultan Bayezid I the Thunderbolt.

There have been ----- great battles in the Ottoman empire. The first was this one of Kosovo Polje. Another was the battle of Sultan Bayezid I the Thunderbolt.[4] Another was the battle of Murad II,

---

[1] "Vineyards and gardens" (*bāġ u bāġçe*) is an often-recurring formula in Evliya's descriptions of towns, and is not to be taken literally in every case; it can mean orchards and greenery in general.

[2] The Llap (Serbo-Croatian Lab, Turkish Klab) is a tributary of the Sitnica and Ibar and does not originate in Albania.

[3] The specific meaning of these terms is not wholly clear. For the first three, see Dankoff 1991b *Glossary*, 76 (*qortela*), 91 (*teybend*), 95 (*varsaq*).

[4] The battle of Nicopolis, 798/1396, when Bayezid defeated the crusading army under King Sigismund of Hungary.

Ebū'l-fetiḥ **[168b]** pederi qoca Murād Ḫānıñ Eflaq u Boġdan ile Varna qurbında Uġraş (?) deresi cengi; biri de Ebū'l-fethiñ Erżurum qurbında Tercān Ovası (2) içre Āẕerbāycān pādişāhlarında Sulṭān Uzun Ḥasan cengi ki tārīḫi "Baṭlān keydü'l-ḫāyinīn"dir, sene -----, ceng-i 'aẓīmdir; biri de sene ----- (3) tārīḫinde Şāh İsmā'īl ile Selīm Şāhıñ Çaldirān cengi 'ibretdir; biri de sene ----- tārīḫinde Süleymān Ḫānıñ Mohac ġazāsında yedi kerre yüz biñ (4) kāfir qatl olup Vlaġoş qıral mürd oldı; biri de sene ----- sālinde Egre qurbında Ḫırıştoş yaylası cengi, bunda da yedi qıral ġā'ib olup (5) yedi kerre yüz biñ kefere-yi fecere mürd oldılar. Ḥamd-i ḫudā, mezkūr olan yedi 'aded ġazālarda cümle küffār qıralları mürd olurlardı, lākin ancaq (6) bu Qos-ova cenginde ba'de'l-ceng āsūde-ḥāl maḥallinde ḥīle ile Ġāzī Murād Ḫān şehīd olup qalb-i şerīfi bu türbe-yi mehbaṭ-ı pür-envārda (7) qalup mübārek cesed-i şerīfleri ḥālā Bursada Eski Qaplıca nām maḥalde cāmi'-i kebīriniñ sāḥasında bir qubbe-yi 'ālī içinde medfūndur kim ziyāretgāh-ı (8) erbāb-ı dilāndır.

Ammā ġarāyib bunda kim bu Qos-ovadaki qubbesine girirken efendimiz Melek Aḥmed Paşanıñ bile dāmeni necāset ile mülevveṡ (9) oldı. Meger cemī'i re'āyā kefereleri eṭrāf qurālardan Priştine ve Vuçitirin şehirlerine bāzārlıġa giderken ihānet içün bu türbeye girüp tebevvül ü (10) teġayyuż[1] éderlermiş. Melek Aḥmed Paşa bu bed-rāyiḥa ve muzaḫrafātları görünce ġażab-ālūd oldı[2]. Ḥaqīr eyitdim: "Sulṭānım, bu pādişāhı (11) şehīd éden menkūs kāfir ise qarşu daġda bir manaṣṭır içinde cevāhir qandīller ile misk ü 'amber-i ḫām rāyiḥalarıyla mu'aṭṭar bir qubbe-yi müzeyyen (12) içre yatup buqadar

[1] Corrected in margin by a later hand to *teġavvuṭ*.
[2] The original word, perhaps *olup*, has been crossed out and replaced above the line in a later hand by *belürdi*.

father of Mehmed the Conqueror, against the Vlachs and Moldavians in the Ughrash valley near Varna.[1] Another was the great battle which took place in the valley of Tercan near Erzurum between Mehmed the Conqueror and Sultan Uzun Hasan, king of Azerbaidjan, in the year ----- dated according to the chronogram *Baṭlān keydü'l-ḫāyinīn* ("Void is the scheme of the traitors").[2] Another was the noteworthy battle of Chaldiran in the year ----- between Shah Ismail and Selim Shah.[3] Another was the battle of Mohács in the year ----- when Suleyman Khan slew king Lajos along with 700,000 infidels.[4] Another was the battle on the Mezö-Keresztes plateau near Erlau in the year ----- when seven kings perished along with 700,000 infidels.[5] Praise be to God that in the seven aforementioned ghazas, the infidel kings were all slain. After the battle of Kosovo Polje, however, Ghazi Murad Khan was slain by a ruse as he took his rest, and his noble heart was placed in this radiant shrine. As for his blessed body, it now lies buried in the sublime mausoleum that is in the courtyard of the Great Mosque in the place called Eski Kaplıca (Old Hotspring) in Bursa and is a place of pilgrimage.

A strange thing occurred as we entered this mausoleum of Kosovo Polje. Even the skirt of our master Melek Ahmed Pasha was besmirched with filth.[6] It seems that all the rayah[7] infidels from the surrounding villages used to stop at this mausoleum on their way to Prishtina and Vushtrria and, as an insult, use it as a privy. Melek Ahmed Pasha became enraged when he saw the stench and the filth.

"My lord," said I, "the inauspicious infidel who slew this sultan lies in a monastery on yonder mountain in a fine mausoleum, lit with jewelled lamps and scented with ambergris and musk. It is supported

---

[1] The battle of Varna, 848/1444. The name Ughrash is otherwise unkown, but *uğraş* means "battle" (see Dankoff 1991b *Glossary*, 93).

[2] The battle of Başkent against the Akkoyunlus, 878/1473.

[3] Sultan Selim I defeated the Safavid Shah Isma'il I, 920/1514.

[4] Sultan Suleyman I defeated Louis II, king of Hungary, 932/1526.

[5] The battle of Hachova (Mezö-Keresztes), 1005/1596, in which Sultan Mehmed III defeated the Emperor Maximilian. For the Mezö-Keresztes (Tk. Ḫırıştoş) plateau, see VII 39a14 (178); also I 58b24.

[6] Elsewhere Evliya says that Melek Pasha was noted for fastidiousness: "his skirts were cleaner than the collars of his peers" (VI 48a22; Dankoff 1991a *Intimate Life*, 278).

[7] Tk. *re'āyā*, taxpaying subjects, here referring to the peasants in the surrounding countryside.

rühbān ḫuddāmları var ve buqadar evqāfları var kim ṣubḥ u mesā buqadar yüz kefere ve müslimler gelüp mihmān olur giderler, ammā (13) bu bizim ġāzī pādişāhımızıñ ne türbedārı ve ne evqāfı olmadıġından cemī'i küffār gelüp ihāneten teġavvuṭ éderler. Gerekdir kim cemī'i eṭrāf (14) qurālar kefereleri gelüp yine anlar bu qubbeyi taṭhīr édüp 'amār édesiz ve İzevçan ḫāṣṣından bir yük aqçe ile 'amār édüp eṭrāfın (15) qal'e-mis̱āl dīvār çeküp bir türbedār ehl-i 'iyāliyle[1] ta'y[ī]n édesiz" dédigimde ehālī-yi vilāyete iki kīse ġuruş verüp cümle qurā kefere(16)lerine qubbeyi taṭhīr édüp bir haftada eṭrāf-ı qubbeye bir yüksek dīvār çeküp bir 'ālī qapu etdi kim atlılar girmeye ve beşyüz mīve diraḫti (17) diküp ve bir āb-ı ḥayāt quyu ḥafr édüp ehl-i 'iyāliyle[2] bir türbedār ta'y[ī]n eyledi kim anda sākin olup İzevçan voyva[da]sından vaẓīfe-yi (18) mu'ayyenesin alup türbe-yi pür-envārda olan ibrīşem ḫālīçe ve şem'dān u buḫūrdān u gülābdān u qanādilleri görüp gözede deyü a'yān-ı (19) vilāyeti bu vaqfu'llāha nāżıru'n-nużżār ta'yīn édüp bir ḫayrāt-ı 'aẓīme oldı. Ḥālā ziyāretgāh-ı ḫāṣṣ u 'āmdır, raḥmetü'llāhi 'aleyh.

Ve bu (20) türbe-yi pür-envār dibinde *ziyāret-i cebāne-yi şühedā* on biñden mütecāviz kibār şühedādırlar[3] ve 'Alemdār Baba ve Şeyḫ Şehīdü'n-nās Dede ve (21) Témürṭaş-paşa-zāde Yaṣavul Beg ve niçe biñ şühedālar daḫi medfūnlardır. ----- Anları ziyāret édüp yine cānib-i şarqa gidüp (22)

Evṣāf-ı ----- ya'nī ----- qal'e-yi *Priştine*. Lisān-ı latince ----- demekdir. (23) Bānīsi Ṣırf qırallarıdır. Fātiḥi yine sene 792 tārīḫinde Ġāzī Ḫüdāvendigārdır. Ba'de'l-fetiḥ qal'esi münhedim olmışdır. Rūm-eli eyāletinde (24) voyvadalıqdır ve yüz elli aqçe pāyesiyle şerīf qażādır. ----- 'aded nāḥiye qurālarından[4] qāḍīlere ber-vech-i 'adālet beş kīse (25) ḥāṣıl olur. Ketḫüdā yeri ve yeñiçeri serdārı ve a'yān [u] eşrāfı ġāyet çoqdur. Şehri Qos-ova ṣaḥrāsınıñ poyraz cānibine vāqı' (26) olmuş cümle ----- 'aded maḥalledir. ----- (27) Ve cümle iki biñ altmış 'aded taḥtānī vü fevqānī kārgīr-binā serāpā kiremitli vāsi' ḥavlılı ve bāġ-ı iremli ma'mūr u müzeyyen ḫānedān-ı (28)

---

[1] Corrected from *iyāliyle*.
[2] Corrected from *iyāliyle*.
[3] Text: *-dır-* repeated.
[4] Text: *-dan* repeated.

by wealthy endowments and ministered by priests who every day and night play host to passing vistors, infidel and Muslim alike. The mausoleum of our victorious sultan, on the other hand, has no such institution or keeper to tend to it, and thus all the infidels come and treacherously deposit their excrement in it. You ought to summon the infidels from the surrounding villages and have them clean and repair the mausoleum. With one load[1] of *akçe* drawn from the *has* of Zveçan, strong walls could be built around it and a keeper could be appointed to live here with his family."

Thereupon the Pasha gave the populace of the *vilayet* two purses[2] of *kuruş* and summoned the rayah from the surrounding area to clean up the mausoleum. In one week they built a high wall with a lofty gate around the mausoleum so that people on horseback could not get in. They also planted 500 fruit trees and dug a well. A keeper was appointed to live there with his family, receiving a regular salary from the *voyvoda* of Zveçan. His duty was to care for the silk carpets, candlesticks, censers, rose-water containers and lamps in the radiant mausoleum. At the same time, the notables of the *vilayet* appointed an official to oversee this charitable institution. Thus a great act of charity was accomplished, and now it has become a pilgrimage site — God's mercy be upon him!

Round about this radiant mausolum lie buried more than 10,000 martyrs and saints, among whom are Alemdar Baba, Sheikh Şehidünnas Dede, Yasavul Beg son of Temirtaş Pasha, and thousands of other martyrs. -----

On finishing our visit here, we advanced slowly eastwards and arrived at *the fortress of ----- i.e., Prishtina.* The name is Latin for ----- . It was founded by the kings of Serbia and was conquered in the year 792 (1389) by Sultan Murad I who razed the fortress. It is administered by a *voyvoda* within the *eyalet* of Rumeli. There is a *kadi* with a salary level of 150 *akçe*, who also derives a legal income of five purses a year from the ----- villages. There is a steward [of the *sipahis*], a commander of the janissaries, and many notables and dignitaries. The town is situated to the northeast of the plain of Kosovo. It has ----- quarters and 2060 attractive one- and two-story stonework houses with tiled roofs. They are all surrounded by

---

[1] One "load" (*yük*) = 500,000 *akçe*.

[2] One "purse" (*kīse*) = 500 *kuruş*.

zībālardır, cümleden qoca budur: alay begi sarāyı ve maḥkeme sarāyı. -----

(29) Ve cümle on iki miḥrābdır, altısı cum'adır, evvelā çārsū içinde ----- (30) ----- mā'adāsı mesācidlerdir. (31) Cümle medāris-i 'ālimān ----- ve dārü'l-ḥadīs̱-i müfessirān -----. (32) Cümle mekteb-i ṭıflān ----- ve tekye-yi dervīşān ----- (33) ve cümle çeşme-yi āb-ı revān ----- ve cümle sebīl-i cān-sitān -----.

(34) Ve cümle ḫān-ı ḫvācegān on bir 'aded ḫānlardır, emmā tārīḫ-i ḫān-ı Ḥācī Beg:

> Dédi tārīḫini lafẓen tārīḫ (?)
> Biñ oṭuz ikide **[169a]** yapıldı bu ḫān. Sene 1032.

Ve çārsū içinde bir qaç ḫānları daḫi var, ammā qurşumlı 'imāretleri yoqdur. -----

(2) Ve cümle ----- 'aded ḥammāmlardır, cümleden çārsū içre Ebū'l-fetiḥ Sulṭān Meḥemmed Ḫān ḥammāmı, ḥālā ziyāretgāh ḥammāmdır, zīrā ṣaġ cānibinde (3) olan ḫalvetde kibār evliyā'u'llāhdan biri ḫalvetde ḫalvet-i erba'īn çıqarup ve du'ā etmiş kim: "İlāhī, bu ḫalvete giren ḫaste girse (4) şifā bula" buyurmuşlar, ilā-hāẕā'l-ān ol ḫalvete marīż girse bi-emri'llāh te'ālā şifā bulur. Çārsū içinde Eski Ḥammām daḫi (5) havāsı ve bināsı ḫūb u müferriḥ ü dilgüşādır. -----

(6) Ve cümle üçyüz 'aded dekākīnlerdir, lākin kārgīr-binā beẕẕāzistānı yoqdur, şehrine göre dükkānları azdır, ammā yine her şey (7) mevcūddır.

Ve āb [u] havāsı laṭīf olduġından maḥbūb u maḥbūbesi ġāyet memdūḥ [u] müstesnā cüvānları var kim diyār-ı Rūmda meşhūrdur. (8) Ve bāġ u bāġçesi firāvāndır, memdūḥātından üzümi ve emrūdı -----. (9) Ve a'yān [u] eşrāfları ġāyet ġarīb-dost ve çirāġ ṣāḥibleri olup bay u gedāya ve pīr [ü] civāna ni'metleri mebzūl olup her géce müsāfirsiz olmazlar. / (11) -----

Andan qalqup *menzil-i qarye-yi Dobroten.* (12) Lisān-ı latince ----- demekdir. Beşyüz ḫāneli ma'mūr u müzeyyen ve maḥṣūldār serbest ze'āmet köyidir.

extensive yards with vineyards and gardens. Among the more prominent buildings are the mansion of the *alay-beg* and the courthouse. -----

There are a total of 12 prayer-niches, of which six are congregational mosques. First of all, in the bazaar, is ----- . The rest are neighborhood mosques. There are ----- *medreses*, ----- hadith schools, ----- primary schools, and ----- dervish *tekke*s. There are ----- fountains and ----- public water-dispensaries.

There are 11 *han*s. The *han* of Hadji Beg has the following chronogram:

> Proudly the date is said in words:
> This *han* was built in 1032 (1623).

There are other *han*s in the bazaar, but no public buildings with leaden roofs.

There are in all ----- bathhouses. In the bazaar is the bathhouse of Sultan Mehmed the Conqueror. It has become a pilgrimage site, because a certain saint once performed a forty-day retreat in a cell to the right of this bathhouse and uttered the following prayer: "My Lord, if anyone sick enters this cell, may he find a cure." To this day, whoever is ill and visits it recovers from his ailment, by God's command. Also in the bazaar is the Old Bathhouse, the construction and atmosphere of which are salubrious and exhilarating. -----

Although there is no stonework *bedestan*, there are 300 shops, which are actually too few for the size of the town. Nonetheless, everything can be found in them.

Because of the fine climate, one finds boys and girls here who are famous throughout the Ottoman lands for their beauty. There are abundant vineyards and gardens, and the grapes and pears are much praised. ----- The notables and better families here take pleasure in receiving guests — rich and poor, young and old — whom they treat with lavish hospitality. Not a night goes by without guests. -----

From here we set off and arrived at the village of Dobroten,[1] which is Latin for ----- . It is a free *zeamet* and is a fair, prosperous and fertile village of some 500 houses.

---

[1] Unidentified.

Andan yine cānib-i şarqa gidüp (13) *evṣāf-ı ----- ya'nī ----- qal'e-yi Qaçanik.* Sebeb-i tesmiyesi oldur kim şehr-i Üskübi bir kerre (14) Arnavud 'aşqıyāları başup qaçarlar, bu maḥalle gelüp qarārdāde (?) olam ẓann édüp cümle qaçanları bu maḥalde qırdıqlarıyçün "Qaçanlar"dan ġalaṭ (15) Qaçanik derler. Ba'dehu bu boġaz aġzına Nehr-i Lipense kenārında sene ----- tārīḫinde fātiḥ-i Yemen Sinān Paşa şekl-i murabba' seng-binā bir sūr-ı ra'nā (16) binā édüp dāyiren-mā-dār cirmi sekizyüz adımdır, ammā bir dere içinde vāqı' olmaġile eṭrāfında ḥavālesi çoqdur. Dizdārı ve elli 'aded neferātlar (17) ve iki ṭopı ve bir qapusı var. Derūn-ı ḥiṣārda qırq elli neferā[t] ḫāneleri var, ġayri 'imāret yoqdur. Ammā ṭaşra varoşı yüz 'aded ḫāneleri var, (18) cümle kiremit örtüli ve bāġçeli evlerdir. Ve bir müferriḥ cāmi'iniñ 'atebe-yi 'ulyāsı üzre tārīḫi budur:

Vallahi dā'ī dédi tārīḫin:
(19) Ma'bed-i ḫūb maqām-ı maḥmūd. Sene 1003.

Ve bir tekye-yi dervīşān-ı Bektaşiyānı var; ve bir mekteb-i ṣıbyānı var; ve bir ḫān-ı 'aẓīmi var, qayalar dibinde (20) vāqı' olmuş; ve bir küçük ḥammāmı var; ammā çārsū-yı bāzārdan bir 'alāmet yoqdur, zīrā şehr-i Üsküb yaqındır. Ve bu Qaçanikden (21) aqan Nehr-i ----- bu dereler içre cerêyān éderek Ġāzī 'İsā Beg kemerleriyle cerêyān éderek énüp şehr-i Üskübüñ ḫān u cāmi' ü (22) ḥammām u medreselerine taqsīm olur, 'aẓīm ḫayrātdır. Ve bu Qaçanik başqa qażādır kim yüz elli aqçe pāyesiyle Üskübī Veysī-efendi-(23)zādeye mü'ebbeden iḥsān olunmuşdur, ve Üsküb sancaġı voyvadalıġıdır.

Andan qalqub Üsküb yolı üzre *ziyāret-i Qırqlar Maqāmı.* Andan ----- sā'atde

[Üsküb]

From here we journeyed eastwards and arrived at *the fortress of ----- i.e., Kaçanik.* The origin of this name is that some Albanian brigands once conducted a raid on Skopje and then fled as far as this point where, expecting to find a halting-place, they were massacred instead. So it was called Kaçanlar ("Fugitives"), which became corrupted to Kaçanik. Later, in the year ----- , Sinan Pasha, the conqueror of Yemen, constructed a beautiful stonework fortress at the mouth of the gorge and on the banks of the Lepenca river. It is square in shape and 800 paces in circumference. One drawback is that it is situated in a valley and so has many higher points surrounding it. The castle has a warden, 50 garrison soldiers, two cannons and one gate. Inside are 40 or 50 houses to accommodate the soldiers, but no public buildings. Outside the wall there are another 100 houses, all with tiled roofs and gardens.

The town contains one delightful congregational mosque, above the threshold of which is the following chronogram:

> By God, a well-wisher has uttered its date:
> A fair temple and praiseworthy site. 1003 (1594).

There is one Bektashi *tekke*, one primary school, one great *han* situated at the foot of the cliff, and one small bathhouse. There is no sign of a bazaar, since Skopje is nearby. The ----- river flows through Kaçanik, continues through these valleys, and is conducted via the Ghazi-Isa-Beg aqueduct to Skopje where the water is distributed to the *hans*, bathhouses and *medreses* — a splendid public work! Kaçanik is the seat of a *kadi* with a salary level of 150 *akçe*, and the office has been granted in perpetuity to the descendants of Veysi Efendi of Skopje. It is governed by a *voyvoda* as part of the *sancak* of Skopje.

From here we set off on the Skopje road and, after visiting the shrine of the Forty Saints, arrived in Skopje after ----- hours.

PART II: NORTHERN ALBANIA, 1662

[VI 33a] Andan Qırraba yaylasın yüz biñ renc [ü] ʻinā çekerek aşup 9 sāʻatde *sitāyiş-i qaṣaba-yı Tiran.* Oẖri sancağı (2) ẖākinde voyvadalıqdır ve yüz elli aqçe qażādır, şehri bir vāsiʻ ṣaḥrāda cāmiʻleri ve ẖān u ḥammāmları ve çārsū-yı bāzārı ve bāğ u (3) bāğçesi bī-ḥisābdır ve cümle ʻimārātları serāpā kiremit örtüli ẖayrāt-ı ḥasanātdır. ----- //

(6) Andan Nehr-i Matiyi atile ʻubū[r] etdik. Bu nehir Omoraṣ (?) dağlarından gelüp Oẖri Buḥeyresine qarışır.

Andan cānib-i ġarba (7) gidüp *menzil-i qarye-yi Omoraṣ.* Bu daẖi Oẖri ṭopragında qaṣaba-mis̱āl üçyüz ẖāneli cāmiʻ ve ẖān u ḥammāmlı (8) bir maʻmūr Arnavud köyidir ve bāğ u bāğçeleri vāfirdir ve reʻāyāları cümle kāfirdir ve ʻavretleri cümle sāḥirdir.

Andan yine 9 sāʻat gidüp // (11) *evṣāf-ı qalʻe-yi ʻatīq-i Leş.* Lisān-ı Arnavudda Leş derler, ammā sene 883 tārīẖinde bu qalʻe Ebū'l-fetiḥ Ġāzī (12) İskenderiyye ġazāsına giderken Venedik Firengi elinden alırken ʻusret çeküp "Bu qalʻa leys̱ gibidir yaʻnī arslan gibidir" deyü (13) nuṭq etdiklerinde baʻde'l-fetiḥ ismine qalʻe-yi Leys̱ dédiler, ġalaṭ-ı meşhūr evlā olmağile Leys̱den ġalaṭ efvāh-ı nāsda (14) Leş qalʻesi dédiler. Ebū'l-fetiḥ Ġāzī taḥrīri üzre Rūm-éli eyāletinde Duqagin sancağı ẖākinde voyvadalıqdır, muḥtesibi ve nāyibi (15) ve bācdārı ve qalʻe dizdārı ve ----- ʻaded ḥiṣār neferātları vardır.

II: JOURNEY THROUGH NORTHERN ALBANIA AND MONTENEGRO, 1662

From there [Mileševa] we crossed the high mountain pastures of Krraba[1] with great difficulty and in 9 hours arrived at *the town of Tirana*. It is administered by a *voyvoda* within the *sancak* of Ohrid and has a *kadi* with a salary level of 150 *akçe*. The town is situated on a broad plain and has mosques, *han*s, bathhouses, bazaars, vineyards and gardens. All the public buildings have fully tiled roofs and are splendid structures. -----

From here we crossed the Mati river on horseback. This river descends from the mountains of Omoras (?) and flows into Lake Ohrid.[2]

From here we continued in a westward direction and arrived at *the village of Omoras*,[3] also in the territory of Ohrid. It is a prosperous village the size of a town, with 300 houses, a mosque, a *han* and a bathhouse, and surrounded by vineyards and gardens. The rayah are all infidels and their women folk are all enchantresses.

From here we proceeded for 9 hours to *the ancient fortress of Lezha*.[4] In Albanian it is called Leş (Lezhë). Sultan Mehmed the Conqueror took over Lezha from the Venetians with difficulty in 883 (1478) when he was advancing on Shkodër. "This fortress is like a lion (*leys*)," he remarked, and after the battle it was called Lion Fortress (Kale-yi Leys), but gradually Leys ("Lion") became corrupted to Leş ("Corpse"). According to the Conqueror's survey register (*tahrir*), it is part of the *sancak* of Dukagjin in the *eyalet* of Rumeli and is administered by a *voyvoda*. It has a market inspector, a deputy *kadi*, a collector of tolls and a castle warden with ----- garrison soldiers.

---

1 As the last places referred to by Evliya on his way from Belgrade and Bosnia are Prijepolje and Mileševa in the sandjak of Novi Pazar, we may assume that substantial parts of the text are missing here.

2 The Mat or Mati river flows to the sea between Tirana and Lezha. We may assume that here again substantial parts of the text are missing, since Evliya does not mention the impressive fortress of Kruja which he must have visited, or at least seen, on his way from Tirana to Lezha.

3 Possibly Mamurras which lies north of the Ishëm river and but 12 km. south of the Mati. The *Relazione di Mariano Bolizza* of 1614 refers to the toponym Omuragni.

4 Noticeable here is the lack of any reference to the Albanian national hero Scanderbeg (1405-68) who was buried in the Church of St. Nicholas in Lezha.

Qal'esi Nehr-i Dirin kenārında bir qaya üzre şekl-i murabba' (16) bir küçük sū[r]-ı üstüvār-ı muṣanna'dır, ammā ma'mūr degildir, lākin Venedik Firengistānınıñ serḥad qal'elerindendir. Bānīsi yine Venedik (17) pirinç pirimleridir.

Bu şehriñ cümle Arnavud ġāzīleri dāyimā fırqatalara süvār olup Venedik diyārların ve İşpanyanuñ Pulya (18) yaqaların yaqa yıqa māl-i ġanāyimler alup küffārıñ esīrleri ve leşlerin qal'e-yi Leşe getirüp Nehr-i Dirine atarlar. Bu qal'e Venedik (19) Körfezi deryāsına ----- ba'īd yerdir, ve Nehr-i Dirin ----- dağlarından çıqup cānib-i qıbleye aqup bu körfez sāḥilinde (20) Sincivan limanı qurbında körfez deñizine maẖlūṭ olur.

Cümle ----- 'aded miḥrābdır ----- / (22) ve cümle ----- 'aded medresedir ----- ve cümle ----- tekyedir (23) ve cümle ----- 'aded mektebdir ----- ve cümle ----- 'aded ẖāndır ----- (24) ve cümle ----- 'aded ḥammāmdır ----- ve cümle ----- 'aded dükkāndır ----- ve cümle 4 (?) 'aded kiremit (25) örtüli bāğlı ve bāġçeli vāsi' serḥad evleridir, ammā qal'e içinde evleri azdır ve bāġçeleri yoqdur, ammā cebe-ẖānesi (26) çoqdur ve şāhāne serāmed bal-yemez ṭopları ve mihter-ẖānesi vardır. ----- / (28) -----

Andan cānib-i ġarba Dirin Nehrin geçüp (29) *evṣāf-ı qal'e-yi İskenderiyye*. İbtidā bānīsi İskender Zū'l-qarneyn bināsı olduġıyçün İskenderiyye (30) derler. Ba'dehu İşpanya ḥākimi destine girüp daẖi tevsī' édüp ba'dehu Pulya qıral elinden Venedik pirinç pirimleri bu qal'eye (31) mālik olup Üsküb ve Priştine ve Vuçitirin cāniblerin nehb ü ġārete başlayınca Ebū'l-fetḥe bu aẖbār-ı müḥiş geldikde hemān niyyetü'l-ġazā (32) deyüp İskenderiyye üzr[e] cüyūş-ı bī-ḥadd [ü] bī-pā[yā]n ile gelüp qırq gün qırq géce muḥāṣara eyleyüp sene 883 tārīẖinde cebren ve qahren (33) Ebū'l-fetiḥ Sulṭān Meḥemmed Ġāzī dest-i Venedikden fetḥ édüp Rūm-éli eyāletinde başqa sancaq begi taẖti édüp ibtidā fetiḥde[1] **[33b]** sancaq ḥākimi olan Meḥemmed Paşanıñ ceddi Yūsuf Beg mīr-livā olup ocaqlıq iḥsān olunduġından ḥālā ḥākimler yine Yūsuf Beg (2) oġullarıdırlar.

---

[1] The text at this point has *ḥālā Yūsuf*, two words from the following line mistakenly placed here as well.

The square-shaped fortress of Lezha is situated on a promontory over the banks of the Drin. Its small ramparts were skillfully fashioned, but they are not in good repair, even though the fortress is on the frontier of the Venetian Franks. It was originally constructed by the doges of Venice.

All the Albanian ghazis from this town cross the sea on their frigates and maraud in Venetian territory and along the coast of Spanish Puglia.[1] They then return with their booty and their infidel captives, alive or dead, to the fortress of Lezha where they throw the corpses into the Drin river. The fortress is at a distance of ----- from the Gulf of Venice (Adriatic Sea). After emerging from the ----- mountains, the Drin continues southwards and flows into the sea near the port of Shëngjin.

Lezha has ----- prayer-niches, ----- *medreses*, ----- *tekkes*, ----- schools, ----- *hans*, ----- bathhouses and ----- shops. It has a total of 4 (?) frontier houses with tiled roofs surrounded by vineyards and gardens. Inside the fortress there are few houses and no gardens, but there are many ammunition depots as well as magnificent long-range battering guns and a military band.

From here we set off westwards, crossing the Drin river, and journeyed to *the walled city of Shkodër*. It was founded by Iskender Zu'l-qarneyn (Alexander the Great) and thus was called Iskenderiyye (Alexandria).[2] It was subsequently taken over and enlarged by Spain, then passed from the king of Puglia into the hands of the doges of Venice. When Mehmed the Conqueror received the dreadful news that the Venetians had begun to loot and plunder the lands around Skopje, Prishtina and Vushtrria, he resolved at once to pacify the region and, arriving with a huge expeditionary force, he conquered the fortress from the Venetians in the year 883 (1478) after a siege of forty days and nights. He then made it the capital of a separate *sancak* in the *eyalet* of Rumeli, bestowing it as a heritary fief (*ocaklık*) upon Yusuf Beg, the first *sancak-beg* of Shkodër. Since that time it has been ruled by that family.

---

[1] Apulia, the region of SE Italy along the Adriatic coast, at this period still part of the Spanish empire.

[2] Shkodër or Shkodra is known in Turkish as Iskenderiyye or Işkodra or Üsküdar, in Italian as Scutari and in Serbo-Croatian as Skadar.

Bu ḥaqīre beg istiqbāle çıqup bizi derūn-ı qal'ede dizdār ----- Aġa ẖānesine qondurup Melek Paşa efendimiñ (3) mektūb-ı maḥabbet-üslūbların verüp qırā'at etdikde vāfir sürūr [u] ḥubūr (?) éder şeklin gösterüp "İnşā'allāh on güne dek qarż-ı ḥasan deynimizi dīnimiz (4) ḥaqqıyçün edā édüp sizi yollar" deyü ḥaqīre ḥammām-behā bir kīse ve bir qat libās iḥsān etdi ve oṭuz 'aded refīqlerime ve ẖuddāmlarıma (5) onar ġuruş in'ām édüp her bār şeref ṣoḥbetleriyle müşerref olup gāhīce Busaṭlar nām qaryede Yūsuf-beg-zāde sarāylarına gidüp (6) zevq u ṣafālar éderdik, ammā dāyimā İskenderiyyeye gelirdik, zīrā Venedik kāfiriniñ ġāyet 'ıṣyān [u] ṭuġyānları var idi.

Evvelā Āl-i 'Os̱mān devletinde (7) İskenderun üçdür: biri budur kim buña Arnavud İskenderiyyesi derler; biri Aq Deñiz kenārında Ḥalebe arayatı Ḥaleb iskelesidir, (8) aña İskenderun derler; biri Mıṣır İskenderiyyesidir. Ammā lisān-ı Yūnāniyānda buña Aleksandire Pırġaz derler; purġaz Urumca qal'e (9) demekdir; ya'nī İskender qal'esi derler.

Ḥālā beginiñ qānūn-ı Süleymān H̱ān üzre ẖāṣṣ-ı hümāyunı 459200 aqçedir ve zi'āmeti (10) 19 ve cümle tīmārı 205. Qānūn üzre üçer biñ aqçede bir cebelüleri ile alay begi ve çeri başı ve ṣu[1] başısı ve paşasınıñ (11) 'askeriyle cümle dörd biñ 'aded güzīde yarar 'askeri vardır. Me'mūr olduqları sefere Rūm-éli vezīriyle yāẖod mīr-livālarıyle sefer eşerler. (12) Ḥattā cümle ġāzīleri bizimle Erdel ġazālarında bile idiler, ḥaqqā ki şecī' ü fetā 'askerdir.

Bu livādan paşasına qırq kīse ḥāṣıl olup (13) biñ 'aded yigit ile bu sancaġı ḥıfż [u] ḥirāset éder. Ḥākim-i şer'-i resūl-i mübīnden şeyẖü'l-islāmı ve naqībü'l-eşrāfı ve a'yān-ı kibār-ı kübbār (14) eşrāfı ve yüz elli aqçe pāyesiyle qāḍīsi ve sipāh ketẖüdā yeri ve yeñiçeri serdārı ve qal'e dizdārı ve qal'e neferātları ve muḥtesibi ve voyvadası ve (15) bācdārı ve mi'mārı ve şehir ketẖüdāsı ve ẖarāc emīni vardır.

---

[1] Text: *bu*.

The present governor, Mehmed Pasha, came out to meet us and accompanied us into the fortress where we were quartered in the house of the castle warden, ----- Aga. When Mehmed Pasha had read the affectionate letters which I gave him from Melek Pasha he expressed delight. "God willing," he cried, "I shall meet my obligations and repay my debt within ten days and you may continue your journey." He gave me a purse of *kuruş* for bath-expenses and a set of clothing, and gave my thirty companions and servants ten *kuruş* each. We frequently resorted to the Yusuf-beg-zade palace in a village called Bushat, where we were well received and had an excellent time. But we always returned to Shkodër because the Venetian infidels were up in arms.

There are three Iskenderuns or Alexandrias in the Ottoman Empire. One is this Albanian Iskenderiyye (Shkodër). The second, called Iskenderun, is on the shore of the Mediterranean one caravan stage from Aleppo and serves as the port for that city.[1] The third is Alexandria in Egypt, which in Greek is called Alexandria Pyrgos or Alexander's Castle.

According to the statute of Suleyman Khan, the *beg* possesses an imperial grant worth 459,200 *akçe*, plus 19 *zeamet*s and 205 *timar*s, and for every 3000 *akçe* he must provide one armed retainer (*cebelü*). These, together with the troops of the *alay-beg*, the *çeribaşı*, the *subaşı*, and the pasha himself, provide a force of 4000 select armored soldiers. In time of war, this force is put under the command of the vizier or else the *sancak-beg*s of Rumeli. And indeed, all of these brave ghazis were with us during the Transylvania campaigns.

The *sancak* also provides 40 purses for the pasha who, with the help of 1000 warriors under his command, guards and defends the *sancak*. Among the *şer'i* authorities in Shkodër are the *şeyhülislam*, the *nakibüleşraf* along with various notables and descendants of the Prophet, the *kadi* with a salary level of 150 *akçe*, the steward of the *sipahi*s, the commander of the janissaries, the castle warden along with the garrison soldiers, the market inspector, the *voyvoda*, the toll collector, the chief engineer, the mayor (*şehir kethüdası*), and the poll-tax official.

---

[1] Formerly Alexandretta, at the eastern end of the Mediterranean coastline of modern Turkey.

Eşkāl-i qal'e-yi İskenderiyye. Buḥeyre-yi 'aẓīm Boyana nām bir gölüñ sāḥilinde (16) bir ṣarp qaya-yı 'ālī üzre çār-gūşeden ṭūlānīce ve muḥarrefce vāqı' olmuş şeddādī[1] seng-ṭırāş bir sūr-ı ṣavaşdır kim aṣlā (17) ḥavālesi yoq bī-ḥāyil ü bī-ġāyil qal'e-yi kāmildir, lākin küçükdür, ammā ṣa'b u metīn ḥiṣār-ı bī-bedeldir, Boyana Göli ṭarâfında (18) ve ġayrinde ḫandaqı yoqdur, burc [u] bārūları ve dendān-ı bedenleri çoqdur. Cümle iki qapusı vardır, biri gün doġusı ṭarâfına, biri (19) Küçük Ovaya nāẓirdir, bu qapu içre ziyāret-i Muyo Baba Sulṭān medfūndur. Ve derūn-ı ḥiṣārda evler azdır, ancaq Sulṭān Meḥemmed (20) cāmi'i kiremit ile mestūr ṭarz-ı qadīm cāmi'-i pür-nūrdur. Ve yedi sekiz ṣarnıçları var, bārān-ı raḥmet ile memlūdur. Ve qal'eden Boyana (21) Göline énecek ṣu yolları vardır kim ehālī-yi qal'e bilir, ṭaşrada düşmen göremez mestūr ṣu yollarıdır, ḥīn-i muḥāṣarada anlardan (22) ṣu alırlar. Ammā bu qal'ede dükkānlar yoqdur, ancaq yüz 'aded neferāt ḫānecikleri ve buġday enbārları vardır. Ammā cebe-ḫānesi ve şāhāne (23) ṭopları vardır, lākin Boyana Göli aşırı Torondoş daġından bu qal'eyi dögdügi daġ sehil bu qal'eye ḥavāledir, ammā (24) qırqar qarış ṭop-ı qal'e-kūb-ı ṭavīl lāzımdır; eger küçük ṭoplar ise bu qal'eye ol ḥavāleden żarar yoqdur, zīrā arada göl (25) vardır. Ve qal'e dibinde qayalar kenārında Boyana Göli içre çam direkleri üzre balıq dalyanları var, başqa emānetdir kim qal'e qulı (26) aqlāmıdır. -----

(27) *Evṣāf-ı varoş-ı qal'e-yi İskenderiyye.* Cümle biñ sekiz yüz 'aded taḥtānī vü fevqānī ḥadīqa-yı ravża-yı rıżvān miṡilli bāġ u (28) bāġçeli kiremit ve qayaġan örtüli kārgīr binā-yı metīn ve ḫānedān-ı müslimīn ve sükenā-yı muvaḥiddīndir. Ve cümle 15 maḥalledir, evvelā (29) Bāyezīd Ḫān maḥallesi ve 'Alī Beg maḥallesi ve Ḥüseyn Beg maḥallesi ve İskele-başı maḥallesi ve Müftī maḥallesi ve Qara Ḥasan maḥallesi ve varoşda (30) bāzār başında Maḥkeme maḥallesi ve -----

(31) *Sitāyiş-i cevāmi'hā-yı muvaḥḥidān.* Cümle on bir miḥrābdır: evvelā çārsū başında Sulṭān Bāyezīd Velī cāmi'i, öñinde bir quyusı

[1] Text: *sdādādī.*

Plan of the fortress of Shkodër. It is situated upon a lofty and very steep cliff overlooking a great lake called Boyana.[1] It is square-shaped, somewhat slanted.[2] The fortress is constructed of chiselled stonework and is fully functional, with no obstructing higher ground in the vicinity. Though small, it is strong and impregnable. It has no moat on the lake side or on any other side, but does have many towers and crenellated battlements. There are two gates, one facing east, the other overlooking Küçük Ova (Small Plain). Inside this second gateway is the shrine of Muyo Baba Sultan. Within the fortress there are few houses and only one congregational mosque, i.e., the radiant mosque of Sultan Mehmed, covered in tiles and constructed in the old style. There are 7 or 8 cisterns which fill up with rain water. Descending from the fortress to Lake Boyana are water channels known only to those in the fortress. They cannot be seen by the enemy outside. It is through these channels that they fetch water during sieges. There are no shops inside the fortress, only 100 houses for the garrison soldiers and storage bins for wheat. There are also ammunition depots and fine imperial cannons. It might be possible for an enemy to bombard the fortress from Mount Tarabosh, which looms above on the other side of Lake Boyana, but they would need cannons forty spans in length. Smaller guns pose no threat, because the lake is in between. At the foot of the fortress, near the cliffs down at the lake, there are fishing weirs built on pinewood pilings. These weirs are administered on commission from the fortress garrison. -----

The open town (varoş) of the fortress of Shkodër. The town outside the walls consists of 1800 one- and two-story stonework houses with slate and tiled roofs and surrounded by vineyards and gardens. The inhabitants are all Muslim. There are 15 quarters, of which the best known are: Bayezid Khan quarter, Ali Beg quarter, Hüseyn Beg quarter, Iskele-başı (Docks) quarter, Müfti quarter, Kara Hasan quarter, and the Courthouse quarter at the end of the bazaar. -----

Mosques of the monotheists. There are 11 prayer-niches (i.e., congregational mosques). First is the mosque of Sultan Bayezid II the Saint at the end of the bazaar. In front of it is a well with delicious

[1] This is Evliya's name for Lake Shkodër, based on the name of the Buna, formerly Boyana, river which flows out of it at the foot of the fortress of Shkodër.

[2] I.e., a parallelopiped? — *muḥarrefce*.

āb-ı {ḥayātdır kim demir zincīri} (32) var kim ġayri cāmi'ler buña göre degil, kiremetli ve cemā'at-i keṡīreye mālik cāmi'-i pür-nūrdur; 'Alī Beg maḥallesinde Ḥüseyn Beg cāmi'i; (33) İskele-başında Müftī cāmi'i; Qara Ḥasan cāmi'i; meşhūr u ma'mūr ve kiremit ile mestūr cāmi'-i pür-nūrlardır.

Bunlardan (34) mā'adā yetmiş 'aded *mesācid-i mü'mināndır*; evvelā -----

[34a] Ve cümle yedi 'aded medrese-yi 'ālimāndır, her cāmi'de birer medrese muqarrerdir, ammā maḫṣūṣ dārü'l-qurrā ve dārü'l-ḥadīṡ yoqdur.

(2) Ve cümle [----- 'aded] mekteb-i ṭıflān-ı ebced-ḫvāndır -----

(3) Cümle altı 'aded tekye-yi ehl-i ṭarīq-ı dervīşāndır -----

(4) Ve cümle ----- 'aded ḫān-ı ḫvācegāndır; cümleden Ulama Paşa ḫānı metīn ü müsteḥkemdir ve cemī'i zī-qıymet eşyālar bu vikālede bulunur.

(5) Ve cümle bir 'aded mükellef ḥammām-ı ṭāhirāndır; ammā ġāyet müferriḥ ve ḫoş-havā ve ḫūb-binā bir ḥammām-ı rūşinādır, ṣuyı dollāb ile Boyana {Gölinden çekilir.}

(6) Ve cümle beşyüz 'aded çārsū-yı beẕẕāzıstāndır, cemī'i ehl-i ṣanāyi' mevcūddur, ammā göl ṭarâfından balıq bāzārı ma'mūr u müzeyyendir.

(7) Sitāyiş-i libās-ı merd-i meydān. Cümle çoqa esbāblar geyüp ṣıqma qopçalı çaqşır ve teybend ḥarīr quşaq ve qūbādī (8) pabuç ve başlarında semmūr Arnavud qalpaqları geyerler; 'ulemāsı ve levendātları qortela bıçaq ṭaşıyup yigitleri qılıç ve qalqan ile dāyim gezerler.

(9) Der beyān-ı libās-ı zenān-ı mü'eddebān. Cümle ḫavātīnleri çoqa ferrāceler geyüp başlarına bostāncı külāhı gibi bir 'acībe-liqā ṭāqıye geyüp (10) üzerlerine beyāż 'izār u dülbend örtünüp ṣarı iç edik ve pabuç geyerler, ammā ġāyet mü'eddebe gezerler.

(11) Der faṣl-i esmā'-ı rācilān -----

(12) Der 'ayān-ı esmā'-ı zenān -----

(13) Der medḥ-i maḥbūbe i maḥbūbān. Eger bintān u püserānları olqadar sīm-endām ve gül-fām maḥbūb u maḥbūbeleri olur kim cümle gül-çehrelerdir.

(14) Tavṣīf-i āb [u] havā-yı cāvidān. Āb [u] havāsı olqadar laṭīfdir kim cemī'i ḫalqı yetmişe seksene yetmiş* daḫi quvvet-i quvāları henūz gitmemiş*

water and an iron chain. It is definitely the finest of the mosques, an exquisite building with a tiled roof, and has a large congregation. Then comes the mosque of Hüseyn Beg in the Ali Beg quarter; the Müfti mosque at the Docks; and the mosque of Kara Hasan. These are all well-known and radiant mosques with tiled roofs. Aside from these, there are 70 other prayer-houses. -----

There are 7 *medreses*, each congregational mosque having its own, but there are no special schools of Koran recitation or Hadith. There are ----- primary schools, 6 dervish *tekkes*, and ----- *hans* of which the Ulama Pasha *han* is the strongest in construction and the most imposing, with all kinds of precious furnishings. There is a single very spacious and attractive bathhouse which gets its water from Lake Boyana by means of a waterwheel. There are 500 shops in the *bedestan*,[1] all the skills and handicrafts being represented. The fish-market at the lakeside is well-maintained and furnished.

Clothing of the manly men. They all wear broadcloth garments and tight buttoned trousers with *teybend* silk waistband and *kubadi* shoes. On their heads they wear Albanian calpacs made of sable. Learned scholars (*ulema*) and rakish youths (*levendât*) alike carry *kortela* knives in their belts, and the youths are never to be seen without their swords and shields.

Clothing of the demure women. They all wear full-length broadcloth coats and a strange conical headpiece, like the caps worn by the imperial guards, and they wrap themselves in white muslin wraps. On their feet they wear soft yellow indoor boots and shoes. They go about very well-mannered.

Men's names. -----

Women's names. -----

Praise of the lovely boys and girls. They have silver limbs and rosy cheeks.

Praise of the salubrious climate. Because of the fine climate, all the people reach the age of seventy or eighty without diminution of their faculties.

---

[1] Omissions here in the printed text (109:21) have led to the mistaken impression that Evliya failed to mention the *bedestan* of Shkodër; see Kreiser 1979, 393.

(15) Ta'rīf-i zülāl-i āb-ı ḥayvān. Bir ṭarâfında Nehr-i Dirin ki gūyā mā'-ı Kevs̱erdir, bir yanındaki Boyana Göli ṣuyıdır kim gūyā şarāb-ı ṭahūrdur.

(16) Eqālīm-i arż-ı beled-i büldān -----

(17) Der zikr-i ṭāli'-i 'amārıstān -----

(18) Bī-medḥ-i kenīse-yi rāhibān -----

(19) Ta'rīf-i ḥubūbāt [u] nebātat -----

(20) Der zikr-i memdūḥāt-ı ṣanāyi'āt -----

(21) Der medḥ-i eṭ'ām-ı me'kūlāt -----

(22) Sitāyiş-i müs̱mirāt-ı mu'teberāt -----

(23) Güzīde-yi envā'-ı meşrūbāt -----

(24) Der beyān-ı 'ibret-numā-yı yed-i qudret-i 'imārāt. Ol ḫallāq-ı 'ālemiñ yed-i qudretiyle bu şehriñ buḥeyresi içre yedi 'aded küçük ve büyük (25) çemenzār cezīrecikler var kim bu buḥeyre-yi kebīreniñ vasaṭında cezīrecikler ḫalq olmuş, her biri bir ḫarman ve iki ve üç ve beş ḫarman (26) cirmi qadar cezīreciklerdir. Ba'żı senelerde her qanqı rūzgār-ı zor-kār-ı şedīd eserse ol cezīreler yerlerinden ḥareket édüp bir semt-i (27) āḫara gider, ba'żı mevsimde mezkūr cezīreler buḥeyreniñ vasaṭında birbirlerine rāst gelüp muttaṣıl olurlar, ve her birinde gūnāgūn ḫorda (28) fidanlar ve çemenzār yerler var, ve ba'żı ehālī-yi vilāyet teferrüc içün bu cezīreciklere qayıqlar ile varup 'īş [ü] nūş éderler. Eger bir rūzgār (29) ġālib eserse cezīreleriñ yā biri yā ikisi yerinden ḥarêket édüp buḥeyre üzre üstinde adamlar ile bir cānibden bir cānibe seyerān u deverān éder, (30) gūyā serīr-i bārgāh-ı ḥażret-i Süleymāndır, ḫalq bu cezīre ḥarêketlerinden ṣafā édüp "Zemānımızda şöyle oldı" deyü tefāḫur kesb éderler, aṣlā (31) bir kimseye żarar iṣābet etmez, ilā-mā-şā'allāh bu cezīrecikler böyle ḫalq olunmuşdur; "İnne'llāha 'alā külli şey'in qadīr." Ammā ġāyetü'l-ġāye rūzgār-ı rīḥ-i ṣarṣar (32) kār-ı şedīd olursa ol cezīreler ḥarêket éder, yoḫsa degme rūzgār ile ḥarêket etmez deyü naql éderler, ammā bu ḥaqīr bu İskenderiyyede (33) iken niçe kerre rīḥ-i 'aẓīmler esdi, ammā cezīre-yi mezbūreleriñ ḥarêkātların görmedim, ammā sekenātların her bār görürdüm, lākin taqrīr olunan māżī ḥāli (34) iḫtiyār kimselerden sü'āl etdim.

"Belī, Sulṭān 'Os̱mān Ḥotin seferine gitdigi sene bir 'aẓīm şiddet-i şitā olup rīḥ-i şedīdler esüp İslāmbol **[34b]** boġazı doñduġı sene bu şehirde rūzgār-ı zor-kārdan qıyāmetler qopup evler yıqılup diraḫt-i müntehālar kökinden çıqup havāda her aġaç (2) peftere gibi uçduġı sene bu cezīrecikler qırq elli gün bu Boyana Göli üzre serserī

Praise of the sparkling water-of-life. On one side is the Drin river, like the water of Kevser, and on the other side is Lake Boyana, the water of which is like "pure wine".[1]

Climes and latitudes of towns and countries. -----

The rising star of auspicious prosperity. -----

Churches of monks. -----

Cereals and plants. -----

Manufactured goods. -----

Meats and foodstuffs. -----

Fruits. -----

Beverages. -----

Natural wonders. The hand of the Almighty Creator fashioned seven grassy islands of various sizes in the middle of the lake, no bigger than one or two or three or five threshing-floors. During some years a violent storm arises and these little islands become dislodged and move to another part of the lake. Sometimes the islands even meet in the middle of the lake and join together. They each have a variety of shrubs and grassy plots. The townsfolk like to sail out to these little islands in their caiques for picnics. Sometimes a strong wind arises and one or two of the islands get dislodged and float from one end of the lake to the other, taking the people with them as though borne on the throne of King Solomon's audience-hall. The people delight in sailing about on the islands, and they boast of their exploits in years gone by. No one ever suffers any harm, for that is the nature of these islands — "God is capable of everything."[2] It takes an extremely strong wind to dislodge the islands, or so it is reported. There were quite a few storms during the time that I was in Shkodër, but I never saw those islands moving, though I did see them *not* moving. In my curiosity I questioned the old people about the past, and they related the following:

"In the year when Sultan Osman II advanced against Chotin,[3] there was a severe winter storm which caused even the Bosphorus in Istanbul to freeze over. Here in Shkodër the storm blew down houses and uprooted large trees, whirling them in the air like falconers' lures. That year, these little islands in Lake Boyana floated about for forty or

---

[1] For Kevser (Kawthar), see Koran 108:1; for "pure wine" see Koran 76:21.

[2] Koran 2:20, etc.

[3] In 1031/1621.

gezüp şināverlik édüp gāh şimāle ve gāh cenūba (3) ve gāh şarqa ve ġarba gezerlerdi" deyü zāl-i zemāne pīr-i fānīler ve kār-āzmūde-yi cihān-bīnler böyle ḥikāye eylediler, ve's-selām.

(4) *Sitāyiş-i buḥeyre-yi āb-ı zülāl-i Arnavud İskenderiyyesi.* Bu buḥeyre-yi āb-ı zülāl İskenderiyye qal'esi dibinde Boyana Göli nāmıyle şöhre-yi (5) şehr olmuş bir lezīz āb-ı ḥayāt göldür, dāyiren-mā-dār cirmi on bir mīl-i kebīrdir, ve şarqdan ġarba ṭūlānīce vāqı' olup Ebū'l-fetiḥ Meḥemmed Ḫān (6) bu qal'eyi dögdügi[1] ḥavāle olan Boyana Göli aşırı Torondoş dağı bir ṭop menzili qarşu yaqındır, mā'adā kenārları ba'īd bir (7) uzunca ḫalq olmuş şehd-i zülālden nişān verir bir ḫalīcdir kim yine qal'e qarşusındaki Torondoş dağında başı vardır, andan (8) çıqar; bir teferrüc-gāh-ı feraḥ-fezā yerdir. Bu maḥalden aşağı bu buḥeyreniñ ayağı dörd sā'at cānib-i ġarba aqup giderek niçe bāġ u besātīnleri rey (9) éderek körfez deryāsına maḫlūṭ olur. Ve qal'eniñ mebnī olduġı qayalarıñ dibinde on 'aded balıq dalyanları var, cümle mīrīdir, (10) bu dalyanlarda ve gölde ṣayd olunan māhīler cümle emīn ṭarâfından żabṭ u rabṭ olunup māli qal'e neferātlarınıñ aqlāmıdır, ve cāmi'-i (11) selāṭīnleriñ e'imme vü ḫuṭabālarınıñ vażīfe-yi mu'ayyeneleri bu dalyanlarıñ maḥṣūlından verilir.

Ve ol qadar māhī-yi munaqqaş-ı gūnāgūnlar çıqar, ḥadd [u] ḥisābın (12) ḫudā bilüp cihānı dutar. Evvelā pisi balıġı ve ṣazan balıġı ve levrek balıġı ve kefal balıġı aşağı deryādan gölüñ ayağıyle gelir, ve niçe biñ elvān māhī-yi (13) gūnāgūnuñ envā'ı bu gölde mevcūddur. Bā-ḫuṣūṣ bu İskenderiyye ḫalīcinde çıqan yılan balıġı ne Göli-kesride ve ne Oḫride ve ne Beşik göllerinde (14) çıqmaq iḥtimālleri yoqdur, bu İskendêriyye Buḥeyresinde çoq çıqar, ve semīn ü lezīz olup balıġı misk gibi qoqar, bu rāyiḥa-yı ṭayyibe daḫi bir diyār (15) göllerinīñ māhīlerine maḫṣūṣ degildir, illā bu İskenderiyye balıġına maḫṣūsdur. Ve ġāyetü'l-ġāye nāfi' yılan balıġıdır kim dünyāda naẓīri yoqdur, ḥummāya (16) ve ağrı ḫasteligine mübtelā olan kimesneler bu yılan balıġın pişirüp yéseler yāḫod başın kendüde götürseler bi-emri'llāh te'ālā ısıtmadan ve ağrı ḫaste(17)liginden ḫalāṣ olup şifā bulur, tā bu mertebe nāfi' yılan balıġı olur kim İskenderiyye şehrinde ḥummā ve ağrı ḫasteligi olmazdır. Ve bu buḥeyreniñ āb-ı nābın (18) dā'imā nūş édeniñ ṭabī'ati müleyyen olup sevdā ve ṣafrā ve balġam ve ṣudā' ve

---

[1] Text: *dögdüdügi.*

fifty days, from north to south and from east to west." This is what the old-timers told me.

Praise of the lake of Albanian Iskenderiyye (Lake Shkodër). The body of pure water at the foot of the fortress is known as Lake Boyana. It stretches lengthwise from east to west and is 11 miles in circumference. Mt. Tarabosh, which looms up on the other side of the lake, is a cannon's range distance. It was from there that Mehmed the Conquerer bombarded the fortress. The other banks stretch lengthwise, forming a kind of fresh-water strait, with Mt. Tarabosh at the mouth of it, where the water runs out of the lake. There is a delightful promenade at that end of the lake. From there a tributary flows westward for four hours until, after passing through vineyards and orchards, it empties into the sea. At the foot of the cliffs on which the fortress is built are 10 weirs for catching fish. These are state-owned; the income deriving from the fish caught in the weirs and in the lake is confiscated by the *emin* on behalf of the garrison of Shkodër fortress and goes to pay the salaries of the preachers and imams of the imperial (i.e., congregational) mosques in the city.

Many kinds of fish are caught in this lake, and in immense quantities. Plaice, carp, sea bass and mullet swim up the tributary from the sea into the lake. Eels are found in quantity and quality that outmatch those in the lakes of Kastoria, Ohrid, and Beşik. They are fat and have a musky scent that is peculiar to the eels of Lake Shkodër and not to be found elsewhere. Also, they are a marvelously beneficial fish. Anyone suffering from fevers and ailments can be cured by cooking and eating these eels, or merely by carrying eel-heads on their persons. Because of the presence of this type of musk-eel, the people of Shkodër suffer from no ills of any kind.

The pure water of this lake, when drunk regularly, brings about a loosening of the bowels and a cure for problems of the spleen and

qabż u inhidār[1] mis̱illi emrāż-ı muḫtelifelerden ḫalāṣ olur, tā bu mertebe (19) ṣuyı daḫi nāfi'dir. -----

(20) *Der beyān-ı kār [u] kesb-i ehālī-yi vilāyet.* Bir ṣınfı buḥeyresinde ṣayyād-ı māhīlerdir; bir bölügi 'askerī ṭā'ifesidir; ve bir zümresi tüccārān-ı berr [ü] biḥārdır; ve bir (21) fırqası ehl-i ṣanāyi'dir; ve bir qabīlesi sūḫtevāt 'ulemālarıdır; ve bir qavmı bāġbāndır, zīrā cümle yigirmi üç biñ 'aded bāġları vardır. Ve ġāyet Ferhād-vār (22) rencberlik édüp kār [u] kesblerine muqayyed şecī' ü fetā Arnavud ġāzīleri var. Ġayri milel[2] bu şehirde yoqdur.

Cümleniñ lisānları Arnavudcadır kim bir lisāna beñzemez, (23) zīrā bu Arnavud qavmınıñ ibtidā aṣl [u] fer'leri Mekke-yi mükerreme Qureyşīlerinden qavm-ı 'Arabdır, anıñiçün Arnavud lisānında ba'żı 'Arab elfāẓları vardır kim ḥālā ara(24)larında isti'māl olınur. Ve bu qavm-ı Arnabud bu İskender ve Avlonya daġlarından ṭulū' édüp lisān-ı Talyan-ı Firengile iḫtilāṭ éderek lisān-ı 'Arab ile (25) lisān-ı Fireng arasında lisān-ı Arnavudı ḥażret-i 'Ömer ḫilāfetinde peydā etdikleriniñ sebêbin ve qavm-ı Arnavuduñ aṣl [u] fer'lerin inşā'allāh maḥalliyle taḥrīr olunur. Ammā şimdi (26) *der faṣl-i lisān-ı Arnavud ve 'Ārnābūd* deyü qavm-ı 'Acem laqab demişler, ve niçe müverriḫler qavm-ı 'Ārnābūd yazmışlar, ammā lezīz lisāndır, (27) birbirlerine i'zāz [u] ikrām ile tevāżu'āne ve ḥilmāne kelimāt éderler. Gerçi kefereleri millet-i mesīḥīden geçinürler, ammā ol daḫi İşpanya [ve] Venedik kefereleriniñ ibrāmlarıdır, (28) yoḫsa mecūsī gibi ne kitāb ve ne ḥaşr u neşirden bir şey bilmezler, bir alay kitāpsız kefere vü fecerelerdir kim lisānları budur.

---

[1] For *inḥidār* "swelling".

[2] Altered from *millet*?

gall-bladder, and for phlegm, headaches, constipation, swellings, and similar illnesses. -----

Professions. There are fishermen, soldiers, merchants who trade on land and sea, handicraftsmen, scholars and ulema, and vintners for the 23,000 vineyards. This place is the home of brave and diligent Albanian ghazis, who, like Ferhad, earn their living by hard toil.[1] There are no other nationalities in this city.

[*Language.*] They all speak Albanian, which is like no other tongue. In origin, the Albanians were one of the Arab tribes of Quraysh in Mecca. That is why there are some Arabic words still in use among them. When these Albanian tribesmen emerged from the mountains of Shkodër and Vlora, they mingled with the Italian Franks, and so, during the caliphate of Omar,[2] produced a language between Arabic and Frankish. We will give an account of the reason for this and of the origin of the Albanians in another place. For now — *Language of the Albanians* — it is called the language of *Arnavud* or, in Persian, *'Ār-nā-būd* ("May there be no shame"),[3] and certain chroniclers write it this way. It is a delightful language which they speak humbly and gently when addressing one another with respect. The infidels among them pass as Christians, although this, too, is at the insistence of the Spaniards and the Venetians. Otherwise, they are a company of scriptureless infidels and fornicators who, like the Zoroastrians, know nothing of the Book or of Judgment Day. Their language is as follows:

---

[1] Ferhad is a figure in Persian and Turkish romance who performs tremendous feats with his pick.

[2] 'Umar ibn al-Khattab, the second caliph (reg. 13-23/634-644)

[3] Evliya is giving a fanciful Persian etymology to explain the origin of *Arnavud* which is the Turkish word for Albanian.

Evvelā: *pörtuni zoti* Allāh ḥaqqıyçün démekdir.

(29) Bey‘ ü şirā maḥallinde aqçe ḥisābları böyle ‘add olunur. Evvelā: *ñe* 1 *dü* 2 *tiri* 3 *qotrá* 4 *pensı* 5 *gâşt* 6 *iştat* 7 *tetı* 8 *nandı* 9 *d̠it* 10.

(30) *falemi müre* selām ‘aleyküm adam *aye şendoş enbahi* ey ḫoş mısın *mir niştıra nişe* ṣabāḥıñ ḫayr ola *miliserde* (31) *palá mizuni* ----- *buq* ekmek *uy* ṣu *miş* et *dele* qoyun *pulı* ṭavuq *bayá müre* gel adam *aha buq* ekmek yer misin (32) *qu qiye* nerede idiñ *miyalt* bal *aqi te ki* arpa var mı *nuqu qám* yoqdur

First, *pörtuni zoti*[1] "For God's sake!" When buying and selling they count coins thus: *ñe*[2] 1 *dü*[3] 2 *tiri*[4] 3 *qotrá*[5] 4 *pensı*[6] 5 *gâşt*[7] 6 *iştat*[8] 7 *tetı*[9] 8 *nandı*[10] 9 *d̠it*[11] 10. *falemi müre*[12] "Greetings, men." *aye şendoş enbahi*[13] "Hey, are you well?" *mir niştıra nişe*[14] "Good morning." *miliserde*[15] ["Welcome."] *palá mizuni*[16] ["Thank you."] *buq*[17] "bread" *uy*[18] "water" *miş*[19] "meat" *dele*[20] "sheep" *pulı*[21] "hen" *bayá müre*[22] "Come, man." *aha buq*[23] "Will you eat bread?" *qu qiye*[24] "Where have you been?" *miyalt*[25] "honey" *aqi te ki*[26] "Is there barley?" *nuqu qám*[27] "There isn't."

---

[1] Mod. Alb. *për tynëzot* "for the Lord's sake."
[2] Mod. Alb. *një* "one."
[3] Mod. Alb. *dy* "two."
[4] Mod. Alb. *tre* (m.), *tri* (f.) "three."
[5] Mod. Alb. *katër* "four."
[6] Mod. Alb. *pesë* "five."
[7] Mod. Alb. *gjashtë* "six."
[8] Mod. Alb. *shtatë* "seven."
[9] Mod. Alb. *tetë* "eight."
[10] Mod. Alb. *nëntë* "nine."
[11] Mod. Alb. *dhjetë* "ten."
[12] Mod. Alb. *falemi, burra* "Greetings, men." The greeting *të falem* is still used by elderly people in Albania.
[13] Mod. Alb. *a je shëndosh, a mbaheni* "Are you well, are you keeping up?" The second verb, in contrast to the first, is in the respectful plural *ju* form. One would normally expect either the familiar singular *a je shëndosh, a mbahesh* or the respectful plural *a jeni shëndosh, a mbaheni.*
[14] Mod. Alb. *mirë ndeshtrasha* "greetings", i.e. *mirë ndesh (ty) të rasha*, a greeting still used in Shkodër dialect. Cf. *ndeshtrashë* n.f. "unexpected occurrence, event, meeting."
[15] Mod. Alb. *mirë se erdhe* "welcome."
[16] Mod. Alb. *të falem shumë.*
[17] Mod. Alb. *bukë* "bread."
[18] Mod. Alb. *ujë* "water."
[19] Mod. Alb. *mish* "meat."
[20] Mod. Alb. *dele* "sheep."
[21] Mod. Alb. *pulë, pula* "hen, chicken."
[22] Mod. Alb. *pa eja, burra* "Come on, men." In Shkodër dialect one often encounters the reduced form *p'eja.*
[23] Mod. Alb. *a ha bukë* "Do you eat bread?"
[24] Mod. Alb. *ku qe* "Where have you been?"
[25] Mod. Alb. *mjaltë* "honey."
[26] Mod. Alb. *elb ti ke* "Do you have barley?" There does not seem to be any trace of an early **aki* for standard *elb* "barley."
[27] Mod. Alb. *nuk kam* "I haven't." The negative form *nuku*, for standard *nuk*, now occurs primarily in the southern dialect of Korça.

ruş üzüm *aqi mebe teşin qurd* (33) arpa getir yoqsa başıñ yararın *pörtuni zoti nuqu qám aqi* Allāh ḥaqqıyçün yoqdur arpa *ṭámu* ana *motrá* qız qarındaş *şoke* 'avret. (34) Yava sözlerdir ammā seyyāḥlara lāzımdır, belki sögeler yāḫod dögeler. *hak mut* boq ye *tıkifşatı ṭámu* anañı filan edeyim *tıkifşatı şoke* 'avrêdiñ **[35a]** filān édeyim *tı pirişte bıhund* burnuña yelleneyim ya'nī ḍarṭa çalayım *tıkifşatı büṯı* edebde götiñi filan édeyim *iç qıvırdım* (2) puşt gidi démekdir. Ḥāṣıl-ı kelām, dervīşler 'ālem-i seyāḥatde böyle lisānları da bilüb kendüye şütūm etdikleri yére varmayup āsūde-ḥāl ola.

(3) *Der vaṣf-ı tetimme-yi şehr-engīz-i şehr-i İskenderiyye.* Varoşı içre Nehr-i Dirinaz üzre iki 'aded cisirleri var, biri Ḥüseyn Beg köprüsidir, ve (4) biri 'Alī Politina köprüsidir, ----- ////

(9) *Der beyān-ı ziyāretgāh-ı İskenderiyye.* Evvelā qal'e qapusınıñ iç yüzinde *ziyāret-i Ġāzī Muyo Baba* quddise sırruhu'l-'azīz. /

(11) Bu qal'eyi seyr [ü] temāşā édüp ve niçe aḥvālātlarına vāqıf-ı esrār olup bir gün mīr-livā Yūsuf-beg-zāde Meḥemmed Paşa ile İskenderiyyeden qalqup (12) cānib-i şimāle 2 sā'at gidüp *sitāyiş-i qaṣaba-yı Buşaṭlar.* Bu rabṭa-yı müzeyyeneye bir alay-ı 'aẓīm ile girüp Meḥemmed Paşa sarāyında mekṡ édüp (13) ba'de'ż-żiyāfe derūn-ı sarāy-ı bihişt-ābād[d]a qonağımıza varup andan bu qaṣabanıñ daḫi seyr [ü] temāşāsına şürū' eyledik. Nehr-i Dirin kenārında bir

ruş[1] "grapes" *aqi mebe teşin qurd*[2] "Bring barley or I'll split your head open." *pörtuni zoti nuqu qám aqi*[3] "For God's sake, there is no barley." *ṭámu*[4] "mother" *motrá*[5] "sister" *şoke*[6] "wife". The following are foolish expressions, but the traveller needs to know them since he might be the object of cursing or a beating: *hak mut*[7] "Eat shit!" *tıkifşatı ṭámu*[8] "I'll fuck your mother." *tıkifşatı şoke*[9] "I'll fuck your wife." *tı pirişte bıhund*[10] "I'll fart in your nose." *tıkifşatı büṯı*[11] "I'll fuck your ass." *iç qıvırdım*[12] "catamite, pimp." In short, when dervishes are travelling, they should know such expressions as well, so that they can avoid trouble by not going to places where they will be abused.

Conclusion of the eulogy (şehrengiz) of Shkodër. In the open town there are two bridges over the Drin river, the Hüseyn Beg bridge and the Ali Politina bridge. -----

Places of pilgrimage. Inside the fortress is the shrine of Muyo Baba, may his mystery be sanctified.

After touring this fortress and learning its ins and outs, we departed Shkodër with the *sancak-beg*, Yusuf-beg-Zade Mehmed Pasha, and travelled 2 hours north to the town of Bushat.[13] We entered this pretty town in grand procession and proceeded to the palace of Mehmed Pasha. After a rest and a sumptuous meal, we were shown our quarters in this paradisiacal palace, then set off to visit the

---

[1] Mod. Alb. *rrush* "grapes."

[2] Unclear, possibly Mod. Alb. **aki më bjerr, të ikën kryet*, i.e. "Bring me *aki*, otherwise your head will be off."

[3] Mod. Alb. *për tynëzot nuk kam *aki* "In the name of our Lord, I have no *aki*."

[4] Mod. Alb. *t'ëma*, Shkodër dialect *e ama, t'ama* "mother."

[5] Mod. Alb. *motër, motra* "sister."

[6] Mod. Alb. *shoqe, shoqja* "wife, companion, comrade (f.)."

[7] Mod. Alb. *ha mut* "Eat shit."

[8] Mod. Alb. *të qifsha të amë* "I'll fuck your mother." First person optative of the verb *qij* "to fuck" plus accusative of *jot amë*. This expression, in the standard form *të qifsha nënën*, is one of the most commonly heard expletives in the Albanian language today.

[9] Mod. Alb. *të qifsha të shoqe* "I'll fuck your wife."

[10] Mod. Alb. *të pjerdhsha mbë hund* "I'll fart in (your) nose," an insult still known in Shkodër. First person optative of the intrans. verb *pjerdh* "to fart" plus the Geg preposition *mbë* for standard *në*.

[11] Mod. Alb. *të qifsha (në) bythë* "I'll fuck your ass."

[12] Mod. Alb. *i shkërdhyem* "fucked." Passive past participle of the verb *shkërdhej* "to fuck" with the Geg ending *-yem*. A common insult in modern Albanian, especially in the Tirana dialect form *shkërdhatë*.

[13] Tk. Buşatlar. Bushat is in fact 15 km. south of Shkodër.

feraḥ- (14) fezā maḥṣūllı ve çemenzār u lāle-ʿizār u marġzār u ḥadīqa-yı cenīn ü ġayṭānlı bāġ-ı irem mis̱āl bir vādīde bir maʿmūr u müzeyyen ü şīrīn rabṭadır. (15) Cümle sekiz yüz ʿaded taḥtānī vü fevqānī cümle seng-binā bir qaṣaba-yı zībādır kim nıṣfı kiremit ve nıṣfı qayaġan örtüli evlerdir. Cümleden sarāy-ı (16) muʿaẓẓam Yūsuf-beg-zāde sarāyıdır kim Ebū'l-fetiḥ Meḥemmed H̱āndan berü cedd-i ʿiẓāmı Qoca Yūsuf Begden berü kendülere irs̱ ile intiqāl etmiş sarāy-ı (17) milk-i mevrūs̱larıdır, qat-ender-qat ḥücre ve qāʿa ve dīvān-ẖāneler ile ārāste* ve maṭbaḫ ve kilar ve tevābiʿāt ḥücreleriyle pīrāste* olmuş sarāy-ı ẖāṣṣadır. (18) Bir cāmiʿ-i müferriḥi ve bir mescidi ve bir medrese ve bir ḥammām-ı dil-güşā ve bir ẖān-ı zībā ve elli ʿaded dekākīn-i raʿnāsı cümle Yūsuf-beg-zādeleriñ ẖayrāt-ı (19) ḥasanātlarıdır. -----

(20) Ḥaqīr bu qaṣabayı daḫi teferrüc édüp Melek Aḥmed Paşa efendimiziñ māli taḥṣīl olunca bunda mihmān olmaq iqtiżā etdikde tażyīʿ-i evqāt olmasın (21) içün ḥaqīr begden yigirmi ʿaded ṭabankeş pür-silāḥ piyāde Arnavud yigitleri refīq alup *Qoṭur ve Qara Daġlara gitdigimiz yolları beyān éder.* (22) Ḥaqīr-i pür-taqṣīr begden ẖarc-ı rāh ve her qalʿe qapudanlarına mektūb ----- alup İskenderiyyeden cānib-i ġarba qara daġlıq içre ----- sāʿat gidüp

(23) *Evṣāf-ı qalʿe-yi intihā-yı serḥadd-i māric, yaʿnī ḥiṣār-ı bī-emān-ı sūr-ı Podġoric.* Lisān-ı Arnavudca ----- demekdir. (24) Sene 883 tārīẖinde Ebū'l-fetḥ-i meġāzī yaʿnī Sulṭān Meḥemmed-i s̱ānī-yi ġāzī qalʿe-yi İskenderiyyeyi fetḥ etdikde ʿArnavud ʿaşqıyāsı ve keferesi Venedik feceresinden (25) İskenderiyye emn ü emān olmaq içün sene-yi mezbūrede bu qalʿeyi bi'z-zāt Sulṭān Ebū'l-fetih binā etmişdir. Qara Daġ nām bir sengistān-ı bī-emān içinde (26) çār-güşe bir seng-binā-yı metīn ve burc [u] bārūları ve dendān-ı bedenleri sedd-i ḥaṣīn bir qapulı ve kesme qaya ẖandaqlı bir qalʿe-yi cedīddir. İçinde dizdārı (27) ve yediyüz ʿaded yarar u bahadır pā-bürehne ve ser-bürehne qotur şehbāz u dilāver ü zorāver u şehnāz yigitleri var, şeb [ü] rūz Qoṭur kāfirleriyle ceng [ü] cidāl (28) ve ḥarb [u] qıtāl etmede mücāhid-fī-sebīli'llāh ġāzīlerdir.

Ammā libāsları ġāyet mużḥikāne libāslardır, sevāhil diyār olmaġile āb [u] havāsı leṭāfetinden (29) ẖalqınıñ qadd [u] qāmetleri çınār-ı bālālar gibi serāmed fidāyī yigitlerdir. Başları Adana qabaġı qadar büyükdür ve bāzūları ṭoẖuma gelmiş dolma qabaġı qadar (30) qalın bāzūları var ve sīne-yi pür-kīneleri ẖusrevānī küp gibi güm gü[m]

town. It is situated on a pleasant fertile grassy plain along the banks of the Drin. The plain is full of gardens, and is as thriving and sweet and pleasant as any garden of paradise. The town has 800 two-story stonework houses, with half the roofs covered in tiles and half in slate. The grandest of these is the palace of the Yusuf-beg-zades, inherited from their ancestor Koca Yusuf Beg who lived at the time of Mehmed the Conqueror. It is a huge multi-storied imperial palace, with many rooms, parlors, halls, kitchens, pantries and servants' quarters. The town also has a spacious congregational mosque, a prayer-house, a *medrese*, a heart-warming bathhouse, a fine *han* and 50 splendid shops, all endowed by the Yusuf-beg-zades. -----

After a pleasant excursion through the town, we took our leave of Yusuf Beg and set off, realizing that he would need much time to fulfil his obligations to Melek Ahmed Pasha, and not wishing to lose time ourselves. As escorts, the *beg* sent us twenty armed Albanian foot-soldiers. *Journey to Mt. Kotor and Montenegro (Kara Dağ).* He also gave me money for the journey and a letter for each of the fortress commanders we would visit. -----

Leaving Shkodër, we journeyed westwards through mountainous terrain (*kara dağlık*) and after ----- hours arrived at *the merciless*[1] *fortress of Podgorica, which is at the extreme frontier.* The name is Albanian and means ----- . It was built by Sultan Mehmed the Conqueror in the year 883 (1478) when he conquered the fortress of Shkodër in order to protect the latter from Albanian brigands and Venetian infidels. It is a new, quadrangular, sturdy stone construction, on a stony tract known as Montenegro (*Kara Dağ*), and has towers, ramparts, serrated battlements, a single gate, and a moat hewn out of the rock cliff.

Inside are the castle warden with 700 garrison troops — bareheaded and barefooted, rough and ready, doughty warriors all! They are ghazis, engaged in the jihad, and battling day and night with the infidels of Kotor. Their uniforms, however, are quite ridiculous. Because it is a coastal region and the climate is mild, these commando warriors grow tall as plane trees, their heads get as big as Adana pumpkins, their upper arms as thick as squashes bursting with seeds, and their chests swollen like imperial crocks[2] which resound when

---

[1] In addition to this epithet, Evliya also uses here *māric* ("flame without fire") for the sake of a rhyme with Podġoric.

[2] *ḫusrevānī küp*; see Dankoff 1991b *Glossary*, 98.

ṣadā verir vāsi‘ [ü] ‘arīż ṣadr-ı mücessemleri var, ya‘nī merd-i kelām bu mertebe (31) cüssede olan ġāzīler olqadar ten-dürüst ve zinde ve cüst ü çāpük ü çālākdir. Cümle silāḥlarıyle qayadan qayaya Baġdād ġazāli gibi (32) pertāb éder, zīrā "Ḫayru's-s̱iyāb qaṣīr" ḥadīs̱i üzre es̱vābları ol mertebede ḫafīfdir kim ol cüsse-yi kebīrleriñ üzerinde gūyā es̱vāb (33) ol[ma]ya. Ayaqlarında cümle ṣıqma çarıqdır ve "Baldır duruda" dédikleri gibi baldırı çıplaqdır, ḥattā donları bile yoqdur, hemān bellerin[d]e birer dimi (34) bol paçaları var. Eks̱eriyyā gömlek nedir bilmezler, eginlerinde birer masḫara daracıq ve qıṣacıq kebe geyerler, gögüsleri ve omuz başları cümle açıqdır. **[35b]** Ve kelem serleri neqadar qazan qadar ise olqadar küçücük ṭāqıyyeleri var kim ancaq bir fincān qadarca ṭāqıyyeyi iplikile iki yanından baġlayup (2) boġazına ipligi geçirüp ṭāqıyyeyi başına geyer, ammā ḫudā ‘ālimdir eyle kelle-yi kebīr üzre ol ṭāqıyye gūyā ‘āriyeti durur, geyilecek ḥāli (3) yoq bir ‘araqıyye-yi siyāhdır.

İşte bu gūne bir alay ġāziyān-ı sipāhdır. Her bār çete ve potura qovup ceng éderler kim Qoṭur kāfiriniñ ve (4) Kilimente[1] ve Qara Daġ Arnavud kāfirleriniñ gözlerin qorqudup ödlerini ṣındırmış ġāziyān-ı Podġoriçsedir. İskenderiyye sancaġı ḫākinde (5) ṣubaşılıqdır ve nevāḥī nāyibi ḥükm éder, ġayri ḥākimleri yoqdur. Derūn-ı ḥiṣārda cümle üçyüz ‘aded daracıq ḫānecikleri ve bir Ebū'l-fetiḥ cāmi‘i (6) ve buġday enbārları ve mükellef cebe-ḫāne ve ṭopları ve ṣu ṣarnıçları var, ġayri ‘imāret ve ḫān ve medrese ve ḥammām ve çārsū-yı bāzārları (7) yoqdur.

Bu qal‘eden Venedigiñ Qoṭur qal‘esine vere ile gidüp temāşā etmek murād édindigimizde qal‘e neferātları rıżā vermediler, (8) meger Qoṭur kāfirleriyle vereleri bozġun imiş. Bir daḫi inşā'allāh fetḥinde bulunup seyr éderiz. "El-ümūru merhūnetün be-evqātihā" deyü Qoṭura (9) gitmeden fāriġ olup Podġoriçden cānib-i şimālde nīm-sā‘at ba‘īd bir püşte-yi ‘ālī üzre ḥaqīr çıqup *qal‘e-yi Qoṭur* Nova Körfezi (10) kenārında bir qaya üzre ḥavālesi çoq bir küçük qal‘e nümāyān idi. Bu qal‘eniñ cenūbında on qonaq yeriñ iki ṭarâfı Venedik (11) Körfezi deryāsıdır, ġarb ṭarâfı Nova Körfezi deñizidir.

---

[1] *K*- altered to *Q*-.

struck. Despite their huge bodies, these well-spoken ghazis are very robust and agile, springing from cliff to cliff with their weapons like Baghdad gazelles. And in accordance with the hadith, "The best garment is short,"[1] their garments are so light, it is as though there were no garment at all on those huge bodies. On their feet they wear tight-fitting rawhide sandals. And in accordance with the expression, *Baldır duruda* ("It is honey when it is still"), they leave their calves uncovered (*baldırı çıplak*),[2] and do not even wear breeches but just a pair of fustian trousers attached to the waist. Most do not know what a shirt is, but instead wear a ridiculous short and narrow felt jacket which leaves their chests and shoulderblades uncovered. Funny-looking also is the tiny headpiece — the size of a cup, to cover their kettle-sized cabbage-shaped heads! — which is tied at the sides and fixed with string around their necks. God knows what a makeshift look those little black skullcaps have atop those huge heads. They are a band of ghazi horsemen who go out raiding and putting the fear of God into the Albanian infidels of Kotor, Kelmendi and Montenegro.

Podgorica is ruled by a *subaşı* in the *sancak* of Shkodër. The deputy *kadi*s hold sway in the surrounding countryside; there are no other officials. Inside the fortress are 300 small houses, a mosque of Sultan Mehmed the Conqueror, several storehouses for grain, artillery depots, and water cisterns. There are no other public buildings, whether *han*s, *medrese*s, bathhouses, or *bedestan*s.

I had planned to go under the banner of truce and tour the Venetian fortress of Kotor, but the garrison soldiers would not permit it, arguing that the truce with Kotor had been broken. So I gave the plan up, hoping that I would be present when, God willing, Kotor was conquered, and tour it then — "Events are hostage to their assigned times." Instead, I climbed to the top of a high hill half an hour north of Podgorica, and from there I caught a glimpse of the fortress of Kotor. It is very small, built on a cliff at the edge of the Bay of Nova, and surrounded by higher points. The Gulf of Venice stretches for ten stages south of Kotor on either side of the peninsula, the Bay of Nova being on the western side.

---

[1] Evliya often cites this Prophetic dictum when discussing fashion of clothing, e.g. I 148a.1, II 341b.29, III 56b29, etc.

[2] *baldırı çıplak*, meaning something like "sans-coulotte," is a well-known expression. Evliya no doubt intends a play on words; however, the expression *baldır duruda* is otherwise unknown, and the meaning suggested here is quite conjectural.

Bu iki deñiz mābeyni on qonaq yere varınca sevād-ı mu'aẓẓam bir burundur kim (12) Mora vilāyetinde Manya burnı gibi cengelistān ve sengistān yalçın ve bī-ḥāṣıl dağlardır kim nıṣfına Qara Dağlar ve nıṣfına Kilimente dağları (13) derler. Qırq yedi biñ tüfeng-endāz zīr[1] [ü] zeber-dest Arnavud kāfirleridir kim muqaddemā İskenderiyyeye tābi'ler idi, cezīre-yi Girid ġazāsından berü (14) bu kāfirler Venedige tābi' olup Qandiye qal'esine imdāda gider. Ve bu Kilimente Burnında yedi pāre qal'eler cümle Venedik ḥükmindedir kim (15) qapudanları Fireng ve 'askerīsi cümle Arnavud kefereleridir.

Bu dağlarda daḫi niçe 'ibret-nümā temāşālar édüp Podġoriçden qalqup cānib-i cenūba (16) sengistān içre pür-silāḥ āmāde giderken *evṣāf-ı qal'e-yi Buduva.* Evvel ü āḫir Venedik Firengi qal'esidir. Leb-i deryāda (17) şekl-i murabba' şeddādī seng-binā bir küçük beyāż qal'e-yi ra'nādır. Bizim 'askeri görüp qal'eden ḫayli ḫaber ṭopları atup bir ṭabyası üzre bir 'ālī (18) gemi sereniniñ zirve-yi a'lāsına bir fılandıra bayraq qaldırdı ve leb-i deryāda olan cümle ——[2] qullelerinde ṭarfetü'l-'ayn içre āteşler yanup (19) dūdları evc-i semāya kehkeşān-āsā 'urūc édüp her qulleden birbirlerine işāret ṭopları atdılar, zīrā bizi çeteci ve nehb ü ġāretci ẓann etdiler.

(20) Bizler daḫi bī-bāk ü bī pervā Buduva qal'esine qurbından ----- (21) *evṣāf-ı sengistān-ı vādī-yi nār, ya'nī sedd-i üstüvār, qal'e-yi Bar.* Lisān-ı Arnavudca ----- demekdir. Bānīsi Pulya (22) qıral bināsıdır kim bu qal'e ibtidā İşpanya qıralı ḥükminde idi, ba'dehu Orḫan Ġāzī 'aṣrında Bunduqani Venedigi destine girüp andan sene 883 de (23) fetḥ-i Ebū'l-fetiḥ Ġāzī qabżasına girdi. İskenderiyye sancağında voyvadalıqdır ve Ülgün nevāḥīlerinden olup niyābetdir. Qal'e dizdārı ve ----- 'aded (24) müke[lle]f ü mükemmel ü pür-silāḥ ġāzī yigitleri cümle şehbāz Arnavud şehnāzlarıdır kim fırqatalarıyle dāyimā Pulya vilāyetleri ve İşpanya ve Qlora (25) qıyıların ve 'āṣī Venedik qal'elerin ve Qara Da[ġ] ve Kilimente[3] Arnavudların qırup qılıçdan geçirüp sālimīn ü ġānimīn qal'elerine dāyimā ṭoq (26) doyum gelirler ve aṣlā boş gelmezler, elbette bir ṭarafdan bir şikār ile gelirler.

---

[1] Text: *dīv.*
[2] Word illegible, perhaps *fırqata.*
[3] Text: *Kimilente.*

Between these two bodies of water there is a large headland, like the Mania peninsula in the *vilayet* of Morea, extending for ten stages. It consists of thickets and barren mountains. Half the mountains are called Montenegro and the other half Kelmendi. They are the home of 47,000 infidel Albanian musketeers. Formerly they were subject to Shkodër, but since the war in Crete they have gone over to the Venetian side and have departed to assist the fortress of Candia. On this Cape of Kelmendi are seven fortresses ruled by the Venetians. While the naval commanders are Franks (i.e., Venetians), the garrison soldiers are all Albanian infidels.

After some pleasant mountain excursions, we set off fully armed in a southern direction over stony ground and arrived at *the fortress of Budva*. This has been in the hands of the Venetian Franks from the very start. It is a graceful little white stone fortress, square in shape, at the edge of the sea. When they saw our soldiers they fired warning shots from their cannons and raised a banner at the tip of a ship's mast above one of the bastions. At once fires were lit in all of the ——[1] towers and smoke rose up like the Milky Way. Supposing us to be a band of armed marauders, they began firing warning shots to each other from every tower. We nonetheless proceeded fearlessly past the fortress of Budva. -----

The rocky Valley of Fire, the impregnable fortress of Bar. The name is Albanian and means ----- . It was built by the kings of Puglia and was initially ruled by the kingdom of Spain. Later, during the reign of Orhan Ghazi, it was taken over by the Venetians. Sultan Mehmed the Conqueror entered Bar in 883 (1478). It is the seat of a *voyvoda* in the *sancak* of Shkodër and of a deputy *kadi* of the district of Ulcinj. It has a warden and ----- garrison soldiers. These are all splendidly-armed and courageous Albanian ghazis who constantly sail across the sea on their frigates to plunder the territory of Puglia, the coast of Calabria and Spain,[2] and the Venetian fortresses. They put the (infidel) Albanian troops of Kelmendi and Montenegro to the sword and return to Bar safe and sound and weighed down with plunder.

---

[1] Illegible, perhaps "frigate."

[2] I.e., Calabria, the region at the extreme SE part of the Italian peninsula, at this period still part of the Spanish empire.

Bu qal'e Venedik Körfezi deryāsı sāḥilinde ----- (27) ----- üzre şekl-i murabba' bir seng-binā-yı muṣanna' qal'e-yi muraqqa'dır. Derūn-ı ḥiṣār[d]a cümle ----- 'aded kiremit (28) ve qayaġan örtüli bāġçesiz neferāt evleridir. Sulṭān Meḥemmed cāmi'i ve mekteb [ü] medresesi ve bir mescidi ve bir ġılāl enbārı ve cebe-ḫāne ḫazīnesi (29) ve ṣu ṣarnıçları ve mükellef iri ṭopları ve ----- qapusı me mihter-ḫāne qullesi ve ḫandaqı ----- /////

[36a] *Evṣāf-ı binā-yı qotur*(?)*-ı gülgūn, ya'nī serḥadd-i intihā-yı qal'e-yi Ülgün.* Lisān-ı ----- demekdir. (2) Ve sebeb-i tesmiyesi ----- ġalaṭdır. Bānīsi yine İşpanya keferesidir kim baş irşeklerinin̄ ḫāṣṣı (3) idi. Ba'de[hu] Venedik bir taqrīb şeyṭanet ile müstevlī olup anın̄ elinden sene 883 Ebū'l-fetiḥ vezīri Hersek-oġlı Aḥmed Paşaya bu qal'e (4) miftāḥların teslīm édüp kendüleri dārü'l- bevār menḥūs ḫānelerine gitdiler. Ba'dehu Meḥemmed Ḫān bu qal'eyi geregi gibi 'amār édüp İskenderiyye sancaġı (5) begi ḫāṣṣı taḥrīr édüp ḥālā voyvadalıqdır ve yüz elli aqçe qażādır. Qal'esi Venedik Körfezi kenārında ----- üzre şekl-i müseddes (6) seng-ṭırā[ş*] berā-yı ṣavaş* perḫāş* bir qal'e-yi ḥāżır-bāşdır. Burc [u] bārūları ve dendān-ı bedenleri ve metīn dervezeleri ve mazġal delikleri ve (7) ḫandaqları ve cemī'ī mühimmāt [u] levāzimātları ile ma'mūr u müzeyyen qal'e-yi zībādır. Ve derūn-ı ḥiṣārda Meḥemmed Ḫān cāmi'i ve cümle ----- 'aded (8) neferāt evleri serāpā ----- mestūr ḫāneciklerdir. Ẓahāyir enbārları ve cebe-ḫāne ḫazāyinleri ve ṣu ṣarnıçları var ve ġāyet mefret bal-yemez (9) ve kāfire emān vermez ṭopları var. Qal'e qapusı ön̄inde dizdār aġa lonca yerinde oṭurup yediyüz 'aded Arnavud ġāzīleri qal'e neferāt(10)larıyle muḥāfaża beklerler. Bunun̄ daḫi yarar u bahadır şecī' [ü] dilāver yigitleri var. Eks̱eriyyā şehbāzları fırqatacılardır. Bu qal'e leb-i deryāda vāqı' (11) olmaq ile yigirmi 'aded fırqataları qal'e limanında mevcūddur. Sāyir qaṣabalardan daḫi şehbāz Arnavud yigitleri gelüp fırqatalara girüp (12) kāfiristān yaqaların yaqa yıqa ḫarāb u yebāb éde bī-ḥisāb māl-i firāvānlar ve esīr-i mümtāzānlar alup manṣūr [u] mużaffer Ülgüne gelirler ve mīr-livāya (13) 'öşür verirler. Ḥatta bū ḥaqīr bu qal'eyi temāşāsında iken yedi 'aded fırqata Pulya kāfiristānında[n] māl-i ġanāyimle gelüp yedi fırqatadan (14) Yūsuf-beg-oġlına yigirmi bir bin̄ ġuruş 'öşr-i sulṭānī ve on yedi esīr düşüp ol daḫi Melek Aḥmed Paşa deynine bu ġazā mālinden (15) verdi-----

The fortress of Bar is a well-constructed, square-shaped stone fortress on ----- on the coast of the Gulf of Venice (Adriatic Sea). Inside are ----- houses of the garrison troops, covered with tile or slate roofs, but without gardens. There is a mosque of Sultan Mehmed the Conqueror, a school, a *medrese*, a prayer-house, a storehouse for grain, an armory, water cisterns, huge cannons, ----- gates, a military-band tower, and a moat. -----

The rose-colored (gülgun) fortress of Ülgün (Ulcinj), which is at the extreme frontier. The name, meaning ----- in the ----- language, has become corrupted to Ülgün (Ulcinj). The fortress was built by the Spanish infidels and was the *has* of their chief cardinal. The Venetians later took it over by a ruse. In 883 (1478) they delivered its keys to Ahmed Pasha Hercegolli, the vizier of Mehmed the Conqueror,[1] and delivered themselves to the abodes of hell. Mehmed Khan in turn registered it as the *has* of the *sancak-beg* of Shkodër. It is now administered by a *voyvoda* and has a *kadi* with a salary level of 150 *akçe*.

The stone-built fortress is hexagonal in shape and is situated on ----- on the coast of the Gulf of Venice. It is well-maintained and embellished with towers, ramparts, serrated battlements, embrasures, loopholes and moats, and is furnished with all major supplies. Inside are the mosque of Sultan Mehmed the Conqueror and ----- small houses for the garrison troops, all roofed with ----- . There are grain storehouses, armories, water cisterns and huge long-range battering guns. The castle warden resides in a loggia in front of the gate and 700 Albanian ghazis stand guard along with the garrison troops, brave and doughty warriors all. Most of them are frigate-men. There are 20 frigates in the harbor, as the fortress is situated on the coast. The Albanians here and from other towns take to their frigates and plunder infidel territory, burning and destroying, then return to Ulcinj with rich booty and choice captives, and give one-tenth of the spoils to the *sancak-beg*. When I was there, 7 frigates had just returned full of booty from the infidel lands of Puglia, and Yusuf-beg-oğlu received a tenth of the spoils, amounting to 21,000 *kuruş*, as well as 17 captives. With this money he paid off the debt he owed to Melek Ahmed Pasha.

---

[1] Hersek-zade Ahmed Paşa actually became a vizier only in 894/1489, during the reign of Bayezid II, and grand vizier in 902/1497. See Süreyyâ 1995-97, I, 195.

[36b] Andan tekrār *menzil-i qal'e-yi İskenderiyye*. Andan tekrār *menzil-i qaṣaba-yı Buşaṭlar*. Bunda bir géce daẖi paşa yanında mihmān olup (2) Melek Aḥmed Paşa efendimiziñ qarż-ı ḥasan verdigi māl içün Yūsuf-beg-zāde ḥaqīre on üc biñ ġuruşluq cümle Venedik altunların (3) ḥużūr-ı şer'de verüp ḥüccet-i şer'iyyeye geçüp bege ḥaqīr temessükātları verüp kibār (?) mümessek şaqq (?) olunduqda begden Melek Paşaya hedāyā (4) üç Fireng ġulāmı ve yigirmi 'aded altun ẓarflı sā'atlar ve bir incü tesbīḥ ve qırq ṭop dībā ve qırq ṭop Ciniviz qaṭīfesi ve muraṣṣa' (5) la'l-gūn mercān qabżalı ẖancer-i zū'l-ficām verüp bunlar daẖi mektūb-ı maḥabbet-üslūba qayd olup begden ḥaqīre üçyüz Venedik altunı (6) ve Bihzād nām bir İşpanya ġulāmı ve bir at ve bir qılıç verüp cümle tevābi' ü ġulāmlarıma onar altun ve birer çoqa ve qumāşlar verüp refīqler verdi. (7) Ertesi ----- *İskenderiyyeden İslāmbola giderken seyr [ü] temāşā etdigimiz qılā' u menāzilleri beyān éder.* //

(10) *Evṣāf-ı dār-ı ḥūt, ya'nī qal'e-yi Mut.* Lisān-ı Arnavudca ----- démekdir. Bānīsi İşpanya (11) qırallarıdır. Ba'dehu sene 884 tārīẖinde Ebū'l-fetiḥ Meḥemmed H̱ān Venedik kāfiri destinden emān ile fetḥ édüp İskenderiyye sancaġı taḥrīr olup (12) niyābetdir. Qal'esi Nehr-i Esim kenārında ----- üzre çār-gūşe ve çār-qulle bir kārgīr seng-binā-yı köhne qal'e-yi 'atīqdir. (13) Bu qal'e altından cerêyān éden Nehr-i Esimde yılda bir kerre olqadar balıq çıqar kim ḥadd [ü] ḥaṣrın cenāb-ı kibriyā bilir. Bazirgānlar bu balıqları ṭorlayup (14) cemī'ī kāfiristāna götürürler. Ġāyet lezīz ḥūtları oldugından niçe müverriẖān-ı Rūm-ı ān merz-ı būm bu qal'eye dār-ı ḥūt deyü tesmiye etdiler. (15) Zemān-ı qadīmde ḥaqqā ki metīn qal'eyimiş. Cānib-i ----- qapusı var ve ḥiṣār içre cümle ----- örtüli bāġçesiz daracıq neferāt (16) evleri ve Ebū'l-fetiḥ cāmi'i ve enbārları ve cebe-ẖāne maḥzenleri

From here we returned to Shkodër and from there to the town of Bushat where we spent one night as guests of the Pasha. Yusuf-beg-zade gave me musk-scented Venetian gold coins amounting to 13,000 *kuruş* to fulfil his obligations to Melek Ahmed Pasha. The transaction was recorded in a legal document, and I gave the *beg* an official receipt. He also gave me, as gifts for Melek Ahmed Pasha, 3 Frankish slaveboys, 20 watches in gold casings, 1 set of pearl prayer-beads, 40 rolls of brocade, 40 rolls of Genoese velvet and 1 dagger with a jewelled coral handle. These gifts were also listed in the letter for Melek Ahmed Pasha. To me he gave 300 Venetian gold coins, a Spanish slaveboy named Bihzad, a horse and a sword, and to each of my retinue and slaves he gave 10 gold coins and a length of cloth. He also furnished us some of his men as escorts.

The next day ----- *Castles and stageposts which we toured journeying from Shkodër to Istanbul.* ----- *The "House of Fish," i.e., the fortress of Mut.*[1] The name is Albanian for ----- . It was built by the kings of Spain and in 884 (1479) was taken from the Venetian infidels by Mehmed the Conqueror. Administratively, it belongs to the *sancak* of Shkodër and is the seat of a deputy *kadi*. Mut is situated on ----- on the banks of the Ishëm river.[2] It is an ancient stonework construction, square in shape and with four towers. Once a year an enormous multitude of fish appears in the Ishëm river flowing below this fortress. They are caught in nets and exported to Europe. The fish are so delicious that some local Greek historians have dubbed this fortress "House of Fish". There was said to be a mighty fortress here in ancient times.

The fortress has a single gate facing toward the ----- ; a total of ----- little houses for the garrison soldiers, with roofs but without gardens; a mosque of Sultan Mehmed the Conqueror; grain

---

[1] Ottoman sources (1560-74) record the toponym as Mus or Musje, site of the fortress of Ishëm, and said to be located at the mouth of the Ishëm river near Kruja (cf. Kornrumpf 1995, 148). Evliya's spelling is perhaps influenced by the rhyme with *ḥūt* "fish" and the like-sounding town of Mut in Anatolia which he mentions below, or perhaps there is a confusion with Mat (given that the mouths of the Ishëm and Mat rivers are very close to one another) or with Milot on the banks of the Mat. Babinger 1930, 56, implausably suggested an identification with the obscure settlement of Motri, which Marinus Barletius, in his 1504 description of the siege of Shkodër, says is 27 miles from Drivasto (Drisht).

[2] Tk. Esim. The Ishëm, ancient Isamnus (Vibius Sequester 149), was recorded in 1302 as Yssamo and in 1622 as Isemi. If Evliya was travelling from here on to Spas and Gjakova, he must have departed up the valley of the Mat, not the Ishëm.

ve kifāyet miqdārı şāhī ṭopları var. Dizdārı ḥākimdir ve voyvadası żābıṭdır (17) ve ikiyüz qadar neferātları var, cümle şehbāz Arnavud ġāzīleridir kim ġarīb-dostlardır, her kim müsāfir gelirse evlerine qondurup ikrām éderler. (18) Ġāyet ġanīmet dār-ı diyārdır kim balıġı meşhūrdur ve bāġ u bāġçeleri ve müşebbek būstānları var, āb [u] havāsınıñ leṭāfetinden maḥbūb u maḥbūbeleri var. (19) Ammā Anaṭolıda Silifke sancaġında bir daẖi Mut qal'esi vardır. ----- // (22) -----

Andan cānib-i şarqa ----- gidüp (23) *evṣāf-ı Yeñi Qal'e*. Sene 883 tārīẖinde Ebū'l-fetiḥ Meḥemmed Ḫān-ı s̱ānī bināsıdır. Rūm-éli eyāletinde Duqagin sancaġı ḥükminde (24) ṣubaşılıq ve niyābetdir, ġayri ḥākimleri yoqdur. Qal'esi bir daġ eteginde vāqı' olup gerçi seng-binādır ammā iç el olmaq ile bu (25) vilāyet qal'eye muḥtāc olmadıġından mürūr-ı eyyām ile qal'esi ẖarābdır, ammā dizdārı ve on 'aded neferātları ve kifāyet miqdārı şāhī ṭopları vardır. / (27) -----

Andan (28) *menzil-i qaṣaba-yı İspas*. Bu daẖi Duqagin sancaġı ẖākinde biñ ẖāneli ve biñ 'aded güzīde tüfengli 'Ārnābūd fetāları (29) var. Bir cāmi'i ve bir ẖānı ve beş on dükkānlı qaṣabacikdir. -----

Andan (30) *evṣāf-ı qaṣaba-yı Yaqoviçse*. Pojeġa sancaġında bir Yaqoviçse daẖi vardır, ammā bu Duqagin sancaġında ma'mūr u (31) müzeyyen iki biñ ẖāneli müzeyyen rabṭadır kim cümle ẖāneleri kārgīr ve ----- örtüli ve bāġçeli büyūtlardır. Ve ḥākimi voyvadadır. Ve yüz elli pāye(32)siyle a'lā qażādır. Cümle 'imāretleri bir ṣaḥrā-yı vāsi'e vāqı' olmuş. İki 'aded mükellef cāmi'i ve mesācidleri ve qurşumlı ẖānları içinde (33) ḥālā Qoṭur seferiyçün cebe-ẖāne ve bekṣumātlar mālāmāldir. Ve bir binā-yı müferriḥ-i dilgüşā ḥammām-ı rūşenāsı ve üçyüz qadar dükkān-ı hezār-āşināsı vardır. (34) Ve āb [u] havāsı leṭāfetinden maḥbūblar vardır.

[Üsküb]

storehouses; ammunition cellars; and a good number of brass muzzle-loading cannons. The warden is the governor (*hakim*) of the fortress and the *voyvoda* is the commanding officer. There are about 200 men, all brave Albanian ghazis and very hospitable to strangers — whenever travellers appear, they host them royally in their homes. Goods are cheap and plentiful. Aside from the famous fish, there are vineyards and orchards and well-kept gardens. Because of the mild climate, the young boys and girls are very pretty. There is another fortress of Mut in the *sancak* of Silifke in Anatolia. -----

From here we set off eastwards ----- and arrived at *Yeñi Kale ("New Fortress")*.[1] It was built by Sultan Mehmed the Conqueror in 883 (1478). It is situated in the *sancak* of Dukagjin in the *eyalet* of Rumeli, and has a *subaşı* and a deputy *kadi* — there are no other magistrates. It is built of stone and lies at the foot of a mountain. Because it is situated well within Ottoman territory, it has fallen into ruins with the passing of time. Nevertheless, it has a warden and 10 garrison soldiers and a good number of brass muzzle-loading cannons. -----

From here we set off and arrived at *the town of Spas*.[2] This also belongs to the *sancak* of Dukagjin. It is a little town, with 1000 houses, 1000 select Albanian musketeers, one congregational mosque, one *han*, and 5 or 10 shops. -----

Continuing on from here we arrived at *the town of Gjakova*.[3] There is elsewhere a Djakovo in the *sancak* of Požega, but this Gjakova is in the *sancak* of Dukagjin. It is a flourishing and attractive town consisting of 2000 houses, all of stone with ----- roofs and gardens. It is ruled by a *voyvoda* and has a *kadi* with a salary level of 150 *akçe*. The public buildings are situated on a broad plain. They include two richly-adorned congregational mosques; several prayer-houses; some *hans* with leaden roofs, which at present are stocked with biscuit and munitions for the Kotor campaign; a delightful bathhouse; and about 300 shops like nightingale-nests. Because of the mild climate, the young boys are very pretty.

[Skopje]

---

[1] Unidentified.

[2] The settlements of Spas and Hani i Spasit, situated on the Drin halfway between Fierza and Kukës, no longer exist, having been submerged with the damming of the river.

[3] In western Kosovo, Serbo-Croatian Djakovica, Tk. Yakoviçse.

PART III: SOUTHERN ALBANIA, 1670

[VIII 352a] (19) *Der taqrīrāt-ı eşkāl-i qal'e-yi Delvine.* Lisān-ı Arnavudca ----- demekdir. İbtidā bānīsi (20) İşpanyadır. Ba'dehu Bunduqani Venedik bir şeyṭanet ile istīlā édüp sene ----- tārīḫinde Sulṭān Bāyezīd-i Velī Venedik elinden (21) fetḥ édüp yine küffār istīlā etdikde sene ----- tārīḫinde Sulṭān Süleymān Ḫān Körfez ġazāsına geldikde 'Arnavudu'l-aṣl Ayas (22) Paşa Delvine qal'esi üzre sipehsālār-ı mu'aẓẓam ta'yīn olunup bi-dest-i vezīr-i a'ẓam Ayas Paşa Delvine qal'esi (23) fetḥ olunup pāy-taḫt-i mīr Delvine oldı. Ḥālā yine Rūm-éli eyāletinde başqa sancaqdır. Beginiñ ḫāṣṣı ṭaraf-ı pādişāhīden (24) 157132 aqçedir ve ze'ametleri 24 'adeddir ve erbāb-ı tīmārı 155 'adeddir. Alay begisi ve çeri başısı var. Ḥīn-i (25) ġazāda qānūn üzre bu livānıñ 'askeri cebelüleriyle ve beginiñ cündiyle cümle iki biñ ikiyüz 'asker olur. Yüz seksen (26) aqçe pāyesiyle qażā-yı āsmānīdir ve nāḥiyesi cümle ----- 'aded qurālardır. Cümle sancağında ----- 'aded qażālardır. Evvelā (27) qaża-yı ----- qaża-yı ----- qaża-yı ----- qaża-yı ----- qaża-yı ----- bunlar meşhūrdur. (28) Şeyḫü'l-islāmı ve naqībü'l-eşrāfı ve sipāh ketḫüd[ā] yeri, yeñiçeri serdārı, qal'e dizdārı [-----] 'aded qal'e neferātları ve şehriñ (29) ṣubaşısı, bācdārı, şehir ketḫüdāsı, muḥtesib ağası, ḫarāc ağası vardır.

Qal'esi bir sivri qayanıñ tā zirve-yi a'lā(30)sında şekl-i muḫammes bir şeddādī seng-binā bir qal'e-yi ra'nā-yı muṣanna'dır kim lā-nażīr qabīlindendir, ammā küçükdür, dāyiren-mā-dār (31) cirmi altıyüz adımdır. Aṣlā bir ṭarâfında ḫandaqı yoqdur, Ve cānib-i şarqa bir demir qapusı var. Derūn-ı qal'ede üç 'aded kire(32)mitli ḫānecikleri var, biri dizdār ve biri ketḫüdā ve biri imām ḫānesi olup bir mescidi ve bir ġılāl enbārı ve bir cebeḫāne (33) maḫzeni ve bir ṣu ṣarnıcı var. Bunlardan ġayri çārsū-yı bāzār ve ḫān ve ḥammām ve cāmi' yoqdur kim ġāyet küçük qal'ecikdir.

(34) Ve qal'eden çıqarken ṣaġ ṭarâfında Ḫünkār cāmi'i kiremitli ve kārgīr minārели çār-gūşe bir müfīd ü muḫtaṣar binālı **[352b]** cāmi'dır. Ve cāmi' dibinde bir uçurum yerde çārsūsı ġāyet daracıq mühmilāt ṣoqaqlı cümle (2) seksen 'aded dükkānlardır, ammā bezzāzistānı yoqdur.

III: JOURNEY THROUGH SOUTHERN ALBANIA, 1670

The fortress of Delvina. In Albanian it means ----- . It was first founded by the Spanish. Later the Venetians brought it under their control by means of a ruse. Sultan Bayezid II the Saint seized it from the Venetians in the year ----- but it once again fell into the hands of the infidels. When Sultan Suleyman went on the Corfu campaign in the year -----[1] the grand vizier Ayas Pasha, an Albanian by origin, was appointed supreme commander and the fortress of Delvina was conquered at his hands and made the capital. Even today, Delvina is an independent *sancak* in the *eyalet* of Rumelia. It is a *has* for which the *beg* receives an income of 157,132 *akçe* from the sultan. It has 24 *zeamet*s and 155 *timar*s. It has an *alay-beg* and a *çeribaşı*. In times of war, the *beg* is obliged, according to statute, to provide 2,200 soldiers, including armed retainers. It has a *kadi* with a salary level of 180 *akçe*. Around the town there are ----- villages and in all of the *sancak* there are ----- *kadi* districts, of which the best known are -----, -----, -----, -----, and ----- . There is a *şeyhülislam*, a *nakibüleşraf*, a steward of the *sipahi*s, a commander of the janissaries, a castle warden plus a garrison of ----- troops, a *subaşı*, a collector of tolls, a mayor, a market inspector, and a poll-tax official.

The fortress is pentagonal in shape and was built of solid stone at the top of a sharply tapering cliff. It is a splendid-looking fortress, without peer, though it is small, only 600 paces in circumference, and has no moat on any side. At the eastern side there is an iron gate. Inside the fortress are three small houses with tiled roofs, one belonging to the warden, one to the steward and one to the imam. Aside from these buildings, there is a prayer house, storehouses for grain and ammunition, and a water cistern. There is nothing else, neither a bazaar, nor a *han*, nor a bathhouse, nor a congregational mosque, because the fortress is very small. On the right side when leaving the fortress is the Hünkâr ("Imperial") mosque. It is a small square building with tiled roof and a stonework minaret. In a canyon just below the mosque, in a small and narrow passageway, there are eighty shops, but there is no *bedestan*.

---

[1] 944/1537.

Der vaṣf-ı varoş-ı Delvine. Qal'eniñ şarq ṭarâfında yoquş (3) aşağı bu varoş cümle yüz 'aded kiremitli ḫānelerdir. Ammā bir düz vāsi' yerde vāqı' olmaġile her evleri (4) birbirlerinden birer oq menzilleri uzaqdır. Bir ḫāneyi 'aşqıyā ḥaydudlar baṣsa ġayri evleriñ adamları ḫaberdār olmaz. (5) Ol ecilden her bir ḫānedānlarıñ birer dāne demir qapulı qulle-yi 'aẓīmleri vardır, ve cümle dīvārları ġāyet metānet üzre binā (6) olunmuşdur.

Ve cümle varoşı ----- 'aded maḥallātlardır. Ve cümle ----- 'aded miḥrāblardır, cümleden çārsū içinde (7) ----- cāmi'i ----- ve ----- cāmi'i ----- cāmi'i ----- cāmi'i ----- . Mā-'adā cümle (8) ----- 'aded maḥalle mesācidleridir, evvelā Laqa maḥallesi mescidi ve Kin Aleksi maḥallesi mescidi, ṭaba-ḫāne maḥallesi mescidi, (9) bunlar meşhūr eynelerdir. Ve cümle üç 'aded medrese-yi sūḫtegānlardır, ammā 'aşqiyā yigit sūḫteleri olur. Andan (10) cümle üç 'aded mu'allim-ḫāne-yi ṣıbyān-ı ebced-ḫvāndır. Ve cümle üç 'aded tekye-yi ehl-i tevhīd-i faqīrāndır. Ve cümle (11) bir 'aded ḥammāmdır. Ve cümle üç 'aded ḫānlardır, ammā cümleden Memo Paşa ḫānı mükellefdir. Ve cümle on 'aded çeşme(12)sārları vardır.

Bu şehir deryāya ----- sā'at yer yaqındır. Āb [u] havāsı ve bināsı ġāyet laṭīfdir. Ve Laqa (13) maḥallesi bir çuqur yerde vāqı' olmuşdur, ammā ġāyet ma'mūrdur. Andan daḫi aşağı gidüp Kin Aleksi maḥallesi ṣāfī (14) bāġ u bāġçedir, maḥkemesi daḫi ġāyet havādār yerdir. Ve Memo Paşa sarāyı ve evlādlarınıñ ḫānedānları ve ketḫüdāsınıñ sarāyı (15) ġāyet ma'mūrdur. Ve limon ve turuncı ve inciri ve zeytūnı ve nārı ve servi ağaçları bī-ḥisābdır kim şehriñ daġ u bāġların (16) zeyn étmişdir. Ve ḫalqı cümle Arnavudca [te]kellüm édüp aṣlā Rūmca bilmezler. Ġāyet şecī' ü bahadır qavmı vardır, ammā (17) ṭā'ūndan ġāyet ḫavf édüp ḫastelerin evlerde bıraġup dağlara qaçarlar, ṭā'ūnı yoq ise de ol adam açlıqdan (18) zār u b[ī]zār elbette ölüp şişüp qalır.

Bu ḫalqıñ geçinişleri cümle bi-şarṭı's-selāmedir. Ekseriyyā kār [u] kesbleri zeytūn ve (19) zeytūn yağı çıqarup vilāyet vilāyet götürüp fürūḫt édüp kār éderler. Reng-i rūyları cümle bay u gedāy ṣaġīr ü kebīr (20) pīr [ü] cüvānıñ yüzleri ḥamret üzredir, zīrā cümle ehl-i ṭarab ve 'ayş [u] 'işrete māyil bir alay ġāziyān-ı mücāhidānlardır. (21) Ammā tāze yigitleriyle sūḫte 'ulemāları ġāyet 'aşqıyālardır, ḥattā sūḫtevātlarınıñ başlarında bir gūne perīşānī serçe (22) yuvalı ṣarıqları var kim gören adamlar gülmeden ḥayrān olurlar. Ve memdūḥāt

The open town (varoş) of Delvina is to the east of the fortress, descending a slope, and consists of 100 houses with tiled roofs. The town is situated on a broad plain and the houses are separated from one another by an arrow's shot distance. If one house is attacked by bandits, the neighboring houses are oblivious of the fact. For this reason, all the houses have a large tower with an iron gate and very strong thick walls. The town has a total of ----- quarters and ----- prayer-niches. Within the bazaar area are several congregational mosques (*cami*), viz. those of ----- , ----- , ----- , ----- , and ----- . Aside from these, there are also ----- smaller mosques (*mescid*) in the various quarters, the most famous of which being those of Vlaka, Gjin Aleksi and the Tanners' quarter. There are 3 *medrese*s, but the students are roughnecks. There are 3 primary schools, 3 *tekke*s, 1 bathhouse and 3 *han*s, the most important of which is the *han* of Memo Pasha. There are 10 fountains.

The town is ----- hours from the sea. The climate is salubrious and the buildings are very fine. The Vlaka quarter is situated in a hollow, but is very well-to-do. Below this is the quarter of Gjin Aleksi, full of vineyards and gardens. The courthouse is in an elevated, breezy part of town. Memo Pasha's palace, as well as his children's houses and his steward's mansion, are very well-constructed. Countless are the lemon, orange, fig, olive, pomegranate and cypress trees which adorn the uncultivated areas and orchards of the town. The inhabitants all speak Albanian and do not know Greek. They are very brave young men, but are very frightened of the plague. Should it happen that a family member falls ill, they take to the hills, leaving the man to become bloated and die of hunger, even though he may not have the plague at all.

The people make an adequate living, most of them with olives and olive oil which they export and sell in other *vilayet*s. Young and old, great and small, rich and poor, they all have ruddy complexions because they are ghazis and fighters given to carousal and drink. The young lads and the theology students are simply brigands. The latter wear a kind of *perişani* turban[1] on their heads, like a sparrow's nest, and whoever sees them cannot help but laugh. Well-known among

[1] In later Ottoman times this was the name of a headdress worn by lower officials; see Mehmet Zeki Pakalın, *Osmanlı Tarih Deyimleri ve Terimleri Sözlüğü* (3 vols., Istanbul, 1971), II, 773.

me'kūlāt [u] meşrūbātlarından beyāż (23) Arnavud simidi ve beyāż poġaçası ve bāde-yi lāle-yi ḥamrāsı memdūḥdur.

Ve bu şehriñ ġarb ṭarâfındaki yüksek Delvine (24) dağından mezkūr Venedik Körfezi aṭası re'ānen (ra'yen?) görinür. ----- /

(26) Ve bu şehriñ cümle yārān-ı bā-ṣafālarıyle vedā'laşup ġarb ṭarâfına gidüp 7 sā'atde dağlı ve ṭaşlı yollar üzre ma'mūr [u] (27) ābādān qurālar geçerek

Evṣāf-ı qal'e-yi Ġalaṭa. Mā-taqaddem Venedik ḥükminde iken sene ----- tārīḫinde Bāyezīd-i (28) Velī 'aṣrında serdār-ı mu'aẓẓam Gedik Aḥmed Paşa fetḥidir. Delvine beginiñ ḫāṣṣıdır kim voyvadası ḥākimdir. Ammā şimdi (29) begini bunda bulup Manya vilāyeti serdār[ı] 'Alī Paşadan getirdigim emr-i pādişāhīleri qırā'at etdirüp mefhūmı ma'lūmları (30) olunca "Fermān Pādişāhıñ" deyüp Manya muḥāfażasına gitmege cümle sancaġı 'askeriyle āmāde olup ḥaqīre üçyüz ġuruş (31) bir at ve beş donluq çoqa ve qumāşlar ve ḫuddāmlarım[a] da yüz ġuruş [ve] birer çoqa verüp şehriñ temāşāsına muqayyed olduq.

(32) Bu qal'e Quryeleş qażāsı bināsıdır. Qal'esi kūh-ı Quryeleş dāmeninde bir düz yerde şekl-i muḫammes bir şeddādī (33) küçük ṭaş-binā qal'ecikdir. Dāyiren-mā-dār cirmi altıyüz adımdır. İçinde ancaq yedi 'aded evleri var ve bir mescidi var (34) ve bir ġılāl enbārı var, ġayri çārsū-yı bāzār yoqdur. Ammā cānib-i şarqa nāẓir bir demir qapusı var. Lākin qal'e eñsesindeki **[353a]** bir sivri ḥavāle dağı var. Dizdārı ve yüz 'aded neferātları vażīfe-yi mu'ayyenelerin Ṣayada emīninden alırlar. Ve bu (2) qal'e dibinden cerêyān éden ----- deresi Quryeleş vilāyeti dağları içinden gelüp mezkūr ḥavāle dağıñ (3) eteginden dolaşup andan bu Ġalaṭa qal'esiniñ ġarb ṭarâfına gidüp leb-i deryā ile tā Avlonya qurbında deryāya girir.

(4) Ba'dehu bu qal'eden qalqup ġarb ṭarâfına leb-i deryā ile tā Avlonya Körfezine varınca bir adama rāst gelmeyüp (5) bu geçidden bir adam [u] ādemī-zād geçmek muḥāldır, zīrā ṣarp dağlar ve bī-emān beller ve sengistān yollar cümle qavmı 'āṣīler olup cümle (6) yetmiş

their food and drinks are white Albanian buns (*simid*), white flatbread (*poğaça*) and red wine. From the lofty mountain which rises to the west of Delvina one can see the Venetian island of Corfu quite clearly. -----

Bidding farewell to all our friends and companions in this town, we set off westwards, journeying over stony mountain roads and passing through many a prosperous and happy village. In 7 hours' time we reached *the fortress of Kalasa*. This was formerly under the control of the Venetians and was conquered in the year ----- by the supreme commander Gedik Ahmed Pasha during the reign of Sultan Bayezid II the Saint. It is a *has* belonging to the *beg* of Delvina and is administered by a *voyvoda*. I met the Beg here and gave him the imperial decreess which I had brought from Ali Pasha, commander of the *vilayet* of Mania[1]. "It is the Sultan's to command," he said, after perusing them, and he made ready all the soldiers of his *sancak* to set off in defense of Mania. He gave me 300 *kuruş*, a horse and lengths of broadcloth and other material enough for five suits, and he gave my servants 100 *kuruş* and one length of broadcloth each. We then set off on a tour of the town.

This fortress belongs to the district of Kurvelesh. Situated on a level site at the base of Mt. Kurvelesh, it is a small, sturdy fortress built of stone, pentagonal in shape, with a circumference of six hundred paces. Inside the walls there are only 7 houses, 1 prayer house and 1 storehouse for grain. There is no bazaar. At the eastern side, there is an iron gate. Looming behind the fortress is a steep mountain. The warden and his 100 garrison troops take their orders from the *emin* of Sajada[2]. Below this fortress is the ----- river which comes down from the *vilayet* of Kurvelesh and, meandering along the skirt of the aforementioned looming mountain to the west of Kalasa, flows into the sea near Vlora.

Leaving this fortress, we followed the coast westward and did not encounter anyone right up to the Bay of Vlora. Indeed, travellers can hardly cross this pass because the roads are steep, rocky and treacherous and the people are all brigands. There are 70 villages

---

[1] Mania or Mani in the southern Peloponnese; see Introduction. Köse Ali Pasha became admiral of the Ottoman fleet in 1082/1671 and died in 1086/1675; see Süreyyâ 1995-97, III, 604.

[2] Town south of Konispol on the Greek side of the present border, across from the port of Corfu.

pāre qul̄alardır kim cümle yigirmi biñ ʻaded fitil[li] tüfeng-endāz ʻĀr-nā-būdları Allāhümme ʻāfinā "Müsülmānız" derler ammā aṣlā dīn [ü] (7) diyānet ve haşr [u] neşr nedir bilmezler.

Der beyān-ı faṣl-ı ibtidā ḥaseb ü neseb-i[1] *qavm-ı ʻĀrnābūd.* Bunlar ol qavmdır kim Mekke-yi (8) mükerremede sākinlerden qavm-ı Qureyş qabāyil-i ʻUrbānı idi. Ḥikmet-i ḫudā, bunlarıñ Cebel-i Elheme nām bir şeyḫü'l-ʻurbānı ki oymaq ṣāḥibi (9) bir qavm-ı kübbār-ı kibār-ı ʻArab idi, ḫaṭa'an bir ʻizzet beginiñ gözin bu Cebel-i Elheme çıqar[ır]. Gözi çıqan beg daḫi ḥażret-i ʻÖmer ḥużū(10)rına gelüp sūre-yi ----- "Ve-ketebnā ʻaleyhim fīhā enne'n-nefse bi'n-nefsi ve'l-ʻayne bi'l-ʻayni" naṣṣ-ı qāṭıʻı üzre Cebel-i Elheme(11)niñ şerʻile gözin çıqarmaġa ṭaleb etdükde ḥażret-i ʻÖmer kitābu'llāh qavlince Cebel-i Elhemeniñ göz[in] çıqarmaġa ḥükm édince hemān (12) ol géce Cebel-i Elheme gözi çıqmāsınıñ ḫavfından üç biñ adam qabīlesin alup doġrı Anṭāqıyyede Ḫırqīl qırala gelüp (13) daḫil düşdükde ol daḫi Cebel-i Elhemeye Cebeliyye daġların verüp anda Cebel sākin olduġıyçün Cebeliyye daġları andan ġalaṭ-ı (14) meşhūr, bu Cebel-i Elhemeniñ bir qarındaşı Keysū ʻNH (?) Seleme (?) çöllerinde sākin olup Keys ʻUrbānı andan qalmışdır. Baʻdehu (15) Hülāgū Āl-i ʻAbbāsiyāndan al-Mustanṣır-bi'llāhı şehīd édüp Baġdādı ḫarāb etdikden ṣoñra Keys ʻUrbānın sürüp Heyhāt (16) saḥrāsı fezālarında meşeyistānlar içre iskā[n] etdirüp Çerākis ʻUrbānı tenāsül bularaq bir lisān-ı āḫar peydā édü[p] Çerākis (17) yaʻnī Çerkes qavmı oldılar, anıñiçün qavm-ı Çerkeziñ aṣılları qavm-ı Qureyşden Keys ʻArabı olup andan Çerkes oldılar. (18) Baʻdehu bu Cebel-i Elhemeniñ bir oymaġı Mekkeden firār édüp Ġazzede ḥażret-i resūluñ ʻammisi ʻArab el-Hāşimiñ yanında gelüp (19) qavm-ı Hāşimī olurlar.

Baʻdehu ḥażret-i ʻÖmer Cebel-i Elhemeniñ Ḫırqīl qıral yanına firār édup mürtedd olduġın istimāʻ etdi(20)kde ʻÖmer ibni ʻAbdü'l-ʻazīzi ve Ḫālid ibni Velīdi ve Esved ibni Miqdādı qırq biñ ʻasākir-i İslāma bunları serdār (21) édüp ceng-i ʻażīm etdiklerinde Cebel-i Elheme Cebeliyyede binā etdügi qalʻede qarār édemeyüp qarārı firā[r]a mübeddel olu[p] (22) cümle tevābiʻātlarıyle Aq Deñiz cezīrelerine fir[ā]r etdiler[2]. Üç nefer evlādlarından ʻAbaza ve Lāziqa ve Migrāl nām evlādları (23) eyyām-ı muvāfıq ile Makiduna yaʻnī İslāmbolda Ġalaṭada sākin Ciniviz qıralına gelüp ol daḫi bunlara Qara Deñiz sā(24)ḥilinde yur[d]lar verüp ʻAbaza Abaza daġlarında qalup lisān-ı

[1] Altered to *ḥasīb ü nesīb.*
[2] Text: *éderler.*

inhabited by 20,000 Albanians, all armed with matchlock muskets — may God preserve us! They claim to be Muslims, but they know nothing at all of religion and the last judgment.

The origins and lineage of the Albanian people. They stem from the Quraysh, the Arab tribe inhabiting Mecca. By God's wisdom, a certain Arab shaykh named Jabal-i Alhama, one of their clan chieftains, accidentally put out the eye of an Arab *beg*. The *beg* who lost his eye went to the caliph Omar[1] and demanded that Jabal-i Alhama's eye be put out in accordance with the definitive Koranic verse "And We prescribed for them a life for a life and an eye for an eye."[2] In accordance with the Book of God, Omar ordered that Jabal-i Alhama's eye be put out. Jabal-i Alhama, terrified that he would be blinded, fled to Antioch, accompanied by 3000 of his tribesmen, and sought refuge with King Heraclius. The king gave him the Jabaliyya mountains — so called because Jabal settled there. One of Jabal-i Alhama's brothers, Keysu, dwelt in the —— (?) Seleme desert and the Kays Arabs are named after him. After Hulagu martyred al-Mustansir-bi'llah, the last Abbasid caliph,[3] and destroyed Baghdad, he drove out the Keys Arabs and forced them to settle in the oak forests of the Kipchak Steppe. From them stem the Cherakis Arabs who started speaking a language of their own. It was thus that the Cherkes or Circassian people came into being — they were originally Keys Arabs of the Qureysh tribe. Meanwhile, another clan related to Jabal-i Alhama fled from Mecca and settled in Gaza with Arab al-Hashim, the uncle of the Prophet Muhammad. This is how the Hashemite people came into being.

When Omar learned that Jabal-i Alhama had taken refuge with King Heraclius and had apostatized from Islam, he sent an expedition against him of 40,000 Muslim warriors, led by Omar ibn Abdalaziz, Khalid ibn Walid and Aswad ibn Miqdad. Jabal-i Alhama could no longer hold out in the fortress he had built in Jabaliyya, so he fled with all his followers to the Aegean archipelago. His three sons, Abaza, Lazka and Migral, fled by fair weather to the Genoese king residing in "Macedonia" — i.e. Galata in Istanbul. The king gave them grazing lands on the coast of the Black Sea. Abaza settled in the Abkhaz mountains where his people started speaking a language of

---

1 'Umar ibn al-Khattab, the second caliph (reg. 13-23/634-644).

2 Koran 5:45.

3 Error for al-Musta'ṣim (reg. 640-56/1242-58).

āḫar peydā édüp ʻAbaza olur, Lāziqa Ṭarabuzan semtinde tavaṭṭun (25) édüp başqa Çiçu lisānı peydā édüp qavm-ı Laz olurlar, Migrāl nām oġlı Gönye qalʻesi dibinde cerêyān (26) éden Nehr-i Çoruġ kenārlarında tā Baṭum sancaġı ḫāklerinde tavaṭṭun édüp Migre[l] qavmı olurlar.

Ammā bu mezkūr Cebel-i Elheme (27) ḥażret-i ʻÖmer ḫavfından bir [yer]de qarār-dāde olamayup āḫir-i kār gemilerile İşpanya qıralına varup ilticā etdikde "Biz qavm-ı Qureyşī(28)lerdeniz" dédikde bunlara arż-ı ḫāliye olan zikri sebqat éden Delvine daġları verüp anda tenāsül bularaq ol (29) ulu ṣarp daġları ʻamār édüp başqa lisān peydā édüp göz çıqarmamaq içün bunlar " ʻĀr nā būd" dédiler, lākin bunlar (30) qavm-ı Qureyşīden olduqlarıyçün ḥālā sākin olduġı daġlara Quryeleş yaʻnī Qureyşī daġları derler. Bī-emān qavmdır. Bunlar (31) dāyimā Venedige günde birer altuna ḫidmet édüp Qandiyede bizimle ceng éden cümle bunlar idi. Yine böyle iken "Müsülmānız" derler. (32) Ammā yarar u tüvā[nā] ve şecīʻ [ü] bahadır fetālardır. İşte ʻĀrnābūd qavm-ı ʻanūduñ aṣl [u] ferʻleri böyle olmuşdur. Ammā ṣoñra Cebel-i Elheme (33) Elbaṣan şehrinde İslāmile merḥūm olmuşdur. Bu qavm-ı ʻArabıñ[1] aḥvāllar[ı] ʻalā't-tafṣīl tevārīḫ-i Tuḥfed[e] mesṭūr. Ve bu Qureyş (34) ṭā'ife[si] ḥaqqā ki ʻArab çehrelidir, cümle silāḥlarından ġayri oqları ve yayları vardır.

Ezīn-cānib Ġalaṭa qalʻesinden **[353b]** yarar refīqler alup 7 sāʻat şimāle sengistān yollar ve çemenzār beller ile gidüp *der tenqīlāt-ı eşkāl-i qalʻe-yi zībā Julad.* (2) Lisān-ı Arnavu[d]ca Julad ----- demekdir. Mā-taqaddem İşpanya qıralı bināsı olup baʻdehu bir ḥīle-yi mekrile Bunduqani (3) Venedigi eline girüp baʻdehu sene ----- tārīḫinde Bāyezīd-i Velī ʻaṣrında bunı daḫi Gedik Aḥmed Paşa fetḥ édüp ḥālā Süleymān Ḫān tahrīri (4) üzre Delvine sancaġı ḥükminde

[1] Text: *qazaqıñ* (?).

their own, becoming the Abkhazians. Lazka settled in the region of Trebizond where his people started speaking a language of their own, known as Chichu, and became the Laz people. The third son, Migral, settled in the *sancak* of Batumi on the banks of the Choruh river, which flows below the fortress of Gönye, and thus the Mingrelian people came into being.[1]

As for Jabal-i Alhama himself, fearing the caliph Omar, he was unable to settle anywhere. Finally, travelling by ship, he took refuge with the king of Spain. When they told him that they were of the tribe of Quraysh, the king gave him the uninhabited mountains of Delvina, mentioned above. After some generations, they populated those rugged mountains and started speaking a language of their own. So as not to have their eyes put out, they used to say *'Ār nā būd* ("May there be no shame"). But since they stemmed from the Quraysh tribe, they called the mountains they now occupied the Quryelesh (Kurvelesh) mountains, meaning Qurayshi. They are a ruthless people. It is they who always sold their services to Venice for one gold coin a day and who always fought us in Candia. Despite this, they still claim to be Muslims. They are indeed brave and capable warriors. Such is the origin and descent of the obstreperous Albanians. Jabal-i Alhama subsequently died as a Muslim in the city of Elbasan. In the *Tuhfa* history, there is extensive information on this Arab tribe.[2] This clan of Quraysh actually do look like Arabs, and in addition to all their other weapons they do use bows and arrows.

Returning to our narrative: from Kalasa we took an armed escort and ventured northwards for 7 hours along rocky roads and verdant ridges and arrived at *the pretty fortress of Zhulat*. In Albanian it means ----- . It was originally built by the king of Spain. It later fell into the hands of the Venetians, by means of a ruse, and was also conquered from them by Gedik Ahmed Pasha in the year ----- during the reign of Sultan Bayezid II the Saint. It is now administered by a *voyvoda* in the *sancak* of Delvina, according to the survey

---

[1] Evliya expatiates on the origin of these Caucasian peoples at II 256a and VII 148b. See Introduction.

[2] As Babinger pointed out (1930, 176, n. 4) there are many histories using this title, and it is hard to pinpoint the one which Evliya had in mind. See also Meşkûre Eren, *Evliya Çelebi Seyahatnâmesi birinci cildinin kaynakları üzerinde bir araştırma* (Istanbul, 1960), 46. At one point, to be sure, Evliya states that the author was a certain Yahya Çelebi, a poet during the reign of Sultan Orhan, but this seems fanciful; see IX 205b3 (454).

voyvadalıqdır. Qal'esi evc-i āsmāna berāber Qahqahā-vār bir qal'e-yi bālādır kim Rūm-élinde (5) eyle bir qal'e-yi bī-hemtā yoqdur, meger Mora cezīresinde Kördüs qal'esi ola, yāḫod Benefşe qal'esi ola. Ammā bunuñ (6) cirmi dāyiren-ma-dār dördyüz adımdır ve ġāyet metīn şeddādī ṭaş-binādır. Şarq ile ġarb mā-beynine nāẓır bir qapusı (7) var. İçinde dizdār evi var, ġayri şey yoqdur. Ve dizdārı ve cümle yüz elli neferātları Ṣayada iskelesi emīninden 'ulūfe(8)lerin alırlar. Ve bu qulların ḫāneleri qal'eden iki biñ [adım] aşağı Nehr-i Yeñice ve Nehr-i Quryeleş ikisi birbirine maḫlūṭ olduġı (9) yerde[dir].

Der beyān-ı varoş-ı Julad. Cümle ikiyüz 'aded ṣaman çöbi örtüli fuqarā evleridir. Ve bu nehirleriñ ikisi (10) daḫi Quryeleş köylerinden gelüp bu qal'e ile varoş mābeyninden 'ubūr édüp ve iki sā'at şarqa gidüp qal'e-yi (11) Qardik qurbından geçüp Ergiri qal'esi ṣaḥrāsından cerêyān édüp Ergiri Nehrine maḫlūṭ olur. Ve bu Julad qal'esi (12) qulınıñ çoġı Quryeleş daġınıñ Arnavud kefereleridir. Ba'dehu Küçük Meḥemmed Paşa "Kāfire qal'e qulı olmaq memnūdur" deyü (13) cümle kefere qulların İslām ile müşerref etdi. Bu varoşda cümle bir cāmi'i var. Yuqaru qal'ede daḫi bir vīrān (14) cāmi'i var. Bu şehirde aṣlā çārsū-yı bāzār ve ḫān ve ḥammām ve tekye ve mekteb yoqdur, ammā cā-be-cā bāġları vardır.

Andan Avlonya (15) begi Memo[1] Beg oġlı 'Oṣmān Paşayı bulup Manya seferine anları da me'mūr édüp emr-i pādişāhīler dīvānda qırā'at olunup (16) cümle "Sem'an ve-ṭā'a" deyüp cümle livāsı 'askeriyle Manya muḥāfażasına gitmege cidd [ü] ihtimām eyleyüp ḥaqīre bir at (17) ve bir köle ve üçyüz ġuruş iḥsān etdi.

Andan şarqa Nehr-i Yeñice kenārınca ----- sā'at çemenzār yerleri ve ma'mūr u (18) ābādān köyleri 'ubūr édüp *evṣāf-ı hey'et-i qal'e-yi ra'nā Qardik.* Lisān-ı 'Arnavudca bu (19) qal'eye ----- derler. Sene ----- tārīḫinde bunı daḫi Bāyezīd-i Velī 'aṣrında serdār Gedik Aḥmed Paşa fetḥ eyle(20)mişdir. Bu daḫi Delvine sancaġı ḫākinde ve Ergiri qażāsı ḥükminde bir sivri depecik üzre şekl-i müdevver bir ṭaş-(21)binā bir küçük sūr-ı üstüvārcikdir, ammā cirmi ma'lūmum

---

[1] Crossed out.

register of Suleyman Khan. It is a lofty, sky-scraping fortress like that of Kahkaha. There is no other such fortress in all of Rumelia; it can only be compared to the fortress of Corinth in the Morea (Peloponnese) or to that of Monemvasia. The circumference is 400 paces. It is a solid and mighty construction of stone. Its entrance is at the side between the east and the west. Inside the fortress is the house of the warden and nothing else. The warden and his 150 garrison troops receive their salaries from the *emin* at the port of Sajada. The houses of the soldiers are 2000 paces below the fortress, at the spot where the Yenice and Kurvelesh rivers[1] meet.

The open town of Zhulat has 200 houses with thatched roofs. The junction of the two above-mentioned rivers, coming down from the villages of Kurvelesh, flows between the fortress and the open town of Zhulat and proceeds for two hours past the fortress of Kardhiq, through the plain of Gjirokastër, and then into the Gjirokastër[2] river. The garrison troops of the fortress of Zhulat used to be mostly Albanian infidels from Mt. Kurvelesh, but Küçük Mehmed Pasha subsequently forbade infidels from serving as Ottoman garrisons and he converted all of them to Islam.[3] There is one congregational mosque in the open town and another one up in the fortress, the latter now being in ruins. There is no bazaar in this town, nor is there a *han*, bathhouse, *tekke* or school. There are some scattered vineyards.

I met Osman Pasha, son of Memo Beg, the *beg* of Vlora, to whom I imparted the imperial decrees for the expedition to Mania. "To hear is to obey," he replied after they were read out publicly, and they prepared to set off as a brigade with all the *sancak* soldiers to defend Mania. He presented me with a horse, a slave and 300 *kuruş*.

From this place we set off eastwards, along the banks of the Yenice river. We travelled for ----- hours through a verdant region and well-kept villages until we arrived at *the lovely fortress of Kardhiq*. In Albanian it is called ----- . This fortress was also conquered by commander Gedik Ahmed Pasha in the year ----- during the reign of Sultan Bayezid II the Saint. It is a small, round, stone fortress, situated on the top of a pointed little hill, and belongs to

---

[1] Probably the Kardhiq river, also known as Belica, and the Zhur river.

[2] Lower part of the Drino river.

[3] Küçük Mehmed Paşa became *begler-begi* of Rumelia in 1074/1663 and died in 1078/1667. See Süreyyâ 1995-97, IV/I, 208. Possibly Evliya is referring to a different person.

degildir, ʿad etmedim. Ancaq dizdārı ve yüz ʿaded neferātları važīfe-yi (22) muʿayyenelerin Ṣayada emīninden alırlar. Ġāyet bahadır ve şecīʿ ve fetā ʿArnavud yigitleri vardır.

Der taʿrīf-i varoş-ı Qardik. (23) Qalʿeniñ aşağısında Nehr-i Yeñice kenārında yüz elli ʿaded kiremitli ve baʿżıları qayağan ve ṣaman örtüli fuqarā evleri ve[1] (24) cā-be-cā müşebbek būstānları ve bāġçecikleri var. Ve bir küçük mināreli ve kiremit örtüli cāmiʿi var. Çārsū-yi bāzārı ve ḫān (25) u ḥammāmı yoqdur; cümle Ergiri qalʿesine muḥtāclardır.

Andan Nehr-i Yeñice kenārınca şarq cānibine 2 sāʿat gidüp Ergiri öñinden (26) aqan Nehr-i Diraġopola Nehr-i Yeñiceye maḫlūṭ olur, ol maḥalle ḥaqīr varup andan gerü cenūb ṭarâfına 3 sāʿat ābādānda gidüp (27) *qarye-yi Tirbuk* ve daḫi *qarye-yi Lab*[2] *Ova*, andan *qarye-yi Qaqoṣ*, bunlar Delvine begi Memo Beg çiftlikleridir. (28) Bunlarıñ öñlerinden temāşā éderek geçüp andan Ergiri bāğları içinden ʿubūr édüp niçe bāğlarda zevq u ṣafālar éderek

(29) *Der tescīlāt-ı ṣūret-i sūr-ı üstüvār, yaʿnī sitāyiş-i qalʿe-yi Ergiri Qaṣri-yi nāmudār.* (30) Lisān-ı Urumda ----- qalʿe demekdir. İbtidā bānīsi Rūm qırallarından Fīleqūs oğlı bināsıdır. Baʿdehu niçe divelden (31) divele intiqāl édüp āḫir-i kār sene ----- tārīḫinde bi'z-zāt Bāyezīd-i Velī Arnavud ʿaşqıyāları elinden fetḥ etmişdir. Ammā niçe yerleriniñ (32) binaları Venedik kāfiri ʿamārıdır; zīrā Ṣanmarqo taṣvīrleri vardır kim Venedik ʿalāmetidir. Süleymān Ḫān tahrīri üzre ḥālā (33) Delvine paşasınıñ ḫāṣṣı voyvadalığıdır ve yüz seksen aqçe şerīf qażādır. Nāḥiyesi ----- ʿaded qurālardır. Şeyḫü'l-islāmı ve (34) naqībü'l-eşrāfı ve aʿyān-ı kibār eşrāfı ve sipāh ketḫüdā yeri ve yeñiçeri serdārı ve muḥtesib ağası ve bācdārı ve şehir ketḫüdāsı **[354a]** ve ḫarāc ağası ve miʿmār ağası ve şehir ṣubaşısı ve qalʿe dizdārı ve ikiyüz ʿaded qalʿe neferātları vardır. (2) Qalʿesi balıq ṣırṭı gibi bir ṣırṭ qayalı püşte-yi ʿālī üzre şeddādī kārgīr ṭaş-binā bir qalʿe-yi qadīmdir. Dāyiren-(3)mā-dār cirmi biñ dördyüz ʿaded adımdır. Ve şarqdan ġarba ṭūlānīce vāqıʿ bir qalʿe-yi bī-hemtādır kim ṭūlı altıyüz (4) ʿaded germe ḥaṭvedir ve ʿarżı yüz adım ensiz qalʿedir. Gūyā hemān qadırġa gibi bir uzun sūr-ı üstüvārdır.

---

[1] Text: *vā* (for *var*?).

[2] Text: *Lat.*

the district of Gjirokastër in the *sancak* of Delvina. I do not know its circumference, since I did not pace it out. It is guarded only by the warden and 100 garrison troops, who are paid by the *emin* at the port of Sajada. They are exceptionally brave Albanian lads.

The open town of Kardhiq is situated below the fortress on the banks of the Yenice river. It consists of 150 miserable houses, some with tiled and others with slate and straw roofs, and with a scattering of flower and vegetable gardens. There is one congregational mosque with a tiled roof and a little minaret. There is no bazaar, *han* or bathhouse; the inhabitants resort to Gjirokastër for these needs.

From here we set off eastwards along the banks of the Yenice and, after 2 hours of travel, we arrived at the Dropull[1] river, which flows past Gjirokastër and into the Yenice river. Turning southwards once again, we proceeded for 3 hours through the prosperous villages of Tërbuq, Labova and Kakoz, which are all farm-estates of Memo Beg, the *beg* of Delvina. From these villages, we continued through the vineyards of Gjirokastër, stopping occasionally for rest and relaxation.

The mighty and famous fortress of Gjirokastër. In Greek it means ----- Castle. Its initial founder was the son of Philip, one of the Greek kings. It later fell into the hands of various rulers and finally in the year ----- was seized from Albanian rebels by Sultan Bayezid II the Saint in person. Many buildings in Gjirokastër appear to have been built by the Venetian infidels because you can see portraits of Saint Mark on them, which is the symbol of Venice. In accordance with the survey register of Suleyman Khan, it is a *has* belonging to the Pasha of Delvina and is governed by a *voyvoda*. It has a *kadi* with a salary level of 180 *akçe*. The district of Gjirokastër has ----- villages. Among the other officials of this town are the *şeyhülislam*, the *nakibüleşraf*, the steward of the *sipahis*, the commander of the janissaries, the market inspector, the collector of tolls, the mayor, the poll-tax official, the chief architect, the *subaşı*, the castle warden and 200 garrison troops. The fortress is an old stonework construction situated along the ridge of a high cliff. The building has a circumference of 1400 paces and stretches from east to west, with a length of 600 broad paces and a width of 100 narrow paces. Its long solid ramparts resemble a galley.

---

[1] Upper part of the Drino river.

(5) Ve qal'e içi şarqdan ġarba ancaq bir ulu şāhrāh ṣoqaqdır. Ve bu yoluñ iki ṭarâfında cümle ikiyüz qadar (6) serāpā qayaġan örtüli fevqānī kārgīr binā-yı muṣanna' evler var. Ve bunda Bāyezīd H̱ān-ı Velī cāmi'i kār-ı qadīm kārgīr minārelī (7) ve qayaġan ṭaşı örtüli rūḥāniyyetli bir büyük cāmi'dir kim ṭūli seksen ayaqdır, 'arżı qırq ayaq enlidir, içinde dörd (8) 'ade[d] 'amelī sütūnları üzre çatma taḫta binālı süṭūḥdur, ammā ṭavanı ġāyet muṣanna' ve munaqqaşdır.

Bu qal'e evce berāber (9) qaya üzre olmaq ile suyı cāmi'iñ mināresi dibinde yol aşırı bir ṣu ṣarnıc-ı 'aẓīmi var. Cümle qal'e içindeki (10) evleriñ ḫalqı ol āb-ı raḥmetden cerêyān édüp cem' olan āb-ı nābdan nūş édüp def'-i 'aṭşān éderler. Deryā-mis̱āl bir ṣarnıc-ı (11) 'aẓīmdir. Bundan mā-'adā elbetde her ḫānedānlarda birer ṣu ṣarnıçları muqarrerdir.

Bu qal'enin iki yerden metīn ü qavī demir (12) qapuları var, ammā cümle üç qat qapulardır. Bir qapusı şarq ṭarafına nāẓirdir kim üç qat qapudur kim bu qapuya ṭaş nerdübānlar ile (13) çıqıldıġından atlı[1] adamlar gücile girüp çıqarlar. Üçünci iç qat qapunuñ ṭaşrasında cihān-nümā bir lonca köşki var (14) kim cemī'i şehriñ yārān-ı ẓarīfān-ı a'yān-ı kibārları anda oṭurup ṣaḥrālardaki ḥadīqa-yı ravża-yı bāġ-ı cinānları teferrüc éderler. Ve bu (15) qapudan daḫi ġarb ṭarâfına namāz-gāh qapusı var, bu daḫi üç qat ḥadīd [ü] cedīd qapulardır.

Bu ṭarafda namāz-gāh meydānıyle (16) qal'e mā-beyninde yüz adım ṭūli ve yigirmi adım 'arżı bir alçaq qal'e ḫandaqı var. Bu qal'eniñ mā-'adā üç ṭaraf cānibleri (17) çāh-ı ġayyā-mis̱āl olmaq ile aṣlā ḫandaqları yoqdur.

Cümle qayaġan örtüli ikiyüz 'aded ḫānedānları cümle qal'e (18) bedenleri üzre binā olunup maqṣūraları ve cümle şāhnişīnleri qal'eniñ yemīn ü yesārındaki çāh-ı ceḥīmde binā olunan (19) varoşa ve ṣaḥrā-yı lāle-zāra nāẓir evlerdir.

Der sitāyiş-i varoş-ı Ergiri Qaṣri. Bu qal'eniñ maşriqa nāẓir qapusı öñinden (20) yoquş aşaġı gidüp bir maḥalle kefere maḥallesi var, Küçük Varoş derler, cümle ikiyüz 'aded vāsi' dār-ı manḥūslardır. Ve qal'eniñ (21) şimālinde qal'e qayaları altında eski çārsūya qal'e çārsūsı derler, cümle qırq 'aded dükkāncıqlardır, iki başında beẕẕāzistān-(22)mis̱āl aġaç qapuları vardır, her géce pāsbān [u] nigehbānları bu qapuları sedd éderler, lākin bu qapular qapandıqdan soñra aşaġı varoşdan (23) qal'eye yol işlemez olur, ancaq namāzgāh

[1] Text: *atları.*

Inside the fortress there is only one main street running from east to west. Ranged on both sides of the street are 200 two-story stonework houses, roofed entirely with slate. Within the fortress is the mosque of Sultan Bayezid II the Saint,[1] with a slate roof and a stone minaret. It is a large old mosque with a spiritual atmosphere and is 80 feet long and 40 feet wide. Inside it there are four carved columns and a wooden ceiling of joined beams with very fine decoration.

Since the fortress is situated on the top of a high cliff, water is collected in a huge cistern at the foot of the minaret. All the houses within the walls get their drinking water from this source, i.e. from rain water that flows into this sea-like cistern. Each house has its own private cistern as well.

The fortress has two gates with three strong and solid iron doorways each. The eastern gate is approached by a stone staircase, and for this reason horsemen have difficulty entering and leaving by this gate. At the third doorway, which is the innermost, there is a loggia pavilion from which one can look out over the whole district. It is here that all the foremost and distinguished citizens assemble and feast their eyes on the gardens and vineyards in the plains below. On the western side is the gate in front of the public prayer-grounds. It also has three iron doors. On this side, between the prayer-grounds and the fortress is a shallow moat, 100 paces long and 20 paces wide. There are no moats on the other three sides as they have very steep cliffs.

Inside the fortress, built over the ramparts, there are 200 houses with slate roofs. These houses have alcoves and bay windows which overlook the town to the left and right and the verdant plain below.

The open town (varoş) of Gjirokastër. In front of the eastern gate of the fortress, down a steep embankment, is the quarter of the infidels, called Küçük Varoş (Little Town). It consists of 200 ill-omened spacious houses. Under the cliffs to the north of the fortress is the old bazaar, called the Fortress Bazaar, consisting of 40 little shops. This bazaar has wooden gates at both ends, much like those of a *bedestan*, which the watchmen close every night. Once the gates are closed, there is no way of getting from the open town up to the fortress on this side. Only the gate on the side of the prayer-grounds

[1] There remains no trace of this mosque.

qapusından işleyüp qal'eye girüp çıqarlar. Ammā daḫi aşağı Büyük Varoşda (24) Memi Beg çārsūsı nev-binādır kim bu maḥaldeki varoşa Memi Beg Varoşı derler. Cümle yüz elli 'aded qayağan örtüli nev-binā-yı (25) muṣanna' bāğlı ve bāğçeli varoş-ı ra'nā evlerdir ve mükellef sarāylardır. Ve maḥkeme-yi şer'-i resūl-i mübīn daḫi bunda olup ol daḫi Memi (26) Begiñ ḫayrātıdır.

Büyük Varoş-ı 'atīq. Qal'eniñ cānib-i erba'asında sekiz 'aded dere ve depeler üzre mālāmāl qat-ender-qat fevqānī kārgīr (27) binālı cümle qayağan ṭaş örtüli bāğlı ve bāğçeli ve her ḫānedānda qulleli büyūt-i ma'mūr [u] müzeyyendir kim bu ḫānedānlarıñ cümle ḥavlılarınıñ dīvārları (28) bir gūne beyāż seng-i ḫārā ṭaşlardan mebnīdir kim gūyā cemī'i ṭaşları Engürü kerpici gibi bir qālıbdan üstād Ferhād kesüp dīvār-ı hemvār (29) etmişler, ammā cümle bay u gedānıñ dīvārları böyledir; bir diyār[d]a böyle çār-gūşe kesilmiş ṭaşlar yoqdur illā Anaṭolıda Tire ve Mağnisa (30) şehirlerinde bu qıṭ'ada dīvār ṭaşları vardır.

Der 'aded-i esmā'-ı maḥallāt-ı Ergiri. Cümle sekiz 'aded varoş maḥallātlarıdır. Evvelā Palor maḥallesi (31) ve Vuṭoş maḥallesi ve Manalat maḥallesi ve Ḥācī Beg maḥallesi, cümleden büyükdür, ve Dundar maḥallesi ve bālāda Memi Beg maḥallesi, bunlar ġāyet ma'mūr (32) maḥallātlardır.

Der 'aded-i vaṣf-ı sarāy-ı ağavāt. Mezkūr sekiz 'aded maḥallātlar içre cümle iki biñ 'aded qayağan ṭaşı örtüli evlerdir. (33) Cümleden Memo Paşa sarāyı mükellef ü nev-binā sarāy-ı ra'nādır, ve oğlı 'O̱smān Beg sarāyı ve alay-beg sarāyı ve Zā'im Beko sarāyı; daḫi niçe sarāylar vardır.

(34) *Der ta'dād-ı cevāmi'hā-yı müslimāt.* Cümle sekiz miḥrābdır. Yuqaru qal'ede Bāyezīd-i Velī cāmi'iniñ bir 'amelī sütūn üzre celī ḫaṭ ile eyle taḥrīr **[354b]** etmiş kim: "Bu şehirden Qandiye ġazāsında yediyüz 'aded ḫānedā[n] ṣāḥibleri şehīd olup ḫāneleri mesdūd qalmışdır. Ve yedi biñ 'aded ḫüdd[ā]mān (2) bu şehirden Qandiyede şehd-i şehādet cāmın nūş etmişlerdir" deyü taḥrīr etmişler. Ḥaqqā ki bu şehirde çoq ḫānedānlar mesdūd qalmışdır, ehillerin ḫuddāmları (3) almışdır.

Ve namāz-gāhıñ ṣağında bir yalçın qaya üzre bir burun uçında cihān-nümā Ḫıżır Ağa cāmi'i, kārgīr mināreli cāmi'-i 'ibret-(4)nümādır.

is accessible. Farther down, in Büyük Varoş (Big Town), is the newly constructed bazaar of Memi Beg, so they call this area Memi Beg Town. It consists of 150 modern houses with slate roofs, embellished with gardens and vineyards. They are magnificent mansions. This quarter is also the site of the *şeriat* courthouse, which was also endowed by Memi Beg.

Old Big Town. The open town is situated on eight hills and valleys all around the fortress with multi-story stonework houses, all with slate roofs and surrounded by vineyards and gardens. Each of these well-built houses has a tower. The walls of the courtyards of these houses are constructed of a kind of white granite, hewn out by master stonecutters as though they were Ankara bricks from a single mold. Both rich and poor have such walls. Such square-cut stone is to be found nowhere else on earth except in the cities of Tire and Manisa in Anatolia.

Names of the quarters of Gjirokastër. There are 8 quarters, including Palorto; Vutosh; Manalat; Hadji Beg, which is the largest of all; Dunavat (Dundar); and, up the slope, Memi Beg[1]. They are all very prosperous.

Mansions of the nobles. In the above-mentioned 8 quarters there are altogether 2000 houses with slate roofs, the grandest of all being the new and magnificent mansion of Memo Pasha, then the mansions of his son Osman Beg, of the *alay-beg*, and of Zaim Beko. There are many others as well.

Congregational mosques. There are 8 prayer-niches in all. Up in the fortress is the mosque of Sultan Bayezid II the Saint. On a column is the following inscription in *celi* script: "Seven hundred householders from this town fell in the battle of Candia as martyrs to the faith. Their houses are closed down. And seven thousand servants from this town also quaffed the cup of martyrdom in Candia." Indeed, many homes are closed down and their servants have married their former masters' wives.

On the right side of the prayer-ground, atop a steep cliff at the end of a promontory, the mosque of Hızır Aga:[2] a fine building with a stonework minaret.

---

[1] Also known as the Tekke or Partizani quarter.

[2] This mosque in the Cfak quarter no longer exists, though there are remnants of a mausoleum (*tyrbe*).

Ve aşağıda ḥammām dibinde Ḥācī Murād cāmi'i, ṭaş nerdübān ile çıqılır bir serāmed kārgīr minare-yi muṣanna'lı ve bir āb-ı ḥayāt çeşmeli (5) ve cāmi' içiniñ munaqqaş ṭavanı ġāyet naqş-ı būqalemūn 'ibret-nümūn cāmi'-i gülgūndur.

Ve Tekye cāmi'i, cemā'at-i keṡīreye mālikdir, ammā (6) minaresi yoqdur, ve cāmi'e altı qademe ṭaş nerdübān ile 'urūc olunur, bir kār-ı qadīm bābāyāne ma'bed-gāhdır. Bu cāmi'iñ ḥarêminde gūnāgūn diraḫt-i (7) müntehālar ile ārāste olup aṣlā güneş te'ṡīr etmeyüp bir āb-ı ḥayāt çāh-ı māsı var, ġāyet lezīz āb-ı ḥayātdır, ḥarêminiñ eṭrāfında Ḫalvetī ṭarīqi (8) tekyesi ḥücreleri var, ve ḥarêmiñ bir cānibinde niçe biñ kibār-ı evliyā'u'llāh a'yān-ı kibārlar medfūndur. Ḥattā bu ḥaqīriñ bir nā-rêsīde ġulāmı merḥūm (9) olup kendim ġusl édüp bu ḥaremde defn etdim. Ḥattā cümle Arnavud ḫalqı "Sen meyyit yıqadıñ" deyü ḥaqīrden nefret etdiler. "Bire vallāhī (10) ṭā'ūnlı degil idi, ishālden merḥūm oldı" deyü niçe biñ yemīn-i muġallaẓalar édüp gücile ḫalqı i'timād etdirdim.

Andan yeñi çārsūda (11) Memi Paşa cāmi'i, içine ancaq yüz adam ṣığar bir teng yerde bir küçük nev-binā bir cāmi'-i ra'nādır kim bir kārgīr muṣanna' minare-yi mevzūnı (12) var. Ammā bir ān cemā'atdan ḫālī degillerdir. Arnavudistānıñ bu maḥalli ġāyet muṣallīlerdir.

Andan Palor[1] cāmi'i, ḫoş-binā-yı ra'nādır.

(13) Andan Vuṭoş cāmi'i, vāsi' binā-yı 'atīqdir. Meşhūr cevāmi'ler bu mezkūrlardır.

Der mesācidhā-yı mü'mināt. Cümle yedi 'aded maḥalle zāviye(14)leri vardır. Evvelā Berqī Efendi zāviyesi ve Vuṭoş zāviyesi ve Memi Beg buq'ası ve alay-beg eynesi, bunlar meşhūr mesācidler[dir].

(15) *Der 'ilm-i dārü'l-ḥadīṡ-i 'ālimān.* Cümle üç 'aded dārü't-tedrīs-i 'ālimān vardır. Evvelā Bāyezīd Ḫān medresesi ve Memi Paşa medresesi.

(16) *Der mekteb-i ciger-gūşe püserān.* Cümle beş 'aded dārü't-ta'līm-i ṣıbyān-ı ebced-ḫvān vardır. Evvelā qal'edē Bāyezīd Ḫān cāmi'i dibinde büyük (17) mekteb ve Palor mektebi ve çārsū mektebi var.

---

[1] Text: *Paloz.*

Below that, at the foot of the bathhouse, the mosque of Hadji Murad:[1] it is reached by way of a stone staircase. It is a lofty stonework building with a well-constructed minaret and a fountain of excellent-tasting water. Inside the mosque the ceiling is finely decorated.

The Tekke mosque:[2] it has a large congregation, but no minaret. This mosque can be reached by way of a six-step stone stairway. It is a place of worship built in the old style. The courtyard is full of various kinds of tall trees and the sun cannot penetrate at all. It has a well with excellent-tasting water. Around the courtyard are the cells of a Halveti *tekke* and on one side are the graves of many saints and notables. It so happened that just at this time a young boy in my retinue died. I washed his body with my own hands and buried him in this graveyard. When the Albanians saw me do so, they were repelled and cried, "You washed the dead!" I replied, "But he did not have the plague. He died of dysentery," swearing to them again and again to convince them.

The mosque of Memi Pasha: built in a rather narrow part of the new bazaar, it is a small, modern and attractive building, holding no more than 100 men. It has a well-proportioned minaret of carved and decorated stonework. It never lacks a congregation. The people in this part of Albania are quite addicted to prayer.

The mosque of Palorto:[3] a very nice building.

The mosque of Vutosh: large and old. These are the best-known congregational mosques.

Neighborhood mosques. There are 7, the best-known being those of Berki Efendi, Vutosh, Memi Beg and the *alay-beg*.

Hadith schools. There are 3 schools training ulema, including the Bayezid Khan *medrese* and the Memi Pasha *medrese*.

Primary schools. There are 5, including Big School at the foot of the Bayezid mosque in the fortress, Palorto school and the bazaar school.

---

[1] No longer extant.

[2] This mosque, rebuilt in the mid-eighteenth century, survived at least until 1967 and was subsequently demolished; cf. Kiel 1990, 142.

[3] A puppet theater now stands at the site of the mosque.

Der zikr-i ḫāneqāh-ı erbāb-ı ṭarīq-i dervīşān. Cümle üç ʿaded tekye-yi ehl-i tevḥīd-i faqīrān-ı (18) zī-şāndır. Cümleden mezkūr Tekye cāmiʿi ḫāneqāhı meşhūrdur, şeyḫi ʿAbdu'llāh Efendi ṣuleḥā-yı ümmetden büyük adamdır.

(19) *Der ʿaded-i esvāq-ı sulṭānī-yi eṣnāfān.* Cümle ikiyüz ʿaded dekākīn-i zībālardır. Ammā yeñi çārsū başqa nev-binā seksen ʿaded dükkānlar inşā (20) olunup iki qatdır ve iki başında iki ʿaded metīn qapulı çārsū-yı ḥüsndür kim şehriñ gūyā bezzāzistānıdır.

Der çeşme-sār-ı teşnegān. (21) Cümle beş ʿaded āb-ı ḥayāt çeşme-yi cān-perverleri var.

Der ʿalāmet-i mihmān-sarāy-ı tüccārān. Cümle beş ʿaded ḫān-ı sevdāgerānlar var, ammā cümleden (22) Memi Paşa ḫānı metīndir.

Der havā-yı ḫūb-ı cāvidān. Bu şehriñ gerçi havāsı laṭīf olduġından ḫalqı ten-dürüst zinde olup maḥbūb u (23) maḥbūbesi memdūḥdur, ammā ṣuyı şehrine göre ġāyet azdır, tā aşaġı ṣaḥrāda cerêyān éden bāġlar içre Nehr-i Diraġopola ṣuyına muḥtā(24)clardır, andan atlarla ve eşeklerle dāyimā ṣu ṭaşırlar. El-ḥāṣıl bu şehre beş çeşme ġāyet azdır.

Der medḥ-ı ḥammām-ı rāḥat-i cān. Ancaq bir ḥammāmı (25) şiddet-i şitāda işler, māh-ı temmūzda mesdūd durur. Bir ḥammām daḫi dāyimā muʿaṭṭaldır. Ammā ev ḥammāmları çoqdur, gahīce anlara ehl-i beled de (26) girüp ġasl éderler.

Bī-medḥ-i deyr-i rāhibān-ı bıṭrīqān. Kefere maḥallātları içre üç ʿaded müfīd ü muḫtaṣar kenīseleri vardır.

Bu Ergiri ṣaḥrāsından (27) cerêyān éden Nehr-i Diraġopol qıble ṭarâfındaki ṣaḥrānıñ öte ucından qarye-yi Żavarahodan çıqup Ergiri ṣaḥrāsından yıldıza (28) gidüp andan Nehr-i Yeñiceye maḫlūṭ olup Depe Delen qalʿesi muqābilinde hemān ol maḥalde sehil gidüp Nehr-i Viyoya maḫlūṭ (29) olup üç nehir bir olup şimāl cānibine cerêyān éderek Avlonya Körfezine qarīb Nehr-i Quru Çaya munṣab olup yine ol maḥalde (30) Avlonya Körfezi deryāsına qarışırlar, ve's-selām.

Der beyān-ı ziyāretgāh-ı Ergiri Qaṣri. Evvelā şehr içre Tekye cāmiʿi ḥarêminde ziyāret-i (31) Berqī Efendi ve Popo Baba Sulṭān ve Baba Ḥasan Dede Sulṭān ve yine Tekye cāmiʿinde ʿAlī Dost Dede. Meşhūr kibār-ı evliyā'u-llāh bunlardır.

Dervish lodges. There are 3 *tekke*s for adepts and dervishes. The most famous is the Tekke mosque lodge, whose sheikh, Abdullah Efendi, is a devout and great man.

Markets and bazaars. There are 200 pretty shops in all. Apart from that, the new bazaar has 80 modern two-story shops. This attractive bazaar has strong gates at both ends like those of a *bedestan*.[1]

Fountains. There are 5 fountains with excellent-tasting water.

Merchant guest-houses. There are 5 *han*s. The best known and most reliable is the *han* of Memi Pasha.

Salubrious climate. The town has a very good climate and, for this reason, its inhabitants have healthy bodies. The boys and girls here are famous for their beauty. But the water supply is not sufficient for the town's needs. The inhabitants resort to the Dropull river which flows through the vineyards down on the plain, where they go continually to fetch water with horses and donkeys. In short, five fountains are far too few for this town.

Baths. There is 1 bathhouse which only operates during the winter and closes in the month of July. Another public bathhouse was abandoned; but there are many baths in private homes which are sometimes used for ritual bathing.

Churches. There are 3 small churches in the quarters of the infidels.

The Dropull river, flowing northwards along the plain of Gjirokastër from the village of Zavaraho[2] at the other end of the plain, is joined by the Yenice river. Later, across from the fortress of Tepelena, they are joined by the Vjosa river. After uniting, these three rivers flow northwards and are joined near the Bay of Vlora by the Kuruçay[3] river and then flow into the Bay of Vlora.

Shrines. Foremost among the pilgrimage sites in the town are the tombs of Berki Efendi, in the courtyard of the Tekke mosque; Popo Baba Sultan; Baba Hasan Dede Sultan; and Ali Dost Dede, also in the Tekke mosque. These are the best-known holy men.

---

[1] Cf. Kreiser 1979, 383.

[2] Unidentified.

[3] Now called the Shushica. When he later reaches this river near Mekat, Evliya calls it the Aksu; see below at VIII 360b12.

(32) {*Menāqıb-ı eş-şeyẖ 'Alī Dost Dede.*} Ḥattā bu 'Alī Dost Dede merḥūm olduqda cümle Ergiri Qaṣri ẖalqı bu 'Alī Dost Dede ṭā'ūndan öldi deyü dağlara ve ġayr[i] qurālar[a] firār (33) éderler, 'azīz-i merḥūmuñ cesed-i pākleri qırq gün qırq géce ṣavma'asında qalup ba'dehu qurālardan niçe adamlar şehre gelüp cür'et édüp ṣavma'a (34) qapusın açup görseler kim na'şe-yi 'Alī Dede ḥücre içre qıbleye müteveccih olup vücūd-ı şerīfi henūz ter ü tāze ve issi olup yatır. Cümle ehālī-yi **[355a]** vilāyet 'ālem-i ḥayretde qalup 'azīz-i merḥūmuñ ṣāḥibü'l-ẖayrātlar techīz-i tekfīnini āmāde édüp tenşūy[1] üstinde ġasl éderlerken 'azīziñ ṣadr-ı münevverinde (2) bir qırmızı et pāresinde qudret qalemiyle 'Alī Dost lafẓı yazılmış. Cümle ẖalq ḥayretde qalup tevḥīd [ü] tezkīr ile ġasl édüp (3) bu Tekye cāmi'i ḥarêminde defin éderler. Ḥālā ziyāretgāh-ı ẖās ı 'āmdır, quddise sırruhu.

Der mesīre-yi ġarībe vü 'acībe. Ḥālā bu Ergiri Qaṣri (4) şehrinde bir adam ṭā'ūndan degil ancaq bir sivrice çıban çıqarsa ṭā'ūndur deyü cümle ẖalq ol adamdan nefret édüp ol (5) adam artıq bir yére varamaz, aña yaqın olan qomşuları cümle firār éderler. Meger ġayri ẖastelik olsa ol adamıñ yanına varup ḥālin (6) ẖāṭırın ṣorarlar. Ve ṭā'ūnlı eve bir iki yıla daq girmezler. Eger girirlerse ol evi sirke ile yıqayup gūnāgūn buẖūrlar tütsi (7) vérüp niçe yerleri münhedim édüp ta'mīr [ü] termīm édüp beyāż kireçler ile her ḥücreleri ağardup andan girirler. Ammā ḥikmet-i ẖüdā, ẖalqı ṭā'ūndan (8) ölmezler, eks̱eriyyā ishāl ve zeẖīr ve ḥummā-yı muḥrıqa ve ağrı ẖasteliginden yollanırlar. Ammā eks̱eriyyā ẖalqı kemāl mertebe müsin ü mu'ammer ve Zāl-i zemān (9) olup quvveti gitmiş ve heybeti yitmiş ve 'ömr-i 'azīzi yüz yetmişe yetmiş kimesneler olup yetmiş seksen sene ṣaqalların (10) ṭırāş éderler, ve eñ ednā pīr-i fānī dédigiñ adamları yine silāḥların quşanup yā at ile yāẖod piyāde olup Quryeleş (11) dāğınıñ 'āṣī Arnavu[d]larıyle yāẖod Venedik kāfirleriyle cenge gider bir alay ġāziyān-ı mücāhidānlardır.

Bunlarıñ ḥaqqında daẖi ḥażret-i (12) Mu'āviyeyi ve Yezīdi sevmez ve sebb éder dérler, ammā görmedim[2], lākin Aydonat ẖalqı gibi

---

[1] Altered from *teneşir*?
[2] Altered to *işitmedim* (and below the line: *ben işitmedim*).

Legend of Sheikh Ali Dost Dede. When this Ali Dost Dede died, the whole population of Gjirokastër, convinced that he had expired of the plague, took to the hills and the villages in the countryside, leaving the blessed body of the great saint unburied in his cell for forty days and forty nights. Later, some of the citizens returned from the countryside and ventured to open the door of the cell. What should they see but the corpse of Ali Dost lying there, pointed in the direction of Mecca, and the blessed body still fresh and warm. All the populace of the province marvelled at this fact. Certain generous benefactors prepared the corpse for burial. While they were completing the ritual cleansing of the body, they noticed the words "Ali Dost" (Ali the Friend) inscribed by some divine pen on a portion of red flesh on the saint's chest. The whole population marvelled at this wonder and washed and buried the saint in the courtyard of the Tekke mosque, to the accompaniment of prayers and incantations. Even today people come from all parts to visit the site — may his mystery be sanctified.

A marvel. If someone in the town of Gjirokastër should happen to have a pimple or a boil, all the people say that he has the plague and flee from him. No one allows him in. Even his closest neighbors take flight. Only when they are assured that he has some other illness will they approach and inquire about his health. No one enters the home of anyone who has had the plague for up to two years, and even when this period has passed, they still cleanse the house with vinegar, disinfect it with aromatic herbs, tear down and rebuild various parts of the house, and whitewash all the rooms with lime before entering. Strangely enough, the inhabitants of this town rarely die of the plague, but rather of dysentery, food poisoning, inflammation and fever. Despite such illnesses, the people here live long lives. There are those who reach 170 years old and are still going strong, though somewhat reduced in vigor. They shave until age 70 or 80. Even the most fragile old men brazenly gird on arms and ride or hike up into the Kurvelesh mountains to put down Albanian rebels or to fight the Venetians infidels. They are courageous ghazis.

I was told that they also despise and curse Muawiya and Yazid,[1] although I never observed this. Like the people of Paramithiá,[2] they

---

[1] Umayyad caliphs. Cursing them would be a sign of fanatical Shiite tendencies.

[2] Tk. Aydonat, a town in northern Greece. In Evliya's description of Aydonat, shortly before the section here translated, there is no mention of these customs; see VIII 350a-b (659-63).

bunlar da aṣlā māvī çoqa geymezler ve Mu'āviye (13) peydā etdi deyü zerde aşın yemeyüp Mu'āviye boza yapup içdi deyü boza daḫi içmezler. Ammā Islāmbolda ekṡeriyyā boza yapan cümle (14) Arnavu[d] qavmlarıdır.

Diger mu'tād temāşā-yı ġarīb-i[1] *qavm-ı Ergiri.* Qırq elli ve seksen yıldan berü ölmüş adamlarıñ esmāların aqrabāları (15) yād édüp elbette her bāzār güni ol merḥūmuñ rūḥıyçün cümle te'alluqātları ücretler ile niçe adamlar dutup amadani bir evde[2] (16) bir feza' u çeza' ve nāliş-i vāveylā qopup bu qāfile aġlayu aġlayu ṣaġular ṣaġlayup feryād éderler kim ol şehirde bāzār günleri (17) feryād u nāliş-i vāveylā qopup feza' u çeza'dan adam bu şehirde duramaz, anıñiçün bu şehre ḥaqīr şehr-i nāliş dédim, ammā ġarābet anda kim (18) ücret ile dutulan 'avretler ve adamlarıñ 'alāqaları yoq iken yüz yıllıq ölü içü[n] aqrâbālarından ziyāde nice aġlayup eşk-i çeşm-i (19) ciger-ḫūn dökebilir. Ba'dehu bunlar aġlaya aġlaya açlıqdan bī-tāb u bīmecāl qalup ba'de'l-bükā gūnāgūn pişiler ve çamuqalar (20) ve qomoştovar nām börek gibi şeyler ve mümessek za'ferānlı ḥalvālar bu şehr içre evden eve birbirlerine gönd[er]üp her bāzār güni şehr içre (21) ervāḥ-ı mevtā şādān ola deyü ni'met-i nefīse bay u gedāya ve cümle müsāfirīn ü mücāvirīne nüzül olunur. Hele bu eyi ḫaṣletdir, ammā yüz (22) yıllıq nāfile aġlamaq bī-ma'nīdir, lākin elbette her diyār ḫalqınıñ birer gūne āyīn-i qadīmeleri[3] vardır.

Ḥattā yine kendüleri naql éder kim (23) bir adam kendi ḫatunıyle cimā' éderken bir münāsib nā-maḥalde[4] ḥerīf eydir: "Canım ḫatun, yarın bāzār günidir" deyince (24) hemān ḥerīf-i ẓarīfiñ altında 'avretiñ ḫātırına biñ qırq üç senesinde Ca'fer Paşa qapudan iken Aq Deñizde İngilis qalyo(25)nlarıyle ceng éderken bu 'avrêtiñ on yedinci qocası ḥerīfiñ altında cimā' maḥallinde ḫātırına ḫuṭūr édüp ol ḥerīfiñ altında (26) yatup zevq éderken hemān 'avret ṣaçı yolup "Hay benim ġazāda şehīd olan on yedinci qırq yıllıq qocacıġımla ben böyle mi (27) cimā' éderdim? Āh sikişine doymadıġım şehīd qocacıġım" deyü eyle feza' u çeza' ve nāliş éder kim girde-bālişde seyl-i eşk çeyḥūn-(28)vār revān olunca faqīr ḥerīfiñ 'aqlı başından gidüp vāveylā vü vāveldā sikişi

---

[1] Altered to *ġarībe-yi* (or vice versa?).

[2] Last three words crossed out, *dutup* altered to *dutulur*, and *ve* added at beginning of next line.

[3] Altered to *qadīmleri*.

[4] sic; for *nā-münāsib maḥalde*?

never wear blue clothes, nor do they eat *zerde*[1] or drink *boza* because these were invented by Muawiya — or so they claim. Despite this, those who sell *boza* in Istanbul are all Albanians.[2]

Another strange custom. The people of Gjirokastër mourn their dead relatives for forty or fifty, indeed up to eighty years. Every Sunday, all the relatives of the dead person gather in a ramshackle house, paying professional mourners who weep and wail and keen and lament, raising a great hue and cry. No one can stand to be in town on Sundays because of all the noise and uproar. For this reason I dubbed Gjirokastër the "city of wailing". It is a great wonder how the professional mourners manage to weep and wail with such feeling — more than for their own relatives — for someone who has been dead a hundred years and to whom they are not even related. And how they lament! It is only when they are exhausted with hunger that they desist. When they finish their lamentations, they have the home owners prepare various pastries, including *pişi, jamuk* and *qumështuar*, and also saffron-flavored sweets to be distributed in town from house to house. These dainties are offered free of charge to rich and poor alike and to all travellers and sojourners on Sundays for the sake of the spirits of the dead. This is a generous deed, to be sure; but mourning for someone who died one hundred years ago seems to me quite pointless. Nonetheless, every country has its own rites and traditions.

They themselves relate the following: One day, while having sex with his wife, a man inopportunely happened to remark, "Tomorrow is Sunday, my dear." His wife, underneath the fellow, suddenly called to mind her seventeenth husband who had been killed in the naval battle in the Mediterranean between the Ottoman admiral Jafer Pasha and some English galleys in the year 1043 (1633-34). While still engaged in intercourse, she began tearing her hair, crying, "Oh, how I long for my poor dear seventeenth husband, with whom I lived for forty years and who was martyred in the ghaza. I had such good sex with him!" She raised such a ruckus and bathed the pillow with so

---

[1] A sweet gelatinous dessert colored and flavored with saffron.

[2] This statement contradicts what Evliya says in his description of the *boza* sellers of Istanbul, that they are Tatars and Gypsies; see I 212b28

cānına geçüp erligi feryād [u] fiġān ile qopup (29) faqīr ḥerīf bāzār güni oldıġına peşīmān olur.

Ol ecilden ḥaqīr vāqıf-ı esrār oldum ki bu Ergiri ḫalqı cümle aġlamış (30) çehreli adamlar olup ḫalq ile ḥüsn-i ülfetleri ve ḥüsn-i zindegāneleri yoqdur. Ammā şecī‘ ü ġāzī şehbāzları çoqdur. Ekṣeriyyā (31) ḫalqı erbāb-ı me‘ārif ve şu‘arā-yı mü'ellifīnlerdir. Bā-ḫuṣūṣ Bükāyī ve Fiġānī ve Nālişī ve Sükūnī ve Fezā‘ī nām şu‘arālar ḥālā bu (32) şehirde mevcūdlardır kim her [bir]i birer fende yed-i ṭūlāların ‘ayān etmişlerdir. Ammā Nālişī penc-beytde ve qaṣīde-perdāzlıqda lā-naẓīrdir.

(33) Ve ekṣeriyyā ḫalqı muḥibb-i ḫānedān olup "Yā 'Alī" der oṭurur ve "Yā 'Alī" der qalqar. Cümle fārsī-ḫān olup muḥibb-i ḫānedān olduqlarından bir (34) fırqası nihānīce Mu‘āviyeye seb édüp Yezīde āşikāre la‘net éderlermiş, ammā istimā‘ etmedim. Ve ḫalqı ġāyet ehl-i zevq u 'ayş u 'işrete **[355b]** māyil olup bāde-yi nāb bī-ḥicāb[1] ve reyḥāniye nām muqavvī şeyleri nūş édüp ser-ḫoş olurlar.

Dīger āyīn-i bed-kār-ı qavm-ı Ergiri. Bunlar (2) dügünlerde ve rūz-ı Ḫıżırda ve nevruz-ı ḫārezm-şāhīde ve qāsım günlerinde ve Ṣarı Ṣaltıq günlerinde ve 'īdeynlerde[2] zer-ender-zere (3) müstaġraq olup la‘l-gūn bādeleri nūş édüp cemī‘i pençe-yi āftāb dilberānlarıyle 'āşıqları el ele verüp āyīn-i kāfir gibi quc-qucaġ (4) olup ḫoros depüp quşaq quşaġa yapışup ḫora depme semā‘ı éderler. Bu daḫi bir bed-sünnetdir kim āyīn-i ke[fe]redir, ammā böyle (5) göre gelmişler, bunı daḫi 'ayblamazız[3].

Der qıyāfet-i qabā-yı ricāl-i insān. İḫtiyārları destār-ı muḥammedī ṣarup māvīden mā-'adā (6) elvān çoqalar geyüp ayaqlarında qopçalı çaqşır olup şecī‘āne gezerler. Ammā cemī‘i tāze cüvānları qıṣa yeñli ve qıṣacıq (7) etekli ve nigendeli qırmızı ḥarīr aṭlas zıbunlar geyüp

---

[1] Crossed out.

[2] Crossed out and replaced by *'īdeynde* above line.

[3] Text: *'ayblamazızız.*

many tears that the poor fellow went limp and, mourning the loss of his virility, now regretted that it was Sunday.

It is for this reason, I divined, that the men of Gjirokastër all have a mournful and somber look. There is hardly any good cheer and friendly feeling, although there are many brave young men among them. There are people of much knowledge here, in particular a good number of poets, of whom Bükâyi, Figani, Nalishi, Sükûni and Feza'i[1] still reside in this city and excel in various skills. Nalishi is without peer in both ghazals and qasidas.

Most of the people of Gjirokastër are devoted to Ali and to the family of the Prophet. They sit down proclaiming "Ya Ali!" and stand up proclaiming "Ya Ali!" They can all read Persian. Because they so love Ali and the family of the Prophet, one group secretly curse Muawiya and openly curse Yazid — at least this is what I was told, although I never heard it myself. These people are very fond of pleasure and carousing. They shamelessly drink wine and other intoxicating beverages, such as the one called *reyhania*[2].

Another bad habit of the people of Gjirokastër. In weddings, on festival days of St George,[3] Nevruz, St. Demetrius,[4] and St. Nicholas,[5] and on the two feasts of Bairam,[6] they put on their finery and drink various alcoholic beverages. Lovers go hand in hand with their pretty boys and embrace them and dance about in the manner of the Christians. This is quite shameful behavior, characteristic of the infidels; but it is their custom, so we cannot censure it.

Men's clothing. The old men wrap a turban around their heads and dress in every color except blue. They stroll about in manly fashion wearing buttoned trousers. Young men wear a short-sleeved shirt and a very short-skirted pleated undergarment of red silk and satin. They

---

[1] All names signifying "Weeper, Lamenter," etc. Only Sükuni (roughly, "Silent") does not fit the pattern.

[2] An alcoholic drink which Evliya later describes as "red grape must produced by boiling grapes of various kinds;" see below at VIII 360a11. It may perhaps have been flavored with sweet basil, Turkish *reyhan*. The drink, Alb. *rehaní*, is still consumed today.

[3] *Rūz-ı Ḫıżır*, i.e. 23 April; cf. F. W. Hasluck, *Christianity and Islam Under the Sultans*, 2 vols. (Oxford University Press, 1929; repr. New York: Octagon, 1973), I, 320.

[4] *Qāsım*, i.e. 26 October.

[5] *Ṣarı Ṣaltıq*; cf. Hasluck, *op. cit.*, I, 55.

[6] *ʿĪdeyn*, the two great Muslim festivals.

qolları ve oyluqları açıqdır. Cümle tenāsüb a'żāları meydāndadır; (8) ancaq ḥarīrden aq kenārlı gömlekleri qaṣıqlarınadaq örter, mā-'adā nā-maḥrem yerleri incecik dondan ve gömlekden nümāyāndır. (9) Donları ise dizlerin ancaq örter bol paçalı serāvīllerdir. Don derler ammā degildir, hemān bir beyāż çarşafı beline bağlamış (10) edebde teşelşül ve teġayyuż maḥallerinde[1] aṣlā uçqur çözmeden donınıñ paçalarından maṣlaḥat görerler. El-ḥāṣıl ġarīb ü (11) 'acīb ṭurfa-libās hey'et-i mecmū'a yigitleri var, ammā ġāyet pāk-dāmenlerdir, anlarda ġulām u zenān qısımlarında fi'l-i şenī' olmazdır, (12) zīrā yigit vilāyetidir ve 'avretleri merḥūme olduqda "Vaḥdehu lā şerīke lehu" ile qapudan ṭaşra çıqar, bir daḫi raḥm-ı māder maṣdarından (13) ṭaşra çıqup dünyāya qadem baṣar. Lākin her bāzār günleri mezkūr üz[r]e feryād [u] fiġānları cihānı dutduqları lā-be'sdir. Yılda bir kerre (14) zenāneleri vālideynleriniñ ḫānelerine gidemez, tā bu mertebe Rābi'a-yı 'Adeviyye mertebesinde ḫavātīnleri vardır.

(15) *Āṣār-ı bināsınıñ ve me'kūlāt [ü] meşrūbātınıñ memdūḥātından.* Evvelā bādesi ve reyḥāniyyesi ve poloniyyesi[2] ve beyāż Arnavud simīdi ve külde (16) pişmiş kül gibi beyāż poġaçası ve ṣaralı nām mümessek üzümi memdūḥdur. Ve cemī'i evleriniñ ṭaş dīvārları (17) ṭarzı rū-yı arżda yoqdur, cümle qırmızı ṣumpara ṭaşından çār-gūşeden ṭūlānīce ṭaş dīvārlardır kim aṣlā çamur (18) ve kireç ve alçısı yoq, ancaq ṭaş ṭaş üzre bir quru binā qadleri yigirmi arşın bālā dīvār kim bālāda sehil memdūḥdur. (19) Tā kāfir zemānından qalmış niçe yüz yıllıq dīvārlar ve ḫānedānlar vardır ve eyle serāmed hemvār dīvār-ı üstüvārlardır kim bir serçe quşı ṭırnaq (20)[3] ildirecek yeri yoqdur. Ve āb [u] havāsı ve bināsı laṭīf yaylaq olduġından limonı ve turuncı ve nārı ve zeytūnı (21) olmaz.

Bu temāşāları etdigimizden ṣoñra naṣb-ı nefes (?) édüp ḫalqile ḥüsn-i ülfet etmege cidd [ü] ihtimām édüp ḫāh-nā-ḫāh bu (22) ḥaqīr anlar ile ālüfte ve āşüftelik éderek maḥrem-i rāz olup Zeynel-paşa-oġlı beg efendimiziñ dügünine biñ yayan ve biñ atlı (23) pür-silāḥ adamlar ile atlanup — *Poġonya feżāsında qarye-yi Jaravinadan qız almaġa gitdigimiz qonaqları 'ayān u beyān éder* — (24) evvelā Ergiri Qaṣriden cānib-i cenūba ol öz içre *Nehr-i Diraġopol* kenārınca ol

---

[1] Phrase beginning *edebde* crossed out and replaced below line by: *derkār olacaq vaqitde.*

[2] To be read thus; mistakenly recorded in *Glossary* (Dankoff 1991) as *belvine (t-?).*

[3] *ṭırnaq* repeated at beginning of line.

leave their arms and thighs uncovered, so their private parts are quite exposed. Only a silk shirt with white hems covers them down to the groin. Other parts of their bodies show immodestly through their very thin shirts and breeches. These breeches — so-called — hardly cover their knees. They are actually trousers, wide in the lower part and like a white sheet tied around the loins. To urinate or defecate — if you will excuse the expression — they do not even need to undo the drawstring. In short the young men have very strange outfits, but they are also very chaste. The men are a race of warriors and do not have illicit relations with either boys or women. As for their wives, when they die they go out the door to the tune of "He is one and has no partner."[1] Otherwise they never leave home from the day they are born until the day they die — I disregard their mourning and wailing every Sunday, as mentioned above. They no not even visit their parents' house, so chaste and virtuous are they, the likes of the saintly lady Rabi'a Adawiyya.[2]

Comestables and construction techniques. The best known foods and drinks are wine, *reyhania,* Polish arrack, white Albanian rolls (*simid*), white flatbread baked in red-hot coals, and aromatic grapes called *saralı.* The manner in which the outer walls of all the houses are constructed has no parallel in all the world. They are all twenty ells high[3] of red sandstone blocks, just stone on stone with no mud, lime or plaster. The walls and the houses are all centuries old, dating from the time of the infidels. The walls are so lofty and solid that not even a sparrow can get a clawhold. Being up in the high mountain pastures, the climate here does not allow for the cultivation of lemons, oranges, pomegranates and olives.

After finishing my tours, I relaxed and began to get acquainted with the people. It was here that I had the good fortune to take part in the wedding of the son of Zeynel Pasha, and accompanied 1000 horsemen and 1000 armed foot soldiers to fetch the bride. *Stages of our journey to fetch the bride from the village of Zharovina in the Pogonia plain.* We set off from Gjirokastër with the entire wedding procession, travelling south along the banks of the Dropull river. On

---

[1] I.e., the funeral prayer.
[2] Ascete and saint, d. 185/801, proverbial for chastity.
[3] Approximately 15 meters.

ṣaḥrānıñ iki ṭarâfı daġlar eteginde cümle (25) altmış sekiz pāre ma'mūr u ābādān ve bāġ u bāġçeli ve cümle qal'e-miṡāl qulleli ve cümle evleri serāpā qayaġan ṭaşı örtüli müzeyyen (26) qurālardır. Ḥikmet bu kim şarq ṭarâfında olan Liboh Ovasındaki ṣıradaki qurālar cümle elli pāre ma'mūr köylerdir kim (27) birbirlerine birer oq menzili qarībdir ve āb-ı ḥayāt ṣuları bī-ḥisābdır, ammā Ergiri Qaṣri ṭarâfında olan qırq pāre qurālar (28) daġlar etegindedir, ammā aṣlā ṣuları yoqdur, 'aceb ḥikmetdir.

Bu temāşāları mezkūr ṣaḥrālar içre éderek 6 sā'atde cānib-i (29) cenūba giderek *der tesvīdāt-ı ṭarz [u] ṭavr-ı qaṣaba-yı Pıṣqopi.* Ergiri qażāsı nāḥiyesinde bir daġ eteginde bāġlı (30) ve bāġçeli ve bir qayalı daġ-ı ser-bülend dibinde cümle üçyüz 'aded qayaġan örtüli evlerdir. Ve qayalar dibinde niçe yüz 'aded (31) ṣu degirmanları yüridir āb-ı ḥayāt ṣular qaynayup çıqar. Ve daġlar üstinde biri biri üzre binā olunmuş ma'mūr u (32) şīrīn kārgīr-binā evlerdir. Ammā aşaġıda degirmenler yanında Memi Paşa nev-binā bir cāmi'-i zībā ve bir kārgīr mināreli ma'bedgāh-ı ra'nā inşā (33) etmiş kim gūyā cāmi'-i Aqṣā olmuş. Cümle qurā ḫalqı bu cāmi'e muḥtāclardır kim 'aceb yerinde binā olunmuş. Ve bir çārsū binā etmiş kim (34) cümle yigirmi 'aded dükkānlardır.

Bu köyden şarq ṭarâfına daġlar içre 2 sā'at gidüp *qarye-yi Eksiri Valtoz.* Elli 'aded **[356a]** ḫānedānları ve bir büyük çiftligi ve yılda bir kerre durur 'aẓīm panayır cem'iyyeti olur, bunda bir 'aẓīm ḫānı ve elli qadar panayır dükkānları (2) var, mā-'adā panayır cem'iyyeti zemānı biñ 'aded çalaş [u] malaş [u] ḫalaşdan külbe-yi aḥzān-miṡāl dükkānlar binā olunup niçe kerre yüz biñ (3) ḫayme vü ḫargāhlar qurılub 'aẓīm cem'iyyet-i kübrā yeri vāsi' çemenzār ṣaḥrā-yı lāle-zārdır.

Andan yine cānib-i şarqa 3 sā'at (4) gidüp ma'mūr qurālar geçerek *qarye-yi Zarovina.* Yüz evli bir ma'mūr köydür ve bir qulleli çiftligi var. Bu qarye Poġonya (5) qażāsı ḥudūdıdır. Ve bundan öteye qıble ṭarâfına artıq Yanya sancaġı qażāsıdır ve bu qaryeden şehr-i Yanya 9 sā'atlik yerdir. (6) Ve bu Zaravina köyi bāġlı ve bāġçeli bir göl kenārında vāqı' olmuş ma'mūr ze'āmetdir. Anda żiyāfet-i 'aẓīmler olup ṭoplar ve tüfengler (7) şādmānları olup bu köyden qızı alup alay ile yollarda niçe yüz kerre tüfeng şādmānları édüp cümle yigitler ṣadā-yı Allāh (8) Allāh gülbāngı çeküp ammā yine kefere gibi ḫoros deperek gidüp ġayri yol ile gerüye dönüp ma'mūr qurālar geçüp 4 sā'atde (9) cānib-i ġarba gidüp

either side of the Dropull valley and in the foothills we viewed 68 prosperous and attractive villages with their vineyards and gardens and their fortress-like houses, all with slate roofs. There are also 50 very prosperous villages in Libohova to the east, all in a line, separated from one another by an arrow's shot, with countless fresh-water streams. On the Gjirokastër side, however, the 40 villages at the foot of the mountain have no water at all — a very curious phenomenon.

Our journey through the plains lasted 6 hours until we arrived at *the town of Peshkëpia*. It lies at the foot of a high rocky mountain in the *kadi*-district of Gjirokastër, with vineyards and gardens and 300 houses with slate roofs. From the cliffs of the mountain flow abundant streams which turn hundreds of water mills.

The houses in this town, of fine stonework, are built one atop the other over the mountains. Down near the water mills, Memi Pasha built a new mosque with a stonework minaret. It is a magnificent prayer-house, recalling the Aqsa mosque in Jerusalem. All the surrounding villages use this mosque, which was built on just the right spot. He also built a bazaar with 20 shops.

From here, we carried on eastwards and, after journeying for 2 hours across the mountains, we arrived at *the village of Ksirovaltos*.[1] It has 50 houses and a large farm-estate. Every year, a huge fair is held here. It has a large *han* and about 50 shops for the fair. When the fair is being held, in a vast flowering meadow, a further 1000 reed huts are built and thousands of tents are set up.

From here, we set off once more in an easterly direction, travelling for 3 hours through prosperous villages until we arrived at *Zharovina*.[2] It is a prosperous village of 100 houses, including a farm-estate with a tower. This village is on the border of the *kadi*-district of Pogonia. Beyond it to the south is the *sancak* of Janina, and the city of Janina is 9 hours away. Zharovina, which is stiuated on the shore of a lake, is a thriving *zeamet* with vineyards and gardens. When we arrived, there were great banquets and volleys of cannons and muskets. Then we set off on the return trip, continuing the festivities along the road with our bridal procession. All the youths shouted "Allah Allah!" and once again danced like Christians.

---

1 On the Greek side of the present border.

2 Exact location unknown, but probably in the vicinity of the Greek villages of Pontikates, Pogoniani, Dolo, and Farangi, all northwest of Delvinaki.

Der müsevvedāt-ı eşkāl-i qaṣaba-yı Delvinak. Bu qaṣaba Poġonya qażāsı ḥudūdında dörd yüz (10) ʻaded kefere evli ve altı biñ ʻaded bāġlı maʻmūr [u] ābādān rabṭa-yı zībādır. Cümle qırq elli qadar dükkānları ve cümle on (11) ʻaded kenīseleri ve cümle üç ʻaded ḫānları var. Cümle kefereleri Arnavuddur. Ve Qapudan Paşa ḫāṣṣı olup voyvadası (12) ḥākimdir, mefrūzu'l-qalem ve maqṭūʻu'l-qadem ḫāṣdır.

Andan 6 sāʻat yine ṭaraf-ı ġarba *qarye-yi Liboh Ova.* Ergiri qażāsı (13) ḥudūdında bāg-ı irem-miṡāl āb-ı ḥayātları cārī vü revān bir daġ eteginde cümle ikiyüz ʻaded qayaġan örtüli ʻĀrnābūd (14) evleridir, ammā ehālīsi müsülmānlardır, bir cāmiʻi ve bir mescidi ve bir ḫānı ve bir küçücük ḥammāmı var. Zeynel-paşa-oġlı (15) bunda çiftligi içre sākindir, ġāyet ḫānedān-ı ʻaẓīmdir kim vaṣfında lisān qāṣırdır. Bunda gelini yüz biñ gūne şādmānlar (16) ile getirüp cumʻa gécesi bege ʻarūsı teslīm édüp ol géce ṣabāḥadaq bir ʻayş u ʻişret ve sāz [u] söz ve hāy [u] (17) hūy zevq u ṣafā-yı Ḥüseyn Bayqara meclisleri oldı kim ṣabāḥısı yetmiş ʻaded şarāb fıçısı boş qaldı ve iki biñ qoyun (18) kebābı tenāvül olundı deyü tefāḫur kesb etdiler. Ḫulāṣa-yı kelā[m] bu ḥaqīr-i ażʻafu'l-ʻibād bu cem[ʻ]iyyet-i kübrāyı bir hafta temāşā édüp (19) bir Arnavud ṭarzı sūr-ı zifāf temāşāları etdim ki vaṣfında lisān qāṣır ve qalemler kāsirdir. Eger bir hafta içre olan temāşā-yı āyīn-i (20) ʻibretnümā-yı ʻaceb-gūyı (?) mā-vaqaʻı üzre taḥrīr etsem bir ṭūmār-ı dirāz zifāf-nāme olur.

Netīce-yi kelām, baʻde's-sūr-ı iḫtitām, (21) begden bir at ve bir köle ve yüz altun ve on qıṭʻa çoqa ve qumāşlar ve bir mīqātlı muṣannaʻ sāʻat iḥsān alup cümle aḥbāb ile (22) vedāʻlaşup cānib-i ġarba 2 sāʻatde tekrār qalʻe-yi Ergiriye gelüp anda daḫi cümle dostānlar ile vedālaşup[1] Ergiri qalʻe(23)siniñ qıblesi ṭarâfındaki evc-i semāya berāber yaylanıñ tā zirve-yi aʻlāsından Delvine şehri dörd sāʻatlik yerdir, ve gün doġduqda (24) havā ḫoşluġında Bunduqani Venedigi Körfezi deryāsı içre cezīre-yi Körfez qalʻesi nümāyāndır. Baʻdehu Ergiri yanından ʻubūr (25) édüp şimāl ṭarâfına bāġlar içre gidüp ve Nehr-i Diraġopol kenārınca gidüp ṣaġ ṭarâfımızda *qarye-yi Qaqoṣ*, Memi Paşa (26) oġlı ʻAlī Beg çiftligidir, gūyā bir qalʻe-yi

[1] Altered to *vedāʻlaşup.*

We returned by another road, passing through prosperous villages. After 4 hours of travelling westwards, we arrived at *Delvinaki.*[1] It is a prosperous town on the border of the district of Pogonia and consists of 400 houses inhabited by infidels — all Albanians — and 6000 fertile vineyards. It has 40 to 50 shops, 10 churches and 3 hans. This town is a *has* belonging to the admiral of the Ottoman fleet and administered by a *voyvoda*. It is exempt from taxation and state interference.

We continued westwards from Delvinaki for 6 hours and arrived at *the village of Libohova*. It is on the border of the *kadi*-district of Gjirokastër at the foot of a mountain with flowing water, like the fabled garden of Irem[2]. It consists of 200 houses with slate roofs and is inhabited by Albanians, who are, however, Muslims. It has a congregational mosque, a prayer house, a *han* and a small bathhouse. Here is to be found the farm-estate of the son of Zeynel Pasha with his indescribably grand villa. We brought the bride to this place with much ceremony on Friday eve (Thursday night) and handed her over to the *beg*. Music and entertainment and noisy festivities continued all night until the next morning by which time, they boasted, 70 kegs of wine and 2000 sheep roasted on skewers had been consumed. In short, I had the pleasure for a whole week of observing an Albanian wedding. It would be impossible to describe such a wedding feast in speech or writing. If I were to record all the marvels I observed during that week, my scroll would turn into a veritable wedding book. To make a long story short, after the wedding the *beg* presented me with 1 horse, 1 slave, 100 goldpieces, 10 measures of broadcloth and other material, and 1 splendid timepiece.

Bidding farewell to all my friends and acquaintances, I set off westwards and returned to Gjirokastër in 2 hours. Here I bid farewell to more of my friends. Just south of the city there is an outlook at the highest point of the summer pasture from which you can see the town of Delvina, four hours away. Also from here, at sunrise and in clear weather, you can see the Venetian fortress on the island of Corfu. We however, after leaving Gjirokastër, headed north through vineyards along the right bank of the Dropull river and reached *the village of Kakoz*, a farm-estate belonging to Ali Beg son of Memi Pasha. It is

---

1 Delvinaki or Delvinakion in northern Greece.

2 Legendary city built by Shaddad ibn ‘Ad in order to imitate paradise. Referred to in the Koran, 89:6.

metīndir. Andan yine semt-i ġarba *qarye-yi Qaryan*. Andan *qarye-yi Lab Ova*. Andan (27) *qarye-yi Tirbuk*, muqābelesinde Nehr-i Yeñice Ergiri Nehrine maḫlūṭ olduġı yerden bir sā'at aşaġı *qarye-yi Horom Ova*, (28) Memi Paşa ze'āmetidir.

Andan *qarye-yi Lekel*. Öñinde Ergiri Ṣuyı üzre Meḥemmed Ṣubaşı cisri bir göz ṭaş-binā cisr-i 'ālī (29) olup iki başlarında birer 'aded küçük gözleri daḫi var. Bu cisri geçüp el-'iyāẕen-bi'llāh[1] 'āṣī Porġonat içidir, bu menzilde (30) giderken bir günde yolumuza iki kerre Porġonat ḥarāmīleri énüp yarar refīqlerimiz olmaġile 'aẓīm ṣavaşlar eyleyüp (31) āḫir refīqimiz Dervīş Rāhī rāh-ı ḥaqqa şehd-i şehādetle gidüp ve benim altımda Ḫamīs nām bir atım ve bir ġulāmım mecrūḥ olup (32) anlardan iki mel'ūn mürd olup silāḥların alup ḥamd-i ḫüdā ḫüdā murġ-ı cānımız āzād édüp Dervīş Rāhīyi şāh-rāh üzre defn (33) eyleyüp iki kelle ile manṣūr u muẓaffer Depe Delen şehrine revāne olduq. Ve bu Porġonat Arnavudı 'āṣīleri içinden yüz biñ (34) renc [ü] 'inā ile 'ubūr éderken elli pāre qurālardır, ve yerleri ġāyet ṣarp ve daġıstān u çengelistān yerlerdir kim ibtidā ḥudūd-ı Avlonya **[356b]** sancaġıdır ve Depe Delen qażāsı nāḥiyesidir.

Bu 'āṣīler içinden selāmetle 2 sā'atde geçüp *qarye-yi Kuzat*. Bu daḫi Depe (2) Delen ḥudūdıdır. Bu qaryeye muqābil Nehr-i Viyo Ergiri Nehrine maḫlūṭ olur. Bu Nehr-i Viyo tā Korça ve Tirḥala (3) daġlarından ve Semerine yaylasından gelir. Andan iki biñ adım cānib-i ġarba ṣarp dereleri ve depeleri ve dere kenārların renc [ü] 'inā çekerek (4) gidüp -----

Der tefhīmāt-ı ṣūret-i qal'e-yi dār-ı emen, ya'nī sūr-ı refī'-i metīn-i Depe Delen. (5) Budin serḥaddinde Nehr-i Ṭuna kenārında qal'e-yi Usturġon-ı meşḥūn muqābelesinde bir daḫi Depe Delen qal'esi var, lākin ol Depe Delen (6) palanqa çit qal'edir, ammā bu seng-binā bir qal'e-yi ra'nādır. Sene 897 tārīḫinde Sulṭān Bāyezīd-i Velī 'aṣrında Gedik Aḥmed Paşa fetḥidir. (7) 'Āṣī Arnavud Venedik Firengiyle bir olup bu qal'e içine qapanup ġuzāt-ı müslimīn daḫi qal'eye ḥavāle ṭabyalar yapup qal'e (8) içindeki küffārlarıñ depelerin deldikleriyçün bu qal'eye ba'de'l-fetiḥ Depe Delen deyü tesmiye etdiler. Ḥālā Avlonya sancaġı ḫākinde (9) voyvadalıqdır ve yüz elli aqçe qażādır,

---

[1] *el-'iyāẕen* altered to *el-'iyāẕu* and *'iyāẕen* written above; but see *Glossary* (Dankoff 1991), p. 7.

built like a strong fortress. From here we continued west to *Karjan, Labova, and Tërbuq*, and hence, from the place where the Gjirokastër river joins the Yenice river, for one hour down to *Hormova*, a *zeamet* of Memi Pasha, and arrived at the village of *Lekël*.

Here, on the Gjirokastër river, is the beautiful one-arched stone bridge of Mehmed Subaşı. There are also smaller arches at either end of the bridge. On the other side of the bridge is the road to Progonat — a rebellious region, God save us! While travelling along this road we were ambushed twice in one day by outlaws from Progonat, but our brave escort fought them off each time. My companion Dervish Rahi was martyred during the second skirmish, and my horse Hamis and one of my servant-boys were wounded. But we did manage to kill two of the outlaws, whose heads we cut off and whose weapons we seized. Praising God for our salvation, we buried Dervish Rahi along the roadside and set off triumphantly toward Tepelena, carrying the two heads.

In this region of Progonat there are 50 villages situated in the mountains and on rugged promontories. It constitutes the border with the *sancak* of Vlora and the *kadi*-district of Tepelena. We came through this rebellious region in 2 hours and arrived safe and sound at the village of Luzat, which is on the border of Tepelena. It is near this village that the Vjosa river and the Gjirokastër river flow together. The Vjosa takes its source in the mountains of Korça and Trikala[1] and in the high mountain pastures of Çamëria.

From here we journeyed some 2000 paces westwards, traversing steep valleys and hillside country until we arrived, after much difficulty, at *the lofty and sturdy fortress of Tepelena (Depe Delen)*. There is another fortress called Depe Delen across from Esztergom on the banks of the Danube, on the Buda frontier. But whereas that Depe Delen is a wooden stockade, this one is constructed of stone. It was conquered by Gedik Ahmed Pasha during the reign of Sultan Bayezid II the Saint in the year 897 (1492). Albanian rebels, allied with the Venetians, locked themselves in the fortress and were besieged and fired upon by Muslim ghazis from the redoubts they had constructed until the latter managed to split open the heads of the infidels within. For this reason, they called this fortress Depe Delen ("Head-splitter"). It is administered by a *voyvoda* in the *sancak* of Vlora and a *kadi* with

[1] Town in northern central Greece which, like Korça, is nowhere near the source of the Vjosa river.

nāḥiyesi cümle seksen pāre qurālardır, ammā çoġı Poġonya daġlarında ʿāṣīlerdir, (10) ġayri ḥākimleri aṣlā yoqdur, ammā qalʿe dizdārı ve cümle yüz ʿaded qalʿe neferātları vardır.

Qalʿesi Ergiri Nehriniñ kenārında (11) evc-i āsmāna berāber bir yalçın qaya üzre bir bayırlı düz yerdedir. Ḥīn-i muḥāṣarada ṭob-ı kūblar ile qalʿesi münhedim (12) olduġından taʿmīr ü termīme imkān olmaġa iqtidārı olmayup anıñ ṭaşı ile aña qarīb yine ol bayırlar üzre sene-yi (13) mezbūrede Gedik Aḥmed Paşa müceddiden şekl-i murabbaʿ bir şeddādī-mis̱āl seng-binā bir qalʿe-yi zībā inşā édüp gūyā sedd-i ʿAdn (14) imiş. Dāyiren-mā-dār cirmi altıyüz adım bir küçük qalʿecikdir, lākin ẖandaqı yoqdur, ammā dīvār[ı] ġāyet qalın ve qırq arşın ʿālīdir. (15) Ve cümle iki ʿaded qapuları vardır, [biri] şarqa ve biri yıldız ṭarâfına nāẓırlardır. Ve qalʿe içinde cümle qırq (16) ʿaded ḥavlısız qırmızı kiremit örtüli küçük neferāt evleridir. Ve ancaq Bāyezīd-i Velīniñ bir küçük cāmiʿi var, ve bir alçaq (17) minārecigi var. Ṣu ṣarnıçları ve cebe-ẖānesi ve darı ile memlū enbārı var. Qalʿe neferātları şeb [ü] rūz ʿāṣī (18) Porġonatlı ʿArnavudıyle ceng [ü] cidāl ve ḥarb [u] qıtāl éderler, zīrā bu qalʿeyi Gedik Aḥmed Paşa ceng-i ʿaẓīm ile fetḥ édüp ḥālā (19) niçe biñ şühedālarımız eski Depe Delen qurbında medfūnlardır.

Ve bizim kelleler ile geldigimizi qalʿe neferātları işidüp (20) alay ile ḥaqīre istiqbāle çıqup tüfeng şādm[ān]larıyle qalʿeye girüp dizdār aġa ẖānesinde sākin olduq. Ammā ġarīb ü (21) faqīr adamlardır. Vażīfe-yi muʿayyenelerin Avlonya zifti maʿdeni emīninden alırlar. Atlarımızı ve baʿżı refīqlerimizi qalʿeden (22) ṭaşra varoşa qondırdılar.

Der vaṣf-ı varoş-ı Depe Delen. Cümle ikiyüz ʿaded ḥavlılı vāsiʿ evleriñ (23) cümlesi qayaġan ve sāz örtüli cā-be-cā bāġçeli evlerdir. Ve yıldız ṭarâfındaki qapu öñinde bir lonca cemʿiyyeti köşki (24) var. Ve cümle altı ʿaded müfīd [ü] muẖtaṣar dükkānları var. Ve cümle bir cāmiʿi var. Ve ẖān u ḥammām u medrese vü mekteb (25) ve ġayri ʿimāretden bir nişān yoqdur, ammā keçileri ve qoyunları ve ṣıġırları çoqdur. Ṭaşra varoş evleri kiremitlidir. (26) Ve aşaġı ṣu kenārında bāġ u bāġçelerinde nārı ve inciri vardır. Ammā ġarb ṭarâfında bu qalʿeye bir ṭop menzili yerde (27) ḥavāleli daġları vardır.

an income of 150 *akçe*. There are 80 villages in this district, most of which form part of the rebel Progonat highlands. The fortress, which aside from the *voyvoda* has no other magistrate, is occupied only by the warden and 100 garrison troops.

The fortress of Tepelena[1] is situated on a level slope at the top of a steep and high cliff above the banks of the Gjirokastër river. During the siege, the fortress was destroyed beyond repair by cannonfire. Using the old stones, Gedik Ahmed Pasha built a new, square-shaped, solid stone fortress like the rampart of Eden near the site of the old one in that same year. The circumference of this small fortress is 600 paces. It is without a moat and has very thick walls, 40 ells high.[2] It has two gates, one facing east and the other north, and 40 small houses for the garrison, with red tiled roofs and no courtyards. Sultan Bayezid II the Saint built a small congregational mosque with a low minaret here. Aside from this there are a water cistern, an armory, and a grain storehouse filled with millet. The soldiers of Tepelena are engaged in constant warfare with the Albanian outlaws of Progonat, because Gedik Ahmed Pasha conquered the fortress after a huge battle and thousands of our men now lie buried near the old fortress.

When the garrison soldiers heard that we had arrived with some heads, they came out to meet me and conducted us into the fortress with a volley of musket shots. We were put up in the house of the warden. The soldiers themselves are alien to the region and quite poor — they receive their salaries from the *emin* in charge of the pitch mines at Vlora — so the horses and some of our companions were accommodated outside the walls in the open town.

The open town of Tepelena. There are some 200 spacious houses with slate or thatched roofs, courtyards, and occasionally gardens. Facing the northern gate of the fortress there is a loggia pavilion where the inhabitants gather. There are 6 tiny shops and 1 mosque. There is no *han*, bathhouse, *medrese*, school or other public building, but there is an abundance of goats, sheep and cows. The open town has houses with tiled roofs. Down near the river are vineyards and gardens with pomegranate and fig trees. One drawback is the mountain which looms within cannon range just to the west of the fortress.

---

[1] For this passage, cf. Kiel 1990, 245.

[2] Approximately 30 meters.

Ve bu Depe Delenden ġayri yarar refīqler alup 'alā'ṣ-ṣabāḥ qalqup gidecek maḥalde (28) qonaġımızıñ qapusı öñinde qal'e qulından ikiyüz 'aded bahadır çatal fitilli ġāzīler bizim ile yola revāne olmaġa (29) mübāşeret etdiler. Ḥaqīr eyitdim: "Ġāzīler, nedir aṣlı, silāḥlanmışsız-a?" dédim Anlar eyitdi: "Va'llāhi sulṭānım, dünki gün (30) siz[1] ceng édüp bir qaç kāfiriñ başların alup niçesini daḫi mecrūḥ etmişsiz. Mel'ūnlarıñ aqrâbāları bu géce şehre gelüp (31) sizi baṣṣalar gerek idi. Qal'e içinde dizdār ḫānesinde yaṭdıġıñızdan bir çāre édemediler. Ba'dehu atlarıñızı (32) oġurlamaġa çalışdılar. Bizler vāqıf-ı esrār olup ṣabāḥadek sizi ve atlarıñızı muḥāfaża etdik ve cenābıñızı ḥużūrıñız (33) uçurmayalım deyü size ve dizdāra ḫaber etmedik. Şimdi ise bu başlar ile sizi bu kāfirler bu yoldan Avlonya paşasına (34) selāmet götürmezler. İleride bir dar boġaz vardır, anda sizi elbette beklerler. Biz bugün sizlerden ayrılmayup refīq oluruz" deyü **[357a]** ikiyüz 'aded pāk müsellaḥ u mükemmel yigitler öñimize düşdiler.

Ḥaqīr daḫi vāfir ḥażż édüp qal'eden yoquş aşaġı yola revāne olup hemān (2) Ergiri Nehr-i 'aẓīmin gemilerle qarşu geçüp ol boġaz dédikleri maḥal Ergiri Nehriniñ öte ṭarâfında qalup qarşu ṭarafda ṣarp (3) daġlara 3 sā'atde çıqup *qarye-yi Damiz*, bir derbend köyi ze'āmetidir. Andan *qarye-yi Qaşist*. Bu qurālar Ergiri Nehriniñ ṣolında qalup (4) yıldız ṭarâfına giden yoldur. Ammā biz beri ṭarafa emn [ü] emān olan Iṣqırapar qażāsı ḥudūdına girüp andan *qarye-yi Marican*. Andan (5) *qarye-yi Qılçoqlar*. Bu mezkūr üç pāre qurālar mu'āf [u] müsellemler ve müsellimlerdir, re'āyāları Arnavud[2] kefereleridir. Bu maḥallerde 'aẓīm çiftlikler daḫi vardır.

Andan (6) 3 sā'atde şarqa gidüp *der teşrīfāt-ı eşkāl-i sūr-ı dār-ı qarār, ya'nī ḥiṣār-ı 'ibretnümā-yı Iṣqırapar.* ----- (7) Zemān-ı qadīmde Rūm keferesi bināsıdır. Lisān-ı ----- demekdir. Sene -----

---

[1] Text: *siziñ.*

[2] Altered to *Arnabud.*

The next morning, we were about to set off with another escort from Tepelena. When we reached the gate, we found 200 of the garrison soldiers waiting for us, armed with matchlock muskets, who refused to let us leave without armed guards. "Ghazis," said I, "why are you armed like this?" "My lord," they replied, "yesterday you did battle on the road with a number of outlaws. You killed some of the infidels and wounded many others. Last night their accursed relatives came into town and tried to attack you, but since you were staying inside the walls in the house of the warden, they found no way to do so. They then planned to steal your horses. We got wind of it and stood guard all night to protect you and your horses. We did not inform you and the warden of this beforehand so as not to disturb your sleep. But now these infidels will not allow you to pass safe and sound with those heads to the pasha of Vlora. There is a gorge[1] you must pass through and it is there that they will surely be waiting for you. Today we will stick with you and escort you." So saying, the 200 splendidly armed warriors set out in front of us, to my great delight.

Leaving the fortress, we set off down hill to the Gjirokastër river, which we crossed without delay by boat, leaving the gorge they had referred to on the other side of the river. Our journey continued for 3 hours up steep mountains until we reached *the village of Damës*, which is a *zeamet* and a mountain pass village. From there, we advanced to *the village of Kashisht*. Leaving these villages and the road heading north on the left side of the Gjirokastër river, we re-crossed the river to the border district of Skrapar. From there we stopped at *the villages of Maricaj and Kiçok*. These three villages are exempt from taxes.[2] The rayah there are Albanian infidels. The villages also contain large farm-estates.

From there, we journeyed for 3 hours and arrived at *the notable fortress of Skrapar*.[3] It was originally built by the ancient Greeks

---

[1] No doubt the Gorge of Këlcyra along the Vjosa river between Tepelena and Këlcyra.

[2] Settlements near mountain passes in the Ottoman Empire were often exempt from taxation in return for their services in guarding the passes. For the Ottoman system of mountain pass forts and villages, see Cengiz Orhonlu, *Osmanlı İmperatorluğu'nda Derbend Teşkilâtı* (Istanbul, 1967; expanded second printing, 1990).

[3] Probably Këlcyra. Here the narrative of the itinerary becomes confused, either because Evliya was not able to reconstruct his routing properly when he wrote or dictated his travelogue or because of omissions in the manuscripts. If he were on his way southwards to Përmet from the pass of Kiçok, having been blocked by outlaws from using the direct route though the gorge, he would no doubt be in Këlcyra which, though not in the present district of Skrapar, best corresponds to the description.

tārīḫinde ʿĀrnābūd ʿaşqıyāsı elinden Sulṭān Bāyezīd-i Velī (8) ʿaṣrında Gedik Aḥmed Paşa fetḥ édüp Avlonya sancaġı ḥudūdında yüz elli aqçe qażādır ve nāḥiyesi qırq yedi pāre qurādır. Yeñiçeri aġalıġından Qandiyeden (9) çıqup İslāmbolda qāyim-maqām olan İbrāhīm Paşanıñ şehridir. Qalʿe dizdārı ve elli ʿaded neferātları var. Ketḫüdā yeri ve yeñiçeri serdārı (10) ve ġayri ḥākimleri yoqdur. Qalʿesi bir depe üzre ḥavāleli ve bir qapulı ve cirmi biñ adımlı bir küçük şeddādī-binā bir qalʿe-yi raʿnācikdir. (11) İçinde cümle qırq beş ʿaded kiremitli ḫāneleri ve bir Bāyezīd Ḫān cāmiʿi vardır. Varoşı aşaġıda yüz ʿaded kiremitli bāġ u (12) bāġçeli evlerdir. Āb [u] havāsı laṭīf olup bāġçelerinde zeytūnı ve inciri cihānı dutmuşdur.

Andan 2 sāʿatde *qarye-yi Vijqar*. (13) Andan bir sāʿatde cānib-i ġarba *qarye-yi Ṭırpan*, Yeñiçeri Ḥasan Aġanıñ bunda bir ʿālī içli ve ṭaşlı mükellef ḥaremli çiftlig-i ʿaẓīmi var, āyende (14) vü revendelere niʿmeti mebzūldur.

Andan ġarba meyyāl ----- sāʿatde gidüp *der şurūʿāt-ı sitāyiş-i qalʿe-yi Piremedi*. Lisān-ı ----- (15) ----- demekdir. İbtidā Rūm bināsıdır ve sene ----- tārīḫinde Gedik Aḥmed Paşa fetḥidir. Dizdārı ve qırq ʿaded merdüm-ı ḥiṣārı var, ammā qalʿe içinde dizdār ḫānesinden ġayri bir şey yoqdur. (16) Cirmi ikiyüz adımdır. Qalʿe içre bir qaya üzre bir ḥavżı var, içinde gūnāgūn māhīleri var; ġarābet anda kim bu yalçın qaya üzre bu ḥavża ṣu nereden gelir kimse bilmez, ve cemīʿi zemānda {aṣlā ṣuyı egsilmez. Aşaġı varoşı cümle yüz elli ʿaded bāġlı ve bāġçeli ve serāpā kiremitli ve baʿżısı sāz örtüli \ evlerdir. Cümle bir küçük cāmiʿi ve bir mescidi ve bir sūḫte medresesi ve bir mektebi ve bir tekyesi ve bir ḫānı var, ammā \ ḥammāmı ve ʿimāreti yoqdur, lākin altı ʿaded dükkāncıqları vardır ve bir qac ev ḥammāmları var, hemcivārları olanlar girirler. Ve bu şehriñ \ āb [u] havāsı ġāyet laṭīfdir. Bu Piremedi qażāsınıñ qıblesi ṭarâfında qażā-yı Poġonyadır.}

and means ----- in the ----- language. In the year ----- Gedik Ahmed Pasha conquered it from Albanian brigands during the reign of Sultan Bayezid II the Saint. It is a *kadi*-district on the border of the *sancak* of Vlora, with an income of 150 *akçe*. In the surrounding area there are 47 villages. This is the town of Ibrahim Pasha, former aga of the janissaries in Candia and now deputy grand vizier (*kayim-makam*) in Istanbul. In Skrapar there is only the castle warden and 50 garrison troops. There is no steward or commander of the janissaries and no other magistrate. The fortress was built on a hill, but there is higher ground overlooking it. It has only one gate and a circumference of 1000 paces. It is a fine small fortress built of stone. Inside, there are 45 houses with tiled roofs and one congregational mosque, that of Bayezid Khan. Down in the open town there are 100 houses with tiled roofs and surrounded by gardens and vineyards. The climate is excellent. The gardens produce olives and figs in vast quantities.

We continued 2 hours beyond Skrapar to *the village of Vizhkor*[1], and 1 hour further west to *the village of Tërpan*[2], where Yeniçeri Hasan Aga has a large estate with an imposing farmhouse whose courtyard is decorated inside and out and which is always open to travellers. West of this, after another ----- hours, we arrived at *the fortress of Përmet*. It means ----- in the ----- language. It was first founded by the Greeks and in the year ----- was conquered by Gedik Ahmed Pasha. It has a warden and 40 garrison troops. There is nothing else inside the walls but the house of the warden. The circumference of the fortress is 200 paces. Also within the walls, up on a cliff, there is a pond with all sorts of fish. The water, strange to say, comes from an unknown source and never runs dry. Down in the open town there are 150 houses with mostly tiled and some thatched roofs, surrounded by vineyards and gardens. It has 1 small congregational mosque, 1 prayer house, 1 *medrese*, 1 primary school, 1 *tekke* and 1 *han*. There is no bath or other public building. It has only 6 small shops and a few private baths used by the local people. The climate in the town is very pleasant. To the south of Përmet is the district of Pogonia.

---

[1] Unidentified.
[2] Tërpan is far to the north, half way between the Kiçok pass and Berat.

(17) Andan cānib-i ġarba yoquş aşaġı ----- sā'atde gidüp *qarye-yi Joṭom*, lisān-ı Arnavudcada ----- demekdir. Bāġlı ve bāġçe(18)li ma'mūr qaryedir kim Raba Nehri cenginde ṣuda ġarq olan yeñiçeri aġası Muṣṭafā Paşa merḥūmuñ köyidir kim sarāyında qal'e-mis̱āl (19) bir qulle-yi 'aẓīm binā etmiş. Ve bu qurāniñ qarşusında yarım sā'at bir dere aşırı Sulṭān Murād ve Sulṭān İbrāhīm ḫān vezīri qatl-i şehīd (20) olan Qara Muṣṭafā Paşanıñ köyi qarye-yi Lavdani ṣaġımızda qalup aña qarīb *qarye-yi Roşinik.* Köpürli Vezīr Meḥemmed Paşanıñ (21) qaṣaba-mis̱āl serāpā kiremit örtüli taḥtānī ve fevqānī kārgīr-binālı ve bāġlı ve bāġçeli cümle ----- 'aded ḫānedānlı rabṭa-yı (22) müzeyyendir. Bir ma'mūr cāmi'i ve bir mescidi ve bir medrese-yi sūḫtegānı ve bir mekteb-i 'irfānı ve bir tekye-yi dervīşānı ve bir nev-binā ḥammām-ı (23) cān-sitānı ve kifāyet miqdār dükkānları var. Āb [u] havāsı ġāyet laṭīfdir. ----- (24) /

(25) Andan yine qarye-yi Joṭoma gelüp andan bir sā'at yoquş aşaġı yıldız ṭarâfına gidüp *qarye-yi Dobrona.* Yüz elli 'aded evli (26) bāġ-ı irem-mis̱āl kefere köyidir. Bundan şehr-i Belġırad ayaq altında ġarb ṭarâfında nümāyāndır.

Andan ġarba yoquş aşaġı bāġlar içre bir sā'at gidüp (27) *der ta'bīrāt-ı sevād-ı mu'aẓẓam-ı dār-ı cihād, ya'nī qal'e-yi irem-ābād, Belġırad-ı ḫurrem-ābād.* (28) Bi-qavl-i müverriḫīn-i Laṭin bu qal'e ibtid[ā] ----- binā édüp niçe divelden divele girüp āḫir-i kār sene ----- tārīḫinde bi'z-zāt Bāyezīd Ḫān (29) ḫilāfetinde serdār-ı mu'aẓẓam

From here, journeying downwards in a westward direction for ----- hours, we arrived at *the village of Zhitom.*[1] It means ----- in Albanian. It is a prosperous village with vineyards and gardens. This village belonged to Mustafa Pasha, the aga of the janissaries, who drowned at the battle of the Raba river.[2] His mansion has a tower which serves as a fortification. Half an hour across a valley from this village is the village of Lavdani[3] on our right, belonging to Kara Mustafa Pasha, the vizier of Sultan Murad IV and Sultan Ibrahim Khan, who fell as a martyr to the faith. Leaving Lavdani on our right we then arrived at *the village of Roshnik.*[4] It has one- and two-story stonework buildings and tiled roofs, with vineyards and gardens, and belongs to Köprülü Mehmed Pasha. There are a total of ----- houses, 1 well-kept congregational mosque, 1 prayer house, 1 *medrese*, 1 primary school, 1 *tekke*, 1 newly-constructed bathhouse, and a sufficient number of shops. The climate is exceptionally pleasant. ----- From here, we returned once again to the village of Zhitom and from there, descending northwards for another hour, we arrived at *Drabonik.*[5] This is an infidel village of 150 houses with vineyards like the Garden of Irem. Looking west from here one can see the town of Berat down in the valley.

From this place we descended westwards through vineyards and arrived in 1 hour at *the imposing region of Jihad, the luxuriant walled town of Albanian Belgrade (Berat).* According to the Latin historians it was first founded by ----- and changed hands many times until, in the year ----- during the reign of Sultan Bayezid Khan, the supreme

---

[1] Zhitom is far to the north, lying between Tërpan and Berat. Obviously some of the text is missing here.

[2] The Battle of Szentgotthárt on the Rába (German: *Sankt Gotthart an der Raab*), now on the Austrian-Hungarian border, took place on 8 Muharram 1075/1 August 1664. Mustafa Pasha is not mentioned in Evliya's eyewitness account, although he does describe vividly the drowning of the janissaries in the river at VII 21a-b (94-97). Indeed, there seems to be a confusion with another Mustafa Pasha who was the nephew of Kara Murad Pasha, became aga of the janissaries during the Raba campaign, then two months later was appointed governor of Shehrizor where he was killed in a battle on the Zab river (see Süreyyâ 1995-97, IV/1, 473).

[3] If Lavdani is half an hour from Zhitom, it cannot be identified with Levan much farther to the west, with Lavdan near Ballsh or with Lavdar on the border between the present districts of Skrapar and Përmet. Perhaps the reference is to Bardhanj, a little settlement near Zhitom i Vogël on the road to Berat. See Babinger 1930, 153, n.4.

[4] There is a village of Roshnik east of Berat, but this would seem rather out of the way, and is certainly not on the road from Zhitom to Berat.

[5] Drabonik, formerly Dobronik, lies between Zhitom and Berat.

Gedik Aḥmed Paşa ʻĀrnābūd[1] ile Rūm ve Bunduqani Firengi elinden[2] fetḥ etmişdir.

Devlet-i Āl-i ʻOs̱mānda ḥālā ----- (30) ʻaded qalʻe-yi Belġırad nām sūr-ı be-nāmlar var. Evvelā bir Ṭuna Nehri kenārında Ṭuna Belġıradı ve biri Budin serḥaddinde Budine bir merḥaleden (31) ziyādece baʻīd Üstülni Belġıradı ve biri de ḥükm-i Āl-i ʻOs̱mānda Erdel Belġıradı, biri de bu dördinci Arnavud Belġıradıdır kim ḥālā Süleymān (32) H̱ān taḥrīri üzre Rūm-éli eyāletinde Avlonya sancaq beginiñ taḫtidir. Ṭaraf-ı pādişāhīden beginiñ ḫāṣṣı 229000 aqçedir ve erbāb-ı zeʻāmet (33) 28 ve erbāb-ı tīmārı 489 dur ve alay begi ve çeri başı vardır. Paşası ḥīn-i seferde qānūn üzre kendü cebelüleriyle (34) ve cümle erbāb-ı tīmār cebelüleriyle dörd biñ güzīde ʻasker olup me'mūr olduqları sefere mīr-livālarıyle giderler. Lākin ġāyet bahadır **[357b]** ve şecīʻ ʻaskeri vardır. Şeyḫü'l-islāmı ve naqībü'l-eşrāfı ve üçyüz aqçe pāyesiyle şerīf qażāsı ve yüz yigirmi pār[e] nāḥiye (2) qurāsı olup ber-vech-i ʻadālet bu qurālardan qāḍīye be-her sene altı kīse ve paşasına oṭuz kīse ḥāṣıl olur. Sipāh ketḫüdā (3) yeri ve yeñiçeri serdārı ve qalʻe dizdārı vē ----- ʻaded qalʻe neferātları ve şehir voyvadası ve muḥtesibi ve bācdārı ve qalʻe (4) ketḫüdāsı ve mihter başısı ve şehir ketḫüdāsı ve miʻmār aġası ve ḫarāc aġası vardır.

Ve Avlonya sancaġında cümle ṭoquz qażā yerdir. (5) Taḫt-i qażā bu Belġıraddır. Ve şimāl ṭarâfında Müzākiyye qażāsıdır kim oṭuz pāre qurādır. Ve şarq ṭarâfında Ṭomoriliçse qaża(6)sıdır. Ve buña qarīb qıble ile maşrıq mābeyninde qażā-yı Işqırapardır. Ve aña muttaṣıl qıble ṭarâfında qażā-yı Piremedidir. (7) Bu qażāya muttaṣıl qıblesi ṭarâfında qażā-yı Poġonyadır. Ve bu qażānıñ ġarbında qażā-yı Ergiri ile müşādır, ammā bu (8) Ergiri qażāsı Delvine sancaġı ḫākidir. Ve bu qażānıñ şimālinde qażā-yı Depe Delendir. Ve anıñ cenūbında qażā-yı Avlonyadır. (9) Ammā bu mezkūr ṭoquz ʻaded qażālar ġāyet maḥṣūllı yerlerdir, ammā baʻżı reʻāyāları ʻāṣīlerdir kim neʻūẕü-bi'llāh.

Ve bu Belġırad qalʻesi (10) Rūm Qusṭanṭīn ile Arnavud elinden fetḥ olmuşdur. *Qalʻeniñ eşkāli*: qıbleden yıldız rūzgārı cānibine ṭūlānī vāqıʻ olmuş bir (11) yalçın boz qaya üzre şekl-i şemʻdān-mis̱āl bir şeddādī mücellā seng-i ṭırāş bir ṣaʻb sūr-ı ṣavaş metīn bir ḥıṣn-ı ḥaṣīn qalʻedir. (12) Lākin iç elde olmaq ile gözden bıraġılup cā-be-cā baʻzı yerleri mürūr-ı eyyām ile münhedim olmaġa yüz dutmuşdur. *Der*

[1] Altered from *Arnavud*?
[2] Text: *altından*.

commander Gedik Ahmed Pasha conquered it from the Albanians, the Greeks and the Venetians. There are ----- fortresses called Belgrade in the Ottoman empire: firstly, Danubian Belgrade on the Danube river; secondly, Stolna Belgrade on the Buda frontier a little more than one stage from Budapest; thirdly, Transylvanian Belgrade which is under Ottoman jurisdiction; and fourthly, this Albanian Belgrade. According to the survey register of Suleyman Khan it is the seat of the *beg* of the *sancak* of Vlora in the *eyalet* of Rumelia. It is a *has* for which the *beg* receives an income of 229,000 *akçe* from the sultan. It has 28 *zeamet*s and 489 *timar*s. It also has an *alay-beg* and a *çeribaşı*. In time of war the *sancak-beg* is obligated by statute to supply the sultan with 4000 armed soldiers including his own armed retainers and those of the timariots. They are very tough and courageous soldiers. Berat has a *şeyhülislam*, a *nakibüleşraf*, a *kadi* with a salary level of 300 *akçe*, and 120 villages, from the annual revenues of which the *kadi* has the legal right to 6 purses and the pasha to 30 purses. It also has the following dignitaries: steward of the *sipahi*s, commander of the janissaries, warden of the fortress and his ----- garrison troops, *voyvoda* of the town, market inspector, collector of tolls, steward of the fortress, chief of the band of musicians, mayor, chief architect, and poll-tax official.

The *sancak* of Vlora consists of 9 *kadi*-districts. The seat of the *sancak* is Berat. North of this is the district of Myzeqe with 30 villages. To the east is the district of Tomorica. Near this to the south and east is the district of Skrapar. Bordering that to the south is the district of Përmet. South of Përmet is the district of Pogonia. West of Pogonia is the district of Gjirokastër which, however, belongs to the *sancak* of Delvina. North of Gjirokastër is the district of Tepelena. South of that is the district of Vlora. These nine districts are very fertile, but some of the rayah are rebellious — may God preserve us from them.

The fortress of Berat was conquered from Constantine the Greek and the Albanians. *Shape of the fortress.* Built like a candlestick on a steep and bare cliff stretching in a north-south direction, it is a mighty, solid and enduring fortress constructed of hewn and polished stone. Since it is in the interior of the country, it has not been kept up and its walls are now damaged in places. The total circumference is 2600

girdāgird-i qılā'āt. (13) Cümle iki biñ altıyüz 'aded germe adım iḥāṭa éder qal'e-yi serāmeddir. Ve cümle dörd 'aded metīn ü qavī dervezeleri var. (14) Evvelā yıldız ṭarâfına çārsūya énecek büyük qapudan çārsū yoquş aşaġı kāmil biñ adımdır. Ve bu qapu üç qatdır, her qatı mābeyni (15) yüzer adım birbirlerinden ba'īd bāb-ı 'aẓīmlerdir. Bu qapularıñ iki 'aded qapusı yıldız ṭarâfına nāẓırdır. Bir qatı içeri qapudur kim şarq ṭarâ(16)ına mekşūfdur. Ve bu qapunuñ iki ṭarâfında temel ṭaşları fīl gevdesi qadar seng-i ḫārālardır, meger bu gūne ṭaşlarıñ emsāli Quds-i (17) şerīf qurbında Ḫalīlü'r-raḥmānda yāḫod Nehr-i Ṭurla kenārında Bender qal'esinde ola. Ve bir qapusı daḫi eski manaṣṭır dibinde cānib-i (18) ġarba nāẓır qapudur kim aşaġı Ḥüseyn Paşanıñ yeñi binā etdügi Murād Çelipa maḥallesindeki cāmi' öñine éner qapu yolıdır. Ve bir qapu daḫi (19) maḥalleler arasında şarqa nāẓır bir küçük oġrın qapudur, ammā olqadar şāhrāh degildir.

Eşkāl-i iç ḥiṣār. Ġarba nāẓır büyük qal'e dīvārınıñ (20) bir köşesine muttaṣıl bir şeddādī seng-binā bir sūr-ı ra'nācikdir kim cirmi sekiz yüz adımdır. Ve iki 'aded qapusı var, biri şarq ṭarâfına meftūḥ (21) qal'e içine nāẓırdır, biri ġarb semtine mekşūf olup ṭaşra aşaġı Çelipa maḥallesine yoquş aşaġı éner iç qal'e qapusıdır (22) kim cenūb ṭarâfına meyyāl qapudur. Ammā bu mezkūr yedi 'aded qapularıñ cümlesi qara aġaç taḫtasından dervezelerdir kim demir (23) qapular degildir, zīrā her bir qapular düşmenden gizli qulleler aralarında pinhān olmuş dervezelerdir. Ḥattā bir iki qapularınıñ taḫta qanaṭları (24) yerde yaṭır, zīrā iç elde ve iç qal'edir, düşmenden aṣlā ḫavf [u] ḫaşyetleri yoqdur. Ve bu iç qal'e içinde cümle qıre elli 'aded (25) kiremit örtüli ḫānelerdir. Ve bir 'aded cāmi'-i Bāyezīd Ḫāndır. Ve cebe-ḫānesi azdır, altı pāre ṭopları vardır. Ve köhne-binā enbārları ve ṣu (26) ṣarnıcları ve dizdār ḫānesi var, ġayri āṡār-ı binā yoqdur.

Sitāyiş-i ṭaşra büyük ḥiṣār-ı Belġırad. Cümle ikiyüz 'aded kiremitli (27) vīrān şekilli evlerdir, ekṡeriyyā Urum keferesi ḫāneleridir. Bāġçeleri ḫarāb ḫayli vāsi' meydānları vardır. Ve cümle bir (28) 'aded kiremetli ve kārgīr minārelı kār-ı qadīm bir vāsi' Bāyezīd Ḫān cāmi'i,

large paces. It has 4 strong and solid gates. First, facing north, is the Big Gate; from it down to the bazaar is a distance of 1000 paces. This gate has three large doorways which are separated from one another by a distance of 100 paces each. Two of these doorways face north and the third, the inner doorway, opens to the east. The foundation stones of the gate are as big as an elephant. Such stones can otherwise only be found in Hebron near Jerusalem and in the fortress of Bender on the banks of the Dniester river. The second gate, below an ancient monastery, faces west and opens onto the road which descends to the front of the new mosque built by Hüseyn Pasha in the Murad Çelepia quarter. The third gate faces east between the quarters; it is a small hidden gate and is not used very much.

Shape of the citadel. It is a splendid small stone citadel, 800 paces in circumference, joined to one corner of the western wall of the great fortress. It has 2 gates. One, opening to the east, faces the interior of the fortress. The other, opening to the west, leads down outside the castle to the Çelepia quarter below, and so it inclines to the south. All 7 doorways of the above-mentioned gates are made of elm wood and not of iron, because they are all concealed behind towers. In fact, the doors of one or two of the gates are lying on the ground, since they are on the inside of the castle and the castle is in the interior of the country, and there is no great fear of attack. Within the citadel there are 40 to 50 houses with tiled roofs, 1 mosque of Bayezid Khan[1], a few munitions stores, just 6 cannons, some outdated grain storehouses and cisterns[2], the house for the warden, and no other buildings.

Outside the castle of Berat there is a total of 200 delapidated houses with tiled roofs, most of them inhabited by Greek infidels. They have very big yards, but the gardens are not kept up. There is one isolated congregational mosque, that of Bayezid Khan[3],

---

[1] The mosque of Bayezid II, also known as the White Mosque, was demolished after the anti-Tanzimat uprisings, although the foundations are still to be seen.

[2] The subterranean cistern is still extant and full of water.

[3] This mosque, which Evliya attributes to Bayezid II, is known as Fethiye Cami (Mosque of the Conquest) and popularly as the Red Mosque. It is the oldest in Berat and, according to Kiel 1990, 74, perhaps the oldest Islamic construction still extant in Albania. It may have been constructed immediately after the conquest of Berat in 820/1417. The foundations, the base of the *minbar* and the outlines of the *mihrab,* as well as the bottom of the minaret, dating from the early 9th/15th century, are still visible.

köhne-binā cemā'atsiz ġarīb cāmi'-i 'acībdir. Ve cümle (29) sekiz 'aded kefere kenīseleri vardır, ammā biri ġāyet ma'mūr u müzeyyen ve büyükdür. Cümle ṣoqaqları qudretden ṭaşlı qaldırımlıdır.

(30) Ve bu qal'eniñ cānib-i erba'asındaki qal'e dīvārına muttaṣıl evlerdir, aṣlā eṭrāfında ḫandaqları yoqdur, zīrā dāyiren-mā-dār yalçın (31) uçurum qanara qayalardır kim cenūb ṭarâfındaki Çeke Beni Qayası nām semti evc-i semāya ser çekmiş şāhīn ve zaġanos ve (32) qara quş āşyānlı ve devlingeç ve çaylaq yuvalı serāmed ü mehīb qayalardır kim adam aşaġı baqmaġa cür'et édemez. Bu maḥalle (33) Çeke Beni Qayası démeden ġaraż oldur kim ba'de'l-fetiḥ küffār-ı ḫāksār-ı dūzeḫ-qarār yine bu qal'e[1] bir vech ile pādişāha feryādcı (34) gönderemezler.

Āḫir-i kār bu qayalardan bir serden-geçdi şehbāz yigidi ip ile ṣarqıdup ol daḫi qayalar dibinden cārī **[358a]** olan Nehr-i ----- şināverlik édüp qaṭ'-ı menāzil ve ṭayy-ı merāḥil éderek Edirneye varup aḥvāl-ı diyergūn-ı muḥāṣarayı bir bir (2) pādişāha taqrīr édüp iḥsānlar alup yine üç günde bir şeb-i muẓlimde bu Çeke Beni Qayası dibine gelüp "Çek-e beni!" deyü feryād (3) édicek bildiler kim qal'eden pādişāha feryāda giden Ġāzī Quṣqıdır kim gelüp qavl-i qarār-ı ma'hūde-yi qadīmeleri üzre (4)"Çek-e beni!" dédi. Derḥāl Ġāzī Quṣqıyı ipler ile qal'eye çeküp "Bire ḫoş geldiñ, ne ḫaber" deyince "Pādişāh-ı 'ā(5)lem-penāh, vüzerā ve vükelā ve 'ulemā ve ṣuleḥā ve şeyḫü'l-islām sizlere selām etdiler, 'Benim ġāzīlerim inşā'allāh te'ālā on günedek elli biñ 'aded (6) 'asākir-i islām ile varup yetişirim. Dīn-i mübīn ġayreti anlarıñdır. Hemān ġayret ü cidd ü ihtimām etsinler, neylerse eylesinler, zinhār-be-(7) zinhār qal'eyi küffāra vermesinler.' İşte cemī'i ser-i kārda olanlarıñ mektūbları" deyüp cümle maḥṣūr olan ġuzāt-ı müslimīne tesellī-yi (8) ḫātır verüp anlar daḫi var maqdūrların ṣarf édüp şeb [ü] rūz ṣavaş-ı perḫāşlar éderken ḥaqīqatü'l-ḥāl on günde (9) yetmiş seksen biñ 'asker amadani qażā ve qader gibi hemān cümle kāfirlere qal'e altında girişüp küffāra bir ṣātūr-ı Bāyezīdi çekerler kim (10) ḥālā Müzākiyye ṣaḥrāsında qarār éden kefereleriñ üstüḫānları çeste çeste ve püşte püşte yıġılup yatdıġı nümāyāndır. Ba'dehu (11) cümle ġāzīler pādişāh-ı cem-cenābdan iḥsān [u] in'āmlar olup ol "Çek-e beni!" deyen şehbāza daḫi bir ze'āmet-i 'aẓīm iḥsān olunur, (12) ḥālā oġullarına Çeke-beni-zādeler deyüp ilā mā-şā'allāh ber-vech-i temlīk ze'āmet köyine mutaṣarrıflardır. Anıñiçün

---

[1] Some words here have dropped from the text. A plausible reconstruction is: *bu qal'eyi muḥāṣara etdiginden qal'edekiler.*

covered in tiles, a large old mosque with a stone-carved minaret, but with no congregation. There are 8 churches of which one is very large and well-built. The streets are paved with unworked cobblestones. On the four sides of the fortress there are houses built against the walls. It has no moat on any side because it is surrounded by sheer gorges.

On the south side is the quarter called Çekebeni ("Pull me up") Rock, a frightful cliff which soars into the sky and shelters the nests of falcons, eagle owls, eagles and kites. The gorge is so steep that no one dares to look down into it. There is a reason why the quarter of Çekebeni Rock bears this name. After the conquest of Berat, the accursed infidels once again laid siege to the fortress, and the Ottoman troops within were unable to alert the Sultan. Finally, one of the brave warriors, willing to risk his life, was lowered down this cliff by a rope. He swam across the ----- river which flows in the gorge below, made his way straight to Edirne, and informed the Sultan of the dire situation that the fortress was being besieged by the enemy. Having been rewarded by the Sultan with gifts, he set off once more and three days later arrived in the middle of the night at the foot of this cliff and shouted: *Çeke beni* ("Pull me up!"). They knew it was Ghazi Kuski — that is the name of the one who had gone to alert the Sultan — who was shouting the agreed-upon password. They immediately drew up Ghazi Kuski with ropes and got him inside the fortress. "Welcome back! What news?" they inquired. "I bring greetings from the Padishah, his viziers and deputies and ulema and *şeyhülislam*. The Sultan informs you that he will arrive in ten days with 50,000 soldiers to make war. Until then, he bids you give proof of your religious fervor and not surrender the fortress to the enemy. Here are the letters from the authorities." Those under siege were encouraged by the news and defended the fortress day and night with all their energy until help arrived, ten days later, like sudden death, in the form of 70,000 or 80,000 soldiers, who cut down the infidels with such a Bayezid-like sword that even today heaps of infidel bones can be seen on the plain of Myzeqe. After this victory, the Sultan rewarded his soldiers for their efforts. He especially rewarded the courageous messenger who had cried out *Çeke beni*, granting him a large *zeamet* with a village of its own, which is still administered by the Çekebeni clan. From that time on, the cliff in question has been known as the

ol sebebden (13) bu qayaya Çeke Beni Qayası derler. Meşhūr-ı āfāq bir ṭāq-ı revāq-miṡāl bir berrāq aq qayadır. Ve bu Çeke Beni qayalarınıñ ba'żı yerinde (14) qulle ve kenīseler ve mesīregāh köşkler vardır.

{*Der faṣl-ı eşkāl-i aşağı ḥiṣār.*} Bu qayalar altında ṣu kenārında aşağıda bir qat qal'e dīvārları daẖi var, ġāyet metīn (15) dīvār-ı sedd-i ḥaṣīndir. Aşağı büyük köprü başındaki qal'e qapusından tā qazancılar çārsūsı qapusınadek cümle sekiz yüz (16) adım uzun çārsūdur kim Nehr-i ----- kenārına vāqı' olmuş sūq-ı sulṭānīdir. Ve bu qal'e içinde cümle yetmiş seksen miqdārı (17) kiremit örtüli sehil ma'mūr evlerdir. Mā'adā hemān bir şāhrāh üzre cümle seksen 'aded vāsi' dükkānlardır kim bir yoldur, ġayri (18) ṭarīq-ı 'ām yoqdur, zīrā bir ṭarâfı qal'eniñ Çeke Beni qayalarıdır ve bir ṭarafı qal'e altından cerêyān éden Nehr-i ----- dir. Ammā üstād (19) Ferhād-ı kūh-ken bu aşağı qal'eden ve yuqaru qal'eniñ Çeke Beni qayalarından oyup kesme qaya nerdübānlar ile bir mināre qaddi qal'e (20) dīvārı ṣu kenārı olmaq ile qal'e temelin ṣu döger, ba'żı yerlerinden ṣuya éner yetmiş seksen qadême ṭaş nerdübānlar (21) ile énilüp qazancılar çārsūsı qapusı dibinde bir 'ażīm ṣu qullesi var, tā ṣuyuñ içinde binā olunmuşdur, tā Çeke Beni qayaları içinden oyma (22) yolları var kim yuqaru qal'eden aşağı ṣu qullesine enince biñ altmış ayaq kesme ṭaş nerdübānlardır kim ḥīn-i muḥāṣarada bu (23) qayalar içindeki yollardan ṣu ṭaşıyup maḥṣūr olanlar aṣlā ṣuya żarūret çekmezler, ve bu yolları düşmenler daẖi görmezler. Ammā (24) qazancılar çārsūsı qayalarından aşağı ṣu yolları alçaqdır, ammā bu yolları daẖi düşmenler göremezler. Ve bu aşağı qal'ede olan dükkānlar cümle (25) qazancılar ve cā-be-cā muṭāflardır. Ve bu qazancılar qapusından ṭaşra merḥum u maġfūrun-leh Uzqurlı ----- bir çārsū-yı (26) 'ażīm binā édüp bu maḥalliñ bir varoş-ı 'ażīm olmasına sebeb olup ḥālā Uzqurlı Varoşı derler. Ve qazancılar çārsūsından şarqa (27) tā muṭāflar başına varınca kāmil iki biñ adımdır ve iki qat şāhrāh yoldur, ve yemīn ü yesārları serāpā her eṣnāfdan pāk ü pākīze (28) dükkānlardır, ekṡeriyyā dekākīnler cümle Uzqurlı oğlı evqāflarıdır kim cümle yediyüz 'aded dükkānlardır, ammā bezzāzistanları (29) yoqdur, lākin yine cümle metā'-ı aqmişe-yi nādir[e] ve dībā ve şīb ve zerbāf-ı fāẖireler cümle mevcūddur, ekṡeriyyā boẖçası ġāyet çoqdur.

(30) *Der vaṣf-ı büyük varoş-ı şehr-i Belġırad-ı Arnavud.* Gerçi bir sevād-ı mu'aẓẓam varoş-ı 'ażīmdir, ammā qal'e dīvārı içinde degildir, (31) yuqaru qal'eniñ cānib-i qıblesi ve şarqīsi ṭarafında bir vāsi'

Çekebeni Rock. It is a landmark, a shining white cliff like a vault of heaven, upon which are situated numerous towers, churches, belvederes and pavilions.

The lower fortress. On the river bank at the base of these cliffs is another row of strong fortress walls. Along the banks of the ----- river, from the lower gate of the fortress at the end of the big bridge all the way to the gate of the kettle makers' market, stretches a bazaar 800 paces long, an imperial market. Inside the fortress, there are 70 to 80 moderately well-built houses with tiled roofs. Aside from these, there is one main street with 80 large shops, and no other public thoroughfare, because there is the Çekebeni Rock on the one side and the ----- river flowing on the other. Master craftsmen carved a staircase into the mountainside from the lower fortress to the upper part. The base of this staircase is in the water and it ascends the fortress wall to the height of a minaret. It is 70 or 80 steps down, and from here leads to the large water tower — built in the water — near the gate of the kettle makers' market. From the Çekebeni Rock down to the water tower there are also paths of hewn stone leading gradually downwards in 1060 steps.[1] Those under siege can use these paths to fetch water from the water tower without being seen by the enemy. The water channels coming down from the kettle makers' market are close to the ground, but they too are invisible to the enemy. The shops in this lower fortress are all kettle makers except for a smattering of goat-hair spinners. Outside the gate of the kettle makers' market, the late Uzkurli -----. constructed another bazaar which attracted a large settlement. This area is called Uzkurli (Skuraj) Town. From the kettle makers' market eastwards to the goat-hair spinners stretches a two-storied[2] main street 2000 paces long. On the left and right are neat shops with tradesmen of all kinds. Most of the shops — 700 or so — are pious foundations which were donated by the Uzkurli family. There is no *bedestan* as such, but one can find all manner of fine fabrics, including brocades, gauzes, and cloth-of-gold. Shawls are especially plentiful.

The large open town of Albanian Belgrade (Berat). It is a huge open town, entirely outside the walls of the fortress. It is situated in a

---

[1] The upper parts of the staircase are still visible today.

[2] I.e., with shops at two levels.

fezāda ve Nehr-i ----- kenā[rı]nda serāpā bāġ u gülistānlı ve müşebbek (32) būstānlı rabāṭ-ı ʿaẓīmdir kim cümle laʿlgūn muṣannaʿ kiremit örtüli beş biñ ʿaded maʿmūr u müzeyyen ravża-yı cinānlı vāsiʿ ve (33) taḥtānī ve fevqānī serāpā kārgīr-binālı ve yedi ʿaded dere ve depeli zemīn-i maḥṣūldārda ġāyet muṣannaʿ dārlar olup yüzden mütecāviz sarāy-ı (34) kāşāneler ile ārāste ve her bir ḫānedānları ḥavż u şāzrevānlar ile pīrāste olmuş şehr-i müzeyyendir kim havāsı ve māsında rūḥ vardır.

[358b] *Der vaṣf-ı sarāy-ı aʿyān-ı aġavāt.* Cümleden Ḥüseyn Paşa sarāyı bāġ-ı merāmdır. Ve paşalara maḫṣūṣ sarāyda vālī-yi vilāyet Çatal-baş (2) Paşa qarındaşı ʿOs̱mān Paşa sarāyında sākin olup getirdigimiz emr-i pādişāhīleri ve Serdār ʿAlī Paşa mektūbların verüp (3) dīvān-ı pādişāhīde Depe Delenden getirdigimiz Porġonatlı[1] ḥarāmīleriniñ kellelerin dīvān-ı pādişāhīde ġalṭān édüp fermān-ı (4) pādişāhīler qırā'at olunduqda mefhūm-ı kelāmları ʿOs̱mān Paşanıñ maʿlūmı olup "Fermān Pādişāhıñ" deyüp Manya (5) muḥāfażasına cemīʿi Avlonya sancaġı ʿaskeriyle āmāde olmaq içün nādīler nidā édüp getirdigimiz kelleler içün ḥaqīriñ (6) başına bir çeleng-i şāhī ṭaqup ve bir ḫilʿat-i fāḫire geydirüp fermān-ı serdār getirdigimiz içün bir kīse ġuruş ve bir at (7) ve bir köle ve ḫuddāmlarıma onar altun ve birer çoqa qumaş iḥsān édüp qonaġımızda bir hafta ṣafālar édüp niçe sarāylar(8)da daḫi zevqler etdik. Andan Meḥemmed-efendi-zādeler sarāyı ve Serdār Aġa sarāyı ve Uzqurlı sarāyı, bunlar meşhūr (9) sarāy-ı ābādānlar[dır].

Der defter-i esmā'-ı ʿaded-i maḥallāt. Cümle oṭuz ʿaded maḥallātlardır. Evvelā qalʿeniñ cenūbında Murād (10) Çelipa maḥallesi ve Uzqurlı maḥallesi, Ḫünkār maḥallesi, Vaqıf maḥallesi, Baba Qāḍī maḥallesi, Paşmaqçılar maḥallesi, Aq Mescid (11) maḥallesi, Eski Bāzār maḥallesi, Gün Görmez maḥallesi, ----- (12) oṭuz ʿaded maḥallātlarıñ meşhūr [u] maʿmūrları bu mezkūr maḥallātlardır. Lākin on maḥallesi keferelerdir ve bir maḥallesi Yahūdīlerdir, (13) ammā Ermenī ve Fireng ve Çingane maḥalleleri yoqdur, lākin Laṭin kefereleri çoqdur kim gelüp bazirgānlıq édüp yine giderler.

[1] Text: *Porġonatları.*

large open area along the bank of the ----- river to the east and south of the upper fortress and is covered in vineyards, rose gardens and vegetable gardens. There are 5000 one- and two-story stonework houses with fine red tiled roofs. They are well-built and attractive houses with gardens and are spread over seven verdant hills and valleys. Among them are over 100 splendid mansions with cisterns and fountains and an invigorating climate.

Mansions of the notables. One is the mansion of Hüseyn Pasha. Another is the mansion reserved for the pashas: this is the residence of Osman Pasha, the brother of Çatalbaş Pasha, who is governor of this *vilayet*. It was to Osman Pasha, in a public meeting, that I presented the imperial decrees and letters sent by Serdar Ali Pasha and displayed the heads of the outlaws from Progonat which we had brought from Tepelena. "It is the Padishah's to command," cried Osman Pasha after the decrees were proclaimed. He immediately sent out heralds to sound the call for all the leaders of the *sancak* of Vlora to muster their soldiers and set off in defense of Mania. For displaying the heads I was awarded a plumed crest and dressed in a robe of honor, and for conveying the Serdar's command I was given 1 purse of *kuruş*, 1 horse and 1 slave, and my servants were given 10 gold coins and 1 length of material each. We then spent a week of rest and recreation in this mansion, where we had our quarters, and in several other fine houses. Among the other famous mansions are those of the Mehmed Efendi family, the Serdar Aga, and the Uzkurli family.

Names of the quarters. Berat has 30 quarters, including Murad Çelepia, south of the fortress; Uzkurli; Hünkâr; Vakëf (Pious Foundation)[1]; Baba Kadi; Paşmakçılar (Slipper Makers); Ak Mescid (White Prayer House); Eski Bazar (Old Bazaar); and Gün Görmez.[2] Then there are 10 quarters belonging to the Christians and 1 to the Jews. There are no Armenian, Frankish, or Gypsy quarters, but there are a lot of Latin infidels who come and go for trading purposes.[3]

---

[1] The Vakëf quarter is known today as the Jani Vruho quarter.

[2] I.e., the quarter which does not see the light of day. This must be the Gorica (Partizani) quarter referred to below. This quarter across the river and in the shade of the Gorica mountain is still known today as a place where the sun does not shine.

[3] By "Latin" here Evliya probably means Slavic-speakers (Serbian, Bosnian, etc.).

(14) *Der 'imāret-i cevāmi'hā-yı ehl-i īmān-ı selāṭīn-i Āl-i 'Os̱mān.* Cümle oṭuz 'aded miḥrāb-ı mü'minān-ı 'ābidāndır. Ammā cümleden cemā'at-i (15) kes̱īreye mālik tā şehriñ vasaṭında Sulṭān Bāyezīd-i Velī cāmi'i, ṭūlı altmış ayaq ve 'arżı elli ayaqdır, ve bir mevzūn u muṣanna' (16) ve serāmed mināresi vardır, ve cümle üç 'aded qapuları olup iki yan qapusı ve bir qıble qapusı. Öñinde bir cāmi' qadar daẖi (17) ṣoffa-yı 'aẓīmi var, ammā ḥarêmi dardır, lākin bir ṭarz-ı qadīm binā olunmuş serāpā kiremit örtüli kār-ı 'atīq cāmi'dir. Miḥrābı öñinde (18) ----- Efendi tekyesi sekiz köşe taḥtānī ve fevqānī tekye-yi H̱alvetīdir.

Andan Uzqurlı cāmi'i, cümle serāmed kārgīr (19) qubbeli ve serāpā raṣāṣ-ı ẖāṣṣ-ı nīlgūn ile mestūr bir cāmi'-i nūrun-'alā-nūrdur kim bir serāmed mināre-yi mevzūnı var kim mis̱li meger (20) Sivas eyāletinde Niksar şehrinde Melik Ġāzī cāmi'iniñ mināresi ola. Ammā bu cāmi'iñ ṭaşra ḥarêmi eṭrāflarındaki (21) yan ṣoffaları üzre beyāż ve mücellā mermer sütūn-ı müntehālar üzre yedi 'aded qurşum örtüli qubāb-ı 'ālīlerdir. Ve cümle (22) medrese ve mekteb ve tekye ve 'imāretleri serāpā qurşum örtülidir.

Andan Ġāzī Murād Paşa cāmi'i, sāde-binā ma'bedgāh-ı ra'nā(23)dır.

Andan yuqaru qal'ede H̱ünkār cāmi'i. Aña Fetḥiye cāmi'i derler.

Andan Murād Çelipa maḥallesinde Qara Murād Paşa yegeni (24) Çelebi Ḥüseyn Paşa cāmi'i, nev-binā bir cāmi'-i zībādır kim bu ḥaqīriñ aña tārīẖi budur kim qıble qapusınıñ 'atebe-yi 'ulyāsı üzre taḥrīr (25) olunmuşdur. Tārīẖ:

> Evliyā penc ism-i a'żamile dédi tārīẖi:
> Ḥay 'Azīz ü yā Başīr ü yā Qavī [ü] yā Metīn. Sene 1081.

Mosques of the Ottoman sultans. Berat has 30 prayer-niches in all, of which the one with the largest congregation is the mosque of Sultan Bayezid II the Saint in the center of town.[1] This mosque is 60 feet long and 50 feet wide with a tall graceful minaret. It has three doors, two at the sides and one in the *kıble* wall. In front of the mosque is a porch which is as large as the mosque itself, though the courtyard is narrow. The mosque was constructed in the old style and has a completely tiled roof. In front of the prayer-niche is the octagonal two-story *tekke* of ----- Efendi. It is a Halveti *tekke*.

The Uzkurli mosque:[2] it has a high domed roof of carved stonework covered entirely in bluish lead. It is a radiant mosque with one tall and graceful minaret which can only be compared to that of the mosque of Melik Ghazi in the town of Niksar in the *eyalet* of Sivas.[3] The porticoes around the outer courtyard have a lead roof of seven lofty domes supported by tall columns of white polished marble. The *medrese*, primary school, *tekke* and soup kitchens also have lead roofs.

The mosque of Ghazi Murad Pasha: a handsome, plain building.[4]

In the upper fortress is the Hünkâr mosque, also known as the Fethiye ("Conquest") mosque.

The mosque of Çelebi Hüseyn Pasha, nephew of Kara Murad Pasha, in the Murad Çelepia quarter: a modern and attractive building. I composed the following chronogram, inscribed, in *celi* script and in Karahisari style, in the lintel over the *kıble* door:

Evliya wrote the date with five divine names:
Living, Glorious, Seeing, Powerful, Steadfast. Year 1081/1670

---

[1] Now known as the Xhamia e Mbretit (Mosque of the King) which we may assume to have been built during Bayezid's Albanian campaign of 897/1492. From an inscription, we know the mosque was restored in 1248/1832 under Mehmed Reshid Pasha. The minaret was torn down some time before 1973 in the wake of the Cultural Revolution. See Kiel 1990, 55-58.

[2] Now known as the Xhamia e Pllumbit (Lead Mosque), said to have been constructed 1553-55.

[3] For Evliya's description of this mosque, see II 283a16 (195). Evliya also compares the minaret of the mosque of Yahya Pasha in Skopje to that of the Melik Ghazi mosque in Niksar; see V 170a20 (555:25 — omitted).

[4] This is possibly again the Red Mosque, referred to earlier by Evliya as the Mosque of Bayezid Khan.

(26) Ammā bir nāzük ü muṣanna‘ ve serāmed ve şeş-ḫāne kārgīr mināre ve bir kāse-yi nīlgūn-mis̱ā[l] müdevver qubbesi üzre la‘lgūn kiremit (27) ile mestūr bir cāmi‘-i ma‘mūrdur, ẓarāfet ü leṭāfet ve ‘ilm-i mi‘mārīde mis̱li yoq bir bī-bedel ve müferriḥ ü dilgüşā cāmi‘-i zībādır.

(28) Andan maḥkeme qurbında nāmına Muşqa cāmi‘i, gūyā ḫuld-i berrīndir. Bu mezkūr cāmi‘ler meşhūr ma‘bedgāh-ı müzeyyenlerdir.

(29) *Der mesācidhā-yı müveḥḥidān-ı mü'mīnāt.* Cümle ----- ‘aded maḥallāt buq‘aları ve zāviyeleri ve mezgitleridir. Evvelā Vaqıf maḥallesi (30) mescidi; Murād Çelipa maḥallesinde üç ‘aded mesācidler var; Baba Qāḍī mescidi; Paşmaqçılar mescidi; Aq Maḥalle mescidi; (31) Eski Bāzār mescidi; Gün Görmez maḥallesi mescidi; ve sekiz ‘aded mesācidleri daḫi var, ammā meşhūr [u] ma‘mūrları bunlardır.

(32) *Der tefhīmāt-ı ‘aded-i dārü't-tedrīs-i müfessirān.* Cümle beş ‘aded dārü'l-‘ulūm-ı ‘ālimāndır, cümleden Sulṭān Bāyezīd-i Velī medresesi; Uzqurlı (33) medresesi; ----- ; bunlar meşhūrdur, ammā başqa dārü'l-ḥadīs̱-i muḥaddis̱ānı ve dārü'l-qırā'-ı (34) ḥuffāẓānı yoqdur, lākin yine her cāmi‘lerde müderris-i ḥasbīler vardır kim cemī‘i fünūn-ı vücūhātlar qırā'at olunur, zīrā ṭalebeleri çoqdur.

[359a] *Der dārü't-te‘allüm-i mekteb-i ciger-gūşe-yi püserān.* Cümle ----- ‘aded dār-ı ebced-ḫvān-ı ṣıbyāndır. Evvelā Bāyezīd Ḫān mektebi ve Uzqurlı (2) mektebi ve Şeyḫ ‘Azīz mektebi ve Murād Çelipa mektebi ve Tekye mektebi -----. Bunlar meşhūrdur.

(3) *Der zikr-i tekye-yi dervīşān-ı erbāb-ı ṭarīq-ı zīşān.* Cümle üç ‘aded ḫāneqāh-ı āl-i ‘abā-yı mecẕūbāndır. Evvelā Ḫünkār cāmi‘iniñ miḥrābı öñinde haẓret-i (4) eş-şeyḫ ----- Efendi ḫāneqāhıdır kim sekiz köşe fevqānī ve taḥtānī bir tekye-yi Ḫalvetīdir kim bir diyārda bu ṭarz [u] ṭarḥ üzre bir (5) tevḥīdgāh-ı maqām-ı ḫāneqāh görülmemişdir; ḥattā cāmi‘iñ ṣaġ ṭarâfında dervīşān ḥücreleri var kim micmer-i tevḥīd ile sūḫte (6) olmuş faqr [u] fāqa ṣāḥibleriniñ ṣavma‘aları nūr-ı tevḥīd ile münevver olup tevḥīd-i erre ‘ıṭriyyātiyle adamıñ demāġları mu‘aṭṭar (7) olur kim cümle qırq ‘aded ḥücrelerdir. Ve Uzqurlı tekyesi; ve -----. Bunlar ma‘rufdur.

(8) *Der medḥ-i ḥammāmāt-ı rāḥat-i cān.* Cümle iki ‘aded germāb-ı ġāsilāndır. Evvelā biri Uzqurlı cāmi‘i öñinde Uzqurlı ḥammāmı, ġāyet (9) laṭīf binā ve naẓīf āb [u] havādır. Ve biri ṭaba-ḫāne çārsūsı içinde binā-yı şāhānī-mis̱āl ḥammām-ı rūşinādır ve ḫuddāmları pākdir.

The mosque has an elegant, tall, hexagonal stonework minaret. Its domed roof is round like a blue bowl and is covered in red tiles, giving this beautiful mosque a particularly pleasing and spacious atmosphere and making it a peerless and elegant architectural monument.

The so-called Mushka mosque,[1] near the courthouse: like a garden of paradise. These are the most famous congregational mosques.

Neighborhood mosques. There are a total of ----- including those in the quarters of Vakëf, Murad Çelepia, Baba Kadi, Paşmakçılar, Ak Mescid, Eski Bazar, and Gün Görmez, plus 8 others, but the ones listed are the most prominent.

Medreses. Berat has 5 schools training ulema, the best known of which are the *medrese* of Sultan Bayezid II the Saint, the Uzkurli *medrese*, ----- . There are no other institutions for instruction in hadiths and Koranic studies, but each mosque has its own learned professors who teach all the religious sciences, since there is great demand.

Primary schools. There are ----- including those of Bayezid Khan, Uzkurli, Sheikh Aziz, Murad Çelepia, and the Tekke.

Tekkes. There are 3. First, that of Sheikh----- Efendi, situated in front of the prayer-niche of the Hünkâr mosque:[2] an octagonal two-story Halveti *tekke*. In plan this *tekke* is quite unlike those seen in other regions. The dervish cells are to the right side of the mosque. It has 40 cells, illuminated with perfumed candles and inhabited by dervishes praising God's name. Also well-known, aside from this one, is the Uzkurli *tekke*. -----

Baths. There are 2 bathhouses with hot water, one being the Uzkurli bath in front of the Uzkurli mosque. This is an extremely pleasant and refined building with good atmosphere. The other is a grandiose building situated at the tanners' market, a clean, bright and airy bath with good service.

---

[1] Perhaps meaning Mosque of the Mule (Alb. *mushka* = "mule").

[2] The present building of the Halveti tekke of Sheikh Hasan was constructed by Kurd Ahmed Pasha in 1785. The building beside it, housing the dervish cells, dates from the 19th century.

(10) *Der vaṣf-ı ḥammāmāt-ı maḫṣūṣ-ı a'yān.* Bi-qavl-i ālüfte vü āşüftegān, bu şehr içre yüz yetmiş 'aded sarāy-ı ḫānedānlarda birer 'aded ḥammāmlar vardır.

(11) *Der 'aded-i çeşme-sār-ı āb-ı ḥayvān-ı āb-ı ḥayāt.* Cümle ----- 'aded çeşme-yi teşnegān-ı 'aṭşāndır. Evvelā cümleden Uzqurlı ḥammāmınıñ qapusı (12) öñinde yol aşırı İslāmbolda mi'mār-ı sulṭān Qāsım Aġa çeşmesiniñ tārīḫidir:

Qāsım Aġa re'īs-i mi'mārān
Yapdı bir ḫayr kim (13) gören éde reşk.
Ḥaq qabūl eyleye çün oldı temām
Biñ elli dörd içinde ga (?) bu çeşme-yi seng. Sene 1054.

Bu tārīḫ (14) çeşme üzre bir qıṭ'a lācverdī kāşī üzre beyāż celī ḫaṭṭ ile taḥrīr olunmuşdur.

Andan sarāc-ḫāne başındaki çeşme (15) daḫi yine Qāsım Aġanıñ olup yine bu merqūm tārīḫ kāşī üzre tenmīq olunmuşdur.

Andan ṭoquz yerde Uzqurlı 'uyūnları cerêyān (16) étmededir.

Der 'aded-i çārsū-yı bezzāzistān-ı qapan. Cümle ----- 'aded bāzār-ı ḥüsn-i sūq-ı sulṭānīdir. Amma cümleden sarāc-ḫānesi ve (17) ḫaffāf-ḫānesi ve debbāġ-ḫānesi ve qazancılar çārsūsı ġāyet ma'mūr u şīrīn ü müzeyyen tertīb üzre binā olunmuş dekākīnlerdir. (18) Ammā nehir kenārında henūz nev-binā bir sūq-ı rānāyı Ḥüseyn Paşa binā etmiş, cümle bir qā'ide bir tertīb bir bāzār yeridir kim mecme'ü'l-'irfāndır kim (19) yüz 'aded dukkān-ı cedīdlerdir kim eṣnāf-ı mütenevvi'e anda mevcūddur. Ortası bir meydān-ı 'aẓīm olup gūnāgūn eşcār-ı sāyedār(20)lar ile āraste olup sāye-yi ẓıl ḥimāyelerindeki ṣoffalarda cümle erbāb-ı ṣanāyi' ve erbāb-ı me'ārif birer gūne kārgīrlik éderler.

Bu meydānda (21) — *der āṡār-ı binā-yı 'ibretnümā-yı 'acāyibāt* — ol çārsū içre bir sā'at qullesi var, evce ser çeküp anda Erdel diyārından gelme bir sā'ati var, (22) nāqūsı içinde on adam oṭurur, vaqt-i ẓuhr olduqda on iki kerre ẓarb édüp ṣadāsı bir qonaq yerde istimā' olunur. Ta'bīr (23) ü tavṣīf ile olmaz, tā ki görmege muḥtāc bir sā'at-i 'ibretnümādır.

Ve bu çārsū qurbında cümle altı 'aded qahve-ḫāneleri var. (24) Cümlesi birer gūne naqş-ı būqalemūn-ı 'ibretnümūn qahāvīlerdir kim her biri birer gūne naqş-ı nigār-ḫāne-yi Çīndir. Bir qaçı şehr içre (25) cerêyān éden Nehr-i ----- kenārına vāqı' olup ba'żı yārān ṣuda

Private baths. There are 170 private baths, thus one in all the great mansions — or so I have been told by the town rakes.

Fountains. A total of ----- . Across the road in front of the door of the Uzkurli mosque is the fountain of Kasım Aga who is architect of the sultan in Istanbul,[1] the date of which can be seen in the following chronogram:

> Kasım Aga, chief of the architects,
> Made a charitable deed to rouse envy in the beholder.
> May God accept it, now that it is complete:
> In 1054 —— (?) this stone fountain. Year 1054/1644.

This chronogram is inscribed in white letters of *celi* script on a dark blue tile over the fountain. There is another fountain, at the head of the saddlers' market, also by Kasım Aga and also containing this same chronogram on a tile. Aside from these, there are 9 fountains donated by the Uzkurli family.

Markets and covered bazaars. There are ----- splendid markets with pleasant and well-ordered shops, including those of the saddlers, the cobblers, the tanners and the kettle makers. Along the river is the beautiful bazaar recently constructed by Hüseyn Pasha with 100 shops, all on the same plan. It is a gathering place of the cognoscenti. Here, in porticoes under the shade of various trees, one finds all sorts of skilled tradesmen and handicraftsmen busy at work in their various professions.

In the middle of this bazaar there is a large square with — *a marvel* — a lofty clock tower. The clock was brought from Transylvania and the bell could hold ten people. It rings out twelve times at noon. The sound of the bell can be heard at the distance of one day's march. The clock tower is so wonderful that it cannot be described; it must be seen to be believed.

In the vicinity of this bazaar there are 6 coffee houses, each one painted and decorated like a Chinese idol-temple. A few of them are on the bank of the ----- river which flows through the city: here some people bathe in the water, some come to fish and others gather

---

[1] He was appointed *mi'mār başı* or chief architect of the Ottoman court in 1055/1645; see art. "Ḳāsim Agha" in *Encyclopedia of Islam, New Edition*, IV (1976), 717-18.

şināverlik éderler, ba'żılar māhī-yi gūnāgūnı ṣayd éderler, ba'żılar (26) niçe gūne aḫbāb u aṣdıqā ve erbāb-ı me'ārifler ile görüşüp bilişüp mübāḥaṣe-yi 'ilm-i şer'iyye ve fünūn-ı şi'riyye görerler, zīrā şu'arāsı (27) ve fuṣaḥā ve büleġāsı ve muṣannifīn ü mü'ellifīnden tekmīl fünūn etmiş baḥr-ı 'ummān-ı me'ānī kimseleri ġāyet çoqdur, ammā meẕheb qaydında degillerdir, (28) ancaq meşreb qaydındadırlar, ẓarīf ü necīb ü reşīd zekiyyü't-ṭab' adamları vardır.

Ve debbāġ-ḫāne çārsūsı nehr-i 'aẓīm kenārında vāqı' (29) olmaġın çınār-ı müntehālar ve bīd-i sernigūn ve engūr-ı gūnāgūn eşcārlarıyle müzeyyen olmuş bir qoyaḫ sāyedār kārḫāne-yi Āh-ı Evrandır kim ġāyet (30) pāk ü ṭāhir mesīregāh yerdir.

Ve qazġancılar çārsūsında gerçi sindān ve çekiçleriñ bir ṭaqa-ṭar-ṭaq ṭaqa-ṭaq ṣadāsı (31) var, ammā ol daḫi uṣul [u] āheng ile nüḥās-ı ḫālıṣı üstādlar dögdükçe ol daḫi bir gūn[e] uṣul [u] āheng ṣadāsıdır. Ammā (32) bu çārsu daḫi ġāyet müzeyyen ve sāyedār dekākīnlerdir kim bir tertīb üzre binā olunmuşdur.

Ve ġazzāzlar çārsūsı daḫi eyle pāk ü laṭīf (33) ü naẓīf bāzār-ı ḥüsndür kim bunda olan maḥbūb pençe-yi āftāb ġazzāz cüvānlarınıñ parmaqlarında özdekleri[1] (?) ilikleri seyr olunup cemāl-i (34) bā-kemālleri müşāhede olunur.

Cemī'i çārsū-yı bāzārından ṣular cerêyān etdiginden olqadar pāk bāzārları var kim adam yollar üzre oṭurup **[359b]** temāşā-yı cemāl etmek ister, zīrā cümle dükkānlar içre olan dilberānları aṣlā güneş yaqmayup her biri gūyā birer gün-görmez pādişāhlarınıñ (2) evlādlarıdır. Ve bu iki ṭaraf dükkānlarınıñ ekṣeriyyā ṣoqaqları üzre taḫta örtüli [dü]kkānlardır, cemī'i yārān-ı erbāb-ı me'ārif-i ṣādıqān-ı (3) 'āşıqānlar cümle dükkānlarda dilberānlar ile muṣāḥabet éderler, 'ayb degildir, zīrā üstādları ve peder [ü] māderleri tefāḫur kesb éderler.

(4) *Der şürū'-ı sitāyiş-i ḫān-ı tüccārān-ı ḫvācegān.* Cümle beş 'aded kiremit örtüli ḫān-ı ḫvācegān-ı sevdāgerānları var, gūyā qal'elerd[ir].

(5) *Der 'aded-i vekāle-yi ġurebā-yı mücerredān-ı ehl-i pīşegān.* Cümle altı 'aded bekār odalarıdır kim içinde ġarībü'd-diyār ehl-i ṣanāyi'ātlar sākin olurlar.

---

[1] The word is crossed out and above it is written: *kemikleri içinde.*

to converse with their friends on matters both religious and secular. There are many poets, scholars and writers here possessing vast knowledge. They are polite and elegant, intelligent and mature, and given more to carousing than to piety.

The tanners' market along the river bank is situated in the shade of lofty plane trees, willows and vines, making it an attractive place for people to come and spend their leisure time, even though it is the workshop of Ahi Evran.[1] The kettle makers' market, with its rhythmic and steady "takatartak takatak" produced by the anvils and hammers of the coppersmiths, is also a shady and pretty market with shops on a single plan.

The silk makers' market, which is also very clean and tidy, offers a view of exceptional beauty with all the handsome young men there. They are so good-looking that the marrow of the bones in their fingers is visible.

Through the entire bazaar flow streams of water which ensure such cleanliness that a man could sit down on the road and let himself be enraptured by the surrounding beauty. The lads in the shops are like royal princes, never struck by the light of the sun. Most of the shops on both sides of the streets have wooden roofs. Here it is that friends, companions and lovers spend all their time chatting up the boys as they work, and there is no shame in it either. Indeed, the master craftsmen and even the fathers and mothers of the boys take great pride in the fact that their apprentices and sons are being courted.

Hans of the great merchants. There are 5 fortress-like *hans* with tiled roofs.

Inns of the unmarried craftsmen. There are 6 inns offering rooms to unmarried tradesmen without houses of their own.

[1] Patron saint of the tanners.

(6) *Der 'aded-i me'kel-i dārü'ż-żiyāfāt-ı aṭ'ām-ı 'imārāt.* Cümle üç 'aded 'imāret-i me'keldir, cümleden Bāyezīd Ḫān ve Uzqurlı ve 'Azīz Efendi 'imāreti meşhūrdur.
(7) *Der beyān-ı enhār-ı zülāl-i cārī-yi āb-ı ḥayvān-ı mā'-ı ḥayāt.* Bu şehr içre cerêyān éden Nehr-i Oṣum tā cenūb ṭarâfında Işqırapar ve kūh-ı Oṣum ve (8) cebel-i bālā Ṭomordan gelüp bu şehr içinden cerêyān édüp ġarb ṭarâfında Morava ṣaḥrāsı içre gidüp Qara 'O̱smān Beg oġlınıñ çiftligi (9) dibinden geçüp Elbaṣan ṣuyı Nehr-i ----- maḫlūṭ olup deryā-mis̱āl ikisi bir yerden cerêyān éderek Müzākiyye ṣaḥrāsından (10) 'ubūr édüp tā yine Başt Ova qal'esi dibinde Venedik Körfezi deryāsına munṣab olup Müzākiyye ṣaḥrāsında yaz u qış bu Nehr-i (11) Oṣum gemilerle 'ubūr olunur.

Der vaṣf-ı 'imāret-i Qoru Varoş. Bu Belġırad şehriniñ bu Oṣum Nehri qarşusında cenūb ṭarâfında (12) ṣu aşırı bir varoş-ı müzeyyen vardır, ismine Qoru Varoş dérler, cümle ikiyüz 'aded evli bāġ u bāġçeli ve cümle kiremitli vāṣı' (13) evlerdir, eks̱eriyyā Rūmlar ve 'Arnavud kefereleri sākinlerdir. Bu varoşuñ eñsesindeki daġa Qoru Daġ dédiklerinde[n] bu qaṣaba anıñ ismiyle müsemmā (14) olup Qoru Varoş dérler, bir 'aẓīm kūh-ı ser-bülenddir kim diraḫt-i müntehā-yı 'aẓīmler ile müzeyyen olup Nehr-i Oṣum üzre olan cisriñ (15) ta'mīr [ü] termīmine diraḫtleriniñ kerastelerin ṣarf éderler. Her kim bu daġdan bir çubuq kesse ḥākim tecrīm édüp ḥaqqından gelirler. Ve şehirde (16) bir adam qan édüp bu Qoru Daga firār édüp daḫil düşse ḥākim elinden ḫalāṣ olup artıq ḥākim aña vaż'-ı yed édemez, ammā ol qātil (17) şehre daḫi gelemez, gelse ol ān qatl éderler. El-ḥāṣıl ḫalāṣ olursa celā-yi vaṭan eyler.

(18) *Der mesīregāh-ı erbāb-ı merām.* Bu şehr-i Belġırad eṭrāflarında cümle yetmiş yedi yerde teferrücgāh [u] mesīregāh yerler vardır. Evvelā yu[qa]ru qal'ede mesīre(19)gāh Çeke Beni Qayalarınıñ maqṣūreleri; aşaġı debbāġ-ḫāne ṣoffaları; yeñi çārsū meydānı diraḫtleri; ve Ṭomor daġı, yigitleriñ ṣayd [u] (20) şikārgāhlarıdır. Ve bu Qoru Daġ mesīregāhı bir çemenzār u lāle-'izār u ḫıyābān-ı 'Acemdir kim gūyā Qonyanıñ Merāmı ve Malāṭıyye şehriniñ Aṣpozusıdır. (21) Niçe yerlerinden 'uyūn-ı cāriye-yi āb-ı ḥayātları revān olup her diraḫt-i 'aẓīm sāyelerindeki ṣoffa ve maṣṭabalarda yüzer adam ṣıġar dikkelerdir. Ḥattā (22) şehriñ 'aşqıyāca ve maryolca olan levendāt maqūlesi cānları bu daġıñ qoyaḫında fısq [u] fücūr édüp bir hafta 'ayş [u] 'işret éderler. El-ḥāṣıl (23) 'acāyib ṭarabgāh-ı 'işretgāh yerdir.

Soup kitchens. There are also 3 soup kitchens, those of Bayezid Khan, of Uzkurli and of Aziz Efendi.

Rivers. Through the city flows the Osum river which takes its source to the south in the mountains of Skrapar, Osum and Tomorr and which, after passing through Berat, flows westwards onto the plain of Morava and, after passing below the estate of the son of Kara Osman Beg, joins the ----- river in Elbasan.[1] The two having joined into one huge river, it passes over the plain of Myzeqe and flows into the Gulf of Venice (Adriatic Sea) near the fortress of Bashtova. The Osum river in Myzeqe is navigable summer and winter.

Koru Varoş (Gorica). Across the Osum river on the south bank stretches another beautiful town, called Koru Varoş, of 200 houses with tiled roofs, surrounded by gardens, orchards and vineyards. It is inhabited mostly by Greek and Albanian infidels. Behind this town is Mt. Koru (Gorica), from which the town derives its name. It is a massive and lofty mountain covered in large, tall trees. The timber from these trees is used for the upkeep and repair of the bridge over the Osum river. Anyone who cuts even a single branch is punished by the authorities. At the same time, anyone who commits a murder and manages to take flight and hide up in the mountain is safe from prosecution, but he may never return to the town. If the murderer returns, he will be executed, so if he does escape he is a permanent exile.

Pleasure-grounds. There are 77 parks and pleasure-grounds in the vicinity of Berat. The foremost of these are: the Çekebeni Rock pavilions in the upper fortress, the tanners' market porticoes in the town below, the square at the new bazaar with its trees, the foothills of Mt. Tomorr where the young men go hunting, and this park on Mt. Koru. The latter, with its meadows and tulip-glades, is a Persian paradise, recalling the gardens of Meram near Konya and of Aspozo near Malatya. Some of the spots are refreshed by flowing water. The benches in the shade of the lofty trees are large enough to sit groups of 100 men each. In some secluded spots on the mountain, the town rakes, like so many libertines, may spend an entire week eating, drinking and carousing. In short, it is an excellent place for having a good time.

---

1 I.e., Devoll river.

Ammā bu Qoru Varoşda ḫān u ḥammām ve çārsū-yı bāzār yoqdur, ancaq iki ʻaded kefere deyrleri vardır. (24) Hemān Belġırad şehriniñ ṣu aşırı bir maḥallesidir ve evleri cümle ṣu kenārlarında balıq dalyanları ile maʻmūrdur, lākin şehr içre cerêyān éden Nehr-i Oṣum (25) ṭuġyān üzre gelse bu Qoru Varoşuñ evlerin ve qarşu ṭarafda Belġıradıñ ṣu kenārında olan mesīregāh debbāġ dükkānların ve niçe evleriñ şāhnişīn (26) ve maqsūra ve qahve-ḫāneler ve derzi dükkānların ṣu ġarq éder, zīrā şehr-i Belġıradıñ ġāyet maʻmūr ḫānedānlarınıñ revzenleri cümle ṣuya nāẓır (27) olup baʻzı zemān ʻimāretlerin ṣu başup geçer, ammā ẓarar etmez, zīrā metānet üzre mebnī binā-yı ʻaẓīmlerdir.

(28) *Der binā-yı cüsūr-ı memerr-i nās-ı ʻacāyibāt.* Evvelā şehr-i Belġıraddan aşaġıc<ay>a qazġancılar çārsūsı başında Nehr-i Oṣum üzre qarşu Qoru Varoşa ʻubūr (29) édecek ṭoquz göz aġaç qanṭara-yı ʻaẓīmdir. Ammā bu cisriñ cümle pāyeleri ṣu içinde kārgīr-binā ʻibretnümā ṭaşlardır, lākin üstleri mezkūr (30) Qoru Daġdan kesme iri meşe ve pelid aġacı direkleri döşelidir. Bir ʻacāyib ü ġarāyib pül-i āṣār-ı ʻacībe vü ġarībedir kim gūyā Hersek (31) vilāyetinde Foça şehrinde Nehr-i Dirin üzre Sulṭān Süleymānıñ bir göz aġaç cisridir. Ammā bū Belġırad cisri ṭoquz gözdür. Ḫüdā ḥıfẓ eyleye, āmīn.

(32) Bu cisr-i ʻaẓīmiñ altında cereyān éden Nehr-i Oṣum Belġırad şehriniñ qarşu ṭarâfındaki ṣaḥrādan cerêyān édüp niçe biñ pirinç ṭarlası ve niçe biñ (33) müşebbek būstānları var. Ekṣeriyyā bu şehr-i Belġırad ḫalqı bu ṣudan istiʻmāl éderler, ġāyet laṭīf ü naẓīf āb-ı ḥayātdır ve ġāyet lezīz pirinci ḥāṣıl olup cümle (34) Arnavudistāna gider.

Der manẓara-yı maqālīd-i cebel-i Ṭomor. Bu Belġırad şehriniñ qıble cānibinde iki sāʻat baʻīd olan Ṭomor daġı **[360a]** eyle yüksek ser-bülend kūh-ı bālādır kim beş altı qonaq yerden nümāyān bir mehīb kūh-ı bālādır. Anda olan nebātāt [u] giyāhāt [u] ʻuşbātıñ (2) envāʻı olur kim cemīʻi Firengistān ve Latinistāndan ḥükemālar bu cibāl-i bālāya ʻurūc édüp niçe biñ yük gūnāgūn edviyeler cemʻ éderler. (3) Bunda olan āb-ı ḥayātlar eṭrāflarında olan on bir qażā yerlere cerêyān édüp qıble ṭarâfındaki ʻuyūn-ı cāriyeler cümle Oḫri Göline aqar. (4) Ve bu kūh-ı bālāda olan ecnās-ı maḫlūqat [u] ḥaşerāt-ı mütenevviʻe meger kūh-ı Bīsütūnda ve kūh-ı Subḥānda ve kūh-ı Demāvend[de] ve kūh-ı Sehendde ve kūh-ı[1] Aġrıda (5) ve kūh-ı Biñ

[1] Text: *kūr*.

Koru Varoş has no *hans*, baths or bazaars, but it does have two churches. It can be considered one of the quarters of Berat, the one across the river. The houses along the water are all outfitted with fishing weirs. At times, when the waters of the Osum river overflow, the houses of Koru Varoş, and also those along the river bank on the other side in Berat proper, get flooded, as do the tanners' market park, many of the private garden pavilions, the coffee houses, and the tailor shops. All the great mansions of the town have their windows facing the river. Usually these houses get flooded too, but they are little damaged because they are strong and well-built.

Noteworthy bridges. Just below Berat at the end of the kettle makers' market there is a bridge across the Osum river to Koru Varoş.[1] It is a large wooden bridge with 9 arches. The supports of the bridge are in the water and are constructed of stone. The surface of the bridge is paved with thick planks of oak cut from trees on Mt. Koru. It is quite a marvelous bridge. The only one comparable to it is the single-arched bridge which Sultan Suleyman built over the Drina river at the town of Foča in the *vilayet* of Hercegovina. But this bridge of Berat has nine arches — may God preserve it. The Osum river, which passes under this majestic bridge, flows through the plain opposite Berat and irrigates thousands of rice fields and vegetable gardens. Most of the inhabitants of Berat get their water from the river, which is extremely clean and good-tasting. The rice is delicious and is exported throughout Albania.

Mt. Tomorr. Two hours to the south of Berat is Mt. Tomorr, a very high mountain which is visible five to six days' march away. There are all sorts of useful plants and herbs and grasses on this mountain. Every year, physicians come here from Western Europe and from Latinistan[2] and climb up the high mountain to collect great quantities of medicinal herbs. The streams which originate in this mountain and flow down its sides sustain 11 surrounding *kadi*-districts. The ones on the south side of the mountain eventually flow into Lake Ohrid. There are also many kinds of creatures and insects on this mountain that are otherwise found only on Mts. Bisutun,

---

[1] The subsequent stone bridge across the Osum was built in 1777-80, during the time of Kurd Ahmed Pasha. It was badly damaged during the flood of December 1888 and during World War I. The present bridge was built in 1928.

[2] I.e., probably the Slavic part of Europe, as opposed to Firengistan, the land of the Franks or Western Europe.

Gölde ve kūh-ı Elbürzde ola. El-ḥāṣıl ġāyet mesīregāh u şikārgāh cibāl-i ʻālīdir.

Ammā bu Belġıradıñ yıldız ṭarâfında olan ṣaḥrā (6) yolıyle şehr-i Elbaṣan beş sāʻat yerdir. Ve bu şehr-i Belġırad yayla éli olmaġile āb [u] havāsı laṭīf olduġından maḥbūb u maḥbūbesi ġāyet (7) firāvān olup cümle ʻāşıq-perestlerdir, ammā ġāyet müʼeddeb ü müʼeddebelerdir. Ve cümle tāzeleri pür-silāḥ gezerler, zīrā el-ʻiyāẕen biʼllāh hodi (8) sedi bilmez Arnavudistāndır, hemān "Işmaṭa ḥaqqıyçün" yaʻnī "Qılıcım ḥaqqıyçün" deyüp gezerler. Ammā ʻaskeri ve levendāt ṭāyifesi olmayup reʻāyā (9) oġlı olanlar ekṯeriyyā bu şehirden İslāmbola gidüp ḥammāmlarda üstād-i kāmil olup dellāklik éderler.

Der beyān-ı memdūḥāt-ı meʼkūlāt-ı ṭaʻām-ı ʻaẓamāt-ı meşrūbāt. (10) Evvelā beyāż ʻArnavud simidi ve noẖudlı çöregi ve ṭavuq böregi ve çamuqa ve qomoştovar nām peynir ü yumurtạlı ṭava böregi (11) ve qaymaq baqlavası ve bādemli ṣamṣası ġāyet memdūḥdur. Ve meşrūbātından üzüm şīresiniñ bir gūne qaynamış laʻlgūn şīresi olur, aña (12) reyḥāniyye derler, bir kāse andan nūş éden serẖoş u sermest olup kāmil bir hafta demāġından reyḥān u ʻamber rāyiḥası zāyil olmaz. El-ḥāṣıl (13) bu şehre maẖṣūṣ reyḥāniyye şerbetidir. Ve darı bozası beyāż elek (?) gibi olup andan nūş éden ṣusızlıġı defʻ éder; gūyā Mıṣrıñ pirinç ṣubya (14) bozasıdır. Ve fevākihāt-ı müṯmirātından adam kellesi qadar lüffān nārı ve zeytūnı[1] ve inciri ve niçe biñ bāġ u ḥadīqa-yı (15) cinānları cihānı zeyn etmişdir, ammā limonı ve turuncı olmaz.

Der kār-ı ṣañyiʻāt-ı maṣnūʻāt-ı mütennevi ʻāt. Cümle ehl-i eṣnāf [u] ehl-i ḥiref (16) mevcūd olup ammā ekṯeriyyā ẖalqı "El-kāsib ḥabībüʼllāh" deyüp kār [u] kesbleri ticāretdir kim vilāyet vilayet metāʻ götürüp getirirler. Bir ṣınfı ʻavāndır. (17) Bir zümresi ʻālimāndır. Bir fırqası ehl-i eṣnāfāndır kim[2] çoġı şehr içre ġazzāz ve ṣarrāc ve quyumcı ve ẖaffāf ve qazġancı ve debbāġdır.

---

[1] In the text here, but crossed out: *ve limonı ve turuncı.*
[2] In text: *kim* repeated.

Süphan, Demavend, Sehend, Ararat, Bingöl and Elburz. In short, this high mountain makes an excellent place for outings and for hunting.

Through the plain to the north of Berat it is a 5 hour journey to Elbasan. With its many alpine pastures, Berat has a very healthy climate, and as a result there are many lovely lads and lasses, adoring to their lovers, yet very well bred. All the young men go about armed because — God help us — this is Albania and no nonsense about it. They swear only by their *shpatë*, i.e., their sword. Those who are not soldiers or sailors but peasants generally leave town and go to Istanbul where they serve as professional attendants in the bathhouses.[1]

Favorite foods and drinks. Among the best known dishes are: white Albanian buns (*simid*), chickpea rolls, chicken *börek*, types of cheese called *jamuk* and *qumështuar,* fried *börek* and eggs, baklava and fresh cream, and almond *samsa*. Of the best known drinks is a red grape must called *reyhania* produced by boiling grapes of various kinds. A glass is enough to make you drunk and will keep your brain perfumed with sweet basil (*reyhan*) and ambergris for an entire week. In short, this town is famous for its *reyhania*. In addition to this, they make a *boza* of millet, like a white sieve, which is thirst-quenching, very much like the Egyptian rice beverage known as *subya*.[2] Among fruits are *lüffan* pomegranates as big as a man's head, as well as olives and figs, the entire region being decked out with orchards and gardens in great numbers, but lemons and oranges do not grow here.

Professions. All types of crafts are to be found here, but most of all they work as tradesmen, based on the Arabic saying, *el-kesību ḥabībü' llāh* ("The businessman is the beloved of God"). They travel from *vilayet* to *vilayet* selling their wares and produce. One group is the commoners or town roughs; another is the ulema; a third is the craftsmen who mainly ply their trades in the town: saddle makers, jewellers, cobblers, silk makers, kettle makers, and tanners.

---

[1] Evliya does not mention them in his description of the Istanbul bath attendants at I 198b11. He does mention Albanian paving-men at I 105a15, and even gives an example of their street cry in the Elbasan dialect (*Evetulata matuzina sulṭana raḥima abur fakite ḥanifese sulṭana yana*); see Dankoff 1991b *Glossary*, 112.

[2] See Dankoff 1991b *Glossary*, 84.

(18) *Der ḥisāb-ı eqālīmāt.* Bi-qavl-i ʿilm-i nücūm-ı ʿilm-i usṭurlāb bu şehir dördinci ıqlīmiñ vasaṭında bulunup arż-ı beledi ----- ve ṭūl-ı (19) nehār ----- bir şehr-i şīrīndir. -----

(20) *Der ṭāliʿ-i ʿamāristān-ı Belġırad.* Bi-qavl-i müneccimīn üstād kehene Padre ve Qolon qavilleri üzre bu şehriñ ṭāliʿ-i ʿimāreti burc-ı sünbüle ve beyt-i (21) ʿUṭārid ve türābīde bulunup şehriniñ maḥṣūlātı ziyāde olup ḫalqı ḫākile yek ḫalūq u ḥalīm ü selīm adamlardır. Ammā bu şehirden çoq aʿyān-ı (22) vilāyet vüze[r]ā ve vükelā ve ʿulemā ve ṣuleḥā kimesneler qopmuşdur.

Der tetimme-yi şehr-engīz-i külliyāt. Evvelā ḫalqı beyne'l-aqrān ġāyet ġayret-keş yarar u bahadır (23) ve şecīʿ [ü] fetā ġāzīlerdir, ve ġāyet müdebbir ü mubaṣṣır u cerī ḥākimlerdir, ve her şeyde ve şeş cihetde pāklerdir. Ve ʿArnavudistānıñ bu qavım ḥasībü(24)'n-nesīb Qureyşī çelebileridir, ammā ehl-i sünnet ve'l-cemāʿat Ḥanefiyyü'l-meẕhebiz derler, ammā bir alay ālüfte ve āşüftegān erbāb-ı meʿārif adamları çoqdur. //

(27) *Der ziyāretgāh-ı Arnavud Belġıradı.* Evvelā ziyāretgāh-ı Vāʿiż Meḥemmed Efendi ve Cim-cim Ḫvāce ve Bāyezīd-i Velī cāmiʿiniñ ḥarêminde ziyāret-i (28) Emīrler Sulṭān ve Uzqurlı cāmiʿiniñ cāmiʿiñ cenūbī ṭarâfı qurbında ziyāret-i Pīr Meḥemmed Efendi ve meydān mezārıstānında (29) cisir qurbında ziyāret-i eş-şeyḫ ʿAlī Dede ----- raḥmetü'llāhi ʿaleyhim ecmaʿīn.

(30) Bu şehriñ şimālī ṭarâfında qarye-yi *Pendi Hondi*den ve daḫi qarye-yi *Duşmenik*den ve daḫi qarye-yi *Lapirda*dan, mezkūr qurālar ġāyet (31) maḥṣūllı beşer altışar yüz evli maʿmūr köylerdir, bunları devr etmeden paşa māl-i ġanāyimiyle şehre bir alay-ı ʿaẓīm ile girüp bir dīvān-ı pādişāhī (32) édüp Manya muḥāfażasına fermān-ı pādişāhī üzre serāperdesiyle ṭuġların çıqarup ḥaqīr ile vedālaşdıqda yine ḥaqīre vedāʿ maḥallidir (33) deyü ḥaqīre ikiyüz ġuruş ve bir siyāh ʿArab kölesi ve bir ʿāṣī ʿArnavud qızı ve bir qat esvāb ve bir at ve ḫuddāmlarıma daḫi tekrār birer çoqa ve (34) birer qumāş ve onar ġuruş iḥsān édüp yüz ʿaded pür-silāḥ tüfeng-endāz şehbāz yigitleri refīq verüp paşa ile öpüşüp vedāʿlaşup **[360b]** anlar vilāyet-i Manyaya, bizler

Vilāyet-i Avlonyaya gitdigimiz qonaqları beyān éder. Evvelā Belġırad içinde mezkūr aġaç cisirden ʿubūr édüp cenūb cānibine (2) maʿmūr qurālar geçüp kūh-ı bülendler üzre 3 sāʿat gidüp *qarye-yi Sineya*; andan *qarye-yi Bobrat;* andan 4 sāʿatde gidüp (3) *qarye-yi Firaqul*, Muḫtār Beg çiftligidir; andan maʿmūr köyler güzer édüp

Clime. According to the science of astrology and astrolabe, this city is in the middle of the fourth clime. The latitude is ----- ; the longest day (i.e., summer solstice) is ----- .

Auspicious star. According to the astrologers and the master diviners Padre and Colon, the rising star of Berat is in the constellation of Virgo, the mansion of Mercury, earthy. As the town has abundant produce, the people are very down to earth, of a sedate and compliant disposition. But also, there are a good number of notables, viziers, deputies, and learned and devout individuals who come from this town.

Completion of the eulogy of Berat. The people are very zealous and courageous ghazis and they are governed by prudent and foresightful agents and administrators. They are neat and clean. This is the Qurayshi clan of gentlemen among the Albanians. They claim to be Sunnis and strict followers of the Hanefi school. But among them are many men who are lax and easy-going and who cultivate the mystical sciences.

Shrines. The mausolea which ought to be visited are those of: Vaiz Mehmed Efendi; Jim-Jim Hodja; Emirler Sultan, in the courtyard of the mosque of Sultan Bayezid II the Saint; Pir Mehmed Efendi, just to the south of the Uzkurli mosque; and Sheikh Ali Dede, in the cemetary of the public square near the bridge. ----- God's mercy be upon them.

North of the town are Perondi, Dushnik and Lapardha, fertile and prosperous villages with 500 to 600 houses each. After we had toured these villages, the Pasha returned to the town in a grand procession with his goods and booty and held a public meeting. In view of the imperial decree, the Pasha prepared to set off in the defense of Mania. He brought out his grand pavilion and horsetail standards and bid us farewell, giving to me on that occasion 200 *kuruş*, 1 Negro slave, 1 Albanian maiden, 1 suit of clothes, and 1 horse; and to each of my servants 1 length of broadcloth, 1 length of fine stuff, and 10 *kuruş*; and sent 100 young men armed with muskets to escort us. I kissed the Pasha goodbye, then he departed for Mania and we ourselves —

Stages of the journey to Vlora — Having crossed the above-mentioned wooden bridge of Berat, we took the road southwards through prosperous villages and over high mountains. After 3 hours of travel, we arrived at the village of Sinja and from there journeyed to the village of Pobrat. 4 hours later, we were in the village of Frakulla,

----- sā'at lodosa gidüp Nehr-i Ergiriyi qarye-yi Miqat altında gemiler ile (4) nehri qarşu ṭarafa 'ubūr édüp

Der beyān-ı temāşāgāh-ı ma'den-i zift-i siyāh. Avlonya sancağı ḫākinde 'aceb ṣun'-ı ḫüdā ma'dendir kim bir dağdan çıqar, (5) ol dağı kūhkenler ferhādī külünkler ile delüp niçe yüz mağārālardan yaṣdıq gibi ve ṣandıq gibi qıṭ'a qıṭ'a zift parçaları çıqarup (6) cemī'i Firengistāndan bāzirgānları gelüp zift emīni bey' éder, yetmiş yük aqçe iltizām-ı māl-i pādişāhīdir kim ġāyet çoq māl-i pādişāhī ḥāsıl olur. (7) Bu ḫidmete me'mūr yigirmi pāre mu'āf [u] müsellem köyleri var, ve neqadar mücrimler var ise qatl etmeyüp bunda mü'ebbed derzincīr zift ma'deninde esīr olup (8) ḫidmet éderler. Ve niçe biñ adamlar bu ma'denlerden kār édüp beslenirler. Ḥālā bir daġ-ı 'aẓīm daḫi var idi, meger bi-emr-i ḫāliq-i kevneyn meger anda daḫi (9) zift ma'deni var imiş, oldaḫi bu maḥalde ẓühūr édüp anı daḫi der-i devlete Avlonya begi 'arż édüp ol daḫi on yük aqçe (10) başqa iltizām oldı. El-ḥāṣıl-ı kelām, cenāb-ı bārī ṣun'ın iẓhār içün cümle bu dağlarıñ üstlerin sebze-zār u çemenzār ḫalq édüp içlerini (11) cümle siyāh zift ḫalq etmiş. Āye-yi sūre-yi ----- "Yef'alü'llāhu mā yeşā'ü bi-qudretihi ve yeḥkümü mā yürīdü bi-'izzetihi."

Bu temāşā-yı 'ibretnümāları édüp (12) hemān bu maḥalle qarīb *Nehr-i Aq Ṣu*, bunı atlar ile geçüp, ammā hemān yine ol maḥalde Ergiriden gelen Nehr-i Ergiriye maḫlūṭ olup ol daḫi (13) ol maḥalle qarīb Avlonya Körfezi deryāsına munṣab olur. Ve bu Aq Ṣudan çeyrek sā'at çemenzār ṣaḥra ile gidüp *qarye-yi Miqat*, (14) bir bayır dibinde bāğlı ve bāğçeli ve bir cāmi'li bir müferriḥ fezā-yı lāle-zārlı qaryedir, ve ma'mūr sarāy-ı 'aẓīm çiftligi var kim Sinān-paşa-zāde Yūsuf (15) Beg efendimizle kāmil bir hafta bu qarye-yi merāmda murād [u] merāmımız üzre cān ṣoḥbetleri édüp yetmiş sene muqaddem pederimiz merḥūm bizim gibi seyāḥatla (16) ol daḫi bu köye gelüp bu ḫānedānda mihmān olup niçe sene sākin olduğı ḥücresinde biz de sākin olup pederimiz rūḥıyçün bir ḫatm-i şerīf (17) tilāvet édüp rū-yı dīvāra yazduğı ḫaṭları ve niçe āṣārların

the estate of Muhtar Beg. After ----- more hours, advancing southwards through prosperous villages, we crossed the Gjirokastër[1] river by boat below the village of Mekat..

The black pitch mine.[2] It is a wonderful natural mine in the territory of the *sancak* of Vlora. The miners dig holes in the mountain with pickaxes and from hundreds of caverns extract pitch in great lumps the size of pillows or caskets. The *emin* or administrator of the mine sells the pitch to European traders who come and buy it on site. The mine is run under a concession and yields 70 loads of *akçe*[3] for the imperial treasury — a very handsome sum. 20 villages are employed at the mine and, as compensation, are exempt from all government taxes. In addition, all the criminals who have been sentenced to death are instead sent for life in prison work at the mine, bound in chains. Thousands of people make their living from this mine. Another large mountain, which also — by God's command — contains pitch, was recently reported to the sultan by the Beg of Vlora, and was awarded as a concession for the sum of 10 loads of *akçe*. In short, in order to reveal His handiwork, our Lord and Creator covered these mountains with greenery and, inside, filled them with black pitch. The Koran, surah ----- states: "God does what He wants by His power and judges what He wills by His glory."[4]

After touring the mine, we crossed the Aksu[5] (White River) on horseback. The waters of the Aksu mix here with those of the Gjirokastër river and then flow into the Bay of Vlora. From the Aksu we went on another quarter hour through a grassy plain to Mekat, a pleasant and verdant village at the foot of a slope and surrounded by gardens and vineyards. It has 1 congregational mosque. There is also a farm-estate here with a large mansion. I spent a week here in the village of our lord Yusuf Beg, the son of Sinan Pasha. We exchanged much pleasant and intellectual conversation and enjoyed ourselves greatly. Seventy years before, my late father, on a journey such as ours, stayed as a guest in this village, where he spent several years. Now I stayed in the very same room and completed an entire Koran

---

[1] I.e., Vjosa river.

[2] The pitch mines of Selenica.

[3] One "load" (*yük*) = 500,000 *akçe*.

[4] Conflation and expansion of two Koranic phrases: "And God does what He wants" (3:40, 14:27, 22:18) and "God judges what He wills" (5:11).

[5] No doubt the Shushica river which flows into the Vjosa near the village of Mekat. Evliya referred to it above as the Kuruçay river.

ve Yūsuf Begde olan yazduğı kitābları cümle temāşā édüp ḫatm-i şerīfiñ (18) ṣavābın pederimiziñ ve Ġāzī Sinān Paşanıñ rūḥ-ı şerīflerine hibe édüp andan beg ile vedā'laşup

Andan qıble ṭarâfına bir öz içre gidüp (19) *qarye-yi Cevherina*, andan yine aña qarīb *qarye-yi Aqça Kilse*, bu qurāları ----- sā'atde 'ubūr édüp yine qıbleye ma'mūr qurālar 'ubūr édüp

(20) *Der ṣūret-i icmālāt-ı dār-ı emāniye, ya'nī sūr-ı cihān-nümā-yı qal'e-yi bālā Qanye.* (21) İbtidā bu qal'e-yi bī-hemtā İşpanya qıralı bināsıdır. Lisān-ı Ṭalyanca ismi Poqrondardır. Sene ----- tārīḫinde 'aṣr-ı Sulṭān Meḥemmed (22) Ḫān Ebū'l-fetiḥde bi-dest-i vezīr Qoca Maḥmūd Paşa fetḥidir. Ba'dehu Venedig-i Bunduqani Firengi bu qal'eye istīlā édüp sene ----- (23) tārīḫinde Sulṭān Bāyezīd-i Velī 'aṣrında Venedik elinden bi-dest-i Ġāzī Küçük Evrenos Beg muḥāṣara ile bu qal'eyi döge döge (24) içinde olan küffārlar vere verüp "Emān, ne yeyelim" deyü sü'āl etdiklerinde Ġāzī Küçük Evrenos Beg "Qan yeyiñ" buyur(25)duqlarından ba'de'l-fetiḥ bu qal'eye Qanye derler, anıñiçün vech-i tesmiyesi Qanye qalmışdır. Ḥālā Avlonya sancağı ḥudūdında (26) vāqı' olup bu qal'eden aşağı leb-i deryāda ġarb ṭarâfında Avlonya qal'esiniñ içindeki qazları ve ṭavuqları cümle (27) görinür.

Bu qal'e-yi Qanye evc-i semāya ser çekmiş bir qal'e-yi serāmeddir kim bir ṭopraqlı ve küfeke ṭaşlı bir kūh-ı bī-(28)hemtā üstinde şekl-i müs̱elles̱ şeddādī-binā bir qal'e-yi bālādır. Cirmi kāmil üç biñ 'aded adımdır. Ve aṣlā bir ṭarâfında bir (29) ḫaṭve qadar bir ḫandaqı yoqdur, zīrā ṣāfī sengistān uçurum qayalardır. İçinde cümle üçyüz kiremitli (30) ḫāne-yi kārgīr-binālar vardır. Ve bir Sulṭān Meḥemmed Ḫān cāmi'i vardır, kiremit ile mestūr bir mevzūn minàreli cāmi'-i ma'mūrı (31) var. Aña qarīb Ġāzī Sinān Paşa sarāyı var, ġāyet cihān-nümādır kim cümle Avlonya ṣaḥrāsı ve Körfez deryāsı ve yüz elli (32) mīl ba'īd Körfez deryāsı içre Körfez cezīresi ve Avlonya Körfezi içi ve Duqat ve Porġonat Körfezi içi (33) ve kenārlarında ----- qal'esi ----- ----- qal'esi (34) cümle bu Qanye qal'esinden nümāyāndır, tā bu mertebe bir zirve-yi 'ālīde binā olunmuş qal'e-yi Qanyedir kim cihān ayaq altında nümāyāndır.

[361a] Ve bu qal'eniñ üç qat qapuları var. Biri qıble ṭarâfına nāẓırdır kim ol ṭarafda olan varoşa açılır. Ve bir qapusı (2) poyraz cānibine meftūḥdur kim aşağı Avlonya qal'esine gider yoldur. Ve biri daḫi cenūb ṭarâfındaki küçük (3) varoşa açılır, ammā bu qapunuñ

recital for the sake of his spirit. On a wall in the room were his calligraphic samples and other inscriptions which he had composed while he was the guest of Yusuf Beg. I offered the blessing derived from the Koran recital to the noble spirits of my beloved father and of Ghazi Sinan Pasha.

Bidding farewell to the Beg, we continued our journey southwards in a valley, passing through Xhyherina and Qishbardha and other prosperous villages, and arrived in ----- hours at *the lofty and peerless fortress of Qanye (Kanina)*. It was initially constructed by the king of Spain. Its name in Italian is Pokrondar. In the year ----- it was conquered by Koca Mahmud Pasha, vizier of Sultan Mehmed the Conqueror. It was later occupied by the Venetians. In the year ----- during the reign of Sultan Bayezid II the Saint, Ghazi Küçük Evrenos Beg besieged the fortress and started to bombard it. When the infidels within had surrendered and cried for mercy, asking "What shall we eat?" Küçük Evrenos Beg replied *Qan ye* ("Eat blood"), thus giving the fortress its name. It is now on the border of the *sancak* of Vlora. From here you can even see the geese and chickens in the fortress of Vlora, which is down by the sea to the west.

Kanina is a lofty fortress rising to the heavens. It was constructed solidly on a mountain promontory of earth and pumice rock. It is triangular in shape and has a circumference of 3000 paces. It has no moat on any side, not even one pace wide, nor does it need one because it is surrounded by sheer rocky cliffs and precipices. Inside there are 300 stonework houses with tiled roofs. Here is also the mosque of Sultan Mehmed II which has a tiled roof and a graceful minaret. Near this mosque is the mansion of Ghazi Sinan Pasha. From the fortress of Kanina one can see the plain of Vlora, the Sea of Corfu (Ionian Sea), the island of Corfu 150 miles away, as well as the bays of Vlora, Dukat and Progonat, and the fortresses of ----- and ----- along the coast. It is such a lofty fortress — the whole world is visible beneath one's feet.

The fortress of Kanina has three gates. The first faces south-east and links the fortress to the open town on that side. The second faces north and opens onto the road which descends to Vlora. The third faces south and opens onto the small extramural settlement (*varoş*).

yanında iç qal'edir kim anıñ bir qapusı şarqa nāẓır olup yine qal'e içre açılır. (4) Bu iç qal'e içinde ancaq yigirmi 'aded kiremit örtüli kār-ı qadīm ḫāneleri ve ġılāl enbārları ve cebe-ḫāneleri ve (5) ṣu ṣa[r]nıçları var.

Ve bu iç qal'e dīvārınıñ ṭaşrasında dīvār dibinde aşağı Avlonya qal'esi limanına nāẓır (6) dörd 'aded ṭoplar var kim bir pādişāh mālik olmamışdır ve bir serḥadd-i metīnelerde mis̱illeri yoqdır. Bu ṭopuñ birinde (7) bir ġarīb adam içinde yaz u qış sākin olup yorġanı ve döşegi ve ṭanceresi ve kebesi cümle bu ṭop içindedir, ḥattā (8) bir ṣāḥibü'l-ḫayr ṭopuñ ağzına bir qapu etdirüp ḥerīf-i ẓarīf ṭopuñ ağzını ḫānesi gibi açup qapayup sākin olur, (9) el-ḥāṣıl bir odadır, ṭopda yaṭup qalqar.

Ve bu poyraz ṭarâfındaki qal'e qapusı üzre bir beyāż çār-gūşe (10) mermer üzre celī ḫaṭ ile Sulṭān Süleymān bu qal'eyi ta'mīr ü termīm etdiginiñ tārīḫi taḥrīr olunmuşdur. Ve bu qal'eniñ (11) cümle ṣoqaqları eniş yoquşdur. Bunda aṣlā çārsū-yı bāzār ve ḫān u ḥammām ve 'imāret yoqdur. Ammā qal'eniñ (12) cenūb ṭarâfındaki varoşda cümle üçyüz 'aded bāğlı ve bāġçeli ve kiremitli biri biri üzre ḥavāleli (13) qat-ender-qat kārgīr binālı evlerdir. Bunda daḫī çārsū-yı bāzārdan bir eser yoqdur, ancaq Ġāzī Sinān Paşanıñ bir (14) müferriḥ cāmi'-i zībāsı ve bir serāmed mināre-yi ra'nāsı ve bir 'aded tekye-yi Ḥācī Bektaş-ı Velīsi var kim ol daḫi Ġāzī Sinān Paşa (15) ḫayrātıdır. Ammā Rūm ve 'Arab ve 'Acemde meşhūr-ı āfāq bir quṭb-ı istiḥqāq Ḥācī Bektaş-ı Velī ḫāneqāhıdır, erbāb-ı me'ārif (16) 'ārifün-bi'llāhdan faqr [u] fāqa ṣāḥibi cānları çoqdur, ve maḥbūb-ı zībā küçükleri vardır kim maḥbū[bu]'l-qulūblardır, ve maṭbaḫ-ı (17) Keykāvūsında ni'metleri āyende vü revendelere mebzūldur, zīrā evqāfı cümle dağlar ve bāğlar ve bāġçeler cümle anıñdır. Ve tekye civārında (18) ṣāḥibü'l-ḫayrāt Ġāzī Sinān Paşa bir qubbe-yi 'ālīde cemī'i aqrâbā [ve] ta'alluqātları ile medfūnlardır, raḥmetü'llāhi 'aleyhim ecma'īn. (19) El-ḥāṣıl cihān-nümā bir ḫāneqāh-ı zībādır kim vaṣfında lisān qāṣırdır.

Near this gate is the citadel which has one gate facing east and communicating with the main fortress. The citadel contains only 20 houses built in the old style with tiled roofs. It also has storage houses for grain and munitions and cisterns for water.

Outside and below the citadel wall there are 4 cannons facing the harbor of Vlora, such as no emperor has ever possessed and no frontier post has ever disposed of. One of the cannons is so large that it is inhabited summer and winter by a homeless man, together with his quilt and mattress, his frying-pan, and his felt jacket. In fact, a kind benefactor had a door made for him in the barrel of the cannon which the fellow can open and close, just like the door of a house. He lives there as if in a room and lies down and gets up inside the cannon!

Above the northern gate there is an inscription in *celi* script on a square slab of white marble indicating the date when Sultan Suleyman repaired and reconstructed the fortress. The roads in this fortress are all up and down. There are no bazaars, *han*s, bathhouses or public buildings inside the walls, but the open town (*varoş*) to the south of the fortress contains 300 stonework houses with tiled roofs and gardens and vineyards, all piled on top of one another. Here, too, there is no sign of a bazaar. There is only the spacious mosque of Sinan Pasha with its tall and elegant minaret. There is also a *tekke* of Hadji Bektash Veli here, also endowed by Sinan Pasha. This *tekke* is famous throughout Turkey, Arabia and Persia. Here one finds many devotees of the mystical sciences and the dervish life of poverty. Among them are lovely young boys. Visitors and pilgrims are fed copious meals from the kitchen and pantry of the *tekke* because all the surrounding mountains, vineyards and gardens belong to it. Near the *tekke*, the benefactor of the endowment, Ghazi Sinan Pasha, lies buried along with all his household and retainers in a mausoleum with a lofty dome — may God have mercy on their souls.[1] In short, it is a rich and famous *tekke*, beyond my powers to describe.

---

[1] The mausoleum, now since disappeared like the other Muslim buildings referred to by Evliya, was still subject of veneration during the visit of Johann Georg von Hahn ca. 1848. Hahn reports, "[The owners of the fortress] are descendents of the first Turkish conqueror of this region, the famous Sinan Pasha of Konya, whose grave can be seen in a small tekke at the base of the castle. People come here on pilgrimage from far off, as the Turks consider Sinan to be a saint;" see Johann Georg von Hahn, *Albanesische Studien*, vol. 1 (Jena 1854, reprint Athens 1981), 72.

Ve bu Qanye qal'esiniñ cümle dörd yüz 'aded qulları ve (20) dizdārı cümle Avlonya emīninden važīfe-yi mu'ayyenelerin alırlar. Bu qal'e qulınıñ daḫi nıṣfın Manya muḥāfažasına me'mūr (21) édüp andan aşagı poyraz ṭarâfındaki qapudan ṭaşra çıqup yoquş aşagı 2 sā'atde enüp cihānı seyr éderek gāh atlı ve (22) gāh yayan gidüp

Evṣāf-ı cā-yı emān-ı limaniye, ya'nī binā-yı sedd-i süleymānī qal'e-yi Avlonya. (23) Sene ----- tārīḫinde Avlonya Körfezini Bunduqani Venediginden ḫalāṣ içün Süleymān Ḫān fermān édüp "Leb-i deryāda bir avlu-(24)mis̱āl bir qal'ecik çeviriñ" deyü işāret buyurduqlarından qal'eyi binā édüp Süleymān Ḫānıñ nuṭq-ı dürer-bārları üzre ba'de'l-itmām (25) qal'eniñ ismine Avlu-ya derler, sebeb-i tesmiyesi oldur kim defter-i ḫāqānīde Avlonya sancagı derler. Qānūn-ı qadīm pāy-taḫt-i livā budur, (26) ammā Belgırad vilāyetiñ ortası olmagile taḫtgāh Belgırad-ı bihişt-ābād olmuşdur. Ammā bu Avlonya qal'esi Avlonya Körfezi ve (27) Duqat Körfezi agzında bur qumsal alçacıq burunda şekl-i müs̱emmen yaṣṣı sekiz köşeli ve şeddādī-mis̱āl binālı (28) bir qal'e-yi müsteḥkem-i üstüvārdır kim ḥaqqā ki sedd-i Süleymān Ḫāndır. 'Os̱mānlı qal'e binā édemez der[ler], Egre serḥaddinde Segedin qal'esi ve (29) Özü serḥaddinde Ṭurla Nehri kenārında Bender qal'e[si] ve bu Avlonya qal'esin görmeyenler Āl-i 'Os̱mān nice qal'e yapdıqlarını bilmezler.

(30) Bu Avlonyanıñ dīvārı kāmil yigirmi arşın yüksekdir ve dīvārınıñ her ṭarâfınıñ qalınlıgı onar arşın enlidir ve sekiz 'aded (31) köşelerinde sekiz 'aded ṭabya-yı 'aẓīmleri var kim her biri birer sedd-i Yācūc ve sedd-i Mācūc olup her birinde yedişer 'aded serāmed balyemez (32) ṭopları var. Bu ṭoplardan mā'adā aşagı yére berāber demir qapular içinde ejder-i heft-serler gibi 'arabalar üzre körfez agzına nāẓır (33) deryāya berāber qırq yedi pāre serāmed şeşḫāne ve burmalı ve

The fortress of Kanina is guarded by 400 garrison troops and the warden, who receive their wages from the *emin* of Vlora. Half of the soldiers of this fortress were ordered to set off in the defense of Mania. For our part, we set off from the northern gate down the mountainside and continued for 2 hours enjoying the view, at times on horseback and at times on foot.

The harbor and fortress of Vlora. Vlora was founded in the year -----[1] by Sultan Suleyman, who ordered a small fortress to be built in the form of a courtyard (*avlu*) overlooking the sea, in order to protect the Bay of Vlora from attack by the Venetians, and so, when it was finished, it was called Avluya. The name figures in the Offices of the Imperial Registry as the *sancak* of Avlonya.[2] Vlora is the capital of the *sancak* according to the old statute, but Berat became capital since it is in the middle of the *vilayet.*

The fortress of Vlora[3] is built on a low sandy spit at the entrance to the Bay of Vlora and the Bay of Dukat. It is octagonal in shape and very strong and solid, a veritable great wall of Sultan Suleyman. People say the Ottomans do not know how to build fortresses, but anyone who has not seen the fortress of Szeged on the frontier of Erlau, the fortress of Bender on the banks of the Dniester on the frontier of Ochakov, and this fortress of Vlora, cannot understand how masterful Ottoman construction work can be. The walls of the fortress of Vlora are 20 ells high and 10 ells thick on all sides. At the 8 corners of the fortress walls are 8 large bastions, each like the wall of Gog and Magog, and each surmounted by 7 great long-range battering guns. Aside from these, inside the iron gates at sea level there are 47 other battering guns with rifled barrels looking out towards the bay and mounted on carriages like seven-headed dragons.

---

1 Sultan Suleyman was in Vlora in the summer of 944/1537 during the Corfu campaign, when he no doubt gave orders for the construction of the fortress. Kiel states that it was still extant in 1906 when its ruins were demolished to provide construction material for the road between Vlora to the port. Only a few fragments have survived, situated on the outskirts of the modern town in the Plaka quarter. Cf. Kiel 1990, 268-74.

2 The Turkish for Vlora is Avlona or Avlunya, thus the folk etymology. The toponym Vlora actually derives from Ancient Greek Aulōn (Ptolemy), related to *aulōn* "gorge, ditch, channel," Lat. Aulon, Aulona. In the accusative case, *eis Aulōna* "to Aulon", the word evolved into Med. Lat. Valona, and in Albanian, with Tosk rhotacism, became *Vëlora and then Vlora, Vlorë.

3 For this section, cf. Kiel 1990, 169-70.

qırmızı çoqa örtüli bal-yemez ṭopları var kim her birine adam ṣığar (34) ṭoplardır, dükeli zemānda ṭıqalı (?) ve ağızlı olup cümle ḫuddāmları şeb [ü] rūz ṭoplarıñ yanında yaṭırlar.

Ve bu qal'eniñ sekiz 'aded köşe **[361b]** siniñ bir köşesinden bir köşesine varınca yüz yigirmişer 'aded adımdır. Bu ḥisāb üzre Avlonya qal'esi dāyiren-mā dār ṭoquz (2) yüz adımdır. Ve içinde Sulṭān Süleymān Ḫān cāmi'i var. Ve tā ortasında Süleymān Şāh qullesi var, yedi qat serāmed ġāyet muṣanna' qulle-yi (3) bālādır kim ṣāfī muṭarraş seng-binā olup üsti qurşum örtüli külāh qubbedir, tā zirve-yi a'lāsında muṭallā 'alemi vardır. (4) Avlonya qal'esiniñ bu qulle iç qal'esi olsa gerekdir. Ġāyet metīn qulle-yi bālādır kim gūyā Selanikde Kele-merye qullesidir, zīrā anı (5) ve bunı Süleymān Ḫānıñ qoca mi'mār Sinānı binā etmişdir. Bu qullede dizdārdan ġayri kimse sākin olmayup cümle cebe-ḫāne ve (6) sāyir mühimmāt [u] levāzimātlar ile ṭabaqa ṭabaqa memlūdur.

Ve bu ṭaşra qal'e içre cümle üçyüz 'aded kiremitli bāġ u bāġçesiz (7) ve ḥavlısız żayyıq evlerdir, ammā ṭarīq-ı 'āmları vāsi'dir, ammā cümle alçacıq ṭarz-ı qadīm yer evleridir. Bunda daḫi çārsū-yı (8) bāzārdan bir şey yoqdur ve ḫān u ḥammām ve 'imāret daḫi yoqdur. Ve cümle iki 'aded qapuları bu dervezeleriñ mābeynleri ṣāfī (9) cebe-ḫāne-yi gūnāgūnlar memlūdur ve şeb [ü] rūz nigehbānları ve dīdebānları mevcūdlardır. Bir qapusı şarqa ve bir bābı ṭaraf-ı ġarba nāẓırdır. (10) Ve dā[yi]ren-mā-dār ṭaşra ḫandaqı ellişer adım enli olup içi leb-ber-leb deryādır ve baṭaqlıqdır. Ve qapularıñ öñlerinde cisirleri maqara(11)lı qanṭaralar olup her géce cisirleri qaldırup qal'e qapularına zincīrler ile bağlayup qapuya siper éderler. Ve cümle ṣağīr ü kebīr (12) beşyüz 'aded ṭopları var ve dizdārı ve on iki 'aded ağaları ve cümle dördyüz 'aded qulları var, nıṣfı Manya (13) vilāyeti muḥāfaẓasına emr-i pādişāhīyle me'mūr etdik. Ve sipāh ketḫüdā yeri ve yeñiçeri serdār[ı] ve üçyüz aqçe pāyesiyle şerīf qażāsı (14) olup nāḥiyesi cümle yüz beş pāre ma'mūr qurālardır. Muḥtesibi ve bācdārı ve gümrük emīni ve ḫarāc emīni ve mi'mār ağası ve qapudan (15) ağası ve liman ketḫüdāsı ve şehir ketḫüdāsı vardır.

Ve bu qal'eniñ şarq ṭarâfında bir zeytūnlı bir bayır ḥavālesi vardır, cemī'i (16) dağ u bāġı ve irağı ve yaqını ṣāfī bāġ u bāġçe ve

They are covered with red canvass and are so big that a man can fit into their barrels. The cannons are ready to fire at all times, and the men guarding them lie right beside them day and night. From one corner to the next of the 8 corners is a distance of 120 paces, so if we add it up we come up with a total circumference for the fortress of Vlora of 900 [sic] paces. Inside the fortress is the mosque of Sultan Suleyman and at the very center is the tower of Suleyman Shah. It is a very tall and finely-wrought tower, 7 stories high, and is built of chiselled stonework with a lead-covered conical dome and topped by a gilded pinnacle. This may be considered the citadel of the fortress of Vlora. It is a very solid and tall tower, like the Kalamaria Tower[1] in Thessalonika, since both of them were built by the great Sinan, the architect of Sultan Suleyman. The tower is inhabited only by the warden and is filled with layer upon layer of munitions and other military equipment and supplies.

Inside the outer fortress there are some 300 squat and narrow old-fashioned earthen houses with tiled roofs and with no vineyard, garden or courtyard. Although the public thoroughfares are wide, there is nothing else but a bazaar: no *han*s, baths or other public buildings. The fortress has 2 gates, the space between them being completely filled with munitions of various kinds. It is guarded by sentries and watchmen day and night. One gate faces east and the other west. The fortress is completely surrounded by a moat 50 paces wide on all sides and filled with sea water, which is, however, swampy. Each of the gates has a drawbridge in front of it which is raised at night and secured with chains to form a protective barrier. There are 500 cannons, small and large. The tower is inhabited by the warden, 12 officers and 400 garrison troops. Half of these soldiers were ordered to depart to defend the *vilayet* of Mania in accordance with the imperial decree. Also here are the steward of the *sipahi*s, the commander of the janissaries, a *kadi* with a salary level of 300 *akçe* and responsible for 105 prosperous villages in the region, a market inspector, a collector of tolls, a customs inspector, a poll-tax official, a chief architect, an officer of the admiralty, the commander of the port and the mayor of the town.

To the east of the fortress and somewhat above it is a slope with olive trees. All the hills and fields in the area are covered in fruit trees,

[1] The famous White Tower.

zeytūnlikdir. Bu ḥavāle burun üzre *ziyāret-i* ----- *Baba Sulṭān*, bir qaç nefer (17) faqr [u] fāqa ṣāḥibi Bektaşiyānları var.

Der vaṣf-ı muṣallā-yı erbāb-ı ḥācāt. Bu qal'e ile varoş qaṣabası mābeyninde bir çemenzār (18) yerde vāqı' bir vāsi' namāzgāhı var kim iki biñ adam alur, ve qal'eden ṭaşra varoşa varınca kāmil biñ adım çemenzār yerdir.

(19) *Evṣāf-ı şehr-i varoş-ı Avlonya.* Bu şehir aṣlā qal'e içinde degildir, hemān bir düz vāsi' çemenzār yerde bāġ u bā(20)ġçeli ve gül-i gülistānlı limon ve turunc ve zeytūn [ve] nār ve incirli bāġ-ı iremler içre cümle biñ 'aded kiremit örtüli taḥtānī (21) ve fevqānī kārgīr-binālı mükellef ü mükemmel ü müzeyyen ü ma'mūr evlerdir.

Ve cümle ----- 'aded maḥallātlardır. Evvelā H̱ünkār cāmi'i maḥallesi (22) ve Mumcı-zāde maḥallesi ve ṭabaqlar maḥallesi ve Ḥüseyn Aġa maḥallesi ve maḥkeme maḥallesi ve çārsū maḥallesi, bunlar meşhūrdur.

(23) Ve cümle ----- 'aded miḥrābdır. Cümleden Sulṭān Süleymān cāmi'i qurşumlı ve kārgīr qubbeli ve bir münhedim olmuş mināreli (24) maḥbūb cāmi'dir. Qıble qapusı üzre tārīḫi böyle taḥrīr olunmuşdur:

İbtidā Ya'qūb şeyḫü's-sālikīn
Etdi mescid fī sebīli'llāh (25) evin
S̱āniyen Sulṭān Süleymānü'z-zemān
Qıldı cüm'a bāreke'llāh āferīn
Dédi Ḥasbī bu maqāmıñ tārīḫin
Nūr-ı (26) ḥaq bu[l] cāmi'ü'l-muqarrabīn. Sene 949.

Bu cāmi' ġāyet rūḥāniyyetli cāmi'-i nūrdur.

Andan çārsū içinde cemā'at-ı kesīreye (27) mālik Mumcı-zāde cāmi'i, kiremitli ve kārgīr mināreli cāmi'-i zībādır. Andan ṭabaqlar başında Ḥüseyn Aġa cāmi'i, nev-binā bir kire(28)mitli ve kārgīr mināre-yi mevzūnlı muṣanna' beytü'llāhdır. Andan qal'e cāmi'i, mevṣūfdur.

Ve cümle beş 'aded maḥalle (29) zāviyeleri vardır kim maḥallātları bālāda merqūmdur.

vineyards and olive orchards. On this high peak is situated the tomb of ----- Baba Sultan[1] with a few Bektashi dervishes.

Prayer-grounds. Between the fortress and the open town there is a broad meadow used for public worship, which can encompass 2000 people. From the fortress to the open town, the meadow stretches 1000 paces long.

The open town of Vlora. The open town is quite separate from the fortress. It is situated on a level grassy plain with gardens and vineyards, roses, lemons, oranges, olives, pomegranates and figs, like the fabled garden of Irem. It has 1000 beautiful one- and two-story stonework houses with tiled roofs.

There are ----- quarters, including those of Hünkâr mosque, Mumci-zade, the tanners, Hüseyn Aga, the courthouse, and the bazaar.

In all, it has ----- prayer-niches. Among them is the lovely Sultan Suleyman mosque[2] with a chiselled stone dome covered in lead and with a fallen minaret. Over the *kıble* door is the following chronogram:

> First, Yakub, sheikh of the devotees,
> Made his house into a mosque (*mescid*), for the sake of God.
> Second, Sultan Suleyman, Solomon of the Age,
> Turned it into a congregational mosque (*cami*) — bravo!
> Hasbi has composed the chronogram of this temple:
> Find the light of Truth, mosque of those drawn near to God.
> Year 949/1542.

This mosque is a site of great spirituality.

Then comes the pretty mosque of Mumci-zade, with a large congregation: it is covered in tiles and has a stone-carved minaret.

The mosque of Hüseyn Aga near the tanners' quarter: a new and well-constructed building covered in tiles and with a graceful stone-carved minaret.

The mosque of the fortress: described above.

There are also 5 neighborhood mosques in the 5 quarters mentioned above.

---

[1] Below he is called Kuzgun Baba.

[2] Now known as the Murad Mosque, built in 949-64/1542-57. This is the only Ottoman monument preserved in Vlora today.

Ve cümle üç ʻaded medrese-yi sūḫtegāndır. Evvelā Yaʻqūb Efendi (30) medresesi ve Mumcı-zāde tedrīsi ve Ḥüseyn Aġa ders-ḫānesi var.

Ve cümle beş ʻaded mekteb-i ṣıbyān-ı ebced-(31) ḫvānı var.

Ve cümle üç ʻaded āstāne-yi ehl-i tevḥīd ḫāneqāhları var. Cümleden Yaʻqūb Efendi tekyesi ḫānedān-ı Ḫalvetīdir (32) kim niçe yüz ʻaded pā-bürehne ve ser-bürehne ḫırqa-yı peşmīne ṣāḥibi ʻabdālānları var. Andan qalʻeye ḥavāle olan daġda bāġlar içre (33) Quzġun Baba tekyesi, bāġ-ı irem-miṡāl bir āstāne olduġı bālāda mevṣūfdur.

Ve cümle bir ʻaded ḥammāmcıġı var. Qarşu(34)sında maḥkeme-yi şerʻ-i resūl-i mübīni var kim ʻAcem Meḥemmed Efendi ḥākimü'l-vaqt iken binā etmiş bir ʻaceb āstāne-yi şerʻ-i resūldur.

Ve cümle **[362a]** dörd yüz on yedi ʻaded çārsū-yı ḥüsn bāzārı var. Cümle ehl-i ḥiref ve cemīʻi metāʻ-ı nevādirāt mevcūddur, lākin (2) bezzāzistānı yoqdur, ammā cemīʻi kālā-yı aqmişe-yi fāḫire-yi bī-qıymet ü bī-minnet (?) bulunur, zīrā Venedik iskelesidir. Ve cümle (3) dörd ʻaded ḫānları vardır.

Ve cümle sekiz ʻaded çeşmeleri var, ammā cümleden Yaʻqūb Efendi tekyesi qurbında (4) İlyās Paşa çeşmesiniñ tārīḫidir:

> Buldum İlyās Paşanıñ tārīḫini yevmü't-tenād
> Çünki dédim tārīḫini ve-hüve ḫayrü(5)'l-ʻibād. Sene -----

Ammā ġayri çeşmeler baṭṭāldır. Bu şehr ehālīsi ġāyetü'l-ġāye ṣuya[1] muḥtāclardır. Mürūr-ı eyyām ile ṣu yolları ḫarāb (6) olmuş, ammā āb-ı ḥayāt ṣuları var, bir ṣāḥibü'l-ḫayrāt sehil şey ile ʻamār etse şehīdān-ı deşt-i Kerbelā ervāḥların şād ve düvāzdeh (7) imāmānlarıñ ervāḥlar[ın] yād éderdi; zīrā bir içim aġız ṣuyı içün nıṣf-ı sāʻat şarq ṭarâfında bāġlar içre ṣıġār u kibār (8) fuqarālar ʻusret çekerek gidüp ṣu getirirler. Ammā ġayri eşyānıñ envāʻı mevcūddur. Bā-ḫuṣūṣ bāġ u bāġçelerinde gūnā(9)gūn meyve-yi ābdārları cihānı dutmuşdur.

Me'kūlāt [u] meşrūbātınıñ memdūḥātından evvelā limanında ṣazan ve ala-kerde ve (10) qolyoz ve kefal ve levrek balıqları ve balıq yumurṭaları olur kim Rūmda olmazdır. Ve reyḥāniyye nām bādesi (11) ve limonı ve turuncı ve zeytūnı ve inciri ve üzümi cihānı dutmuşdur. Ve Duqat köylerinde qırmızı çoqa boyası (12) kökleri ve

---

[1] Text: *şehre*.

There are 3 *medreses*: Yakub Efendi, Mumci-zade, and Hüseyn Aga-zade.

There are 5 primary schools.

There are 3 dervish convents, including the Halveti *tekke* of Yakub Efendi[1] with hundreds of devout dervishes, barefooted and bareheaded, with patched woolen cloaks; and the above-mentioned *tekke* of Kusum (Kuzgun) Baba on a hillside overlooking the fortress, set amidst vineyards, like the fabled garden of Irem.

There is 1 small bathhouse — a marvellous structure — across from which is the *şeriat* courthouse built by Acem Mehmet Efendi when he was a town magistrate.

There is a fine bazaar with a total of 417 shops where one can find all sorts of trades and goods. There is no *bedestan*, but one finds all kinds of fine fabrics and precious cloth here because it is a Venetian *scala* or emporium. There are 4 *han*s and 8 fountains, the best known of which is that of Ilyas Pasha near the *tekke* of Yakub Efendi, with the following chronogram:

On the day of assembly I found the date of Ilyas Pasha,
Since I pronounced its chronogram: "And he is the best of God's servants". Year ----- .

All the other fountains are no longer functioning, so the people of the town have a pressing need. Water sources exist, but the channels have become ruined with the passage of time. A benefactor could improve the situation with a bit of effort and cheer the martyrs of Kerbala and recall the spirits of the twelve imams. As it is, everyone in the town — rich and poor, great and small — has to walk for half an hour out to the vineyards east of town in order to get a sip of water. Apart from this, there is plenty of everything. They have a great abundance and variety of fruits in their gardens and vineyards.

Important foods and drinks. In the bay one finds carp, bonito, chub mackerel, mullet and bass, as well as fish roe, better than we get in Turkey. There are great quantities of the wine called *reyhania*, and of lemons, oranges, olives and grapes. In the villages of Dukat, they

[1] "[He] is known to have propagated the 'Path of Seclusion' in Southern Albania in the third decade of the 16th century" (Kiel 1990, 273).

rāvend-i rūmī ḥāṣıl olup ḥükemālar cem‘ édüp Firengistāna götürürler.

Ve Avlonya zifti gibi bir lezīz [ü] pāk (13) zift bir diyārda yoqdur, ḫuṣūṣan bir yeñi bardaq içre zifti qaynadup bardaq içine qoyup çalqanup artanın yine (14) ṭaşra döküp ol bardaqdan ṣu içeniñ vücūdında aṣlā ṣafrā ve sevdā ve belġam ve ṣovulcandan[1] bir emrāż-ı muḫtelife (15) qalmayup pāk-vücūd olur.

Ve Yuqaru Qanye qal‘esi altındaki qayalardan degirman ṭaşları ma‘deni var, göz göz (16) sünger gibi bir ṭaşdır kim anıñ degirman ṭaşları Dib Firengistāna gider kim Aq Deñiz içre Degirmenlik cezīresi ṭaşından laṭīf (17) seng-i ḫārā degirman ṭaşları olur.

Ve bāġlar yolı üzre alçı ṭaşı ma‘deni ve demir ma‘deni ve niçe gūne me‘ādinler daḫi çoqdur. (18) El-ḥāṣıl kān-ı me‘ādināt bu vilāyet-i Avlon[y]adır.

Ve leb-i deryād[a] olqadar bī-ḥisāb balıq dalyanları vardır kim miṡli meger Anaṭolquz (19) deryāsında ola.

Ḫulāṣa-yı kelām bu Avlonya sancaġı maḥṣūl cihetinden bir gizlice Mıṣır manṣıbıdır ve bunda ḥāṣıl (20) olan misk [ü] ‘amber-i ḫām rāyiḥalı ‘asel-i muṣaffā beyāż u berrāqı Atinede ve cezīre-yi Giritde olmazdır, bir filcān balı yigirmi (21) fincān ṣu götürüp yine lezīz şerbeti ve lezīz pālūde-yi teri olur.

Der sitāyiş-i liman-ı ‘aẓīm-i Avlonya. Avlonya qal‘esi (22) ile Yeñgeç qal‘esi mābeyni cümle liman-ı ‘aẓīmdir kim biñ pāre gemi alır, ḥattā Sulṭān Süleymān Ḫān eyyām-ı ḫilāfetinde bu Avlonya (23) qal‘esini binā etmesi bu limanda yatan gemileri muḥāfaża etmek içün binā édüp ba‘dehu donanma-yı hümāyūnı bunda qoyup (24) andan Venedigi Körfüs cezīresi qal‘esine ṣarıldı, ammā iri barça qalyonlar Avlonya altına gelemeyüp nīm mīl (25) alarqada lenger-endāḫt olup yaṭırlar.

Ve bu şehr-i Avlonya ile deryā mābeyninde *qarye-yi İzvoric*, yüz elli ‘aded kefere (26) ḫāneli köydür. Bir mu‘aẓẓam u ma‘mūr kenīsesi vardır. Cümle fecereleri balıqçılar ve ṭuzcılardır. Bunda olan (27) ṭuz ma‘deni başqa emānetdir. Cümle kefereleri tekālīf-i ‘örfiyyeden berī olup ṭuz çıqarma ḫidmetine me’mūrlardır. (28) Ammā ṭuzi ġāyet lezīz ü beyāż ṭuzı olup niçe yüz gemi yüki ṭuz Firengistāna götürürler.

[1] The word is crossed out and below it is written: *ṣoġcan.*

grow red-colored madder roots and Anatolian rhubarb, which physicians collect and export to Europe.

There is no pitch as pure and delicious as that of Vlora. If you pour boiling pitch into a new cup, then rinse it out thoroughly and drink water from the cup, it will cure ailments such as yellow and black bile, phlegm, worms, etc., and will cleanse your body.

Good millstones, with pores like sponges, are to be quarried from the cliffs below the upper fortress of Kanina. These millstones are exported to Western Europe. They are better than those produced on the Aegean island of Milos.

Along the road to the vineyards there is a gypsum mine, an iron mine, and various other mines. Indeed, the Vlora region is a mine of mines.

Along the seashore there are countless fishing weirs, of the sort only to be found elsewhere off Anadolguz.[1]

In short, the *sancak* of Vlora is a hidden Egypt — potentially a source of great wealth to its governor. The pure white honey produced here, with its aroma of musk and ambergris, is better than that made in Athens and on the island of Crete. One cup of honey mixed with twenty cups of water makes a delicious sherbet or pudding.

The great harbor of Vlora. It lies between the fortress of Vlora and the fortress of Jengjeç, and can hold 1000 ships. It is said that Sultan Suleyman built the fortress of Vlora in order to protect the ships anchored in this harbor. Later he anchored the imperial fleet here, and it was from here that he attacked the Venetian island of Corfu. Big bargia galleons cannot enter the harbor, but rather lay anchor half a mile out in the water.

Between the town of Vlora and the open sea is *the village of Zvërnec*, containing 150 infidel houses and a large and thriving church. All these dissolute Christians make their living by fishing and extracting salt. The saltworks here is an independent concession (*emanet*): the infidels are all exempt from the customary taxes and are charged instead with the task of extracting salt. This salt, which is very white and tasty, is loaded onto hundreds of ships and exported to Europe.

---

[1] Near Mesolongion, at the mouth of the Gulf of Corinth; see Evliya's description at VIII 341a14 (624).

Ve bu köyüñ cānib-i ġarbīsinde (29) leb-i deryādan biñ adım ba'īd bir burunda *qal'e-yi Yeñgeç*, bir vīrān sūrdur ammā ġāyet büyük limanı var, liman aġzındaki qulleleri (30) ve qal'esini cümle Gedik Aḥmed Paşa fetḥ édüp cābecā münhedim édüp Süleymān 'aṣrında ṭaşıyle Avlonya qal'esi binā olunmuşdur. (31) Bu Yeñgeç qal'esi limanınıñ cümle cānib-i erba'ası balıq dalyanlarıdır.

Ve bu limanıñ ġarb tarâfında on sekiz mīl alarqada (32) *cezīre-yi Ṣazandır*, her sene cümle Venedik kāfiri donanması bu cezīrede qışlayup yaġlayup ne cānibe isterse bu cezīreden (33) teveccüh éder. Ve Avlonya qal'esiniñ lodos ṭarâfında Qara Burun démek ile ma'rūf bir menzilgāh yelken yeri oldur (34) ve lodos ile qıble cānibinde 'āṣī Duqat Arnavudistānı cümle yüz pāre 'āṣī qara başlı ve qara şapqalı qara **[362b]** keferelerdir, ammā kefere deseñ adamı qatl éderler, lākin yine her bār Girid kāfirine bunlar imdāda giderler. Bunlar ġāyet şecī' [ü] (2) bahadır Arnavud adamlarıdır. Ve bu Avlonyanıñ daḫi cemī'i ḫalqı bahadır ve ġāzī dilāver server hünerver yigitlerdir (3) kim on pāre fırqatalarıyle cemī'i Firengistān kāfirlerin qorutmuşlardır, qal'elerin ol fırqatalar ile qorutmuşlar , ḥattā şimdiki (4) ḥālde qal'e neferātlarınıñ nıṣfı Manya muḥāfażasına fırqatalarıyle revāne oldılar.

Ve bu Avlonyanıñ havāsı ġāyet laṭīfdir, (5) ammā ṣuyı nażīf degildir, zīrā quyu ṣuyı içerler. Ammā maḥbūbı ve maḥbūbeleri ḫüdā ḥaqqıyçün ġāyet laṭīflerdir, lākin tāze yigitleri (6) ġāyet 'aşqıyā olurlar. Ve esbābları cümle cezāyirli gibi qıṣa ve da[ra]cıq es̱vāb geyüp baldırı çıplaq başı fesli ve ayaqlar[ı] (7) siyāh fillar pabuçlı, arqaları beyāż iḥrāmlı ġāzī mücāhidün-fī-sebīli'llāhlardır. Eks̱eriyyā başları dāġlı ve sīne-yi 'üryānları bāġlı (8) olup sīne-yi pür-kīneleri çāk çāk şerḥa şerḥa olup bī-pīrêhen pā-bürehne ve ser-bürehne 'abdāl-ı qalenderī-ṣıfat ġāzīleri var kim dāyimā (9) lisānlarında vird-i zebānları oṭursa [ve] ṭursa ve qalqsa "Yā Muḥammed! Yā 'Alī!" deyü ḥarêkāt [u] sekenāt éder bir alay muḥibb-i ḫānedān cānlar(10)dır kim cümle fārsī-ḫānlardır. Ve reng-i rūyları cümle ḥamret üzre olup ten-dürüst ü ten-perver bir alay serverlerdir. Ḫüdā cümlesinden (11) rāżī ola, eyi cānlardır.

Andan cümle eḥibbā ve dostānlar ile vedā'laşup ve yarar vesīle yigitler alup andan ġarb ṭarâfına 2 sā'at gidüp (12) *qarye-yi Çirqona*,

West of this village, on a cape 1000 paces from the seaside, is *the fortress of Jengjeç*. It is now an abandoned ruin with a large harbor. Gedik Ahmed Pasha partially destroyed the fortress and the towers at the mouth of the harbor when he conquered it. The stones left over were used to construct the fortress of Vlora during the reign of Sultan Suleyman. In the four corners of the harbor of Jengjeç are fishing weirs.

West of the harbor of Jengjeç, 18 miles offshore, is *the island of Sazan*. Each year, the fleet of the Venetian infidels spends the winter at this island greasing their ships. Then whatever direction it heads out for, it sails from here. South of the fortress of Vlora there is a place for setting sail called Kara Burun (Black Cape). To the southeast is the region of Dukat with 100 rebellious Albanian villages. The inhabitants are black infidels with black head and black hats, but if you call them infidels, they will kill you. Despite this, every year they assist the infidels of Crete. They are among the most valiant warriors of the Albanians. However, the people of Vlora are no less brave and valiant warriors and, with their 10 frigates, they can defend the coastal fortresses against all the infidels of Europe. At the moment, to be sure, half of the garrisons of these fortresses departed on these very frigates in order to defend Mania.

Vlora has a mild climate but does not have good water, since the people drink well water. Nevertheless, by the grace of God, the lovely boys and girls are very attractive. The young men, however, are all brigands. They wear short skin-tight clothes, as is the fashion throughout the Mediterranean Archipelago, with bare calves, fezzes on their heads, black Circassian-style shoes on their feet, and white Bedouin-style cloaks on their backs. They are ghazis always ready for jihad. Most of these ghazis look like Kalenderi dervishes: shirtless, barefoot and bareheaded, with brand marks on their heads and gashes on their bare chests, and their hearts rent with anguish. Whenever they sit down or stand up, or whatever they do, they exclaim, "Oh Muhammad, oh Ali!" They are devoted to the Prophet's family, and can all read Persian. They have ruddy complexions and are of a lively and robust nature. May God be pleased with them, for they are good souls.

Bidding farewell to all our friends and companions, and taking with us a number of guards as escorts, we journeyed westwards for 2 hours to *Cerkovina*, a large and well-developed village and an

ḫünkār ḫāṣṣı olup ʿaẓīm maʿmūr qaryedir. Anı ʿubūr édüp Nehr-i Ergiri Venedik Körfezi deryāsına maḫlūṭ (13) olduġı maḥalde atlarımızla cümle bir keştiye süvār olup Nehr-i Ergiriyi qarşu ṭarafa geçüp Müzākiyye ṣaḥrāsı fežāsına dāḫil (14) olup ol ṣaḥrā içre maʿmūr u ābādān qurālarda zevq [u] ṣafālar édüp 5 sāʿat daḫi cānib-i ġarbda qurālarda gidüp

(15) *Der qayd-ı ḥudūd-ı vilāyet-i Elbaṣan, yaʿnī eşkāl-i qalʿe-yi Başt-ovaṣan.* (16) Lisān-ı Arnavudca ----- demekdir. Bānīsi Bunduqani Venedigi pirinç pirim qıralı bināsıdır. Baʿdehu sene ----- tārīḫinde bi'z-zāt (17) Ebū'l-fetiḥ Sulṭān Meḥemmed Ḫān Arnavud İskenderiyyesi ġazāsına giderken bu qalʿeyi bi-dest-i Ġāzī Maḥmūd Paşa ve Ġāzī Semendireli (18) Bali Beg fetḥ etmişlerdir. Ḥālā Elbaṣan sancaġı ḫākinde leb-i deryāda Venedik Körfezinden şarq cānibine girmiş bir körfez daḫi (19) vardır, ol küçük körfeziñ aġzında Elbaṣan şehri içinden cerêyān éder Nehr-i Vāʿiẓ ve Nehr-i Uşqumbi bu Başt-ova (20) qalʿesi dibinde deryā-miṡāl olup deryāya deryā-miṡāl maḫlūṭ olduġı maḥalde qalʿeniñ bir dīvārın mezkūr nehr-i ʿaẓīm (21) münhedim édüp Venedik Körfezi baḥrına munṣab olduġı maḥalliñ bir qumsal yerinde şekl-i murabbaʿ bir küçük qalʿecikdir. Dār-ma-(22)dār cirmi yediyüz adımdır. Dizdārı ve yetmiş ʿaded neferātları vardır. Diraç qalʿesi emīni ḥükminde olup cümle dalyanları (23) ve sāyir maḥṣūlātları cümle mīrīdir, zīrā iskele-yi ʿaẓīmdir kim qarşu İşpanya ve Qlora ve Pulya ve Körfüs [ve] Venedik şehir(24)leriniñ bender-ābād iskelesidir. Derūn-ı qalʿede bir kiremitli cāmiʿi ve qırq elli qadar neferāt evcügezleri vardır. Bir qaç kerre Malṭa küffārı (25) fırqataları bu qalʿe yıqıqlarından girüp iḥrāq édüp gitmişlerdir. Çārsū-yı bāzārı ve ḫān u ḥammāmı yoqdur, ammā cābecā bāġları vardır. (26) Ve ḫalqı ġāyet ġarīb ü ġarīb-dost Arnavudlardır. Balıq ṣayd édüp kifāflanırlar ve Fireng ile beyʿ [ü] şirā éderler, zīrā Elbaṣanıñ (27) bir iskelesi daḫi budur, ammā ṣıġ ve qumsal deryā olmaq ile iri qalyonlar limanına gelemez, ammā ufaq gemilere laṭīf yataq (28) yeri limandır.

Andan şimāle ----- sāʿatde yine Müzākiyye ṣaḥrāsı ābādānı içre qalʿe-miṡāl qulleli çiftliklerde zevq u ṣafālar éderek

(29) *Evṣāf-ı dār-ı emānet-i bāc, yaʿnī köhne-binā qalʿe-yi ʿaẓīm-i Dirac.* (30) Zemān-ı qadīmde sirāc-ı bedr-i münīr gibi şaʿşaʿa verir bir qalʿe-yi münevver imiş kim bi-qavl-i müverriḫān-ı Latin bu qalʿe Rūm-ı Yūnāniyān bināsı (31) olup baʿdehu İşpanya destine girüp baʿdehu bir ḥīle ile Bunduqani Venedigi eline girüp andan sene -----

imperial *has*. Just beyond, at the point where the Gjirokastër river flows into the Gulf of Venice (Adriatic Sea), we boarded boats and, taking all our horses with us, crossed over to the other side and entered the open territory of the plain of Myzeqe. We had a pleasant time in the fine and prosperous villages there, continuing our journey westwards for 5 more hours.

The fortress of Bashtova, at the border of the vilayet of Elbasan. Bashtova is Albanian and means ----- This fortress was founded by the doges of Venice. Later, in the year ----- it was conquered by Ghazi Mahmud Pasha and Ghazi Bali Beg of Semendria when Sultan Mehmed the Conqueror was on his way to Shkodër. Bashtova now belongs to the *sancak* of Elbasan. It is situated on another small bay on the east coast of the Gulf of Venice, into which flows the great river Shkumbin which comes from Elbasan after joining the Vajza. The river has destroyed one of the walls of the fortress. It is a small square fortress on a sandy spot where the river flows into the sea. The circumference of the fortress is 700 paces. It is guarded by a warden and 70 garrison troops. It is under the authority of the *emin* of Durrës, and all the fishing weirs and other sources of income belong to the state, because it is a great *scala* or emporium used by ships coming across from Spain, Calabria, Puglia, Corfu and Venice. Inside the fortress there is a mosque with a tiled roof and 40 to 50 little houses for the garrison. The Maltese infidels have penetrated the ruined wall and set fire to the fortress on several occasions. There is no bazaar, *han* or bathhouse. But there are vineyards scattered around the area. The local Albanian inhabitants, although very poor, are friendly and hospitable. They fish for a living and trade with the Europeans, because this also serves as a minor emporium of Elbasan. Big galleons cannot enter the harbor because it is too shallow and sandy, but it is a fine and suitable place for smaller ships to lay anchor.

From here we continued northwards for ----- hours, passing agreeably through the towered farm-estates of the plain of Myzeqe, until we arrived at *the large and ruined fortress of Durac (Durrës), emanet of the toll (bac)*. In ancient times it shone brightly, like the lamp (*sirac*) of the full moon. According to the Latin historians, it was the Greeks who built the fortress. Later it fell into the hands of the Spanish, from whom it was taken over by the Venetians by means

tā[r]īḫinde Ebū'l-fetiḥ Meḥemmed Ḫān (32) Ġāzī İskenderiyye[1] ve Ülgün ve Bar ve Leş qal'elerin fetḥ etdikde bi-dest-i Maḥmūd Paşa bu Dirac[2] qal'esin daḫi zor-bāzū ile (33) Bunduqani Venedik elinden fetḥ édüp ba'dehu küffār-i Fireng-i bed-reng-i pür-ceng yine bu qal'eye istīlā édüp ba'dehu cülūs-ı Bāyezīd Ḫānda (34) sene ----- tārīḫinde yine bu qal'e fetḥ olup ḥālā Süleymān Ḫān taḥrīri üzre Élbaṣan ḫākinde voyvadalıqdır. Ve yüz elli aqçe pāyesiyle şerīf **[363a]** qażādır. Ve nāḥiyesi ----- 'aded qurā olup ḥālā ḥükūmeti ḫāṣṣ-ı hümāyūndur kim maqṭū'-ı qalem ve mefrūzü'l-qadem oṭuz yük aqçe iltizām (2) ile başqa emīni var, ikiyüz adamıyle ḥükūmet éder, zīrā Elbaṣanıñ ve ġayri vilāyetleriñ 'aẓīm iskelesidir, zīrā Venedik (3) Körfezi içidir ve Elbaṣanıñ şāhrāh-ı emn-i emān yolıdır kim dāyimā 'arabalar işlediginden cümle bāzirgānlarıñ gemileri bunda (4) yanaşırlar. Ve 'aẓīm ṭuz ma'deni vardır kim başqa muqāṭa'adır, cümle Rūm-éliye ve cemī'i Firengistāna 'arâbalar ve gemilerle (5) ṭuz bundan gider, zīrā ġāyet lezīz ṭuzlası vardır kim iskele başında daġlar gibi ṭuzlar yıġılıdır.

Der ṣıfat-i qal'e-yi Dirac. Bir (6) düz ṭuz ṣaḥrāsınıñ deryā kenārında Venedik Körfezinden bir küçük körfezcik daḫi yetmiş seksen mīl içeridir, anıñ kenārında (7) şekl-i murabba' bir qal'e-yi 'aẓīm imiş. Mürūr-ı eyyām ile niçe divelden divele[3] intiqāl édüp ḥıfẓ [u] ḥirāseti mümkin olmadıġından gözden (8) düşüp vīrān olmuşdur. Ammā dāyiren-mā dār cirmi beş biñ adımdır. Zemān mürūrıyle içinde adam az qalup kefere ṭuġyānından (9) anlar daḫi sākin olmaġa iqtidārları olmamaġın sene ----- tārīḫinde Bāyezīd Ḫān-ı Velī 'aṣrında bu qal'eniñ qıble cānibinde bir köşesin (10) bölüp şekl-i murabba' bir küçük qal'ecik binā etmişler kim cirmi sekiz yüz adımdır. Ve iki qapusı var, biri cānib-i şarqa nāẓır Elbaṣan (11) qapusıdır; biri cānib-i ġarba meftūḥ leb-i deryāda emīn-i iskele qapusıdır. İçinde yüz elli 'aded alçacıq binālı ve kiremitli evlerdir. Çārsū-yı bāzārı ve ḫān u ḥammāmları yoqdur, ancaq bir cāmi'i kiremitli ve kārgīr mināreli Bāyezīd-i Velī cāmi'idir. Ve bāġ u bāġçe(13)leri olqadar yoqdur, zīrā alçaq ṭuzlı şūre yerlerdir. Dizdārı ve yüz elli qadar neferātları 'ulūfelerin emīnden alırlar. (14) Ve yüz elli aqçe qażādır, gāhīce Elbaṣan qażāsına ilḥāq éderler. Sipāh ketḫüdā-yeri ve yeñiçeri serdārı

---

[1] Altered from *İskenderūn*?
[2] Text: *Dirarc.*
[3] *Divelden divele* is crossed out and replaced above the line with: *devletden devlete.*

of a ruse. Thereafter, in the year -----[1] when Mehmed the Conqueror took the fortresses of Shkodër, Ulcinj, Bar and Lezha, Mahmud Pasha took this fortress of Durrës from the Venetians by force. It was subsequently reoccupied by the cunning and warlike infidels and, in the year ----- after the accession of Sultan Bayezid II[2] was definitively conquered by the Ottomans. According to the survey register of Suleyman Khan, it is ruled by a *voyvoda* in the *sancak* of Elbasan. It has a *kadi* with a salary level of 150 *akçe* and disposing of ----- villages. It is an imperial *has*, administered by an independent *emin* and his 200 employees, and free from government intrusion and taxation. The revenue farm is fixed at 30 loads of *akçe*, because it serves as the major emporium for Elbasan and other *vilayet*s. It lies directly on the Gulf of Venice, and is connected to Elbasan by a highway which is served at all times by carriages, and so trading vessels prefer to land here. There is a large saltworks here which is an independent concession. The salt is exported to Rumelia and Europe by boat and by carriage, since it is a very tasty saltworks, and at the docks the salt is piled up like mountains.

Description of the fortress of Durrës. In a level salt plain on the coast of the Gulf of Venice a smaller bay penetrates 70 or 80 miles inland. On the shore of this bay there is a large square fortress, 5000 paces in circumference. With the passage of time and the change of many ruling families, it became defenseless, fell from favor, and now lies in ruins. Most of the inhabitants fled and those who remained could not withstand the rebellions of the infidels. In the year ----- during the reign of Sultan Bayezid II the Saint, a small square castle was built in the southern corner of the fortress, 800 paces in circumference and with 2 gates: the Elbasan gate facing east and the docks' agent (*emin-i iskele*) gate at the shoreline facing west. It has 150 squat houses with tiled roofs. There is no bazaar, *han* or bathhouse, but there is 1 congregational mosque, that of Sultan Bayezid II the Saint, with a tiled roof and a minaret of chiselled stonework. There are no vineyards or gardens to speak of because it is a low-lying, salty and brackish region. The warden and 150 garrison troops receive their salaries from the *emin*. It has a *kadi* with a salary level of 150 *akçe*, who is sometimes attached to the jurisdiction of Elbasan. The steward of the *sipahi*s and the

[1] 883/1478.
[2] 886/1481.

cümle Elbaşandadır. Ve cümle (15) on bir ʿaded ẖurde ṭobcuġazları var. ----- / (17) El-ḥāṣıl ʿacāyib emānetdir, ammā olqadar şehr-i maʿmūr degildir.

Andan qalqup cānib-i şarqa ----- sāʿat çemenzār düz yerlerde maʿmūr u ābādān (18) qurāları deryādan bir körfez girmiş anıñ kenārınca yemīn ü yesārda olan qurāları ve qulleli ābādān çiftlikeri seyr [ü] temāşā éderek

(19) *Evṣāf-ı şehr-i bāzār-ı maḥmiyye, yaʿnī qaṣaba-yı metīn Qavaya.* (20) Sene ----- tārīẖinde ----- bināsıdır. Élbaşan ḥudūdında bu daẖi Dirac emīni ḥükminde başqa voyvadalıqdır. (21) Dirac qalʿesi leb-i deryāda bir cezīre-yi bī-ḥāṣıl yerde olmaġın Dirac qāḍīsı bunda sākin olup emīni Diracda sākin olur. (22) Yüz elli aqçe qażādır. Nāḥiyesi yetmiş üç pāre qurādır. ʿAmāristān şehri bir düz vāsiʿ zemīn-i maḥṣūldārda ve bir ẖalīc-i körfez (23) nihāyetinde bāġ u bāġçeli müferriḥ ü dilgüşā bir şīrīn qaṣaba-yı raʿnādır. Cümle dördyüz ʿaded taḥtānī ve favqānī ve ḥadīqa-yı (24) ravżalı kārgīr binālı ḥavż u şāzrevānlı serāpā kiremit ile mestūr qalʿe ve şāhnişīn ve maqṣūreler ile maʿmūr u müzeyyen ü (25)[1] mükemmel sarāyları vardır. Aʿyān-ı kibārı ve kibār eşrāfı çoqdur; evvelā Ḥarīṣ-zāde ve Paşo-zāde ve ----- .

(26) Ve cümle dörd ʿaded maḥallātlardır, evvelā ----- maḥallesi ve ----- . Ve cümle dörd ʿaded miḥrābdır, (27) evvelā çārsū içinde ----- cāmiʿi ----- ve cāmiʿi ----- meşhūrlardır. Cümle 4 ʿaded (28) maḥalle mescidleridir, ammā kārgīr-binā mināreleri yoqdur, cümle alçaq mināreciklerdir. Ve cümle iki ʿaded medreselerdir, ammā sūẖte(29)vātları ṭālib-i ʿilm degillerdir. Ve cümle üç ʿaded ders-ẖāne-yi ṣıbyāndır. Ve cümle iki ʿaded āstāne-yi ṭarīq-ı dervīşāndır. (30) Ve cümle ikiyüz ʿaded maʿmūr u ābādān u müzeyyen çārsū-yı bāzār dükkānları var kim her şāhrāhda gūnāgūn tut meyvesi (31) aġaçları ile müzeyyen olup sāyedār bir sūq-ı sulṭānīdir. Cümle ehl-i ḥiref mevcūd olup cemīʿi metāʿ-ı zī-qıymet-i bī-qıymet ü (32) bī-minnet bulunur, zīrā Başt-ova qalʿesi ẖalqı ve Dirac qalʿesi ẖalqı bu şehriñ çārsū-yı bāzārına muḥtāclardır, anıñiçün (33) bāzārı maʿmūr u müzeyyendir. Ve cümle iki ʿaded ẖān-ı tücccārānı vardır, bunlar daẖi kārgīr-binā olup gūyā bezzāzistān gibi her qumāş-ı (34) kālāy-ı vālāy mevcūddur.

Ammā çārsū ḥammāmı yoqdur, lākin sarāy ḥammāmları qırqdan ziyādedir deyü naql etdiler; ammā Ḥarīṣ- **[363b]** zāde Aġa bir çārsū

---

[1] *ü* repeated at beginning of line.

commander of the janissaries also reside in Elbasan. There are altogether 10 small cannons. ----- In brief, it is a noteworthy *emanet*, but not a very flourishing town.

From here, we set off eastwards along the coastal plain of the bay, viewing well-developed, verdant villages to the left and right of the road and prosperous towered farm-estates, and in ----- hours we reached *the well-protected and mighty town of Kavaja*. It was founded in the year ----- by ----- . Kavaja, at the border of Elbasan, is ruled by an independent *voyvoda* under the jurisdiction of the *emin* of Durrës. Since the fortress of Durrës is located in an isolated and unproductive place on the coast, the *kadi* of Durrës resides here, whereas the *emin* still lives in Durrës. The *kadi* has a salary level of 150 *akçe* and has authority over 73 villages. Kavaja is a charming town on a broad, flat and fertile plain at the end of a bay projecting from the gulf, and is surrounded by gardens and vineyards. It has 400 one- and two-story stonework houses with tiled roofs and embellished with delightful gardens, ponds and fountains. There are also exquisite mansions with towers and pleasure-domes. Many noble families live here, such as the Haris-zade family and the Pasha-zade family.

Kavaja has 4 quarters, including ----- and ----- ; and 4 congregational mosques, including ----- in the bazaar, ----- and ----- . There are also 4 neighborhood mosques, all with squat minarets lacking stonework. There are 2 *medrese*s, but the students are not much interested in learning. There are 3 primary schools and 2 dervish *tekke*s, as well as 200 prosperous and well-kept shops in the bazaar. On both sides of the main streets grow mulberry trees which provide the bazaar with shade. All the trades are represented here and one finds all kinds of valuable and invaluable goods. The bazaar is wealthy and bustling, since people from Bashtova and Durrës come here to buy their goods and produce. There are 2 *han*s for travelling tradesmen, also built of carved stonework, in which all sort of fabrics are to be found, as if they were *bedestan*s.

There are no baths in the bazaar, but over 40 private baths are to be found in the better homes — or so I have been told. Haris-zade Aga

ḥammāmı inşā etmege ta'ahhüd édüp çārsū içre zemīnin daḫi görüp tedārük eyledi; ḫüdā itmāmın (2) müyesser éde. Lākin bu şehriñ a'yān-ı kibār ḥammāmlarına aqrâbā ve ta'alluqātlar kirüp çārsū ḥammāmına iḥtiyācları olmadığından çārsū ḥammāmı (3) yapmağa bir kimesne sa'y etmemişlerdir. Amma 'anqā ve bāzirgān u mün'im ḫānedān ṣāḥibi adamları vardır. Ve āb [u] havāsı ġāyet (4) laṭīf olup ḫalqı ġāyet ġarīb-dostlardır.

Andan yine şarq ṭarâfına düz yollar ile Elbaṣan Nehri kenārınca 3 sā'at gidüp (5) *Evṣāf-ı sūr-ı üstüvār-ı metīn, ya'nī qal'e-yi ma'mūr-ı Pekin.* (6) Sene ----- tārīḫinde Dirac ve Qavaya ve Başt-ova qulları 'Arnavud 'aşqıyası elinden Elbaṣan yolları emn [ü] emān olma(7)ġıyçün Sulṭān ----- 'aṣrında ol yollar beklensün deyü bu qal'eyi binā édüp ismine Beklin qal'esi derler, ba'dehu (8) ġalaṭ-ı meşhūr evlā olup Beklinden ġalaṭ Pekin qal'esi derler. Vech-i tesmiyesi böyledir. Ḥālā taḥrīr-i Süleymān Ḫān üzre Elbaṣan (9) beginiñ ḫāṣṣı voyvadalığı ḥükminde olup Elbaṣan qażāsı nāḥiyesidir.

Qal'esi bir bayır altında bir vāsi' düz yerde ve (10) Elbaṣan Nehri kenārında şekl-i murabba' bir küçük qal'edir. Cirmi kāmil dāyiren-mā dār beşyüz 'aded ḫaṭvedir, ammā ḫandâqı (11) yoqdur, ammā çār gūşesinde çār yār 'aşqına çār 'aded ṣa'b qulleleri var. Ve qıble ṭarâfına bu qal'e sehil yoquşdur. (12) Cümle temelleri qayalar üzre vāqı' olmuşdur. Ancaq bir qapusı şimāl ṭarâfında ṭaşra varoşa açılır. Dīvārınıñ qaddi (13) on iki arşın bālādır. Dizdārı ve yetmiş 'aded neferātları ve beş 'aded şāhī ṭopları var. Ḥālā iç eldir kim ġāyet (14) emn [ü] emāndır. Derūn-ı qal'ede cümle oṭuz 'aded ufaq daracıq kiremit örtüli dārları vardır. Ve qapusı üzre (15) bir küçük cāmi'i var, ammā mināresi yoqdur. Ve qal'eniñ ṣolında dīvāra muttaṣıl bir çemenzār yerde namāzgāhı var.

(16) *Der ta'rīf-i ṭaşra varoş-ı müzeyyen.* Qal'eniñ şimāli ve şarqı ve ġarbında cümle dörd yüz 'aded kiremitli mükellef ü (17) mükemmel sarāy-miṣāl bāġlı ve bāġçeli ve ḥavż u şāzrevānlı cümle taḥtānī ve fevqānī kārgīr-binā evlerdir. Cümle yedi 'aded (18) maḥallātlardır. Ve cümle dörd 'aded kiremitli cāmi'lerdir, üçi kārgīr ve muṣanna' ve serāmed minārelidir, ammā bir (19) mināresi alçaq minārelі cāmi'dir. Ammā cümleden çārsū içre Qandiye fetḥine bā'iṣ ü

has promised to construct a public bath and has secured a lot for it in the bazaar — may God fulfil his intention. No one until now has undertaken such a project; it was deemed unneccessary because the noble families allowed their relatives and retainers to use their private baths. There are many rich businessmen and generous home owners. Kavaja has a mild climate and the people are very hospitable.

From here, we set off in an eastward direction on flat roads along the Elbasan river and in 3 hours we reached *the fortress of Peqin with its solid ramparts*. It was built in the year ----- during the reign of Sultan ----- by the garrisons of Durrës, Kavaja, and Bashtova, in order to safeguard (*beklen-*) the road connections to Elbasan from Albanian bandits; so it was dubbed Beklin, which gradually became corrupted to Pekin (Peqin). In accordance with the survey register of Suleyman Khan, it is a *has* belonging to the *beg* of Elbasan and is administered by a *voyvoda* under the jurisdiction of the *kadi* of Elbasan.

The small fortress[1] is situated at the foot of a slope on a flat, open site on the banks of the Elbasan river.[2] It is square with a circumference of 500 paces. It has no moat, but has 4 sturdy towers, one in each corner, to commemorate the four companions of the Prophet. To the south there is a slight upward slope. All its foundations are built over rock cliffs. There is 1 gate facing north which opens onto the extramural settlement. The walls of the fortress are 12 ells high. Inside live the warden and 70 garrison troops, and there are 5 *shahi* cannons. Being situated in the interior of the country, it is at present a very secure fortress. Inside the walls there are a total of 30 small and narrow houses with tiled roofs. Above the gate there is a small mosque, but without a minaret. Adjoining the wall to the left of the fortress is a grassy square for public worship.

The open town of Peqin occupies the area east, north and west of the fortress and has 400 exquisite one- and two-story houses, which are more like mansions, constructed of chiselled stonework and covered with tiled roofs. They are embellished by vineyards and gardens as well as by ponds and fountains. The open town has 7 quarters and 4 mosques with tiled roofs, three of which possess tall, finely-carved stone minarets. Among the latter, in the bazaar, is the

---

[1] For this section, cf. Kiel 1990, 208.

[2] I.e., the Shkumbin.

bādī olan yeñiçeri aġası vezīr-i Āṣaf-(20)delīr 'Abdu'r-raḥmān Paşa cāmi'i gerçi kiremitlidir, ammā ġāyetü'l-ġāye cemā'at-i keṣīreye mālik cāmi'-i müferriḥdir, qıble qapusınıñ (21) 'atebe-yi 'ulyāsı tāki üzre müẕehheb celī ḫaṭ ile taḥrīr olan tārīḫi budur:

Ḥamdü lillāh[1] çün bu cāmi'-i cedīd oldı (22) temām
Her naẓar édenlere oldı maqāmı dilgüşā
Nevbahārıñ evsaṭında çün temām oldı bu cāy
Bāreke'llāh oldı (23) ra'nā tārīḫi: Hey aġniyā. Sene 1077.

Andan çārsūnuñ öte başında Ḥarīṣ-zāde cāmi'iniñ qapusı üzre lācverd ü müẕehhebli (24) tārīḫidir:

Ḥażret-i ḥaqdan olupdur işbu cāmi' bī-gümān
Qaṣaba-yı Beklin içre oldı bir 'ālī niṣān
Her gören ḫayr-i (25) du'ā ile dédi tārīḫini
Ḥamdü lillāh çün yine luṭf eyleyüp ol müste'ān. Sene 1076.

Meşhūr cāmi'ler bunlardır.

(26) Ve cümle yedi 'aded maḥallātlarda yedi 'aded mesācidler vardır. Ve cümle üç 'aded yerde medrese-yi ṭālibān-ı sūḫte(27)gān vardır. Ammā ehl-i 'ırż ḥāl ṣāḥibi mü'eddeb adamlardır, zīrā bu diyārıñ sūḫtevātlar cümle 'aşqıyālardır, anlarıñ irtikāb (28) etdiklerin qavm-ı 'avān etmezlerdir. Ve cümle beş 'aded mekteb-i ṣıbyān-ı cigergūşe püserān vardır, zīrā ġāyet zekiyyü'ṭ-ṭab' necīb ü (29) reşīd ġulāmları vardır, ekṣeriyyā manẓūm kitābları ḥıfẓen oqurlar. Ve cümle iki 'aded tekyegāh-ı fuqarā-yı āl-i 'abā-yı dervīşānı(30)dır.

Ve cümle yedi yerde āb-ı ḥayāt çeşmesārları var, cümlesi yeñiçeri aġası 'Abdu'r-raḥmān Paşa ḫayrātıdır ve ġāyet lezīz āb-ı ḥayāt-ı (31) ḫoş-güvār ṣulardır kim bu şehri mā'-ı cārīler ile saqy édüp 'amār

---

[1] Text: *Allāh.*

mosque of Abdurrahman Pasha[1], who was commander of the janissaries and a courageous vizier who initiated the Candia campaign. It has a tiled roof, but is nevertheless a spacious mosque with a huge congregation. On the arch over the *kıble* door is the following chronogram in *celi* script:[2]

> Glory be to God that when this new mosque was completed
> All who cast their eyes on it rejoiced.
> Its construction was completed in the middle of spring.
> May God bless it and may the date shine in splendor:
> Oh wealthy ones. Year 1077/1666-67

At the other end of the bazaar is the Haris-zade mosque. Above the door is a chronogram in dark blue and gold:

> This mosque was made with the help of God, no doubt.
> It has become a lofty landmark in the town of Beklin.
> All who saw it uttered a benediction and its chronogram:
> Glory be to God that He whose aid is sought has again
> been gracious. Year 1076/1665-66

These are the famous congregational mosques.

Each of the 7 quarters of the town has a prayer house. There are 3 *medreses* with honorable and well-behaved students, unlike those elsewhere in this region who are bandits and commit outrages that the town bullies would not dream of. There are 5 primary schools with very clever, literate and mature pupils. Most of them can recite from books of verse off by heart. There are also 2 dervish *tekkes*.

There are 7 fountains in this town, all of which were endowed by Abdurrahman Pasha, commander of the janissaries. Their water is very sweet and salubrious, and serves to irrigate the land around the

---

1 Abdurrahman Pasha, also known as Abdi Pasha, became commander of the janissaries in 1079/1669, served as governor of Baghdad and Egypt, and eventually became the last Ottoman governor of Buda, where he died defending the city against Christian forces in 1098/1687; see Süreyyâ 1995-97, III, 357. The mosque of Abdurrahman Pasha, which was finished four years before Evliya's arrival, was reconstructed between 1834 and 1841 after a fire, when a clock tower was also added. The mosque and minaret were torn down ca. 1967 and the remains of the building were subsequently used as a coffee shop until 1991, when the mosque was rebuilt. Cf. Kiel 1990, 203-07 (with photo).

2 Cf. Kiel 1990, 206.

etmişdir. Zīrā bu ʻAbdu'r-raḥmān Paşanıñ aṣlında bu şehir mesqaṭ-ı (32) re'sleri olduğında[n] ʻamār édüp daḫi niçe gūne ḫayrāt-ı ḥasenātlara şürū' etmişdir.

Muqaddemā sene ----- tārīḫinde Sulṭān (33) İbrāhīm Ḫān cülūsında ve Sulṭān Meḥemmed Ḫān-ı rābi' iclāsında qul ketḫüdāsı bulunan Çelebi Muṣṭafā Ketḫüda bu şehirli olup ʻAbdu'r-raḥmān (34) Paşa Çelebi Ketḫüdanıñ qız-qarındaş-zādesi olup yegenidir, Muṣṭafā Ketḫüda {ʻAbdu'r-raḥmān Paşanıñ dayısıdır kim Buruşuq oğulları nāmıyle meşhūr idi, ol} merḥūm yerde sa'īd ü şehīd yatdıqca cenāb-ı kibriyā ʻAbdu'r-raḥmān **[364a]** Paşa gibi müdebbir ü mubaṭṭın u mübehhir ġāzī vezīre cenāb-ı bārī ʻömr-i ṭavīller vére, zīrā Köpürli-zāde Fāżıl Aḥmed Paşa ile yek-dil yek-(2)cihet olup anıñ re'y [ü] tedbīriyle Qandiye üç yılda fetḥ oldı, yoḫsa qırq yılda fetḥi müyesser olacaq qal'e degil idi.

Ve cümle (3) bir ʻaded laṭīf ḥammāmı var, bu daḫi ʻAbdu'r-raḥmān Paşa ḥammāmıdır, ġāyet āb [u] havāsı ve bināsı laṭīf bir küçük rūşen-binā bir (4) ḥammām-ı rūşenādır. Ve cümle iki ʻaded ḫāncügezlerdir. Ve cümle ikiyüz ʻaded qal'e öñi meydānında dükkānlardır, ekṡeriyyā (5) muṭāfları ve pāypūşcıları çoqdur. Ve çārsu-yı ḥüsn içre gūnāgūn diraḫt-i müntehā sāyedār eşcārından mā'adā ābdār u lezīz ṭut (6) diraḫtleri ve üzüm aṣmaları ile bu çārsū-yı ḥüsn sāyedār olmuşdur kim cümle diraḫtleri tertīb üzre dikilüp sūq-ı sulṭānīyi (7) tezyīn etmişdir.

Ve bu şehriñ āb [u] havāsı ve bināsı ġāyet laṭīf olduğından maḥbūbı ve maḥbūbesi ġāyet çoqdur. Ve cümle ehālīsi ġarīb-(8)dostlardır kim āyende ve revendeye ni'metleri mebzūldur. Ve ġāyet ehl-i sünnet ve'l-cemā'at ṣalāḥ-ı ḥāl ile meşhūr adamları vardır. Ve bāġ u (9) bāġçeleri cihānı dutup zeytūnı ve nārı ve inciri ve cābecā limon ve turuncı bulınur. Ekṡeriyyā bāġlarınıñ ḫandaqlarında bīd-i ser-(10)nigūnlar ve qavaq diraḫtleri dikilidir. El-ḥāṣıl ġāyet şīrīn ü müzeyyen qaṣaba-yı ra'nā ve qal'e-yi zībādır kim cümle eşyā bu rabṭada mevcūd(11)dur.

Ba'dehu bunda cümle aḥbāb ile vedā'laşup ve ʻAbdu'r-raḥmān Paşa efendimize a'yān-ı vilāyetden mektūblar alup andan nīm sā'at şarqa gider[ken] (12) ----- deresi üzre ʻAbdu'r-raḥmān Paşanıñ bir göz ṭaş cisr-i muṣanna'ından ʻubūr édüp andan bayırlar dibinden gidüp *menzil-i qarye-yi Çi Çöl*, (13) ʻAbdu'r-raḥmān Paşa efendimiziñ eben-ʻan-ced vaṭan-ı aṣlīsi olan köyidir kim ḫānedānında qarındaşı Maḥmūd Aġa da sākin olup zevq u (14) ṣafālar etdik. Bir depe başında bir mürtefi' zemīn-i cihān-nümā havādār yerde bir

town. As this town is the birthplace of Abdurrahman Pasha, he has undertaken many other charitable works as well. He is the maternal nephew of Çelebi Mustafa Kethüda, also of this city, who was deputy of the janissaries (*kul kethüdası*) in the year -----[1] under Sultan Ibrahim and at the accession of Sultan Mehmed IV, and who was known as Buruşuk-oğulları ("Sons of the Wrinkled One"). As long as he lies in the ground as a blessed martyr, may God grant long life to such a capable and illustrious ghazi and vizier as Abdurrahman Pasha who, lending his expertise and experience, together with Köprülü-zade Fadil Ahmed Pasha, conquered Candia in three years.[2] Otherwise Candia would probably not have been conquered in forty years.

This town has 1 delightful bathhouse which was also constructed by Abdurrahman Pasha. It has very good atmosphere and water. The building is small, but charming and well-lit. There are also 2 small *han*s and 200 shops on the square in front of the fortress. There are especially many goat-hair spinners and slipper makers. Apart from the lofty shade trees, the splendid bazaar is adorned with juicy and delicious mulberry trees and vine trellises planted at regular intervals.

Because the town has a pleasant climate and fine buildings, there are many lovely boys and girls. The populace is extremely hospitable. They are good Sunnis, famous for their piety. The town is filled with vineyards and gardens. There are olive trees, pomegranates, figs, and here and there also lemons and oranges. Most of the ditches around the vineyards are planted with willows and poplars. In short, it is a delightful and charming town, where you can find everything you want.

Bidding farewell to all our friends and acquaintances, and taking letters for Abdurrahman Pasha from the notables of the *vilayet*, we set forth. After travelling eastwards for half an hour, we crossed the ----- river over the finely-wrought one-arched stone bridge built by Abdurrahman Pasha, and advanced along the foot of the hills to the first stage, *the village of Çiçul*.[3] It is the ancestral home of our lord Abdurrahman Pasha. We had a pleasant time with his brother, Mahmud Aga, who resides here in his dynastic homestead, a

[1] 1058/1648.

[2] The final conquest was in 1080/1669. See Evliya's description at VIII 288a-302b (396-457).

[3] Unidentified; possibly Çengelaj on the Shkumbin.

ma'mūr çiftlikdir. Bunda bir şāhnişīnde sākin olup kāmil (15) bir hafta ṣoḥbet-i ḫaṣlar édüp Pekin şehrinden gürūh gürūh aḥbāb gelüp Ḥüseyn-Bayqara cem'iyyetleri éderdik. Ba'dehu Maḥmūd Aġa ile vedālaşup[1] (16) andan yine cānib-i şarqa Elbaṣan Nehri kenārınca giderken gemiler üzre binā olunmuş un degirmanların seyr [ü] temāşālar etdik kim bu daḫi böyle (17) bir diyāra maḫṣūṣ degil bir ṭarz muṣanna' degirmenlerdir kim göreniñ 'aqlı gider, ve ġāyetü'l-ġāye sür'at üzre işler āşyānlardır.

Andan yine nehir (18) kenārınca ma'mūr qurālar ve bāġ u bāġçeler güzer édüp *qarye-yi Lolat*, andan *qarye-yi Pay-ova*, andan *qarye-yi Peşkim*, andan *qarye-yi Quras*, (19) andan *qarye-yi Bürdaşiş*. Bunlar cümle Elbaṣan nāḥiyesi köyleridir, kimi tīmār ve kimi ze'āmet ve kimi mu'āfdır. Ammā mezkūr Bürdaşiş[2] köyi (20) Elbaṣan Nehri üzre olan aġaç cisriñ ta'mīr [ü] termīmi içün mu'āf [u] müsellem bir ma'mūr köydür.

Bu mezkūr köyleri 4 sā'atde 'ubūr édüp (21) şehr-i Elbaṣan ḫāricinde Ḫışım Meḥemmed Paşanıñ çiftliginde sehil ilerden énüp şehirde Rūm-éli eyāletine mutaṣarrıf olan Çorum Muṣṭafā Paşa (22) qāyim-maqāmına Manya muḥāfaẓasıyçün emr-i pādişāhīler ile geldigimiziñ ḫaberin gönderüp qāyim-maqām daḫi cümle a'yān-ı kibār zu'amā (23) ve erbāb-ı tīmār ve ġayri 'asākir-i bī-şümār[3] ile ḥaqīriñ istiqbāline çıqup alay-ı 'aẓīm ile şehirde beglere maḫṣūṣ sarāy-ı 'aẓīmde nüzūl (24) édüp dīvān-ı pādişāhī olup emr-i pādişāhīler qırā'at olunup mefhūmı cümle a'yān-ı kibārıñ ma'lūmları olup "Emir pādişā(25)hıñ" deyüp ba'de'd-du'ā ve's-s̱enā şehr içre nādīler nidā édüp herkes Manya muḥāfaẓasına gitmege āmāde olmaġa mübāşeret (26) édüp ḥaqīrden on gün mühl[et] ricā etdiklerinde ḥaqīr eyitdim: "Eyle olsun, ammā on birinci gün elbette bu şehirden çıqmaq (27) gereksiz" dédikde cümle "Fermān pādişāhıñdır" deyü herkes işlerine meşġūl oldı.

Meger Çorum Muṣṭafā Paşanıñ (28) bu müsellimi olan kimesne Cemālī-zāde nāmıyle ma'rūf bir mīr-i kelām ve ālüfte ve āşüfte çelebi adam meger Elbaṣan şehrinden imiş, (29) hemān ḥaqīri paşalar sarāyından qaldırup kendünüñ sarāyına qondurup ḫānedān-ı 'aẓīmde cümle ḫuddāmlarımla ḥücreler ta'yīn (30) édüp şeb [ü] rūz üç nevbet ṭa'ām-ı firāvān mümessek ni'met-i 'uẓmālar yeyüp şehr-i Elbaṣanıñ

---

[1] Altered to *vedā'laşup*.
[2] Text: BRK'ŞŞ.
[3] Crossed out.

prosperous and pleasantly breezy farm-estate situated at the top of a hill, with a view of the surroundings. We took up quarters in a gallery, and spent an entire week here partying and conversing. Friends of the *beg* arrived from town in groups, and we had several musical soirées.

Then, bidding farewell to Mahmud Aga, we continued eastwards along the banks of the Elbasan river, where we inspected the flour mills, skilfully mounted on boats and turning at an amazing speed. I have not seen mills like this anywhere else. We proceeded along the banks of the river through *the prosperous villages of Lolaj, Pajova, Bishqem, Murras and Bradashesh*, with their gardens and vineyards. They are all in the jurisdiction of Elbasan, some *zeamet*s, some *timar*s, and some exempt from taxes. Thus, Bradashesh is a prosperous village which has been exempted from all taxes because it is responsible for the upkeep and repair of the wooden bridge across the Elbasan river. We passed through these villages in 4 hours and arrived at the farm-estate of Hısım Mehmed Pasha just outside Elbasan where we dismounted for a while.

From here, we sent word to the deputy, representing the governor of the *eyalet* of Rumelia, Çorum Mustafa Pasha, that we had arrived and had brought with us imperial decrees to assemble troops for the defense of Mania. The deputy assembled all the nobles and other dignitaries of Elbasan as well as the *timar* and *zeamet* holders, and came out to meet us with a large cortege of soldiers. We were then escorted in a grand procession to a large palace in the city reserved for the *beg*s. A meeting of council was held, during which the imperial decrees were read out. All the nobles and other dignitaries acknowledged the decrees, saying, "It is the Padishah's to command," and uttering prayers and benedictions. Heralds were then sent out into the town to inform all the people to prepare themselves for the defense of Mania. They asked me for ten days respite. I acquiesced, but insisted that they must lose no time and by all means must be ready to leave on the eleventh day. "It is the Padishah's to command," they replied, and set about their tasks.

It turned out that this deputy of Çorum Mustafa Pasha was himself a native of Elbasan named Cemali-zade, a good-humored gentleman and a ready wit. He conducted me forthwith from the pashas' palace to his own large mansion, where he put me and all of my entourage up in special guest rooms, offering us three lavish meals a day. We

ālüfte ve āşüfteleriyle ḥüsn-i ülfetler (31) éderek şehriñ kibār evliyā'u'llāhların ve niçe biñ gūne temāşā-yı 'ibret-nümālar seyr-i seyerān etmege bezl-i ihtimāma sa'y-ı tām etdik.

(32) *Evṣāf-ı şehr-i bezek-ārā-yı 'arūs-ı cihān, ya'nī belde-yi 'aẓīm-i qadīm-i qal'e-yi Élbaṣan.* (33) Ḥaqqā ki Anaṭolıda 'Arâbistānıñ bezekistān 'arūsı şehr-i 'Ayntābdır, ammā Rūm-élinde Arnavudistānıñ gelincik şehri bu belde-yi Elbaṣandır. (34) Bi-qavl-i müverriḫīn-i Latin bu şehr-i qadīmiñ ibtidā bānīsi İskender-i kübrā 'aṣrında Qavala qal'esi ṣāḥibi Fīlequs-ı Yūnān bināsıdır. **[364b]** Niçe biñ ḥükemā-yı qudemā-yı kühenā-yı qūhen-ı (?) selef bu şehri cā-yı vaṭan édinüp 'amār etmişler. Netīce-yi merām niçe yüz gūne (2) mülūkden mülūke ve melikeden melikeleriñ (?) destlerine, ba'dehu Rūm-éli diyārları ṭavāyif-i mülūk şeklinde olup bu şehr-i (3) 'aẓīm Ṣırf qıralı Dest-pot nām qıral-ı żāllıñ Banya nām bir oğlı ve Baṣanya bir veled-i pelīdi ellerinde bu şehr iştirāk söyler (?)[1] (4) üzre mutaṣarrıflar iken iki nefer qarındaş-ı pelīd-i 'anīdler ḥüsn-i zindegāne édemeyüp birbirleriyle ceng-i 'aẓīm édüp āḫir-i kār Baṣanya (5) nām şehzāde-yi āzāde ceng [ü] cidāl [ü] ḥarb [u] qıtāldan ḫalāṣ olup doğrı Ebū'l-fetiḥ Sulṭān Meḥemmed Ḫān Ġāzīye gelüp şehādet parmağın (6) qaldıru[p] ḫüdā-yı bir-i bī-zevāli birleyüp kelime-yi tevḥīd getirüp ḥużūr-ı pādişāhīde Aq Şemse'd-dīn ḥażretleriniñ ta'līm [ü] telqīniyle[2] şeref-i (7) İslām ile müşerref olup bi'z-zāt Ebū'l-fetiḥ Sulṭān Meḥemmed şehr-i Üskübden Arnavu[d] İskenderiyyesi fetḥine 'azīmet etmişken (8) 'aṭf-ı 'inānın bu Élbaṣan üzre çevirüp qırq biñ 'asker ile Qoca Maḥmūd Paşa ṭalī'a-yı 'asākir-i kerrār olup Baṣanya nām (9) müslim olan Meḥemmed Begiñ delāletiyle bir géce şehri buqadar él baṣılup Baṣanya Meḥemmed Beg qarındaşı Banya nām qıralı cāme-ḫābında (10) baṣup dib-diri dutup qatl édüp Āl-i 'Osmān i'ānetiyle İslāma geldüginden babası şehrin Maḥmūd Paşa ile ma'an fetḥ éderler (11) ve içinde olan Rūm ve Fireng kāfirlerin cümle qırarlar. Anıñiçün bu şehir él vilāyet ḫalqıyle baṣıldığından ve Baṣanya Meḥemmed Beg (12) fetḥinde bulunduğundan Elbaṣan şehri derler. Yoḫsa lisān-ı Rūmda ismi ----- , lisān-ı Firengde nāmı ----- , (13) lisān-ı Arnavudda ----- dır.

---

[1] Vocalized *şunlar* in the text, but neither form makes sense.
[2] Text: *telqīniniñ.*

enjoyed ourselves immensely with the rakes of Elbasan, and also took care to pay our respects to the saints of the city, and to tour the sights.

The great and ancient fortress of Elbasan, bride of the world. Just as the city of Antep is the bride of Anatolia, so is this city of Elbasan the bride of Albania in Rumelia. According to the Latin chroniclers, this ancient city was first founded by Philip the Greek, ruler of the fortress of Kavala, in the period of Alexander the Great. Countless philosophers and sorcerors of olden days took up residence in this city, causing it to flourish. Eventually, after being ruled by hundreds of kings and queens, the lands of Rumelia fell into anarchic conditions and this great city was taken over by the two sons of the Serbian Despot, named Banya and Basanya, and was ruled by them jointly. But the two obstreperous brothers were unable to get along and quarrels and fighting broke out between them. In the end, Basanya grew weary of the fighting and took refuge with Sultan Mehmed the Conquerer. In the Sultan's presence he raised his index finger and uttered the monotheistic creed, thus converting to Islam according to the instruction of Ak Şemseddin.[1]

When Sultan Mehmed the Conqueror was on his way from Skopje to conquer Shkodër, he turned his reins against Elbasan and sent in advance a force of 40,000 men under the command of Koca Mahmud Pasha. With Basanya, now under the Muslim name Mehmed Beg, showing them the way, and having subdued the surrounding countryside (*él bas-*), they entered the town one night. Mehmed Beg found his brother Banya asleep and slew him, thus conquering his father's city with the assistance of Mahmut Pasha and the Ottomans. All the Greek and European infidels within the town were put to the sword. Once the town, the surrounding countryside (*él*), and the population of the *vilayet* were brought under the sway (*bas-*) of Basanya, also known as Mehmed Beg, the town was renamed Elbasan ("He who subdues the province").[2] But it is called ----- in Greek, ----- in Frankish and ----- in Albanian. The Latin chronicles

---

[1] Renowned scholar and mystic who served as a kind of chaplain to the army at the siege and capture of Istanbul. He died in 863/1459 and is buried in Göynük in western Turkey; Evliya claimed to have visited his tomb forty time; see I 98b (336), II 368a-b (461-63).

[2] This Turkish etymology for the present city of Elbasan, founded in 870/1466 on the site of the ancient Scampis, is doubtful in view of the earlier French form Val d'Elbu recorded in 1180; see Aimon de Varennes, *Floriment*, lines 4875, 4877 (ed. Alfons Hilka, Gesellschaft für Romanische Literatur, Band 48, Göttingen 1932).

Tevārīḫ-i Latinde mufaṣṣal ḥikāyetleri vardır, ammā biz iḫtiṣār üzre taḥrīr etdik.

Ba'dehu (14) bu qal'e fetḥi müjdesiyle Başan[ya] Meḥemmed Beg ḥużūr-ı Meḥemmed Ḫāna ılġar ile varup müjde etdikde Ebū'l-fetiḥ Ġāzī kelām-ı mu'ciz-(15)nuṭuqlarından buyururlar kim "Āferim élin başan Meḥemmed Beg saña! Başdıġıñ babañ taḫtini iḥsān etdim. Anda benim nāmıma gümüş (16) ma'deninden sikke kesdirüp daḫi eṭrāf vilāyetlerin qabża-yı tesḫīr[e] al" buyurduqlarında Aq Şemse'd-dīn ve Emīr Buḫārī (17) ve Monlā Gürānī ḥażretleri "Ol memleketler fetḥ [ü] tesḫīre ḥayyiz-i sühūletle girmegiçün bu niyyete el-fātiḥa" dénilüp ḥaqīqatü'l-ḥāl (18) cemī'i Arnavudistān ve Hersekistān Sulṭān Meḥemmed-i Fātiḥ ve Sulṭān Bāyezīd-i Velī-yi Nāṣıḥ zemānlarında fetḥ-i fütūḥ olmuşlardır.

Ba'dehu (19) bu Élbaşan Süleymān Ḫān taḥrīri üzre Rūm-éli eyāletinde başqa sancaq begi taḫtidir. Ṭaraf-ı pādişāhīden beginiñ ḫāṣṣ-ı hümāyūnı (20) 201963 aqçedir ve ze'āmeti 18 dir ve cümle erbāb-ı tīmārı 138 'adeddir. Alay begi ve çeri başı vardır. Ḥīn-i seferde (21) qānūn üzre cümle erbāb-ı tīmārı dörd[1] biñ altıyüz pür-silāh güzīde 'asker olur. Rūm-éli vezīri qanqı sefere giderse bunuñ (22) daḫi mīr-livāsı me'mūr olduġı sefere giderler. Ve üçyüz aqçe pāyesiyle taḫta başı manṣıbıdır. Ve nāḥiyesi cümle ----- 'aded (23) ma'mūr qurālardır, be-her sene qāḍīye ber-vech-i 'adālet on kīse ḥāṣıl olur, begine oṭuz kīse ḥāṣıl olur. Ve şeyḫü'l-islāmı (24) ve naqībü'l-eşrāfı ve a'yān-ı eşrāfı ve şehir nāyibi ve muḥtesib nāyibi ve muḥtesib aġası ve bācdār aġası ve ḫarāc aġası ve sipāh (25) ketḫüdā yeri ve yeñiçeri serdār[ı] ve qal'e dizdārı ve cümle ----- 'aded qal'e neferātları ve beş 'aded qal'e aġaları ve mi'mār aġası (26) ve şehir ketḫüdāsı ve mu'āf qal'e ḫuddāmı kefereleri var. Ve re'āyālar üzre portoyoroz kefereleri vardır kim cümle yigirmi 'aded ḥākimlerdir. Ve ġāyet (27) ma'mūr u mażbūṭ ḥükūmet yeridir kim cümle re'āyā ve berāyāları muṭī' [ü] münqādlardır.

Ve sancaġı ḥudūdı içre cümle ----- 'aded (28) qażālardır. Evvelā cenūb cānibinde Başt-ova qażāsı, Müzākiyye qażāsı, cānib-i ġarbda Dirac qażāsı ve ----- (29) ----- meşhūr qażālar bunlardır. (30) Ve cümle sancaġı ḥükminde beşyüz yigirmi altı 'aded qurālardır, ammā çoġı mu'āf u müsellem ve çoġı mīrī köylerdir, begler müdāḫale éde(31)mezler.

---

[1] Altered to *dört*.

have many long tales to offer about the town, but we have recorded its history in summary fashion.

Basanya Mehmed Beg went by forced march to bring the Sultan the good news of his conquest of the town. The latter was delighted to hear the wonderful news and, congratulating him, offered Mehmed Beg rule over the town which had belonged to his father. The Sultan also authorized him to mint silver coins in his name, exploiting the silver mine, and to pacify the surrounding region. Then the blessed Ak Şemseddin, Emir Buhari, and Molla Gürani prayed for the easy conquest of this land, reciting a Fatiha for the intention expressed by the Sultan. And shortly thereafter, during the reigns of Mehmed the Conqueror and Sultan Bayezid II the Saint, the conquest of all of Albania and Hercegovina actually took place.

Subsequently, in accordance with the survey register of Suleyman Khan, Elbasan was made the residence of a *beg* for a separate *sancak* in the *vilayet* of Rumelia. For this imperial *has*, the *beg* was allotted an income of 201,963 *akçe* by the sultan. Elbasan has 18 *zeamet*s and 138 *timar*s with an *alay-beg* and a *çeribaşı*. In time of war, the timariots are required by statute to muster a force of 4600 select and armed soldiers. Whenever the vizier of Rumelia goes on campaign the *sancak-beg* of Elbasan goes with him. The chief magistrate (i.e., the *kadi*) has a salary level of 300 *akçe* and supervision over ----- villages. The annual income of the *kadi* is 10 purses and that of the *beg* is 30 purses. Other high-ranking officials include the *şeyhülislam*, the *nakibüleşraf*, the notables, the substitute-*kadi* of the town, the market inspector, the collector of tolls, the poll-tax official, the steward of the *sipahi*s, the commander of the janissaries, the warden of the fortress and a total of ----- garrison troops, 5 agas of the fortress, the chief architect, the mayor, and the infidel servants of the fortress who are exempt from taxes. The infidel rayah are governed by 20 town elders (*portoyoroz*). Elbasan has a strong and well-disciplined administration. Both the rayah and the free Muslim citizens are respectful and obedient to the authorities.

The *sancak* of Elbasan has ----- *kadi*-districts, including Bashtova and Myzeqe in the south, Durrës in the west, and ----- . In all, the *sancak* has 526 villages under its jurisdiction. Many of them are exempt from taxes and many are state property and the *beg*s cannot intervene in their affairs.

Der girdāgird-i eşkālāt-ı qılā'āt-ı Elbaṣan. Qal'esi bir düz zemīn-i maḥṣūldārda şimālī rub' sā'at ve qıble cānibi rub' sā'at ba'īd (32) bayırları ve dağları cümle bāğlı bir vāsi' öz içinde Nehr-i Uşqumbi kenārında şekl-i murabba' bir şeddādī bir köhne-binā qal'edir kim (33) qaddi on beş arşındır ve dendān-ı bedenleri ġāyet muṣanna' ve eṭrāfında elli 'aded ebrācları var ve cānib-i erba'asında ḫandaqı iki (34) adam qaddi qadar 'amīqdir, ammā elli arşın 'arīżdir, ve ḫandaqı içi ṣāfī bāġ u bāġçelerdir. Qal'eniñ dāyiren-mā-dār cirmi iki biñ dörd[1] **[365a]** yüz adımdır.

Ve cümle üç 'aded demir qapuları vardır, biri şarqa ve biri ġarba ve biri çārsū ṭarâfında qahveler (2) öñinde qıbleye nāẓır işlek bāb-ı 'aẓīmdir. Ve bu qapu iki qat qapudur, öbürleri daḫi ikişer qatdır, zīrā qal'e daḫi gird[ā]gird iki qat ḥiṣār dīvār(3)lıdır, anıñiçün qapuları ikişer qatdır. Ammā bu qıbleye nāẓır çārsū qapusınıñ kemeri üzre Ebū'l-fetiḥ Sulṭān Meḥemmediñ tā 'Os̱māncıġa[2] (4) varınca ecdādları bir beyāż memer üzre celī ḫaṭṭ ile taḥrīr olunmuşdur ve tārīḫ-i Elbaṣan yazılmışdır: sene 859.

Ve bu qapu üzre (5) üç 'aded çār-gūşe beyāż mermer-i ḫāṣṣ üzre oq ve qurşum ẓarbları urulmuş 'alāmetleri zincīr ile aṣmışlar, cümle āyende (6) ve revendegānlar temāşā éderler. Ve bu qapu üzre bir fevqānī Ḫünkār cāmi'i var, kiremitli bir kār-ı qadīm cāmi'-i kerīmdir. Bu cāmi'e qarīb (7) bir serāmed sā'at qullesi var, ġāyet muṣanna' ve dürüst sā'ati var kim aṣlā daqīqa ve derīce fevt etmez, cümle cevāmi'leriñ mü'ez̠z̠inān-ı (8) bilālīleri aña nāẓırlardır.

Ve bu qal'e içre cümle dörd yüz altmış 'aded kiremitli bāġsız ve bāġçesiz sehil vāsi'ce taḥtānī ve fevqānī (9) kār-ı qadīm köhne-binā ḫāneleri var. Dizdār ḫānesi bundadır, ammā iç el olmaq ile neferātlarınıñ kendüleri ve evleri daḫi yoqdur, (10) ancaq qal'eye mu'āf [u] müsellem kefereler ḫidmet éderler.

---

[1] Altered to *dört.*
[2] Text: *Āl-i 'Os̱māncıġa.*

The fortress of Elbasan is situated on a level fertile plain which stretches northwards and southwards for a quarter of an hour. The surrounding hills and mountains are covered in vineyards. This square and solidly built, ancient construction is situated in a broad valley on the banks of the Shkumbin river. It is 15 ells high. The outer ramparts of the fortress are skilfully constructed and have 50 towers.[1] It is surrounded on all sides by a moat the depth of which is equal to the height of two men. It is 50 ells wide and filled with gardens and vineyards. The circumference of the fortress is 2400 paces.

It has 3 iron gates, one to the east, one to the west, and one to the south in the direction of Mecca, across from the coffee houses in the bazaar. This large gate is much used and has double doorways, as do the others. The fortress itself has double walls and this is why the gates have double doorways. On the vault[2] over the southern or bazaar gate there is a block of white marble on which are inscribed, in *celi* script, the names of the forefathers of Mehmed the Conqueror back to Osmancik[3] and the date of the conquest of Elbasan: 859 (1455).[4] Also above this gate are three quadrangular blocks of white marble, suspended on chains, and showing traces of arrow and bullet shots; all who go in and out the gate remark on them.[5] Over the gate at the second story level is the Hünkâr mosque, an old stonework building with a tiled roof. Near the mosque is a high clock tower.[6] The clock was very skilfully constructed and is quite accurate, never losing a minute or a second, so the muezzins of all the mosques follow it faithfully.

Inside the fortress are 460 old, rather spacious one- and two-story houses with tiled roofs but without vineyards and gardens. The warden's house is located here, but since Elbasan is in the interior of the country, there are no garrison troops or houses for them. Instead, there is a contingent of infidels serving the fortress, who are thus exempt from taxes.

---

[1] Actually there were only 26 towers. On the figures here, see Kiel 1990, 111.

[2] For this section, cf. Kiel 1990, 116.

[3] Sultan Osman I.

[4] A mistake for 870/1465.

[5] The three blocks of marble mentioned still hang from the southern gate (1997).

[6] This clock tower may be the one that was destroyed by fire around the time of the death of Sultan Mahmud II in 1839.

Der vaṣf-ı ṭaşra varoş-ı ʻimāret-i ḫānedān-ı aʻyān-ı aġavāt. Evvelā bu Élbaṣan qalʻesiniñ (11) cānib-i erbaʻasında bayırlar dibine birer sāʻat meṣāfe yerleredek cümle maʻmūr u ābādān u müzeyyen ve bāġ u bāġçe-yi besātīn-i cinān mis̱illi (12) cihān sarāylarıyle āräste ve gūnāgūn qaṣr-ı Ḫavarnaq ve şahnişīnler ile pīrāste olmuş serapā laʻlgūn u muṣannaʻ u hemvār kiremit (13) örtüli ḫānedān-ı büyūt-ı raʻnālardır kim cümle kārgīr-binā ikişer üçer qat şāhāne şahnişīnli maʻmūr[1] büyūt-ı raʻnālardır (14) kim elbette her ḫāne-yi raʻnālarda birer ʻuyūn-ı cāriyeler cerêyān édüp ḥavz [u] şāzrevān u selsebīl-i fevvārelerden pertāb éder ḥadīqa-yı (15) ravża-yı rıżvānlı kāşāne-yi zībālardır. Ammā aṣlā cāmiʻleriñ mināre külāhlarından ġayri qurşum örtüli binālar yoqdur. (16) Hemān cümle aḥmer-levin kiremitler ile mestūr büyūt-ı maʻmūrlardır.

Evvelā aʻyān-ı kibār-ı kübbārdan müteʻaddid sarāy-ı ʻaẓīmleriñ biri Ḫışım (17) Meḥemmed Paşa vezīr sarāyı ve paşalara maḫṣūṣ sarāy ve Muṣṭafā Aġa sarāyı ve Memi Aġa sarāyı ve Cemālī-zāde sarāyı ve Qara ʻOs̱mān Aġa (18) sarāyı ve Ḫışım Meḥemmed Aġa sarāyı ve Ḫışım Ḥasan Aġa kāşānesi ve Bıçaqçı-zāde ḫānedānı ve Paşo-zāde beyti ve sipāh aġası (19) āstānesi, niçe yüz sarāy-ı zībālar vardır. Netīce-yi merām, şehir ketḫüdāsı defteriyle cümle biñ yüz elli ʻaded sarāy ve ḫānedānlar ve (20)[2] büyūt-ı raʻnālar vardır. Māʻadāları yine bāġçeli vasaṭu'l-ḥāl kimesneleriñ büyūt-ı rāḥatlarıdır. Ammā cemīʻi ḫānedānlarınıñ qapuları (21) ṣubḥ u mesā güşādedir, ḥattā niçe qapular üzre bu ʻarabī ebyāt celī ḫaṭ ile taḥrīr olunmuşdur. Beyt:

Ṣabāḥüke meqrūnün bi-ʻizzin ve (22) devletin
Ve bābüke meftūḥün li-ehli'l-ḥavā'ici

deyü niçe dervezeleriñ ʻatebe-yi ʻulyāları üzre taḥrīr olunmuşdur. Ve niçe sarāyıñ (23) dīvān-ḫānelerinde bu ebyāt taḥrīr olunmuşdur:

Şerefü'l-beyti bi-ehlihi
Ve şerefü ehlihi bi-seḫā'ihi.

Niçe biñ bunuñ ems̱āli ebyātlar (24) terqīm olunmuşdur. Bu ebyātlar mażmūnı üzre bu şehirde qapuların qapamaq ve ḫānedān ṣāḥibi başlı başına misāfirsiz ḫuddāmlarıyle ṭaʻām (25) yemek ġāyet

---

[1] Text: *maʻmūr ve*.
[2] *ve* repeated at beginning of line.

The open town outside the walls extends on all sides of the fortress to the foot of the hills at a distance of one hour's march. The prosperous and cheerful-looking mansions in the open town are adorned with beautiful vineyards, paradisiacal gardens and parks with their pavilions and galleries. They are two or three stories high, made of stonework and with tiled roofs. Each of them has a source of pure flowing water, a pool and a fountain with water spurting from jets. They are luxurious dwellings like those in the gardens of paradise. In the open town only the spires of the minarets of the congregational mosques have leaden roofs; all the other buildings have red-colored tiled roofs.

Fine houses of the great notables include the vizierial mansion of Hısım Mehmed Pasha; the mansion reserved for the pashas; the mansions of Mustafa Aga, Memi Aga, Cemali-zade, Kara Osman Aga, Hısım Mehmed Aga, Hısım Hasan Aga, Biçakçi-zade, Pasho-zade, and the steward of the *sipahis*. In short, according to the mayor's registry, Elbasan has 1150 mansions and splendid houses. The rest are confortable houses with gardens for the middle class. The doors of all these houses are open day and night; indeed, on the lintel over many of the doorways you can find this Arabic couplet written in *celi* script:

> Your morning is blessed by glory and prosperity,
> Your door is open to all the needy.

In the reception halls of some of the mansions, one finds the following couplet instead:

> The honor of the house depends on its owner,
> And the honor of its owner depends on his generosity.

As one can see from these and thousands of similar verses, home owners in this town consider it shameful to close their doors and to be without guests or to eat alone in the presence of their servants only.

'aybdır. Anıñiçün elbette her ḫānedānda āyende ve revende müsāfirīn eksik degildir. Ve her dergāhda buqadar müsāfirīn atıyle (26) ve ḫuddāmlarıyle bir ay yaṭup qalqsa istis̱qāl etmezler. Yıl başında bulunursa ḥāline münāsib elbette 'īdiyye bir kisve (27) verirler. Bu ḥüsn-i ḥālleri qırq yıldan berü bir diyārda görmedim, illā Şām Ṭarâbulūsında yeñiçeri aġası Ḫıẓır Aġada gördüm, bir de (28) bu Elbaṣanda kördüm.

Der 'aded-i esmā'-ı müzeyyenāt-ı maḥallāt. Bu varoş-ı irem cümle on sekiz 'aded maḥalle-yi müslimīndir, ve cümle (29) on 'aded maḥalle-yi Rūm ve Arnavud ve Latin keferesi maḥallātları vardır, ammā aṣlā Yahūdī ve Fireng ve Ermenī ve Ṣırf ve (30) Bulġar ve Voyniq kefereleri yoqdur, lākin ticāret ṭarīqıyle gelüp ḫānlarda meks̱ édüp yine giderler, yoḫsa tavaṭṭun édelim (31) deyü qalırlar ise o ān emān u zemān vermeyüp qatl éderler, tā qadīmden böyle göre gelmişlerdir. Evvelā ----- maḥallesi ve ----- (32) ----- . Meşhūrı bunlardır.

(33) *Der beyān-ı 'aded-i cevāmi'hā-yı selāṭīn-i Āl-i 'Os̱mān-ı ṣāḥibü'l-ḫayrāt.* Cümle qırq altı 'aded miḥrābdır. Cümleden qadīm Ebū'l-fetiḥ Sulṭān (34) Meḥemmed Ḫān Ġāzī cāmi'idir kim qal'e qapusı üzre fevqānī vāqı' olup cemā'at-i kes̱īreli cāmi'-i qadīmdir. Ve qal'e ortasında **[365b]** Ġāzī Sinān Paşa cāmi'i, taḥtānīdir ammā binā-yı 'aẓīm ü 'atīqdir, ve çār-gūşe dīvārlarınıñ ṭaşra rū-yı dīvārında bir noqṭa qonacaq (2) qadar ḫālī yer yoqdur, cümle ebyāt [u] eş'ār [u] qaṣāyid ü ḥadīs̱ ü müfrādlar taḥrīr olunmuş kim Rūm ve 'Arab ve 'Acem seyyāḥānlarınıñ birer (3) qıṭ'a ḥüsn-i ḫaṭları var kim yüz

For this reason, there are no homes without guests and wayfarers. They do not grow weary of them even when the latter arrive with servants and horses and stay for an entire month. Should guests happen to be here at the end of the year, they are given a holiday garment suitable to their circumstance. In the forty years I have been travelling, I have never encountered this kind of good will except in the person of Hızır Aga, the commander of the janissaries in Syrian Tripoli,[1] and here in Elbasan.

Quarters. The open town, which is like the fabled garden of Irem, has 18 Muslim quarters and 10 infidel Greek and Albanian and Latin quarters. There are no quarters for Jews and Franks and Armenians, or for Serbs and Bulgarians and Voyniks. The latter groups only come here to do business, lodging in the *han*s and then departing. If they come with the idea of taking up residence, they are slain immediately — this is an ancient custom. The famous quarters are ----- and ----- .

Mosques of the Ottoman sultans and benefactors. Elbasan has 46 prayer-niches,[2] of which the oldest is the mosque of Mehmed the Conqueror[3] built over the gate of the fortress, a two-story building with a large congregation.

In the middle of the fortress is the large old mosque of Sinan Pasha[4], a one-story construction. The outer sides of its four walls are completely covered[5] with couplets, poems, qasides, hadiths, and single verses inscribed by travellers from Turkey, Arabia and Persia,

---

[1] This Hızır Aga is mentioned twice in the course of Evliya's description of Tripoli, with nothing about his hospitality; see IX 187b10, 188b7 (412, 414).

[2] According to Elbasan scholar Lef Nosi (1873-1945), there were still 31 mosques in Elbasan in 1931. Of the five mosques which survived the Cultural Revolution of 1967, four were destroyed in the following decade. Only the Naziresha Mosque, outside the center of town, survived the dictatorship in a recognizable state.

[3] According to Kiel (1990, 116), "This mosque was destroyed in the last century, perhaps with the suppression of the Albanian revolts against the Tanzimat reforms and together with the dismantling of the fortress." A photograph from 1920, however, shows a construction still above the main gate.

[4] Known as the Xhamia e Mbretit (Mosque of the King), this largest and oldest mosque in Elbasan was constructed ca 1490-1500. In 1970-71, it was mutilated beyond recognition and used initially as a painter's studio, then by the Democratic Front as a "Center for the Political Instruction of the People" and finally as a puppet theatre. It has been reconstructed recently, though without the minaret it once had. Cf. Kiel 1990, 114-17 (and photo).

[5] The outer walls of the mosque were still covered in red-colored Arabic script in the 1960s.

mücelled kitāb olur, zīrā niçe biñ şuʿarānıñ bu cāmiʿ-i qadīm menzilgāhıdır, anıñiçün herkes (4) teberrüken birer gūne qalem ile ʿarż-ı maʿrifet édüp niçe kerre yüz biñ āsār terqīm eylemişler, zīrā ġāyet muṣayqal u mücellā vü müşaʿşaʿ dīvār[lardır]. (5) Ḥattā ḥaqīriñ her vardığım qurā ve qaṣabātlarda ve bir cemʿiyyet-i kübr[ā] olacaq yerde birer āsār taḥrīr etmek deʾb-i qadīmim olmaġile (6) bunda daḫi ḥaqīr güstāḫāne bir ebyāt taḥrīr édüp "Ketebehu seyyāḥ-ı ʿālem Evliyā sene 1081" deyü tenmīq etdik. Her şehre ʿalā(7)ʾl-ittifāq cemīʿi müverriḫīn esmā tevzīʿātına bir isim qomuşlar; bu şehr-i Elbaṣana Dār-ı Şuʿarā deyü tesmiye etmişler.

Ve bu (8) qalʿe içre bu Sinān Paşa cāmiʿi cemāʿat[i] çoq maʿbedgāh-ı rūḥānīdir, ammā içinde leb-ber-leb Venediġiñ Qoṭur qalʿesine gitmek içün (9) ʿasker-i İslām bekṣumātı me[m]lūdur, ḥattā Manya muḥāfażasına giden ʿasker-i İslāma bundan biñ qanṭār bekṣumāt Diraca ʿarabalar ile gidüp (10) andan gemilerle Manyaya gitdiler.

Andan Uzun Çārsū içinde Ḥasan Bali-zāde cāmiʿi, qapusı üzre tārīḫi budur. Tārīḫ:

> Yapup (11) Ḥasan Bali-zāde ḫüdāyçün
> Bu beytüʾllāh[ı] çün mānend-i cennet
> Bi-ḥamdiʾllāh temām etdi bu ḫayrı
> Qabūl éde bi-ḥaqq-ı zāt-ı vaḥdet
> (12) Ne devletdir bu kim tā rūz-ı maḥşer
> Deyeler rūz [u] şeb rūḥına raḥmet
> Manaṣtīrī Leʾālī dédi tārīḫ
> Zihī oldı (13) ʿibādetgāh-ı ümmet. Sene 1017.

Andan taḫıl bāzārında Bıçaqçı-zāde ----- Aġa cāmiʿi, ʿaceb mevzūn mināreli bir cāmiʿ-i cedīd-i (14) zībādır.

each of whom wrote in his own hand, in fine calligraphy. If one were to collect all the inscriptions, they would make up 100 volumes. This mosque has been visited by thousands of poets who have vied in displaying their skill, and so the exceptionally smooth, polished and shiny walls are covered in countless works of art. Indeed, in accordance with my old practice of leaving my mark in whatever village or town or place of worship that I visit, I too had the impertinence to write a couplet, and signed it: *Ketebehu seyyāḥ-ı 'ālem Evliyā sene 1081* (Written by the world traveller Evliya, year 1081/1670). The chroniclers have given special names to each city, and this Elbasan is known as Abode of Poets.

This Sinan Pasha mosque inside the fortress with its large congregation has a spiritual atmosphere, but it is now full of biscuits stocked for the Ottoman army preparing to attack the fortress of Kotor in Venetian territory. In fact, 1000 quintals of these biscuits were loaded onto carts and sent to Durrës and from there to Mania by ship for the Ottoman troops there.

The mosque of Hasan Bali-zade[1] in the Long Market: over the gate is this chronogram:

> Hasan Bali-zade constructed for the sake of God
> This house of God resembling paradise.
> Praise to God that he completed this charitable work:
> May God accept it for the sake of the essence of Unity.
> How fortunate it is that, until the day of judgment,
> Day and night people will pray: "Mercy on his spirit."
> Leali of Manastir[2] uttered the chronogram:
> Splendid became the place of prayer of the community.
> Year 1017/1608

At the grain market is the beautiful new mosque of ----- of Bıçakçı-zade[3] Aga with a marvellously well-proportioned minaret.

---

[1] Known as the Xhamija e Balliës (Ballia Bosque), dating from 1017/1608. This mosque was finely restored in 1965, but demolished in 1970-71. According to Kiel (1990, 120), only the *mihrab* and part of the *mihrab* wall were still standing in 1978 as a ruin in the back yard of a department store. Cf. Kiel 1990, 120-23 (and photo).

[2] Possibly Le'ali Hasan Efendi, poet and scholar from Manastir, of whom little is known.

[3] Known as the Xhamia e Agait (Aga's Mosque) and dating from approximately 1660-70, it was situated at the the western end of the Long Market, i.e. at the grain

Andan Tavşan cāmi'i, maḥbūb [u] muṣanna' cāmi'-i pür-envārdır. Andan maḥkeme qurbında Sinān Beg cāmi'i. Cemā'at-i kes̱īreye [mālik]. (15) Meşhūr [u] ma'mūr bildigimiz cevāmi'ler bunlardır.

Der vaṣf-ı ma'bedgāh-ı mesācid-i maḥallāt. Cümle yigirmi 'aded maḥalle zāviyeleri ve buq'a(16)ları ve mezgitleri eyneleridir. Evvelā ----- mescidi ----- . Bunlar meşhūrdur.

(17) *Der 'ilm-i dārü't-tefsīr-i 'ālimān-ı 'āmilān.* Cümle ----- 'aded medrese-yi ṭālibāndır. Cümleden ----- .

(18) *Der 'aded-i dārü'l-ḥadīs̱-i muḥaddis̱ān-ı peyġamberāt.* Cümle ----- .

(19) *Der defter-i dārü'l-qurrā'-ı ḥuffāẓān-ı mücevvidān.* Cümle ----- .

(20) *Der mekteb-i ṣıbyān-ı ebced-ḫvān-ı ṭıflān.* Cümle ----- .

(21) *Der tekye-yi erbāb-ı ṭarīq-ı āl-i 'abā-yı dervīşān.* Cümle on bir 'aded ḫāneqah-ı faqīrāndır. Cümleden qal'e içinde Sinān Paşanıñ (22) tekye-yi Ḫalvêtīsi bir şehirde yoqdur, fuqarāsı ve evqāfı çoqdur. Ve anda Ḫünkār cāmi'i tekyesi, faqr [u] fāqa ṣāḥibi (23) çille-yi merdān ṣāḥibi 'ārifün-bi'llāh terk [ü] tecrīd cānları var. Andan Ḥācī Ḥasan tekyesi, bir ḫāneqāh-ı fuqarādır kim niçe (24) riyāżat-keş ḫalqdan münzevī gūşe-nişīn merdleri var, kendü der[d]leriyle ciger-ḫūn ile tevḥīd-i erreye meşġūllerdir. Andan (25) ----- . Ma'rūf [u] benām tekyeler bunlardır.

(26) *Der me'kel-i dārü'ż-żiyāfāt-ı 'imārāt.* Cümle üç 'aded me'kel-ḫāne-yi müsāfirīndir kim ṣubḥ u şām bay u gedāya ve pīr [ü] cüvān ve (27) gebrā vü tersā vü muġāna ni'metleri mebzūldür. Evvelā Ḫünkār 'imāreti ve Sinān Paşa 'imāreti ve tekye 'imāreti var. Bunlar meşhūr 'imāretlerdir.

(28) *Der qāyime-yi ḫān-ı ḫvācegān-ı tüccārāt.* Cümle on bir 'aded ḫānlardır. Evvelā ----- ḫānı ----- /

(30) *Der şerḥ-ı çārsū-yı bezzāzistān.* Cümle ṭoquz yüz 'aded sūq-ı sulṭānī dekākīnleridir. Gerçi bir şāhrāh üzre degildir, ammā (31) her ṭarīq-ı 'āmda olan dükkānları tertīb üzre binā olunmuş ma'mūr u müzeyyen ve pāk ü pākīze ve üzerleri örtüli sāyedār çārsū-yı (32) bāzār-ı ḥüsndür. Cümleden ṣarrāc-ḫānesi ve ġazzāz-ḫānesi ve zergerān çārsūsı şīrīndir. Ve yedi 'aded qahve-ḫāneleri var kim gūyā her (33) biri birer gūne münaqqaş nigār-ḫāne-yi Çīndir kim cemī'i erbāb-ı me'ārif ehl-i dil şu'arālar anda mevcūdlardır. Eger bu qahāvīleriñ her birin mā-vaqa'ları (34) üzre taḥrīr etsek taṭvīl-i kelām olur. Ammā bu şehriñ ābādānına göre kārgīr binālı bezzāzistānı

The mosque of the Hare: fair and radiant.[1]

The mosque of Sinan Beg near the courthouse: it has a large congregation. These are the best-known congregational mosques.

Neighborhood mosques. There are 20 smaller prayer houses, including ----- .

Institutes for Koran interpretation and the training of ulema. there are ----- *medreses*, including ----- .

Institutes for the study of hadiths. ----- .

Institutes for the training of Koran reciters and memorizers. ----- .

Primary schools. ----- .

Dervish tekkes. There are 11, including the Halveti *tekke* of Sinan Pasha inside the fortress, with numerous dervishes and endowments, unmatched anywhere else; the famous *tekke* of the Hünkâr mosque, with its masters of poverty and mystics engaged in withdrawal and isolation; the *tekke* of Hadji Hasan, where men of God retire into a corner and engage in quiet meditation; and ----- .

Soup kitchens. There are 3 public guest-houses which every morning and evening feed rich and poor, young and old, Christian and Zoroastrian. They are: the Hünkâr soup kitchen, the Sinan Pasha soup kitchen and the Tekke soup kitchen.

Hans of the merchants. There are 11 *hans*, including ----- ; ----- .

Bazaars. The grand bazaar of Elbasan has 900 shops, although they are not all on one main street. Rather, the shops are laid out along all the public thoroughfares. These attractive markets are well-stocked, clean, orderly and well-kept, roofed and shaded. The nicest markets are those of the saddlers, the silkmakers and the goldsmiths. And there are 7 coffee houses, like painted Chinese idol-temples, gathering places of scholars and poets. If I were to describe each one of them it would be very tedious. The city has no stonework *bedestan* adequate

---

market. Restored in 1935-36, it was demolished in 1970-72. Cf. Kiel 1990, 123-24 (and photo).

[1] Known as the Xhamia e Lepurit (Mosque of the Hare) just to the east of the main hotel, where the monument to Aqif Pashë Elbasani is presently situated.

yoqdur, ammā cemī'i dünyāda olan eşyā-yı z[ī]-qıymet **[366a]** la'l [u] yāqūt u elmās u zümürrūd ve dībā vü şīb ü zerbāf u kāmḫā-yı dārāy ve niçe biñ gūne aqmişe-yi fāḫireleri mevcūdlardır.

(2) *Der kār [u] kesb-i ehl-i işġālāt.* Cemī'i ehl-i ṣanāyi' ve erbāb-ı ḥiref mevcūddur, ammā ġazzāzları ve 'Arnavud qalqancıları ve oqcıları ve yaycıları (3) ġāyet çoqdur ve ġāyet memdūḥ ālāt [u] silāḥlar işlerler. -----

(4) *Der şināḫ-ı 'ulemā-yı ebdān-ı ḥāziqān.* Cümle qırq yedi 'aded ṭabīb-i nebbāżı vardır, ammā cümleden Firanqul-ı Laṭin 'ilm-i nebiżde yegāne-yi (5) 'aṣırdır, ve Ḥakīm Muḥyī Çelebi gūyā Mesīḥ-enfāsdır, ve. -----

(6) *Der kāmil-i ṣāḥib-naẓar-ı keḥḥāl-ı üstādān.* Cümle üç 'aded keḥḥāllardır, ammā -----

(7) *Der medḥ-i cerrāḥ-ı feṣṣādān-ı 'āmilān.* Gerçi 'ilm-i cerāḥatde çoq kimesneler vardır, ammā cümleden ----- üstād-ı müsellemdir.

(8) *Der vaṣf-ı rūz-ı bāzār-ı cem'iyyet-i ādemiyyān.* Bu şehr-i Elbaṣan içre her bāzār günleri bir germiyyet cem'iyyet-i kübrā bāzār olur kim bu şehriñ (9) cānib-i erba'asındaki qurālardan ve qaṣabāt u qılā' u şehirlerden niçe biñ 'aded ṣıġār u kibār ve 'avret ü oġlan gelüp bu şehr (10) içi adam deryāsıyle mālāmāl olup omuz omuzı sökmeyüp cemī'i maḥbūb u maḥbūbeler 'arż-ı cemāl édüp bī-dirīġ (11) ü bī pāk ü bī-pervā seyr [ü] temāşālar olunup gizli metā'ların bey' ü şirā éderler. Ammā ṭaşra köylerden olqadar bedr-i münīr ṭal'at (12) Arnavud qızları gelir kim gūyā her biri bir bānū-yı perī-peyker ve melek-manẓar duḫter-i pākīze-aḫterler gelir. Ḫulāṣa-yı kelām, her bāzār günleri (13) bu Elbaṣan şehri benī-Ādem ile pür olup cemī'i kālā-yı metā' ile şehir bezenüp cümle Rūm diyārınıñ ve cemī'i Arnavudistā(14)nıñ gelincik çārsūsı olur, ve cemī'i çārsū-yı bāzār soqaqları serāpā qaldırım döşeli olup iki ṭarâfındaki yaya (15) qaldırımlarınıñ kibārlarından birer gūne lezīz āb-ı ḥayāt ṣular cerêyān édüp cemī'i şāhrāhları ṣuları pāk éder. Ḫuṣūṣan (16) çoqacılar çārsūsında ve oqcılar ve yaycılar ve bıçaqcılar ve qılıççılar çārsūları içre yollar üzre ṣıra ṣıra dikilmiş tūt (17) aġaçları ve serāmed çınār-ı müntehālar ve bīd-i sernigūnlar ve niçe biñ gūne üzüm aġaçları tertīb üzre yollarda dikilüp (18) şehr içi diraḫt-i sāyedārlar ile müzeyyen olup cümle bāzār ḫalqı ol diraḫtleriñ ẓıll-i ḥimāyelerinde oṭurup metā'-ı nādire(19)lerin fürūḫt éderler. Ve ġayri çārsūlarda daḫi gūnāgūn diraḫtler dikilmişdir kim cümle dükkān ehālīlerine mezkūr şecerler (20) sāyebānlar olup aṣlā çārsū-yı ḥüsne güneş te'ṡīr etmez. Gūyā bu

to its prosperity, but precious goods from all over the world can be found, including garnets, rubies, diamonds, emeralds, embroidered silks, gauzes, brocades, velvets, and other fine fabrics.

Professions. All the craftsmen and tradesmen are to be encountered here. In particular, there are many silk makers, Albanian shield makers, arrow makers, and bow makers. The place is famous for the manufacture of fine weapons.

Physicians. There are 47 doctors and pulse-takers, the most outstanding of whom is the Latin doctor Frangulis; and the physician Muhyi Çelebi is like the breath of the Messiah.[1]

Oculists. There are 3 eye doctors, notably ----- .

Surgeons and phlebotomists. There are quite a number of surgeons, but especially ----- is a great doctor; ----- .

Market day. A large public market is held in Elbasan every Sunday. On this occasion, thousands of people, great and small, men and women, come in from the villages and surrounding areas, towns and fortresses. You can hardly make your way through the streets. All the lovely boys and girls gather here, too, displaying their hidden wares, ogling and haggling without stint and without scruple. On such days, fair Albanian maidens also come in from the villages, each one with the face of a nymph and the form of an angel. Every Sunday, in short, Elbasan is crowded with people and decked out with merchandise, making this market town the bride of Albania and of Rumelia. All the streets in the bazaar are paved with cobblestones, and along the gutters on either side flow sparkling streams which cleanse the roadways. The streets in the textile market in particular, and in the markets of the arrow makers, bow makers, knife makers and sword makers, are lined with mulberry trees, lofty plane trees and weeping willows and thousands of vine trellises, so that all the merchants can sell their wares while sitting in the shade. The other markets are planted with various types of trees, too, providing shade for all the shop owners. The sun cannot penetrate into this beautiful bazaar at all. Being like the fabled garden of Irem, this town can be compared to Košice in the *vilayet* of Kurs in Hungary.[2]

---

[1] In that he can bring the dead to life.

[2] Košice (Germ. Kaschau, Tk. Qaşşa) is now in eastern Slovakia. See Evliya's description at VI 13a-15a (46-52).

şehir Macaristānıñ Qurş vilāyetinde hemān Qaşşa şehri gibi bāġ-ı iremdir.

(21) *Der sitāyiş-i ḥammāmāt-ı rāḥat-ı cān.* Cümle üç ʿaded ḥammām-ı dilsitānları var. Evvelā biri qalʿe içinde şarq ṭarâfındaki qalʿe (22) qapusınıñ iç yüzinde Sinān Paşa ḥammāmı, kār-ı qadīmdir ve āb [u] havāsı ve bināsı ġāyet laṭīfdir, ṣuyı ḫandaq üzre cisr ile (23) ṭaşradan gelir. Andan ṭaşra varoşda çārsū ḥammāmı, vāsiʿ ü ḫoş-binā ve pāk ü pākīze maḥbūb ḫuddāmları ve bisāṭları var. (24) Andan -----

(25) *Der beyān-ı ʿaded-i ḥammāmāt-ı maḫṣūṣ-ı kibār-ı aʿyān.* Bi-qavl-i şehir ketḫüdāsı bu şehr içre yüz altmış ʿaded sarāy ḥammāmları vardır deyü feraḥ kesb éderler.

(26) *Der faṣl-ı enhār-ı zülāl-i āb-ı ḥayvān.* Bu şehr içre cerêyān éden nehr-i ʿaẓīm Uşqumbi tā Korça ve Lanqada daġlarından gelüp niçe biñ (27) ʿaded bāġları ve müşebbek būstānları rey édüp niçe biñ āsyāblar çevirüp bālāda taḥrīr olduġı üzre Bunduqani Körfezi (28) içre ----- qurbında maḫlūṭ olur. Ammā şehriñ eṭrāfında olan daġlardan niçe yüz ʿaded ʿuyūn-ı cāriyeler cerêyān édüp (29) şehriñ eṭrāfında olan niçe biñ ʿaded cenīn-i ġaytānları rey etdiklerinden māʿadā her ḫānedānlarda birer ve ikişer ʿaded āb-ı revānlar (30) cerêyān etdikilerinden māʿadā

Der ʿaded-i çeşmesār-ı āb-ı ḥayāt. Bu şehr içre cümle dörd[1] yüz oṭuz ʿaded çeşme-yi cārīler va[r]dır, (31) cümleden ḫandaq kenārında İslāmbolda Sulṭān Aḥmed Ḫānıñ at meydānındaki Yeñi Cāmiʿi binā éden miʿmār başınıñ bu şehr içre qırq ʿaded (32) çeşme-yi āb-ı ḥayātları vardır; cümle çeşmesārlarıñ kemerleri üzre kāşī-yi Çīnde taḥrīr olunan tārīḫ budur:

Ḥażret-i miʿmār (33) başı oldurur bir rū-yı pāk
[―――――――――――――――――――――]
Deh düşüp tārīḫini dédi Ḥüseynī-yi ḥaqīr
ʿAşqına geldi Muḥammed Muṣṭafānıñ māʾ-ı pāk. Sene ----- .

---

[1] Altered to *dört*.

Baths. Elbasan has 3 heart-relieving bathhouses. First of all is the bathhouse of Sinan Pasha[1] inside the fortress near the eastern gate in an old building. Its water and atmosphere and construction are quite pleasant. It gets its water from outside by means of an aquaduct crossing the moat. In the open town is the Bazaar bathhouse,[2] a spacious, agreeable and clean building with lovely serving-boys and furnishings. ----- .

Private baths. According to the mayor, the town has 160 baths in the mansions of the well-to-do.

Rivers. Through the town flows the great river Shkumbin, which takes its source in the mountains of Korça and Lankada[3] and which serves to irrigate thousands of vineyards and fruit and vegetable gardens. It also drives thousands of water mills in the vicinity of -----, as mentioned above, before flowing into the Gulf of Venice. From the mountains around the town flow hundreds of streams which water the thousands of gardens in the town and also provide each house with one or two sources of fresh running water. In addition — *Fountains* — there are 430 fountains in the town, 40 of which were built by the Chief Architect who constructed the New Mosque of Sultan Ahmed on the hippodrome in Istanbul.[4] The following chronogram is inscribed in faience on all of these fountains:

He is the revered Chief Architect, a pure face.
[————————————————]
The humble Hüseyni uttered its chronogram minus ten:
Pure water has come for the sake of Muhammad Mustafa.
Year ----- .[5]

---

1 This bathhouse, still preserved, was founded around 1500 and restored in 1989; cf. Kiel 1990, 127-28.

2 This bathhouse, next to the hotel, was still being used in the 1940s. It was situated at the entrance of the Long Market, surrounded by narrow shopping streets. It was rehabilitated and preserved during the dictatorship, but in the early 1990s was transformed into a bar and then briefly into a bingo parlor. Cf. Kiel 1990, 126-27.

3 The town of Langadas, east of Thessalonika in Greece, is nowhere near the source of the Shkumbin river.

4 The reference is to Mehmed Aga, d. ca. 1032/1622, who was perhaps a native of Elbasan; see Howard Crane, Introduction to *Risāle-i mi'māriyye: an early-seventeenth-century Ottoman treatise on architecture* (Leiden: Brill, 1987), 7, 12. The construction of the New Mosque, now known as Sultan Ahmed (or the Blue Mosque), began in 1018/1609-10 and was completed in 1026/1617.

5 The editor of the printed edition (Istanbul, 1928, 724) derives 1056 - 10 = 1046 (1636) from this chronogram. From the next one, with *nāb-ı pāk* substituted for *mā'-ı*

(34) Dīger tārīḫ: bir çeşmesiniñ tārīḫi "nāb-ı pāk" vāqı' olmuşdur. Ve Bıçaqçı-zāde çeşmesi ve Cemālī çeşmesi ve Vā'iẓ 'aynı vardır.

[366b] *Der qayd-ı ḫān-ı ġurêbā-yı mücerredān.* Cümle ṭoquz 'aded bekār-ḫāne odaları var kim içinde ehl-i ṣanāyi' ġarībü'd-diyār kimesneler kār édüp işlerler.

(2) *Der reng-i rū-yı pīr [ü] cüvān.* Havāsınıñ leṭāfetinden pīr-i nātüvānları zinde olup yüz yaşında iken yüzleri ḥamret üzre olup tāzeleri hemçünān eylecedir.

(3) *Der medḥ-i ṣıfat-i maḥbūb [u] maḥbūbān.* Maḥbūbı ve maḥbūbeleri eyledir kim her biri ḥüsn [ü] cemālde ve luṭf [u] i'tidālde olup ḫālleriniñ her dānesi ḫāl-i hāşemī vardır.

(4) *Der esmā'-ı eşrāf-ı kibār-ı a'yān.* Cümleden velī-ni'metimiz Cemālī-zāde ve Ḫışım-Meḥemmed-Paşa-zāde ve Bıçaqçı-zāde ve Çavuş-zāde ve dizdār aġa, bunlar meşhūr a'yāndır.

(5) *Der menāqıb-ı ṣuleḥā-yı meşāyiḫān.* -----

(6) *Der şi'r-i güzīde-yi muṣannifīn-i şā'irān.* -----

(7) *Der nāmhā-yı iḫvān-ı ḫoş-ṣoḥbet-i yārān.* -----

(8) *Der ṣāḥib-ḥāl-i ehl-i ṭarīq-i mecāzibān.* -----

(9) *Der qabā-yı eşkāl-i ricāl-i merd-i meydān.* Cümle ḫalqı çoqa ferrāce ve dolamalar geyüp ṣarıq ṣararlar. Tāzeleri qırmızı 'araqıyye ve baġır yeleki ve qopçalı çaqşır ve qubādī pabuc geyerler.

(10) *Der lisān-ı ıṣṭılāḥāt-ı merd-i süḫendān.* Cümle Arnavudca kelimāt édüp ekṣeriyyā faṣīḥ Türkī bilüp 'ulemāsı Fārsī-ḫānlardır, tüccārları Rūmca ve Firenkçe daḫi bilirler.

(11) *Der nāmhā-yı delīrān-ı fetā-yı şecī'ān.* Ekṣeriyyā isimleri Cemālī-zāde ve Qāsım-zādedir, ammā 'avānları Çelo [ve] Meto ve Paşo ve Afo ve Ḥamzo ve Qoçi nāmlılardır.

(12) *Der esmā'-ı ḫuddāmān-ı ḥalqa-begūşān.* Ekṣeriyyā köleleriniñ esmāları ----- .

(13) *Der libās-ı gūnāgūn-ı bintān-ı nisvān.* Ekṣeriyyā ḫātūnlarınıñ libāsları çoqa ferrāceler ve yaṣṣı başlı ṭāqıyyeler üzre beyāż dülbend örtüp gezerler.

(14) *Der esmā'-ı ḫavātīn-i qavm-ı zenān.* Ekṣeriyyā ḫavatīnleriniñ isimleri Selīme ve Sālime ----- .

(15) *Der benām-ı cevāriyegān-ı ehl-i 'ıṣyān.* Ekṣeriyyā qaravaş ḫalāyıqlarınıñ esmāları Cānisi ve Ḥanifi ----- .

(16) *Der binā-yı 'ibretnümā-yı 'amāristān-ı ābādān.* Evvelā Elbaṣan qal'esi ġāyet muṣanna'dır ve cāmi'leri ve zīr-i zemīnde ṣu yolları ve serāmed mināre ve ḫānları metīn binālardır.

On another of the fountains the chronogram has *nāb-ı pāk* ("pure and clear"). There are also the fountains of Bıçakçı-zade, Cemali and Vaiz.

Hans of the bachelors. Elbasan has 9 *hans* which offer rooms to unmarried transients. They are used by skilled tradesmen away from home.

Complexion of young and old. Because the climate of the town is agreeable, even people over 100 years old still have ruddy faces, not to speak of the youths.

Lovely boys and girls. They are famous here for their beauty and grace, and they have beauty-marks like that of the Hashemite.[1]

Names of the notables. The foremost families of Elbasan are firstly that of our patron Cemali-zade, Hısım Mehmed Pasha-zade, Bıçakçı-zade, Çavuş-zade, and that of the warden. These are the most famous.

Sheikhs. ----- .

Poets. ----- .

Companions and lovers. ----- .

Mystics. ----- .

Men's dress. They all wear long broadcloth robes and turbans. The young men wear red felt caps, vests, buttoned trousers and *kubadi* slippers.

Language and technical terms. All the people speak Albanian. Most also know good Turkish, and the ulema can read Persian. Greek and Frankish are used by the merchants.

Men's names. Most of the names are like Cemali-zade, Kasım-zade, etc., but the town rough have names like Çelo, Meto, Paşo, Afo, Hamzo and Koçi.

Slaveboys' names. ----- .

Women's dress. Most of the women and girls wear broadcloth robes and go about in flat headpieces which they cover with white muslin kerchiefs.

Women's names. Common names are Selime, Salime, etc.

Slavegirls' names. Among the names for female slaves are Canisi, Hanifi, etc.

Fine buildings. First, the fortress of Elbasan is very well constructed. Also sturdy constructions are the mosques, underground water channels, lofty minarets and *hans*.

---

pāk, he derives 1066 - 10 = 1056 (1646). Both of these dates appear to be too late for Mehmed Aga.

[1] I.e., the Prophet Muhammad.

(17) *Der medḥ-i havā-yı ḫūb-ı cāvidān.* Āb [u] havāsı ve bināsı memdūḥ-ı ʻālem olup ṣayf [u] şitāsı dāyimā iʻtidāl üzre olup ḫalqı tendürüstlerdir.

(18) *Der ʻaded-i çāh-ı āb-ı ḫoş-güvār-ı ḫānedān.* Cümle şehr içre bi-qavl-i şehir ketḫüdāsı iki biñ altmış ʻaded āb-ı ḥayāt ṣu quyuları vardır kim qullanırlar.

(19) *Der ḥisāb-ı eqālīm-i arż-ı beled-i şehristān.* Be-ʻilm-i usṭurlāb bu şehr ıqlīm-i rābiʻde bulunup arż-ı beledi ----- dir, ṭūl-ı nehārı ----- .

(20) *Der qavl-i müneccimān-ı tāliʻ-i ʻamāristān.* Bu şehriñ ṭāliʻ-i ʻimāreti bi-qavl-i kühhān-ı qudemā burc-ı mīzān beyt-i zühre ve havāyīde bulunup ḫalqı mesrūrdur.

(21) *Bī-medḥ-i kenīse-yi rāhibān-ı qıssīsān.* Bu şehr içre cümle ----- ʻaded kenīseler vardır. Evvelā ----- .

(22) *Der faṣl-ı ḥubūbāt-ı sebzevāt-ı maḥṣūlāt.* Her gūne maḥṣūlātları olur, ammā dānedār buğdayı ve darısı ve arpası ve mercimegi ----- bī-ḥisāb olur.

(23) *Der niʻmet-i ʻuẓmā-yı envāʻ-ı meʼkūlāt.* Evvelā beyāż çöregi ve bahārlı ve şekerli firançile çöregi ve noḫudlı simidi ve qırq gūne ṭaʻāmı memdūḥdur.

(24) *Der ṣunʻ-ı ḫüdā güzīde-yi fevākih-i müs̠merāt.* Evvelā bir vaqıyye gelir amrūdı ve elması ve ābdār kirazı ve ayvası ve qızılcığı ve kestānesi meşhūrdur.

(25) *Der gūnāgūn-ı cān-perver-i meşrūbāt.* Evvelā laʻl-gūn bādesi ve ḫardāliyye ve reyḥāniyye müs̠elles̠i ve vişnābı ve bal ṣuyı ve bozası memdūḥdur.

(26) *Der cüsūr-ı memerr-i nās u cemīʻi ḥayvānāt.* Evvelā şehr içre cerêyān éden Nehr-i Uşqumbi üzre ḫaşeb cisri ġāyet muṣannaʻ evqāf-ı ʻaẓīmdir.

(27) *Der taʻdād-ı bāġ u besātīn-i ḥadāyıqāt.* Bi-qavl-i bācdār bu şehr eṭrāfında yigirmi bir biñ bāġ u bāġçe dölüm ḥaqqı verir deyü naql etdi, ammā çoġı muʻāfdır.

(28) *Der muṣallā-yı ʻibādetgāh-ı erbāb-ı ḥācāt.* Bir müferriḥ namāzgādır kim duhāvī yeşil qaṭīfe gibi çemenzārda elli yedi ʻad[ed] serv-i serāmedler ile müzeyyen ʻibādetgāhdır.

(29) *Der sitāyiş-i mesīregāh-ı kibār-ı aġavāt.* Bu Élbaṣan şehriniñ endêrūn [u] bīrūnı cümle teferrücgāh-ı ārāmgāh yerlerdir, ammā ḫāṣṣ u ʻāmlara (30) maḫṣūṣ olmuş çemenzār u lāle-ʻizār yetmiş yerde merāmgāh [u] mesīregāhları var.

Climate. The town has an excellent climate, always temperate in winter and summer.

Wells. According to what the mayor told me, there are 2060 operative wells with good-tasting water.

Clime. According to the science of the astrolabe, this city is in the fourth clime. Its latitude is ----- and longest day is ----- .

Rising star according to the astrologists. This city's rising star, according to the ancient sorcerors, is in the constellation of Libra, mansion of Venus, airy, so the people are cheerful.

Dispraise of the churches. There are a total of ----- churches, including ----- .

Cereals and vegetables. All kinds of crops are grown here, of which wheat, millet, barley, lentils, and ----- are very abundant

Foods. White *çörek* cakes, spiced and sweet breadrolls, chickpea buns, and 40 other kinds of food are highly praised.

Fruits. The pears weighing 1 okka[1] apiece are very famous, as are the apples, juicy cherries, quinces, cornelian cherries, and chestnuts.

Beverages. The drinks which are consumed here include red wine, grape juice flavored with mustard, *reyhania*, sour-cherry juice, honey mead, and *boza*.

Bridges for people and animals. The main bridge is the well-constructed wooden bridge over the Shkumbin river which flows through the town; its upkeep is supported by large endowments.[2]

Vineyards and gardens. According to the toll collector, there are 21,000 vineyards and gardens; some pay tax per *dönüm* but most are exempt.

Prayer-grounds. There is a delightful public prayer-grounds situated in a meadow shimmering like green *duhavi* velvet and adorned with 50 tall cypress trees.[3]

Pleasure-outings for gentlemen. Elbasan has numerous spots for leisure and relaxation, both in town and out. Indeed there are 70 private and public parks with grass and flowers, suitable for picnics and outings.

---

[1] 1 okka = 1.28 kg.

[2] This wooden bridge was replaced ca. 1780 by a twelve-arch stone bridge built by governor Kurd Ahmed Pasha, of which photos remain.

[3] A couple of cypress trees are all that remain of what was once the *namazgjah* of Elbasan. The square is now (1997) covered by kiosks, parked cars and refuse.

Cümleden şehir ḫāricinde Lonca Köşki nām (31) olan yerde her gün ba'de'l-'aṣr şehriñ cümle aḥibbā vü dostān-ı 'āşıqān-ı ma'şūqānları bu çemenzār-ı ḫiyābān-ı diraḫtistān fezāsında gūşe-be-(32)gūşe herkes āşnāları ile gūnāgūn cilveler éderler; ġāyet laṭīf mecma'u'l-'irfān yeridir.

Ve mesīregāh-ı 'Aynü'l-ḥayāt, şehriñ cānib-i şimālinde(33)ki bāġlı bayırlar dāmeninde bir şarāb-ı ṭahūr-ı ṣāfī qaynaġı kenārında ḥavż u selsebīl ü şāzrevānlı ma[q]ṣūreler ve çemenzār ṣoffalı yerdir.

(34) Ve teferrücgāh-ı Büzürg Seng,[1] şehriñ qıble ṭarâfı ḫāricinde Nehr-i Uşqumbi ṣuyı aşırısında bir diraḫtistān naḫlistān gül-i **[367a]** gülistān ḫıyābānistān içre bir çemenzār vāsi' fezāda Büzürg Seng nāmıyle meşhūr-ı āfāq bir naẓargāh-ı 'uşşāqdır. Ammā Arnavud qavmı (2) lehcesiyle bu mesīregāha Boz Eşek derler, ġalaṭ-ı meşhūr evlā olup böyle qalmışdır, ammā aṣlı Büzürg Sengden ġalaṭdır. (3) Meṡelā (?) bu çemenzār mesīregāhıñ tā ortasında bir ulu qaya vardır, anıñiçün Büzürg Seng deyü şöhre-yi şehr olmuş bir temāşāgāhdır kim Rūm (4) ve 'Arab ve 'Acemde miṡli yoq bir naẓargāh-ı ḫüdādır kim evc-i āsmāna ser-çekmiş niçe yüz 'aded ber-qā'ide vü tertīb dikilmiş diraḫt-i müntehā(5)lardan çınār ve qavaq ve mīşe ve pelīd ve servi ve bīd-i ser-nigūnlar ile müzeyyen olmuş cānib-i erba'ası gül-i gülistān ve bāġ u būstān ḥadīqa-yı cinānlı (6) bir mesīregāhdır kim gūnāgūn maqṣūreler ve neşīmen ṣoffalar ve niçe fışqıyye ve ḥavż u şāzrevān [u] fevvāreler pertāb édüp cerêyān (7) etmede, ve niçe maṭbaḫ-ı Keykāvūslar ve müte'addid kilar ve ḥücreler ile ārāste ve gūnāgūn qameriyye ve dikkeler ile pīrāste olmuş merāmdır, (8) ve her fevvāreleri çınārlarıñ ḫaşeblerine érer āb-ı ḥayātdan nişān verir āb-ı şāzrevānlardır.

Ve niçe biñ 'aded pençe-yi āftāb maḥbūb-ı cihān gül-fem (9) u la'l-gūn kiraz dudaqlı kerrūbiyyān ṣıfatli dilberānlar içün 'uşşāq-ı müştāqān hezār hezār nāle vü efġān édüp hezārān hezārı (10) naġamāt etmeden firāġat etdirüp her 'uşşāq 'andelīb-āsā nevāsāz u ḫānendelikler ile ḫoş elḥān ve aṣvāt-ı ḥazīn etdiklerinde bülbülān-ı (11) çemenistān dembeste vü ḥayrān olurlar, her ṭarafda gūşe-be-gūşe cemī'i 'uşşāqān ma'şūqlarıyle cilveler édüp bir hāy (12) hūy [u] ṭarab u 'ayş [u] 'işretler olur kim gūyā rūzları rūz-ı nevrūz-ı Ḫārezm-şāhī olup şeb [ü] rūz Hüseyn-Bayqara meclisleri olur, (13) ve her ṭarafda gūnāgūn ḫānende vü sāzende ve muṭribān u meddāḥānlarıñ ser-āġāze-

---

[1] In the text, vocalized throughout as: *Bezreng Seng*.

One such site is the so-called Lonca Köşki (Loggia Pavilion), outside the town, where every afternoon lovers gather behind the tall trees and in the shady spots and flirt with their beloveds. It is a delightful gathering-place for men of culture.

Another is Aynü'l-Hayat (Spring-of-Life) Park, a grassy meadow with pavilions amidst ponds and fountains of sweet water, like wine from paradise. It is located among the vineyards and slopes to the north of the town.

Büzürg Seng (Big Rock) Park, outside the town on the south side across the Shkumbin river, is a resort for lovers in a large open meadow full of palm trees and rose gardens. The Albanians call this spot Boz Eşek (Grey Donkey), a corruption of Büzürg Seng; and indeed, there is a big rock in the middle of this meadow, which is why it is known as Büzürg Seng.[1] It is a beautiful natural setting, without its like in Turkey, Arabia and Persia. Rising into the heavens are hundreds of plane trees, poplars, oaks, cypresses and willows, planted in rows. On all sides are orchards and gardens of roses and other flowers. Water flows continually through the various pavilions and pleasure-domes with their pools and fountains fitted with water jets. These buildings are equipped with many kitchens and well-stocked pantries and the park is ornamented with numerous wrought-iron trellises and bowers. The water from the jets is projected up into the branches of the plane trees, like the Water of Life.

Here countless love-stricken young men come to sing love songs to the handsome boys they adore, whose red lips are like roses and cherries. They pour out their emotions so sweetly and sadly that the

---

[1] Today it is Byshek, in the direction of the village of Shushica. The rock, spring water and a few ancient plane trees still exist. The site was retransformed into a little park with ponds ca. 1985 and a hotel complex was begun in 1989, though never finished.

yi hengāmelerinden cemī'i hezārān ḫāmūş-bāş olup (14) dem çekmezler.

Ve bu mesīregāh meydānında olan Büzürg Seng ya'nī ulu qayanıñ altından bir āb-ı ḥayāt şu qaynayup pertāb édüp (15) çıqar kim gūyā ṭurna gözi gibi billūr-vār şa'şa'a verir, cemī'i zemānda eyle ḥayāt-ı cāvidānī zülāli gibi cerêyān etmededir. (16) Māh-ı temmūz rūz-ı nevrūzda degme 'uşşāq bu 'ayn-i zülāliñ içinden üç qıṭ'a ṭaş çıqarmaġa cür'et édemez, meger bir (17) 'āşıqıñ ma'şūqası "Gel[1] şu ṣuda ġusl eyle" déyü fermān éde, ol zemān ṣuya girmek muqarrerdir. Ya'nī tā bu mertebe (18) bürūdet üzre ḫalq olunmuş āb-ı zülālden nişān verir şarāb-ı ṭahūrdur.

Ve bu mesīregāha şehirden ve eṭrāf [u] eknāf qurā ve qaṣabā(19)tlarından niçe biñ a'yān-ı kibārlar ḫayme ve ḫargāhlarıyle gelüp niçe biñ 'aded külbe-yi aḥzānlar binā olunup yılda bir kerre bir cem'iyyet-i kübrā bir adam (20) deryāsı bāzārı olur kim bunuñ daḫi vaṣfında diller lāldir, gūyā hemān Dolyan ve Maşqolur ve Alaṣonya ve Mizistre panayurları (21) gibi bāzār-ı 'aẓīm düzüb olqadar bey' ü şirā olur kim on gün on gécede beş Mışır ḫazīnesi māl cem' olup niçe ḫazīne māl itlāf (22) olup ehālī-yi Elbaṣan bunda zevq u ṣafālar édüp felekden sehilce kām alup géceleri qadar rūzları rūz-ı 'īd-i aḍḥā olup ṣoḥbet-i (23) ḫāṣṣu'l-ḫāṣ olur.

Andan mesīregāh-ı ----- (24) -----. Niçe teferrücgāhları var, ammā bunlar meşhūrdur.

(25) *Der tetimme-yi şehr-engīz-i külliyyāt-ı şehr-i Elbaṣan.* Evvelā bu şehriñ cānib-i erba'asındaki yollar ile gelirken bu Elbaṣan şehriniñ aṣlā 'amāristān (26) 'imāretleri tā şehr içine girmeyince bir 'alāmet görünmez, hemān eflāke ser-çekmiş diraḫt-i müntehālar içre ve bāġ u bāġçeler içre pinhān (27) olmuş bāġ-ı irem-mis̱āl bir şehr-i 'aẓīmdir. Elḥāṣıl bu şehir ma'mūre-yi qadīm mecma'-ı 'ulemā ve menba'-ı fuẓalā ve mesken-i şu'arā ve ıqlīm-i 'acībe vü ġarībedir. (28) 'Ulemā ve ẓurêfāları 'ulūm-ı kes̱īreye ve fünūn-ı ġarībeye māliklerdir. ----- //////

[367b] *Der beyān-ı ziyāretgāh-ı merāqıd-ı pür-envār-ı kibār-ı evliyā' u'llāh-ı şehr-i Elbaṣan.* Evvelā qal'e ḫandaqı muqābelesinde Çelebi Efendi merḥūm qabr-ı şerīfi (2) seng-i mezārındaki celī ḫaṭṭ-ı müẕehheb ile taḥrīr olunan tārīḫ-i muṣanna'dır:

---

[1] Text: KR (?).

nightingales get tongue-tied with admiration. In every corner there is flirtation and fun and drinking and carousing, with music and singing and other entertainments day and night, like New Year's eve.

There is a crystal clear stream of water continuously bubbling out from beneath Büzürg Seng or Big Rock, in the middle of this park. Even in July none of the lovers dares to reach into the water and bring out three stones — only if his beloved were to command him to jump in the water, of course he would do it — so cold is the water from this spring, betokening the wine of paradise.

Once a year, a huge country market is held in this park, and thousands of notables from town and from the surrounding villages come and pitch their tents. It is a huge fair with a sea of people like the fairs in Dojran[1], Mashkolur[2], Elassonos[3] and Mistra[4]. Trading flourishes at this time; in 10 days and nights money is spent equivalent to 5 Egyptian treasures.[5] The people of Elbasan get some pleasure out of life and spend their days and nights feasting and merrymaking, like the feast of Kurban Bayram [6].

The park of -----; ----- . There are other parks and spots for leisure, too, but these are the most famous ones.

Completion of the eulogy of the city of Elbasan. If one arrives by road from any direction, one cannot see the buildings at all until one actually enters the city. The entire metropolis is concealed amidst tall trees and vineyards and gardens. In short, it is a prosperous and ancient city, the home of scholars and virtuous men, poets and mystics. ----- //////

Pilgrimage sites. Across from the fortress moat is the tomb of Çelebi Efendi. On the gravestone in gilded lettering and *celi* script is the following chronogram:

---

[1] Tk. Dolyan; south of Strumica in the present-day Republic of Macedonia; see Evliya's description at VIII 375b (757).

[2] In Greece between Trikala and Levadhia; see Evliya's description at VIII 242a (215).

[3] Tk. Alasonya; see Evliya's description at VIII 234b (188).

[4] Tk. Mizistre; see Evliya's description at VIII 274a (341).

[5] See Dankoff 1991a *Intimate Life*, 236 (n. 9).

[6] Muslim feast of sacrifice.

Devr-i ʻālemden eger şeker (?) saña eger āh
Hīç mümkinmi ki taġyīr oluna (3) ḥükm-i ilāh
Dédiler ḥāl-i firāqında aḥibbā tārīḫ
Göçdi āh kevn-i fenādan Çelebi ṭābe s̱erāh. Sene 1027.

Tārīḫ-i türbe-yi Vaqıyye-zāde:

Dirīġ (4) eyledi tārāc mülk-i maʻrifeti
Hemīşe böyle sitemḫīz olur felek dād-ā
Efendiler bu duʻā ile deyelim tārīḫ
Vaqıyye-zādeye ḥaq (5) raḥmet eylesün ebedā. Sene 1074.

Tārīḫ-i meşhed-i Yaḥya-beg-zāde:

Yaḥya-beg-zāde ʻubūdiyyet ile ṣāliḥ idi
Rūhına raḥmetiñi (6) eyle ʻaṭāyā maʻbūd
Bu duʻā ile ilāh-ā dédi Rūmī tārīḫ
Cennet-i ʻAdn ola luṭfuñla maqām-ı maḥmūd. Sene 1073.

Andan (7) tārīḫ-i ṭāʻūn:

Dédi Zevqī bī-ṣafā tārīḫ
Qıldı vīrān şehri ṭāʻūn āh. Sene ----- .

Bu tārīḫ Sinān Paşa cāmiʻi (8) dīvārında merqūmdur. Tārīḫ-i merqad-i Ḥasan Şāh der baḥr-ı müstezād:

Ger evc-i semāya éresiñ qaʻr-ı semekden Hīç umma emānı
Kim (9) arż [u] semāvāta gelen ins ü melekden Hep olmada fānī
Gūş eyleyicek dédi Hilālī bu beyiti Hem ola bu tārīḫ
(10) Cām-ı eceli içdi Ḥasan dest-i felekden Ṣū-yı du-cihānı.
Sene 1072.

Whether sugar (?) or sighs come to you from the revolving world
Is it possible to change the judgment of God?
When he departed, his friends uttered the chronogram:
Ah, Çelebi has migrated from the transitory realm;
may his earth be sweet. Year 1027/1618.

Chronogram on the tomb of Vakıyye-zade:

Alas! the kingdom of knowledge has been plundered.
Justice! fate is always so cruel.
Gentlemen, with this prayer let us utter the chronogram:
May God have mercy on Vakıyye-zade for ever.
Year 1074/1663-64.

Chronogram on the tomb of Yahya Beg-zade:

Yahya Beg-zade was pious in worship.
O worshipped One, bestow the gift of Your mercy on his spirit.
With this prayer, O God, Rumi uttered the chronogram:
With Your grace may the Garden of Eden be his station.
Year 1073/1662-63.

Chronogram of the plague:

Zevki uttered the chronogram without joy:
Ah, the plague has ruined the city. Year ----- .

This chronogram is inscribed on the wall of the mosque of Sinān Pasha. Chronogram on the tomb of Hasan Shah in *müstezād* meter:

Though you reach the zenith from the lower depths,
hope not for mercy.
Men and angels, all who come to heaven and earth
are transitory.
Hearing this, Hilali uttered this couplet, which also serves
as chronogram:
Hasan quaffed the cup of death from the hand of fate,
water (?) of both worlds. Year 1072/1661-62.

Ve niçe biñ böyle muṣanna‘ tārīḫler cemī‘i ḫān u cāmi‘ (11) ve mesācid [ü] medreselerde manẓūrumuz olmuşdur, ammā taḥrīrinde ‘aczımız olup seyāḥatimize māni‘ olur ve taṭvīl-i kelām olmasın içün buqadar (12) ile iktifā etdik.

Ve *merqad-ı pür-envār-ı emīr sulṭānlar* qal‘e içinde Sinān Paşa tekyesinde medfūnlardır kim ziyāretgāh-ı erbāb-ı dilāndır. Andan eş-şeyḫ (13) İlhām Sulṭān ziyāreti. Andan eş-şeyḫ quṭb-ı āfāq, maḥbūb ‘alā’l-iṭlāq, ‘āşıq-ı ḥayy-ı vedūd, ya‘nī eş-şeyḫ Dede Maqṣūd, ḥālā (14) vücūd-ı şerīfleri Ebū’l-fetḥ ‘aṣrından berü qabr-i münevveri içre bir seccāde ḫırqasıyle dest-i şerīfinde tesbīḥiyle vücūdı ter ü tāzedir deyü naql (15) etdiler, raḥmetü’llāhi ‘aleyhim ecma‘īn.

Der beyān-ı ecdād-ı qadīm-i qavm-ı ‘Ārnābūd, ya‘nī qabr-ı Cebel-i Elheme-yi nā-maḥmūd. Elbaṣan şehri (16) ḫāricinde ----- nām maḥalde ----- bir mesīregāh yerde medfūndur kim cemī‘i ‘Arnavud qavmları cedd-i ‘iẓāmımız(17)dır deyü ziyāret éderler. Qabri üzre zemān-ı qadīm üzre iri ṭaşlar qomuşlardır. Niçe bir kerre münāsebêtiyle aḥvāli terqīm (18) olunmuşdur, ammā şimdi bu maḥalde medfūn olduğıyçün bir şemme sergüzeşt-i firārın taḥrīr édelim. Bu Cebel-i Elheme bi’z-zāt (19) qavm-ı Qureyşden ḥażret-i risālet-penāhıñ ṣaḥābe-yi kirāmından olup Tebūk ve Uḥud ve Tābūt (?) ve Ḫaybar ve Bedr-i Ḥuneyn ġazālarında bile (20) olup niçe ġazālar édüp ḥużūr-ı resūl-i kibriyāya niçe kerre baş ve diller getirir bir ġāzī vü şecī‘ ü tüvānā mīr-i ‘Arab imiş. Ba‘dehu ḥażret-i (21) ‘Ömer ḫilāfetinde bir şeyḫü’l-‘Arâbıñ yā ḫaṭa’en yā qaṣden gözin çıqar[ır], şeyḫü’l-‘Arâb daḫi bir gözi çıqmış gözin eline alup ḥużūr-ı ḥażret-i (22) ‘Ömere gelüp “Yā ‘Ömer, emir şer‘-i resūl-i mübīniñdir, gözüm yerine Cebel-i Elhemeniñ gö[zi]n isterim” dédikde Cebeli ḥażret-i ‘Ömer ḥużūrına (23) da‘vet édüp sü’āl olunduqda Cebel eydir: “Yā ‘Ömer, kendü qabīlemden bir ‘Arâbımıñ gözidir, ben çıqardım” dédikde iqrārı sicill-i (24) şer‘e tescīl ü terqīm olup sūre-yi ----- “Ve-ketebnā ‘aleyhim fīhā [enne] ’n-nefse bi’n-nefsi ve’l-‘ayne bi’l-‘ayni” naṣṣ-ı qāṭı‘ı (25) fehvāsınca Cebel-i Elhemeniñ gözi çıqması fermān olunca Elheme ilhām-ı nā-şer‘ī ile rıżā vermeyüp

We saw thousands of such chronograms on all the *hans*, mosques, prayer houses and *medreses*. To record all of them is beyond our capacity, and furthermore would hinder our travels and would be considered loquaciousness, so we will stop here.

The *mausoleums of the saints* are in the fortress at the *tekke* of Sinan Pasha and are visited by many pilgrims. One is the shrine of Sheikh Ilham Sultan. Another is that of the pole of the horizons, the absolute beloved and lover of the Living and Beloved One, Sheikh Dede Maksud, of whom they say the body, wrapped in his patched cloak and a prayer rug and with prayer beads in his hand since the time of Mehmed the Conqueror, is still fresh. May God have mercy on them all.

Mausoleum of Jabal-i Alhama, ancestor of the Albanian people. He is buried in the ----- park in a place called ----- outside the city of Elbasan. All the Albanians visit the grave, claiming him as their ancestor. Over a long period they have placed large stones on his grave. An account of his life was given in an earlier chapter.[1] Now, because he is buried here, we would like to write in more detail about his adventures. Jabal-i Alhama himself was of the Quraysh tribe and a companion of the Holy Prophet. He took part in the ghazas of Tabuk, Uhud, Tabut (?), Khaybar and Badr-i Hunayn.[2] He also fought in other battles and was a courageous Arab chieftain and ghazi who offered the holy Prophet the heads and tongues of many prisoners. Later, during the caliphate of the blessed Omar, he put out the eye of an Arab sheikh, either wilfully or by accident. The Arab sheikh, holding his gouged eye in his hand, went to Omar and said, "Oh Omar, it is my right under the law of the Prophet to demand the eye of Jabal-i Alhama for my own." They summoned Jabal who, when asked about the matter, replied, "Oh Omar, it is the eye of an Arab of my own tribe. I put it out." His confession was recorded in the *şeriat* register, and it was ordered that Jabal's eye be put out in accordance with the definitive Koranic verse in surah ----- (5:45) "And We prescribed for them a life for a life and an eye for an eye." Unwilling

---

[1] VIII 353a.

[2] This list (with the exception of Tabut which, if read correctly, is perhaps just a jingle with Tabuk) agrees with two others where Evliya lists the ghazas in which the Prophet Muhammad participated. I 19b9-11: Bedr, Uḥud, Khandaq ("the Trench"), Benū Ferīṭ (recte: Qurayẓa), Benī'l-Muṣṭaliq, Khaybar, Mecca, Ḥunayn, Ṭāyif; IX 288a25-26 (630): Bedr, Uḥud, Khandaq, Benū Qarbaṭ (recte: Qurayẓa), Benī'l-Muṣṭaliq, Khaybar, Mecca, Bedr-i Ḥunayn, Ṭāyif.

'ār-nā-būd édüp cümle (26) ta'alluqāt-ı oymağıyle firār édüp doğrı qayṣar-ı Rūm Ḫırqīle gelir, andan Cebeliyye dağların 'amār etdiginden Cebeliyye derler, anda (27) daḫi ḥażret-i 'Ömer Qudsi fetḥ édince duramayup gemilere süvār olup İşpanya qıralına daḫil düşüp İşpanya daḫi dest-i (28) ḥükminde olan Arnavudluq olan Avlonya ve Delvine ḫāklerinde Duqat ve Podġorad[1] ve Ferengis dağların Cebel-i (29) Elhemeye temlīk verüp arż-ı ḫāliye iken az zemānda mesken-i me'vā édüp Fireng ile [i]ḫtilāṭ éderek 'Arab lisānından 'Arna(30)vud lisānın peydā édüp tenāsül bularaq ḥālā ibtidā vaṭan édindikleri yére Quryeleş dağı derler, zīrā bunlarıñ aṣlı (31) qabāyil-i 'Arabdan Qureyşīlerdir, anıñiçün Arnavud ṭāyifeleri "Biz aṣḥāb-ı güzīn evlādlarından Qureyşīleriz" deyü tefāḫür kesb éderler.

Lākin Cebel-i (32) Elheme taḥaqquq-ı İslām üzre merḥūm olduqdan ṣoñra vaṣıyyeti üzre bu ḫiyābānda defn olunup ba'dehu evlād evlādları Fireng-i bed-reng (33) ile qız verüp qız aldıqlarndan bir fırqası Fireng olup kitābı olmamaq ile kimse (?) ve Qara Dağlar ve Quryeleş ve Porġonat ve (34) ----- dağlarınıñ cümle Arnavudları kitābsız kefereler olup şeb [ü] rūz yine aqrâbāları olan musülmān Arnavud ile şeb [ü] rūz ceng éderle **[368a]** ve esīr olur. Tā Ebū'l-fetiḥ Ġāzīye gelince çoq Arnavudistān qavmı mürtedler idi. Ba'de[hu] İskenderiyye ve Leş ve Ülgün ve Bar ve Leş ve Dirac (2) ve Arnavud Belġıradı ve bu Elbaṣan ve Avlonya ve Delvine qal'eleri cümle dest-i Āl-i 'Oṣmāna girüp Arnavudistān cümle İslām ile müşerref olup (3) ancaq Kilimente ve Qara Dağlar ve Quryeleş ve niçe dağlarıñ kefereleri 'ıṣyān üzre geçinirler, "Cebel-i Elheme ḥāşā bizim mezhebimiz üzre mürted oldı" (4) derler. Ammā tevārīḫ-i Tuḥfede İslām ile gitdigine zāhib olup qaçan gözin çıqarmağa 'ār édüp firār etdikde Qayṣar Ḫırqīl yanında iken (5) qayṣar üzre cenge gelen ṣaḥābe qayṣar keferelerinden baş kesse nihānīce iḥsānlar édüp kendi qayṣara imdād etmeyüp cenge girmezmiş. (6) Andan ba'dehu Qusṭanṭīne gelüp anıñla daḫi Anṭāqıyye üzre 'Arab cengine gidüp yine kefereye imdād etmeyüp ṣavaş-ı perḫāş etmez (7) imiş, ol ecilden 'Arnavudlar "Ceddimiz Cebel-i Elheme aṣḥāb-ı güzīnden olup İslām ile merḥūm oldı" derler. Ḫulāṣa-yı kelām Arnavud qavmınıñ (8) aṣlı qavm-ı Qureyşden Cebel-i Elheme olup ḥażret-i 'Ömer ḫilāfetinde

---

[1] sic; for *Porġonat*.

to comply, on the grounds that “There should be no shame” (*‘ār-nā-būd*), Jabal-i Alhama fled with his entire clan to the emperor of Byzantium, Heraclius. He settled in the Jabaliyya mountains and that is why these mountains bear his name. When the blessed Omar conquered Jerusalem, Jabal could not remain any longer in that place, so they boarded ships and took refuge with the king of Spain. Jabal-i Alhama was given the mountains of Dukat, Progonat and Frengis in the Albanian regions of Vlora and Delvina to live in, which were then under Spanish rule. These lands were previously uninhabited and, within a short period of time, he settled them and, mingling with the Franks, they created the Albanian language from a mixture of Frankish and Arabic. The place they originally inhabited, and where they still reside after many generations, is now called the mountain of Quryelesh (Kurvelesh), since they are descended from the Quraysh tribe of the Arabs. Accordingly, the Albanian people boast that they are descended from the Quraysh, the companions of the Prophet.

Although Jabal-i Alhama died as a Muslim and was buried at this site according to his last will and testament, his descendents intermarried with the treacherous Franks and became Frankish and bookless themselves. The Albanians of Kelmendi, Montenegro, and the mountains of Kurvelesh and Progonat and ----- became infidels and people without a book. They do battle day and night with the Muslim Albanians, who are their own kinsmen, and take one another prisoner. Many Albanians had abandoned their faith before the arrival of Mehmed the Conqueror. Then, when the Ottomans conquered Shkodër, Ulcinj, Bar, Lezha, Durrës, Berat, this fortress of Elbasan, Vlora and Delvina, all of Albania once again converted to Islam. Only the infidels of Kelmendi, Montenegro, Kurvelesh, and some other mountain ranges continue to resist, saying, “God forbid that Jabal-i Alhama should have converted to Islam.” In the *Tuhfa* history, however, it is written that he did become a Muslim. Even when he fled in shame because of the gouged eye, and when he was staying with the emperor Heraclius, he refused to join his own emperor in battle when the Prophet’s companions attacked the infidels and cut off their heads, but secretly aided the Muslims. Later, when he joined Constantine, he refused to assist the Christians in the battle of Antioch against the Arabs. For this reason, the Albanians claim that their ancestor Jabal-i Alhama was a companion of the Prophet and that he died a Muslim. In short, Jabal-i Alhama of the Quraysh tribe is the

Arnavudistānı ʻamār etmiş nevpeydā keferesi bī-kitāb, müsülmānları pür-ṣavāb, (9) bir alay ġāziyān-ı mücāhidān-ı ḥāżır-cevāb, şecīʻ fetālardır, ve's-selām. -----

(10) Bu şehr-i müzeyyeni daẖi seyr [ü] temāşā édüp cümle aḥbāb ile vedāʻlaşup yarar refīqler alup *Oẖri sancağına gitdigimiz qonaqları beyān éder* (11) evvelā bismi-ilāh ile Elbaṣandan çıqup cānib-i şarqa ----- sāʻatde Babya nām yaylağın aşdıq. Ammā ne ʻacāyib şāhrāh (12) olmış, meger merḥūm Beñqo Paşa Rūm-éli eyāletine mutaṣarrıf iken Qotur Venedigi kāfiri üzre sefere me'mūr olduqda bu (13) yollardan bal-yemez ṭoplar ve ʻasākir-i İslāmlar refāhiyyet üzre ʻubūr etsünler deyü bu yolları taṭhīr édüp cemīʻi (14) cengelistān u ẖiyābān dağlarıñ meşeyistānların qırup cümle āteşe urup qayalara ṣar[p] sirkeler dö[kü]p şāhrāhlar etmiş kim anlar (15) ile cirid oynayaraq ʻubūr étdik, aṣlā ḥaydud keferelerine bir kemīngāh yerler qalmayup emn [ü] emān üzre ḥamd-i ẖüdā selāmetle (16) 4 sāʻatde

Menzil-i qarye-yi Babya, ḥālā bu derbend-i calenderi fermān-ı pādişāhīle emn [ü] emān édüp taṭhīrine me'mūr olmuşlar (17) iken (?) maʻmūr Arnavud u Rūm u Bulġar keferesi köyidir.

Andan yine şarq ṭarâfına ʻaẓīm diraẖt-i müntehālar ve kūh-ı bī-sütūn-miṡāl (18) evc-i āsmāna ser-çekmiş qayalar üzre cerêyān éden āb-ı ḥayātlar içerek ve taṭhīr olmuş yollar ile geçerek 4 sāʻat gidüp (19) *qarye-yi Çora*, bu daẖi derbend içün muʻāf [u] müsellem olmuş kefere köyidir.

Andan yine cānib-i şarqa 8 saʻat gidüp Elbaṣan (20) Ṣuyın bir daẖi geçüp andan Domuz Ovasın daẖi ʻubūr édüp *der ḥudūd-ı sancaġ-ı Oẖri* hemān Babya dağınıñ ġarb ṭarâ(21)fı Elbaṣan ẖākidir. Bu şarq ṭarafı yér aşağı Oẖri livāsı ḥüdūdıdır. Baʻdehu bu maḥalde qoca yaylasın baş aşağı (22) şarq ṭarâfına 5 sāʻat énüp Oẖri Gölin şarq ṭarâfımıza alup Oẖri Göli kenārınca çemenzārlı maʻmūr fezāları geçüp

ancestor of the Albanian people. At the time of the caliphate of the blessed Omar, he populated Albania and his descendents, be they bookless infidels or bookish Muslims, are a race of militant ghazis, brave warriors and clever souls. -----

Having toured this beautiful town, we bid farewell to all our friends and, with an armed escort — *Stages of our journey to the sancak of Ohrid* — set off from Elbasan with a *besmele* heading east and in ----- hours we crossed the alpine pastures of Babja. We travelled on a surprisingly broad military road.[1] It appears that, while he was governor of the *eyalet* of Rumelia, the late Benko Pasha built this broad road when he was ordered to wage war on the Venetian infidels of Kotor. He put through wide roadways, after digging out the trees and burning the thickets and levelling the rocks with vinegar, in order to transport his long-range battering guns and to move the Ottoman troops more easily. So we crossed over the pastures on this royal road, playing *jerid*[2] as we went. There are no longer any places for infidel bandits to lie in ambush.

Thus, thanks be to God, we arrived safe and sound 4 hours later at the *stage of the village of Babja.* This steep mountain pass was cleared of bandits by order of the sultan, and it is a prosperous village of Albanian, Greek and Bulgarian infidels.

From here we set off eastwards again along roads cleared of bandits, passing beneath great and lofty trees and drinking the sweet water flowing over towering cliffs, until we arrived 4 hours later at *the village of Xhyra.* This is another infidel village which, as a mountain pass, is exempt from taxes.

From here, we continued our journey eastwards for 8 hours and, after crossing the Elbasan river once again, arrived at Domosdova[3]. This is the border of the *sancak* of Ohrid. The western side of the Babja mountain range belongs to Elbasan, while this eastern side and down the mountain belongs to Ohrid. From here we descended precipitously in an eastward direction for 5 hours down the huge alpine pasture. With Lake Ohrid to our right, we passed some villages situated on a grassy field at the edge of the lake.

[1] Remnants no doubt of the Via Egnatia, the ancient Roman road linking Rome and Constantinople, which in Albania ran from the port of Durrës through Kavaja, Peqin and Elbasan to Lake Ohrid.

[2] Turkish *cirit,* a game played on horseback with wooden javelins.

[3] Turkish Domuz Ova, lit. "Valley of Pigs", near Përrenjas.

(23) *Evṣāf-ı qal'e-yi bend-i māhī Usturqa.* (24) Zemān-ı qadīmde Oḫrin nām qıralıñ ṣayd [u] şikārgāhı olmaq içün Ustu[r]qa nām bir v[ez]īri qal'e inşā eyledügiyçün anıñ nāmıyle (25) müsemmā olup Usturqa derler. Lisān-ı ----- da ----- demekdir. Oḫri Göliniñ boġazı üzre şehr içinde çār-gūşe (26) şeddādī-binā bir qal'e-yi ra'nā imiş. Ġāzī Evrenos sene ----- tārīḫinde Destpoṭ qıralı oġlı elinden fetḥ édüp bu qal'eyi münhedim (27) etmiş kim bir daḫi küffār istīlā etmege ṭama' etmesin deyü ḫarāb etmiş. Ba'dehu Ġāzī Evrenos bu qal'e boġazından Oḫri Gölin (28) qarşu geçüp Poġradas şehrin ve Iṣṭar-ova şehirlerin ḫarāb [u] yebāb éder, küffār yine 'askeriñ ardın almaġiçün bu göl kenā(29)rında Usturqa qal'esine gelüp görse kim qal'e ḫarāb olup müteḥaṣṣın olacaq bir cā-yı menāṣ yoq, hemān küffār ḫāyib ü (30) ḫāsir gerü dönüp Ġāzī Evrenos selāmetle yine Oḫri boġazın geçüp Usturqa qal'esinde qarār éder. Ammā ḥaqqā ki göl (31) boġazında bir qal'e-yi zībā imiş. Eger 'amār olsa göl boġazından qarşu bir maḫlūq-ı ḫüdā 'ubūr édemezdi. Ve yine bir ferd-i āferīde (32) geçemez, géce ile qapuları qapanır.

Bu Usturqa qaṣabası ve qal'esi Oḫri sancaġı ḫākindedir, ammā ḥükūmetiniñ ṣalb [u] siyāseti ve (33) cürm [ü] cināyeti Oḫri Göli emīni ḥükminde olup maqṭū'-ı qalem ve mefrūzü'l-qadem qırq yük aqçe ḫāṣṣ-ı hümāyūn māl-i pādişāhīli emānetdir kim (34) gökde uçan ve yerde gezen ve gölde yüzen cemī'i maḫlūqāt [u] mevcūdāt emīniñ iltizāmında olup cümle qaçqın köleler ve cemī'i yuvalar **[368b]** ve bāc u bāzār ve 'aded-i aġnām ve ispençe ve qışla ḥaqqı ve tütün ḥaqqı ve dölüm ḥaqqı ve beytü'l-māl ve ḫāṣ ve ḫarāc ve ḫāne-yi 'avāriż, (2) el-ḥāṣıl cemī'i tekālīf-i 'örfiyye-yi ṣāqqalar cümle Oḫri Göli emīniniñ ḥükminde olup Oḫri beginiñ aṣlā 'alāqası yoqdur. (3) Büyük emānetdir kim ikiyüz 'aded neferātlarıyle bu ḥükūmeti fermān-ı pādişāhīle żabṭ [u] rabṭ-ı taṣarruf édüp şeb [ü] rūz gölün eṭrāfların (4) 'askeriyle dolaşup ḥıfẓ [u] ḥirāset édüp gölün eṭrāflarında ṣayd olunan māhīleriñ 'öşr-i sulṭānīlerin alup anıñ izniyle (5) ṣayyādlar balıq ṣayd éderler; eger emīniniñ izinsiz bir kimesne nihānī bir şibr māhī ṣayd éderse tecrīm édüp siyāsetler éderler. (6) Ve cümle Usturqa qażıyyesiniñ re'āyāları ve yedi pāre köy re'āyāları bu emīniniñ qabża-yı taṣarrufında olup mu'āf [u] müsellemler(7)dir kim mīrī balıq ṣayd

The reservoir of fish, the walled town of Struga. It was built in ancient times by the vizier Usturka as a hunting-grounds for his king named Ohrin, and it was called Usturka (Struga) after him. It means ----- in the ----- language. The fortress is a pleasant, quadrangular-shaped and solidly built construction situated in the town at the mouth of the river of Lake Ohrid. It was conquered in the year ----- from the son of the Serbian Despot by Ghazi Evrenos[1] who had it demolished so that the infidels would never try to occupy it again. Ghazi Evrenos later crossed to the other side of Lake Ohrid and razed the towns of Pogradec and Starova. The infidels returned to the fortress of Struga at the mouth of the lake in order to block the Ottoman troops. When they saw that the fortress was in ruins and that it would provide no refuge or defense, they immediately lost heart and returned home. Evrenos got back to the fortress of Struga safe and sound and camped there. It is indeed a pretty ruined castle at the lakeside. If it were to be restored, not a soul would be able to cross the mouth of the river. And indeed no one can, for the gates are closed at night.

The town of Struga is in the territory of the *sancak* of Ohrid, but it is under the command of the *emin* of Lake Ohrid, who has sole authority over punishments and fines. It is an imperial *has* and an *emanet*, the income from which has been fixed at 40 loads of *akçe*, and the state has no power to tax or intervene. All creatures that fly in the sky and creep on the ground and swim in the lake are in the *emin*'s jurisdiction. All levies on fugitive slaves and bird nests, all tolls, sheep taxes, poll taxes on slaves (*ispençe*), levies on winter pastures, tobacco taxes, farm taxes, royal taxes, poll taxes and special fees — in short, all the customary impositions are administered by the *emin* of Lake Ohrid, and the *beg* of Ohrid has nothing to do with them. It is a large *emanet*, administrered by the *emin* according to imperial decree with the help of 200 employees. He and his henchmen patrol the lake day and night, exacting the royal tithe for all fish caught in it. Fishing in the lake is only allowed with the *emin*'s permision. Anyone caught fishing without a licence, even if the fish he catches is no longer than a span, is severely fined. All the rayah in the *kadi*-district and the 7 surrounding villages of Struga are in the service of this *emin* and are thus exempt from taxes. They are employed in

[1] Commander of Ottoman forces in Rumelia under Sultans Murad I and Bayezid I, d. 820/1417; see art. "Ewrenos" in *Encyclopedia of Islam, New Edition.*

etmege me'mūrlardır. Her géce cümle re'āyālar on on beş dāne qayıqlara süvār olup qayıqlara meş'aller (8) yaqup balıq şebekeleri ve ıġribleri çeküp ṣayd etdikleri māhīleri qayıq qayıq emīne teslīm éderler, old[aẖ]i cümle (9) Rūm-élinden gelen bāzirgānlara balıqları fürūẖt édüp anlar daẖi ṭuz ile ṣalamora édüp vilāyet vilāyet Oẖri balıġın götürürler.

(10) *Der vaṣf-ı eşkāl-i buḥeyre-yi Oẖri.* Ba'żılar Ohri yazarlar. Vech-i tesmiyesi ----- dir. (11) Bu buḥeyreniñ girdāgirdi kāmil on beş mīldir. Ṭūle māyil müs̱elles̱ü'ş-şekildir kim kāmil yigirmi dör[d] sā'atde devr olunur bir (12) āb-ı ḥayāt şīrīn göldür. Bir kerre Tirḥālalı Fā'iq Paşanıñ şāṭır-başısı baḥis ile devr etmişdir, ammā ol gün gelemeyüp ba'de'l-ġurūb (13) gücile gelüp bir günde serī'an devr etmişdir. Eṭrāfında dörd pāre qal'esi vardır: evvelā biri bu Usturqa qal'esidir; ve (14) biri Poġradas qal'esidir; cümleden büyügi göl kenārında evce ser-çekmiş qaya üzre Oẖri qal'esidir kim gölün şimāl ṭarâfına vāqı' (15) olmuşdur. Ammā gölün cānib eṭrāfı ġāyet ma'mūr [u] ābādān çiftlikler ile müzeyyen olmuşdur.

Ve bu buḥeyrede olan gūnāgūn mā'ideler (16) bir diyār buḥeyresinde olmazdır, bā-ẖuṣūṣ yılan balıġı müşk [ü] 'amber-i ẖām gibi rāyiḥa-yı ṭayyibesi vardır, ġāyet semīn ü ter ü (17) tāzesin tefne yapraġıyle kebāb édüp tenāvül édeniñ bedênine olqadar quvvet-i quvā verüp olqadar mu[q]avvīdir kim ehli ile pehlivān-(18)āsā güleş etse ehlini beş altı kerre yeñüp eline alup ġalebeler éde, tā bu mertebe ṣaqanqūr-ı berrī-mis̱āl yılan balıqları olur. (19) Ve aġrı ẖasteligine yeyüp başını ṭuzlayup balıq başın kendü başında götürse bi-emri'llāh ol adam aġrı ẖasteliginde ẖalāṣ (20) olur. Ve uştuq balıġı ve misarya balıġı ve ṣazan balıġı ve ala balıġı, bunlar daẖi lezīz mā'idelerdir. Ammā niçe biñ gūne (21) māhīleri olur, ammā bu mezkūr beş 'aded balıqlarda bi-emr-i ḥayy-ı qadīr aṣlā balıq rāyiḥaları yoqdur. Ve bu māhīleri emīn aġa [----- ?]

(22) Usturqa qaṣabasınıñ çaq ortasında bir boġazda on iki 'aded göz aġaç cisir yüz elli adım ṭavīl bir (23) cisr-i 'aẓīmdir, ol qanṭara-yı ṭavīl üzre emīn aġanıñ sarāy-ı 'aẓīmi büyük qazıq direkler üzre binā olunmuş ẖānedān-ı 'aẓīmdir, (24) bu sarāy ortasında cisr üzre bir aġaç qapu vardır, her géce bu cisir qapusın pāsbān [u] bevvābānlar mesdūd édüp öteden beriye (25) ve beriden öteye bir adam 'ubūr édemez, zīrā her géce bu cisir qapusı üzre tā ṣabāḥadek qırq elli 'aded pür-silāḥ dīdebānlar (26) cāsūsluq édüp keşik ya'nī nevbet beklerler, zīrā qaçqın köleler ve ḥarāmīler ve qanlılar ve balıq oġrıları 'ubūr etmesün

fishing for the government. Every night, rayah fishermen go out in 10 to 15 caiques, spread their nets by torch-light and catch fish which they deliver up to the *emin* by the caique-load. The latter sells the fish to traders who come from all over Rumelia. The traders salt the fish in a brine and export it throughout the various *vilayet*s as fish from Lake Ohrid.

The form of Lake Ohrid. Some call it Okhri, some Ohri. The reason for its name is ----- . This lake is 15 miles in circumference and triangular in shape, tending to the oblong. It is possible to go around this sweet-water lake in 24 hours. The chief runner of Faik Pasha of Tirhala once did so on a wager: he did not return that night, but did get back just after dawn the following day. So it can be circumambulated in a single day if one runs fast enough. There are 4 [sic] fortresses along its shores: Struga, Pogradec, and Ohrid. Largest of all is the fortress of Ohrid which, built on a high cliff, rises into the sky over the lake. It is situated at the northern end of the lake. All sides of the lake are adorned with prosperous farm-estates.

The fish caught in Lake Ohrid cannot be found anywhere else. The eels, in particular, have a delightful fragrance of musk and ambergris. They are very oily. If caught fresh, wrapped in bay leaves and roasted, they make a very nutritious meal. Anyone who eats this dish will be able to have intercourse with his wife five or six times — so invigorating are these eels, like skinks. Anyone with consumption who puts a salted eel head on his own head will be cured of his ailments, by God's command. There are also pike, *misarya* (?), carp and trout, all of which make delicious dishes. There are a thousand different kinds of fish in this lake, but the 5 kinds that I have named are the best — they never have a fishy smell!

Right in the center of Struga, where the lake narrows into a river, there is a large wooden bridge 150 paces long and with 12 arches. Atop this long bridge is the spacious mansion of the *emin*, built on wooden piles in the water. In the middle of the mansion there is a wooden gate which is shut at night by the sentries, so no one is allowed to cross. Every night 40 or 50 armed watchmen patrol the bridge until dawn. Indeed, this mansion gate was built on the bridge in order to stop fugitive slaves, brigands, murderers, and fish

(27) maṣlaḥatiyçün bu cisr üzre bu sarāy qapusı binā olunmuşdur. Ve bu gölüñ ayaġı tā on qonaq 'Arnavudlıq içinde İskenderiyye (28) sancaġında Leş qal'esi dibinde körfez deryāsına Sincivan limanı içinde maḫlūṭ olur. Bir ṭarafdan aṣlā geçit (29) vermez. Oḫri Göli bu vilāyet ortasında sed olmış bir buḥeyere-yi 'aẓīmdir, ve iki yerden daḫi ayaġında cisirleri vardır, (30) anda daḫi emīniñ adamları bekleyüp āyende ve revendegānlardan bāc u bāzār ve 'öşr-i māhīler alup ḥükūmet ile quş uçurmazlar. (31) Ammā memerr-i nās şāhrāh bu Usturqa cisridir. Bu qanṭaranıñ alt yanında niçe yüz 'aded balıq dalyanları var kim ta'bīr (32) olunmaz, görmege muḥtācdır. Ve bu cisriñ altında göli ayaġı ol mertebe aqar kim göz görmez, yaz u qış Nehr-i Dirava (33) gibi dörd qoldan aqar, aṣlā egsilmez. Ḥikmet ol kim bu gölüñ içine 'aẓīm nehirler maḫlūṭ olmaz, yine böyle iken (34) ṣayf [u] şitāda bu gölüñ ayaġı Nehr-i Ceyḥūn gibi aqar, ve ġarb ṭarâfına cerêyān édüp qaṣaba-yı ----- uġrar, **[369a]** andan ----- uġrar, andan ----- uġrayup mezkūr Leş qal'esi dibinde Sincivan limanında Bunduqani Körfezine (2) munṣab olur. Bir āb-ı ḥayāt göldür, ammā yaz günleri ġāyet isidir, ammā sehil bardaqda durup kesb-i havā etse buz (3) pāresi olur, lākin qaçan bu göl ṣuyı isi olduqda ol zemān balıqlar ziyāde ṣayd olunur.

Ve bu Usturqa qaṣabası (4) Oḫri qażāsı niyābetidir. Ve göl kenārında bir qumsal yerde ve çemenzār vādīleriñ düz yerinde cümle üçyüz 'aded (5) kiremit örtüli kārgīr binālı taḥtānī ve fevqānī bāġ u bāġçeli āb [u] havāsı laṭīf qaṣabacikdir. Cümle üç maḥalledir, (6) ammā Bulġar ve Rūm kefereleri çoqdur. Ve cümle dörd 'aded miḥrābdır; evvelā çārsū içinde Oḫri-zāde cāmi'i, qurşum ör(7)tüli ser-āmed qubbe vü minare-yi bālālı cāmi'dir. Bir ḫānı ve bir 'imāreti ve bir medresesi ve bir ḥammāmı var, cümle Oḫri-zāde ḫayrātıdır. (8) Ve cümle üç 'aded mesācidleri vardır. Ve cümle beş 'aded ṣaġīr ü kebīr ḫān-ı mihmān-sarāyları vardır. Ve cümle (9) qırq 'aded dükkānları var, ammā bez̠z̠āzistānı yoqdur, hemān kifāyet miqdārı dekākīnlerdir. Ve bu çārsū içinde gölden bir qol (10) ṣu daḫi aqar, anıñ üstinde bir aġaç cisir daḫi var, 'imāret ve medresesiniñ pençereleri ol ṣuya nāẓır olup 'imāretiñ ṭa'āmın (11) tenāvül édenler pençerelerde oṭurup kesb-i havā éderler. Ve cümle şehriñ ve gölüñ qayıqçılar qayıqları bu şehr içre olan (12) ṣuda qayıqların limana baġlarlar.

poachers from escaping. From this end of the lake, the river flows through Albania for 10 stages and, passing below the fortress of Lezha in the *sancak* of Shkodër, it empties into the sea at the harbor of Shëngjin. It cannot be forded anywhere. Lake Ohrid is a great wall of water in the middle of this *vilayet*. There are two other bridges at the other tributaries where the *emin*'s agents are posted to collect both tolls on merchandise and levies on fish — not even a bird can fly by without the authorities noticing. But the major crossing-point is this bridge at Struga. Under this bridge there are hundreds of fishing weirs. They have to be seen to be believed. This outlet flows so swiftly under the bridge that you can hardly see it. It flows at full strength summer and winter, like the Drava river, and never diminishes. One strange thing is that no big rivers flow into the lake,[1] and yet this outlet is constantly flowing just like the Oxus river. It flows west passing the town of -----, then -----, then ----- until it finally empties into the Gulf of Venice (Adriatic Sea) at the harbor of Shëngjin below the fortress of Lezha, as I mentioned above. The lake has good drinkable water. It is very warm in the summer, but if you fill a cup with it and leave it out in the air, it turns cold as ice. As the water in the lake warms up, more and more fish are caught.

The town of Struga is part of the *kadi*-district of Ohrid. This little town, with a delightful climate, lies along a sandy stretch of the lakeside and in the flat bottoms of the stream beds. It has 300 one- and two-story stonework houses with tiled roofs and surrounded by gardens and vineyards. There are 3 quarters, the populace being mainly Bulgarian and Greek infidels. There are 4 prayer-niches. Foremost is the mosque of Ohri-zade in the bazaar, with its lofty dome and minaret and lead-covered roofing; and there is 1 *han*, 1 soup kitchen, 1 *medrese* and 1 bath, all of them charitable gifts of the Ohri-zade family. There are also 3 neighborhood mosques and 5 large and small *han*s for travellers. There are 40 shops, but no *bedestan*; the shops are quite sufficient. One arm of the lake flows through the middle of the bazaar. Over it is a wooden bridge. The windows of the soup kitchen and the *medrese* overlook the water, and people sit here to have their meals and relax in the fresh air. This creek also serves as a harbor for all the caiques of the town and the lake.

---

[1] Evliya is quite right. The lake is fed by water which flows underground from Lake Prespa.

Ve bu şehr içre yılda bir kerre panayur-ı ʿaẓīm yaʿnī bāzār durup qırq elli biñ adam cemʿ olup on (13) gün on géce bir hāy [u] hūy bāzār-ı cemʿiyyet-i kübrā olur kim vaṣfında lisān qāṣırdır. Şehir ḫāricinde cümle üçyüz ʿaded (14) panayır dükkānları vardır ve niçe biñ dükkān daḫi bāzār maḥallinde çalaş [u] malaş [u] balaşdan dükkānlar binā édüp kār [ü] kesb édüp (15) giderler.

Bunda aʿyān-ı kibārdan ḫānedān ṣāḥibi Ḫalīl Aġa ve ʿÖmer Aġa ve İmām Efendi ṣofra ṣāḥibi kimesnelerdir. Bunda daḫi (16) cümle aḥbāb ile vedāʿlaşup yarar refīqler alup Usturqadan cānib-i qıbleye göl kenārınca bāġlar ve bāġçeler geçüp ve Uşṭuq (17) yaylaġından énen āb-ı ḥayāt ṣu Oḫri Göline qarışdıġı maḥalde Oḫri-zādeniñ balıq avlayacaq dalyanın geçüp (18) bu maḥalden tā Oḫriye varınca göl kenārınca sekiz biñ adım kārgīr-binā beyāż ṭaşlı vāsiʿ qaldırımdır, anı geçüp 3 sāʿatde

(19) *Der beyān-ı evṣāf-ı dār-ı māhī, yaʿnī qalʿe-yi ḫurrem-ābād-ı Oḫri.* (20) Sebeb-i tesmiyesi ----- dir. Bānīsi bi-qavl-i müverriḫān-ı Latin ibtidā Rūm pādişāhlarında[n] Melik Racʿīm (21) ibni ḥażret-i Süleymān ʿaṣrında Melik Racʿīmiñ Oḫri nām bir ḥekīmi ʿilm-i ḥikmet ile bu qalʿeyi binā édüp niçe divelden divele intiqāl etdügin (22) İslāmbolı binā éden Yanqo ibni Madyanıñ qarındaşı Yanvan ve müverriḫ-i Latin Ban bu qalʿeniñ evṣāf [u] ʿimāretin ġāyet (23) mufaṣṣal yazmışlar, ammā biz iḫtiṣār üzre güzer édelim. Çünki bu şehir bu Oḫri Buḥeyresi kenārında Medāyin ve Baġdād ve Mıṣır ve (24) Buzanṭa ve Makedonya ve Qavala ve Qusṭantiniyye qadar maʿmūr bender-i sevād-ı muʿaẓẓam olup balıġıñ maḥṣūlāt-ı menāfiʿinden niçe yüz ʿaded (25) ḫazāyin taḥṣīl olduġın yedi qıral istimāʿ etdiklerinde cümlesi birer yüzden ṭamaʿ-ı ḫāmlara düşüp bu şehre niçe (26) kerre her biri istīlā etdiklerinden şehir ḫarāba müʾeddī olduġından yazıqları gelüp āḫir-i kār yedi qıral iştirāk-i sevī (27) üzre bu Oḫri şehrin żabṭ u rabṭ etmege ʿahd-i mīs̱āq édüp yedi qıralıñ vezīrleri oṭururdı. Evvelā biri (28) Rūm tekurı ve biri Fireng-i Bunduqani ve biri Ṣırf Dest-poṭ ve biri Bulġar ve biri Hersek-i Latin ve biri İşpanya (29) ṭarâfından Arnavud ve biri Voyniq Ban, bu mezkūr yedi ʿaded qırallar bu şehri iştirāk-i sevī üzre taṣarrufda ikenler (30) sene ----- tārīḫinde qoca Sulṭān Murād Ḫān-ı s̱ānī yedi

A great market fair is held once a year in this town, where 40,000 to 50,000 people gather and there is an indescribable commotion for 10 days and nights. There are 300 permanent shops for the fair outside the town and several thousand wicker huts and stalls are set up annually for transient traders.

Among the better homes open to visitors here are those of Halil Aga, Ömer Aga and Imam Efendi.

After bidding farewell to all our friends in Struga, we took an armed escort and set off southeastwards along the lake shore, passing through vineyards and gardens to the fishing weirs of Ohri-zade. These are situated where the waters of the lake are joined by the stream rushing down from the mountain pastures of Istok. From here to Ohrid, a distance of 8000 paces along the lakeside, there is a wide pavement of white cobblestones. In 3 more hours we entered

The abode of fish (mahi), the felicitous fortress of Ohrid (Okhri). The reason for its naming is ----- . According to the Latin historians it was founded during the reign of King Rehoboam, son of Solomon. This King Rehoboam, who was one of the ancient Greek emperors, had a philosopher named Okhri who constructed this fortress according to philosophical principles. It then passed from one dynasty to the next. There is an elaborate description of it in the history of Yanvan,[1] who was the brother of Yanko son of Madyan, the founder of Istanbul, and also in the history of Latin Ban; what I am giving here is a mere summary. Because of its position on the shore of Lake Ohrid, the city became a large and prosperous emporium, comparable to Ctesiphon, Baghdad, Cairo, Byzantium, Macedonia, Kavala and Constantinople. The Seven Kings — i.e., the Byzantine emperor, the Doge of Venice, the Despot of Serbia, the kings of Bulgaria and of Hercegovina, the king of Spain as represented by Albania, and the Ban of Voyniq — hearing of the vast treasures accruing to the city from the fishing trade, each coveted it for himself, and each of them conquered it several times. As a result, the city became ruined. Finally, taking pity, the seven kings agreed together and decided, according to a pact drawn up by their viziers, how to rule it in concert. This was the situation when Sultan Murad II conquered

[1] Evliya's name for *Kitāb al-'Unwān* by Agapios (10th cent.), Evliya's source for the legends of Yanko ibn Madyan and Constantinople; see Stéphane Yerasimos, *La fondation de Constantinople et de Sainte-Sophie dans les traditions turques* (Paris 1990; Tk. tr. Istanbul 1993), ch. 2.

qıral ellerinden feth édüp Edirnede qul ġulū-yı ʿām édüp "Murād Ḫān qocadır" (31) deyü ḫilāfetden ḫalʿ édüp Ebū'l-fetḥi ḫalīfe etdikleri maḥalde yedi qıral fürce bulup bu qalʿeyi dest-i İslāmdan alup dest-i (32) küffārda bu qalʿe qaldıqda yine qul ġulū édüp "Ebū'l-fetiḥ küçükdür, iş görmemiş ġulāmdır, yine Murād Ḫān qoca qurnazdır, (33) düşmenden intiqām alur" deyü yine sene ----- tārīḫinde tekrār ḫalīfe olduqda ibtidā yine ġazāsı bu Oḫri qalʿesi olup cümle yedi (34) qıral-ı żāl banlarınıñ ʿaskerlerin dendān-ı tīġ-i āteş-tābdan geçirüp andan ikinci fetḥi taḫt-i Qaydefā İzmir qalʿesin feth édüp ḥikmet-i ḫüdā **[369b]** defʿa-yı s̱āniyede yine Murād Ḫānı ḫalʿ édüp yine tekrār Ebū'l-fetiḥ müstaqil qarār-[dā]de pādişāh-ı cem-kişver olduqda ol aralıqda küffār-ı feccār (2) Oḫri qalʿesine istīlā édüp bi'z-zāt Meḥemmed Ḫān Siroz ve Zihne ve Manaṣṭır semtlerine geldikde ʿaṭf-ı ʿinānın Oḫri qalʿesine (3) çevirüp sene ----- tārīḫinde tekrār dest-i İslāma girüp ilā-mā-şā'a'llāh qabża-yı İslāmdadır.

Ḥālā Süleymān Ḫān taḥrīri üzre Rūm-éli (4) eyāletinde sancaq begi taḫtidir kim başqa ḥükūmetdir. Beginiñ qānūn-ı qadīm üzre ḫāṣṣı 235299 aqçedir ve zeʿāmeti 60 ve (5) tīmārı 342 ʿadeddir. Alay begi ve çeri başısı vardır. Qānūn-ı pādişāhī üzre cemīʿi erbāb-ı tīmārları cebelüleri ile (6) yedi biñ ʿaded güzīde pür-silāḥ ʿasker olup Rūm-éli eyāleti vezīri sancaġı altında me'mūr olduqları sefere giderler. Ḥākimlerinden sipāh (7) ketḫüdā yeri, yeñiçeri serdārı, qalʿe dizdārı, yetmiş ʿaded qalʿe neferātları var, ammā baʿżı neferātları qānūn üzre qalʿeyi vere (8) ile veren Rūm kefereleri neferātlardır kim cemīʿi tekālīflerden berīlerdir, ve qalʿeniñ taʿmīr ü termīmine me'mūr olduqlarından her şāqqadan (9) muʿāf [u] müsellemlerdir, ammā ġayri-müslimlerdir. Ve ḥākim-i şerʿī şeyḫü'l-islāmı ve naqībü'l-eşrāfı ve aʿyān [u] eşrāfı. Ve üçyüz aqçe pāye ile şerīf (10) qażāsı, ve cümle nāḥiyesi üç ʿadeddir, biri Usturqadır ve biri Rasnadır ve biri Oḫridir, ġayri nāḥiyeleri yoqdur. Ve cümle (11) sancaġı yüz qırq pāre maʿmūr u ābādān qurālardır kim Rūm-élinde Yanya livāsından ṣoñra bu Oḫri sancaġı ġāyet maʿmūr u müzeyyendir. (12) Ḥākimān-ı ʿörfīleri muḥtesib aġası ve şehir voyvadası ve bācdār aġası ve balıq emīni aġası ve ḫarāc aġası ve pandur aġası (13) ve martolosān aġası ve yedi ʿaded qalʿe aġaları ve şehir ketḫüdāsı ve miʿmār aġası ve kefereler üzre portoyorozları vardır.

it from the Seven Kings in the year ----- . Then the janissaries rebelled in Edirne, removed Murad II from the sultanate on the grounds that he was too old, and appointed Mehmed II. During this period of disorder the Seven Kings recaptured Ohrid. The janissaries rebelled again, this time on the grounds that Mehmed was too young and inexperienced, and so they reappointed Murad II as a sly old sultan who would take revenge on their enemies. When he became sultan for the second time in the year ----- his first campaign was to recover this fortress of Ohrid and put to the sword all the troops of the errant Seven Kings. After his second campaign, the conquest of Izmir and the throne of Queen Candace, by God's wisdom Murad was removed from the sultanate a second time and Mehmed reappointed, and the tricky infidels once again occupied Ohrid. As Sultan Mehmed approached on his campaign against Serres and Zihna and Manastir he turned his reins toward Ohrid. It passed into the hands of the Muslims for the third and final time in the year ----- .

According to the register of Sultan Suleyman, Ohrid is an independent *sancak* in the *eyalet* of Rumelia. It is a *has* for which the *beg* receives an income of 235,299 *akçe* from the sultan. It has 60 *zeamet*s and 342 *timar*s. It has an *alay-beg* and a *çeribaşı*. In times of war, according to statute, the timariots, including their armed retainers, provide 7000 soldiers and march under the banner of the governor of Rumelia. Magistrates include a steward of the *sipahi*s, a commander of the janissaries and a castle warden plus a garrison of 70 troops. Some of the latter, according to statute, are the Byzantine troops who surrendered the fortress to the Ottomans and who, although they are Christian, are exempt from all onerous impositions, in exchange for maintaining the fortress in good repair. *Şeriat* magistrates include a *şeyhülislam* and a *nakibüleşraf*, plus the town notables and descendants of the Prophet. There is a *kadi* with a salary level of 300 *akçe* and there are 3 *kadi*-districts: Struga, Resen and Ohrid. The *sancak* contains 140 prosperous villages — indeed, in the *eyalet* of Rumelia, this *sancak* of Ohrid is second in prosperity only to that of Janina. Secular magistrates include a market inspector, a *voyvoda*, a collector of tolls, an *emin* of the fisheries, a poll-tax official, a chief of the gendarme corps (*pandur*), a chief of the Christian militia corps (*martolosan*), 7 garrison officers, a town mayor, a chief architect, and several Christian community leaders (*portoyoroz*).

(14) *Der ṣıfat-i eşkāl-i girdāgird-i qal'e-yi Oẖri.* Evvelā Oẖri Göliniñ şimāli kenārında bir yalçın qırmızı qaya püşte-yi 'ālī üzre şekl-i (15) muẖammes bir şeddādī binā-yı 'atīq seng-ṭırāş qal'e-yi ṣavaş kār-ı qadīm ve bir sūr-ı üstüvār rabāṭ-ı 'aẓīmdir kim dāyiren-mā dār cirmi (16) dörd biñ dörd yüz adımdır. Ve bir bayır üzre ṭaşra qal'esi içinde şimāle nāẓır bir köşedeki qal'e-yi kebīr dīvārına muttaṣıl (17) biñ adım cirminde bir ṣa'b iç ḥiṣārı vardır, dīvārınıñ qaddi kāmil qırq arşın 'ālīdir, ve şīrīn-kārlıq ile (18) üstād-ı mühendis gūnāgūn muṣanna' ebrāclar ve gūnāgūn metīn bedenler tertīb eylemiş kim miṡli bir qal'ede yoqdur. El-ḥāṣıl bir sedd-i (19) metīn iç qal'edir. Ve cümle iki 'aded qapusı var. Biri qıbleye nāẓır büyük qapudur kim Ḫünkār cāmi'ine nāẓırdır, ve bu qapu (20) üzre qullede bir taẖta örtüli serāmed köşki vardır, şeb [ü] rūz mihter-ẖāne anda çalınır, ve bu qapunuñ ṭaşrasında daẖi bir lonca (21) qaṣrı var, cihān-nümādır. Ve bir qapusı daẖi şimāl ṭarâfında aşağı varoşa açılır. Ve derūn-ı qal'ede bir mescid ve dizdār ẖānesi ve ġılāl (22) enbārı va[r], ġayri şey yoqdur, mā-'adā yerleri bāġçelerdir.

Ammā ṭaşra büyük qal'e dīvārı on arşın yüksekdir, ve cümle qırq (23) 'aded qulle ve dirseklerdir, ammā dendān-ı bedenleri ṣaymadım, lākin dīvārı on beş ayaq enli ve metīn ü müstaḥkem dīvār-ı şeddādīdir. (24) Ve cümle üc 'aded qapuları vardır, biri iç qal'e altında şimāle nāẓır göl ṭarâfındaki varoşa enilir büyük qapudur, ve biri (25) şarq ṭarâfına ṭabaqlar qapusıdır, ve biri büyük göl qapusıdır. Ve bu ṭaşra qal'eniñ maşrıqdan şimāle ve yıldız cānibinde ve (26) ġarbında ṣa'b u metīn qal'e dīvārları vardır, ve ol ṭaraflar cümle bayırlardır, ammā göl ṭarâfı ki qal'eniñ qıble ve cenūb ṭaraflarıdır (27) kim ol semtler yalçın qanara serāmed qayalar olmaġile maẖūf u muẖāṭara uçurum bī-emān çāh-ı esfelleri yerler olup bu ṭaraflarda aṣlā (28) qal'e dīvārları yoqdur ve lāzım da degildir, lākin gāhīce ḥayvānlar düşüp pāre pāre olurlar, tā bu mertebe evce ser-çekmiş qayalardır. (29) Zemān-ı evāyilde bu uçurum ṭaraflarına qorquluq şekilli dīvārlar binā eylemişler, ammā mürūr-ı eyyām ile cābecā yerleri münhedim olmuş.

(30) Ve bu büyük qal'e içinde cümle yüz altmış 'aded la'l-gūn muṣanna' kiremit örtüli cihān-nümā kefere ẖāneleri vardır, cümle(31)siniñ daqqa ve revzenleri cenūb cānibinde göle nāẓır şīrīn-kārlı ma'mūr evlerdir ve cümle biri biri üzre mürtefi' dār-ı menḥūslardır. (32) Ammā aşağı göl kenārında paşa sarāyı yaẖşı sarāydır kim üçyüzden mütecāviz içli ve ṭaşralı ve ḥammāmlı ve vāsi'

Shape of the fortress. It is an ancient and solidly-constructed pentagonal fortress, 4400 paces in circumference, situated atop a bare red rock cliff on the northern shore of Lake Ohrid. On one slope, within the outer fortress walls and attached to the great wall at one corner facing north, is a mighty citadel, 1000 paces in circumference. The citadel walls are 40 ells in height and outfitted with all sorts of embrasures and crenels of incomparable workmanship. It has 2 gates. The larger one, facing north toward the Hünkâr mosque, is topped by a tower with a high wood-ceilinged portico where the military band plays day and night, and outside the gate is another portico, or loggia, affording a view of the surroundings. The smaller gate, also on the northern side, opens to the lower town. Within the citadel, other than a prayer-house, the warden's house, and a grain-storage bin, there are only gardens.

As for the great walls of the outer fortress, they are 10 ells in height, and include a total of 40 towers and battlements. I did not count the crenelations, but the walls are 5 feet thick and very solid. There are 3 gates: one, the Great Gate, faces north below the citadel and heads down to the lower town in the direction of the lake; another, the Tanners' Gate, faces east; the third, also large, is the Lake Gate. This outer fortress has strong defense walls running from east to north on the north-western and western sides, where there is open country. But no walls are necessary along the lake, or on the south-eastern and eastern sides where there are sheer cliffs dropping precipitately — so steep, in fact, that sometimes animals tumble down and are dashed to pieces. In ancient times a kind of parapet wall was built, but over the centuries it has largely collapsed.

Within the great outer fortress are 160 Christian houses roofed with red tiles, all nicely built with balconies and windows facing south overlooking the lake, inauspicious abodes piled one atop the other. Below, on the lake shore, is the Pasha's palace, a fine and grand mansion completely covered with tiles and having over 300 rooms, including indoors and outdoors, baths, and a large courtyard.

meydānlı ve müte'addid (33) ḥücreli ve serāpā kiremit örtüli ẖānedān-ı 'aẓīmdir. Derūn-ı qal'ede bundan ma'mūr sarāy-ı kebīr yoqdur, lākin 'avān ẖānesidir kim ẖarābe (34) olmadadır. Ve cümle 3 'aded miḥrāblardır.

Der esmā'-ı cevāmi'-i selāṭīn-i qal'e-yi 'aẓīm-i iremizāt. Evvelā paşa sarāyı dibinde göl **[370a]** kenārında Aya Ṣofya cāmi'i, ġāyet ulu cāmi'dir kim mis̱li meger Selanikde ve Qara Deñiz sāḥilinde Ṭarab-efzūnda ve İslāmbolda Küçük (2) Aya Ṣofya cāmi'leri ola. Ammā bu Aya Ṣofya cāmi'i hażret-i Süleymān oğlı Melik Rac'īm 'aṣrında Yanvan qarındaşı Oẖr[i] nām qıralıñ (3) bināsıdır, ol binā etmek ile anıñ ismiyle müsemmā olup bu şehriñ ismi Oẖri Bandır, ammā lisān-ı Rūmda ismi ----- -[a]ndir ve (4) ve lisān-ı Latinde ----- -i fülāndır, lisān-ı Firengde ----- dir. Ammā bu ol 'aṣrıñ keferesi 'aṣrında bilā-teşbīh Qudüsleri imiş. Ḥamd-i (5) ẖüdā şimdi ma'bedgāh-ı müslimīndir. Lākin ba'żı zemān kefereler bevvāblara nihānīce bir qaç aqçe verüp cāmi'e girüp fī'l-ḥāl teberrüken āyīn-i 'İsāyı (6) édüp ṭaşra çıqarlar. Cümle ṣaġīr ü kebīr on yedi 'ad[ed] qubbe-yi 'aẓīmlerdir, ammā cümle qırmızı kiremit ile ve ẖorâsānī kireç ile mestūr (7) cāmi'-i pür-nūrdur. Bunda olan ās̱ār-ı qadīmeleri ve 'amūd-ı müntehāları birer birer ta'bīr ü tavṣīf etsem tażyī'-i evqāt olup ve vaṣfında (8) lisān qāṣır ve qalemler kāsirdir, ammā ġarīb cāmi'-i vīrāne yüz dutmuşdur. Niçe muṣanna' pirinc qapuları ve ṣadefkārī pencere qanatları fenā bulmuşdur, (9) zīrā aṣlā cemā'ati yoqdur, cümle kefere içinde qalmışdır. Eger müstaqillen kefere elinde qalsa bu cāmi'i ürdibihişt éderlerdi. Ancaq haftada (10) bir kerre cum'a gün qapuları açılup ẖuddāmları silüp süpürüp beş on 'aded pāsbānlar cum'a namazın qılup yine qapuların sedd (11) édüp giderler. Ve ḥīn-i fetiḥde Fetḥiyye cāmi'i bu idi, ẖüdā 'amār eyleye.

Andan yuqaru iç qal'e öñinde bir mürtefi' yerde cāmi'-i Oẖri-zāde. (12) Bunlar ḥasīb [ü] nesīb ẖānedān ṣāḥibi qıral-zādeler imiş, ḥālā bu şehir anlarıñ ḥükminde fermān-berdir. Bir qurşumlı ve taẖta qubbe örtüli (13) ve bir kārgīr mināreli bir müferr[iḥ] cāmi' binā éderken Allāhu a'lem Sulṭān Bāyezīd-i Velī bir ġazāya giderken bu cāmi'i görüp "Poh bāreke'llāh (14) ne güzel cāmi' olmuş" dédikde hemān

There is nothing this fine within the town walls, only rough houses going to ruin. The town has a total of 3 prayer-niches.

Imperial mosques. First is the Aya Sofya congregational mosque, situated on the lake shore at the foot of the Pasha's palace. It is very large, comparable to the congregational mosques in Thessalonika and in Trebizond on the Black Sea, or to the Little Aya Sofya in Istanbul. As for this Aya Sofya, it was built by the king named Okhri, the brother of Yanvan, during the reign of King Rehoboam, son of Solomon. Since he built it, the city was named after him Okhri Ban, in Greek ----- *-an*, in Latin ----- *-i fulan*,[1] in Frankish ----- . In those Christian days this was their Jerusalem — saving the comparison! — but now, God be praised, it is a prayer-hall of the Muslims. Occasionally, however, Christians manage to enter the mosque by slipping a few *akçe*s to the doorkeepers; they hold a quick prayer-service in honor of Jesus, then depart. This light-filled mosque contains 17 great domes and is totally covered with red tiles and mortar. It would take too long to enumerate all of the ancient remains and the lofty columns on the inside — tongues fall short and pens are too weak to describe them — but it is an isolated mosque, slowly going to ruin. Several finely-wrought brass doors and wooden shutters with inlay mother-of-pearl are in a terrible condition. The reason is that the mosque is stranded in the midst of the Christians and has no Muslim congregation. Were it to be completely abandoned to the Christians they would turn this mosque into a month of April.[2] Only once a week, on Friday, the doors are opened, the servants sweep it out, and five or ten guards perform the Friday noon prayer. Then they shut the doors again and leave. At the time of the conquest this was the Fethiyye or "Conquest" mosque — may God restore it to prosperity!

Above, on a hill in front of the citadel, is the congregational mosque of Okhri-zade. These Okhri-zades are a dynasty which trace their ancestry back to kings, and even now the city is under their sway. The story goes that during the construction of this cheerful mosque, with its lead-covered wooden domes and one stonework minaret, Sultan Bayezid II passed through Ohrid while on campaign and remarked, "God bless, what a beautiful mosque!" The quick-

---

[1] *Fülān* ("such-and-such") here is a jocular addition, as though in all languages the original name of the city ended in *-an*.

[2] Ürdibihişt. The import of this phrase is unclear.

'āqıbet-endīş [ü] dūr-bīn-fikir Oḫri-zāde zemīn-būs édüp "Ḫüdā qabūl eyleye, ṣavābı ve bināsı (15) pādişāhıma hibe olsun" déd[ikd]e pādişāh ḥażż édüp "Tīz ṣaġ ṭarâfına bir mināre-yi 'ālī daḫi binā etsinler" deyü fermān etdiklerinde binā édüp (16) ol ecilden ḥālā iki mināreli olup Ḫünkār cāmi'i derler. Ġāyet evqāfları metīn cāmi'-i cihān-nümādır. Cümle göl cenūb ṭarâfında nümāyān olup (17) cemī'i keştīleriñ ve cümle balıqcı qayıqlarınıñ şināverlik etdikleri nümāyāndır. Ve qıblesi öñinde revzenlerinden buḥeyre ve ṣaḥrā-[yı] bī-pāyān içre (18) cümle 'amāristān ẓāhir ü bāhirdir. Ve ḥarêminde kehkeşān-āsā semāya ser-çekmiş diraḫt-i müntehālar var kim her biriniñ ẓıll-i ḥimāyesindeki (19) çemenzār yerlerde cümle eḥibbā vü[1] yārān-ı bā-ṣafā-yı erbāb-ı me'ārifāt oṭurup kesb-i ṭarāvetler édüp mübāḥaṣe-yi 'ilm-i şar'iyyeler édüp bir ṭarafda (20) daḫi levendāt maqūlesi tāze cüvānlar gūnāgūn lu'bede-bāzlıqlar ve silāḥşorluqlar ta'līm etmededirler. Ve bu cāmi'-i pür-envārıñ qıble (21) qapusınıñ 'atebe-yi 'ulyāsı üzre celī ḫaṭ ile "Lā ilāhe illā'llāh, Muḥammedün resūlü'llāh" şehād[et]i taḥrīr olunmuşdur.

Ve bu qal'ede bunlar(22)dan ġayri cümle iki 'aded maḥalle mesācidleri vardır. Anlar daḫi cemā'atden ġarīblerdir. Ammā altı 'aded kefere manaṣṭırları var, (23) eyle ma'mūrdur kim ve eyle müzeyyen ü ābādāndır kim her birinde qırqar ve ellişer 'aded rühbān paṭriqleri vardır. Cümleden Patirgāh deyri ve (24) Latin deyri ġāyet ma'mūrdur kim ṣubḥ [u] mesā maṭbaḫ-i mesīḥiyyesinde papaslara ni'metleri çıqdıça müsülmānlara daḫi ni'met-i firāvān (25) bezl éderler. Ve bu qal'ede aṣlā ḫān u ḥammām ve çārsū-yı bāzār yoqdur. Mā-'adā arż-ı ḫāliye yerleri cümle bāġ u bāġçe ve niçe dölüm (26) arż-ı ḫāliye yerleri vardır, zīrā büyük qal'edir.

Der sitāyiş-i aşaġı şehr-i 'aẓīm-i iremzāt. Ġāyet ma'mūr u müzeyyendir kim (27) gūyā Şām-ı cennet-meşām-ı merāmdır, vaṣfında lisān qāṣırdır. Uşṭuq yaylasından énerken bu şehri gören adamlar Edirne ve Bursa (28) qadar vardır derler.

Ammā der 'aded-i esmā'-ı maḥallāt-ı Oḫri. Cümle on yedi 'aded maḥallātlardır, onı müsülmān maḥallesidir, (29) yedisi kefere-yi Rūm ve Bulġar ve Latin maḥallātlarıdır. Evvelā cümle maḥallātlardan ma'mūr u müzeyyen Oḫri-zāde maḥallesi ve Tekye (30) maḥallesi ve Qul-oġlı maḥallesi ve Ḥaydar Paşa maḥallesi ve Qoca Siyāvuş Pa[şa]nıñ medrese maḥallesi ve Ẓulmiyye maḥallesi ve (31) Ḥācī

[1] Text: *veyā*.

witted and far-sighted Okhri-zade immediately kissed the ground and cried, "Please God, let all the merit for it go as a gift to my Padishah!" This pleased the Sultan greatly. "Have them construct another lofty minaret on the right side," he commanded. For this reason it has two minarets and is the Hünkâr ("Imperial") mosque. Its endowments are very sound. To the south it commands a view of the entire lake, with all its commercial and fishing boats, and through the windows in front of the prayer-niche one can see the lake as well as the broad plain and all the fields and buildings. The courtyard is graced by huge lofty trees, in the shadow of which are grassy knolls where the town's cognoscenti and mystics sit to enjoy the fresh air and to engage in religious debates, while to one side the young bloods of the town engage in sports and military exercises. Above the lintel of the prayer-niche door, in *celi* script, is written the witness formula: "There is no god but God, Muhammad is the messenger of God."

Aside from these there are also 2 neighborhood mosques within the fortress walls, but these too are isolated from their congregations. And there are 6 churches, so lively and pretty that they have 40 or 50 priests each. Two of these — the Church of the Patriarch and the Latin church — are so wealthy that their Christian kitchens provide meals morning and evening to the priests, and even to the Muslims. There are no *han*s or public baths, and no bazaars within the fortress; rather, the large space is filled with vineyards and gardens and several *dönüm*s of open fields.

The lower city. It is very handsome and prosperous, like Damascus the paradisiacal, at which the tongue falls short. Descending from the mountain pasture of Istok, one would believe it to be as large as Edirne or Bursa.

Town quarters of Ohrid. There are 17 of which 10 are Muslim and 7 are Greek, Bulgar and Latin. The richest and finest is the quarter of Okhri-zade. Others include the quarters of the Tekke, Kul-oghlu, Haydar Pasha, the Koca Siyavuş Pasha *medrese*, Zulmiye, Hadji

Ḥamza maḥallesi ve İskender Beg mescidi maḥallesi ve Yūnus Voyvada maḥallesi ve Küçi Beg maḥallesi ve Emīr Maḥmūd (32) maḥallesi ve Qara H̱oca maḥallesi, netīce-yi kelām on yedi ʻaded maḥallātlarıñ eşbehi ve maʻmūr u ābādānları bunlardır.

(33) *Der faṣl-i cevāmiʻhā-yı selāṭīn [ü] vüzerā vü kibār-ı aʻyān.* Cümle on yedi ʻaded miḥrāb-ı qıble-yi erbāb-ı ḥācātdır. Evvelā (34) cümleden cemāʻat-i kesīreye mālik göl kenārında Ḥācī Qāsım cāmiʻi, nīlgūn raṣāṣ-ı ẖāṣ qurşum örtüli çār-gūşe **[370b]** taẖta qubbe örtüli bir ṭurfa ṭarz-ı qadīm mināreli cāmiʻ-i zībādır. Andan Tekye cāmiʻi, Sulṭān Süleymān H̱ānıñdır, bir ʻaceb müferriḥ (2) cāmiʻ-i pür-nūrdur. Andan Qul-oġlı cāmiʻi, ṭarz-ı qadīmdir. Andan Ḥaydar Paşa cāmiʻi, maʻbedgāh-ı qadīmdir. Andan Ẓulmiyye (3) cāmiʻi derler ammā münevver cāmiʻdir, lākin iḥtimāldir ẓulm ile binā olunmuş ola. Andan Ḥācī Ḥamza cāmiʻi. Andan yuqaru (4) qalʻede çifte minareli H̱ünkār cāmiʻi. Andan qalʻede Aya Ṣofya-yı kebīr cāmiʻi. Bu mezkūr cevāmiʻler meşhūr-ı āfāq maʻbedgāhlardır.

(5) *Der defter-i mesācidhā-yı mü'mināt-ı ʻābidāt.* Cümle 17 ʻaded maḥallāt buqʻalarıdır. Evvelā cümleden İskender Beg mescidi ve (6) Yūnus Voyvada mescidi ve Küçi Beg mescidi ve Emīr Maḥmūd mescidi ve Çārsū mescidi ve Çınārlı mescid ve Qara H̱oca (7) mescidi, el-ḥāṣıl on yedi ʻaded cāmiʻ olmaġa müstaʻid mesācidler vardır,[1] her biriniñ evqāfları metīn olup ẖuddāmları mevcūddur.

(8) *Der vaṣf-ı sarāy-ı aʻyān-ı aġavāt ve ġayri büyūt-i mü'mināt.* Cümle sicill-i şerʻde merqūm olduġı üzre dördyüz (9) ʻaded kiremitli kārgīr binālı taḥtānī ve fevqānī cümle ravża-yı rıżvān mis̱illi bāġ-ı cinānlı vāsiʻ ẖānedān-ı şehr-i ʻaẓīmdir kim (10) bāġ u bāġçesiyle Oẖri ṣaḥrāsın zeyn etmişdir, gören bu şehri on on beş biñ evlerdir der. Ve bu şehr-i muʻaẓẓam eṭrā(11)fında aṣlā qalʻe yoqdur, hemā[n] şimāli ve ġarbı ve cenūbı ve qıblesi ṭarâfı Oẖri Göli olup şarq ṭarafı tā Uştuq (12) yaylası eteklerine varınca serāpā ẖıyābān-ı gül-i gülistān içre bir şehr-i merāmdır, eṭrāfına qalʻe olmaq muḥāldir, zīrā bāġçe(13)leri ve müşebbek būstānları cihānı zeyn etmişdir. Cümleden mükellef ü mükemmel sarāy-ı ʻaẓīm Oẖri-zāde sarāyı qalʻe-(14)mis̱āldir, müteʻaddid dīvān-ẖāneleri ve ıṣṭabılları ve göl kenārında maqṣūreleri [vardır]. Ve qarındaşınıñ sarāyı daẖi ʻibretdir. Bunlar meşhūrdur.

(15) *Der qāyime-yi medāris-i ʻālimān-ı müfessirān.* Cümle iki ʻaded dārü't-tedrīs-i ʻālimāndır. Evvelā[2] göl kenārında (16) mezkūr

---

[1] Text: *vrardır.*

[2] *Evvelā* twice in the text.

Hamza, the Iskender Beg mosque, Voyvoda Yunus, Küçi Beg, Emir Mahmud, Kara Hoca. These are the most important and most prosperous of the 17 quarters.

Congregational mosques of the sultans, viziers, and notables. There are a total of 17 prayer-niches. First, and possessing the largest congregation, is the Hadji Kasım mosque, situated on the lake shore. It is a handsome square building surmounted by a wooden dome and roofed with fine blue-colored lead; it has one quaint old-fashioned minaret. Others include the Tekke mosque, built by Sultan Suleyman, full of light and good cheer; the Kul-oghlu mosque, old-fashioned; the Haydar Pasha mosque, quite new; the Zulmiye or "Oppression" mosque, so-called, but it is a splendid mosque, even though probably it was constructed with oppression; the Hadji Hamza mosque. Also, up in the fortress, is the Hünkâr mosque with two minarets; and the great Aya Sofya mosque. Those listed here are the most famous.

Neighborhood mosques. These are 17 in number, beginning with that of Iskender Beg, and including the Voyvoda Yunus mosque, the Küçi Beg mosque, the Emir Mahmud mosque, the bazaar mosque, the mosque with the plane tree, and the Kara Hoca mosque. All 17 are solidly endowed and well kept up; indeed, any of them might also serve as a congregational mosque.

Mansions of the notables and other houses. The *şeriat* court register lists 400 two-storied tile-roofed stone houses. These large houses with their lush vineyards and gardens are spread over the Ohrid plain so attractively that one judging from afar would say the city had ten or fifteen thousand houses. This large urban area is completely unwalled. Rather, it is bounded by Lake Ohrid to the north, west, south, and south-east, and by the foothills of the mountain pasture of Istok to the east, like one big rose garden. Indeed, it would not be possible to surround it with a wall, so extensive are the flower gardens and the vegetable gardens. Finest of all the mansions is the huge Okhri-zade palace, like a castle with its numerous audience halls and stables and its pleasure-domes and gazebos along the lake. His brother's palace is also quite remarkable. These are the best known houses.

Medreses. There are 2 colleges for training religious personnel. The first is the old Siyavuş Pasha *medrese*, situated on the lake shore across the street and to the left of the Hadji Kasım mosque, like a

el-Ḥācī Qāsım cāmi'iniñ ṣolında yol aşırısında eski Siyāvuş Paşa medresesi, gūyā bāġ-ı Ṣudaqdır, (17) ḥarêminiñ eṭrāfında müte'addid ḥücreleri var, ders-i 'āmmı ve ṭalebeleri mevcūd olup her ḥücreniñ ṭalebelerine cānib-i vaqıfdan (18) laḥmiyye ve şem'iyyesi mu'ayyendir. Andan Süleymān Ḫānıñ tekye medresesi, bu daḫi ma'mūr. Ve niçe zāviye medreseleri daḫi vardır.

(19) *Der şarḥ-ı dārü'l-ḥadīs̱-i muḥaddis̱ān.* Cümle bir yerde 'ilm-i ḥadīs̱ ve 'ilm-i tecvīd tilāvet olunur, ammā muḥaddis̱i ve ḥamele-yi (20) ḥāfıẓ-ı Qur'ānı meşhūr degildir, 'ilm-i tecvīdde ancaq Ḥafṣ qırā'ati tilāvet olunup 'ilm-i ḥadīs̱de kitāb-ı Buḫārī oqunur.

(21) *Der ta'rīf-i mekteb-i ciger-gūşe-yi püserān.* Cümle yedi 'aded dārü't-ta'līm-i ebced-ḫāndır. Evvelā Oḫri-zāde mektebi ve Aġa mektebi var.

(22) *Der şehr-engīz-i ḫān-ı ḫvācegiyān-ı tüccārān.* Cümle üç 'aded ḫān-ı zībālardır, ammā ṣāḥibü'l-ḫayrātların sü'āl etmedim.

(23) *Der ta'rīf-i ḥammām-ı ġāsilān-ı rāḥat-i cān.* Cümle iki 'aded ḥammām-ı ḫāṣṣ [u] 'āmları vardır. Evvelā biri Oḫri-zāde (24) ḥammāmı, ṭarz-ı qadīmdir ammā ḫoş-havādır. Ve biri Ġāzī Ḥüseyn Paşa ḥammāmıdır, havāsı ve bināsı laṭīf ḥammām-ı rūşenādır.

(25) *Der tavṣīf-i ḥammām-ı maḫṣūṣ-ı kibār-ı a'yān-ı vilāyet.* Ālüfteleriniñ naqılları üzre cümle yetmiş yedi 'aded sarāy ḥammāmlarımız (26) vardır deyü tefāḫür kesb éderler, ḥaqīqatü'l-ḥāl vardır. Evvelā Oḫri-zāde Beg-cuġazıñ sarāyında iki ḥammāmı var, (27) ve qarındaşı ----- Efendi sarāyı ḥammāmı var, ve -----

(28) *Der taḥrīr-i 'aded-i çārsū-yı bezzāzistān.* Cümle yüz elli 'aded dükkānlardır, ve yedi 'aded mükellef ü müzeyyen mecma'ü'l-'irfān (29) qahve-ḫāneleri vardır, ammā boz[a]-ḫāne ve meyḫāneleri āşkārede yoqdur, lākin qal'ede kefere maḥallelerinde bāde-yi nābı ġāyet çoqdur, (30) lākin bezzāzistānı yoqdur, yine her gūne metā'lar firāvāndır, lākin çārsūsı dörd yerde pārekende ve perīşāndır. Ve (31) şāhrāh çārsūsı ṣoqaqları içre 'aẓīm diraḫt-i sāye-dār çınār-ı müntehālarla zeyn olmuşdur, ammā eks̱eriyyā çeşmeleri mu'aṭṭaldır (32) ve şuya daḫi iḥtiyācı yoqdur, zīrā göl ṣuyı gibi āb-ı ḥayāti var iken çeşme-sārlar lāz[ım] degildir, anıñiçün cümle 'uyūnları baṭṭāldır (33) ve eks̱eriyyā ḫānedān-ı 'aẓīmleri göl kenārına vāqı' olmuşdur. -----

(34) *Der temdīḥ-i āb [u] havā-yı ḫūb-ı cāvidān.* Āb [u] havāsınıñ leṭāf[et]inden maḥbūbı ve maḥbūbeleri ġāyet çoqdur, cümle sīm-ten ü nāzik- **[371a]** endām ehline nerm [ü] rām maḥbūbü'l-qulūb cüvānları

garden of Sudak.[1] The courtyard is surrounded by numerous cells. There are classes of public instruction, and the *medrese* students occupying the cells are appointed rations of meat and candles by the endowment. The second is the Tekke *medrese*, built by Sultan Suleyman, also thriving. There are several other *medreses* attached to the dervish lodges.

Hadith schools. There is 1 school devoted to instruction in hadith and Koran recital, but neither the hadith scholars nor the Koran reciters are very prominent. In recital, only the reading according to Hafs is followed, and in hadith, Bukhari.

Primary schools. There are 7, including those of Okhri-zade and Aga.

Hans of the merchants. There are 3 fine *hans*, but I did not inquire after their endowers.

Baths. There are 2 baths open to the public: the Okhri-zade bath, old-fashioned but pleasant; and the Ghazi Hüseyn Pasha bath, with fine atmosphere and furnishings.

Private baths of the notables. The town rakes boast that there are 77 baths belonging to the large mansions, and this is true. My dear friend Okhri-zade Beg has two in his palace, and his brother ----- Efendi has one, and ----- .

Bazaars. There are 150 shops and 7 imposing and beautiful coffee houses which serve as gathering places for the cognoscenti. There are no taverns for *boza* or wine, at least none visible, but there is no lack of wine in the Christian quarters inside the fortress. Although the bazaars are spread over four different parts of the city, and there is no *bedestan*, nevertheless all types of merchandise are readily available. The bazaar in the alleys off the main highway is lined with stately shade-providing plane trees. Most of the fountains are not functioning, but indeed there is no need for them, since the lake water is pure and delicious, and most of the larger houses are situated along the shore.

Perpetually fine climate. Owing to the delightful climate there are numerous lovely boys and girls, with silvery limbs and loving

---

[1] A city in the Crimea famous for its gardens and orchards; see Evliya's description at VII 136a24-29 (654-55).

olur kim ḥüsn [ü] cemālleri ile cihān-ārā olmuşlardır, niçe cānlar bunda qalmışlardır.

(2) *Der medḥ-i ṣun'-ı ḫudā-yı güzīde-yi fākihāt.* Memdūḥātından ṭoquz gūne ayvası ve baba ayvası ve ekmek ayvası ve (3) bā-ḫuṣūṣ yigirmi dörd gūne al-alal ālūsı ve yigirmi dörd elvān emrūdları sicillātlarda mesṭūrdur kim böyle (4) ābdār [u] ḫoş-ḫv[ā]r emrūdlar Malāṭıyye şehrinde ve Kürdistānda Bitlis şehrinde ve Tebrīz vilāyetinde Tesu ve Ordubar şehir(5)lerinde böyle ābdār emrūdlar görmedim, cümleden beg emrūdı olqadar lezīz ü ābdārdır kim gūyā bir ṭolum qaṭr-ı nebātdir, lākin (6) ẓālim (?) şehriñ meyveleri bir yerden bir yére hedāyā gidemez, zīrā ġāyet terdir, ammā elması quṭularla her diyāra gidüp (7) henūz leṭāfet [ü] ḥalāveti bāqī qalup ṭūl-i zemānda tüffāḥınıñ rengine ve rāyiḥa-yı ṭayyibesine aṣlā taġayyür gelmez, ammā ġayri meyve(8)leri bir fersaḫ yére gitmez, ammā bu ḥaqīr ayvasından tā Uṣṭurumca şehrine dek pembe içinde ayva-yı sefer-celīsin getirdim.

(9) *Der vaṣf-ı ni'met-i 'uẓmā-yı me'kūlāt.* Bu şehr a'yānına maḫṣūṣdur kim qış géceleri cümle ṣıġār u kibār bir birlerine żiyāfet-i (10) 'aẓīmler édüp bir ṣoḥbetde yenilen ṭa'ām-ı nefīse bir ġayri ṣoḥbetlerde yenmeyüp her bir żiyāfetde ṭarz-ı āḫar mümessek (11) ṭa'ām-ı gūnāgūnlar yenmek bu şehre maḫṣūṣdur. Ḥulviyyātı ve gūnāgūn ḫoş-āblari keẕālik bir ṣoḥbetdeki ḫoş-āblara ve (12) ḥulviyyātlara aṣlā ve qaṭ'ā müşābehetleri yoqdur. Ḥattā Oḫ[r]i-zāde żiyāfetinde yigirmi altı gūne ḫoş-āblar yenüp bu ḥaqīr (13) ḫoş-ābdan şehīd ola yazdım. Rūm diyārında Oḫri żiyāfeti ve ḫoş-ābları meşhūr [u] memdūḥdur.

(14) *Der tektīb-i 'imāret-i dārü'l-me'kel-i sūḫtevāt.* Cümle üç 'aded yerde dārü'ż-żiyāfet-i faqīrān vardır. Evvelā yuqaru (15) qal'e öñinde Oḫri-zādeniñ pādişāha iḥsān etdügi cāmi'-i dilgüşānıñ 'imāreti ṣubḥ u mesā bay u gedāya ve (16) pīr [ü] cüvān ü gebr ü tersāya birer ṣaḥan çobrası ve birer nān pāresi faqīrāna mebzūldür. Ve biri Tekye cāmi'i 'imāreti var.

(17) *Der tasṭīr-i mihmān-sarāy-ı kārbān-revān.* Cümle üç 'aded mihmān-ḫāne-yi ḥasbīlerdir. Cümleden küçük bāzārda çınār (18) aġaçları sāyesinde qırq ocaqlı kārbān-sarāy-ı ma'mūrdur. Ve Oḫri-zāde mihmāndār-sitānı binā-yı metīndir.

(19) *Der terqīm-i binā-yı 'ibret-nümā-yı ābādān.* Cümleden cāmi'-i Aya Ṣofya-yı kebīr vācibü's-seyrdir. Ammā yuqaru qal'e öñinde (20) Oḫri-zādeniñ pādişāha hibe etdügi cāmi' öñinde bir āb-ı ḥayāt ṣu

dispositions. The beauty of the inhabitants is famous and has attracted settlers from abroad.

Fruits. Among the natural products in high repute are 9 varieties of quince, including the "father" quince and the "bread" quince; and 24 varieties each of plum and of pear are listed in the registers. Indeed, I have not seen such luscious pears even in Malatya or in Bitlis in Kurdistan or in Tesu and Ordubar in the region of Tebriz. The "*beg*" pear is so sweet and delicious that each one is like a sack of candy. Unfortunately, however, the fruits of this city do not travel well, since they are picked very fresh, and so are unsuitable for gifts. Only the apples are shipped abroad in boxes and retain their sweetness and color and fragrance. All the other fruits spoil if they are shipped just a few miles away. I was able to bring some quinces along with me wrapped in cotton as travelling companions[1] as far as Strumica.

Foods. The notables of Ohrid have the custom of feasting one another, great and small, on winter nights, and their specialty is not to repeat any of the dishes served at one party at another. The same holds true for their sweets and their sherbets: the kinds served at one gathering are never served at another. In fact, at one of the Okhri-zade feasts we were served 26 different kinds of sherbets — I was nearly sherbeted to death! The feasts and sherbets of Ohrid are famous throughout the Ottoman empire.

Soup-kitchens. There are 3 of these. One belongs to the delightful mosque in front of the fortress which Okhri-zade gave away to the Sultan as a gift. Here, morning and evening, a bowl of soup and a piece of bread are provided to the poor — indeed to everyone, rich or poor, young or old, Christian or Zoroastrian. Another belongs to the Tekke mosque.

Caravansarys. There are 3 adequate guest-houses. One is the fine 40 hearth caravansary in the shade of the plane trees in the small bazaar. Another is the sturdy Okhri-zade guest-house.

Noteworthy buildings. The great Aya Sofya congregational mosque is especially remarkable. Another impressive sight is the well of sweet water in front of the mosque which Okhri-zade presented to the

---

[1] *Sefer celīsi*, play on words with *sefercil* "quince."

quyusı var kim üstād Ferhād bu çāh-ı (21) māya eyle ferhādī külünkler urup bir bi'r-i 'ibret-nümā qazup 'umqı kāmil seksen qulaçdır. Ġarāyib anda kim (22) üstād-ı kūh-ken qayaları lağım ile delüp tā Oḫri Gölinden 'ilm-i hendese ile ṣu girüp āb dollāblarıyle ṣuyı (23) çekilüp 'imārete ve cāmi'iñ ḥavżı ve ḥanefī çeşmelerine ve ġayri yerlerde isti'māl olunur. Bir temāşāgāh-ı vācibü's-seyrdir.

(24) *Der taqrīr-i mesīregāh-ı müferriḥāt.* Bu şehriñ cānib-i erba'asında cümle on iki 'aded yerde teferrücgāh-ı erbāb-ı merāmlar var kim (25) bir diyāra maḫṣūṣ degildir illā Oḫridedir. Evvelā qayıqlar ile göl içre eyyām-ı müvāfıq ile bādbānlar açup çiftliklere (26) gidüp gūnāgūn māhīler ṣayd édüp deryā üzre 'īş [ü] 'işretler etmek bu şehre maḫṣūṣdur. Biri daḫi qal'eniñ (27) qıble ṭarâfında yol aşırı bir ṣazlı göli vardır, beş ḫarman cirminde vardır, ammā ġāyet 'amīqdir derler, anda olan gūnāgūn (28) qaz ve ördekleriñ ṣayd [ü] şikārı 'acāyibdir. Andan balıq dalyanları zevqi, andan Uştuq yaylası mesīreleri 'acāyibdirler.

(29) *Der tenqīl-i lehce-yi maḫṣūṣ-ı ehālī-yi bilād.* Cümle ḫalqı Bulġarca ve Urumca tekellüm éderler, ammā Arnavudca bilmezler, zīrā (30) Rūm-élidir, Arnavudistān degildir, lākin faṣīḥ ü belīġ lisān-ı türkī bilirler. Ġāyet şehrī ẓarīf nüktedān nükte-şināsān erbāb-ı (31) ma'ārif adamları vardır.

(32) *Der eşkāl-i libās-ı fetā-yı şecī'ān-ı delīrān.* Cümle tāze yigitler qırmızı ṣaya çoqalı semmūr ve zerdevā qalpaqlar ve gūnāgūn (33) çoqa dolamalar ve qopçalı daracıq ṣıqma çaqşırlar geyüp ayaqlarında ṣarı qubādī pāy-pūş geyüp bellerinde pala bıçaqlar (34) ṭaqup reftār éderler. Ammā iḫtiyārları başlarına gūnāgūn muṭallā destār-ı muḥammedīler ṣarup ve gūnāgūn çoqadan **[371b]** serḥaddi ve qonṭoşlar ve ferrāceler geyerler. Ammā tāzeleri gūnāgūn bol yeñli ferrāceler geyüp ve yaṣṣı başları üzre (2) dülbend çemberler bağlayup çārsū-yı bāzārdan ġayri sūq-ı sulṭānīlerde mü'eddebāne gezerler.

(3) *Der faṣl-i tetimme-yi şehr-engīz-i külliyāt-ı şehr-i Oḫri.* Evvelā bunda daḫi Manya vilāyeti muḥāfaẓasıyçün getirdigimiz emr-i pādişāhī dīvān-ı (4) pādişāhīde Oḫri begi 'Alī Beg ḥużūrında tilāvet olunup "El-emrü emrüküm" deyüp cümle 'asākir-i İslām Manya vilāyetine gitmege (5) āmāde oldılar. Bu ḥaqīre beg ikiyüz ġuruş ve bir at ve bir 'āṣī Arnavud ġulāmı ve bir qılıç iḥsān édüp ḫuddāmlara daḫi onar altun (6) iḥsān etdi. Yine zevq [ü] şevqimize muqayyed olup anlar daḫi 'asker cem'ine cidd [ü] ihtimām etdiler.

Sultan, the one in front of the fortress. The skilled miner like Ferhad who excavated it went to a depth of 80 fathoms. The marvelous thing is that, using his geometric and engineering skills, he bored a channel through the rocks so that he could draw water all the way from Lake Ohrid, using water wheels, and thus provide water for the ablutions basin and the fountains, for this mosque and others as well. It is an attraction not to be missed.

Pleasure-grounds. There are 12 delightful excursions in the vicinity of Ohrid such as are not to be found elsewhere. First, when the wind is right, you can take a sailboat on the lake and go to the farm-estates along the shore, or else go fishing, or just have a party. Then, across the road south-east of the fortress there is a lake with bullrushes, not larger than five threshing-floors, but very deep, so people say, and a marvelous hunting-grounds for geese and ducks. Other marvelous excursions are to the fishing weirs and to the mountain pasture of Istok.

Language. All the people speak Bulgarian and Greek. They do not know Albanian, since this is Rumelia not Albania. But they do speak elegant Turkish, and there are some very urbane and witty gentlemen.

Dress. The young men wear sable and martin calpacs lined with red broadcloth, and varicolored broadcloth jackets, and tight trousers fastened with hooks and eyes, and strut about with yellow *kubadi* slippers on their feet and scimitars at their waist. The old men wind varicolored gold-ornamented Muhammadan turbans on their heads and wear *serhaddi*, *kontoş*, or *ferace* cloaks of varicolored broadcloth.[1] But the young men wear *ferace* cloaks with ample sleeves and bind round turbans on their flat heads and go for elegant strolls about the bazaars.

Completion of the eulogy of Ohrid. Here too, the imperial orders which we had brought concerning the defense of Mania were read out in the imperial council in the presense of the *beg* of Ohrid, Ali Beg. "It is yours to command," he cried, and all the Ottoman troops prepared to go off to Mania. The *beg* presented me with 200 *kuruş*, 1 horse, 1 rebellious Albanian slaveboy, and 1 sword, and to my servants he gave 10 goldpieces each. Then he attended to mustering troops, and left us to our own devices.

---

[1] The specific meaning of these terms is not wholly clear. For the first two, see Dankoff 1991b *Glossary*, 82 (*serḥaddi*), 75 (*qontoş*).

(7) *Der temāşā-yı sikkegāh-ı ḍarb-ḫāne-yi qadīm.* Bu şehr-i ʻaẓīm Ebū'l-fetḥiñ taḫtgāh-ı qadīmi olup bunda cemīʻi ʻasākir-i İslām ile Bāyezīd Ḫān-ı Velī bir sene (8) meştā etdiginden taḫtgāh-ı Āl-i ʻOs̱mān olup tā Sulṭān Murād Ḫān-ı rābiʻ ʻaṣrına gelince bu şehirde sikke kesilirdi. Ḥālā ḍarb-ḫānesi (9) aşağı qalʻede paşa sarāyı ve qurbında bir kārḫāne-yi ʻaẓīmdir kim ḥālā qapusı mesdūd durur, cemīʻi ālāt [ü] bisāṭları ve cümle enkāzı (10) ve sikkeleri mevcūd durur. Ḥattā ḥaqīr ḫāliṣü'l-ʻayār aqçesin görmek olup (?) "Sulṭān Aḥmed bin Meḥemmed Ḫān ʻizze naṣruhu ḍarb Oḫri" (11) deyü sikkesi var idi. ----- /

(13) *Ziyāretgāh-ı Oḫri.* Evvelā merqad-i Oḫri-zāde ve Ġāzī Beg, yuqaru qalʻede Ḫünkār cāmiʻi miḥrābı öñinde medfūnlardır. Ve Şehīd Ḫazīnedār, paşa sarāyınıñ (14) yanında Aya Ṣofya cāmiʻi ṣağında göl kenārında bir qaya üzre kiremitli bir qubbede medfūndur. Ve -----

(15) Baʻdehu Oḫri-zādeler ile niçe yüz adamlar atlarımıza süvār olup Uşṭuq Yaylası teferrücgāhına revāne olduq. Evvelā Oḫriden (16) *qarye-yi Çeri Baş*, Oḫri ṣaḥrāsında Bulġar reʻāyālı maʻmūr bāġçeli ve ikiyüz ḫāneli müzeyyen köydür. Andan baş yuqaru cānib-i şarqa (17) 5 sāʻatde eflāke ʻurūc édüp

Der sitāyiş-i yaylaq-ı ʻaẓīm Uşṭuq. Bu yaylaq ʻArab u ʻAcemde meşhūr-ı āfāq bir yaylaq-ı (18) nüh-ṭāqdır kim her cānibde yedi qażā yerleriñ daġ u ṭaşları cümle nümāyāndır. Ḥattā bu yaylaqdan cānib-i ġarba Oḫri şehri cenūb (19) cānibine meyyāl 8 sāʻatlik yerdir, buḥeyresiyle ve cemīʻi hāmūn-ı vāsiʻatü'l-aqṭār müzāraʻātlarıyle pāymāl-i rimāl gibi nümāyandır. (20) Ve bu yaylada velī-niʻam Oḫri-zāde Beg-cügez efendiniñ kāmil üçyüz ʻaded egrek qoyunları oṭlayup yaylalanır kim cümle yetmiş (21) biñ ʻaded gūsfend-i gūnāgūndur. Diyār-ı Rūmda Alaman yaylasından ṣoñra ve Zile (?) ve Dest-poṭ ve Siroz ve Viṭos (?) yayla(22)larından ṣoñra bu Usṭuq yaylası meşhūrdur. Bunda ḫaymātlar ile qoyun ṣayalarında ve egreklerinde qonup göçüp qaymaq (23) ve yoġurd ve teleme peynirleri ve ağız ve añızlar ve gölemezler ve hoşmerimler ve ballı qaymaq ve ballı qayqanalar ve tāze peynirler yeyüp (24) ve ṣarı keçileriñ surutqa nām ciger tāzeler mā'-ı cibin ṣuların içüp ve ṭoqlı quzu kebābları ve ala balıqları yeyüp günā(25)gūn buz pāresi āb-ı ḥayāt ṣuların nūş édüp

The ancient mint. This city was one of the capitals of Sultan Mehmed II, and during one year Sultan Bayezid II used it as the winter quarters for the Ottoman army. It is therefore an Ottoman capital, and coins were struck here up until the reign of Sultan Murad IV. The mint still stands, a large building in the lower fortress near the Pasha's palace, and while the building is closed up, all the dies and minting tools are in place. In fact, I used to have an *akçe* in mint condition stamped with the following: "Sultan Ahmed son of Mehmed Khan, may his victory be glorious, mint Ohrid."

Shrines. First are the tombs of Okhri-zade and of Ghazi Beg, both in front of the prayer-niche of the Hünkâr mosque. Şehid Hazinedar (The Martyred Treasurer?) is buried in a tile-covered dome on a cliff on the lake shore to the right of the Aya Sofya mosque next to the Pasha's palace. -----

After visiting these tombs, we joined a party of several hundred mounted men in the company of the Okhri-zades and set off on an excursion to the mountain pasture of Istok. Our first stop was Çeri Baş, a pretty Bulgarian village with prosperous gardens and 200 houses. From there we started our ascent, in an eastward direction, and in 5 hours arrived at

The great mountain pasture of Istok. It is a pasture-of-paradise whose far-flung fame has reached the Arabs and the Persians. From the summit one can view an expanse covering 7 *kadi*-districts. In fact, one can see the city of Ohrid to the south-west, 8 hours away, also Lake Ohrid and its vast agricultural hinterland, spread out at one's feet. In this pasture our dear friend and patron, Okhri-zade Beg, has 300 sheepfolds comprising a total of 70,000 sheep of various kinds. In all the Ottoman lands, this Istok pasture nearly rivals those of Alaman and Zile and the Despot and Serres and Vitos.[1] We went from fold to fold, staying in tents, eating the yoghurt and cheeses and beestings and curds and cream with honey and omelets with honey, drinking the buttermilk and whey, savoring the kebabs of roasted lamb and trout, quaffing water from the ice-cold streams and various kinds of honeyed sherbets, snacking on a thousand kinds of herbs

---

[1] Of these *yaylas* or summer pastures, only that of Serres is readily identifiable; see Evliya's description at VIII 221b-222a (137-38). The reading of Vitos is quite uncertain. Zile is a town in Anatolia near Tokat, but Evliya's description (at III 91a11) does not suggest a *yayla*. The list of Anatolian *yaylas* at III 89a15-24 does not include any of these names. A list of Rumelian *yaylas*, if there is one, has not been located.

niçe biñ gūne nebātāt [u] giyāhātdan reybās ve ışğın ve çilek ve yer vişne(26)leri yeyüp gūnāgūn ʻasel-i muṣaffaʻ şerbetleri nūş édüp zevq ü ṣafālar etdik. Bu yaylada olan sünbül ve müşk-i rūmī ve lāle ve zerrīn (27) ve nergis meger Erżurum diyārında Biñ Göl yaylasında ve kūh-ı Bī-sütūnda ve kūh-ı Demāvend ve kūh-ı Ercişde ola.

Bu yaylada (28) bir hafta zevq [ü] ṣafālar édüp andan cānib-i şarqa gāh yoquş aşağı piyāde ve gāh esb-süvār 5 sāʻatde *qarye-yi Pazı* geçüp (29) yine cānib-i şarqa 2 sāʻat gidüp

Evṣāf-ı qaṣaba-yı maʻmūr Rasna. O͟hri ṭoprağında niyābetdir ve serbest zeʻāmetdir. (30) Qaṣabası bir vāsiʻ öz içinde ----- deresi cerêyān éder, bir vāsiʻ yerde. Cümle yüz seksen ʻaded kiremitli (31) maʻmūr bāğçeli evlerdir. Cümle iki maḥalledir, nıṣfı müslim ve nıṣfı keferelerdir. Cümle iki miḥrābdır, biri çārsū (32) içinde Manaṣṭır şehirli Ramażān Beg cāmiʻi, kiremitli ve kārgīr minārelі ve ḥarêminde bir mektebli cāmiʻ-i laṭīfdir, ve biri Ḥācī (33) Murād cāmiʻidir. Ve cümle bir medrese-yi sū͟htegān; ve cümle bir tekye-yi dervīşān; ve cümle bir ḥammāmı var, Ṣavur-(34)zāde ͟hayrātidir; ve cümle bir ͟hānı var; ve cümle yigirmi ʻaded müfīd [ü] mu͟htaṣar dükkānları var. Ammā haftada bir gün cemīʻi **[372a]** eṭrāf qurālarından niçe biñ benī-Ādem cemʻ olup bir cemʻiyyet-i kübrālı bāzār-ı ʻaẓīm durup germāgerm beyʻ ü şirālar olur. Ḥaqīr (2) bu bāzārda Manya muḥāfaẓasına me'mūr olanlar bir ān durmayalar deyü dellāllar nidā etdirüp bu şehr aʻyānlarından Qoçi Beg (3) ve Murtażā Beg ʻacāyib ͟hānedān ṣāḥibleridir, anlar ḥaqīre ve O͟hri-zādelere ʻaẓīm żiyāfetler édüp ertesi gün Manya (4) seferine revāne oldılar.

Bu qaṣaba-yı Rasnanıñ memdūḥātından kestānesi ve qış emrūdı ve dağlarında qırmızı iḥrām (5) boyası kökleri ve çoqa boyası egirler ʻacāyib meşhūr temāşā boyalardır. Ve cümle ͟halqınıñ kār [ü] kesbleri bu boya kökleridir kim (6) Firengistāna götürürler, ğāyet rāyicdir, cemīʻi vilāyetlerden bāzirgānları gelüp niçe biñ kök boya kökleri bağlayup vilāyet (7) vilāyet boya köki götürürler.

Bu maḥalden Priştine qażāsı ṣolumuzda ğāyet yaqın qalup andan yine gerüye ʻavdet édüp (8) defʻā *menzil-i yaylaq-ı Uşṭuq*, bir gün bir géce da͟hi anda zevq édüp[1] andan cānib-i ğarba yoquş aşağı yayladan énüp (9) 5 sāatde yine *qarye-yi Çeri Başı* geçüp defʻā *menzil-i şehr-i ʻaẓīm-i O͟hri*. Bunda bir géce da͟hi mihmān olup ertesi gün (10) cümle aḥbāb ile vedāʻlaşup O͟hri begi mihter-͟hānesin çalaraq cümle

---

[1] *édüp* twice in the text.

and tendrils and sorrel and wild strawberries and sour cherries, and generally having a good time. The hyacinth and spikenard and poppy and jonquil and narcissus growing here rival those of the summer-pastures of Biñ Göl in the Erzurum region and of Mounts Bisutun and Demavend and Erciş.

After one week of savoring the delights of this mountain pasture we descended in an eastward direction, dismounting when it became steep. We passed the village of Pazi in 5 hours, then proceeding eastward for 2 more hours we arrived at

The prosperous town of Resen. It is a *kadi*-substitute district in the territory of Ohrid and a free *zeamet*. The town is in a large valley through which flows the ----- river. There are 180 tile-roofed houses with fine gardens, divided evenly between a Muslim and a Christian quarter. There are 2 congregational mosques. One, in the bazaar, named for Ramazan Beg from the city of Manastir, is a pretty mosque with tiled roof and stone minaret and a Koran-school in the courtyard. The other is named for Hadji Murad. There are 2 *medreses*; 1 dervish lodge; 1 bathhouse, endowed by Savur-zade; 1 *han*; and 20 small shops. But once a week thousands of villagers from the surrounding districts set up a large and bustling market. I took the occasion of such a market to have criers remind the officials charged with the defense of Mania not to delay. Two excellent householders, Koçi Beg and Murtaza Beg, mounted great feasts for myself and for the Okhri-zades, and the next day they went off on the Mania campaign.

Among the famous products of Resen are its chestnuts, its winter pears, and its marvelous dyes — a red dye extracted from roots in the mountains, and a broadcloth dye from orris root. These dyes provide the main living for the people of Resen, who export them to Western Europe. Merchants from all the surrounding provinces come for these dye roots, which they bind together and transport from province to province.

From here the *kadi*-district of Prishtina is very near by. But we turned back to spend one more day and night enjoying ourselves on the mountain pasture of Istok, then descended in a westward direction, passed through Çeri Baş once again after 5 hours, and returned to Ohrid where we were entertained for one more night. The next day we took leave of all our friends. The *beg* of Ohrid, playing his military band, went off with all his soldiery to the defense of

'askeriyle Manya muḥāfaẓasına revāne olup (11) *ḥaqīr-i pür-taqṣīr Oḫriden İslāmbola gitdigimiz qonaqları 'ayān u beyān éder* (12) evvelā ulu yolumuz yine Uştuq Yaylası iken anda gitmeyüp Oḫri sancağında Manya ġazāsına me'mūr olan erbāb-ı zu'amāları (13) ve erbāb-ı tīmārları sefere sürmek içün ba'żı qurā ve qaṣabātları devêrān u seyerān etmek içün Oḫriden yine cānib-i (14) şimāle gidüp qaṣaba-yı Usturqayı 'ubūr édüp Oḫri Göli kenārın devr éderek cānib-i cenūba 5 sā'at gidüp (15)

Evṣāf-ı qaṣaba-yı şīrīn Poġradas. Bu daḫi Oḫri begininñ ḫāṣṣı voyvadalığı ḥükminde İstar-ova (16) qażāsı niyābetidir. Bu şehrinñ qarşu göl aşırı qaṣaba-yı Usturqa ve qal'e-yi Oḫri nümāyāndır, mābeynehümālarında hemān (17) göl vardır. Bu qaṣaba cümle dörd 'aded maḥalle ve cümle dörd 'aded miḥrābdır. Evvelā çārsū içinde ----- (18) cāmi'i, kiremitli ve kārgīr mināreli cāmi'-i zībādır. Ve ----- cāmi'i, cemā'at-i keṡīreye mālikdir. Cümle iki 'aded ma'mūr (19) maḥalle mesācidleridir. Ve cümle bir 'aded medrese-yi sūḫtegāndır. Ve cümle iki 'aded mekteb-i ṣıbyān-ı ebced-ḫvāndır. (20) Ve cümle bir 'aded tekye-yi dervīşān-ı 'abdālāndır. Ve cümle üç 'aded ḫānları vardır. Ve cümle bir 'aded ḥammām-ı (21) muḫtaṣarı vardır. Ve cümle altı yüz 'aded bāġ u bāġçeli ve serāpā kiremit örtüli ḫānedānlarda yigirmi 'aded ev ḥammāmları (22) daḫi vardır. Ve cümle yüz elli 'aded dükkānları vardır, ammā kārgīr binālı bez̲z̲āzistānı yoqdur, lākin göl kenārında pāk (23) debbāġ dükkānları çoqdur.

Ve bu şehir göl kenārında vāqı' olmaġile ba'żı ḫānedān-ı 'aẓīmlerinñ şāhnişīn ü maqṣūreleri göl (24) kenārında olup cümle revzenleri ṣuya nāẓırdır. Ba'żı yārānlar pençerelerde oṭurup gölden nāzik balıq avlarlar. Ammā her géce nisā (25) ṭāyifesi evlerinde balıq avlayup her bār lezīz balıq yerler.

Āb [u] havāsı laṭīf olduġından bāġ u bāġçelerininñ gūnāgūn (26) ābdār [u] ḫoş-ḫvār meyvelerinden emrūdı ġāyet lezīz ü terdir. Ve şehri daḫi meyvesi gibi şīrīn rabṭa-yı zībā olup başqa (27) bir rūḥ vardır. Bu qaṣabanınñ cānib-i qıblesinde şehr-i Korça 8 sā'atlik yerdir. Muqaddemā sene ----- tārīḫinde şehr-i Korçayı (28) ve şehr-i Horpuşta ve şehr-i Bilhişta ve şehr-i Göli-kesriyi görmek ile ol cāniblere teveccüh etmeyüp yine Oḫri Göli kenārınca (29) cānib-i şimāle 2 sā'at düz vāsi' maḥṣūldār fezālı bāġ u bāġçe ve çiftlikli yerlerde meymene vü meysere emn [ü] emān yerlerde ṣafā ile gidüp

(30) *Evṣāf-ı qaṣaba-yı ma'mūr Iṣṭar-ova.* Bu rabṭadan Poġradas qaṣabası ġāyet nümāyāndır. Ve bu qaṣaba daḫi (31) Oḫri sancağı

Mania, while we — *stages of our journey from Ohrid to Istanbul* — shunning the main road through the mountain pasture of Istok, began our tour of some of the villages and towns in the *sancak* of Ohrid in order to impel the *zeamet* holders and the timariots who were charged to join the Mania campaign to set out. Heading north from Ohrid we passed through Struga, followed the shore of Lake Ohrid around to the south, and after 5 hours arrived at

The sweet town of Pogradec. This too is part of the *kadi*-district of Starova and is a *has* of the *beg* of Ohrid, administered by a *voyvoda*. From here, across the lake, one can see the town of Struga and the fortress of Ohrid. This town has 4 quarters and 4 prayer-niches. Foremost among them is the beautiful mosque of ----- in the bazaar, with a tiled roof and a stonework minaret. Then there is the mosque of ----- with a large congregation. There are 2 *medreses*, 2 primary schools, 1 dervish *tekke*, 3 *hans* and 1 tiny bathhouse. Of the 600 houses with tiled roofs, surrounded by vineyards and gardens, 20 have private baths. There are 150 shops, though there is no stonework *bedestan*. At the lakeside there are several immaculate tanneries.

Because the town is situated on the lake, some of the balconies and pavilions belonging to the great houses are on the shore and all their windows overlook the water. Certain of the gentlemen enjoy sitting at their windows and catching fish from the lake, and in the evening the women-folk make delicious meals of these fish. Pogradec has a mild climate, and so the various fruits growing in the vineyards and gardens are very fine. The pears, especially, are fresh and delicious. Indeed, the whole town has a special atmosphere, as sweet and lovely as its fruit.

The city of Korça lies 8 hours to the southeast of Pogradec. Since I had already visited Korça, Hoçişt, Bilişt and Kastoria in the year ----- I decided not to go in that direction. Instead, setting out northwards along Lake Ohrid, we journeyed pleasantly for 2 hours over a broad, flat and fertile plain, with vineyards and gardens and farm-estates to the right and the left.

The prosperous town of Starova. From here one can see the town of Pogradec quite clearly. Starova too is part of the *sancak* of Ohrid and is a *has* of the *beg* of Ohrid, administered by a *voyvoda*. It has a *kadi* with a salary level of 150 *akçe* and jurisdiction over 70 villages.

ḫākinde beginiñ ḫāṣṣı voyvadası ḥākimdir. Yüz elli aqçe pāyesiyle qażādır. Nāḥiyesi yetmiş pāre qurālardır. (32) Cümle re'āya ve berāyāları Bulġardır.

Ve qānūn-ı Süleymān Ḫān üzre sarāy-ı ḫāṣṣaya se'ādetlü pādişāh içün bu şehre yeñiçeri (33) ocaġından bir çorbacı degşirme aġası gelüp bundan niçe yüz 'aded güzīde Bulġar ve Rūm oġlanların degşirüp başlarına (34) qırmızı şebkülāhlar ve eginlerine qırmızı 'abā ḫil'atler geydirüp der-i devlete degşirme ġulāmları götürürp ġāyetü'l-ġāye maḥbūb olup **[372b]** aṣıl-zāde olanları ġılmān-ı ḫāṣsa édüp daḫi fenālarını būstān ocaqlarına ve yeñiçeri ocaqlarına daḫi zeber-destlerin ṭopḫāne (2) ve cebe-ḫāne ocaqlarına verirler. Ammā ġayri qażāların̄ degşirme ġulāmların her ocaqlara ve a'yān-ı kibārlara defterler ile verüp 'ilm ü (3) kemāl [ü] ma'rifet ögrendiklerinden ṣoñra 'acemī oġlanı 'ulūfesine geçirüp andan yeñiçeri qapusına, andan sipāh qapusına çıqarup, eger kim (4) taqdīr-i ḫüdā olursa niçeleri vezīr-i a'ẓamlar ve müftī ve monlālar olmuşlardır. Ya'nī bu Iṣṭar-ova şehri kān-ı cüvānān-ı degşirme-(5)gān yeri bir mübārek rabṭa-yı zībādır kim Oḫri Gölinden dörd biñ adım içeri qarada alarqadır.

Ve cümle dördyüz (6) 'aded kiremitli ma'mūr [u] ābādān ḫānedānlardır. Ba'żıları fuqarā evleri olmaq ile ṣaz örtülidir, ammā her evde bāġ u bāġçeler muqarrerdir. (7) Ve cümle dörd 'aded maḥallātdır, nıṣfı müslim ve nıṣfı ġayri-müslim maḥalleleridir. Ve cümle dörd 'aded miḥrābdır, ikisi cāmi'dir, (8) çārsū içinde ----- cāmi'i kiremitli ve bir minārelidir, ve ----- cāmi'i müzeyyendir. Ve cümle iki maḥalle zāviyesi (9) vardır. Ve cümle bir 'aded medrese-yi sūḫtegānı var. Ve cümle bir 'aded mekteb-i püserānı var. Ve cümle bir 'aded ḫāneqāh-ı (10) erbāb-ı ṭarīqi var. Ve cümle yüz 'aded dükkānları var, ammā bezzāsistānı yoqdur, lākin meṭā'ları çoqdur ve yine her şey mevcūddur. (11) Ve cümle üç 'aded ḫānları var. Ve cümle bir 'aded ḥammāmı var, ammā bunuñ daḫi ev ḥammāmları vardır. Ve bāġ u bāġçe(12)leri firāvāndır. El-ḥāṣıl şīrīn qaṣaba-yı bāġ-ı cihāndır.

Bunda ḫānedān ṣāḥibleri zu'amālardan ----- Aġayı ve ----- (13) Aġayı ve ġayrilerin fermān-ı pādişāhī üzre Manya muḥāfażasına me'mūr édüp anlar ol ṭarafa bizler der-i devlet ṭarâfına bu şehirden qalqup

All the rayah peasants are Bulgarians.

It is here, in accordance with the statute of Sultan Suleyman, that a colonel from the janissaries arrives in the name of the sultan and collects hundreds of select young Bulgarian and Greek boys for the Devshirme.[1] They are all dressed in red conical hats and red woollen robes and are sent to the court. The ones who are extremely handsome and well-born are made court pages; the poorer sort are given to the palace guards and janissaries corps; and the worst ones to the artillery and munitions corps. The boys of other regions are sent to other units and to various notables, according to registers. After being well educated and trained, they serve as recruits, then enter the service of the janissaries, then graduate to the service of the *sipahi*s. If God determines it, some of them can go on to become grand viziers, *müfti*s and mullahs. So this town of Starova is the mine of Devshirme boys and a blessed and beautiful place.

It lies 4000 paces inland from Lake Ohrid and has 400 wealthy and prosperous houses with tiled roofs. Some of the houses, to be sure, are poor and have thatched roofs, but every one of them has its garden and vineyard. There are 4 quarters, half Muslim and half non-Muslim. There are 4 prayer-niches, 2 of which are congregational mosques — the mosque of ----- in the bazaar, with tiled roof and 1 minaret, and the fine mosque of ----- — the other 2 being neighborhood mosques. There is 1 *medrese*, 1 primary school, 1 dervish *tekke* and 100 shops, though no *bedestan*, but one can find all manner of products and merchandise here. There are 3 *han*s and only 1 bathhouse, though here too there are baths in private homes. There are numerous vineyards and gardens. In short, it is a delightful town.

Here we left ----- Aga and ----- Aga and others, officers and householders, in charge of raising troops for the defense of Mania, according to sultanic decree. They went that way, while we, departing from this city, headed in the direction of the capital.

---

[1] The levy of young Christian boys as tribute from the Balkan countries. The boys were taken away, educated as Muslims and trained for the sultan's service in the palace and army. Many rose to lofty positions in the Ottoman administration. At I 195b8 Evliya says that every seven years a colonel of the janissary corps with 500 to 600 men takes 7000 to 8000 Bulgarian, Albanian, Serbian and Greek boys from Rumelian villages to Skopje where they are dressed in the distinctive red robe and conical hat before being sent on to Istanbul. By the time Evliya was writing, the practice was in steep decline; see V. L. Ménage, art. "devshirme" in *Encyclopedia of Islam, New Edition*.

BIBLIOGRAPHY

Babinger, Franz (1930). "Ewlija Tschelebi's Reisewege in Albanien." *MSOS* As., 33, 138-78. [repr.: *Rumelische Streifen* (Berlin, 1938), 1-40; *Aufsätze und Abhandlungen zur Geschichte Südosteuropas und der Levante* 2 (Munich 1966), 51-89.]

—— (1931). "Die Gründung von Elbasan." *MSOS* As., 34, 1-10. [repr.: *Rumelische Streifen* (Berlin, 1938), 53-62; *Aufsätze und Abhandlungen zur Geschichte Südosteuropas und der Levante* 1 (Munich 1962), 53-62.]

Bruinessen, Martin van and H. Boeschoten (1988). *Evliya Çelebi in Diyarbekir*. Leiden: Brill.

Cheiliadikēs, Nikos (1991). *Taxidi stēn Hellada. Eblia Tselempi*. Athens: Hekatê.

Cialicoff, C. J. (1919). "Din descrierea călătoriei lui Evlija Celebi," *Arhiva Dobrogei* 2, 139-46.

Čohadžić, Dim. S. (1905). "Putopis Evlije Čelebije o srpskim zemljama u XVII veku" *Spomenik. Srpska Kraljevska Akademija* (Belgrade) 42, 1-34.

Danişmend, İsmail Hami (1961). *İzahlı Osmanlı Tarihi Kronolojisi*, III. Istanbul.

Dankoff, Robert, (1989). "The Languages of the World according to Evliya Çelebi." *Journal of Turkish Studies*.

—— (1990). *Evliya Çelebi in Bitlis*. Leiden: Brill.

—— (1991a). *The Intimate Life of an Ottoman Statesman: Melek Ahmed Paşa*. . . . State University of New York Press.

—— (1991b). *An Evliya Çelebi Glossary: Unusual, Dialectal and Foreign Words in the Seyahat-name*. Cambridge, Mass. [In: Sources of Oriental Languages and Literatures, ed. Şinasi Tekin & Gönül Alpay Tekin.]

Dankoff, Robert and Klaus Kreiser (1992). *Materialien zu Evliya Çelebi* II (incl. *A Guide to the Seyahat-name of Evliya Çeleb* and *Bibliographie raisonnée*). Beihefte zum Tübinger Atlas des Vorderen Orients B 90/2. Wiesbaden: Reichert.

Delić, M. R. (1948). "Evlija Čelebija o Skoplija." *Sbornik Skopskog naučnog družstva za istoriju južne Srbije i susjednih oblasti* (Skopje) 1, 311-25.

Dimitrov, Strašimir (1972). *Evlija Čelebi. Pătepis*. Sofia: Izd. na Otečestvenija Front.

Duda, Herbert W. (1949). *Balkantürkische Studien*. In: Österreichische Akademie der Wissenschaften. Philosophisch-historische Klasse, Sitzungsberichte Vol. 226, Abhandlung 1. Vienna.

Elezović, Gliša (1953). "Evlija Čelebija o Skoplja." *Zbornik Skopskog naučnog društva za istoriju južne Srbije i susjednih oblasti* (Skopje) 1, 311-25.

Elsie, Robert (1997). "Leksiku shqip i Evlija Çelebiut i vitit 1662 dhe ç'duhet të dijë dervishi shtegtar." *Studime* (Prishtinë) 4, 239-49.

—— (1998). "Das albanische Lexikon des Evliya Čelebi (1662) und was ein Derwisch auf der Durchreise alles wissen muss." *Südost-Forschungen* (Munich), 57.

Gadžanov, D. G. (1909). "Pătuvane na Evlija Čelebi iz bălgarskite zemi preză sredata na XVII vekă." *Pečatano v Periodičesko spisanie na bălgarskoto kniževno družestvo* (Sofia) 70, 639-724.

Giannopoulous, Iôannos G. (1969). "Hē periēgēsis tou Evlia Tselempē ana tēn Sterean Heliada." *Epetēris Hetaireias Stereohelladikōn Meletōn* (Athens) 2, 139-98.

Hodo, Adem (1973). "Kujtimet e Çelebiut. Turist turk në Shqipëri," *Koha jonë* (Paris) 1, 39-40.

Kaleshi, Hasan (1955). "Kosova e Metohija n'udhëpërshkrimin e Evlija Çelebis," *Përparimi* (Prishtinë) 7-8, 422-34.

Kemura, Sejfudin Fehmi (1908). "Iz Sejahatname Evlije Čelebije," *Glasnik Zemaljsko Muzej* (Sarajevo) 20, 181-201, 289-341.

Kiel, Machiel (1990). *Ottoman Architecture in Albania, 1385-1912*. Istanbul: Research Centre for Islamic History, Art and Culture.

Kornrumpf, Hans-Jürgen (1995). *Territoriale Verwaltungseinheiten und Kadiamtsbezirke in der Europäischen Türkei (ohne Bosnien und Ungarn). Ein Versuch*. Stutensee-Fr.

Krasniqi, Mark (1982). "Shqiptarët në udhëpërshkrimin e Evlija Çelebiut," *Gjurmë e gjurmime* (Tiranë), 320-26.

Kreiser, Klaus (1979). "Bedesten-Bauten im Osmanischen Reich," *Istanbuler Mitteilungen* 29, 367-400.

Mazov, Ivan (1978). *Razmeani kolepki. Po tragite na Evlija Čelebi*. Skopje: Sovremenost.

Radonić, Jovan (1910, 1911, 1912). "Putovanje Evlije Čelebije po srpskim i hrvatskim zemljama." *Godišnjak Nikole Čupića* (Belgrade) 29, 33-101; 30, 259-91; 31, 233-97.

Šabanović, H. (1954). *Evlija Čelebija. Putopis. Odlomci o jugoslovenskim zemljama*. Sarajevo. [repr. 1967, 1979, 1996.]

Šehapi, Behidžudin (1988). "Evlija Čelebi i drugi patepisci vo Skopje," *Takvim* (Sarajevo), 45-55.

Sulēs, Christo (1944). "Taxidi turku periēgētu stēn Ēpero," *Ēpeirōtika Grammata* 1, 162-66, 197-200, 246-52.

Süreyyâ, Mehmed (1995-97). *Sicill-i Osmanî*, 6 vols. Istanbul: Sebil Yayınevi. [Romanization of the original publication, Istanbul, 1308 (1893).]

Vuçitërni, Salih (1930). *Shqipnija para dy shekujsh. Përkëthye nga libri turqisht "Evlija Çelebi Sejjahatnamesi."* Tirana.

Wolfart, Ulrich (1970). *Die Reisen des Evliyā Čelebi durch die Morea*. München.

Zamputi, Injac (1989, 1990). *Dokumente të shekujve XVI-XVII për historinë e Shqipërisë*. Tirana: Akademia e Shkencave. 4 volumes.

Zoto, Odise (1993). "Evlija Çelebiu dhe disa përshkrime të tij për qytetet shqiptare të shekullit XVII," *Jehona* (Skopje) 3, 89-95.

GLOSSARY

ağa	aga, title of officials
akçe	asper, a small silver coin, the basic unit of the older Ottoman monetary system
alay-beg	deputy officer of the *sancak-beg* responsible for marshalling the *sipahis* of a sancak
bedestan	covered market, an enclosed stone structure in the center of a bazaar with shops for precious textiles and jewelry
beg	a military title (= *emir*), governor of a *sancak*
begler-beg	governor of an *eyalet*
besmele	Basmalah, the formula "In the name of God the Compassionate the Merciful," recited when undertaking an activity
beg	bey, governor of a *sancak* or *eyalet*
boza	a beverage made of fermented millet
celi	a kind of large cursive script, generally a variant of *sülüs*, used for inscriptions on mosques, etc.
çavuş	chaush, pursuivant or messenger
çeribaşı	a local military official
defterdar	director of the financial administration of a province
divan	1) a council; 2) a collection of poems
dönüm	about 2000 hectares or a quarter of an acre.
emin	customs officer or other agent appointed by the sultan to carry out a public work with financial responsibility; the customs district is called *emanet*
eyalet	an Ottoman province
Fatiha	the first surah or chapter of the Koran, often recited as a prayer
ġazā	ghaza, holy war or jihad, a term used for Ottoman military campaigns
ġāzī	ghazi, one who engages in ghaza, a term used for an Ottoman soldier
ḥadīs̱	Hadith, a traditional saying attributed to the Prophet Muhammad
han	khan, an inn or caravansary
has	an imperial grant to a governor, a *timar* providing an annual income of over 100,000 *akçe*

imam	1) prayer-leader; 2) one of the twelve successors to the Prophet recognized by the Shiis, and also honored by the Sunnis
kadi	qadi, judge in a *şeriat* court and administrative governor of a *kadi* district (*qażā*)
kıble	qibla, the direction of Mecca, south
kuruş	piaster, a foreign (Venetian or Spanish) silver coin worth about 80 *akçe*
medrese	theological school
müfti	mufti or jurisconsult and head of a legal school in a region
nakibüleşraf	superintendent of descendants of the Prophet
pādişāh	Padishah, the Ottoman sultan; a great ruler
paşa	Pasha, title of high-ranking members of the Ottoman elite
sancak	sandjak, a sub-province or county of an *eyalet*
sancak-beg	sandjak-bey, governor of a *sancak*
sipahi	timariot cavalryman
subaşı	commander of a *sipahi* regiment with police functions
şeriat	Shari'ah, the Islamic sacred law, administered by a *kadi*
şeyh	Shaikh, title of the head of a religious order
şeyhülislam	the chief *müfti* of a region
tekke	dervish lodge
timar	a grant of land in exchange for military service (see *zeamet*)
'ulemā	Ulema, religious personnel, including *kadi*s, *müfti*s, *imams*, etc.
vilayet	same as *eyalet*
voyvoda	voyvode, a military agent appointed by a governor to oversee tax collection in a *kadi* district
zeamet	a *timar* providing an annual income of over 20,000 *akçe*

INDEX

'Abaza (Abkhazians), VIII 353a22, 24
'Abdu'llāh Efendi, VIII 354b18
'Abdu'r-raḥmān Paşa, VIII 363b20, 30 - 364a3, 11-13
'Acem (Persians), VI 34b26; VIII 359b20, 361a15, 365b2, 367a4, 371b17
'Acem Meḥemmed Efendi, VIII 361b34
Adana, VI 35a29
Adriatic Sea: see Venedik Körfezi
Aġrı (Ararat), VIII 360a4
Āh-ı Evran, VIII 359a29
Alaca Ḥiṣār, V 167b12
Alaman, VIII 371b21
Alaşonya (Elassonos), VIII 367a20
Albania, Albanian: see Arnavud, Arnavudluq
'Alemdār Baba, V 168b20
Aleppo: see Ḥaleb
Alessio: see Leş
Alexander the Great: see İskender Zū'l-qarneyn
Āl-i 'Abbāsiyān (Abbasids), VIII 353a15
Āl-i 'Os̱mān, 'Os̱mānlı (Ottomans, the Ottoman dynasty), V 167a29-32, 168a34; VI 33b6, 357a29, 31, 358b14, 361a28-29, 364b10, 365a33, 368a2, 371b8
'Alī (the Prophet's cousin and son-in-law, caliph, reg. 644-56), VIII 355a33, 362b9
'Alī Beg (in Shköder), VI 33b29
'Alī Beg (in Kakoz), VIII 356a26
'Alī Beg (in Ohrid), VIII 371b4
'Alī Dede, VIII 360a29
'Alī Dost Dede, VIII 354b31 - 355a3
'Alī Paşa (Serdār = Kapudan Köse 'Alī Paşa [I 87a4]), VIII 352b29, 358b2
'Alī Politina, VI 35z4
Anaṭolġuz (Anadolguz), VIII 362a18
Anaṭolı (Anatolia), VI 36b19; VIII 354a29, 364a33
Ankara: see Engürü
Anṭāqıyye (Antioch, Antakya), VIII 353a12, 368a6
Aq Deñiz (Mediterranean, Aegean), VI 33b7; VIII 353a22, 355a24, 362a16
Aq Ṣu (Aksu, river), VIII 360b12-13
Aq Şemse'd-dīn, VIII 364b6, 16
Aqça Kilse (Qishbardha), VIII 360b19
Aqṣā (al-Aqsa mosque in Jerusalem), VIII 355b33
'Arab, 'Urbān (Arabs), VI 34b23; VIII 353a8-9, 15-17, 33-34, 361a15, 365b2, 367a4, 367b21, 23, 29, 31, 368a6, 371b17
'Arab (Negro), VIII 360a33
'Arab al-Hāşim, VIII 353a19
'Arabistān, VIII 364a33
Armenian: see Ermenī
Arnavud, Arnabud, 'Arnavud, 'Ārnābūd; Arnavudluq, Arnavudistān (Albanian; Albania), V 167b1, 168a24, 169a14; VI 33a8, 17, 33b7, 34a8, 34b4, 22 - 25, 35a21, 24, 35b4, 13, 15, 24-25, 36a9, 11, 36b17, 28; VIII 352a21, 352b23, 353a6 - 34, 353b12, 22, 31, 354b9, 12, 355a11, 13, 355b15, 356a11, 13, 19, 33, 356b7, 18, 357a5, 29, 31, 357b10, 359b13, 34, 360a6, 10, 23, 33, 362a34, 362b2, 17, 26, 363b6, 364a33, 364b7, 18, 365a29, 366a2, 12-14, 367a1, 367b15-16, 28, 31, 34, 368a1-2, 7, 17, 368b27, 369a29, 371a30, 371b5
Arnavudca, Arnavud lisānı, lisān-ı Arnavud (Albanian language), V 168a26; VI 33a11, 34b22 - 35a2, 23, 35b21, 36b10; VIII 352a19, 352b16, 353b2, 18, 357a17, 362b16, 364b13, 366b10, 29-30, 371a29

Aswad ibn Miqdad: see Esved ibni Miqdād
Atina (Athens), VIII 362a20
Avlonya (Vlora) VI 34b24; VIII 353a3, 353b14, 356b8, 21, 33, 357a8, 32, 357b4, 8, 358b5, 360b1, 4, 9, 25-26, 31, 361a5, 20, 23 - 362b11, 367b28, 368a2
Avlonya Körfezi (Bay of Vlora), VIII 353a4, 354b29-30, 356a33, 360b13, 32, 361a23, 26
Aya Sofya, VIII 370a1-11, 370b4, 371a19, 371b14
Ayas Paşa, VIII 352a21-22
Aydonat (Paramithiá), VIII 355a12
'Ayntāb (Antep), VIII 364a33
Āẕerbāycān (Azerbaijan), V 168b2
'Azīz Efendi, Şeyḫ 'Azīz, VIII 359a2, 359b6

Baba Ḥasan Dede, VIII 354b31
Baba Qāḍī, VIII 358b10, 30
Baba Sulṭān: see Quzġun Baba
Babya (Babja), VIII 368a11-17, 20
Bedr (Badr), VIII 367b19
Baġdād (Baghdad), VIII 353a15, 369a23
Banya + Başanya (sons of Serbian king Dest-pot), VIII 364b3-11
Bar, VI 35b21-29; VIII 362b32, 368a1
Başt Ova, VIII 359b10, 362b15-28, 363a32, 363b6, 364b28
Baṭum, VIII 353a26
Bayezid Khan: see Sulṭān Bāyezīd II
Beklin: see Pekin
Bektaşi (Sufi order; see Ḥācī Bektaş-ı Velī), V 167b4, 169a19; VIII 361b17
Belġırad (Berat), VIII 357a26 - 360b1, 360b1, 361a26, 368a2
Belġırad (Belgrade), VIII 357a30
Bender, VIII 357b17, 361a29
Benefşe (Monemvasia), VIII 353b5
Beñqo Paşa, VIII 368a12
Berat: see Belġırad
Berqī Efendi, VIII 354b14, 31
Beşik (lake), VI 34b13
Bıçaqçı-zāde, VIII 365a18, 365b13, 366a34, 366b4
Bilhişta (Bilisht), VIII 369a28
Biñ Göl (mountain in Anatolia), VIII 360a5, 371b27
Bīsütūn (mountain in Iran), VIII 360a4, 371b27
Bishqem: see Peşkim
Bitlis, VIII 371a4
Bitola: see Manaṣṭır
Black Sea: see Qara Deñiz
Bobrat (Pobrat), VIII 360b2
Boġdan (Moldavians), V 168b1
Bosna, Bosnevī (Bosnia, Bosnian), V 167b5, 8-13, 168a26
Boyana Göli (Lake Shkodër), VI 33b15, 17, 20-21, 23, 25, 34a5, 24 - 34b19
Boz Eşek, VIII 367a1
Bradashesh: see Bürdaşiş
Buda: see Budin
Budin (Buda), V 167b12; VIII 356b5, 357a29
Buduva (Budva), VI 35b16-20
Buḫārī, VIII 370b20
Bulġar (Bulgarian), VIII 365a30, 368a17, 369a6, 372a32-33, 369a28, 370a29, 371b16
Bulġarca (Bulgarian language), VIII 371a29
Bunduqani: see Venedik
Bursa, V 168b7; VIII 370a27
Burun Qullesi, V 167b10
Buruşuq oġulları, VIII 363b34
Buşaṭlar (Bushat), VI 33b5, 35a12-20, 36b1
Buzanṭa (Byzantium), VIII 369a23
Bükāyī, VIII 355a31
Bürdaşiş (Bradashesh), VIII 364a19
Büzürg Seng, VIII 366b34 - 367a8, 14

Ca'fer Paşa, VIII 355a24
Calabria: see Qlora
Candace: see Qaydefā

Candia: see Qandiye
Cebel-i Elheme (Jabal-i Alhama), VIII 353a8-21, 26, 32, 367b15 - 368a9
Cebeliyye (Jabaliyya, mountain and fortress in Syria [see IX 179a14 (392)]), VIII 353a13, 21, 367b26
Cemālī-zāde, VIII 364a28, 365a17, 366a34, 366b4, 11
Cerkovina: see Çirqona
Cernik, V 167b11
Cevherina (Xhyherina), VIII 360b19
Ceyḥūn (Oxus), VIII 368b34
Chotin: see Ḥotin
Cim-cim Ḫvāce, VIII 360a27
Ciniviz (Genoese), VI 36b4; VIII 353a23
Circassians: see Çerkes
Constantine: see Qusṭanṭīn
Constantinople: see Qusṭantiniyye
Corfu: see Körfez
Corinth: see Kördüs
Crete: see Girid
Ctesiphon: see Medāyin

Çaldirān, V 168b3
Çamëria: see Semerine
Çatalbaş Paşa, VIII 358b1-2
Çavuş-zāde, VIII 366b4
Çeke Beni Qayası (Çekebeni Rock), VIII 357b31 - 358a14, 18-19, 21, 359b19
Çelebi Efendi, VIII 367b1-3
Çelebi Ḥüseyn Paşa, VIII 358b23
Çelebi Muṣṭafā Ketḫüda, VIII 363b33-34
Çeri Baş, VIII 371b16, 272a9
Çerkes, Çerākis, Çerkez (Circassians), VIII 353a16-17
Çi Çöl (Çiçul), VIII 364a12-17
Çiçu, VIII 353a25
Çingane (Gypsy), VIII 358b13
Çirqona (Cerkovina), VIII 362b12
Çora (Xhyra), VIII 368a19
Çoruġ (Choruh), VIII 353a26
Çorum Muṣṭafā Paşa, VIII 364a21, 27

Damiz (Damës), VIII 357a3
Danube: see Ṭuna
Dede Maqṣūd, VIII 367b13-14
Degirmenlik (Milos), VIII 362a16
Delvinak (Delvinaki), VIII 356a9-12
Delvine (Delvina), VIII 352a19-352b26, 26, 353a28, 353b4, 20, 27, 32, 356a23, 357b8, 367b28, 368a2
Demāvend (mountain in Iran), VIII 360a4, 371b27
Depe Delen (Tepelena), VIII 354b28, 356a33, 356b1-2, 4 - 357a1, 357b8, 358b3
Derviş Meḥemmed Ẓıllī (Evliya's father, not named in the text), VIII 360b15-18
Derviş Rāhī, VIII 356a31-32
Dest-pot (Despot, title of Serbian king), VIII 364b3, 368a26, 369a28, 371b21
Dirac, Diraç (Durrës), VIII 362b22, 29 - 363a17, 20-21, 32, 363b6, 364b28, 365b9, 368a1
Diraġopola (Dropull, river = Upper Drino), VIII 353b26, 354b23, 27, 355b24, 356a25
Dirava (Drava, river), VIII 368b32
Dirin (Drina, river in Hercegovina), VIII 359b31
Dirin, Dirinaz (Drin, river in N Albania), VI 33a15, 18-19, 28, 34a15, 35a3, 13
Dniester: see Ṭurla
Dobra-venedik (Dubrovnik), V 167b9
Dobrona (Drabonik), VIII 357a25-26
Dobroten, V 169a11
Dolyan, VIII 367a20
Domuz Ovası (Domosdova), VIII 368a20
Drabonik: see Dobrona
Drin, Drina: see Dirin
Drino (river in S Albania): see Diraġopola, Ergiri Ṣuyı
Dropull: see Diraġopola
Dubrovnik: see Dobra-venedik

Dundar (Dunavat), VIII 354a31
Duqagin (Dukagyin), VI 33a14, 36b23, 28, 30
Duqat (Dukat), VIII 360b32, 361a27, 362a11, 34, 367b28
Durrës: see Diraç
Duşmenik (Dushnik), VIII 360a30

Ebū'l-fetiḥ: see Sulṭān Meḥemmed II
Edirne, VIII 358a1, 369a30, 370a27
Eflaq (Vlachs), V 168b1
Egre (Erlau), V 168b4; VIII 361a28
Egypt: see Mıṣır
Eksiri Valtoz (Ksirovaltos), VIII 355b34 - 356a3
Elassonos: see Alaşonya
Elbaşan, VIII 353a33, 360a6, 362b18-19, 26, 34, 363a2-3, 10, 14, 20, 363b4, 6, 8-9, 364a19, 21, 28, 30, 32 - 367b15, 368a2, 10-11, 21
Elbaşan nehri, şuyı, etc. (Elbasan River), VIII 359b9, 363b10, 364a16, 20, 368a19-20
Elburz (mountain in Iran), VIII 360a5
Emīr Buḫārī, VIII 364b16
Emīr Maḥmūd, VIII 370a31, 370b6
Emīrler Sulṭān, VIII 360a28
English: see İngilis
Engürü (Ankara), VIII 354a28
Erciş, VIII 371b27
Erdel (Transylvania), VI 33b12; VIII 359a21
Erdel Belġıradı (Transylvanian Belgrade), VIII 357a31
Ergiri Qaṣri (Gjirokastër), VIII 353b11, 20, 25, 28 - 355b24, 27, 29, 356a12, 22-24, 357b7-8, 12
Ergiri Ṣuyı, nehr-i Ergiri, etc. (Gjirokastër River = Lower Drino), VIII 35b11, 356a27-28, 356b2, 10, 357a2-3, 360b3, 12, 362b12-13
Erlau: see Egre
Ermenī (Armenian), VIII 358b13, 365a29
Erżurum, V 168b1; VIII 371b27
Esim (Ishëm, river), VI 36b13
Esved ibni Miqdād (Aswad ibn Miqdad), VIII 353a20
Esztergom: see Usturġon
Evliyā Çelebi (self-reference as *ḥaqīr* "this humble one," translated "I"), V 168b10-15; VI 33b4, 34a32, 35a21-22, 36a13, 36b2-3; VIII 352b30, 353b26, 354b8-10, 356a31, 356b29, 357a1, 358b5, 25, VIII 360b15-18, 364a26, 29, 365b5-6, 371b5, 372a1
Evrenos: see Ġāzī Evrenos

Fārsī (Persian), VIII 366b10
Ferengis (Frengis), VIII 367b28
Ferhād (legendary mountain-digger), VI 34b22, VIII 354a28, 358a19, 371a20
Fezā'ī, VIII 355a31
Fiġānī, VIII 355a31
Fīlequs (Phillip of Macedon), VIII 353b30, 364a34
Firanqul (Frangulis), VIII 366a4
Firaqul (Frakulla), VIII 360b3
Fireng, Firengistān (Europeans, Europe), VI 33a12, 16, 34b24-25, 35b15-16; VIII 356b7, 357a29, 360a2, 360b4, 22, 362a12, 16, 28, 362b3, 26, 33, 363a4, 364b11-12, 365a29, 366b10, 367b29, 32-33, 369a28, 370a4, 372a6
Foça (Foča), VIII 359b31

Ġalaṭa (Kalasa), VIII 352b27 - 353a4
Ġalaṭa (Galata, in Istanbul), VIII 353a23
Ġāzī Beg, VIII 371b11
Ġāzī Evrenos, VIII 368a26-27, 30
Ġāzī Ḥüseyn Paşa, VIII 370b24
Ġāzī Ḫüdāvendigār: see Sulṭān Murād I
Ġazze (Gaza), VIII 353a18
Gedik Aḥmed Paşa, VIII 352b28, 353b3, 19, 356b6, 13, 18, 357a8, 15, 29, 362a30
Genoese: see Ciniviz
Girid, Girit (Crete), V 168a21; VI 35b13; VIII 362a20, 362b1
Gjakova: see Yaqoviçse

Gjin Aleksi: see Kin Aleksi
Gjirokastër: see Ergiri Qaṣri
Gog and Magog: see Yācūc ve Mācūc
Gorica: see Qoru Daġ, Qoru Varoş
Gölikesri (Kastoria), VI 34b13; VIII 372a28
Gönye, VIII 353a25
Greek, Greeks: see Rūm, Rūmca, Yūnāniyān
Gypsy: see Çingane

Ḥācī Beg, V 168b34
Ḥācī Bektaş-ı Velī (see Bektaşi), VIII 361a14-15
Ḥācī Ḥamza, VIII 370a31, 370b3
Ḥācī Ḥasan, VIII 365b23
Ḥācī Murād, VIII 354b4, 371b32-33
Ḥācī Qāsım, VIII 370a34, 370b16
Ḥafṣ, VIII 370b20
Ḥaleb (Aleppo), VI 33b7
Halveti: see Ḫalvetī
Ḥanefī (Sunni legal school), VIII 360a24
Ḥarīṣ-zāde, VIII 363a25, 34 - 363b1, 23
Ḥasan Bali-zāde, VIII 365b10-11
Ḥasan Şāh, VIII 367b8-10
Ḥasbī (poet), VIII 361b25
Hāşimī (Hashemite), VIII 353a9
Ḥaydar Paşa, VIII 370a30, 370b2
Hebron: see Ḫalīlü'r-raḥmān
Hersek, Hersekistān (Hercegovina), VIII 359b30, 364b18, 369a28
Hersek-oġlı Aḥmed Paşa, VI 36a3
Heyhāt Ṣaḥrāsı (Kipchak Steppe), VIII 353a15-16
Hilālī (poet), VIII 367b9
Horom Ova (Hormova), VIII 356a27
Horpuşta (Hoçisht), VIII 369a28
Ḥotin (Chotin), VI 34a34
Ḥuneyn, VIII 367b19
Hülāgū (Hulagu), VIII 353a15
Ḥüseyn Aġa, VIII 361b22, 27, 30
Ḥüseyn Beg, VI 33b29, 35a3
Ḥüseyn Paşa, VIII 357b18, 358b1, 359a18
Ḥüseynī (poet), VIII 366a33

Ḫālid ibni Velīd (Khalid ibn Walid, Arab commander, d. 642), VIII 353a20
Ḫalīl Aġa, VIII 369a15
Ḫalīlü'r-raḥmān (Hebron), VIII 357b17
Ḫalvetī (Halveti, Sufi order), VIII 354b7, 358b18, 359a4, 361b31, 365b22
Ḫaybar (Khaybar), VIII 367b19
Ḫırıştoş (Mezö-Keresztes), V 168b4
Ḫırqīl (Herakil, [i.e., Heraclius, Byzantine emperor, reg. 610-41]), VIII 353a12, 19, 367b26, 368a4
Ḫışım Ḥasan Aġa, VIII 365a18
Ḫışım Meḥemmed Paşa, VIII 364a21, 365a16-18, 366b4
Ḫıżır Aġa, VIII 354b3, 365a27

İbrāhīm Paşa, VIII 357a9
İlhām Sulṭān, VIII 367b13
İlyās Paşa, VIII 362a4
İmām Efendi, VIII 369a15
İngilis (English), VIII 355a24
İpek (Peja, Peć, town and mountains), V 167b1
'İsā Beg, V 169a21
İskender (Skënder) VI 34b24
İskender Beg, VIII 370a31, 370b5
İskender-i Kübrā, İskender-i Zū'l-qarneyn (Alexander the Great), VI 33a29, 33b9; VIII 364a34
İskenderiyye (Shkodër, Scutari), VI 33a12, 29 - 35a11, 25, 35b4, 13, 23, 36a4, 36b1-7, 11; VIII 362b17, 32, 364b7, 368a1, 368b27
İskenderiyye (Alexandria), VI 33b8
İskenderun, VI 33b7-8
İslāmbol (Istanbul), VI 34a34, 36b7; VIII 353a23, 355a13, 357a9, 359a12, 360a9, 366a31, 369a22, 370a1, 372a11
İspas (Spas), VI 36b28-29
İspilit (Split), V 167b10

İşpanya (Spain, Spanish), VI 33a17, 30, 34b27, 35b21, 24, 36a2, 36b6, 10; VIII 352a20, 353a27, 353b2, 360b21, 362b23, 31, 367b27, 369a28
Işqırapar (Skrapar), VIII 357a4, 6-12, 357b6, 359b7
Istanbul: see İslāmbol
Işṭar-ova, İstar-ova (Starova), VIII 368a28, 372a15, 30 - 372b13
Italian: see Talyan
İzevçan (Zveçan), V 167b5-8, 13, 168a9, 168b14, 17
İzmir, VIII 369a34
İzvoric (Zvërnec), VIII 362a25-28
İzvornik (Zvornik), V 167b12

Jabal al-Himma: see Cebelü'l-himme
Janina: see Yanya
Jaravina, Zaravina, Zarovina (Zharovina), VIII 355b23, 356a4-8
Jengjeç: see Yeñgeç
Jerusalem: see Quds
Jewish: see Yehūdī
Joṭom (Zhitom), VIII 357a17-19, 24
Julad (Zhulat), VIII 353b1-14

Kaçanik: see Qaçanik
Kahkaha: see Qahqahā
Kakoz: see Qaqoş
Kalasa: see Ġalaṭa
Kanina: see Qanye
Kardhiq: see Qardik
Kaschau: see Qaşşa
Kashisht: see Qaşist
Kastoria: see Gölikesri
Kavaja, Kavala: see Qavaya, Qavala
Kerbelā, VIII 362a6
Keys (Arab tribe), VIII 353a14-15
Khalid ibn Walid: see Ḫālid ibni Velīd
Khaybar: see Ḫaybar
Kiçok: see Qılçoqlar
Kilimente (Kelmendi), V 167b9; VI 35b4, 12, 14, 25; VIII 368a3
Kin Aleksi (Gjin Aleksi), VIII 352b8, 13
Kipchak Steppe: see Heyhāt Ṣaḥrāsı
Keysū, VIII 353a14
Klāb (Llap, river), V 167a24, 167b1, 168a24, 29, 31
Kevs̱er (river in Paradise), VI 34a15
Korça, VIII 356b2, 366a26, 372a27
Kosovo: see Qoş-ova
Košice: see Qaşşa
Kotor: see Qoṭur
Köpürli (Köprülü) Meḥemmed Paşa, VIII 357a20
Köpürli-zāde (Köprülü Zade) Fāżıl Aḥmed Paşa, VIII 364a1
Kördüs (Corinth), VIII 353b5
Körfez, Körfüs (Corfu), VIII 352a21, 356a24, 360b32, 362a24, 362b23
Krraba: see Qırraba
Ksirovaltos: see Eksiri Valtoz
Kurras: see Quras
Kurvelesh: see Quryeleş
Kusum Baba: see Quzġun Baba
Kuzat, VIII 356b1
Küçi Beg, VIII 370a31, 370b6
Küçük Evrenos Beg, VIII 360b23-24
Küçük Meḥemmed Paşa, VIII 353b12
Küçük Ova, VI 33b19
Kürdistān, VIII 371a4

Lab Ova (Labova), VIII 356a26
Lajos: See Vlaġoş
Lake Shkodër: see Buyana
Lanqada, VIII 366a26
Lapirda (Lapardha), VIII 360a30
Laqa (Vlaka), VIII 352b8, 12
Laṭin, Latince, Latinistān ("Latin", Slavic, Serbian, Eastern Europe), V 167a21, 168a10, 168a22, 169a12; VIII 357a28, 358b13, 360a2, 362b30, 364a34, 364b13, 365a29, 366a4, 369a20, 28, 370a4, 24, 29
Latin Ban, VIII 369a22
Lat Ova (Latova), VIII 353b27
Lavdani, VIII 357a20
Laz, VIII 353a25
Lāziqa (Lazqa), VIII 353a22, 24

Lekel (Lekël), VIII 356a28
Leş (Lezha, Alessio), VI 33a11-28; VIII 362b32, 368a1, 368b28
Liboh Ova (Libohova), VIII 355b26, 356a12-22
Lipense (Lepenca, river), V 169a15
Llap: see Klāb
Lolat, VIII 364a18

Macaristān (Hungary), VIII 366a20
Maġnisa (Manisa), VIII 354a29
Maḥmūd Aġa, VIII 364a13-15
Maḥmūd Paşa: see Qoca Maḥmūd Paşa
Makedonya (Macedonia), VIII 369a24
Makiduna (Macedonia, name of Istanbul), VIII 353a23
Malāṭıyye (Malatya), VIII 359b20, 371a4
Malṭa, VIII 363b24
Manalat, VIII 354a31
Manaṣṭır (Bitola), VIII 369b2, 371b32
Manaṣtīrī Le'ālī, VIII 365b12
Manisa: see Maġnisa
Manya (Mania), VI 35b12; VIII 352b29-30, 353b15-16, 358b4, 360a32, 360b1, 361a20, 361b12, 362b4, 364a22, 25, 365b9-10, 371b3-4, 372a2-4, 10, 12, 372b13
Marican (Maricaj), VIII 357a4
Maşqolur, VIII 367a20
Mati (river), VI 33a6
Medāyin (Ctesiphon), VIII 369a23
Mediterranean: see Aq Deñiz
Meḥemmed Aġa (chief architect, not named in the text), VIII 366a31-33
Meḥemmed-efendi-zāde, VIII 358b8
Meḥemmed Paşa, VI 33b1, 35a11-12
Mekke (Mecca), VI 34b23; VIII 353a7, 18
Melek Aḥmed Paşa, V 167b6-7, 168b8-19; VI 33b2-4, 35a20, 36a14, 36b2-6
Melik Ġāzī, VIII 358b20
Memi Aġa, VIII 365a17
Memi Beg, Memi Paşa, Memo Beg, Memo Paşa, VIII 352b11, 14, 353b15, 27, 354a24-26, 31, 33, 354b11, 14-15, 22, 355b32, 356a25, 28
Mezö-Keresztes: see Ḫırıştoş
Mışır (Egypt), VI 33b8; VIII 362a19, 367a21, 369a23
Migrāl, Migrel (Mingrelian), VIII 353a22, 25, 353a26
Milos: see Degirmenlik
Miqat (Mekat), VIII 360b3, 13-18
Mitroviçse (Mitrovica), V 167a21, 32, 167b2, 4, 168a24
Mizistre (Mistra), VIII 367a20
Mohac (Mohács), V 168b3
Moldavians: see Boġdan
Monemvasia: see Benefşe
Monlā Gūrānī, VIII 364b17
Montenegro: see Qara Daġlar
Mora (Morea), VI 35b12; VIII 353b5
Morava (river, plain), V 167b1, 168a25; VIII 359b8
Mu'āviye (Muawiya I, caliph, reg. 661-80), VIII 355a12-13, 34
Muḥammed, Muḥammed Muṣṭafa (the Prophet), VIII 362b9, 366a33
Muḥyī Çelebi, VIII 366a5
Muḫtār Beg (Frakulla), VIII 360b3
Mumcı-zāde, VIII 361b22, 27, 30
Murād Paşa, VIII 358b22
Murtażā Beg, VIII 372a3
Murād Çelipa (Murad Çelepia), VIII 357b18, 21, 358b9-10, 23, 30, 359a2
Murād Ḫān: see Sulṭān Murād
Muṣṭafā Aġa, VIII 365a17
Muṣṭafā Baba, V 167b4
Muṣṭafā Paşa, VIII 357a18
al-Mustanṣır-bi'llāh (caliph, reg. 1226-42), VIII 353a15
Muşqa, VIII 358b28
Mut, VI 36b10-22
Muyo Baba, VI 33b19, 35a9
Müzākiyye (Myzeqe), VIII 357b5, 358a10, 359b9-10, 362b13, 28, 364b28

Nāliṣī, VIII 355a31-32
Niksar, VIII 358b20
Nova (bay), VI 35b9
Nova Borda (Novobërda, mountains), V 168a23

Ochakov: see Özü
Oẖri (Okhri, philosopher or king, founder of Ohrid), VIII 369a21, 370a2
Oẖri (Ohrid), VI 33a1, 6-7, 34b13; VIII 368a10, 20-21, 32, 368b2, 14, 369a4, 18 - 371b16, 18, 29, 372a9-13, 15-16, 31
Oẖri Göli, Oẖri Buḥeyresi, Oẖri Boġazı (Lake Ohrid), VI 33a6; VIII 360a3, 368a22, 25, 27, 30, 33, 368b2, 9-21, 29 - 369a3, 17, 23, 369b14, 370b11, 371a22, 372a14, 28, 372b5
Oẖri-zāde, VIII 369a6-7, 17, 370a11-15, 29, 370b13, 21, 23, 26, 371a12 (?), 15, 18, 20, 371b11, 15, 20, 372a3
Oẖrin (Ohrin), VIII 368a24
Ordubar, VIII 371a4
Omar: see 'Ömer
Omoraṣ, VI 33a6-8
Orẖan Ġāzī: see Sulṭān Orẖan
'Os̱mān Beg, 'Os̱mān Paşa, VIII 353b15, 354a33, 358b2-8
'Os̱mānlı: see Āl-i 'Os̱mān
Ostoq: see Uşṭuq
Oṣum (river, mountain), VIII 359b7, 11, 14, 24, 28, 32
Ottomans: see Āl-i 'Os̱mān
Oxus: see Ceyḥūn

'Ömer (Omar I, caliph, reg. 634-644), VI 34b25; VIII 353a9-11, 19, 27; VIII 367b20-23, 27, 368a8
'Ömer ibni 'Abdü'l-'azīz (Omar II, caliph, reg. 717-20), VIII 353a20
'Ömer Aġa, VIII 369a15
Özü (Ochakov), VIII 361a29

Padre (diviner; see Qolon), VIII 360a20
Palor (Palorto), VIII 354a30, 354b12, 17
Paramithiá: see Aydonat
Paşo-zāde, VIII 363a25, 365a18
Patirgāh, VIII 370a23
Pay-ova (Pajova), VIII 364a18
Paz, VIII 371b28
Peć, Peja: see İpek
Pekin, Beklin (Peqin), VIII 363b5 - 364a11, 15
Pendi Hondid (Perondi), VIII 360a30
Përmet: see Piremedi
Persians: see 'Acem
Peşkim (Bishqem), VIII 364a18
Peshkëpia: see Pışqopi
Phillip: see Fīleqūs
Pışqopi (Peshkëpia), VIII 355b29-34
Pīr Meḥemmed Efendi, VIII 360a28
Piremedi (Përmet), VIII 357a14-16, 357b6
Pirmojya (Primorje), V 167b10
Podġorad (error for Porġonat), VIII 367b28
Podġoriçse, Podġoriç (Podgorica), V 167b9; VI 35a23 - 35b9, 15
Poġonya (Pogon), VIII 355b23, 356a4, 356b9, 357a16, 357b7
Poġradas (Pogradec), VIII 368a28, 368b14, 372a15-27, 30
Pojeġa (Požega), V 167b11; VI 36b30
Popo Baba, VIII 354b31
Porġonat (Progonat), VIII 356a30-34, 356b18, 358b3, 360b32, 367b33
Priştine (Prishtina), V 168b9, 22 - 169a23; VI 33a31; VIII 372a7
Progonat: see Porġonat
Pulya (Puglia), VI 33a17, 30, 35b21, 24, 36a13; VIII 362b23
Pupuşqa (Pupuška), V 167b10

Qaçanik (Kaçanik), V 169a13-23
Qahqahā (fortress in Iran, proverbial for impregnability), VIII 353b4
Qandiye (Candia), VI 35b14; VIII 353a31, 354b1-2, 357a8, 363b19
Qanija (Kanija), V 167b11

Qanye (Kanina), VIII 360b20 - 361a21, 362a15
Qaqoṣ (Kakoz), VIII 353b27, 356a25
Qara Burun, VIII 362a33
Qara Daġlar, Qara Daġ (Montenegro), V 167b9; VI 35a21, 25, 35b4, 12, 25; VIII 367b33, 368a3
Qara Deñiz (Black Sea), VIII 353a23, 370a1
Qara Ḥasan, VI 33b29
Qara Ḫoca, VIII 370a32, 370b6
Qara Murād Paşa, VIII 358b23
Qara Muṣṭafā Paşa, VIII 357a20
Qara ʿOs̱mān Aġa, VIII 365a17
Qara ʿOs̱mān Beg, VIII 359b8
Qardik (Kardhiq), VIII 353b11, 18-29
Qaryan (Karjan), VIII 356a26
Qāsım Aġa, VIII 359a12, 15
Qāsım-zāde, VIII 366b4, 11
Qaşist (Kashisht), VIII 357a3
Qaşşa (Kaschau, Košice), VIII 366a20
Qavala (Kavala), VIII 364a34, 369a24
Qavaya (Kavaja), VIII 363a19 - 363b4, 6
Qaydefā (Candace), VIII 369a34
Qılçoqlar (Kiçok), VIII 357a5
Qırqlar Maqāmı, V 169a23
Qırraba (Krraba), VI 33a1
Qishbardha: see Aqça Kilse
Qlora (Calabria), VI 35b24; VIII 362b23
Qoblaki (assassin of Sultan Murad I), V 167a24, 168a32
Qoca Maḥmūd Paşa; VIII 360b22, 362b17, 32, 364b8-10
Qoca Siyāvuş Paşa, VIII 370a30, 370b16
Qoçi Beg, VIII 372a2
Qolon (Colon [i.e., Christopher Colombus], diviner; see Padre), VIII 360a20
Qonya, VIII 359b20
Qoru Daġ (Gorica, mountain), VIII 359b16, 20, 30
Qoru Varoş (Gorica), VIII 359b11-28
Qoṣ-ova, Qos-ova, Qos-ovası (Kosovo), V 167a23, 33, 167b2, 7, 168a9, 23, 34, 168b6, 8, 25
Qoṭur (Kotor), V 167b9; VI 35a21, 27, 35b3, 7-14, 36b33; VIII 365b8, 368a12
Quds (Jerusalem), VIII 357b16-17, 367b27, 370a4
Qul-oġlı, VIII 370a30, 370b2
Quras (Kurras), VIII 364a18
Qureyş, Qureyşī (Quraysh), VI 34b23; VIII 353a8, 17, 27, 30, 33, 360a24, 367b19, 31, 368a8
Qurṣ (Kurs), VIII 366a20
Quru Çay (river), VIII 354b29
Quryeleş (Kurvelesh), VIII 352b32, 353a2, 30, 353b10, 12, 355a10 367b30, 33, 368a3
Quṣqı, VIII 358a3-4
Qusṭanṭīn (Constantine), VIII 357b10, 368a6
Qusṭantiniyye (Constantinople), VIII 369a24
Quzġun Baba (Kusum Baba), VIII 361b16, 33

Raba (Raab, river), VIII 357a18
Rābiʿa-yı ʿAdeviyye, VIII 355b14
Racʿīm (Rehoboam, son of King Solomon), VIII 369a20-21, 370a2
Ramażān Beg, VIII 371b32
Rasna (Resen), VIII 369b10, 371b29 - 372a7
Rehoboam: see Racʿīm
Resen: see Rasna
Roşinik (Roshnik), VIII 357a20-23
Rūm, Urum (Greeks, Ottomans, Turks), V 169a7; VI 36b14; VIII 353b30, 357a7, 15, 29, 357b10, 27, 359b13, 361a15, 362a10, 362b30, 364b11, 365a29, 365b2, 366a13, 367a3, 368a17, 369a6, 20, 28, 369b8, 370a29, 371a13, 371b21, 372a33

Rūmca, Urumca, lisān-ı Rūm, lisān-ı Urum (Greek language), VI 33b8; VIII 352b16, 353b30, 364b12, 366b10, 367b26, 370a3, 371a29
Rūm-eli (Rumelia), V 167b5, 12, 168a8-9, 12, 25, 29, 168b23; VI 33a14, 33b11, 36b23; VIII 352a23, 353b4, 357a32, 363a4, 364a21, 33, 364b2, 19, 368a12, 368b9, 369b6, 11, 371a30
Rūmī (poet), VIII 367b6

Ṣavur-zāde, VIII 371b33-34
Ṣayada (Sajada), VIII 353a1, 353b7, 22
Ṣazan, VIII 362a32
Scutari: see İskenderiyye
Segedin (Szeged), VIII 361a28
Sehend (mountain in Iran), VIII 360a4
Selanik (Thessalonika), VIII 361b4, 370a1
Seleme (? - desert), VIII 353a14
Seleşti (Serbian king), V 167a22
Selīm Şāh: see Sulṭān Selīm I
Semendireli Bali Beg, VIII 362b17-18
Semerine (Çamëria), VIII 356b2
Serbian: see Ṣırf
Serdār ʻAlī Paşa: see ʻAlī Paşa
Serem (Sremska), V 167b2, 12
Shëngjin: see Sincivan
Shkumbin: see Uşqumbi
Ṣırf (Serbia, Serbian), V 167a22, 168a11, 168b23; VIII 364b3, 365a29, 369a28
Silifke, VI 36b19
Sinān (architect), VIII 361b5
Sinān Beg, VIII 365b14
Sinān Paşa, V 169a15; VIII 360b14, 18, 31, 361a13-14, 18, 365b1, 8, 21, 27, 366a22, 367b7, 12
Sincivan (Shëngjin), VI 33a20; VIII 368b28, 369a1
Sineya (Sinja), VIII 360b2
Siroz, VIII 369b2, 371b21
Sivas, VIII 358b20
Siyāvuş Paşa: see Qoca Siyāvuş Paşa
Skënder: see İskender
Skopje: see Üsküb

Skrapar: see Işqırapar
Solomon: see Süleymān
Spain: see İşpanya
Spas: see İspas
Split: see İspilit
Sremska: see Serem
Starova: see Işṭar-ova
Struga: see Usturqa
Strumica: see Uşṭurumca
Subḥān (mountain in Anatolia), VIII 360a4
Ṣudaq, VIII 370b16
Sulṭān Aḥmed I (reg. 1603-17), VIII 366a31, 371b10
Sulṭān Bāyezīd I = Yıldırım Ḫān (reg. 1389-1402), V 168a33-34
Sulṭān Bāyezīd II = Velī "the Saint" (reg. 1481-1512), VI 33b29, 31; VIII 352a20, 352b27-28, 353b3, 19, 31, 354a6, 34, 354b15-16, 356b6, 16, 357a7, 11, 28, 357b25, 28, 358a9, 358b15, 32, 359a1, 359b6, 360a27, 360b23, 362b33, 363a9, 12, 364b18, 370a13-15, 371b7
Sulṭān İbrāhīm (reg. 1640-48), VIII 357a19, 363b32-33
Sulṭān Meḥemmed II = Ebū'l-fetiḥ (Mehmed the Conqueror, reg. 1451-81), V 168a34, 168b1, 169a2; VI 33a11, 14, 31-33, 33b19, 34b5, 35a16, 24-25, 35b5, 23, 28, 36a3-4, 7, 36b11, 16, 23; VIII 360b21-22, 30, 362b17, 31-32, 364b5-7, 14-16, 18, 365a3, 33-34, 367b14, 368a1, 369a31 - 369b3, 371b7
Sulṭān Meḥemmed IV (Mehmed, reg. 1648-87), VIII 363b33
Sulṭān Murād I = Ġāzī Ḫüdāvendigār (reg. 1362-89), V 167a22-32, 168a11, 18, 30-168b20, 23
Sulṭān Murād II (reg. 1421-51), V 168b1; VIII 369a30 - 369b1
Sulṭān Murād IV (reg. 1623-40), VIII 357a19, 371b8

Sulṭān Orḫan (reg. 1326-62), V 167a23, VI 35b22
Sulṭān ʻO̱smān I = ʻO̱smāncıq (reg. 1299-1326), VIII 365a3
Sulṭān ʻO̱smān II (reg. 1618-22), VI 34a34
Sulṭān Selīm I (reg. 1512-20), V 168b3
Sulṭān Süleymān I (Suleyman the Magnificent, reg. 1520-66), V 168b3; VI 33b9; VIII 352a21, 353b3, 32, 357a31-32, 359b31, 361a10, 23-24, 28, 361b2, 5, 23, 25, 362a22, 30, 362b34, 363b8, 364b3, 19, 370b1, 18, 372a32
Sulṭān Uzun Ḥasan (Akkoyunlu, reg. 1453-78), V 168b2
Sükūnī, VIII 355a31
Süleymān (Solomon), VIII 369a21, 370a2
Süleymān Ḫān: see Sulṭān Süleymān I
Syria: see Şām

Şāh İsmāʻīl (Safavid shah, reg. 1501-24), V 168b3
Şām (Syria), VIII 365a27, 370a27
Şehīd Ḫazīnedār, VIII 371b13
Şehīdü'n-nās Dede, V 168b20
Şeyḫ ʻAzīz: see ʻAzīz Efendi
Şibenik (Šibenik), V 167b10

Tābūt (?), VIII 367b19
Talyan, Ṭalyanca (Italian), VI 34b24; VIII 360b21
Tarabosh: see Torondoş
Ṭarabulūs (Tripoli), VIII 365a27
Ṭarabuzan, Ṭarab-efzūn (Trebizond, Trabzon), VIII 353a24
Tebrīz, VIII 371a4
Tebūk, VIII 367b19
Témürṭaş-paşa-zāde Yaṣavul Beg, V 168b21
Tepelena: see Depe Delen
Tercān, V 168b1
Tesu, VIII 371a4
Thessalonika: see Selanik
Ṭırpan (Tërpan), VIII 357a13
Tiran (Tirana), VI 33a1-3
Tire, VIII 354a29
Tirḥala (Trikala), VIII 356b2
Tirḥālalı Fā'iq Paşa, VIII 368b12
Tirbuk (Tërbuq), VIII 353b27, 356a27
Ṭomor (Tomorr, mountain), VIII 359b8, 19, 34 - 360a5
Ṭomoriliçse (Tomorica), VIII 357b5
Torondoş (Tarabosh, mountain), VI 33b23, 34b6-7
Transylvania: see Erdel
Trebizond: see Ṭarabuzan, Ṭarab-efzūn
Trikala: see Tirḥala
Tripoli: see Ṭarabulūs
Tuḥfe (title of a history), VIII 353a33, 368a4
Ṭuna (Danube), V 168a25; VIII 356b5, 357a30
Ṭurla (Dniester), VIII 357b17, 361a29
Türk, Türkī (Turk, Turkish), V 168a26; VIII 366b10, 371a30

Uġraş (?), V 168b1
Uḥud, VIII 367b19
Ulama Paşa, VI 34a4
Ulcinj: see Ülgün
Urum, Urumca: see Rūm, Rūmca
Usturġon (Esztergom), VIII 356b5
Usturqa (Struga), VIII 368a23 - 369a16, 369b10, 372a14, 16
Uşṭurumca (Strumica), VIII 371a8
Uşqumbi (Shkumbin, river), VIII 362b19, 364b32, 366a26, 366b34
Uşṭuq (Ostoq), VIII 369a16, 370a27, 370b11, 371a28, 371b15, 17-28, 372a8, 12
Uzqurlı, Uzqurlı-oġlı, VIII 358a25-26, 28, 358b8, 10, 18, 32, 359a1, 7-8, 11, 15, 359b6

Ülgün (Ulcinj), VI 35b23, 36a1-15; VIII 362b32, 368a1
Üsküb (Skopje), V 169a13, 20-23; VI 33a31; VIII 364b7

Üstülni Belġıradı (Stolna Belgrade), VIII 357a31

Vā'iẓ, VIII 366a34
Vā'iẓ (Vajza, river), VIII 362b19
Vā'iż Meḥemmed Efendi, VIII 360a27
Vaqıyye-zāde, VIII 367b3-4
Varna, V 168b1
Venedik, Bunduqani (Venice, Venetians), VI 33a12, 16-17, 30, 33, 33b6, 34b27, 35b9, 14, 16, 22, 25, 36a2, 36b2, 5, 11; VIII 352a20, 352b27, 353a31, 353b2-3, 32, 355a11, 360b22-23, 361a23, 362a2, 24, 362b16, 23, 31, 33, 365b8, 368a12, 369a28
Venedik Körfezi, Bunduqani Körfezi ("Venetian Gulf", Adriatic Sea), VI 33a18-19, 35b10-11, 26, 36a5; VIII 352b24, 356a24, 356b7, 357a29, 359b10, 362b12, 18, 21, 363a2-3, 6, 366a27, 369a1
Veysī Efendi (author, d. 1627), V 169a22
Vijqar (Vizhkor), VIII 357a12
Viṭos (?), VIII 371b21
Viyo (Vyosa, river), VIII 354b28, 356b2
Vlachs: see Eflaq
Vlaġoş (Lajos, Hungarian king), V 168b3
Vlaka: see Laqa
Vlora: see Avlonya
Voyniq (Voynuk), VIII 365a30, 369a29
Voyvada (voyvod), V 167b8, 168b24, 169a23; VI 33a.2, 14, 33b14, 35b23, 36a5, 36b16, 31; VIII 352b28, 356a11, 363a20, 369b12, 372a31
Vuçitirin (Vushtrria, Vuçitërna), V 167b13, 168a9-29, 168b9; VI 33a31
Vushtrria: see Vuçitirin
Vuṭoş, VIII 354a31, 354b13-14

Xhyherina: see Cevherina

Yācūc ve Mācūc (Gog and Magog), VIII 361a31
Yaḥhā-beg-zāde, VIII 367b5
Yanqo ibni Madyan, VIII 369a22
Yanvan, VIII 369a22, 370a2
Yanya (Janina), VIII 356a5, 369b11
Yaqoviçse (Gjakova)
Ya'qūb (sheikh), VIII 361b24
Ya'qūb Efendi, VIII 361b29, 31, 362a3
Yehūdī (Jewish), VIII 358b12, 365a29
Yemen, V 169a15
Yeñgeç (Jengjeç), VIII 362a22, 29-31
Yeñice (river), VIII 353b8, 17, 23, 25-26, 354b28, 356a27
Yeñiçeri Ḥasan Aġa, VIII 357a13
Yeñi Qal'e, VI 35b23-26
Yezīd (Yazid I, caliph, reg. 680-83), VIII 355a12, 34
Yūnān, Yūnāniyān (Greeks), VI 33b8; VIII 362b30, 364a34
Yūnus Voyvada, VIII 370a31, 370b6
Yūsuf Beg, Yūsuf-beg-zāde, Yūsuf-beg-oġlı, VI 33b1, 5, 35a11, 16-19, 36a14, 36b2-6
Yūsuf Beg (Sinān-paşa-zāde), VIII 360b14-15, 17

Zadra (Zadar), V 167b10
Zā'im Beko, VIII 354a33
Zaravina, Zarovina: see Jaravina
Żavaraho, VIII 354b27
Zevqī (poet), VIII 367b7
Zeynel-paşa-oġlı, VIII 355b22, 356a14
Zharovina: see Jaravina
Zhitom: see Joṭom
Zhulat: see Julad
Zihne (Zihna, town in Macedonia), VIII 369b2
Zile (?), VIII 371b21
Zirin (Zrin), V 167b11
Zvërnec: see İzvoric
Zvornik: see İzvornik

FACSIMILES

ظالوغی جانب جنوبیده تا آرناوود لتوالجنبده بحوزر قلعه سی نواحیلرنده مسیر صحراسنده برکولدن ظالوغ ایدوب
اندن نهر ایژره یه قریشوب اندن نهر راشقه نهر یوشانیچسه و نهر ترنوویچسه دخی نهر یوشانیچسه مخلوط
اولوب نهر راشقدن دورد عدد آرق عظیملر شهرک باغلرینه و دکرمانلرینه تقسیم اولنور و برآرقی دخی آشغی باغچه لره
و مشبک بوستانلره بعده بو مذکور یدی عدد انهارلر اوکز ایشتر بلغراد دیولنده نهر موراوایه مخلوط اولور نهر موراوه دخی
قلعهٔ کوپلوجه قربنده نهر طونایه منصب اولور و بو شهرک زمینی برقوممال بر اولمغله شدت شتاده ایله اصلا چامور اولماز پاک و پاکیزه شهردر
در وصف تتمهٔ شهر ... شهرک بازارلری بالاده بو شهر اوچ قفل ایله منشا اولوب بو شهر اچره هفته بازاری کونلری اوچ قاضی
بر یره کلمه سی مقرر در کم اوچ حصه حصه شهر در اولا بوسنه سنجاغی قاضیسی و بو شهر قاضیسی روم ایلینده بر قوور شته
~~قاضیسی و ... قاضیسی دخی بوسنه قاضیلری دخی شهر قاضیسیله لوردعدد قاضیلر~~ بو شهرده عضو ...
غیری شهرلرده استماع اولنمامشدر و السلام و بو شهر قضاسنده منشا اولان قلاعی بیان ایدر

اوصاف زیارتکاه بکیم بازارده الشیخ ولی افندی حاجی خرم جامعنده مدفوندر

بو شهردن ... ایدوب بالعافیه قزاره ... اوجه برابر ... پانزده قالوغ
اندن ۸ ساعتده اوصاف ... کرماتینسقه یعنی قلعهٔ ... بانسقه ۱۰۲۸ سنه تاریخنده قورشونجی زاده مصطفی
پاشا سلطان عثمان ثانی فرمانیله ارناوود عشقیالر دفعیچون بو بوغاز آغزنده بو قلعه شکل مربع سنگ بنا برالجاق قیا اوزره برقلعه
رعنا انشا ایتدی اما سهل حوالهسی واردر بوسنه ایالتی خاکنده واقع اولوب درون حصارنده دزداری و محترخانه و اللی
عدد نفرایکی وکفایت مقداری جبه خانه سی وشاهی طوپلری وغلال انبارلری وبر کوچوک جامعی وار غیری عمارتندن برشی
یوقدر اما آشغی وار وشی اوچیوز مقداری باغچه کچه قفراخانه لر وار جمله کیره متی ایله مستوردر بر جامعی مصطفی
پاشانکدر برخانی عصمتی وار اما چارشوسی یوقدر لکن باغلری چوقدر کرخیم حمامی یوقدر اما اوصاف ... قاوزا یعنی
ایلیجه قدرت حمامی بش آلتی یرده حوضلری وکوچوک قبه لو ایلیجه لر وارکم جمله دیاردن جذام وکر و کچیسک اولان اهل درد
کلوب یدی سکز کون آب گرمادن نوش ایدوب بش اون کره کرسه بامرالله اول اهل مرضک وجودی درتبعضه دن تو شفا بولور
اندن ساعتده اوصاف ... یعنی قلعهٔ بالا ... نچسه ... دمکدر
بانیسی صرف مرالریدن سکشتی قرال بناسیدر تاریخی بالزا ... تاریخنده غازی خداوندکار یعنی سلطان مراد اول ابن
اورخان غازیدرکم بو قلعهٔ فتح ایدوب بعده قوص اووا جنکنده یدی کره یوز بیک کفاری دنحان تیغدن کچروب
باده جه لشلری سیر ایدوب شهداری کلاتهری کنارنده بر یره یبغارکن کفار لشلری اچندن منکوس مولاک
تام برکفره فالعقوب سلطان مرادی شهید ایدر بر روایتده بعدالجنک جدال مرکور کافر الحیله تقربیله دست بوس
پادشاهیه کلنجه داء الخنزیر والجام اولوب مرادخان غازی شهید ایدنجه آننه بنوسفرار ایدرکن بو قدر عسکر اسلام بو قدر
سلاح اوشرلرله اصلا بیقه مازلر برفرعتوته عورت ایدر بیره آتیمطرنفیدن اوروله بوخسه آتی بیله جله دم
یکم ایجنده در دیبنجه برقولی قونلی آتند طرنقنه براوق اورنجه آیله کافر یره زیرا اولنجه غازیلر اوشوب دیمرکیمک
یتعاسندن کوجیله یول یولوب کافری بوغازلیوب دیه لرلر حالا اول رمانندن برو آل عثمانه کافر دن برالجی کلسه
پادشاه تختی اوزره قرار داده اولوب پادشاهک خلعتنده متصل براوزون بکم الجیلر اویرکن ایکی طرفندن الجیلری
برک لدوتوب ابتدا براوید برو صکره سکز آدم اوزون بکم اویدروب پادشاه یانته قومالتلر غازی خداوندکارک
شهید اولدوغی کوندن قانون آل عثمان قالمشدر انکیچون بو منترو ویچسه قلعه سنه قلعهٔ منحوس درلرکم بوقلعهٔ بالا
قوس اووا صحراسنک مغربی جانبی نهایتنده حواله سز یومورطه مثال شکل مدور سنک طاشی برقلعهٔ صوش
متریس ولغم قبول ایتمز برحصن حصین وسد متین در الحاق برقپوسی وار ایچنده اصلا معمور اندن براو بنا یوقدر

امابو قلعه دیبندن جاریدر ارناود لقده ایبک داغلرندن کلوب نهر کلاد ایله براولوب اینر بونهر مورا اورته غلوجه اولور بو قلعه یه بو دیارلرده قوس اوداء منزویجه سمی درلر برینه دخی سرنز منرو وتیجه سمی درلر اما انلک تکلمه سی خرابدر

وبو قلعهٔ منزویچسیه براوق منزلی بعید زیارتگاه مصنیه نوربابا تکیه سنده فقرای بکتاشیانی وار بعضی آینده وروندکان قونار وبو تکیه یه متصل اوجقسا آخر لحدود اینزویچه دن ایالت بوسنه بو علده تمام اولوب جمله روم الی اعیانلری بنک چقینده اولانلری بو علده پاشا افندیمزه الای عظیم ایله استقبال ایدوب مبارک باد قوربانلر کسلوب فقرالره بزل اولندی وپاشا افندیمز ایزوچا جامعنده ایکی رکعت نماز قلوب فقرایه تصدقلر اتدی بو ربطه معموره قوس اوداء صحراسنده اوچیوز کیره مت ایله مستور خانه لر وجامع وحمام وخان وبر تمام فاخر دکانلی وحاماتی مزوبو ادالیده معمور قصبه در بوسنه ایالتنک براوجی بو علده وبراوجی قره داغلرده وبرطرف دوبدغور چسه وکلمسه وقلعه قطورده بر سمتی دوبره وینه دیکده وبراوجی بورن قله سنده وعالمده وبراوجی بوبوشقه دیبرمورریه واسپیلنده وبرجانب غریده شبه نیک وزادره وسمتی شماله زیرین اوغلنده وبرطرف فی مرسک سنجاغنده ماینره ایله مسادر وبرطرف فی موزعه ایله مسادردر سمتی بودین ایالتیله وبراوجی ازوورنیکده سرمسنجاغیله مسادر وجانب شرقیسی روم الی الاجه حصار ایله مسادر وبراوجی بوقبله سمتنده دوابروجانبده ووجدرسنجاغیله مسادر سواد معظم ایالتدر کبیردر کم بونده اولان قلعه لر بو دیارده

اولا بوسنه ایالتنده یدی سنجاق بکی اولان قلاع علک مقرالرینه

بوسنه دفتردارینک علوفه لری ویردیکی یوز یتمش انتیار قلاع اغلری

اولاجانب شمالده چرنیک سنجاغنده اولان قلاع اغلردن قلعهٔ چرنیک وقلعهٔ ولیقه وقلعهٔ بلوسیتنا وقلعهٔ پاقرچسه وقلعهٔ سرچه وقلعهٔ اوستونچاپچسه وقلعهٔ دوبره قوکه وقلعهٔ زانچه وقلعهٔ زاغراب وقلعهٔ حسین وقلعهٔ لونجارکه وپوژغه سرحدی قلعه لرنی بیلن بعد قلعهٔ ووکین وقلعهٔ ویروویتیچسه وقلعهٔ ما ضلوون وقلعهٔ پوژغه وقلعهٔ راهوویچسه وقلعهٔ والپا اووا وقلعهٔ اوسک وقلعهٔ یاق اووا وقلعهٔ بروو وقلعهٔ غزه دیشقه وقلعهٔ یاسه نوچسه وقلعهٔ متین دوبچسه وقلعهٔ قوسدا پچسه وقلعهٔ قوی قوق نووی وقلعهٔ بهکه وقلعهٔ پوریلیج نیک وقلعهٔ بلای قرقه سنجاغی قلعه لریدر قلعهٔ اوذوینا وقلعهٔ لقا ویکی حصار وقلعهٔ سیبنقه وقلعهٔ قوزیا وقلعهٔ اوبورجه بالا وقلعهٔ اوبورجه زیر وقلعهٔ بوداق وقلعهٔ درشلاق وقلعهٔ قریم وقلعهٔ زرین وقلعهٔ ولیم وقلعهٔ راقنیچه وقلعهٔ قورلادو قلعهٔ روزای زادره جانبنده اولا قرقه سنجاغی قلعه لریدر قلعهٔ پوروق وقلعهٔ بابا احمد وزادوورنیه قلعه سی اورمش قلعه سی وقلعهٔ سین قلعهٔ کلیش کافرده قالدی وقلعهٔ تروغیر وقلعهٔ اسپلت کافرده قالدی وقامن قلعه کری قلعهٔ ونرلیقه بومزکورلر کلیس خاکنده درلر وقلعهٔ کنین قرقه سنجاغی تختیدر وقلعهٔ نادین وقلعهٔ اشغرادین وقلعهٔ سداکلک وقلعهٔ ایوارینه وقلعهٔ قارین وقلعهٔ پوسه دارنیه وقلعهٔ زمونیک وقلعهٔ اوزرین وقلعهٔ پرودین وقلعهٔ نوطارلر وقلعهٔ زادره کافرکیدر وقلعهٔ زمونیک وقلعهٔ نین وقلعهٔ وره نه وقلعهٔ اوستوروچه وقلعهٔ قره اورمان وقلعهٔ هلونه کلیس خاکیدر وقلعهٔ غلاموخ وقلعهٔ ربچسه قرب شبه نیک وقلعهٔ ماندالینا وقلعهٔ ماربنا قرب شبه نیک وقلعهٔ قامن غراد وقلعهٔ دزنیش وقلعهٔ صولین وانیرین قلعهٔ خراب دوره وقلعهٔ خراب کلپ وقلعهٔ آق حصار وقلعهٔ دیسچاز وقلعهٔ یایچسه وقلعهٔ کول حصار وقلعهٔ بانیه لوقه وقلعهٔ نوتنیا ق وقلعهٔ تراونیک وقلعهٔ ووجتش وقلعهٔ سرای وقلعهٔ ویسه قو وقلعهٔ وشغراد بونلر سرای سنجاغی قلعه لریدر تمام قلعهٔ خلانه وقلعهٔ صقول وقلعهٔ سره برنچسه وقلعهٔ قولشا وقلعهٔ ازووزنیق وقلعهٔ طوزله وقلعهٔ قستل وقلعهٔ بلینه وقلعهٔ راچه ازوونیق قلعه لری تمام اولدی ۵ هرسک سنجاغی بیان ایدر قلعه لو بوشقه وقلعهٔ پرسوزیه وقلعهٔ اموچقه وقلعهٔ قونچسه وقلعهٔ لیته وقلعهٔ موسطار وقلعهٔ بولقای وقلعهٔ پوچه تل وقلعهٔ غباله وقلعهٔ نورن وقلعهٔ قوریه

قلعهٔ

قلعهٔ پره زووتلهٔ اصلنه وقلعهٔ دوبره ونه دیکه کافرده بر وقلعهٔ نووادقالهٔ روصا وقلعهٔ قوموبوز وقلعهٔ رشنا و
قلعهٔ دریفه وقلعهٔ براشته کافرده قالدی وقلعهٔ قطوز کافرده قالدی وقلعهٔ کلمنته آرناووده قالدی وقلعهٔ پودغورجسه
آرناووده قالدی وقلعهٔ قله بوق عاصی داغلر ایچره قلعهٔ پیوه وقلعهٔ نکشیك وقلعهٔ بانکا وقلعهٔ زطرناق وقلعه
دوررونناق وغاچقه صحراسنده قلعهٔ کولوچ بوز میدر وقصبهٔ لوبن وقصبهٔ اصطولچه وقصبهٔ نوه سین وقصبهٔ اولوق وقلعهٔ بلچ
وشهر فوچه وقصبهٔ اوستی قولینا وقصبهٔ چاینچه وشهر طاشلیجه وقلعهٔ بیلکه شوقا وقصبهٔ پره پولو قلعهٔ قوودین و
قصبهٔ رودا نك ایچندن اقان لیم صوینك قرشو جانبنه اوصطاری راولاه خاصکی بوستانجی باشیلر حکمنده در روم ایلی ایالتی
خاکیله مشا اولان قلعه لرکم مقدما ذکری سبقت ایدن قلعهٔ بانسقه وقلعهٔ فزلر وقلعهٔ مترووچسه نام قلعه لرده بوسنه
ایالتنك یدی عدد یکجاغی قلعه لری دخی بو آراده تمام اولنجه [illegible] روم ایلی ایالتنی قراده سیاق تکرو ملازم شهرلرن بیان ایکر
اولا ابتدا روم ایلی حکمنده ذکر اولنان قصبهٔ ایپز وچایدن قالتقو جانب قبلیه قوس اووا صحرا سینه یایانی ایچره ٧٠ ساعتده
اوصنـا یعنی لواء قدیم قلعهٔ ووجه تسمیه لسان لاسیحه
دمکدر بانیسی صرف قراللریدر ٧٩٢ سنه نار رنجنده بالکرا غازی خداوندکار فتحیدر بعدالفتح بردخی کفاره جای امان اولماسن ایچون قلعه سی منهدم
اولنوب حالا قمالری ظاهر وباهردر روم ایلی ایالتنده سنجاق بکی تختیدر یکینك طرف پادشاهیدن خاص همایونی الجه دك
ولواسنده زعامتدر و عدد تیماردر الای بکیسی وچری باشیسی ویوزباشیسی واردر بوطائفه لرك قانون اوزره جبه
لولرایله بکینك عسکرایله جمله بولرسیك عسکر اولور مفتیسی ونقیبی ویوز اللی اقچه پایه سیاله قاضیسی وار عددناحیه
قرالری عمار سپاه کتخدا یری ویکیچری سرداری ومحتسبی وباجداری وخراج اغاسی واعیان اشرافکر واردر
جمله عدد محله اولا شهدا محله سی الای بکی زاده محله سی اسکی محله بوقاروعله اشقو محله معلوم بونلرك
وجمله عدد کارکیر بنا تحتانی وفوقانی وسرایا کیره مت اورتولی ایکی بیك معمور خانه لری اسملردر
وجمله عدد محرابدر اولا چارسو ایچره اسکی جامع خنکار اوقافیدر واسملردر
بونلردن ماعدا مساجدلر
مدرسه وتکیه لری ومکتبلری ومتعدد خانلری وعکمه قربنده برکسیف حمامی وار اما چارسوی آزدر بنا آزستانی
وماکول عمارتی یوقدر اما هر خانده آینده ورونده به نعمتلر مبذولدر جزیرهٔ کرید فتحی آچلمازدن مقدم بو شهر ایچره
یوز اللی خاندان صاحبی اعیان کبار سرایلری قبا تمشدر حالا انکچون بو شهر خرابه یوز دوتمشدر اما انشاالله ینه عمار اولور زیرا
قوس اووا کبی محصولدار زمین واسعت الاقطاره واقع اولوب آب وهواسی لطیفدر زیرا زمینی نووه بروده کاغکر دامننده
باغ وباغچه لی شهر غریبدر نهر کلا صحراسندن جریان ایدر ابتدا طلوعی آرناوود لقدن کلوب مذکور منزوویجسه قلعه سی
دیبنده نهر مخلوط اولوب اندن نهر موراوه ایله نهر طونایه منصب اولور بو شهر خلقی جمله روم ایلی قومیدر
جوغلوق لسان بوسنوی تکلم ایدرلر اکثریا آرناوود لسانن وطورك لسانن تکلم ایدرلر جمله چوقه انوابلر گیوب سنرجه لی
کوردك وسمور الجاق ناحلی قرمزی قلپاق گیوب قلپاغی کورکن چوبروب قلپاقلری کنارنده سیاه دارایی بروازلری کوریننور
سسند قوساق ومور ساله وار ساقچاق طشیوب قرمزی صیقمه کومش قوجالی چاقشیرلرایله قوبادی نازوك بابوج
گیرلرکم ایالت روم ایلی انسانی بو بیله لباس فاخره لرده بو شهردن قالنقو جانب قبلیه قوس اوا صحراسی ایچره نهر کلا کنارینه
کیدرکن اوصاف تربهٔ پر انوار زیارتگاه سعید الشهید وغازی داوند کار طاب ثراه وقدس الله سره العزیز
نهر کلا کنارنده بیابان ایچره قالمش بر قبهٔ عالی ایچنده مبارك قلب شریفلری وجمیع اخلاط فضلاتیکر بو محلده ٧٩٢ سنه تاریخنده
جنك عظیم اولوب بالاده غزا اولدوغی اوزره منکوس قوتلاکی نام لعین وبیدین بو بیله بر پادشاه جم جاهی شهید ایدوب بطن شریفن
یاردقلرنده جمیع یوراکلر بوبره کوچیکر وقلبن بو محله دفن ایدوب بعده بو قبهٔ علیایی یلدرم بایزید خان بنا ایتمشدر
دولت آل عثمانیه هنده عدد جنك عظیم اولمشدر اولا بری بو قوس اووا جنکیدر بری یلدرم خان جنکیدر بری ابوالفتح

جم جاهی بر

بذر فتوحه مراد خانك اول قوصوه وبغداد ایله وارینه قربنده ادعراش دره سی جنگی بریده ایوالملك رضه روم قربنده برجای اووا

ابجره آذربایجان پادشاهلرندن سلطان اوزون حسن جنکیکه تاریخی بطلان کید الخائنین در سنه جنگ عظیمدر بریده سنه

تاریخنده شاه اسماعیل ایله سلیم شاهك چالدران جنکی غیر بدر بریده سنه تاریخنده سلیمان خانك مهاجم غزاسنده یدی کره یوز بیك

کافر قتل اولنوب ولا غوش قرال مورد اولدی بریده سنه سالند اکره قربنده حرسوس پیلاسی جنکی بونده ده یدی قرال غزا اولنوب

یدی کره یوز بیك کفرهٔ فجره مردار اولدیلر حمد خدا مذکور اولان یدی عدد غزالرده جمله کفار قراللری مرد اولنورلردی لکن اتفاق

بوقوصوه اووا جنکنده بعد الجنك آسوده حال عالمنده حیله ایله غازی مراد خان شهید اولوب قلب شریفی بو تربهٔ مهبط پر انوارده

قالوب مبارك جسد شریفلری حالا بورسه ده اسکی قاپلیجه نام محلده جامع کبیرینك ساحه سنده بر قبهٔ عالی ایچنده مدفوندر زیارتگاهدر

ازدیاد اولنمز اما غرایب بونده کم بوقوصوه اووا ده کوردیکمز شهرك امینی ملك احمد پاشانك بیله دامنی غباست ایله ملوث

اولدی مکر جمیع رعایا کفره لری اطراف قرالردن پرشتنه و وحسرت شهرلرینه بازارلغه کیدرلرکن اهانت ایچون بو تربه یه کروب تبول ره

تنقیص ایدرلرمش ملك احمد پاشا بو بد رایحه و مزخرفاتلری کوروب غضب آلود اولوب حقیر اینده سلطان مراد بو پادشاه

شهید ایدن منکوس کافر اسه قرشوده بر منصب ایچنده جواهر قندیللر ایله مسك و عنبر خام بر انجه لر ایله معطر بر قبه مزین

ایجره یتوب بو قدر رهبان خدا ملکدار و بو قدر اوقاف وارکن جمیع رسما بو قدر بوز کفره و مسلمانلر کلوب مهمان اولوب کیدیلی اما

بوبزم غازی پادشاهمزك نه تربه داری و نه اوقافی اولمادیغندن جمیع کفار کلوب اهانت تغوط ایدرلر کرکدر کم جمیع اطراف

قرالکفره لری کلوب بونده انلر بوقبه تطهیر ایدوب عمار ایده سز و اروحاتی خاصه بر بیوك اقچه ایله عمار ایدوب اطراف

قلعه مثال دیوار چکوب بر تربه دار اهل عیالیله تعیین ایده سز دیو بکمده اهالی ولایته ایکی کیسه غروش کوروب جمله قرالکفره

لرینه قبه تطهیر ایدوب بر هفته ده اطراف قبه یه بر بوکسك دیوار چکوب بر عالی قپو اتدیکم آنلیدر کرمیه و یمشوز میوه درختی

دیکوب بو بر آخبانی موحش ایدوب اهل عیالیله بر غوبدار تعیین ایلدیکم اینده ساکن اولوب ارواحی و یوم سنندن و ظیفهٔ

معینه سن آلوب تربه پر انوارده اولان ابریشم حالیچه و شمعدان و بخوردان و کلابدان و قندیللری کوروب کوزه ده دیوا عبا

کلاسو بوقف اللهه ناصر المصار تعیین ایدوب برخیرات عظیمه اولدی حالا زیارتگاه خاص و عامدر رحمه الله علیه و بو

تربه پر انوارده یه زیارت جانه شهدا اون بیکدن متجاوز کبار شهدا اولدیلر و علمدار بابا و شیخ سعد الماسردده و

تیمور پاشا شوپاشازاده مصارلری و پچه بک شهد الرحمن مدفونلردر انلری زیارت ایدوب بنه جانب شرقه کیدرک

اوصاف قلعهٔ پرشتنه لسان لاتنیجه یعنی دمکدر

بانیسی مرف قراللردر ماعوسنه ۷۹۲ تاریخنده غازی خداوندکار در بعد الفتح قلعه سی منهدم اولمشدر روم ایلی ایالتنده

وموادا العمر و یوز اللی اقچه پایه سیله شریف قضادر عدد ناحیه قرارلندر قاصیره بر وجه عدالت بش کیسه

حاصل اولور کتخدا یری و یکیچری سرداری و اعیان اشرفی اغاچو قدر شهری قوصوه اووا صحراسینك پویراز جانبنده واقع

اولمش جمله عدد ۲۰۰۰ در

و جمله ایکی بیك آتمش عدد تحتانی و فوقانی کارگیر سراپا کیره متلملر و اسع حولیلی و باغ ارملی معمور و مزین خانه دان

زیبالردر جملتا قوجه بوندلر الایبکی سرای و محکمه سرای

و جمله اون ایکی ایدر آلتیسی جمعه در اولا چارسوایچنده

ماعدا مساجدلرد

جمله مدارس عالمان	ودار الحدیث مفسرن
جمله مکتب طفلان	و تکیهٔ درویشان
و جمله چشمه آزوان	و جمله سبیل جانبستان

و جمله خان خواجه کان اون بر عدد خانلردر اما تاریخ خان حاجی بك دیدی تاریخی لفظا تاریخ بیك و یوز ایکیده

یاپلدی

١٧٦ ١٦٩

یا یلدیرم بوخان ۱۰۳۲ سنه‌ده وچارسو ایچنده بر قاچ خانلری دخی وار اما قورشونلی عمارتلری یوقدر

وجمله ... عدد حماملردر جمله‌دن چارسو ایچره ابو الفتح سلطان محمد خان حمامی حالا زیارتگاه حمامدر زیرا صانع حمامینک اولان خلوتده کبار اولیاء اللهدن بری خلوتده خلوت اربعین چیقاروب دعا ایتمشکم الهی بو خلوتنه کیرن خسته کیرسه شفا بوله بیورمشلر الی هذا الان اول خلوتنه مریض کیرسه بامر الله تعالی شفا بولور چارسو ایچنده اسکی حمام دخی هواسی و بناسی خوب و مفرح و دلکشادر

وجمله ... عدد دکاکینلردر لکن کارگیر بنا بدستانی یوقدر شهرینه کوره دکانلری آزدر اما ینه هر شی موجوددر و آب و هواسی لطیف اولدوغندن محبوب و محبوبه‌سی غایت ممدوح مستثنا جوانلر وار کم دیار رومده مشهوردر و باغ و باغچه‌سی ... اوزومی و امرودی ... و اعیان اشرافلری غایت غریب دوست و چراغ صاحبلری اولوب ... نعمتلری مبذول اولوب هر کیجه مسافرسز اولمازلر

اندن تا القوی منزل قریهٔ ...

لسان لاتینده ... دیمکدر بشیوز خانه‌لی معمور و مزین و محصولدار سربست زعامتلو بندر اندن ینه جانب شرقه کیدنه

اوصاف ... یعنی قلعهٔ قچانیک سبب تسمیه‌سی اولدر کم ... اسلوبی ... ارناوود عشقیالری ... بو قلعه ... جمله قچانلر ... قچانلردن غلط قچانیک دیرلر بعده بو بوغاز اغزینه نهر ... کنارنده ... تاریخنده فاتح ... پاشا شکل مربع ... بنا ایدوب ... اما بر دره ایچنده واقع اولمغیله اطرافنده حواله‌سی چوقدر دوردار ... عدد نفراتلری و ایکی طوپی و بر قپوسی وار درون حصارده قرق اللی نفرات خانه‌لری وار غیری عمارت یوقدر اما ... واروشی یوز عدد خانه‌لردر

جمله کیره‌مت اورتولو و باغچه‌لی اولردر و بر مفرح جامعی ... وزیره ... تاریخی بودر ... معبد خوب مقام محمود ... سنه‌ده ... و بر تکیه‌ٔ درویشان بکتاشیانی وار و بر مکتب صبیانی وار و بر خانی ... واقع اولمش و بر کوچوک حمامی وار اما چارسو بازاری یوقدر ... شهر اسکوب ... و بو قچانیکدن اقان نهر ... بودره‌لر ایچره جریان ایدوب ... عیسی بک ... جریان ایده‌رک ... شهر اسکوبده ... جامع و حمام و مدرسه‌لرینه تقسیم اولنور عظیم خیراتدر و بو قچانیک باشقه قضادر ... اسکوب ... زاده‌یه ... احسان اولنمشدر و اسکوب سنجاغی ... اسکوب ... ساعتده

اوصاف روضهٔ ریاض بلدان یعنی قلعهٔ اسکوب مرام جهان نیجه کونه وجه تسمیه‌سی واردر اما ... آلتون بولنوب ... اسکوب غلط مشهور اسکوب دیرلر اما لسان لاتینده اسمی ... در بعضی مورخان رومک ... قلعه‌سی ... عیسی ... بوط ... بنا ... جبل ... داغلرینه ... بو کوعارتا ... ارناود ... قوم عارنا بودر ... الرند ... اولدیلر ... صوفیه جانبلرینه ... یلدیرم ... فتح اولمشدر آل عثمان دیارنده خسارته باشلدقلرنده تاریخ ... یلدیرم بایزید خان ... غازی اورنوس ... بعده ... بایزید خان ... هواسنی حفظ ایدوب ... تخت ثانی ... بو شهر اسکوبده ... فتح فتوحاتلر ایدردی حاکمان بیان ایدر اولا سلیمان خان تحریری اوزره روم ایلی ایالتنده باشقه سنجاق بکی تخت ... لوا ... میرمیران ... اولنوب ... عسکر ایله حکومت ایدر ... مامور اولدوغی سفره کیدر بر وجه عدالت اون سکز ... کیسه حاصل اولور پاشا ... پادشاهیدن قانون اوزره خاصی ۰۰۰ ... زعامت ۱۵

اندن قرآبه بيلاسن بوزبيك برنج غناچكرك آشوب ٩ ساعتده سيستانه يش مصبته تيرات اوغريكاغي خاكنده وروادالقدر وبورالليراتجه قضادر شهري بر واسع صحراده جامعلري وخانلري وحماملري وچارسوى بازاري وباغ و باغچه سي بحساب در وجمله عماراتلري سراپا كرميت اورتولي خيرآ حسناتدر

اندن نهرى ماى اسلامى عبور اتدك بونهر اوغراغنده داغلردن كلوب اوغري غيره سنه قريب شرابدن جا غزبه كيدر منزل قرينه او... ضروري دخي اوغري طوپراغنده قصبه مثال اوچيوز خانه لي جامع وخان وحماملي ومعمور آرنا ووده كويدر وباغ وباغچه لري وافردر ورعايا كرجمله كافردر وعورتلري جمله ساحره در اندن بنه ٩ ساعت كيدوب 6

وصف قلعه عتيق [illegible] اولمشدر اما سنه ٨٨٣ تاريخنده بوقلعه ابو الفتح غازي 11 اسلامبوله عراسنه [illegible] بوقلعه ليث كيدر يعني آرسلان كبيدر ديو نطق ايتدكلرنده بعد الفتح اسمنه قلعه ليث ديديلر غلط مشهور اولا ارلما غيله ليشدن غلط افواه ناسده لش قلعه سي ديديلر ابو الفتح غازي غزاسي وزره روم ايلي اياتنده درمه لش كاعمجا لده ويوادالقدر محتسبي ونايبي وباجدارى وقلعه دردارى و عدد حصار ايرانلري واربر قلعه سي نهر درين كنارنده رمل اوزره سكل مربع بركوچوك سوانستوار مستحكمدر اما معمور دكلدر لكن ويره دار سرحد قلعه لرندندر بانسي يه ويره ديك پرنج پرلربيدر بوسهر جمله اربا وود عاريلري دايما بربنه اره سوار اولوب ويره ديك ديارلرن واسپانيه نك پوليه يتالرن يقه يبقه مال غنايمله اكوب [illegible] تلعه [illegible] نهر درينه آتارلر بوقلعه ويره ديك كورفزى درياسنه بعيد يردر ونهر درين داغلردن حصوب جانب قبله يه آقوب بوكورفز ساحلنده سنجوآلي اماني قربنده كورفزدكزينه مخلوط اولور جمله عدد ابنيه

وجمله تكيه در وجمله عدد مدرسه وجمله

وجمله عدد خانه وجمله عدد دارالتعليم

وجمله عدد كيره ميت وجمله عدد دكاكين وجمله عدد حمامي

اورتولي باغلي وباغچه لي واسع سرحد اولوربدر اما قلعه ايچنده اولرى آزدر وباغچه لري يوقدر اما جبه خانه سي چوقدر ومساحه سي سرامند با السم صويلرى ومهتر خانه سي عاردر

اسنجا غزبه درين نهرين كچوب وصف قلعه اسكندريه ابتدا بانيسي اسكندر ذوالقرنين بنا سي اولديغيچون اسكندريه درلر بعده اساسه حاكم دسسه ... ديوب اسعد دى قران ... بوقلعه يه مالك اولوب اسلوس ... ابو الفتح بو اسكندريه اوزرينه ... سنه ٨١٣ تاريخنده جبرا وقهرا ابو الفتح سلطان محمد غازي ... روم ايلي ايالتنده ... ابتداخانده حالا بو

سنجاق وجانبنه اولاق محمد پاشا بوجوه یوسف بک مرلوا اولوب اوجاقلق احسان اولنوب وعدوب حالا حاکملرینه یوسف بک
اوغوللری درلر بوجمعه بدل اسعنابله حصوب برکی دروب قلعه ده دردار اغاجانه سنه موبدروب ملک پاشا افندیمک
ملوب عساکر سلوبلرینه دروب سقزان آتکده زاد سرور حور ایدر سجل لسروب انشاالله اولوب توبه دل مرص حسدینمز بیدینمز
حقیچون ادا ایدوب سر بولرد یوجمعه حمام بهار لنسه وبیر نمانلبا شراحسان انتدیم دا وصعدعدد رمعار نسه وحدا ملریمه
اونار غروش انعام ایدوب هربار سر مصحب بله مسرف اولکوتا هیچ توسا طراپام فریده بوسعبل زاده سرایلرینه لسدوب
روی وصفالر ایدردل اما داعما اسکندریه دلرد لزیرا وبه دیک کافرینك غایت عصیان طغیانکزوار ایدی اولة العما دولتنه
اسکندرون اوچ دریه مودم لم بوله اریاتوبه اسکندریه سمدلری اودر لداریده حلقه اره مصرحلبا اسکله سیدر
اکه اسکندرون دنزلر بری مصر اسکندریه سیدر اما لسا سوبا سانجه بوکه آلگستانثوره بزغازدرلر سورغاز اوره قلعه
نمالدر مصر اسکندر قلعه سمیدرلر حالا بسک مانوس سلماها اودره حاصر هما یونتی ٢٠٠٢٥٤٠ اقچه لدر دعامتی
١٩ وجمله تیمار ٣٠٥ مانور اودره اوچر یبد اقچه بر جبه لوکر ایله الایبکلمودری پاسود یوا سسمو پاسنک
عسکر یله جمله دور دیک عدد گزیده برار عسکر عساردرما هور اولدقلر سمره روم ایلمده بریله راحود مرلوالریله سعراشرلر
حتی جمله غازیلرکر بزمله اردل غزالرینه بیله ایدیلر حتاکه شجیع ونتا عسکر در بولواوب باشا سه مروب لسه حاصل اولور
مدعدد بلد ایله یوسکاعی جمعاعه راسه اندر حاکم شرع رسول مبیندن شیخ الاسلام ونقیب الاشرافی واعیان کبار
اشرافی ویوز اللی اقچه بانه سیله قاضی سمدساه لیحدار غد یکچری سردار وقلعه دزداری وقلعه ثمراکری عسسی ووبوادا سی
باجداری ومعماری وسهر امیتی اسمو جراح امینی واردر اشکال قلعة اسکندریه محروه عظیم بویانا نام برکوکك ساحلنده
رصارمانند عالی اودره حارلوسه دمعولا سحه دورحجه واقع اولمش سداد ادی سنك طراش رسوب صواسدرلم اصلا
حواله سی یوق لمحالدوبی عاید قلعة مالدر لکن تو حولسدر اما صعصوصی حصاری بیدلدر بویانا لوکمه فیند
وعزیده صعصو بومدر سورجبار ولری ودندانه بدنلری جوقدر جمله اللی صوکساردر بری کوندوغو طرفنه بری
تو حوداودانه ناظردر بوقپو ایچره زیارت سویتو بابا سلطان مدفوندر ودروب حصارده اولرآزدر اعمام سلطان محمد
جامعیلرینه اللهمستور طرز قدیم جامع پرنوردر ویدی سکز ضار بجکر وار بابانه رحمه الله بهلودر وقلعه بویانا
کولنه اینه جک صویولکری واردر کم اهالی قلعه بلر طشره ده دشمن کوره مز مستور صویولری ایله حیس ضاصره آلردن
صو آلرلر اما بوقلعه ده کاندر یوقدر انجاو یوز عدد ثمر اجانه حمامکری ویوبغدای انبارکری واردر اما جبه خانه سی پادشاهانه
طوپلری واردر لکن بویاناکولی آشری تورندنش د اغدن بوقلعة دوکنغو کی داغ بسهل بوقلعه یه حواله در اما
قرقرشر طوپ قلعه کوب طویل لازمدر اکر کوچوك طوپلر ایلسه بوقلعه یه اول حواله دن ضرری یوقدر زیرا آرا ده کول
واردر وقلعه دبنده قیالر کنارنده بویانا کولی ایچره چام درکلکری اوزره بالق دالیانلری واردر باشقه اماننده کیم قلعه متولیسی
اقلا مینذر
اوصاف وار وشیرة ... اسکندریه جمله بیك سکز یوز عدد تحتانی وفوقانی حدیقة روضة رضوان مثللو باغ و
باغچه لی کیره متو قیاغا اودرتولی کارکیر بنایی متین وخاندان مسلمین وشکنای موحدیندر وجمله ٥ اعلام درا اولا
بایزیدخان محله سی وعلی بك محله سی وحسین بك محله سی وا اسکله باشی محله سی ومفتی محله سی وقره حسن محله سی ودار رشده
بازار باشنده عکمه محله سی
ستایش جوامع ... جمله اون بر محرابدر اولا چارسو باشنده سلطان بایزید ولی جامعی اوکنده بر قیو سی
وار قدیم عتیق جامعدر بوله نوره دکل لسه مملو جماعت لسه ماکه جامع پرنوردر علی بك محله سنده حسین بك جامعی
اسکله باشنده مفتی جامعی مره حسن جامعی مشهور ومعمور ولنره مت الله مستور جامع پرنورلردر بونلردن
ماعدا یتمش عدد مساجد مؤمنانلدر اولا

وجمله

وجمله یدی عدد مدرسهٔ عالمانی در هر جامع معده بر مدرسه مقرر در اما مخصوص دار القرا و دار الحدیث یوقدر

وجمله مکتب طفلان ابجد خوانی در

جمله التی عدد تکیهٔ اهل طریق درویشانی در

وجمله عدد خانات خواجگانی در جمله اولا ما پاشلی خانی متین و مستحکمدر وجمیع ذی قیمت اشیالر بوخانلرده بولنور

وجمله بر عدد مکلف حمام مقامی اندر اما غایت مفرح و خوش هوا و خوب بنا بر حمام روشنا در صنعتلرلا ایله یوپیانا

وجمله بشیوز عدد چارسوی بزازستانی در جمیع اهل صنایع موجود در اما کول طرفنده بالق بازاری معمور و مزیندر

ستایش لباس مرد میدان جمله [illegible] اسبابلری جمله [illegible] سمور [illegible] و قوبا دیبا

[illegible] عبا سمور [illegible] ملی و مالعا ایله دایم گزرلر

در بیان لباس زنان [illegible] جمله [illegible] فراجه [illegible] کلاه [illegible] تاتیه کیوب

[illegible] بیاض عزار دولبند اورتنوب [illegible] ایدر [illegible] مستوره گزرلر

در فصل اسماء رجالان

در بیان اسماء زنان

در مدح محبوبه محبوبان اکر بنتان و پسرانلری اولقدر سیم اندام و کمال فام محبوب و محبوبه لری اولور کم جمله گل چهره لردر

توصیف آب و هواسی جانب [illegible] هواسی اولقدر لطیفدر کم جمیع خلقی [illegible] [illegible] قوت [illegible] کیمه مشهور

تعریف زلال آب حیوان بر طرفنده نهر [illegible] کویا ماء کوثردر بر یاننده کم [illegible] صویی [illegible] کویا شراب طهور

اقالیم ارض بلاد بلدات

در ذکر طالع عمارستان

بمدح کعنیسهٔ راهبان

تعریف حبوبات نباتات

در ذکر محدوده صنایعات

در مدح اطعام ماکولات

ستایش ثمرات معتبرات

گزیدهٔ انواع مشروبات

در بیان عبرت نمای قدرت عمارات اول حلاق عالمک نه قدر تبلیغ بو شهرک بحیره سی انجره [illegible] عدد [illegible]

[illegible] جزیره [illegible] بو بحیرهٔ کبیره [illegible] وسطنده جزیره [illegible] خلق اولمش [illegible]

[illegible]

[illegible]

[illegible]

[illegible]

[illegible] بر کیمسه [illegible] ان الله علی کل شیٔ قدیر اما تا الکفایه روزگار [illegible]

[illegible]

[illegible] اما اسکندر [illegible] کوردم لکن تقریراولنان ما فی حالی

[illegible] سلطان عثمان [illegible] اسلامبول

بوغازی ینه کلدوکی سنه‌سنده بو شهرده روزکار زورکار دنیا متلر قوپوب اولریکلوکی درخت منتهالر کوکندن چیقوب هواده چراغ
پغتره کبی اوچدوغی سنه‌سنده بو جزیره جکلر قرق اللی کون بو بویانا کولی اوزره سرسری کزوب شناورلک ایدوب کاه شمالدن کاه جنوبه
وکاه شرقدن غربه کزرلردی بو زال الزمانه پیرفانیلر وکارآزموده جهان بینلر بویله حکایه ایله دیلر والسلام
ستایش بحیرهٔ آب زلال آرناؤد اسکندریه‌سی بو بحیرهٔ آب زلال اسکندریه قلعه‌سی دیبنده بویانا کولی نامیله مشهور
شهر اولمش بر لذیذ آب حیات کولدر دائرا مادار جرمی اون بر میل کبیردر وشرقدن غربه طولانیجه واقع اولمشدر ابو الفتح محمد خان
بو قلعه‌یی دوکدوکی حواله اولان بویانا کولی آشری توررونداش داغی بر طوب منزلی قرشو یقیندر ماعدا اکناری بعید بر
اوزونجه خلق اولمش شهزرلا اللذ نشالر وار بر خلیجدر کم بو قلعه قرشوسنده کی تورزونداش داغنده باشی وار درزاندن
چیقار بر تفرجکاه فرح فزا یردر بو حالات آشقی بو بحیره‌نک آیقی دورت ساعت جا غربه آقوب کیده رک نیجه باغ وبستانلر کی
ایده رک کور فرزه دریاسنه مخلوط اولور وقلعه‌نک مبنی اولدوغی تپه‌لرک دبنده اون عدد بالق دالیانلری وار جمله میریدر
بو دالیانلرده وکولده صید اولنان ماهیلر جمله امین طرفندن ضبط وربط اولنوب مالی قلعه نفراتلرینه اقلامیدر وجامع
سلاطینلر ائمه وخطبا ارینک وظیفهٔ معینه‌لری بو دالیانلر محصولندن ویریلر واول قدر ماهی منقش کوناکون لر چیقار حد حسابن
خدا بلور جهانی دیقاره اولا پسی بالغی صازان بالغی توزک بالغی کفال بالغی آشقی ده یادن کولک آیاغیله کلر ونیجه بیل الوان ماهی
کوناکونلر انواعی بو کولده موجوددر باخصوص بو اسکندریه خلیجنده چیقان یلان بالغی نه کولی کسیزیده ونه اوخریده ونه بیشک کولده
چیقماق احتماللری یوقدر بو اسکندریه بحیره دبنده چوق چیقاره وسمین ولذیذ اولور بالغی مسک کبی قوقار بو رائحهٔ طیبه دخی بر دیار
کوللرینک ماهیلرینه مخصوص دکلدر الا بو اسکندریه بالغنه مخصوصدر وغایت الغایه نافع یلان بالغیدر کم دنیاده نظیری یوقدر حمایه
وآغری خسته لکنه مبتلا اولان کمسنه‌لر بو یلان بالغی پشروب ییسه‌لر یاخود باشن کندوده کتورسه‌لر بامر الله تعالی استماد وآغری خسته‌
لکندن خلاص اولوب شفا بولور تا بو مرتبه نافع یلاندر بالغی اولور کم اسکندریه شهرنده حما وآغری خسته لکی اولمازدر وبو بحیره یلان آب بناس
دائما نوش ایده‌نک طبیعتی ملین اولوب سودا وصفرا وبلغم وصداغ وقبض وانحدار مثللی امراض مختلفه‌لردن خلاص اولور تا بو مرتبه
صو بو دخی نافعدر

در بیان قوارت حسب اتنالیمی ولایت بر صنعی بحره سنده صیادماهیلردر بر بلوکی عسکری صانعه سیدر وبرزمره سی عمار ارباب دروبر
فرزنه سی اهل صنایعدر وبر قبیله سی شوخنته واعلمالرلری در بر قومی باغبانلردر برا جمله ملرمی اوج بیک عدد باغلری واردر وعاشر هادوا
رنجبرلک ادوب کار کسبنلری مقید سلیم وقنااری اولور لهاریکری وار عربی مالی بو شهرده یوقدر جمله‌نک لسانلری ارباب وجاندیم بر لسانه بکزر
زیرا بو آرناؤد قومنده ابتدا اصل فرعیلری مکهٔ مکرمه قریشیلرندن قوم عربدر انکیچون آرناؤد لسانندە بعضی عرب الفاظلری واردر کم حالا آره
لرنده استعمال اولنور وبر قوم اربابو بو اسکندر داولوسه داغلرندن صلوحا ایدوب لسانمالنا قریله احلاط ایدوب لسان عرب ایله
لسان فرنک ارکسده لسان ارباب وودی جفرسی عمر ثلاثه سدا امد ابر مسعه سی وقوم ارباوودلی اصل وعرب اسالله علیه عربی اولنور اما شهدی
در فصل لسان آرناؤد وعارنا بوید دیو قوم عجم لقب دمشلری وجه بو حرفلر قوم عارنا بوذیا مشلری اما الومن لسانده
بو لرسه اعرار اکرام الله سواصا وحلمی کلمات ایدلر رحیم لرمله مسحمد کحز امر اول دحی اسساسه وبه دیل نبره لرمله ارناملرده
بو حسه عوسی لیمیه کبا وبه حضر ومنزیلر بر شیپرلر ایو الانخ کتاپسز کفره وفجره لردر کم لسانلری بوداولا پرتونیه زوتیمه آه جیچوت دینکلر
بیع وشرا عددنده اقچه حسابلری بویله عد اولنور اوقه که دی تری قوتره پیسی کاشت اشتات تتی نانپد ذیت
فائمی موره سلام علیکم آدم آیه شندوش انا مراء خوش مسن میز نشطا نسته صباح الخیر اوله ملیسرد
یاالله میرزونی بوق اکمک ادنی صو میشرات دله قیون پولی طاوق بایه موره کل آدم آها بوق آکمک یومین
قوقیه بزه ده ایدلش منیالنت بال آقی تهکی آربا داری نوتوتم یوقدر روش اوزوم آقیمته تتشن قورد
آربا کیتر یو قسه باشلک یرارم برتوتیه نودی یوتوتم آتی الله حیچوت یوقدر آربا طهوکانا سوتره قرزه ندابی شوکه عورت
یاوه سوزلردر اما سیاحلره لازمدر بلکی شوکه لرنا خود دوکه ره هاک موت بوق یه تکفشات طهوانا لیولا ایدیم تکفشات شوکه عورته

ملان

ئيلان ايدوم رنجيده پريشان بوزنكه ياتدوم بعض حرطه چلايم يلكوشا بستونى اردم گوزيكم يلان ايدوم ايچ تپوزدوم پوشت پيچيده مكمر حاصل كلام درويشان عالم سياحتده بو بلالسانلريده بلكه كندويه شنوم اندكم بيره وار ميوب آسوده حال اوله درويش ضعف تمنّه شهزا انكيز شهر اسكندريه وارديغمز ايچره نهر بنار آرزه ايكي عدد جسر كجار بري خسين بك كوپريسيدر و بري علي پوليتنا كوپريسيدر

در بيان زيارتگاه اسكندريه اولا قلعه متوسط ايچ بورنده زيارتگاه منوچ بابا قدس سره العزيز

بو قلعه سرحد ساليمده ... احوالاتدر رسه واقف اسرار اولوب بركون ميرلوا يوسف بك زاده محمد پاشا ايله اسكندريه فتالتو حاسماله ٢ ساعت كيدوب سمت بايش صبحه بو شاطر بو رنجه مرسسه رالاء عظيم ايله كروب محمد پاشا سرايده مكث ايدوب بعد الضيافه درون سرايي بهسا باده ساعره وارد ايدوب بو محسنه بلده سر بما ساسه شروع ايلدك ... دربندلريده روح فزا عمو للى وحمدارو لاله عرار ومرعرار وحديقه حسن وعسعا للى باغ ارم مثال ... محمود ومرس وسدس بربطكه جمله سلر بور عدد بو ... جمله سند سار رصنه زيبا در كم نصفي ... ساعات اورتوب اولر در جملدا سرايي معظم يوسف بك زاده سرايدر ابو الفتح محمد خان ... يوسف بك ... ارث الله انتقال ايتمش سراي ملك ... ما آيدر ما حجره و قاعه ... آراسته و مطبخ وكلار و توابعات حجره لريله پيراسته اولمش سرايي خاقانيدر ... جامع منزحي ... مسجدي ... مدرسه ... حمام دلكشا ... زيبا اللي عدد دكانلر ... جمله يوسف بك زاده كر خيرات حسناتلريدر

حقير بو محسنه ... ملك احمد پاشا ... مهمات اوطاق ... تضييع اوقات اولمش ايچون حقير بكلدن يكرمي عدد طبان كشتي پور سلاح پياده آرنا وودي يكتلر ... آمو قسطوريه ... داغلره ... حقير پر تقصير بالسحر راه ... قلعه قپودانلر بينه مكتوب ... ساكيعوت اوصنست ... قلعة انتهاي سرحد ... يعني حصاري ... ديكر سنه ٨٨٣ تاريخنده ابو الفتح ... سلطان محمد ثاني غازي قلعه اسكندريه فتح ايتدكده ... اسكندريه ... اوصاف ... بو قلعه بالذات سلطان ابو الفتح بنا ايتمشدر ... چار كوشه برسنك بناء متين و برج و بارولي ... قلعه ... بدن و سور عدد ... و هر ... مال ... مجاهد ... سبيل الله غازيلر ... آب و هواسي لطافتندن قلعه ... قالن باز وكر و ... وسينه ... جسيم ... كلام ... جمله ... بعدا ... اوله ... جمله ... اولا ... حتى دونكبله ... بالغريبه بردي ... بو الجالري واركنز ... كوكوسلري ... جمله اچقدر

ودکلم شهرلری معمور وآبادان اسمه اولمدی بوحوجه نامه گرفتارکم الحاق برمخان مندرجه نامه ی بالله ایکی یانندی بغلیوب
بو عارضه اهاللو یحزور نامه نامه لرایا ما هدا عالمه دایله ولله لسر اوزره اول طاقیه کویا عاربتی دور کمیله جک حالی
یوق بر عرصه سیاهدر اسمه بولوبه برالاب غازیان سپاهدر هر بار چته و پوستوره قووب جنگ ایدرلرکم مصور دامرسلو
قلیمنته و قره داغ اربا وود دامرلسلو بودار فورموده اودلرسی مسن عاریاب یوخ مو چمسه در اسلمدر بکتاغی خاکنده
صوباسلعدر و سواحو یاسی حالم اندر عدی حاکملری یوقدر درون حصارده جمله او حوریعد دار احق خانه محکم و برابو الفتح جامی
ذبوعدا انبارلر و مطعه خانه و صو یکر و صوصار جلیری وار غیری عمارت و حات و مدرسه و حمام و حار سوعمارتلری
یوقدر بو قلعه دن وبه دیحل مصور قلعه کسه وبره الله لسدوب تماسا ایلمه مراد ایدیکلمر ده قلعه یه شهرلر رضا و بر مدیلر
مصور دامرلسیله وبره گرپورغدی ایمیس بردحی انشاالله محمده بولنوب سرانده رز الا مورمرهونة باوقاتها دیو قطعی
کتمدی تمارز اولوب پودلعور چون جانب شماله یتم ساعت بعیدیر پشته عالی اوزره حقیر چیقوب قلعه یه ... یوره کوردم
کنارنده برقبا اوزره حوالده چوق بر کوچوک قلعه نمایان ایدیب بو قلعه بد حمو بعده اودماو برلر ایلو مره فی وبه دیک
بودمور دریاسیدر عرب مره مه بوول یودموری دکیزیدر بوالی دریاسی اودماو بره قاریخه سواد معظم بر سور ودیدلم
موره ولایتده ماسه بور بو لیو هنطاسات وسلسان بالحو بمی حاصلدا علردرلم بصمسه مره داغلر و دصمه کیلمنته داغلر
سرلر مره صعسل بوصل ابدار دیوریردسی ارناوود دامرلریدرکم معدما اسلمدرسه نامطرا بدعی حریرهٔ لزید عراسدن بروز
بو دامرلر وبه دیله باسم اوکوفاند بسه قلعه سه امداده کیدر و بو کلمنته بور سده تعساره قلعه لر حمله وبه دلحکمندرکم
موداکلروبل و عسار سو حمله آرناوود کفره لریدر بوداغلرده وحمی جمله عبرت نما تما شالرایتدک بودغور حدب ماکمو حابر جنو
سلستان ابحره برسلاح آماده کیدرکن اود فسب ! قلعه بنوید... اولکوآخر ونه دیک فرنکی قلعه سید لب دریاده
شکل مربع شدادی سد نابر بوحول بیاض قلعهٔ زعادیر بر عسکری بودروب قلعه حمله حمر طوبلر ایوب بر طابیای اوزره بر عالی
لیمو سره نینک ربوه اعلاسنه برفلاندیره بیراق قالدردی ولسدریاده اولاب حمله بوبه قلعه لرده صوصالعمر ابحره اسلمدایو
بود لرعا و حرسمایه کهکشان آسا عروج ایدوب هر بارهدن بر بر ارتبه اسار صویکر ایدلمر بیر ابزیسی حصه حو و بهم وعارتحو صوانیلر
مارد حوبمیالس دبو بروا بود بودوا قلعه سی قربندن
اوومتمسسا ... یعنی سدتر استوار قلعه ... لسان ارناوودچه دماکلر یاسی بولیه
ورال ساسمدرلم بو قلعه اسدا اشپانیه قرالی حکمنده ایکن بعده اورحان غازی عصرنده بو یحو مانی وبه دیلی دسسه اروسانه ۸۹۳ سنه ده
فتح ابوالفتح غازی منصه سه اردی اسلمدریه خاعده وبوا دلعدر واولکون بو احلر بدن اوکو نیابتدر قلعه دزداری و عدد
قلعه مکمل وبرسلاح غازی بکلری حمله شهباز آرناوود شهباز لریدرکم فرقته اریله دائما بو لسه ولاسلری واسماسه و ملوره
مسلرب و عاصیم ونه دیک قلعه لر ووره داو لیملمسه ارناوودلر فروسی قلمحد گجروب سالمین و غانمین قلعه لرنه دائما طوق
دو بیوم گلرلر ما صلا بوس دلمرلر السه برطرفدن برشکار ایله گلرلر بو قلعه وبه دیک بودمور دریاسی ساحلند
اوزره شکل مربع برسنگ بنای مصنع قلعهٔ مرتفعدر درون حصاره حمله عدد کرومت
و صناعا آوربولی نامحه سر بعرا اولریدر سلطان محمد جامعی و مکتب مدرسه کی و بر مسجدی و برغلال انباری و جبه خانه خزینه سی
و صوصاریجلر و مکلف ابری طوپلری و قبوسی و مهترخانه قله رخندسی

اوصاف بنای سور کلکوین یعنی سرحد انتهای قلعهٔ اولکوین لسان ... دیمکدر
وسبب تسمیه‌سی ... غلطدر ... یاسر ... خاصی
ایدی بعده ... مسعود ... سنه ۹۶۳ ابو الفتح وزیری ... احمد پاشا بو قلعه
... دار السرور ... خانه‌لرینه کتدیلر بعده محمد خان بو قلعه ... اسکندریه ...
... حالا ... الحمد لله ... قلعه ... اوزره شکل مثمن
... برقلعهٔ حاضر ...
خندقی ... قلعهٔ زیبا ... عدد
... خزانه ... حضرت بالیمز
... اما ... قلعه ... قلعه ...
... واقع
اولماغ ایله ... موجود ... قلعه ... کروب
... مصور ...
... قلعه ...
یوسف بک اوغلنه ... احمد پاشا ... بوغزاما اللدن
ویردی

اوصاف بنای سور تکلکویت یعنی سرحد انتهای قلعه‌سی اویکوار لسان دیمکدر
وسبب تسمیه‌سی غلطدر با نسبه اسبابنه لوره سندرکم باس ارسلان بند خاصی
اند نعدوبه دیل بر معتبر شسصه الله مسولی اولوب ایل النذن سنه ۵۹۳ ابو الفتح وزیری هرسک اوغلی احمد پاشا بو قلعه
معماهکر سلیم اعدوب کندولرب دار البوار منحوس خانه لرینه کتدیلر بعده محمد خان بو قلعه‌لره لی لسی عمار ایتدی اسلنه بو سنجاغی
بلوغامی عمرا ایدوب حالا وسوادلعدر قدور اللی احمد قضا نسر قلعه سوریه دیل دورموی لا ربده اوزره شکل مثنی
سسلطرا اسرای صواش پرخاش برقلعهٔ حاضر باشدرو برحر باروری و بدان بعلری و مس دروره‌سی و ماربعال دکاکلرو
خندقلری وجمعو بهما کواز ماتکری ایله معمور ومزین قلعهٔ زیبا دور و دردن حصارده محمد خان جامعی وجمله عدد
نفرات اوکرسرایا مسفور خانه حکادبه صمار اسارلری وجبه خانه خزاینلری وصوصار غلری وار وعا نفرت بالبیز
قدامره اما وزیر طوبلری وار قلعه منوسی اوکنده بردارا اعا لوعد برده اوصوروب بد سور عدد اربا وودعار بکر قلعه نفرات
لر ایله محافظه بحارلر سول دحورار وبها در شجیع دلاور بلدلرعدوارا اندربا سهلارکی فرمه حالردر بو قلعه لب دریاده واقع
اولماق ایله یلر می عدد فرقه‌کر قلعه لیماسده موجود در سایر مصنه لر بد دحی سهمار اربا وود بلدلری کلکو فرمنه لره کروب
ماهرسان نعه لر نعه سعه جرا وسا آنده لحسا ما لعراوالر واسیر مهمارلر الکی مسعور مصعر اولکونه کلرلر دمیرلکوا
عسرو زرلر حصی برحصر بو قلعه مما ساسحه ایلوسدی عدد فرقه بولنه ماهرسا بعده مال غنا بمله کلکو بعصرمسه‌دن
یوسف بک اوغلنه یلر می ربد عروس عسر سلطانی وادر بدی اسیر دوسوب اولدحی ملا احمد پاشا دیننه بو غزا مالندن

اندن تکرار منزل قلعهٔ اسکندریه اندن تکرار منزل قصبهٔ بوشاطلر بونده بر لحظه دم نیاساسنده مهمات اوتوب ملک احمد پاشا امدیمزه کورجسو وردیلر مال الجون یوسف بلاده حقیره ایراوج سلسعروسولو جمله ویه دیل السولرف حضورشرعده ویروب حجت شرعیه کچوب بکه حقیر مسکاتلرب ویروب لیار بمسل بشق اولندقده بالله ملل یاساسه هدایا اوچ فرنل علای وبلرمی عدد الیور طرفلی ساعتلر مبرانجو تسبیح وبرو طوب دسا وبرو طوب جنیوز قطیفه کچه برمرقع لعلکون مرجان قبضه لی خنجر رولمه لم ویروب بوبارده ملوسعمد اسلوبه قیداولوب بلاد حقیره اوحسور ویدیلر التوبنی ویمرادیام یراساسه علامه ویراب ویرمکم ویروب جمله توابع وعلاملرمیه اوبارالیون ویرر حوده وعماسلرویرکرمشعلورده ارتسی اسکندریه دن املامبونه دیه دن سیرتماشا اندکمزه قلاع ومناقلر بیان ایدر

اوصاف دار حنوت یعنی قلعهٔ موست لسان ارناووده بیکمکدر یا دسیواساده قرال لزنیه بعده ۸۸۴ تاریخنده ابوالفتح محمدخان وندیک کافرینک الندن دستندن امان ایله فتح ایدوب اسکندریه سنجاغی تحریر اولنوب نیابتدر قلعهٔ سی نهر اسیم کنارینده اوزره چار کوشه وچار قلعه برکار کیرسنک بنالی کهنه قلعهٔ عتیقه در بوقلعه السدحره را ایدر نهر اسیمده بلاده بردره اولعدر بالوحیمالرم حجرعماکیرالر باری جاللر مو العلرعصوراسو جمیع کافرستانلر کربرلر غاتز برحو سکرا اولدوعمد مجمد مورخان روم ان مرزبوم بوقلعیه دار حنوت دیو تسمیه ایدلر رماید مدیده حقاکه متین قلعه ایمش جامع موسی وارد حصار ایچره جمله اونوقلی یا محمد سرداراجوق بعزا اولرابو ابوالفتح جامعی واتباز لری وجبه خانه عزبلری وکفایت مقدار شاهی طوپلری وار دزداری حاکمدر ونوبواتلی ضا بطه وایلیوزقدر نفراتلری وار جمله شهباز ارناوود غازیلریدر لیم عرب دوستلردر هرکیم مسافر کلسه اولرسه قوبدورق اکرام ایدرلر عالی غنیمت دار دیاردرکم بالغی مشهوردر وباغ وباغچه لری ومشتبک بوستانلری وار اب هواسنک لطافتندن محبوب ومحبوبه لری وار اناطولیده سلفکه سنجاغنده بر دخی بوشت قلعه وار در

اندن جانب شرقه کیدوب

اوصاف تکیه قلعه ... سنه تاریخنده ابوالفتح محمدخان ثانی بناسیدر روم ایلی ایالتنده دوقه کین سنجاغی حکمنده صوباشلقدر نیابتدر عمری حاکمی بوقدر قلعه سی بر داغ اره کنده واقع اولوکرجو سدساد اما اعمال اولمالی ایدر بوقلعه عماری اولماد بعده مرور ایام ایله قلعه سی خرابدر اما دزداری وار وعدد نفراتلر ومقدار شاهی طوپلری وار در

اندن

منزل قصبهٔ اشپانه بودمحمد دوه لرسکا غمحا کنده سدحاته لی وبلنغود کزیده بومحلی عمارنابوده ازکی وار بر جامعی وبر خانی وبش اون دکانلی قصبه جکدر

اندن

اوصاف قصبهٔ یاقوت حبیبه سورعه سکاعنده ریامووحسه دحموار در اما بو دوقه کین سنجاغنده معمور مزین المو سلحانه لو مزین رمصه درنم جمله خانه لر دار لیرو اوز بولی و باغچه لی سولردر رحا نمی ووبو ایادر و بور اللی تاسیله اغلا قضاییدر جمله عمارتلر برصحرای واسعه واقع اولمش ایکی عدد مکلف جامعی ومساجد لری ومعمور سولو خانلر ایچنده هالاقطوز سفر چوبجه خانه وبکصماتلر مالامال در وبربنای مفرح دلکشا حمامی روشناسی وار وچیوز قدر دکانی هزار آشناسی وار در واب وهواسی لطافتندن محبوبلری وار در

تورمورو دریاسی اجره روم ایلی قسمنه ایلی سلم بر سر شرقدن غربه طولانی واقع اولوب کاینات طقسان میل احاطه
ایدر بر صعب و مرس جزیره ویمی سالدر باسعدو حصور حرالبه بو تسوب سر مله وار مصاحبلر ایلدی بر رامنده
حرالیه ایلی سعدالعج مدینه معمور سولماسده هربار سرایند واروب اسالو لسسا ابمسد دسمده سه بو تورکوند
حرالصال بولوب سره بر مسره تاه مساف وبردب قلعه بروام لوکسمر بما سالر اتدکب اوکلاکتمانی اسکندریه قلعه دلك
صاغنجه و بریم صولسده اولوب المسی سکر زوزکار ده امنلردر وهر سرسه سنر سو بار ه تعمل وبارجه مالنوبلر
صعار و قلعه کر بر المس سا اوزره تورمور دریاسه داوند نده ناظر ایلکی ماسسح اسلمدر مال اولمسر عدد
ماسه لری فصعمی وار قلعه دیرلر اکدروب سرو یی حالا نحه سد لوبه محکم مسصلر اییله ارامسه ویده سوز عدد مالمر
صعمیلر اییله راسده اولمسر قلعه سد ماهو حمدر وحالا بخه سد نعار بر عالا الرفساو سوز بخه سالر احیفا الکف دحمی
نسالیه عمار اتمیه ندرلر حالا وبسلا وامر لرسد ملدالحمد قلعه ربسا دیرلرسد سلصولی بر تورمور دریاسند
اعربده واقع اولمسو ماسعدر الرسد وحوره لرندب وقلعه ماسسه لب نعمدر رعایا حمعلر دیا سه بو جزیره
ایجره اسکان ایدیروز آنم دریاسی اولمش

بوحسن حصار وامرایعاملر اییله سسد روزوصات عمیلر ایدوب ریدمام تو لریده برصوب ساده مالری اندیلم رمحی
اسمانریدر وسره ورسا امه جبخو لور بوحعمدی برما بعه قنوب مار مله حصرال ودا عملسوب سه قرسودالبات
بلعکسه کلوب ابدرسه رسمعلر الوب ۱۰ ساعت کاملر شماله کیدوب نعمی صاسلحو سعیمی محل الرده مرس قرالحره
عبور ایتدک در تقریرات اشکال قلعهٔ ذکونیته لسان اریاووده دملکدر اسدا ابانسو
اسساسه در بعده نوبدوما نمو یدید تر سلطنت ایله استیلا ایتدی سسه ماربحمکه سلطا ماربدولی بو یدبلا الدوب
فتح ایدوب سه نعار اسسلا ایدلده سسه مار بحمکه سلطان سلیمان خان تورمور عراسه کلدکن عرباوعده الا صلا ماس
پاسا دلوسه قلعه کادر ر سپهسالار صعیلم بعمس اولنوب ندسسعود پراعصم اناسر پاشا لوبسه قلعه کـ
فتح اولنوب یاعت تخت مصردلوسه اولدعی حالا سه روم ایلی ایالتنده یاسعه سنجاقدر بکینک خاص طرف پادشاهیدن
۳۰۳۱۵۷۱ اقچه در ودرعاملری ۴۲ عدد در وار باب تیمار ۱۰۰ عدد در الای بکیسی وجری باسسی وارحس
عراده ماسوسا اوزره بولنوب السعسکر وحیه لولرناله وبکسد جندیله جمله ایلی سکا السسودعسکر اولور بوز سلسن
آقچه پایه سیله قضادر اسا سندر ناحیه سی جمله عدد قرالری جمله سحا عدده عدد مصالرندراولا
قضاسی قضاسی قضاسی قضاسی قضاسی بولر مسهور در
شیخ الاسلامی و نقیب الاشرافی وسپاه کتخدا یری یکیچری سردارب قلعه دزداری عدد قلعه نفراتلری و شهر
صوباشیسی باجداری سهر کتخداسی محتساغاسی حرام اغاسی وار در قلعه سی بر سیوری عمالی باریرو اعلا
سنده سحابحمسر برسدا اته سبسار قلعه رعایای مصصعدر لم لاحصر سلسلدر اما لوحو لدر بار ارامادار
جرمی التیوز آدمدر اصلا برصره مده خندقی یوقدر وجامع سرونه یرجر متوکسد وار در ورقلعه اوچ عدد کره
ملو خانه مکلری وار بر غدر نلری وبرسجدا ویریامام خانه سا اولوسندر مسیحدی ویرعلا کلار بر دیر خسحا
عربی و بر صوصای عجووار سولرده عدی عار سوی بازار وحان وحمام وجامع یوقدر لم عاسی تورمول قلعه جکلم
وقلعه حصارلی صاعرصره یده حصار رعامعورلره قلورده بر ساره لری حار لوسه برمفید عکشتر بنالی

حاصلیدر وخاصیتی بیلنده برار اوچیشور ومیردره حار سوسن عاسد دار اجق مسملا صنوماقلی جمله
سلس عدد دکانلردر اما نحار نساس موجدر دره وصنف اروش کلونیه ملحه ملسر وسعرهمده بتعوش
اشغی بوارو سن جمله بورعدد دره ملر جانه لردر امار بعدودانسیج برده دابیع اولماغله هر اولسره
بوحلو بسدر انفعی مالرعساوراومسر برجانهٔ عسعما مالحودلر با مستند غیرفیافکر کاد ملر یغجر دار اولماز
اول احلید هرنره دانلرلسی بردانه نعرسولی ملهٔ عمملر صفار ندر وجمله دسوار لرسعاً میانسه اوددر بینا
اولنمشدر وجمله دارو سن عدد علاملردر وجمله عدد عمرانلردر جملدا حار سولعدد
حامعی و حامعی حامعی حامعی ماعدا جمله
عدد علا ~~مساحد مسجد~~ اولا لامه محله سی مسجدی ولنز الدسی محله سی مسجدی صدعانه محله سی مسجدی
بوالرمسهور اسه لردر وجمله اوچ عدد مدرسه سوجه کانلردر اما عسما بلاسوجه لر صاولمدر اندر
جمله اوچ عدد معلم خانهٔ صبیان انجد خواندر وجمله اوچ عدد تکیهٔ اهل توحید فقیرانندر وجمله
بر عدد حمامدر وجمله اوچ عدد دکانلردر اما حملدا مشهور پاشا خانی مکلفدر وجمله اون عدد حسمه
سارلر سعارندر بوسهر دربانه ساعد رمصدر اب هوا سی وسا سی عابت لصیفدر ولاقه
علاسی زحمدر برده دابیع اولمسدر اما عامشهور دیر ابید دعاسی لسعد کبین الکسی محله سی صامی
باعی وباغچه دیر علسه کند حماسه هوادلر بردر ومسهور پاشا سرای عالولاد لرسد جانه انلرسعیدا بسد سرای
تماشی مشهوردر ولحمسد سورتجه واتحه عدد سوتی وباری وسروعا عاعلر غنجسا بدر لم سهر لسدالچی وباغلر
زبن اتمشدر وحلم جماله اربابو وجهه ملم امدی اصلار وبکه ملر لرعاسد سحیح ومسادر مو مصعار درراما
جماعوبید عاسعو اندی مسسه لرب اولرده براعوسد اعلر ومحارلر مارعوبی مور انسده اول انم احلعد
بار و سرار العبه اولکوشش شوب تالر بو حلعلمشلر جماله بسرطا السلاسلدر الدر باحار لسلره رسدنعه
رسومی باعی جسمارغ علا ولا کسوروب فروخت ایدرکار ایدرلر بریله رو بلری جمله باعی وکداعی صعبدر ولبدر
بسو هوا بدید لر بسحرب اوددره دیر بر راجماله اهل طرب وشمس عشرسه ما ایل برالا فسعاریان مجاهد المردر
امامارده بلمارمله سوجه علما لرب عاسد عسعار لردر جمی سوجه والمرلسد باسلرده برلوسه بر بسا بجی بسرچه
نوقالی چمار ولری عار کم کورن آدملر کمو لسعَنّ حیران اولورلر و مصنوعات ما لولاب مسروبا المرندره ساص
ارمانوکه مصعد ساص بوعا حاسه وبادهٔ لالده حمراسی مصدوحدر وبو سهر لرعرسهره مده لی بو لسدکلونه
تاعهدیب مرلور وبدنذ کور قبوزی آطه سی تاآنا کورینور

وبوسهر لرجمله بلراب باصمالرده وداعلسو غربه طرف فنه کیدوب مرساعده دلعلموه حاسلی بولر انددر ومسهور
انادان مرالرکجرک اوصفا قلعهٔ غلطه ما بعدم وبدیلد جلسه الدر سه بارجده بار بد
ولی عصریده سردار معظم کدککا احمد پاشا تحقیقدر دلوسه بلسد حاصید لم وبحا داسعا ثمه ار اماسمدی
بلسی بو بده بولوب ماسه ولا سعید سردار علی پاشاب بحردلر امر با دسا هلر فرامار ندرو سعمو مصلوملکر
اولنجه فرماب پادشاهلمدیرب ماسه محاصصه لمله جمله محاعی عسا ملسه اماده اوکوحصره اوحید عرد سی
برانسدس لدیلوب جمعه وموماسلر وبعدا ملرسمه بوز عرس بر حوصه ده روب شمر کی تماشاسنه مشید اولدق
بوملحه موز بلس مصاسو پاسیدر ملحه کی نوه موز بلسی پامسده بر بعد بردده شکل مخمّس برشدادلی
بوحو لسعاس ساملع حلدر دارا ما تارهر می البنور آنمدر الجمله اخلاف بسعیدد اولر عدلر وبر مصدعار
وبوهلالد اسار لسعار عدر عار سعدر بعدر اما حاسیعرفه باطرردم زنبر جبعار الحرملمه السکسده لی

رسولنه حواله داعی وار [illegible] وصیعه معینه لرن صیه ذا امیننده آرلر ایله
ملعه دستور [illegible] آندر دره [illegible] لا ینتفع ذا علرینا محمود کلوب [illegible] حواله داعی
اتکندن [illegible] اندر [illegible] لسدیر با الله ما آوتوبه قربنده ذریا ایه کیرر
نعده [illegible] ما الله ما اولوسه [illegible] بر ادمه راست کلمیوب
[illegible] ادمی الحمل [illegible] اصار داعلر [illegible] اولکر حمله [illegible] اولکو جمله
[illegible] اللهم عاما مسلما [illegible] اصلا دس
[illegible] نشر ندر بلمزلر در بیان فصل ابتدا حسیب ونسیب قوم عارنا بوذ [illegible] مکه
[illegible] جبل الحمه نام [illegible] العرب انیله اوتماق صاحب
برقوم کبار کبار جزت ایدی خطا [illegible] بکیند کوزن بوجبل الحمه [illegible] کوزی جیقان بك دخی [illegible]
[illegible] کلوب سوره ولسنا علیهم [illegible] بالعس والعس بالعس [illegible] اودره حبل الحمه
[illegible] کوزن جیقارمغه [illegible] حبل الحمه [illegible] حلیم [illegible]
اول [illegible] حبل الحمه [illegible] ادم [illegible] کلو
[illegible] اولدی حبل الحمیه [illegible] داعلر [illegible] داعلری [illegible]
مسهور بو حبل الحمه [illegible] ما المسدر [illegible]
هلا [illegible] المسمر بالله [illegible]
[illegible] اسکا [illegible]
[illegible] اللحود [illegible]
نعده بو حبل الحمه [illegible] الفاسمک [illegible]
[illegible] حبل الحمه [illegible] اسماع اند
کده [illegible] اسلامه [illegible]
[illegible] حبل الحمه [illegible] مسجد [illegible]
[illegible] عشره ولاره [illegible] مکر الشام اولادری
امام موافق الله [illegible] اسلامو [illegible] کلوب اولدیم [illegible]
[illegible] عکبارا اولور لاره [illegible] توطن
اندک [illegible] مکر الشام [illegible] ملعه [illegible]
[illegible] توطن [illegible] اما بو [illegible] حبل الحمه
[illegible] اولمیوب [illegible]
[illegible] اوکاب [illegible] داعلر [illegible]
اولوصکر داعلری [illegible] عارنا بوذ [illegible]
[illegible] قریشه داعلری [illegible]
[illegible] بویله ایکن مسلمانلرلر
[illegible] تقالرین [illegible] عارنا بوذ [illegible] اما [illegible] حبل الحمه
[illegible] اسلامیه مرحوم اولمسدر [illegible] محمد [illegible] دبو قریش
[illegible] اوقلرو [illegible] ازین جانب [illegible] ملعه [illegible]

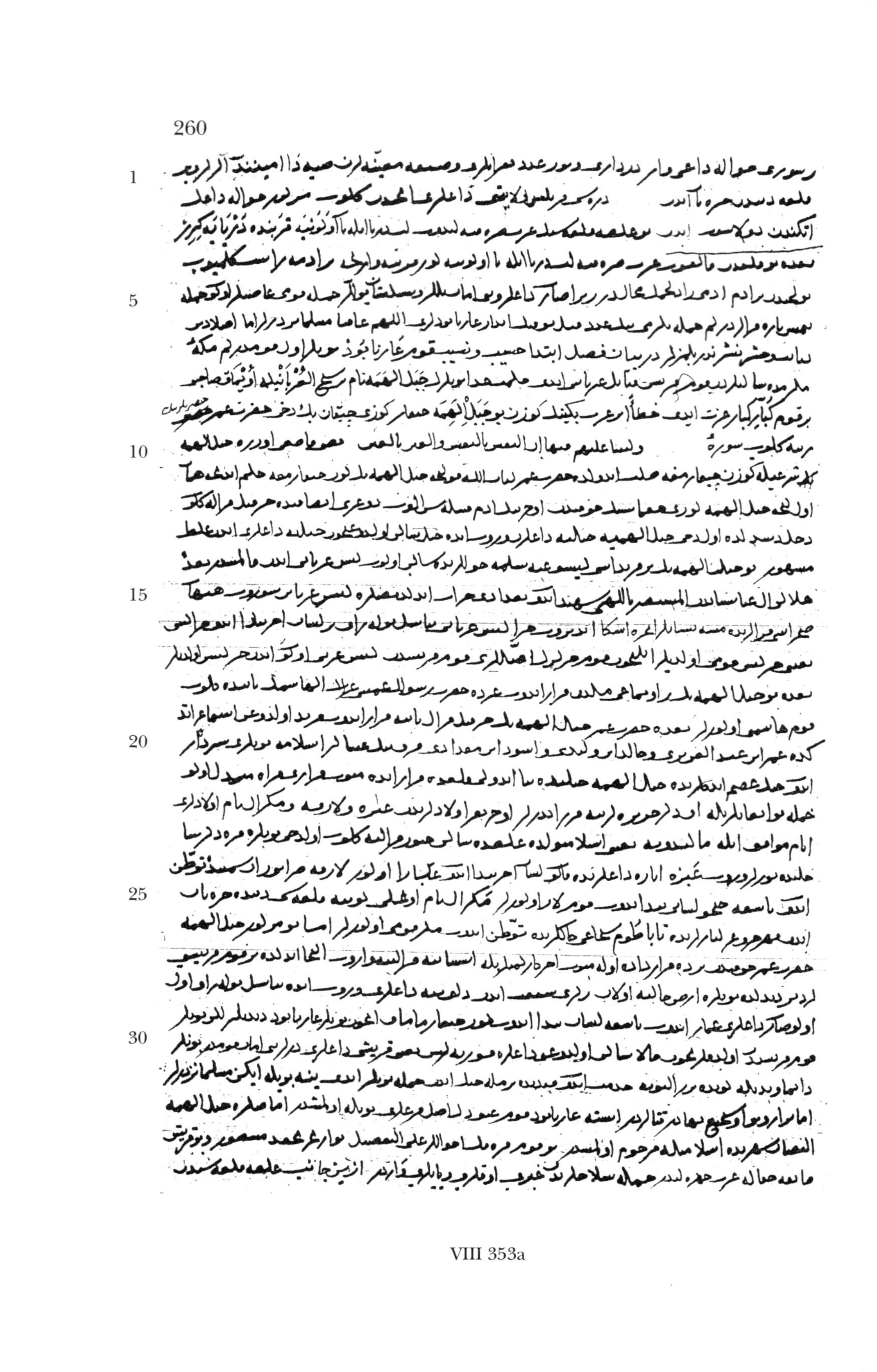

برابر فیقلر اکوپ ۱ ساعت شماله سنلسمک تولر وحمدلر بللر ایله کیدوب درتنقیلا آشکال قلعهٔ زیبا ژولاد
لسان اریا وعجه رولاد ۱ دیمکدر مانعدم اساسه مرالوساسی اولور بعده برحمله ملر بله نوبت حومامی
ونیکی اینه کروب بعده سنه ۱ تاریخنده مار یدولی عصرنده یونی دخی کتکک احمد پاشا مع اسکو حالا سلطان محمد غزیر
اوزره دلونیه بغاغیه حکمنده وبواد القدر ملحس اوحر اسمایه اثر مهمها وار بر قلعه بالادر لم روم ایلده
ایله بر قلعهٔ بی همتا یوقدر ملر موره حوره سنده کوز تکدش قلعهسی اوله یاحود ممسه قلعهسی اوله اما بنوك
جرمی ذا ایراماتار دور دیوز آدمدر وغایت متین سدادی حاوی تما درسرف ابله عرب ما بیننده تام بر موک
دار انجمنه لدرلار اوی غار غیر وشو یوقدر ویدلاری وحمله نوراللی بعر ابلاری صدمه اسطه سی امسک علوفه
لرن اکرلر ویومولر حاله اری ملعودر الحوبه اسعوبه بالحه ویهر ویلسو ایلسوبر بر سه مخلوط اولدقلر
سده دربانی واروش ژولاد حمله ایلسور عدد صار حوبی اوز بولی معمرا اولرندر ویومرلرا ایلسو
دحو عورنلسو لوبلر یدیدلو بو قلعه ایله وارورس ما نسدی عمور ایتمک والمو ساعتی سرحه لدور قلعه
مار بلسفر برید یلعوس ازکری قلعهکی صحرا اسک حره یاما ایتمک ارلری سهر سه مخلوط اولدر دیو ژولاد قلعه
تولینك جوفنی قبور بلسو آغلار ناوود کفره لر یدر بعده کوجک محمد پاشا کافره ملکه قولی اولماق ممنوعدر دیو
جمله کفره قولرن اسلام ایله مشرف اتدیب بو وارو شده حمله برجامع وار بوملر وقلعه ده حو بو سرار
جامع وار بوسهرده اصلا چارسو بازار وخان وحمام ودکان و مکتب یوقدر اماجا جا باغلر وباغلر در انداز دلونیه
بکمک دریک ادغلو عثمان پاشایه بلوب مانیه سفرینه انلر بده مأمور ایدیب امر پادشاهیله دیوانده قرآت اولنوب
حمله سمعنا واطعنا دیوب حمله لوازم عسکریله مانیه صاقصه سه کمال جد اهتمام ایلیوب معمور
دیر لوله واوضو عروس احسا ایدی ابدای سرحه نهر بالیه لنار نجه ساعت معمورلر یولر وقشو معمور
آبادان کویلری عبور ایدوب اوصاف هیئت قلعهٔ رعنا قاردیک لسان عار یاوو دحه بو
قلعه
لرلر سنه تاریخنده یونی دحی تاریخیدولی عصرنده سردارلرلدی احمد پاشا مع الله
مسلمر بوده دلونیه سلطان محمد خان عصر ما سو حکمنده برسوری دپه جکا وزره سطح مدور برصانش
مایر لوجود سور استوار ملدر اماحرمی معلوم دکلدر هذا انتدم الحاق ددداری وبور عدد نعر ابلری وظیفهٔ
معینه لرضبطه امیننداکرلر غایب دهالیر وجمیع دفتاغار یاوو دیلبلری غاز یدر درتعرینعقاروش قاردیک
قلعه نك آشغیسی سنده نهر بالیه لنار یده یورالی عدد لره ملر ومصبطری دباغان وصبار لوز بولی معمرا اولری وا
جامع مسجد بوستانلری وباغچه حملری ولر دیرلوجول مناره لی دره مسی اوز بولی جامع وار چارسو بازاری وحا
وحمامی یوقدر حمله ازکری قلعهسنه غنا جلردر اندن نهر بالیه کنار نجه شرق جانبنه ۲ ساعت کیدوب ازکری اوکندن
آقان نهر براغو بولیه نهر بالیه مخلوط اولور اول محله حقیر وار وب اندن کرو جنوب طرفنه ۳ ساعت آباد آبادان کیدوب
قریهٔ ترزبوک ودخی قریهٔ لاتا ادقا اندن قلرسیهٔ قاقوش بوبلر دلونیه بلرمو بد جمله جلرددر
بولرل اولار یدر تماشا ایده رکچوب اندن ازکری عاغر قلعهسی عبور ایتمک بحه باغلرده روم وصعالر ایده رک
در تسجیلا صورت سور استوار نهر سنایش قلعهٔ ازکری قصر بنا مدار
لسان اورومده قلعه دیمکدر اسکلایا نحوی روم مر الرید قلعوس اولغی بنا سندر بعده قلعه دولت
دوله انتقال ایدوب امرکار سنه تاریخنده مالوکا تاریدو لمار یاوو دعسعار الندن فتح ایتمشدر اما بحیره برانسان
تاتاری عوسمید کاهر عبار ید ربرا صاتما بو مصور لرعیار لدر کم وندیک علا متیندر سلطان محمد خان غزیر دورنده
دلونیه پاشا سند جامع وبواد الغیندر وبور سلسو ایحه سربع مصادرناحیه ک عددم الرتم سی الاسلامی
بعنیه الاسر لمو ولعما لنار اسرامی وساه لحدادی ویلهر ونیرداری دعسیم اعاسی و یا حذاری وسم لحداسی

وهر ایام آغاسی و معمار آغاسی و سهر صوباشیسی و قلعه‌یه ذکر اولنان ... ایلسون عدد قلعه نفراتلری وار در
قلعه‌سی بالتقصیر طولی کبیر بر حصار صالی بشته عالی اوزره بنا اولنمش کارگر حصار بر قلعه قدیمدر بابرًا
ما دار جرمی بیك نفر دیوز عدد آدمدر و سرونده غربه طوغری واقع شو قلعه‌نك همیا در لم صول ایلسون
عدد کرمه خطوه در و عرضی یوز آدم انیز قلعه در کویا هان قدرغه کبی بر اوزون سور استوار در
و قلعه‌نك سرونده غربه الحاق بر اولو شاهراه صوقاقدر ولی بو یول ایلمه و منده جمله ایلسون
سرایا صاغات اوز بولی مها نحار لر بلا مصنع اولوار و بونده بارید صاسولی جامع کارقدیم بار لم منارهلی
و صاغ آغاسی اوز بولی بر و جانیتلی بر سول جامعدر لم بولی سکسن ایاقدر عرضی ... الحمد لله نور
عدد علی سوالری اوزره چابتمه تحته سالی سطوحدر اما صولی غایت مصنع و منقشدر بو قلعه اوجه برابر
قبا اوزره اولماق ایله صوبی چامنك مناره کبی دبنده یول آشرمی بر صوصار عظیمی وار جمله قلعه الحمد لله
اولر جلیلی اولان ... اما الله حمی اولان ... دفع عصیان ... دریا مثال بر صارنج
عظیمدر تویید ماعدا السده هر جانبلرده بر صوصارنجلری مقرر در بو قلعه‌نك ... مسن و موصوم
سولر ... اما جمله لری جرّتا قپولر در بر قپوسی شرق طرفنه ناظر در لم اوج قات قپو در کم بو قپو یه طلاش نرد بانلر ایله
جمله ... آتلیه ... کوچیله کرونچ چیقارلر او ... شو قلعه ... چیقار ... بو سلو وار
لر خشمی ... اعجاب ... وصه ... باغ ... الله لر ... بو
قپودن دخی غرب طرفنه نمازگاه ... اوج ... جدید جدید قبولر در بو طرفنده نمازگاه میدانیله
قلعه مابیننده یوز آدم طولی ... عرضی بر الحاق قلعه ... وار بو قلعه ... اوج ... جاسلری
چاه غیا مثال ... ایله اصلا ... جمله ... ایلسون عدد ... جمله قلعه
بنالری اوزره بنا اولنوب معصوره ... سا ... قلعه‌نك ... جامع ... اولمان
وار ... ناظر اولمادر در ... قصری بو قلعه‌نك مشرقه ناظر ... کندن
... محله ... وار ... جمله ایلسون عدد واسع دار ... قلعه
... قلعه قپالری السده ... قلعه ... جمله ... عدد ... اسلی ... بستان
... قپولری ... جمله ... بو ... لر اسمی ...
قلعه‌یه یول ... قلعه‌نك ... جمله ... اسمی ... وار
... بك چارشوسی ... محله ... ایلسون عدد صاغات اوز بولی
مصنع ... وار ... اول ...
بكلك خیر ... عتیق قلعه ... عدد ...
بنالی جمله صاغات ... جمله ...
... جمله ...
... اما جمله ...
... جمله ... عدد ... محله ...
و ... محله ... محله ...
محله‌لر در ... عدد ... سرای اغوات ... جمله ... عدد محله‌لر
جمله ... سرای ... سرای ... سرای ... بکوك سرای ... سرایلر وار در
در تعداد جوامعها مسلمان جمله ... قلعه ... حفظ الله ...

ایمش بو شهرده قنده عمارتی بو شهر عدد خانه‌لری اصحاب‌لری مشهورلر مسجد ومعابد مشهور وبو قلعه‌نک عدد جامعی
بو شهرده عدد شهر سوادی جامع بورس ایمش بو شهر برابرلر جماعه کوشه‌ده جوامع‌لر مسجد مالمسجد اهالی جماعت
آلمیشدر ونمازکاه اهالی صاحبنده ر باغچه‌لی اولور بر جامع مقبول وجنده . جماعت صاحب اعیان جامع کارکیر مناره‌لی جامع عتیق
ساده‌در واشبو حمام دبنده حاجی مراد جامعی صاحب بنا اولان الله حسین رسوله مدفون مناره مصنعلی ودراعنا جشملی
وجامع اچینده منقش طوانی عادت بعض بوملمع عمرت نمونه جامع کلکوندر وبلده جامعی جماعت ابتدا بنا اللدراما
مناره یکی یوقدر وجامعه التوبدمه صاحب بر بنا آل الله عزوجل اولنمش کار قدیم بابا بانه مقیدکاهدر بوجامع حرمنده لوبالودرحی
مسعالر الله ارامسه اولونمامسلا کونش پاره انبوه براسحاق آغا جامعیلر عالی آب حیاتدر حرم منداصامده حلو بطریق
بلده کی محرولری وار وحرم ملس جامعیده یعنی بله اولیا اللهعات لدار ارمنقودر حسن بو جعفر برار کسده غلامی مرحوم
اوکولدم عقل انک بوحرمده دفن اتدم حتی جمله ارناوود خلقی سن میت بیقادک دیو حقیر دن نغرت انتدیلر بیره واللهی
طاعونلی کلدی ایدی اسلام الدن مرحوم اولدقده دونیه سلبیر مطلع اللحد لوجمله طلبه اعتماد ایدرلر آندن یکی چارسوده
مهمد پاشا جامعی الحمد الحاق بوراده صحابه رسنده برده بر لوجولی بوسار جامع رغادرلم بر کارلر مصنع مناره موزونی
واراماران جماعتی حالودکللر درار باوره دستانه بوجملگی غایت مصنعلر در آندن پالوزر جامعی خوش بنا جمیع عنادر
آندن وصوص جامعی واسع بنا عتیقدر مشهور جوامعلر بونلردر در مساجد ها مسجدنا جمله بش عدد محله زاویه
لریغاردر اولارمصامددر زاویه وصوص زاویه وپیو بکر بلقنه یی والاعلا اشکی بونلر مشهور مساجدلر
در علم دار الحدیث عالمان جمله اوچ عدد دار التدریس عالمان واردر اولا بابنه مفتی مدرسه‌سی ومیمو پاشا مدرسه‌سی
در مکتب جکر کوشه پسران جمله بش عدد دار التعلیم صبیان ابجد خوان واردر اولا قلعه‌ده باربوجا جامعی دیده سود
مکتب وپالوز مکتبی وچارشو مکتبی واردر در ذکر خانقاه ارباب طریق درویشان جمله اوچ عدد بلده اهالی بو عدد معمر
زیبا اندر جمله‌دن مذکور بلده جامعی خانقاهی مشهوردر کلی عبدالله افندی حلاجی امدسوله ایمدر
در عدد اسواق سلطانی اصناف جمله الی عدد دکاکین زسالردر اما بیلی چارسو باشده بوسا سکسن عدد دکانلر انسا
اولنوبالی جامعدر والی بلیسده الی عدد معمور چارسو بتسندر کم شهرک کویا بر آرستانیدر در چشمه سار تشنه کان
جمله بش عدد انهار جسمه جارندر ورعمار در علامت مهمان سرای تجارات جمله بش عدد خان سودا کرانلر وار اما جمله‌دن
میمو پاشا خانی متیندر در هواء خوب جاودان بو شهرلرده هواسی لطیف اولدقدر جلبی بر در بسته ربده ارکو محبوب و
محبوبه‌کی مصدودرلر اماصوی سهرسنه لوره عاشارلر بالاسی مطراده حره بالاسی باعلر اجره نهر دراغوبول صویه محتا
جلدر اجدا المرله واسکرله دارحا صوصرلر الحاصل بو شهر سرچشمه عاشقاردر در مدح حمام راحت جان الحاق بر حمام
سدوسباده اسلم باه بمورده مصدود بعدر بر حمام دخی اما مصلعلر اما او جاملری جوقدر فاتحه انلره اهل بلده
لوسعسل ایدرلر بیمه مدح ذیر راهبان بطریقان لعره محلالری اعجره اوچ عدد معبد مختصر کنیسه لری وارزیر بوار لری صحرا
حره بالا نهر دراغوپول فیله مرسده لیمص المادو به اوجمله قریه ضاوره هکوریحمو اولری صحرا اسدی کلدره
کسدانلر نهر بلیجه مخلوط اولور دیبه دلوین قلعه‌سی معابلنده همان او محلده سهل کیدوب نهر ویسویه مخلوط
اولور اوچ نهر اولور سهال جانسه حره ما انده رک آولونیه کور فزینه قریب نهر قورزچایه منصب اولوبنه اولحلا
اولوسه لور مرز دریا سنه قریبشرلر والسلام در بیان زیارتکاه ارکری قصری اولا سهر اجره بلده جامعی حرمنده زیارت
بر قبو افندی وپیو پیو بابا سلطان وبابا حسین دده سلطان وبلده جامعنده علی دوست دده مشهور کبار اولیاء الله بونلردر
وبر حسن بو علی دوست ده مرحوم اولدقده جمله ارکری قصری جلبی بو علی دوست دده جامعنده اولدقده بو داعلره وعدم ار معرار
ایتمامدرلر غرررمرحوم الحسنه اطلاع عمرو بودور قرقلمه صومعه‌سنده تلک بعده مرارد رسکله ایملر سهره تلوسحرام الله صومعه
یولسلم اموب لودرسه ارلم بعسه علی دده حرم اجره بلده مسجد اوکو وجود سر بو حصوربزبارده واسعها اولوب بو جمله اهالی
ولایت

٢٥٥

تنسوی

نكه عالم هجرنده ماكو حزينز قومك صاحب الخيرات لر جهيز تكفينه آماده ايدوب تشييع ايدوب وسنده و غسل ايدرلر كه عزيز كه صدر منور
بر فرمز عماشا پاره كسندن قدرت قلميله على دوست لبطي بار لمش جمله خلق هجرنده مالوب توحيد تكبير ايله غسل ايدوب
بو تكيه جامع حجره سنده دفن ايدرلر حالا زيارتگاه خاص و عامدر قدس سره در مسيرهٔ غريبه و عجيبه حالا انوار لرى قصرى
شهرنده بر آدم طاعوندن دكل الخلاف بر سور رعيه جبات چيقمار سه طاعوندر دير جمله خلق اول آدمدن نفرت ايدوب اول
آدم ار تغير ير ه ور ماز اگه يقين اولنان موشلو لرى جمله فرار ايدرلر مكر غير خسته لر اولسه اول آدمك باشنه اوكو حالكن
حاضر نصير لر و طاعونلى او ه بر ايكى بالاد تذكره لر اكر كير لر سه اول او ه ستر كه ايله بيقمبوب كونا كون بحور لر تتونسو
و بو سكه يرلرى منهدم ايدوب تعمير ترميم ايدوب يبا ضو كرجله ايله هر حجره لرى آغرد وب ايندكر لرى اما حكمت خدا خلقى طاعوندن
اولمزلر اكثر يا اسهال و ذخيره و حماى محرقه و آغرى خسته لكندن بوللر اما اكثريا خلقى كمال مرتبه مسن و معمر وزا ...
اوكو موتى كتمش دهيستو يتمش و عمر عزيز لرى بوزه يتمشه يتمش ... كمسه لر اولوب بهمه كسى سنه صفالرن
طرانغو ايدرلر واك اذنا بيرقانى ديديكك آدملرى بينه سلاحلرن موشنوب يا آت ايله يا حود پياده اوكو مقور يلمش
داعيد عاصى ارناو ولر جله ياجود ونديك كافرلر ايله منكله ايدر براينكه غازيا جها ايدرلر بو نلر الحنفنه دخى حضرت
معاويه و يزيده سو مزوسب ايدرلر اما تقدم لكن آيدوياتى خلقى كبى بونلرده اصلا عقيده كيمزلر و منكه
بيدا اندعه بو زرده آشنو بهيوب معاويه بوزه يپوب الجند لبو بوزه دخى الجمزلر اما اسلام بولنده اكثريا بوزه بيا جمله
ارناوو قوملر ديكر معتاد تماشا غريبه قوم اركرى فروالمور سلس بلد نيز واولمشلر آدملرى اسالرى امرالرى
يا يا يتنق السه هر بارلر لويوب اول مرحومك مرضنى جمله ... اوجرتلر ايله بعده آدملر دوعلى ...
وبر فرعوجر خروبا لنفى و اويلا موت بوماله اعليو اعلبو صاعو لر صاعليو هر باد اندر لرلم اول سهرده بار ار لولى
فرياد يا لنسو و اويلا مثو مرجر و جرعون آدم بو شهرده تدرير ماراتلمو بو شهره حمد سمر يالسو دندم اما عراسا اندكم
اوجرسا ايله دو بولو عو ير لر و آدملر لعلامه لرى بو اكر مو ر يلليعا اولو امحوا امره نالر ينده زياده مجه اعليو اسا حيم
جكر خون دوكه بلر بعده بو نلر اعلمه اعلمه احلعدب يموباس دمبيجا ما ماكون بعدا لنكا لويالور بسملر وجاموقيه لر
وموموسسوا ريام بو ر لنو سلو وعميسد رشعر الملو حلوا الر بوسمرا لحمره اود ناده سر لر بينه لونددن هر يارلر لو لو سهر لحره
امر واح حوريانالر آوله ديو تعيين نقسمه لايميد كدايه وجمله مساعز ترك نزك اولنور حلقه بو آنى خصلتدر اما بونلر
يلمو يامله آعلماق بم معيندر لكن ابنه هر دمار حلعند ير كوره ايلينه قديمدر اراده حتى بينه كنده لرى نقل ايدرلر
بر آدم لندعه ما و نبله حماعر ايدر كن ...
حماعر بغشر بغليا لتنده عوير بلحا مرنيه ...
بلر يله خبليا ايدر كى بو عور ...
يا ع زووا ايدر كن ...
جماعر ايدر دم اجى سكستنه ...
داد رواد اوليه ...
فقيد حر يف بار لر لو ...
هر هره لي ...
خلقى ارباب معارف و شعرايى ...
شهرده موجود ...
والد ربا حلى ...
فرقه كي ... معاوينه سب ايدوب ...

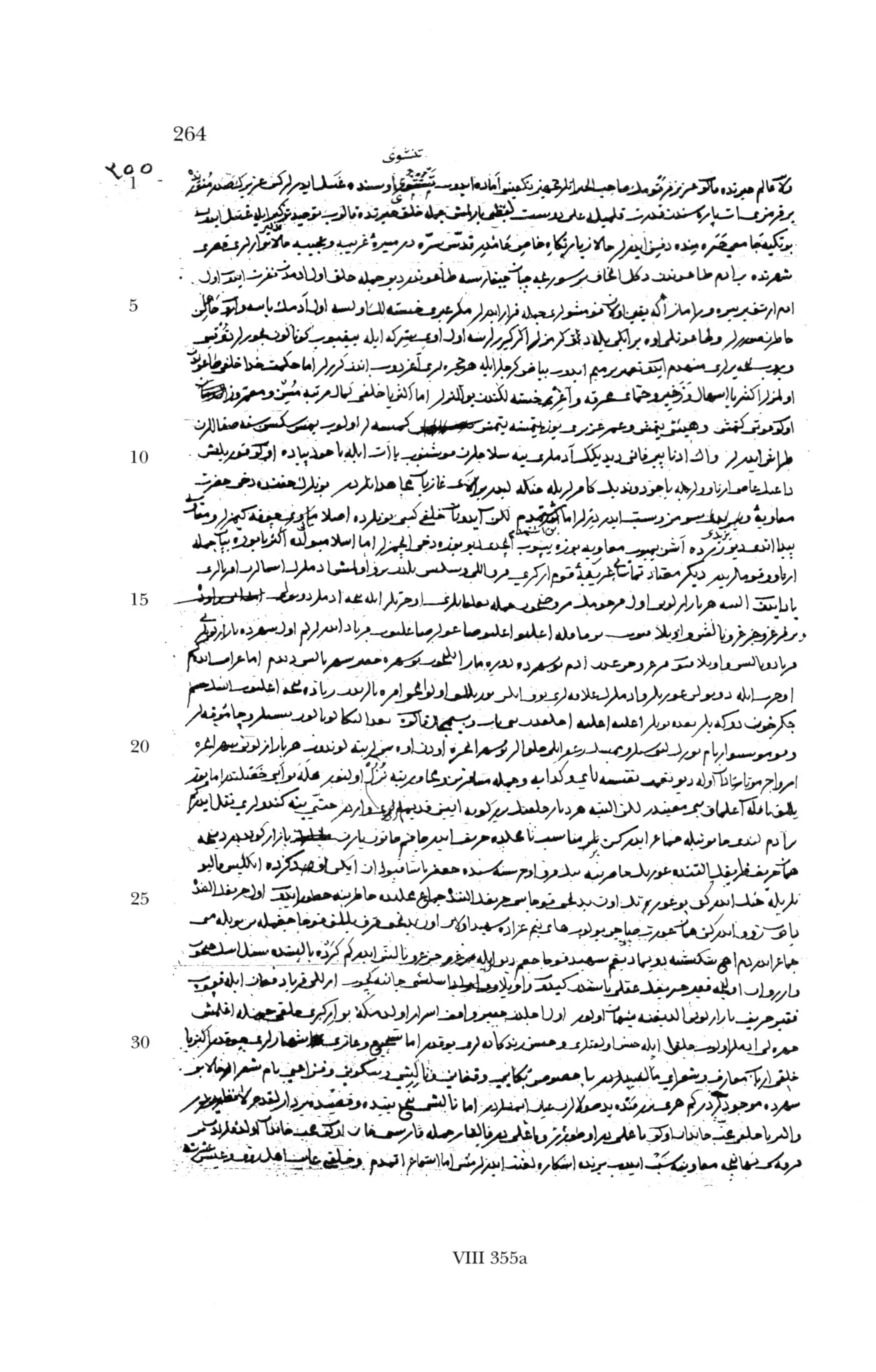

مابلا اولقی [illegible] کتاب [illegible] نام [illegible] دیکر آیین بدکار قوم ارکری بونلر
[illegible] و [illegible] کونلرنده وصاری [illegible] وعید [illegible] جمله [illegible]
[illegible] آل الله و [illegible] آیین کافر کبی [illegible]
اولکن [illegible] ایدرلر [illegible] ایین کره [illegible]
کوبر [illegible] رجال النسا [illegible] محمد [illegible] ماعدا
[illegible] اما [illegible]
[illegible] احمدر [illegible]
[illegible] ماعدا [illegible]
[illegible]
[illegible] اصلا [illegible] مصطفی [illegible]
عجیب [illegible] اما [illegible] علام [illegible]
[illegible]
[illegible]
[illegible]
آثار بنا [illegible]
[illegible]
[illegible]
[illegible]
[illegible]
[illegible]
[illegible]
[illegible] قریهٔ [illegible]
[illegible]
[illegible]
[illegible]
[illegible]
[illegible]
[illegible] اما اصلا [illegible]
[illegible]
[illegible]
[illegible]
[illegible] جامع زیبا [illegible] مناره [illegible]
[illegible] جامع [illegible]
جمله [illegible] قریهٔ [illegible]

خانه‌لری انلر عمدیر بو شهرده چفتلکی ویلده برکره‌لدر بر عظیم بنا بر جمعیتی اولنور بر بده بر سقلم جامع والجی قدیم بنا بیکانلر دار ماعدا بنا بر جمعیتی زمانی بلنعدد چلاش ملاشی حلاسدن دلمه امرات مبالدها لر سالوسعه لره نور سلطان حمه وجرما هلر موریلدن عظیم جمعیت لسا بریده واسع جمله ارمو اکاله زار لر اندن بنه جانب شرقه ٣ ساعت لسک معمور مزارکمرلر قریه زازو و بینا بو اوله معمور لودم و مرمله‌لو حصلکی ولر قبو قریه بپونغونیا قصابو حدودیدر بوینا اوسه مسله مرومه ارسن ماسه کتامو قصابسندر و بو قریه سهریاسه ٩ ساعت کیدر دیورارا و بسا لوبی یا علمو یا محه‌لی برکول کنارنده واقع اولمش معمور زعامتدر اینه صابه عصملر اوکوصو لر و بو محلر سابقا لر سا اولنور بولو سعمو الوسلا اعسالو لو لرده محه مولرلره بو معد سنا دمالری اندن جمله بلیلر حمد الله الله بلما لو حلو اماسه لعره لسی مروس دیرلر لعمعمولی لرینه دوستو معمور مزارکمو ٤ ساعت جانب غربه کیدوب در مسودات اشکال قصبه دلونیاک بو قصبه بو عوسا معمور حدودنده لعرد معمور عدد لوره اولی والمو سید عددا علی معمور آباد دانر بلطه زیبا لر جمله مرو الل معدد دا لر سه جمله او عدد لسسه لره جمله اوج عدد جا لرسه ولر جمله لو ملری اربا ووردیلر ومودان باساحاص اولوب و سواد اسمی جالندر معمور العلم و مقطوع القدم خاصدر اندن ٦ ساعت منطرف غربه قریه لیمبوه اوه‌وا ارز مقفقاک حمد الله ماعرار مال اسما لر وعاره ودروات برداعر المده جمله البلسمو عدد ساعات اوریرتو لجی علرنابو اولر لسدر اما اهالسی مسلمانلردر برجامع و برمسجد و برحامی عبر لو جوحد حمام علی رسلما سا اوغلی بوده جمعا الوالجره سالمدرعا جاند اعقیدهم لر وصعمه لسا ماحر در بو بده دلسی بو بوید بو یه ساد مالر ایله کشرو سب جمعه لیحه که بله عمروسی بسلم اندسه او لیحه صناحداف برعسو و عشرت و نشاط سرور و صفا عمره روعو وصفا حسینی بیتر لشکلسلری اهلیدیکم صباحسی بمشرعدد شرا محبسو بو سق ما الدف و ایکی یتعون لبابو نیادر اولدی دیو تعام کسب اندیلر خلاصه کلام بو حقیر اضعف العباد بو حمیت لبراعی بر هفته تماسا اند زارباو ودطرزی سور زفاف تماشالری انیمکه وصعمه لسا سما مر و قلعملر کاسر لر الر برهمه اعره اولا تماسا اسی عرس ماعمه لو عسما و معی اندره عربر اسم بر عومار درار زفاف مامه اولنور لحه ملام بعد آکسویر احتشام ملدد مراسعدر لو له و مودالعسعه او عصمه حمو نه و ما سلر در مساللی مصبح ساعت اهمال الوب جمله احبا ایله وداغلشوب جانب غربه ٣ ساعت تکرار قلعه اکر بیه کلوب اندن دهی جمله دوستلر ایله وداعلشوب ارزیر مقلعه سدر بله سو مراه نده کیاو حسابه برابر بیلاند با زروه اعلا سیدن دلونه شهرینه دوردساعتلک یردر وکو بی بوغرمه هوا خوشلنمند بوسده ما می و بد بکلی بور مرو بدرباسو الجره حو بره بو قرمو ملحه که صابا لدر بعده ارزیر باسد سنو اندن شمال طرفنه باغلر ایچره کیدوب و شهر برزغو پول کنارنجه کیدوب صاغ صو مهرده قریه قاقوصی محو یلما اوصلمو علی بلر چقتلکیدر کوبا بر قلعه متیندر اندن بلسمت غربه قریه قریان اندن قریه لاکوا اندن قریه برتوکی معا اله سیده بو یلده ارزیر شهرینه علوط او للمغی بر دنبر ساعت اشقو قریه هوزوم اوه‌وا مو باسارغامسدر اندن قریه لکان اولدها ارزیر قصوبه اوزره عمد صوباشی حسرتی برکور طاس بنا جسر عالی اولکو آنلی باشلرنده بر عدد کوچوك کوزلر دهی وار بو حسر ملحوس الع الناذ بالله عاصی پوغونات ایچیدر بو منزلده کیدرکن بر کوینده بولو مزه ابکی کره پوغونات حرامیلری ابنوب بیلدر رفیقلر بمزاو لما عیله عظیم صوا اشلر اللمه آخر رفیقمز بدرویش برا هیمر راه حقه شهید سعادتله لسدوب و بم النهده خمیس نام برآتم و بر غلامم مجروح اولوب جملر بوله آتلی ملعون مرداوکو سلاحلر الوب حمد خدا خدا معین جانمز آزاد ایدوب بدرویش برا هیم شاهراه اوزره دفن ایلیوب ایکی کله ایله منصور و مظفر دیبه دلن شهرینه روانه اولدق و بو پوغونا آرناود دیمک عاصیلری الجده‌لرنده بر ملعون عنا ایله عبور ایدر کوف الکی پاره قرالردر و بر لرغعا صلب و دا غستان و جنکلستان برلردر کم ابتداسلطعو ذا ولونیه

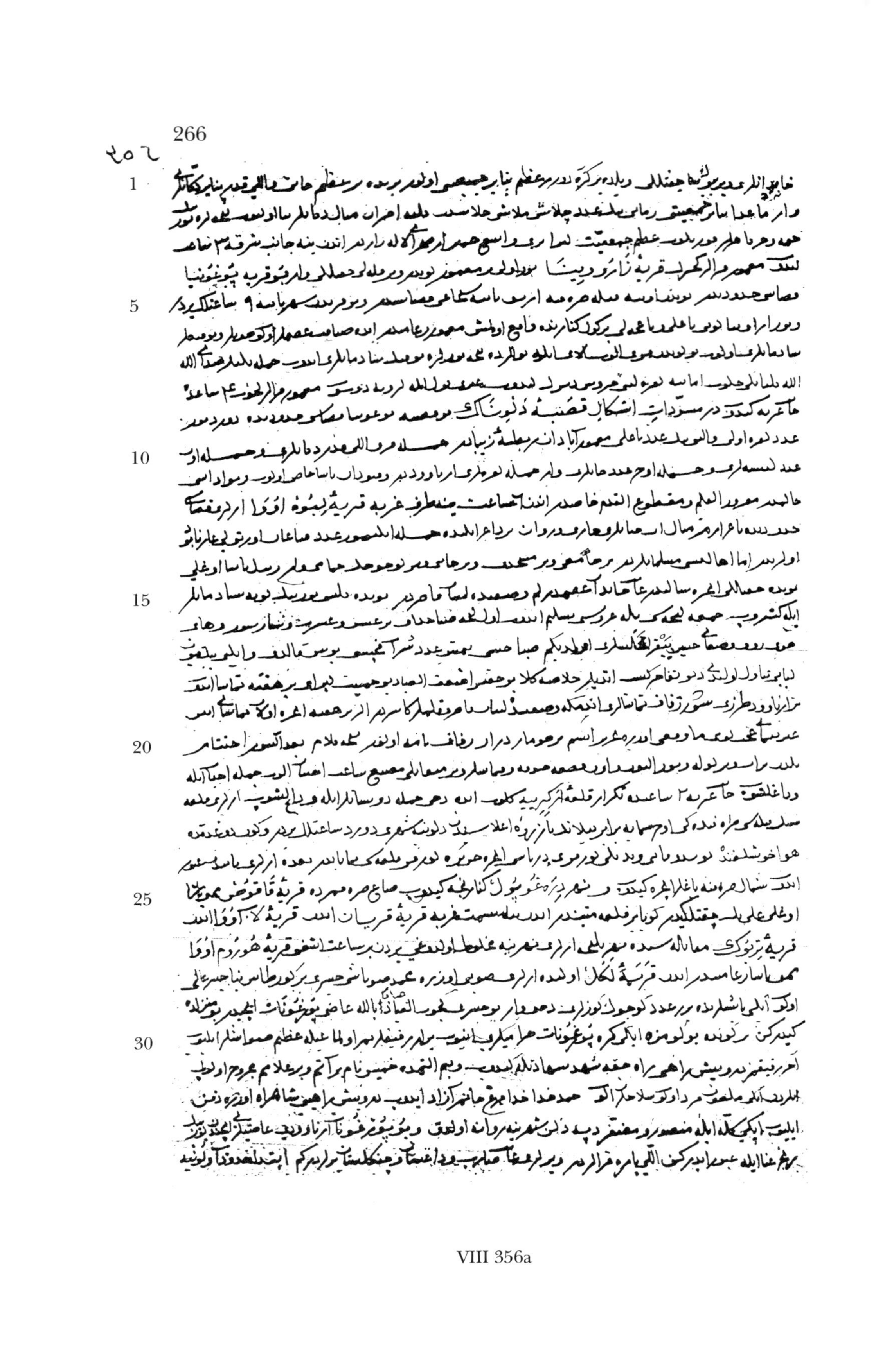

سنجاغنده ووده دلو مصالح ناحیه سیدر بو عباس الحمد سلامتله ٢ ساعتده بجوب قریه کوکنات بودمودیه
دلو حمد دیدر بو قربیه مقابل نهر بیتو ارکی نهرینه مخلوط اولور سو سحر و بیستونا کوروجه ترحالده
داغلرده وشهرینه بیلا سندنکلر انده اتلو بیلادم جا عزیه صادر دره لرده وده له لیارلرده رم عنایجکگ
کیدر درنعیما صورت قلعهٔ دارامن یعنی سور رفیع متین ذیه دلن
بودر سرحدینده نهر طورنا کنارنده قلعه اسمر غوب مسحور معالله سده بو دحودسه دلو قلعه سو وار اولو اولدیه دلن
پلانقه چیت قلعه در اما بو سند ما بو قلعه بر عمارتدر ٩٧ تاریخنده سلطان بایزید عصرنده لدا احمد پاشا محمد
عاصی ارباودده ویند و ملتله بر اولوب بو قلعه الحسه ما بوسر آسلمه دحو قلعه جواله صاحبه لر یابو قلعه
الحمده لیو لیار لرنده لر بیلدرلر بوب بو قلعه بعد الفتح دیه دلو دیو سمینه انقدیلر حالا اولو یه صحا عر حاکنده
موبوادا لعند و بود اللمه المعصا در ناحیه سو حمله سلسماره وراردر اما حواعو بوغو نیا داغلرنده عاصیلردر
عنری جانبلری اصلا بوقدر اما قلعه درداری وحاله یوز عدد قلعه نفرالعیادر قلعه سی ارری نهر نیلکنارنده
اوج اسناده براتو بریالحو ما اوده بوماری یور برده در جمعا صره ده حو تو لرایله قلعه سی سهدر
اولدو عندی تمعمو برمیه امحاب اولماعه امدادری اولمو ایلحا صاسه ایله الهه قریب سه اول مارزرا اودری سه
مو بورده لدا احمد پاشا محمد پاشا سحل مربع بوسد اتعمال سند یا رقلعه ریا اسما ابروب بوبا سو عدی
ابهش دار اما دار حرمه السور انم بر بو جوار قلعه حالدر للوجه بومدر اما دیوار جامالونه قراز شیرغالیه
وحمله ایلو عدد مولری واردر سرمه وبری بالد طره قنه ناظرلردر وقلعه ایچنده حمله العرب
عدد جولیسز قیمز کرمید ابد بولب کوچوک نفرات اولردر والحاق بایزید ولینک برکوچوک جامع وار ویرالچاق
مناره جکی وار صو حصار بجلری وجبه خانه بجو داری ایله مملو انبار ری وار قلعه نفرانلری شب وروز عاصی
بورغو نا تلو غارتلو دیلله جنک جدال و حرب قتال ایدرلر برا بو قلعه کدک احمد پاشا جنک عظیم ایله فتح ایتدکده الا
نیجه بیک شهدا لر بیز اسکیه دیه دلو قربنده مدفونلردر و بزم کلدکلر ایله کلدیکمزی قلعه نفرانلری ایشدوب
الای ایله حضره استقبال چیقوب توفنک شادمانه ایله قلعه یه کروب بزدار اغا خانه سنده ساکن اولدق اما فریبه
فقیرادملر در وضیفهٔ معینه لر اولونیه زرقتو معدنیا میندنکی آرلر آنلر بیز بو بعضی رفیقلر بیزی قلعه دن
طشره وار وشه قوندیردیلر دیر وصف واروش ذیه دلن حمله ایلسور عدد جولیلی واسع اولرلر
حمله سی وباغ ارحوسار اوربولو حاعا باغچه لی اولردر وبلادصره صده لو مو اولمده برلونجه جمعیتی کوتسکی
وار وحمله اللی عدد معبد مختصر دکانلری وار وحمله بر جامع وار وخانه حمام ومدرسه ومکتب
وعنری عمارتلر برسان بومدر اما الحمله بره قمولری وضعلری جوقدر مسره واروشی اولری کره تللیدر
واسعو صو لیارنده باغ وباغچه لرمده بازی دانجیری واردر اما عرصره صده بو قلعه برصحوسر منزلی بردر
حواله لی داغلری واردر وبودنه داخلده عنری عمارتر برصلر اول علی المصباح تاالقوه لسدن قلعه دن
فاغمزله مقوسی اولمده قلعه مولدر ایلسور عدد بها لر جمال صالح عاریلر برم ایله ایله بر رانه اولماعه
مماسر سا ارنلر خمعر اسدم عاریلر بدرا اصلی سلاحلمسی سره ددم ایلرا اسدیعه و اللهم سلطانم بو ترکی لوب
سرلحیدا ایلدکده برماج طام باسلرب الوسکه سودحم عروح اهمیسر قلعه لر اشاره مالری بو نلکه سمره کلو
سرنی بصه لرلرا انده قلعه ایچنده دردار جاله سده ایطه بحمله ده برحاره انده صدیلر بصده ایلر بلری
اوعو لحمه حال سمدلر بر لر واقعه اسرار اولو صاحدل سرمعا الرلری صاصه اتلک وحالری حضوریکر
اوحو رمه لم دیو سمره ودردار ره خبرا تحملک سمدی اسه دو ناسلر ایله سوی بو عا فرار بو بولدی کوتونیه پاتشاننه
سلامت کتخدر تمزکر ایلر بده برنارنجغا زوار بهر انده بیزی البته بکلار وسولوت سزلرزنگیر لمیوب رمص اولور ردیو

ایکیوز عدد باغ مبلغ و مکمّل یکنلر اولکمزه د و رشدیلر حقیر دخی وافر حظ ایدک قلعه‌دن یقوش اشغی یوله رأوانه اولکوهمان
اکر کری نهر عظیمن کمیلرله قرشو کچوب اول بوغاز دبدکلری محل اکری نهرینک لونه طرفنده قالور قرشو طرفده صارپ
داغلره ٣ ساعتده چیقعه قریه‌ده امیز بر در بند کوپریه زعامتدر اندن قریهٔ قاششت بو قرالر اکری نهرینک صولنده قالوب
یلدز طرفنه کیدن یولده ا تمام بری طرفه امزامات اول اصفره بار قصاسی حدودینه کروب اندن قریهٔ مازیجان اندن
قریه تلیچو قلر بونز کفر ادم باره قرال معاف مسلملر و مسلملر در رعایالری ارنامیدر بو محللرده عظیم جفتلکلر دخی وار
٣ ساعتده شرقه کیدوب در شتریفا آشکال شولر کبار قرا یعنی حصار عبر تنهای اصفره بار
زمان قدیمده روم کفره سی بنا ایتمشلر امان تعمکدر بسته نا بجنده ارابعه عشقیا سم اللندن سلطان بایزید ولی
عصرنده کدلی احمد پاشا فتح ایتدی بو بنیه سناغی حدودنده بوز اللی اقچه قضادر وناحیه‌سی قرق بیک پاره قرادر بکجیری اغالغندن تنبید
جیقعنا سلامبولده قائم مقام اولان ابراهیم پاشانک شهیددر قلعه دزداری عالی عدد نفراتلر عمار کتخدایی و یکجری سرداری
وغیری عاکملری یوقدر قلعه‌سی بر دیه اوزره حواله لو ویرقبولی و حرم بیداد ملی بر کوجوک سنداتعنا بر قلعهٔ رعنا حکمدر
ایچنده جمله قرق بش عدد کره متلم خانه لر و بر بایزید خان جامعی واردر وارشی آشغیده یوز عدد کره متلم باغچه
باغچه لو اولدر آب و هواسی لطیف اولدوغی باغچه لرنده زیتونی و انجیری جهانی بوتستدر اندن ٣ ساعتده قریهٔ ویشقار
اندن بر ساعتده جانب غربه قریهٔ طرپان بکجری حسن اغانک بونده برعالی انجلی وطشلی مکلف محلی جفتلکی عظیمی واراینده
درونده اره نعمتی مبذولدر اندن جانب غربه مثال ساعتده کیدوب در شروعات سیتایش قلعهٔ برزه مقدمی بیان
تعمکدر اندن روم بنا سیدر وسنه تاریخنده کدیک احمد پاشا فتحیدر نزد اکرد قرق عدد مرد حصاری وار اما قلعه لکنده دزدار خانه عنبر برسو بیه قدیم
جزایکینه اوضهد قلعه ایچره برمیا اوزره بر حوض وار ایچنده کونا کون ماهیلر وار غرایت انده کم بو ایلچی غیا اوزره بر حوض صوزره تدکلر کمسه بلمز و جهیمز ماندی
اندن جانب غربه بوقوش آشغی ساعتده کیدوب قریهٔ ژرو طوم لسان باوود دخی ده دمکدر باغلی و باغچه
لی معمور قدریه درکم رابه نهری جنکنده صونده غرق اولان بکجری اغاسی مصطفی پاشا مرحومک کوبیدر کم سراینده قلعه مثال
برقلعهٔ عظیم بنا اتمش دیو مرانک قرشوسنده یارم ساعت برزده قواسترین سلطان مراد و سلطان ابراهیم خان وزیری قتل شهید
اولان قره مصطفی پاشانک کویی قریهٔ لادانی صاغمزده قالوب اکد قریب قریهٔ روشنیک کوپرلی وزیر محمد پاشانک
قصبه مثال سرای کره متلو تولو تحتانی و فوقانی کارکیر بنالی باغلی و باغچه لی جمله عدد خانه لی رابطه سی
مزینندر بر معمور جامعی ور مسجدی و بر مدرسه سوحته خانه سی و بر مکتب صبیان خانه سی و بر تکیهٔ درویشانی و بر بو بنیا حمام
خان ستانی و کفایت مقدار دکانلری عمار آب و هواسی غایت لطیفدر

اندن ینه قریهٔ رود طومعه کلوب اندن بر ساعت یقوش آشغی بلغراد طرفنه کیدوب قریهٔ زوبزد سنه بوز اللی عدد اولی
باغلر ارم مثال کفره کوییدر بوندن شهر بلغراد آیاق آلتنده غربی طرفنده نمایاندر اندن غربه یقوش آشغی باغلر ایچره بر ساعت کیدوب
در تعبیر آسمان معظم دار جهاد یعنی قلعهٔ ارم آباد بلغراد خرم آباد
بقول مورخین لاطین بو قلعه ابتدا بنا ایدن ینجه بوکفندوکه لروپ اخر کار رسته تاریخنده بالرا بلیر دخی
خلافتنده سردار معظم کدک احمد پاشا انرناود ایله روم و بونیدوقاشی فرنکی النده فتح اتمشدر دولت عثمانیه ده هلا
عدد قلعهٔ بلغراد نام سوربنا ملر وار اولاری طونا نهری کنارنده طونا بلغراد عسوری بو بنیز سرحد دیده بو بنیه بر محلک
زیاده بعید استولنی بلغراد و بریده حکم العثمانیه اردل بلغرادی بریکه بو دو دو دیجی ارناو و دبلغرادی درکم حالا سلطان
فاتحی عادره روم ایلی ایالتنده آونونیه سنجاق بکینک تختیدر طرف پادشاهیدن بکینک خاصی ٢٢٩٠٠٠ اقچه در و ارباب زعامت
٢٨ و ارباب تیماری ١٨٩ ٤ دبر والای بکجری باشی وار در پاشاسی حین سفرده قانون اوزره کندو تابعی لوا ایله
و جمله ارباب تیمار تابعیه لوا ایله دورد بیک کزیده عسکر اولوب تابعی اولدقلری سفره میرلوا ایله کیدر لر لکن قاعاهاک

وجمیع عسکری واردر شیخ الاسلامی ونقیب الاشرافی واوچیوز اقچه پایه سیله شریف قضاسیدر ویوز یکرمی پاره ناحیه قرابسی اولور بو وجهله کتخدا ایری وقفلری واردر حاکمنه بو سنه الترکیسه وپاشاسنه اوطوز کیسه حاصل اولور سپاه کتخدا یری ویکیچری سرداری وقلعه دزداری عدد قلعه نفراتلری وشهر وویوداسی ومحتسب وباجداری وقلعه کتخداسی ومهتر باشیسی وشهر کتخداسی ومعمار اغاسی وخراج اغاسی واردر وآولونیه سنجاغنده جمله طقوز قضادر تحت قضا بو بلغراددر وشمال طرفنده مزاکیه قضاسیدر کم اوطوز پاره قرادر وشرق طرفنده طموربلیچیسه قضاسیدر وبوکه قریب قبله ایله مشرق مابیننده قضای اصقره پاردر وانکه متصل قبله طرفنده قضای پره مدید بو قضایه متصل قبله سی طرفنده قضای پوغونیادر وبو قضانک غربنده قضای ارکری ایله مشادر اما بو ارکری قضاسی دلونیه سنجاغی خاکیدر وبو قضانک شمالنده قضای دیه دلندر وانک جنوبنده قضای آولونیه در اما بو مذکور طقوز عدد قضالر غایت محصوللیلردر اما بعضی رعایالری عاصیلردر کم نعوذ بالله وبو بلغراد قلعه روم مسطنطینی ایله ازاووینا الندن فتح اولمشدر قلعه نک اشکالی قبله‌دن یلدیز پوزکاری جانبنه طولانی واقع اولمش بر بالجن تپه زقیا اوزره شکل مسدس ان مثال برشداد عجلا سندطراش برصعب سور صعواش متین برحصن حصین قلعه در لکن ایچ ایل‌ده اولمق ایله کوزدن براغیلوب جابجا بعضی برلری مرور ایام ایله منهدم اولمغین یوز یدی تمنشدر کرکاکردی قلاعات جمله ایکی بیک التیوز عدد کرمه ادم احاطه ایدر قلعه سرامددر وجمله یدی عدد متین وقویجه برج وزه لری واردر اولا یلدیز طرفنه چارشویه اینه جک یول قپودن چارشو یقوش اشغی کامل بیلداد مدر وتوفنکدار اوچ قات تدرهر قاتی مابینی یوز ادم برلرندن بعید باب عظیملردر بوقپولرک ایکی عدد قپوسی یلدز طرفنه ناطردر بر قاتی ایچری قپودر کم شرق طرفنه مکشوفدر وبوقپونک ایکی طرفنده تمل [illegible] قیل کوپه سی قدر یشک چارالریدر مکر بوکون بطا شلرک امثالی قدس شریفده قرنده حلیل الرحمن یا خود نهر طوبرله کنارنده بندر قلعه سنده اولا وبر قپوکه دخی ایچکی منصورد بنده محبه غربه ناظر قپودر کم اشغی حصین پاشانک یکی بنا اتدوکی مرادچلبیا محله سنده کیجا معی اوکننه اینر قپو یولیدر وبر قپودخی محله لرارسنده شرقه ناظر برکوچوک اوغرین قپودر اما اولقدر شاهراه دکلدر اشکال ایچ حصار غربه ناظر بیوک قلعه دیوارنک برکوشه سنه متصل برشدادی سندنبا برسور رحنا حکدر کم جرمی سکز یوزاد مدر وایکی عدد قپوسی واربر شرق طرفنه مفتوح قلعه ایچنه ناظردر بری غرب سمتنه مکشوف اولوب طشره اشغی چلبیا محله سنه یقوش اشغی اینر ایچ قلعه قپوسیدر کم جنوب طرفنده میالد قپودر اما بومذکور یدی عدد قپولرک جمله سی قره اغاج تخته سندن دروزه لردر کم دمر قپولر دکلدر زیرا هربر قپولر دشمندن کزلی قله لر آره لرنده پنهان اولمشدر وزه لردر هیچ برایکی قپولرنک تخته قناطلری برده یوقدر زیرا ایچ ایل‌ده واقع قلعه در دشمندن اصلا خوف خشیتلری یوقدر وبو ایچ قلعه ایچنده جمله قرق الی عدد کیره مستاوبر تولی خانه لردر وبرعدد جامع بایزید خاندر وجبه خانه لری ازدر التی پاره طوبلری واردر وکهنه بنا انبارلری وصو صارنجلری ودزدار خانه سی وغیری اثار بنا یوقدر مستاپش طشره بیوک حصار بلغراد جمله ایکیوز عدد کره متلی ویران شکللی اولردر اکثریا اوروم کفره نک خانه لریدر باغچه لری خراب خیلی واسع میدانلری واردر وجمله بر عدد کرمتلی وکارکیر مناره لی کارقدیم برواسع بایزید خان جامعی کهنه بنا جما عتسز غریب جامع مجیددر وجمله سکز عدد کفره کنیسه لری واردر اما بریغا مهجور وسرزین وتنکدر جمله صو قاقلری قدرتدن طاشلی قالدرملیدر وبو قلعه نک انجاری آره سنده کی قلعه دیوارنه متصل اولدر اصلا اطرافنده خندقلری یوقدر زیرا دائرا ما دار بالجن اوچوروم قناره قیالردر کم جنوب طرفنده کی چکه قیاسی نام سمتی اوچ سایه سرچکمش شاهین وزغنوس وقره قوش اشیانلی وبوده لنکیج وچیلاق یوواری سرامیدی مهیب قیالردر کم آدم اشغی باقمغه جرات ایده مز بر محله چکه قیاسی بهدن فرض اولدیکم بعضا تتبع کفار خاکسار تعوذ قرار بینه بو قلعه بروجه ایله پادشاهه فریادجی ایکن بکی کفارله ... آخرکار بوقیالردن صورسر دنیکره شهبازتکندی اشبه ایله حارقدب اولادخمه قیالردبندن چاغرین

اوّلا نهر شناورلسا یعبب فطیح منازل عاصی مراحل ایده رك آدرنیه واروب احوال دیرکوف عاجزه بیر
پادشاهه تقریر ایدوب احسانلرا اولدینه اوچ کونده برشب مظلمده بو چکه بنی قپاسی دینه کلوب چکه بنی دیو فریاد
ایدیجك بلدیلرکم قلعه‌دن پادشاهه فریاده کیدن غازی قوصقیدرکم کلوب قول قرار معهوده قدیمه لری اوزره
چکه بنی دیدی درحال غازی قوصقیی ایپلر ایله قلعه‌یه چکوب بیره هوش کلدلك نه خبر دیجه پادشاه عا
لمپناه وزرا و وکلا و علما و صلحا و شیخ الاسلام سزلره سلام ایتدیلر بنم غازیلرم انشاالله تعالی اون کونه دك الله ایلد عدد
عساکر اسلام ایله وارو بشترمر دین مبین غیرتمانلرکدر همان غیرت وجدا هتمام ایشلر تیلرسه ایله سنلر رنعار به
زنهار قلعه کفاره ویرمکسنلر اشته جمیعیسر کارده اولنلر مکتوبلری دیوب جمله عصیان اولان غزات مسلمینه تسلیم
حاطروروب انلر دخی وار مقدورلرن صرف ایدوب شب وروز صواش پرخاشلر ایدرکن حقیقت الحال اون کونده
یتمش سکسن بیك عسکر امدادی قضا وقدر کبی همان جمله کافرلره قلعه التنده کرشوب کفاره بر صاتمور بازیدیوب جکراکم
حالا مرا لنه صحرا سنده قرار ایدن کفره لر استخانلری جسته جسته وپشته پشته یغیلوب یاتدیغی نمایاندر بعده
جمله غازیلر پادشاه جم جنابدن احسان انعاملر اولوب اول چکه بنی دین شهبازه دخی برزعامت عظیم احسان اولنمش
حالا اوغوللرینه چکه بنی زاده لر دیوب الحمد الله بروجه تملیك زعامت کوینه متصرفلردر انکیچون اول سببدن
بو قپایه چکه بنی قپاسی درلر مشهور آفاق بر طاق رواق مثال بر برّاق آق قپادر و بو چکه بنی قپالرینك پیشخوارنده
فله و کنیسه لر و میره کاه کونشکلر وار ایدی بو قپالر التنده صوکنارنده اشقیه برقات قلعه دیوارلری دخی وار غایت متین
دیوار سندهصیندر اشقو بیول لوپروپا شنده کی قلعه قپوسندن تا قرانجیلر چارشوسی قپوسنه دك جمله شکیز یوز
ادم ادروی چارشودرکم نهر کنارینه واقع اولمش سوق سلطانیدر و بو قلعه‌ایچنده جمله یتمش سکسن مقدار
کره متاورتولی سد معمور اولردر ماعدا همان بر شاهراه اوزره جمله سکسن عدد واسع دکانلردرکم بر بولدرغیره
طریق عام یوقدر زیرا بر طرفی قلعه ندچکه بنی قپالریدر و بر طرفی قلعه التندن جریان ایدن نهر
فرهادکوه کسن بو اشقو قلعه‌دن و یوقاری قلعه ندچکه بنی قپالرندن اولوب کیسمه قپانرد بانلر ایله بر منارده قلعه
دیوار پیچه صوکنارینه واطاقه ایله قلعه تیمه لی صولوکر بعضی یرلرنده صویه اینر یتمش سکسن قدمه طاش نردبانلر
ایله اینیلوب قرانجیلر چارسوی قپوسی دینده بر عظیم صوقله سی وار تا صویه ایچنده بنا اولنمشدر تا چکه بنی قپالرینه ایچنده ادیمه
بولری وارکم یوقاری قلعه‌دن اشقو صوقله سنه ایچنده بینا اولنمش یاق کیسمه طاش نردبانلردرکم حین محاصره ده بو
قپالر ایچنده کیجه یولردن صو طلشیوب محصور اولنلر اصلا صویه ضرورت چکمزلر و بو یولری دخی شهرلر دخی کوروزلر اما
قرانجیلر چارسوی قپالرندن اشقو صوییو لری الحاقکه اما بو یولر دخی دشمنلر کوره مزلر و بو اشقو قلعه‌ده اولان دکانلر جمله
قرانجیلر و جانجا مطافلردر و بو قرانجیلر قپوسندن طشره مرحوم و مغفور له اوزون قوزلی بر چارشوسی
عظیم بنا ایدوب بو محله‌ده بر و لار وش عظیم اولماسنه سبب اولوبحالا اوزون قوزلی چارشو دیرلر و قرانجیلر چارشوسندن شرقه
تا مطافلر باشنه وارنجه کامل ایکی بیك ایلهدر و ایکی قات شاهراه یوللر و یمین و یسارلری سراپا هر اصنافك پاك و پاکیزه
دکانلردر اکثریا دکچیا کیشلر جمله اوزقورلی اوغلی اوماقلریدرکم جمله لد تیوز عدد دکانلردر اما بذازستانلری
یوقدر لکن بینه جمله متاع اقمشه نادر و دیبا و سنسو و زریاف فاخره لر جمله موجوددر اکثریا موجحسو غایت چوقدر
در وصف بیوك وارونیش شهر بلغراد آرنا و دکرچه بر سواد معظم دارونش عظیمدر اما قلعه دیوارلری ایچنده یکدر
بو قاری قلعه ندجانب قبله سی و شرقیسی طرفنده بر واسع مراده و نهر کنارنده سراپا باغ و کلستانلی و مشبك
بوستانلی بر باط عظیمدرکم جمله لعلکون مصنع کره مت اورتولی بنش بیك عدد معمور و مزین روضهٔ جنانلی واسع و
تحتانی و فوقانی سراپا کارکیر بنالی و بیك عدد در مود پنه لی زمین محصول لدرده غایت مصنع دارلر اولوب یوزدن متجاوز سرای
کاشانه‌لر ایله آراسته و هر بر خانه‌لری حوض و شاذروانلر ایله پیراسته اولمش شهر مزیندرکم هواسی بلاسنده روم دارك

سرفصل سنکاز آشقو حصار

در وصف سرای اعیان اغوات جملهٔ حسین پاشا سرایی باغچه سرایدر و پاشالره مخصوص سرایدر والحالة هذه چتال باش
پاشا قرانداشی عثمان پاشا سراینده ساکن اولوب کترد بکلر امر پادشاهیله و سردار علی پاشا مکتوبلرین ویروب
دیوان پادشاهیده ونه دکدن کترد بکلر یوزعوبالری حرامیلرینک کلّه‌لرن دیوان پادشاهیده غلطان ایدوب فرمان
پادشاهیلر قرائت اولندقده معهود کلاملری عثمان پاشانک معلومی اولوب فرمان پادشاهیله دیوب مانیه
محافظه‌سنه جمیع اولونیه سنجاغی عسکریله اماده اولماق ایچون نادیلر ندا ایدوب کترد بکلر ملعونلر ایچون حقیر
پاشنه برچلنک شاهو طقوب و بر خلعت فاخره کیدروب فرمان سردار کترد بکلر ایچون بر کیسه غروش ویرات
ویر کوله و حذاملر بیله اوزر التونی ویر چوقه قومش احسان ایدوب قماغزده بر هفته صفالر ایدوب نیجه سرایلر
ده ذوق زوقلر ایدوب آندن محمد افندی زاده‌لر سرایی و سردار اغا سرایی و اوردقوریم سرایی بلوکلر مشهور
سرایلر ابادانلر دفتر اسماء عدد محلات جمله اوطوز عدد محلاتلردر اولا قلعه‌نک جنوبنده مراد
چلبیا محله‌سی و اوروموزلو محله‌سی حطاب محله‌سی وقف محله‌سی بابا ماصم محله‌سی پاشاقجیلر محله‌سی آق جامع
محله‌سی اسکی بازار محله‌سی کون کورمز محله‌سی
اوطوز عدد محلاتلر مشهور معمورلری بو مذکور محلاتلردر لکن اون محله‌سی کفره لردر و بر محله‌سی یهودیلردر
اما ارمنی و فرنک و چنگانه محله‌لری یوقدر لکن لاطین کفره لری چوقدر کم کلوب بازرکانلق ایدوب بنه کیدرلر
در عمارت جوامع مفهمات اهل ایمان سلاطین آل عثمان جمله اوطوز عدد محراب مومنانی عابدانیدر اما جمله جماعت
کثیر جماعتلک نانشمزده سلطنتده سلطان بایزید ولی جامعی طولی التمش ایاق و عرضی التمش ایاقدر و بر موزون و مصنع
و سرامد مناره‌سی واردر و جمله اوچ عدد قپولری اولوب ایکی یان قپوسی و بر قبله قپوسی اولوب کنده بر جامع قدر دخی
صفهٔ عظیمه‌سی وار اما حرمی یوقدر لکن بر طرز قدیم بنا اولنمش سراپا کره مستاوی تولی کار عتیق جامعدر محرابی اوکنده
افندی تکیه‌سی سکز کوشه تحتانی و فوقانی تکیه خلوتیدر آندن اوزقورلی جامعی جمله سرامد کارکیر
قبه‌لی و سراپا رصاص خاص بکلکونیله مستور بر جامع نور علی نوردر کم بر سرامد مناره موزونی وارکم مثلی مکر
سیواس ایالتنده یکسار شهرنده ما السفار جامعنده مناره‌سی اوله اما بو جامعک ملثر حجره‌سی اطرافلرنده کی
یا نصیفه‌لری اوزره بیاض و مجلا مرمر ستون منتهالر اوزره بیش عدد قورشوم اورتولی قبه‌لرلیلر در و جمله
مدرسه و مکتبی و تکیه و عمارتلری سراپا قورشوم اورتولیدر آندن غازی مراد پاشا جامعی سیاده بنا معبدگاه رعنا
در آندن یوقاری قلعه‌ده خنکار جامعی اکه فتحیه جامعی درلر آندن مراد چلبیا محله‌سنده قره مراد پاشا یکه نیمه
چلبی حسین پاشا جامعی بو بنا بر جامع زیبادرکم بو حقیره اکا تاریخ بودرکم قبله قپوسی عتبهٔ علیاسی اوزره محرر
اولمشدر تاریخ اولیا پنج اسم اعظم الله دیدی تاریخنی ۵ حتی عزیز و یا بصیر و یا قوی یا متین ۸ سنة ۱۰۸
اما بر بارلی و مصنع و سرامد کشش مانه کارکیر مناره و بر کاسه سلکون مثال مدور قبه‌سی اوزره لعلکون کرمیت
ایله مستور بر جامع معمور در ظرافتده لطافت و علم معمارنده مثلی یوق بر بدیل و مجروحدر لکشا جامع زیبادر
آندن محکمه قربنده نامنه منوشقا جامعی کویا خلدبریندر بو مذکور جامعلر مشهور معبدگاه مزینلردر
در مساجدهای موحدان مؤمنان جمله عدد محلات تفحص اوزره لرندر اولا وقف محله‌سی
مسجدی مراد چلبیا محله‌سنده اوچ عدد مساجدلر وار بابا ماصم مسجدی پاشاقجیلر مسجدی اق محله مسجدی
اسکی بازار مسجدی کون کورمز محله‌سی مسجدی و سایر عدد مساجدلر دخی وار اما مشهور معمورلری بونلردر
در تفهیم اعدد دار التدریس مفسران جمله سی عدد دار العلوم عالمانیدر جمله اسلحه تاریخ ولی مدرسه‌سی اوزقورلی
مدرسه‌سی بونلر مشهوردر اما ماسبه دار الحدیث سعدناملی و دار القراء
خدامانی یوقدر لکن بعضه هر جامعلرده مدرس حسبیلر واردرکم جمعه ایرتسی حقها الفراشی اولعمدر زیرا طلبه کرچوقدر

در دار التعلیم مکتب جگرگوشه پسران جمله ؟ عدد دار الحدیث صبیاندر اولا [illegible] اوقونور
مکتبی و شیخ [illegible] مکتبی و مراد چلبی مکتبی و [illegible] بونلر مشهوردر

در ذکر تکیهٔ درویشان ارباب طریق زنشان جمله اوچ عدد خانقاه آل عبادر اولا خنکار جامعی [illegible] ادهم
السیح ابتدای خانقاه هیدر کم سکز گوشه قوتانلی و [illegible] مولوی خانه در [illegible] اوزره بر
توحیدگاه و مقام حایعاه [illegible] صاغ طرفنده درویشان حجره لریدر [illegible] توحید الله سوخته
اولمش [illegible] نور توحید الله منور اولوب توحیدایتی عطریاتیله آکنمک دماغلری معطر
اولور کم جمله قرق عدد حجره لردر و اوزرلری قورشونلی تکیه‌در بونلر مشهوردر

در مدح حمامات راحت جان جمله ایکی عدد گرمابه غسالاندر اولا [illegible] اورتلری جامعی اولدیغی اوزره [illegible] غسالت
لطیف سافی [illegible] هواسی [illegible] سودی [illegible] حمام روشنادر و جانلری پاکدر
در وصف حمامات مخصوص اعیان [illegible] عدد سرای حمامی وار در
در عدد چشمه سار آب حیوان آب حیات جمله [illegible] عدد چشمه [illegible] اولا جملدن اورتلری جامع [illegible]
اوکنده [illegible] معمار سلطان قاسم آغا چشمه سیدر تاریخیدر قاسم [illegible] معماران یا بیع خیر کم
کورن ایده ز شکر حق قبول ایلیه چونکه اولدی تمام سل الی [illegible] بو چشمه سنه ۱۰۵۴ بلو تاریخ
چشمه اوزره [illegible] لاجوردی کاشیلر اوزره [illegible] عزیز اولمشدر [illegible] چشمه
در [illegible] قاسم آغا [illegible] قاسم آغا [illegible] اولمشدر [illegible] اورتلری [illegible]
ابتدای در ذکر عکدچار سوی بزازستان قپان جمله [illegible] عدد [illegible] سرای جامعی [illegible]
[illegible] دباغ خانه [illegible] چارسوی [illegible] اوزره [illegible]
اما [illegible] جمله [illegible] جمیع [illegible]
[illegible] موجوددر [illegible]
[illegible] جمله ارباب صنایع و ارباب معارف [illegible] بو میدانده
در آثار بنای عبرت نمای عجایبات [illegible] ساعت [illegible] ساعت [illegible]
[illegible] استماع اولنور [illegible]
[illegible] ساعت [illegible] جمله [illegible] عدد [illegible]
[illegible] حمام [illegible]
[illegible] کتاره [illegible] بعضیلر [illegible] بعضیلر
[illegible] احباب و اصدقا و ارباب معارفلر ایله کورشوب بیلشوب مباحثه علم شرعیه و فنون شعریه [illegible] اشعار
و فصحای بلغای و مصنفین و مؤلفیندن [illegible] اما مذهب [illegible]
[illegible] طریق [illegible] دباغ خانه چارسوی [illegible] کنار [illegible] واقع
[illegible] اشجارلر [illegible] کارخانه [illegible]
[illegible] طرفنه [illegible] طرفنه [illegible]
[illegible] اولدیغی [illegible] اما
[illegible] و غازلر [illegible] لطیف
و [illegible] ایلکلری [illegible]
[illegible] چارسوی [illegible] آنلرکم [illegible] اوزره [illegible]

ماتم جمال ابطال ایسور زیرا جمله ده دکانلر اجره اوله دکانلری اصلا کوسی یا ممسوح هر برینه نوبتلر نوبت نوبت مزین ساهلر
اولدقلرندن و بو اهل صرف ده دکانلر سد ایدر پاصوماملری اوزره بجمله اور سولی دکانلر در همیشه یاراسلر اریکه معمار منقا دعاب
عاسمانلر جمله دکانلرده دکانلر ایله مصاحبت ایدرلر عسده دکانلر زیرا اسماد لری و بدر ماندلری معامر قسمت احمرلر
در شروع متایشی خان تجاران خواجه کان جمله سوعد ذکره مت اوزتولی جانب خواجه داب سودا کرانلر عمارتی ایله قلعه کی
در عدد وکالهٔ عزه بایمی بهر تجاران اهل پیشه کان جمله الوعدد بلار اوداری ترکم الحمد سرپرسه اللدار اهل صبانعانلر سلسو اولورلر
در عدد ماکل دار الضیافت اطعام عمارات جمله اون عدد عمارت ماکلدر جمله باربحا واورمورلی و عزیزا شعب عمارتی مشهور در
در بیان انهار زلال جاری آب حیوان ما حیات بو شهر اجره جریان ایدن نهر اوصنوم باشی صرمده اصمره باروک اوصوم و
جبل بالا طولومتوردن کلوب بو شهر المجنون جره یا ایدن عرسحره سده حوادث اصحر ایجره کیدوب مره عماکدلو علیلچقتلکی
نیندن کچوب البصای صونورنهر ملعوط اولوب دریا مال ایلنسو [illegible] تمراکیه صحراسندن
عبور ایدن تاینه ناسماه اوقلمیسی دسده ویحدل [illegible] اوکو تمراکیه صحراسنده باروحسن بونهر
اوصوم نهرلا عبور اولنمز در وصف عمارت قنطرهٔ وارقوش بولنمز اسهر بدل بو اوصوم نهری عبور [illegible] مده
صو اشربی [illegible] در اسمنه قنطره وارقوش ذرکر جمله [illegible] دجله لره [illegible]
اولور اکثریا رومللو [illegible] سرکنار در [illegible] موقعیه اهالی اسهال سما
اوکو [illegible] در عصم بوه سربلند درکم درخت منتهای عظیملر ایله مزین اولوب نهر اوصوم اوزره اولا [illegible]
[illegible] هر بیم [illegible] کمشسه حالم بیم اکه حقیقتکلرلر [illegible]
رادیم ما آنی [illegible] حالم الله [illegible] صحیح [illegible]
[illegible] الحاصل [illegible]
در میسره کاه ارباب [illegible] میسره کاه [illegible] اولا [illegible] میوه
[illegible] معصور [illegible]
تسکار کاهلر [illegible] مسیره کاه [illegible] ملاطفت شهرینک آصبوزو [illegible]
نجه [illegible] درخت عظیم سایه [illegible] صفه [illegible] مصطبه [illegible]
سهر [illegible] الحاصل
[illegible] اما بو [illegible] حمام [illegible]
[illegible] شهر [illegible]
طعیا اوزره [illegible] مسیره کاه [illegible]
ومقصوره [illegible] ناظر
اوکو [illegible] اوزره [illegible] عظمادر
در بیان جسور [illegible] عجایبات [illegible] نهر اوصوم اوزره [illegible]
[illegible] قنطرهٔ عظیمه [illegible]
[illegible]
[illegible] آمین
[illegible] نهر اوصنوم [illegible]
[illegible]
[illegible] قنطرهٔ متعالیه جبل طولومتور [illegible] اولا طولومتور داغی

الله بو كسكن سر بلند دوه بالادر كه هنوز صاف بردن نمایان بر مهیب كوه بالادر انده اولان شتاده قشلا انك
انواع میوه لری كرم جیم فرنكستانده كی تنسستانده چمنلر صحرالری بالاده عروج ایدوب نیجه بیك بیوك كونا كون ادویه لر جمع ایدرلر
بوینده اولان ابصارلر اطرافلرنده اولان اوزبر مغارلرده جره بابا اتك مبلغ صو منبع بو عیون جاریه لر جمله اوخر نه كوكلنه آثار
دیو بوده بالاده اولان اجناس مملو ما حضر آسوده مكركوه بیستونده وكوه شمانده بولنه دنیا و نده نیجه سهیده و لوراغ ریده
معلوم تبدیل اولنه عجب بو البرز ده اولان الحاصل عاصی مسیره كاه وشكاركاه جبال عالیه در اما بو بلغراد بلده مطره منه اولان صحرا
سعادت الله شهر البصات سوی ساعت سیر یدر و بو شهر بلغراد ایلیلا ابلر اولما علاء آب هواسی لطیف اولدوغندن محبوب و محبوبه سی عاشق
مراولی اولكه جمله عاشق بر صیلر در اما عاشق مائل و مائده لرد و جمله ماره لرغ سور سلاح لوزلر زرا الصادا الله هو دیو
ستدی بلمرا ریاو رساندهر هبار اسما طلا حبیب بصو ملح حبیب دیو سوزلر اما عسكری و لوندات طایفه سیما و لباس رعایا
او علمه اولانلر اهر یا بو شهرده اسلامبوله لسان حاملرده انشا ایله كاملا اولوردلر كلكیا ایدر اما درپیا ممدوح ما كولات طعام عطعم مشروبات
اولا ساحرعاریا و ورد سمندی و محمودی حدوره لمو صادق بوره لمو حیا مو تلمو قبو منشتو ار زنام پنیرو بنو منو قطه لی سلوه بورك
وقیماق تعلواسی و بادملر صمصه كی عاشق ممدوحه در و مسویات اوزوم شیر كسنك بر كوزنه قیقنا مثل لعلكون شیره سی اولور آكه
آكه تر كمانیه دیرلر بر دانه سی انبوس اكه سر موسی وسر مسا اوكو بامل بر حصه دنیا عدن بر حما و سمنی الحك انا ایل وملل كامل
بو شهره مخصوص تر كمانیه شیرین بتیدیر و دا یوره كه باص اللی او كو اكه نوش اینن صوینی لعو نفع ایدر لو با مصرلر بوصوره
بوزه سیلیر وقووا كیما شمرا اندن ادم هلاسو عذر لعاب بارعو رسویو و لمو ممدوحی و الحاصل بلباغ و حدیقه
هابلرعصها بو رسا انمشدر اما الموید بور محرا او لمار درگار صنایع مصنوعات متنوعات جمله اهل اصناف اهل حرف
موجود اولكه اما اندریا حلما الكاسب حبیب الله دیو دارلسلر عطار لر اولا سلا سا مایع لسرو لودلر ر صیع عوائدر
رد ومره كه عالمانده بزم قسمی اهل اصناف لر لمه و سعرالحمه عز اره صراج و صومكی و خفاف و مر عاجمه و دباغلر
درحسنا اقالیمات تعلواعلم لمو علم اسمر لا بو شهر بدری لحوا ملماه كه صند و لبوس ارص بلده وصول
نهار رسم سر یدر
در طالع عمارستان بلغراد بعول مهمن استاد كهنه پادره و قلمون موالدیل اوده بو شهر كه طالع عماریتی برج سنبله و بیت
عطارد و ترابیه بولنمغین شهرینك عمولاتی زیاده اولوب خلقی خاكیله بلخلوقه حلیم و سلیم آدملردر اما بو شهرده نیجه علما
و لا ورا و حلا و علما و صلحا لمسنه لر قو بمشدر درتتمه شهر انگیز كلیات اولا هلمی لوز لا امرات عاعتمرنس مارو سعادت
و كیبع مماعاریلرد و عاسه در و منم و حرم عاكملرد و هر سنده و شش حصه دیه كلرد و عبر باو ودسانده بو قوم حسیب
النسیب مرسی حلیلردر اما اهل سنت و الجماعت حنفی لكه هبز در لر اما را لائی الحمد لله كان اربا معار ادملركو قدر

در زیارتكاه آرناوود بلغرادی اولا زیارتگاه واعظ محمد افندی و جیم جیم خواجه و یاریدنلی جامع صاحبیدر مدد زیارت
امیر لر سلطان وار و ربولی جامعنك جامع جنوب طره فی قریبنده زیارت پیر محمد افندی و میدان قلعه ستاننده
حسن مرسده زیارت البسیع علی دده رحمة الله علیهم اجمعین
بو شهر لسان لو طره مدده قریه پندی هونیدن و دخی قریه دوشمه نكدن و دخی قریه لابرزا نومنز كو قرالر عالن
محصولی بشر الغشر مترا اولیو مسهور لوبلر در بو بلد عدلر ا... باسا مال عالمه لسیره ولا عصم الملو بردیو با دشاهی
ایتك ماسه مال محصله مر ما نادیاه لعدره سرار لرنكسلره صو ... حمد الله و النعمده ده حصره دیلی عملدر
بو حمدره اللمو غرویش و دیرساه عرب كوله سیوی عاطر باو ودقتریه ... اسوا و براسو هدا ملرنه دهر ... بوغعه و
ور مجاس و اولر عروس احسانلارك نور عددر سلاح موحدلر ... سیها ... الساالله او بو سعود اعلشوب

اهالیسی ماسه برلره محتاج اولوب سنه لرده بر مرتبه باغ اولور اولا بلغراد الحمده مذکور آغاج جسردن عبور ایدوب جنوب جانبنده
معمور البحر کوه بلندلر اوزره ٣٣ ساعت کیدوب قریهٔ بیسینه یا آندن قریهٔ بوشتراتا اندن ٤ ساعتده کیدوب
قریهٔ فیراقتول مختارلی چفتلکلری اندن معمور یوللر ایله ایدوب ساعت لودوسه کیدوب نهرلر قریهٔ میقاآلتنده شهرالله
نهری بر سوصر عبور ایدوب دربیان تماشاگاه معدن زفت سیاه اولوسکلرعالده عجب صنع خدا معدندرکم یرلرداغدن چیقار
اولداغ بوجهله مرهانی گلنکلرالله دلوسنده دور معاالرلب باصیدو لوصید لو بصعصعه روسابرجدار منمور
حبوبریلسانده بارکانلر مکو روسا اسوسع انده نفس بو الحمالرام مال دساهدر لم عاده هو مالدسا هم حاصل اولور
بو حدسه ماصور بلر مماره معاف سلم لوبلرعوار و بعده عجر ملروار اسنه قبل امسور بوده مانده ریطر روسمعدنی اسرلوکی
خدمت ایدرلر وسیحه سدادملر بو معدنلردن گارایتدیکلرلر حالا مرداغی عصم دمعار انده ملر بام حالو لوس ملرانده حب
روسمعدن مار اسلو اولدم بوعلده صهور انده اسم دمود بو لسه اولوسه تلی عرض انده اولدم اور بولسه
بانشقه المرام اولدی الحاصل کلام هاتاری صمصر اصحار الحور جمله بو داغلرده اوسبلرسمر مرابو همرارحلوانده احمر
جمله سیاه روسحلو انمس آیهٔ سورهٔ یفعل الله مایشاء بقدرته ویحکم مایرید بعزته بو تماشای عبرتنما الرایدوب
هماتو علده مربس منهر آق صو بو بی ایلر الله لحوس اما هاسه اولعلده ارکر یرین گلن نهرلرکرسه مخلوط اولور اولدم
اولعله مرسه اولونیه کور نزی نهر باسنه منصب اولور دیوار صوده حمرد ساعت حمدار حمرالله کیدوب قریهٔ میقات
بربارده مده باغلی و باغچه لی دیرها معلی رمسح مرالکلر الدار لرمریه در و معمور سرای عصم همالی وارلر بسار ماسارانه یوسف
بلالمعمله باملی همده بومربه مرامده مراد مرامه لرورد حاف حمصلرانده لمس سسه معدم بدر بمرحوم برم ایمو یسلی جنله
اولدر بو لوبه لکو بوجاندلده مهما اگوسحه سه سالو اوانده عمحمر کسده برده سالی اولو مدر بمر بر حلو بو حم بمربعه
بکلام انده بروعدد دواره باردو عو حصار و بحه امارلری و مو سمه بلی اولا بارد وعی لسانلری جمله بمانسا انده حصم سرعلی
صواتر بدریمرلعاکرسار اسالی روح سرعلرسه همسه انده ابدین اله ودا عکنو ای اله صلعمره مسه بر اولاعره کیدوب
قریهٔ جو هرینا اندن بنه اکه قریب قریهٔ اجمه کلنسه یوملری ساعده عبور ایدوب سه سالمه معمور مرالرعبور انده

در صورت احمال الاستحکام امانیه یعنی سور جهانمای قلعهٔ بالاتانیه

اسما بو قلعه بو جما اسما اسا و الرسا سیدر لسان الیانجه اسمی یو قرونداردر سنه ما بحمده عمر سلطان محمد
خان ابو الفتحنه بدسه ودرر مو حمد محمود پاشا فتحندر بعده و بدیل بونده وماس مرملی بو قلعه اسملا انده سنه
ما بحمده سلطان بایزید ولی عصرنده و بدیلا انده بدسه غازی کوچوک داورنوش بک محاصره الله بو قلعهٔ نوکه نوکه
الحمده اولا لهلر اوره ور روسه امارسه لم دوسوال انده بده عاری لوحول اوروسی یدقان یه بدسور
دملر بده بعدا الفتح بو قلعه عارسه درزا المحمور و جه سمه سی قانیه قامشدر حالا اولوبه کیل عمر حدودنده
واقع اولور بو قلعه اسمی لیه دریا کنارسه صره قنده اولوسه ملحه کسه الحمن لرمارلر عوها و ملرع جمله
لور سو بو قلعه ماسه اوج سمایه سر جلمس بر قلعه سرامد درلرم رصو پرافلی و لو عله ما سلمی پر لوبی
جمنا اوستنده سحل مملی سنادی بار قلعه بالا در حرمی کاملا اوچ بیک عدد ادمدر واصلا رصره مذکور
حصو مذر بر جمدمو بودر زیرا صافی سنکستان اوچ بوروم قیالرید الحمده خندق اولوموز کره متلی
حالته کار لیدریا لر وار در ور سلطان محمد خان جامعی واردر بره معه الله مسمور ر موروو منارهلی جامع عمری
وار الله مرس عازی بسار پاسا سرا عمر عاس حمان بماد رلم جمله اولوسه حیرگو لورمو درباسو و بور اللی
مملی بعد بورمو دریا سو اعمره لوبرمو حو بوره که وار اولوسه بور مرعی احمو ودو ما و برعوبات بور مو عالمو
دکانلر بدده قلعه سی

قلعه سی

جمله بو قلعه ملحه کسه بماییدر بابو مریه زیروهٔ عالیده سا اولمسر قلعه ماسه درلم حمان اباق السده نمایاندر

و بو قلعه‌نك اوچ قپوسی وار بری قبله طرفنه ناظردر اول قپودن ایچرو اولا واروشنه آچیلر و بر قپوسی
واروشه قپودر اسمی اولوب قلعه‌یه گیدر یوللر و بر قپو دخی صو قپوسی دیدکلری کوچوک
واروشه آچیلر اما بو قپونك یاننده ایچ قلعه‌دن ایلرو بر قپوسی دخی وار اولوب ایچ قلعه ایچره آچیلر
بو ایچ قلعه الحمد لله آبادان بیوتلر عدد لره مسافه یولی وار قدیم خانه‌لری و علالی انبارلری وجه خانه‌لری
صو صاقلری وار و بو ایچ قلعه‌ده دیوارلره کرسیده اسمی اولوب قلعه‌نك ماه
یرد عدد صو یولی وار زیاده ... مسجدلر و برسر حدثینه گرده مثللری یوقدر صو یولی بر
ادم الحمد لله سالم اولوب بورغاز و دوسته لو صیره که قلعه الحمد لله درجه
صاحب الخیر صو یوللری ... صو اولوب ساکن اولور
الحاصل بر اوباد ... قلعه قپوسی اوزره بر تاریخ کوشه
مرمر اوزره جلی خط ایله سلطان سلیمان بو قلعه‌یی تعمیر و ترمیم ایدوب ... تحریر اولنمشدر و بو قلعه‌نك
جمله صو قلعه‌سی اتش یقتوشمدر بوده اصلا چارسوی بازار و خانلر و حمام و عمارتلر یوقدر اما قلعه
... ده کی واروشده جمله اوچ عدد ... واردر
... اوچاق عاری ...
... عاری ... اولدقده عاری ...
... اما روم و عرب و عجمده مشهور ... حاجی بکتاش ... ارباب معارف
عارف باللهدر فقر فاقه صاحبی ... و محبوب زیبا کوچکلری وار ...
... جمله شاعر و ... اللهدر
صاحب الخیر ... رحمة الله علیهم اجمعین
الحاصل ... ‌تقاه زیاده کم و ضیقنده لسان قاصردر و بو ... جمله دور ... عدد ...
دردارلری جمله اولوسه امیننده وظیفهٔ معینه‌لری ... بو قلعه ...
... طشره ... ساعتده ... آتلیوب
اوصاف جای امان لیمانیه یعنی بنای ... قلعهٔ آولونیا
... بابا ...
... سلطان ... زیاده ...
... بو قلعه ... سلطان ... اوزره ...
قلعه ... آولونیا ... اولوسه ...
اما ... اولوسه ... اولوسه ...
... آغزنده بر قوم ... ایلچی ... سکل ...
بو قلعه مسلم ... سلطان ... قلعه ... سرحد ... قلعه ...
اورو سرحد ... قلعه ... اولوسه قلعه ... کل عثمان ... قلعه یاپیلر ...
بو اولوسه ... قالنلغی ... و ... عدد
... عدد ... عدد ...
... ناظر
... صغار
... و بو قلعه‌نك ... عدد کوشه

سنه بر لو سنه سنه بر لو سنه وارنجه نوبتلر محصور عدد ادمدر بو حصار آوده اولوب قلعه‌ده دار امام دار حضور بولنمایمدر والحمد کسلطان سلیمان خان جامعی وار و بو اوربا سنده سلیمان شاه قلعه سی وار بدعت اسرار مدعا مصیح قلعه بالادر لیمانی مصرسی سنه لرسا اولوب اوسی و بر سوم اوربولی قلعه مسه در باد روه اعلا سنده مطلا علمی وار در اولوب قلعه کیسه بو قلعه ایچ قلعه کی اولسه لر لیدرعاسه قلعه بالادر لیمان لوبا سلا بلده قلعه مرینه قلعه سعدرن آتی و بو سلیمان خانک توجه معمار سنانی بنا ایتمشدر بو قلعه ده درد اردرعمو لمسه ساکی اولمیوب جمله جامعی سار معمار لعارمانلر ایله طبقه طبقه مملودر و بو طشره قلعه ایچره جمله اوچیوز عدد ثره ملی باغ و باغچه لی وحولیسر صنعا اولرلدر اما صربوعنا ملرعنا سعدر اما جمله الجاجق طرز قدیم یترا و اریدیر بو نده دخی چار سوی بازاری بر شی یوقدر و چارو حمام و عمارت دخی یوقدر و جمله ایکی عدد قپولری بودر و ره لرلیماسکر صاغی همچنانه لوبا لوبلر مملودر وسسرو ریحانلر عدد بده باتکر موجودلردر برمنوکه سروه و ریا محصور عربه ناظردر و دار امام دار صسره هدهما اللعسر انم اللهی اوکوز الحی لدبرلسه دریا در و مصا قلعه در و مولرلر اولرینه حصرلری مره لی سمره لرا و لوسه هر لعمسر کرم الدروسه قلعه مولرینه لعمر را الله بعلمو قپوینه سبز ایدرلر وجمله صمروسر بشیوز عدد طوبکروار و دد ارمعوا و سالمو عدد اغالری و جمله لور دیوز عدد مولری وار بعصمو ماسه ولاسه محافظه سسه امر باد سا هسله مامور ادسلو سباه لحدارمو و بلمری سردار و اوچیوز الجماسه سله سرمعمعصاکی اولو قنا جیه کی جمله بوربسی باره معمور مرا لردر حصمو باحدار و بو بر ولسا ممسو حرام امسو مهار اغاسی و صود آغاسی و لها ریکتاسی و شهر کتخداسی وار در و بو قلعه نک شرق طرفنده ... ربار حواله سی وار در جمیع دام و باغی و ارا غمو بعسو صاف یالر و باغچه و ربو بالدر بو حواله بودوب اودیره زیارت بابا سلطان برجاج نفر مرماممصاحبی بکتاشیانلری علر در وصف مصلای ارباب حاجات بو قلعه الله وار وس مصسه کما بیننده رجمنرار بودره واسع و اتسع بمارها هصارلم ایلچی سلسادم الوبر وقلعه سعسره وار و بشه وارنجه کامل بکتاشیانلر حینزار یدر اوصناف شهر وار و بشر آو لوبنیشه بو سمرا صلا قلعه الحده دکلدر همان بر دور واسع حمرار بروده باغ و باغچه لی و کل کلستانلی لمعسد و برو رسوب مار ولحده لی باغ ارملر ایچره جمله سد عدد لره مسلو و بولی لجامی وموقالی کارلردیالی محله و ململ دمرمر و معمور اولردر و جمله عدد محلالردر اولا صحار جامع محله سی و مو محوراده محله سی و صاملر محله سی و حسن اغا محله سی و عامس محله سی و چارسو محله سی بو بلر مشهوردر و جمله عدد محرابدر جمله‌دا سلطان سلیمان جامعی مور سو ملی و کارگیر قبه لی و بر مسقف اولمسی مناره لی محمودسجامعدر بیله موسکه اوزره تاریخی بو بله تحریر اولنمشدر ابتدا یعقوب شیخ السالکین ۵ اندی مسجد مو سبل الله ادین ۵ ثانیا سلطان سلیمان الکرمان ۵ قلدی جمعه بارک الله آفرین ۵ دیدی حسبی بو معامله تاریخ ۵ نور حق بو جامع المتقین ۵ سنه ۹۴۹ ۵ سو جامع عاسرو جاسلمی جامع بو بدر آندن چارسو ایچنده جماعت کثیره مالک مو محمدزاده جامعی لره قلعه عمار لیر مناره لی جامع زیادر آندن صاملر باسنده حسن اغا جامعی بو سار کره قلعه و کارگیر مناره معمور و بلر مسیح بیت اللهدر آندن قلعه جامعی مو صنو فدر و جمله سی عدد محله زاویه لر معارلردر ایم محلالر سالاده مرقوم مدر و جمله اوچ عدد مدرسه سی جمله دانلر اولا معمور امدی مدرسه کی و مو محمود زاده مدرسه‌سی و حسن اغا درسخانه سی وار و جمله سی عدد ملت ... الحد حوالی وار و جمله اوچ عدد اسانه اهل بو حیدخانه اهل عمار جمله‌دا معمور امدی یلده کی خانه دار حلوسدر لم مکتب عدد دار هسوسر برهم حرمه سمسه صاحب عبدالله الری عمار آندن قلعه حوالی اولا داعده باغلر ایچره مورعوسا مادلله کسه باغ ارم مال راسانه او لدوغی بالاده موصوفدر و جمله بر عدد حمام محمود و ارقاشو سنده محکمه شرع رسول مبینی وارکم عجم محمد امدی حاکم الوصال المیسا امسو بر عجیب استانه شرع رسولدر و جمله

دورد

بو شهرده هوا اوبن تدبیر ایتدکده جارسوی بزستانی بازاری یوقدر اما جمله اهل حرف وجمیع متاع بو ادراکده موجوددر لکن
بازارلری بوقدر اما جمیع ولایتلرینه ماهر صنعتکارلر بولنورلر آوینه دکانلری اسکله نسندر وجمله
دنیزده عدد خانلری واردر وجمله سکز عدد چشمه لری وار اما جمله اسمعول امدی بالمنه کم قوبنده
الناس باشا حسیمه کسب تاریخیدر مولدم الیاس پاشانک تاریخی یوم البناء حو بله دیدم تاریخی وهو خیر
العبادة سنه اما عددی مسمه لری صالدر بوشهرها المسجد العالیه شهر مساجدلر مرور ایام ایله سومالری
اولمشلر اما جمله صوکماری صاحب الخیرات سهل سو ایله عمارنسه ابدی شهرلا اروا هلری شاد ودواده
اما معنالری اهل بادل ایدنلرلا اوالحم اعلی ونوب الخیر مصمم ساعت شهر بنده باعلر الخیره مصاروللری
ممالک عمر جهلری صوکترلر اما عددی اسماری معلوم موجوددر مخصوص باغ وباغچه لرنده کونا
کون میوه ابدالری جملانی دوتمشدر ماکولات مشروباتنده وحاتندن اولا لهجه اسی صاری وکالا قرده و
موللو روحماللرک بالطرمه بانک بومورده لری اولورم روده اولمازدر ورنجابه ماهر باده سی
دلمو برچون ربو واللحوری واورنی جمالری دوتمشدر و دوقات کوبلرنده قرمزی عجوه بنو باسی
کوکلری دراوسدر بومو حاصل اولور حکمالر جمیع ابتدا فرنکستانه کتورلر اولوسه لرینه سوی یاک
زفت بیناده بو مدنی حضوصا بکری بار داق الجره زفت خاینالری باردا الحسنه فنوت جالعوت آثار نینه
طشره دوکوب اول بار دافدن صواخند وحودنیده اصلا صفراو سوداو بلغم وصونک اعلی برامراضی فتلغه
مالمیوب پاک وجود اولور ومونا وقانه ملمسی السده کی قیالرده درمان سومعالی شکر معدنی وارکوز کوز
سونکر کی برطاشدر کم ایله درمانی طاشاری دبیو فرنکستانه کیدرکیم احذ ایاکره درملالحریره سی جاسدی لصف
سبد جارادزمان جاسکراولور وباغلر بولنوب اولدره الحو باسو بعد ووحم مصدر عجیبه نویه معادنلر حمو جود در
الحاصل جان معادنلری بو ولایت آولونیا در ولیت دریاده اولنمز بحر مالی دالالری وارد کم مثلی مکر آناطولی
دریاسنده اوله خلاصهٔ کلام بو آولونیه بجاغی عمورلی جمهتندن بر کزیده مصر منصبیدر ومونده حاصل
اولان مشک عنبر جام رایحه لوسی عسل مصمی باجو وزاتیمی اسده وصوبره لرده اولمازدر بر ملحان بانو بکرمی
قیما صونلو بروسه لوپر شربتی وبلور باده اولور بر اولمرد رشاپش لیمان عظیم آولونیه اولوسه ملسمی
الله یکلکچ ملحه سی باسی جمله لیمان عمده لر بر باره لیمان الرحیم سلطانی سلیمان خان ایام هلاکنده بو اولوسه
ملحه سی بیا امیمک بولمانده معاف لیملری مامسه ایمالا الحمون بالکون نصده دوسیاع جمالونوبه بوندو
اسمعو بلکی کورفوس جزیره سی قلعه سنه ضاری لیمانی اما اری بارجه ملسمیلر اولوبسه النته کله میوب بیم میل
الارمده لنگر انداختن اولور بطالر دیو شهر آولونیه ایله دریا ما بینده قرینهٔ ازودیرج بور الله عددکمره
جابه لو بولیدر بر معظم ومعمور کنیسه کی باردر جمله جمره لری بالحمله مرور جهلر دربوده اولان
صورمعد بر باسمه اما سدر جمله لیمره لری ایطالیه عرمده بری اولکو صور چیقارمه مدسه ماموردر
اما صورعنا کسربو وبیاض صوری اولوسیچه لور لیمو بوله طوزی فرنکستانه کتورلرلر وبو بولده ماهر بعسده
لسمر بارلر بدادم نعمه برورویده قلعهٔ یکلکچ بوزبران سوردر اما عاسمول لیماسوارلر لیمان اعرضه نوماره
وملحه سی جمله لدر احمد باسابع اعور ماعا مسهدم اعرسلطان عصرنده عاشله آولونیه قلعه سی بنا اولنمشدر
بوملم ملحه سی لیماسل جمله جانسار بصنی بالود الثالثریدر وبو لیمانک عرصه سنده اوردی مل الارقده
جزیرهٔ صازاندر هرسه جمله وبعدت کامر دوساسی بوجزیرده مسلمو سبا علمو به جاسه اسیر سه بوجزیره دن
توجه ایدر و آولونیه قلعه سنک لودوس طرفنده قره بروب دینکا ایله معروف برمیرلجاه بلمنوبرملواللر
ولودوس ایله صله جاسده عاصی دو عا ابر باوود سمای جمله بوز پاره عاصی قرمباشلی معقره شاپتالی قره

نعره‌لر ادر اما نعره دسک ادمو عقل اندرلر لکن سه هربار لرند دامر سه نوبلر امداده کیدرلر موبلرعا سحیح
مهانیر اربا وود ادملری در دیو اولو سه بلد دخی جمیع جلبی بهادر و غازی دلاور سرور هر روز بللردر
لم اوب ماره مرمه لرایله جمیع مرسلسات دامرلر مروی مسلردر ملعه‌لر اولعر مه لرایله مرو مسلر حتی سمدیکی
حالده ملعه نعرالر بلد یعنی ماسه عا قنطیه سنه فرقته لرایله روانه اولدیلر دیو اولو سه بلد هوا سی عا لطیفم
اما صوبی نظیف دکلدر زیرا موصوبی الحمرلر اما محبوب و محبوبه لری حدا حمحوب عا کثصملر در لکن تازه یکیتلری
عاشق مسما اولورلر وا سالاری جمله هوا لری لمو صه و داحی اسواب لموسالدری جملاو ماسی فشلی و اناملر
ساه قبلار رامو حلی ارمالری بیاض احرامللی غازی مجاهد فی سبیل الله لر اکثریا ماسلری داغلی و سسه عربا بلری عا علی
اوکو سسه برلسنه لری حال سرحه سرحد اوکو نمی نیره هی با رهسه و سر برهسه عند العلدری صنعت عاربلر و عارلم دایما
لسا بلربحه و ر در بانلری او صور سه صور سه و ملعسه دامجد باعلی دبوحره دار سلدات اندرلر الاعقب حانداسحالر
در لم جملعارسی جیللر در و رنک رنکری جمله مهر سا اوره او کو سدر سسو سر برهر بر الای سرورلر در حدا حمله سندن
راصولیله الرحالردر اندی جمله احماو دوستانلرایله وداعلشوب و برار وسیله بللرالوب اندن غرب سمره مده ٢ ساعت کیدوب
قریهٔ جزقسونیا حصار حاصل اوکو عمم معمور قریه در آنی عبور ایدوب نهرلری و یدید لوموری دریاسه مخلوط
اولدوغی محلده انلر نهرله جمله برلسنه سوار اولوب نهرلر سعر سو صرمه لحوب منزاکیه صحراسی قضاسنه داخل
اولوب اول صحرا ایچره معمور و آباد دانعرالرده زوق و صفالر ایدوب ٥ ساعت دخی جانب غربه قرارده کیدوب

در وصف حدود ولایت البصان یعنی اشکال قلعهٔ باشت اووا صان

لسا آرناوودجه دملدر باسمی بونحوم ما و ویدبلی برع برمرالی باسمر نعده سنه تاریخنده با آثار
ابو الفتح سلطان محمد خان ارناوود استمدید کو عراسه لدرلن بو ملعه بدست غازی محمود پاشا و غازی سعدولی
بالمولیفح امسدلر حالا البصان کتاعی حا لسه لسدرباده و ندیک کورفزیمدن سرو حا اسه لرمس برکورفز دخی
واردر اول لوحول لورفزک آغزنده البصان سهری الحمد حره باب اندرمهر و اعظ و نهر اوشقو نبی بو باسلاووا
قلعه‌کی دینبه دریا مثال اولوب دربایه دریا مثال مخلوط اولدوغی محلده ملعه بلد برد مولرب مرلو بر نهر عظیم
منهدیم ایتدی و یدبلد لوموری طره سه مصب اولدوغی محلده زمو مسال بر نده سطح مربع بر لوحول ملعه بحکدر دارما
دارحرم بحسو ر ادمدر دردارم و سمسو عدد نهرالری واردر دراج ملعه کما امسو حلصده اوکو جمله بالعالر
وساریحصولالری جمله میریدر زیرا سجاله عصمدر لم مرسوا اشبانیه و قلکوره و پولیه و کورفوس و ندیک شهر
لرینه بندر کابا دا اسکله سیدر درون ملعه ده برده ملرها می و قرق اللی قدر نفرات اوجکرلری واردر برماج لره ما لطه کفار
فرقتنه لری بو قلعه یقلتر ندن گروبا احراق ایتدیکه تکمنلر در حارسو یعار ارعو حان و حمامی یوقدر اما اجابجا باغلر بیواردر
و حلمی عا عرسو عرب بدس ارناوودلردر بالوصید ایدوب کفا فلترلر و مرید الله سع سرا اندرلر زیرا البصان
دراسحاله سمدحه بودر اما مسع و مو مسال دریا اقلما قالله ارمی عا النو بلر لمنا سه دله مرا ما او ماف نهلره لصمه یناق
تمک تماندر اند سماله ساعت ده سه مرا لسه صحراسی آباد انه الحمره قلعه مثال قلّه لر حقیقتلکلر به زوق و صفالر ایدرک

اوصاف دار امان تیرانه یعنی کهنه بنا قلعهٔ عظیم دراج

زمان سعد نمده سراج بدر منیر لنوشنمه دررو ملعهٔ معمور آمسلم بقول مورخان لاتین بو قلعه روم مویاسنا ساس
اوکو نعدره اسا اسه دستنه لروسا بعده برحمله الله مویدما مو و یدبلی السه لروسا اندن سنه ما لمعده ابو الفتح محمد خان
غازی استمدید برده و او للوب و ما ر و لسو ملعه لرب فتح اندکده بدست محمود پاشا بومرارح ملعه کس دخی بوربار و الله
بو بدعا ممعدله اللدفتح ایدوب بعده نصارا فریک بدرید برحل سه بو ملعه اسیلا ایدوب بعده حلوس بابر سعادته
سنه بارحمده سه بو قلعه فتح اوکو حالا سلطان حاکمده اوره البصان حا لسه و سواد القدر و یدبلد الله لحبه با به کسیله نشرف

قضادر وباجه‌سی عددقرا اولوب حالا حکومت حاصر حابونلردرکیم مقطوع القلم ومفروز القدم اولمشدر یوک آقچه التزام ایله باشقه امینی واردر ایکیوز آدمیله حکومت ایدر زیرا البصانك وعمره‌سی لیمانی اعظم اسکله‌سیدر زیرا وندیك کورفزی ایچنده در والبصانك شاهراه امن‌الامان یولیدرکیم دائما عربه‌لر اشلدیکندن جمله بازرکانلر کمیلری بونده یناشرلر وعظیم طوز معدنی واردرکیم باشقه مقاطعه‌در جمله روم ایلیه وجمیع فرنکستانه عربه‌لر وکمیلرله طوز بوندن کیدر زیرا آغ‌کوز طوزلسی واردرکیم اسکله باشنده داغلر کبی طوزلر یغیلیدر در صفت قلعهٔ دراج بر بعد طوز صحراسنك دریا کنارینده وندیك کورفزندن برکوچوك کورفزجك دخی یتمش سکسن میل البحر بندر آنك کنارنده شکل مربع برقلعهٔ عظیم ایمش مرور ایام ایله ایچنده دولتلو دولت (دوکتن درته) اسعال ایدوب حفظ حراسته یمکی اولمادیغندن کوزدن دوشوب ویران اولمشدر اما دائرا مادار جرمی بشیوز آدیمدر زمان مروریله ایچنده ادم آزاولوب کفره طلغیان ایدند انلر دخی ساکن اولمغه اقتدارلری اولمامغین سنه تاریخنده بایزید خان ولی عصرنده بوقلعه‌نك قبله جانبنده برکوشه‌سی بلوب شکل مربع برکوچوك قلعه‌جك بنا اتمشلرکیم جرمی سکز یوز آدیمدر وایکی قپوسی واردر بریسی شرقه ناظر البصان قپوسیدر بریسی جانب غربه مفتوح لب دریاده امین اسکله قپوسیدر ایچنده یوزاللی عدد الحاجیق بنالو کرمیتلو اولردر چارشوی بازاری وخان وحماملری یوقدر الحاق برجامع کرمیتلو وکارکیر منارهٔ‌لی بایزید ولی جامعیدر وباغ وباغچه‌لری اولمغدر یوقدر زیرا الحاق طوزلو سعوره یرلردر دزدارعی یوزاللی قدر نفرلری علوفه‌لرینه امنیدنالرلر ویوزاللی آقچه قضادرکه هیچه البصان قضاسنه الحاق ایدرلر سپاه کتخدایری ویکچری سرداری جمله البصانده در وجمله اون برعدد خورده طوبجغزلری وار

الحاصل عجب آماندر اما اولقدر شهر معمور دکلدر اندن تمالیغوب جانب شرقه سلطنت چیفتلر ده بردرلرده معمور وآبادان قرالری دریانك برکورفزکرمشدر انك کنارنجه یمین ویسارده اولا قرالری وقبله‌لو اباد انچفتلکلری سیر تماشا ایدرك اوصاف شهر بازار محمیه یعنی قصبهٔ متین قواسیه

سنه تاریخنده بناسیدر انلبصان حدودنده بوده‌جی دراج امینی حکمنده باشقه ووبوادالقص دراج قلعه‌سی لب دریاده برجزیره‌یی حاصل برده اولمغله دراج قاضیسی بونده ساکن اولور امینی دراجده ساکن اولور یوزاللی آقچه قضادر ناحیه‌سی یتمش اوچ پاره قرادر عمارستان شهری بریعنی واسع زمین معمولداردر برچلیج کورفز نهایتنده باغ وباغچه‌لی مفرح ودلکشا برشیرین قصبهٔ رعنادر جمله دورت یوز عدد تحتانی وفوقانی وجدید نقش روضه‌لی کارکیر بنالی حوض وسازلر وانلی سرایاکره مقابله مستورقلعه وشاهنشین ومقصوره‌لر ایله معمور ومزین ومکمل سرایلری واردر اعیان کبارعی کبار اشرافی چوقدر اولا حرمیصری زاده وپاشوزاده و جمله دورت عدد محراب

وجمله دورت عدد محلانلردر اولا محله‌سی د

اولا چارشو ایچنده جامع وجامعی مشهورلردر جمله اعی عدد محله مسجدلریدر اما کارکیر بنا مناره‌لری یوقدر جمله الحاق مناره جکلردر وجمله ایکی عدد مدرسه‌لردر اما آسوختنه وانلری طالب علم دکللردر وجمله اوچ عدد درسخانهٔ صبیاندر وجمله ایکی عدد آستانهٔ طریقت درویشاندر وجمله ایکیوز عدد معمور وآبادان ومزین چارشوی بازار دکانلری وارکیم هرشاهرا هده کوناکون تورت میوه‌سی اغاجلر ایله مزین اولوب سایه‌دار بر سوق سلطانیدر جمله اهل حرف موجود اولور جمیع متاع ذی قیمت بی قیمت بولنور زیرا ناسب اوواقلعسی حلفوی دراج قلعه‌سی حلقی بوشهرك چارشوی بازارینه محتاجلردر انکیچون بازاری معمور ومزیندر وجمله ایکی عدد خان تجارانی واردر بونلر دخی کارکیر بنا اولور کویا بزازستانکبی هرقماش مالامال لالیعدر اما چارشو جامعی یوقدر لکن سرای حماملری قرقدن زیاده در دیو نقل اتدیلر اما حریص موجود

راده اغالر چارسو حمامی انشا ایتمکه تعهد ایدوب چارسو ایچره رصد ایدوب سعادتلو ایلبصان اعیانی من
بعد الله بو شهر الیصان چارشو حمامی بنا ایلدیلر بو چارسو حمامی احیا حلری اولمادقچه چارسو حمامی
یا یمغه برکیمسنه سعی ایتمه مشلردر اما عمارتلری رعایا منتفع اولدقلری صاحب آدملری وارد رواحسن هوا سی عالم
لسماوتلو چاتی غایت غریب دوستلردر اندن سیر ومسیر ومعمور بولار ایله ایلبصان نهری کنارنده ۳ ساعت کیدیلوب

اوصاف سور استوار متین یعنی قلعهٔ معمور ایلبصان

سنه تاریخنده دیرام وجوانبه ... بولدقلری چاربا اورد غسماسی ایلبصان ایلبصان بولدقلری اما اولا
عصر بوسلطان عمرنده اول بولدقلری بوقلعه بنا ایدوب اسمنه ... قلعه کبی در بعده
غلط مشهور اولا اوکو ... غلط ... قلعه کبی اول وجه تسمیه کیم بویله درحالا تحریر سلطان خان اوزره ایلبصان
بکلکیدر خاصی ویوادالغی حکمنده اولوب ایلبصان قضاسی ناحیه سیدر قلعه سی بربابر النسخه برواسع یرده در
ایلبصان نهری کنارنده شکل مربع برکوچوک قلعه در جرمی کامل دایرا ما داربشیوز عدد خطوه در اما خندقی
یوقدر اما چار کوشه سنده چاریار عشقنه چار عدد صعب قله لری وار وقبله طرفنده بوقلعه سهل یقوشدر
جمله تهالری قبالر اوزره واقع اولمشدر الحاق برقبوسی شمال طرفنده طشره واروشه آچیلر دیوارینک قدی
اون ایکی ارشین بلادر دزدار ی ویتمش عدد نفراتلری وبش عدد شاهی طوبلری وار حالا ایچ ایلدرکم غایت
امن امانده در درون قلعه ده جمله اوتوز عدد اوقافدار اچیق کرمت اورتولی دارلری واردر وقبوسی اوزره
برکوچوک جامعی وار اما مناره سی یوقدر وقلعه نک صولنده دیواره متصل برچمنزار یرده نمازگاهی وار
در تعریف طشره واروش مزین قلعه نک شمال وشرقی وغربنده جمله ... یوز عدد کره متلی مکلفی
مکمل سرای مثال باغلی وباغچه لی وحوض وسلسبیل وانلری جمله تختانی وفوقانی کارکیر بنا اولردر جمله یدی عدد
محله لردر وجمله ... عدد کره متلی جامعلردر اوچی کارکیر ومصنع ومرصع مناره لیدر اما بر
مناره سی الحاقی مناره لی جامعدر اما جمله دن چارسو ایچره تنده سنه فیحه باعث ... اولا یکیچری اغاسی وزیر آصف
دلبر عبد الرحمن پاشا جامعی کرچه کوه متلیدر اما غایت الغایه جماعت کثیره مالک جامع منوردر قبله قپوسی
عتبهٔ علیاسی پایلی اوزره مذهب جلی خط ایله تحریر اولان تاریخی بودر ۞ حمد الله چونکه بو جامع جدید اولدی
تمام ۞ هر نظر ایدنلره اولدی مقام دلکشا ۞ بو شهرک اورتاسنده چونکه تمام اولدی بو جامع ۞ بارک الله اولدی
رعنا تاریخی هو الغنیا ۞ سنه ۱۰۷۷ ۞ آندن چارشو اورته یانسنده حریمی زاد جامعی قبوسی اوزره لاجورد ومذهبلی
تاریخیدر حضرت حقدن اولوبدر اشبو جامع بی کمان ۞ قصبهٔ بجالین ایچره اولدی بو عالی نشان ۞ هر کورن غیر
ثنا ایله دیدی تاریخنی ۞ حمد لله چونکه لطفا یلیوب اول مستعان ۞ سنه ۱۰۷۶ مشهور جامعلر بونلردر
وجمله یدی عدد محله لرده یدی عدد مساجدلر واردر وجمله اوچ عدد یرده مدرسه طالبان سوخته
کان واردر اما اهل عرض حال صاحبی مادت ادملردر زیرا بو دیارک سوخته وانلری جمله عشقیالر در انلرک ارتکاب
ایتدکلری قوم عوانلردر وجمله بش عدد مکتب صبیان جگرکوشه پسرانی وار در زیرا غایت زکی الطبع نجیب
رشید غلاملری وار در اکثریا منظوم کتابلری حفظ اوقورلر وجمله ایکی عدد تکیه کاه فقرای آل عبا درویشانی
وار وجمله یدی عدد آب حیات چشمه سارلری وار جمله سی یکیچری اغاسی عبد الرحمن پاشا خیراتیدر وغایت لذیذ آب حیات
خوشگوار صولاردر کیم بو شهر سماء چارپارلر ایله سعی ایدوب عمار ایتمشدر زیرا بو عبد الرحمن پاشانک اصلنده بو شهر مسقط
راسیدر اولادغنده عمار ایدوب دخی نیجه کونه خیرات حسناته شروع ایتمشدر مقدما سنه آثار رحمده سلطان
ابراهیم خان جلوسنده وسلطان محمد خان رابع احلاسنده قول کتخداسی بولنان چلبی مصطفی کتخدا بو شهرلی اولوب عبد الرحمن
پاشا چلبی کتخدانک قرنداشی زاده سی اولوب یکیچه نیجه در مصطفی کتخدا مرحوم بردکه شهید باتیجه جنا کبری عبد الرحمن
عبد الرحمن پاشانک دایسیدر کیم برو شوق
اوغورلری نامیله مشهور ایدی اول
پاشا

پاشا کبی مدبر و مقبل و متبصر غازی وزیره جفا ایدوب عمر طویل اولوره زیرا کوپرلی زاده فاضل احمد پاشا ایله بیله دل بیر
جهت اولوب انلر ایله تدبیر ایله قندیه ادچ بلده فتح اولدی یوخسه قرق بلده ده فتحی میسر اوله جق قلعه دکل ایدی و جمله
بر عدد لطیف حمام وار بودخی عبدالرحمن پاشا حمامیدر غایت آب هواسی و بناسی لطیف برکوچوک روشن بنالر
حمام روشنادر و جمله ایکی عدد خانلردر و جمله ایکیوز عدد قلعه اولی میدانی ده دکانلردر اکثریا
مطافلری یابوس پنجکی جوقدر وچارسوی حسن ایچره کوناکون درخت مشمشلر اشانیدر امتجار ندن ملعدا اندازولر طوت
درختلری غایت اوزوم اصالری ایله بوچارسوی حسن شاندار اولمشدر کم جمله درختلر ترتیب اوزره دیکلوب سوق سلطانی
برکیف اتمشدر و بوشهر کنار هواسی و بناسی غایت لطیف اولدوغندن محبوب و محبوبه سی غایت چوقدر و جمله اهالیسی غریب
دوستلردر کم اینده و رونده یه نعمتلری مبذولدر و غایت اهل سنت و الجماعت صلاح حال ایله مشهور ادملری واردر و باغ
باغچه لری جهان دوتوب زیتونی و نار و انجیری و جابجا لیمون و تورنج بولنور اکثریا باغلرینده خندقلرنده بیسوسنر
نکونلر و قواق درختلری دکیلیدر الحاصل غایت شیرین و مزین قصبه رعنا و قلعه زیبادر کم جمله انشا بوربطده موجود
در بعده بونده جمله احبا ایله وداعلشوب عبدالرحمن پاشا افندیمزه اعیان و لایتدن مکتوبلر الوب اندن نهر ساعت شرقه کیدر
درهکیا اوزر معبد الرحمن پاشانک برکوزل طاش جسر مصنعیدن عبور ایدوب اندن یارلر دبندن کیدک منزل قریهٔ چیچوک
عبدالرحمن پاشا افندیمزک ایا غوجه وطن اصلیسی اولا کوییدر کم خاندانیده قرنداشی محمود اغا ده ساکن او لوب نوقدر
صغار اتدلر بر دیه باشنده برم تفیع زمین جهان نما هوادار یرده بر معمور جفتلکلر بونده برشاهنشین مساکن اولوب کامل
بر هفته صحبت حاصل ایدوب نکیو شهرندن کروه کروه احبا کلوب حسین بیقر اجمعیتلری ایدردک بعده محمود اغا ایله وداعلشوب
اندن بنه جانب شرقه البصان نهری کنارنجه کیدرکن کمیلر اوزره بنا اولنمش اوندکرمانلرک سیر تماشالر ایتدکم بودخی بویله
بر بیاره مخصوص دکل برطرز مصنع دکرمنلردر کم کورمه عقل کیدر دغایت الغایه سرعت اوزره ایشلر اشیانلردر اندن بنه نهر
کنارنجه معمورالرباغ و باغچه لرکذر ایدوب قریهٔ لوکلاث آندن قریهٔ پاپی اروا آندن قریهٔ پشکم آندن قریهٔ قورش
آندن قریهٔ بزکا ششش بونلر جمله البصان ناحیه سی کوئلریدر کمی تیمار و کمی زعامت و کمی معادندر اما منور بوز کاششوکوی
البصان نهری اوزره اولان اغاج جسرک تعمیر ترمیمی ایچون مقاف میلم بر معمور کوییدر بومزکور کویلرک ۴ ساعتده عبور ایدوب
شهر البصان خارجنده خصم محمد پاشانک جفتلکنده سهیل ایلرنه اینوب شهرده روم ایلی ایالتنه منصرف اولان بچوق مسلم و بر پاشا
قایم مقامنه ما نیه محافظه سی یحیون امر پادشاهیلر ایله کلدیکمزی خبرن کوندروب قایم مقام ادم جمله اعیان کبار زعما
و ارباب تیمار و غیری عساکر ایله حقیرک استقبالنه چیقوب الای عظیم ایله شهرده بکلره مخصوص سرای عظیمده نزول
ایتدوب دیوان پادشاهی اولوب امر پادشاهیلر قرائت اولنوب مفهومی جمله اعیان کبارک معلوملری اولوب امر پادشاهی تیسمار
هلک دیوب بعدالدعا والثنا شهر ایچره نادیلر ندا ایدوب هر کس ما نیه محافظه سنه کتمکه اماده اولمانغه مباشرت
ایتدی حقیردن اون کون مهلت رجا ایتدکلرنده حقیر ایتدم ایله اولسون اما اوزبرنجی کون البته بو شهردن چقماق
کرکسز دیدکده جمله فرمان پادشاهکدر دیو هرکس اسلاحنه مشغول اولدی مکر حیدر وم مصطفی پاشانک
بو مسلمی اولان کمسنه حمالوزاده نامیله معروف بر مهر کلام و آلفته و اشفته چلبی ادم مکر البصان شهرندن ایمش
همان حقیری پاشالر سراینه نقل ایدوب کندونک سراینه قوندوروب خاندان عظیمده جمله جهلو املرملر حجره لر تعیین
ایدوب شب و روز اوچ نوبت طعام فراوان ممسک نعمت عظما لر بیورت شهر البصانک آلفته و اشفته لری ایله حسن القلم
ایدرک شهرک کبار اولیا اللهلرن زیارت ایدوب کونه تماشای عبرت نما لر سیر سیران ایتدکم برزبان هتامه سی تمام ایتدک

اوصاف شهر نزکه رای عروس هفت یعنی بلدهٔ عظیم قدیم قلعهٔ البصان

حقا که اناطولیده عروس بستان بزه کتشا عروس شهر عینتابدر اما روم ایلنده آرنا و دستانک کلچک شهری بو بلدهٔ البصاندر
بقول مورخین لاتین بو شهر قدیمک ابداعی یانیسی اسکندر کبرا عصرنده قوال قلعه صاحبی فیلقوس یونانی بناسیدر

نیجه بیلگ حکمای قدمای کهنادن قوقمش سلف بو شهری جای وطن ایدینوب عمارت ایتمشلر نتیجه مرام نیجه یوز کونه
ملوکدن ملوکه و ملکه دن ملکلکه دستلرینه بعده روم ایلی دیارلری طوائف ملوک شوکتلندن اولوب بو شهر
عظیم صوفی قرالی دستنده بو بنام قرال ضالک بانیه نام براوغلی و بتصانیه برولدی بلندی الّرنده بو شهر اشتراک سویلر
اوزره متصرفلر ایکن ایکی نفر قرنداش بلند عبیدلر حسن زندکانه ایده میوب بر برلریله جنک عظیم ایدوب آخرکار بتصانیه
نام شهزاده آزاده جنک جدالدن عاجز قالدقده خلاص اولوب بو شهری ابو الفتح سلطان محمد خان غازیه کلوب شها دت باز ماغن
قالدرغدای بیو توزوالحیه ارلیوب کلمهٔ توحید لتروب حضور پادشاهیده اق شمس الدین حضرتلرینک تعلیم بلعسد شرف
اسلام ایله مشرف اولوب بالذات ابو الفتح سلطان محمد شهر اسکوبدن ارناود اسکندریه کمفتینه عزیمت اتمشکن
عطف عنان بو ایلبصان اوزره جو بروب قرق بیک عسکر ایله قوجه محمود پاشا طلیعه عساکر کرار اولوب بتصانیه نام
مسلم اولان محمد بکک دلالتیله بر کیجه شهری بو قدر ایل بطلوب بتصانیه محمد نک قرنداشی بانیه نام قرالی حامه خانه
بصوب بدوب درعقب دوب قتل ایدوب العثمان اعانتیله اسلامه کلدوکنفدن پاشا شهرن محمود پاشا ایله مفاتیح ایدرلر
وا لجمله اولان روم و فرنک کافرلرن جمله قرارلرا ایکچون بو شهر ایلدکلری استخلاصیله بصلدیغندن و بتصانیه محمدنک
فتحنده بولندوغندن ایلبصان شهر عدلر یوخسه لسان رومده اسمی لسان فرنکده نامی
لسان ارناوودده در تواریخ لاتینده مفصل حکایتلری واردر اما بر اختصار اوزره تحریر ایتدک بعده
بو قلعه فتحی سوزده کسیله بصان محمد نک حضور محمد خانه اتفاق ایله واروب معذره ایدکده ابو الفتح غازی کلام معجز
نطقلرندن بیورلرکم آفرین ایلدی بصان محمدنک سکا با صدیغک باباک قتوا احسان ایتدم اینده نیم نامه کوسش
معدنندن سکه کسد روب دخی اطراف ولایتلرن قبضه تسخیره الیوب دقلرنده اق شمس الدین و امیر بخاری
و منلا کورانی حضرتلری اول مملکتلر فتح تسخیره حیدر سعود لتله کرملیچون بو نسته الفاتحه دیتلوب خفیفت الحال
جمیع ارناوود دیستان و هرسکستان سلطان محمد زمانم و سلطان بایزید ولی ناصح زمانلرنده فتح متوحی اولمشلردر بعده
بو ایلبصان سلطان خاقان تحریری اوزره روم ایلی ایالتنده پاشا شهنه سنجاق بکی تقیدی صرف پادشاهیدن بکلیکنک خاص همایونی
۲۰۱۹۶۳ اقچه در و زعامتی ۱۸ در و جمله ارباب تیماری ۱۳۸ عدد در الای بکیسی و جری باشیسی واردر حین سفرده
قانون اوزره جمله ارباب تیمارلری دوبرتیلیا اکثیسی زرسلاح کزیده عسکر اولورلر روم ایلی وزیری قتنی سفره کیدرسه بونک
دخی میرلواسی مأمور اولدوغی سفره کیدرلر و اوچیوز اقچه پایه سیله تحته باشی منصبیدر و ناحیه جمله عدد
معمور قرالردر بدیسنه قاضیه بر وجه عدالت اون کیسه حاصل اولور بکینه اوقوز کیسه حاصل اولور و شیخ الاسلامی
و نقیب الاشرافی و اعیان اشرافی و شهر نائبی و محتسب نائبی و محتسب اغاسی و باجدار اغاسی و خراج اغاسی و سپاه
کتخدا یری و یکیچری سردار و قلعه دزداری و جمله عدد قلعه نفرلری و سر عدد قلعه اغالری و معمار اغاسی
و شهر کتخداسی و سائر متعینلری کفره کروار و رعایالر اوزره پیوز تویوز کفره لری واردر کم جمله بکرمی عدد حاکملردر وغیره
معمور و مضبوط حکومتلردر کم جمله رعایا و برایالری مطیع منقادلردر و سنجاغی حدودی ایچره جمله عدد
قضالردر اولا جنوب جانبنده باشمت اوره قضاسی مزاکیه قضاسی جانب غربیده دراج قضاسی و
مشهور قضالر بونلردر
و جمله سنجاغی حکمنده بش یوز یکرمی التی عدد قرالردر اما چوغی معاف و مسلّم و چوغی میری کویلردر بجار مداخله ایده
منزل درکر داکرد اشکالات قلاعات ایلبصان قلعه سی بر یوز زمین عضوادارده شمالی ربع ساعت و قبله جانبی ربع ساعت بعید
بایرلر و عدا اغلی و جمله باغلی بروا سیع اوزلغنده نهر اوشقوم نهری کنارنده مشکل مربع بر شدادی بر کهنه بنا قلعه درکم
قدیمی اون بش کرشنمه و دندان بدنلری غایت مصنع و اطرافنده التمش عدد ابراجلری واردر و جانب اربعه سنده خندقلری ایکی
ادم قدی عمیقدر اما التمش ارشن عریضدر و خندقی ایچی صاقی باغ و باغچه لردر قلعه نک دایرا ماداری جرمی ایکی بیک دورت
یوز ادیم

٢٦٥

بو شهرآبادمدر و جملهسی اوچ عدد دمیر قپولری واردر بری شهره و بری عربه و بری حارس و صره مده مشهورلر
اولمغه قلعه ناصر اسلام بابی عظیمدر و بو قپولری آهن قپولر اولوب ایکی عدد حواله ایلمشلردر بو قلعه دمیرلردر آهن قپولی حصار دیواری
لسان انگیجو قپولری ایکیشر قاتدر اما بو قلعه ناصر حصار بو قپو سند تهرینا اوده ابو الفتح سلطان محمد خان آل عثمان فتحه
فتحنه اعدادلری بر ساعت صوم مراد اوده ملوح خط ایله تحریر اولنمشدر و تاریخ السعادات ارلمسدر سنه ٨٥٩ ٥ و بو قپو اوزره
اوچ عدد چارگوشه ساعت مرحوم اولدره اوده قورشوم قبه لری اوزرنده علامتلری رچداللهم اصحاب جمله اسمه
ودرونده کانلر تماشا ایدرلر و بو قپو اوده برموجب حصار جامع وار کیره مثلی بر کار قدیم جامع کریمدر بو جامعك تقریب
بر ساعت ملکه کوه وارد مصنع و درسب ساعتی وارکم اصلا دمعه وردیحه متی ایدر جمله حوائجلری منزلنات
بلالیلر که ناظرلردر و بو قلعه ایچره جملهسی نعره دیوار المسی عدد لره ملوی باغسوز باغچه سز سعلو واسعی طبانی فوقانی
کار قدیم تهمه ساحانه لر عمار ردار حانه سی بوعجه دراما اعتدال الهوا اله مع ایلرسه لسولر صاو لردحو حعودر
لمکان ملاحت مسلم کفر مرد خدمت ایدرلر درو صنع طلشره و اروش عمارتخانه لری اعیان اغوات اولا بو ایلمکانی مکه سیك
حاسار عکسنده نارلر دینکه بر ساعت مصافه برلره دل جمله معمورو آبادان و مرتفع و باغچه سانس عمارتنلی
حمام سرایلر بله آراسته و گویا لور عصرحور بو ساهنسملر ایله سرایسه اوملش سرایات العالیه مصنع و همواره
اوبر توللی خانداران سوسه حمالردرکم جمله کار کیر بنا ایلمسر او بر قات شاهانه شاهنشینلی معمور بو سی عالردر
تم الحدره هر خانه عمارده بر عمود حاربه لر حره باب اددره حوض سارروانك سلسبیل صوارهلری بر باب اعدرحدنعه
روضه رضوانلی کاشانهٔ زیبالریدر اما اصلا حامعلر بنا ره بلا هلردر عمره عور بر سوم اوپر بلی سالم بودر
هار جمله احمرلون تره ملا ایله معمور سوس معمورلردر اولا اعیان کبار کبارلرندن مسعود سرای عضملردر بر حصم
محمد پاشا او ربر سرای و پاشاره عصوصو سرایی و مصطفی اغا سرایی و مصطفی اغا سرایی و حمالی زاده سرایی و مره عمار اغا
سرایی و حصم محمد اغا سرایی و حصم حس اغا پاشایك و یحا محمد زاده خاندانی و پاشو زاده بیتی و سیاه اغانك
اسنانه سی نیجه نور سرای رجالر واردر نیجه مرام سر نجدا اسم دیمر بله جمله سل نور اللمعدد سرایمی خاندانلر و
حسنی عالی وار در ماعدا اره رسه باغچه لی و سط الحال نمسه لر سوس راحتلی مجد اما حصم خاندانلر پسندیده لر
مبلغ و مثال سادهدر حصوصا سولر اوده بو عمر بو اسلحلی خط ایله تحریر اولنمشدر بیت صباحك مقرون بعز و
دولة ٥ و بابك مفتوح لاهل الحوائج ٥ دو بیجه بر دره لر سعسه علمالری اوده تحریر اولنمشدر و نیجه سرایلر
دیوار عانه لرده بو ابیات تحریر اولنمشدر شرف البیت باهله ٥ و شرفا اهله بسخائه ٥ بیجه سل سولرا مالی ایالتلر
ترقیم اولنمشدر بو ابیاتلر مصبوب اوده بو سهرده سولر قمامالی خانداران صاحبی پاسلی یاسه مسافر سر حدا ملر بله طعام
نه ثمه عاسه عسدر اللحوب السه هر خاندانده اسده و ردوده مسافرس اصلد طلدر و هر در باغچه ده بودر مسافر سرایله
و حدا ملر بله برای بمعو حالمسه اسمعا ال نمرلر بل باسده بولور حالنه مناسب السه عدده برلره
و یرلر بو حسها الیری فرق بلادر بوربرد باره ده لور مدم الاسلام صره بلوسنده بلیمری اعاسی حصر اعاده لور دم برده
بو کسماده کورنم در عدد اسماء مزیناتی محلات بو وار روس ایر جمله اوبسار عدد محله مسلمیندر و جمله
اوبعدد محله روم وار باوو دوکلاموس لوره سی محلالری واردر اما اصلا یهودی و فرنك وار بو وصرف
بلعار و و بیتیق بوره لری بودر للو محار سصر بعله بلوبو حالرده بلمسا ابعه سه لیدار بوحسنه سوص الاسلام
دیو عالرلرایسه اوراب اما ور عماد وربو سعد اندر لر بامدیمد بوبله بوره کلمشلردر اولا محله سی و
مشهوربی بونلردر

در بیان عدد جوامع معابد سلاطین آل عثمان صاحب الخیرات جمله حرف السعد عدد محرابدر جمله امدم ابو الفتح سلطان
محمد خان غازی جامعیدر تم قلعه سو عسا اندره و مو باسی و جامع اولکه جماعت کثیره لی جامع قدیمدر و قلعه اوزرینده

خارج سوردن تا ساحل جامع شريفه اما ساير عظيم عنبر و چيلر گوتنمه ديوار زنبيل طاشره روي صو دوارنده برنقطه قونمشدر
قدر حالي بر يوقدر جمله ابيات اشعار قصايد حديث و مفردات تحرير اولنمشلر روم و عرب و عجم سياحتلرنده بر
تصحيحسز خطلر يازمشلردر نور علا لسان اولور ريزاليه سدسور اهل بو جامع ديبم منبر لطافتده ر المحمود هر كس
تحرير اولنمه ملهم الله عرض و معرض ساري نخه لره يوريسا ايلر رحيم الله مسلر برابر اعماسه مصيقل و مجلا و مسبحه دولت
حسن مصور هر واردينم مراد و مصيانتلرنده و برحضرت لر اوله جهونده ديراينه امداد اسعد همم اوليا غايله
نوبت دهر حصر لسانحانه برابات تحريراللدوب نسبه سياح عالم اولنان سنه ١٠٨١ ده نوبت ساعت ادلدي هر بشره على
الاتفاق حسنچه مورحس اسمانور بعانه براسم تونمش بو شهر البعنانه دار شعرا ديو تسميه اتمشلردر بو
ملحمه الحمد بوسان بلتا جامع جماعتسز حوض معصد ما ء روحاندر اما الحمد لله برلن و پر بلك مطور ملحكمه لساني
علماء اسلام بلتصاب ملودر حسو ماتنه بعا مصلحت سنه سنسز علماء اسلامه نوبت سلطان بلصما ادراجمعه لرينه ايلدي
الله كميلله ماتنيه كنديلر آندن اوزون چارسو اچنده حسن پاشازاده جامعي قپوسي اوزره تاريخيدر تاريخ تاموس
حسن پاشازاده حدا لحمدت ه بو بيت الله چوز ملتنده جنت ه لحمد الله مام اسعد بو حسرت ه قبول ايده لحقوق آوحد ه
به تعالدر بو كتم تاروز محشره ديه لر روز شب بو جينه رحمت ه منصطيرو لاكي بيعيتا تاريخ ه زهي اولدي
عباد تكاه امت ه سنه ١٠٧٢ ه آندن حلبل بار اردن لحاجي راده اغا جامعي محب موروث منارلي جامع جديد
ريادر آندن ملوسان جامعي محرر مصبع جامع را نوار در آندن محلمه مرده سنان بك جامعي جماعت كثيره
مسطور معمور بلدنلر خوا مطابونلردر در وصف معبدگاه مساجد محلات جمله بلر بر عدد محله رلوينه اوج بقعه
لر اوج كتابه اينه لردر اولا مسجدي
سوبلر مسعوردر
در علم دار التفسير عالمان عاملان جمله عدد مدرسه حالياندر جملدا
در عدد دار الحديث محدثان پيغمبرات جمله
در دفتر دار القراء حفاظان مجودان جمله
در مكتب صبيان ابجد خوان طفلان جمله
در تكيهٔ ارباب طريق آل عبا درويشان جمله اون بر عدد خانقاه فقيراندر جملدا ملحمه الحمد سنان پاشا
تكيهٔ ملوه تنيمه رسمرده بو مدرمدر اسواو عمامه چوقدر و آنده هجار جامع تكيه مدر ماسه صاحب
چلهٔ مردان صاحبي عارف بالله برلن مرحدا بلدر واردر آندن حاجي حسن تكيه سي رحانماه معرادرلم بعه
رياضت كش ملددر معروف لويسه سبي مرد لر مواردر و درلبله حلرجوب الله توحيد اريه مسغوللردر آندن
معروف بنام تكيه لر يوقدر
در ماكل دار الضيافات عمارات جمله اوچ عدد ماحل خانه مسافر يدرلم صبح و شام تاعيد لداته و بيرجوانه
لدراو برسا و معانه بعمليدر مسولدر اولا حطار عمارت و سنان پاشا عمارتي و بلنه عمار سعادر بوبلر مسعور عمارتلر
در قيامت خان خواجه كان تجارات جمله اوبر عدد خانلردر اولا خانيف
در شرح چارسوي بنا زستان جمله معمور بو ر عدد سوق سلطاني دكانلر ردير لر حمو بر ساهراه اوزره دكانلر اما
هر هر بو غامده اولا دكانلري ترتيب اوزره بنا اولنمش معمور و مرتب و باذو بالدره و اوزرلرين اورتولو سانه دار چارسو
بازار جستدر جملدا مرام خانه سمه و عزار خانه كمسه بيلر لران چارسوي سعريدر و بدي عدد قهوه خانه لر موارلم بوباهر
ريعدرلويه ممنس نجار رحا نه جمسدرلم حمعي ارباب معارف اهل دل سحر الرانه موجود لردر ار بو مهاوبلده هر نوع ماو معارف
اوزره محبر لسد نصيل كلام اولور اما بوسعادتنا اماداسه لوبره مارلقرينالي بلا رساله بوبدر اما حمي دساه اولاسه اساس قيمت

لعل یاقوت والماس و زمرد و دیبا و سندس و زرباف و کامخای دارای و تیجه نیك گونه اقمشه فاخره‌لر موجودلردر
دکاکین کسب اهل اشغالك جمیعی اهل صنایع و ارباب حرف موجوددر اما غزازلری غازی یاوودقالتاقجیلری و اوقجیلری و یایجیلری
غایتده قدر و غایتده مصدح آلات صلاحلر ایشلرلر

در مشاخ علمای ابدان حاذق حکمای جمله قرق قدر عدد طبیب نباض واردر اما جمله‌دن افلاطون علم طبده یکانه
عصرلر و حکیم محب چلبی گونا مسیح انفاسدر و

در کحالان صاحب نظر کحال استادان جمله اوچ عدد کحاللردر اما

در مدح جراح فصادان عاملات گرچه علم جراحتده چوق کیمسه‌لر واردر اما جمله‌دن استاد مقلد

در وصف روز بازار جمعیت آدمیان بو شهر العتیقان ایلیجه هر بازار گونلری بر گرمیت جمعیت کبرا بازار اولور کیم بو شهرده
جانب اربعه‌سنده که عمارلردن و قصبات و قلاع و شهرلردن نیچه بیك عدد صغار و کبار و عورت و اوغلانلر گلوب بو شهر
ایلیجه ادم دریاسیله مالامال اولوب اوموز اوموزه سوکیشوب جمیع محبوب و محبوبه‌لر عرض جمال ایدوب بو دریغ
بیع و بیکلوب بیهوده سیر تماشالر اولنوب کیندلی متاع غلات بیع و شرا ایدرلر اما حشره گونلردن اولقدر بدر منیر طلعت
ازناوود قزلری گلورکم گویا هر بری بر بانوی بر مه پیکر و ملك منظر دختر پاکیزه اخترلر کلر خلاصه کلام هر بازار گونلری
بو ایلیجه شهری بنی ادم ایله پر اولوب جمیع کالای متاع ایله شهر بزه بوب جمله روم دیارینده جمیع ارناوودکستا
نك گلجلی چارسوی گلور و جمیع چارسوی بازار سوقاقلری سرا پا قالدرم دوشنمش اولوب ایکی طرفنده گویا
تالاردر بند کبارلردن بریز گونه لنزیر آب حیات صولر جریان ایدوب جمیع شاهراه‌لری صولر باد ایدر خصوصا
جوقه‌جیلر چارشوسنده و اوقجیلر و یایجیلر و پاچاجیلر و قلجیلر چارسولری ایلیجه یوللر اوزره چیره چیره دیکلمش توت
اغاجلری و سرامد چنار منتهالر و بید سرنگونلر و نیچه بیك گونه اوزوم اغاجلری ترتیب اوزره یوللرده دیکلمش
شجر المجر درخت سایه‌دارلر ایله مزین اولوب جمله بازار خلقی اول درختلر ظل حمایه‌لرنده لحوطر و سیمتاع نادره
لرین فروخت ایدرلر و عنبری چارسولرده دهر گونا گون درختلر دکلمشدرکم جمله دکانلرها ایلدریه مذکور شجرلر
سایه‌بانلر اولوب اصلا چارسوی حسنه گونشك تأثیر اتمز گویا بو شهر چارسنالر قورص و کلایشدی هما قشله شهری کبی باغ ارمدر

در ستایش حمامات راحت جان جمله اوچ عدد حمام دلستانلری وار اولا بری قلعه ایچنده شرق طرفنده کی قلعه
قپوسنك ایچ یوزنده سنان پاشا حمامی کار قدیمدر و آب و هواسی و بناسی غایت لطیفدر صوی خندق اوزره جسر ایله
طشره‌دن گلور اندن طشره واروشده چارسو حمامی واسع و خوش بنا و پاك و پاکیزه محبوب حمام‌لری و شیاطلری وار
انوت

در بیان عدد حمامات مخصوص کبار اعیان بقول شهر کیخداسی بو شهر ایلیجه یوز التمش عدد سرای حماملری واردر دیو فرح کیمسه‌لر ایلر

در فصل انهار زلال آب حیوان بو شهر ایلیجه جریان ایدن نهر عظیم اوشقه میوتا گورجمولانند داغلردن گلوب نیچه بیك
عدد باغلری و مشك بوستانلری بری ایدوب نیچه بیك آسیابلر چویروب بالاده تحریر اولندیغی اوزره بو نهر قانی گوله منصب
ایلیجه قربنده مخلوط اولور اما شهرك اطرافنده اولان داغلردن نیچه یوز عدد عیون جاریه‌لر جریان ایدوب
شهرك اطرافنده اولان نیچه بیك عدد جنات غبطه المزری بریان اتدکلرندن ما عدا هر خاندانلرده بررر ایکشر عدد آب روانلر
جریان اتدکلرندن ما عدا درون عدد چشمه‌ساران آب حیات بو شهر ایلیجه جمله یوز یتمش عدد چشمه جاریه‌لری
جمله‌دن اعتق کنارنده اسلامبولده سلطان احمد خانك اتمیدانده کی چشمه معمار پاشا بو شهر ایلیجه ترك عدد
چشمه آب حیوانلری واردر جمله چشمه‌ساران کمرلری اوزره کاشی چینیده تحریر اولنان تاریخ بودر حضرت معمار
باشی اولدی بر بروی پاك ه ده دشوب ... حسنو حقیره عشقنه کلدی محمد مصطفی بك ماه پاکه سند
دیگر تاریخ بر چشمه سنك تاریخ ناب پاك واقع اولمشدر و جا الحمد زاده چشمه کرد هما الزخشمه کی وقوا عقلا عشیقلارنه

در قید خانغره بای بحردات جمله طقوز عدد بکارخانه اوداری وارکم ایچنده اهل صنایع غریب البدایع کمسنه‌لر کار ایتمکده‌لر

در رنگ روی پیر جوانان هواسی لطافتدن پیر یا توانکر رنده اولقده یوز یاشنده ایکن یوزلرکم حمرت اوزره اولقتارة لرعجبا ایله جقدر

در مدح صفت محبوب محبوبان محبوب ومحبوبه‌لر ایله درکم هر بری حسن جمالده ولطف اعتدالده اولقدر حالکرنیده هردانه بر حالها شعر واردر

در اسامیء اشراف کبار اعیانات جمله اولیا نعمتدر جمالی زاده وخصم محمد پاشازاده وقپاقجی زاده وچاوش زاده ودزدار اغا دوتلر مشهور اعیاندر

در مناقب صلحای مشایخان

در شعر گزیدهٔ مصنفین شاعران

در نامهای اخوان خوش صحبت یاران

در صاحب حال اهل طریق مجازیان

در قبای اشکال رجال مردمیدان جمله خلقی چوقه فراجه وبدیله ایکید صارق صارارلر تازه لر قرمزی عرقیه وباغرلیه کی وقونیالی چاقشر وقبادی بابوج کیرلر

در لسان اصطلاحات دستحندان جمله ارناوودجه کلمات ایدر اکثریا فصیح رلی بلور سیلما رسمی فارسی حالدر تجارلری رومجه وفرنکجه ذمی تلرلر

در نامهای دلبران عبتانای شیمعان اکثریا اسملر جمالی زاده وقاسم زاده در اما اغوانلری خلوو متو یاشو آفو وحمزو وقوچو نامیلردر

در اسامیء خدامان خلقه بکوشام اکثریا کوله لرینک اسملر

در لباس کوناکون بتان نسوان اکثریا چاتونلرینک لباسلر چوقه فراجه لردر وبعضیلری شیلی طاقیه لر اوزره بیاض چینی لبند اورتوب کزرلر

در اسامیء خواتین قوم زنان اکثریا خواتینلرینک اسملر سلیمه وسالمه

در بنام جواریه کان اهل عصیان اکثریا قرآواش خلایقلرینک اسملر جانیمی وحانیمی

در بنای عبرت نمای عمارستان آبادان اولا ابنیهٔ قلعه کوبای مسعود جامعی وزیر زمنده صوبولکر وسرامد منارة وجامع متینی بنالردر

در مدح هوای خوش جاودان آب هواسی وبناسی ممدوح عالم اولوب صیف شتاسی یانمیا اعتدال اوزره اولقده خلقی تن درستلردر

در عدد چاه آب خوشکوار خاندان جمله شهر ایچره معمول شهر کحد اسمایلکم بیله التمش عدد آیچنا صوقیولر واردر کم قوله زلر

در حساب اقالیم ارض بلد شهرستانه علم [illegible] بو شهر اقلیم رابعه بلغنار شیکلدر در صول انهار

در قول منجمان طالع عمارستان بو شهرک طالعی عمارتی موقعیکمان قدما برج میزان بیتش زهره وهوا ینده بولنمغله خلقی مسروردر

بیم مدح کنیسهٔ راهبان تبستان بو شهر ایچره جمله عدد کنیسه لر واردر اولا .

در فصل حبوبات سبزوات محصولات هر کونه محصولاتلر اولور اما دانه دار بوغدای وارپه‌سی والاچه‌سی مرحوکی بحساب اولور

در نعمت عظمای انواع ماکولات اولا بیاض چوره کی وپهار یموشکرلر فراچالیه چوره کی وخودلی شهدی وقره کونه طعام ممدوحدر

در صنع خدا کزیده فواکه مثمرات اولا برومیه کلا امرودی والماسی وانداری کرازی وانواسی وقزلجیق وکستانه‌سی مشهوردر

در کوناکون جان سرور مشروبات اولا لعل کون باده‌سی [illegible]

در جسور مهرتاسی وحمیم حیوانات اولا شهر ایچره [illegible]

در تعداد باغ وبساتین حدایقات [illegible]

در مصلای عبادتکاه ارباب حاجات [illegible]

در ستایش مسیره‌کاه کبار اغوات [illegible]

[illegible]

اولا [illegible]

[illegible]

[illegible]

[illegible]

[illegible]

گلستان خیابانستان ایچره بر چمنزار واسع فزاده بر بزرك شنلك نامیله مشهور آفاق بر نظرگاه عشاقدر اما ارناوودقومی لهجه‌سیله بو مسیره گاهه بوز اشك درلر غلط مشهور اولا اوکوبویله قالمشلر اما اصلی بر زنك شنلکدر غلطدر مثلا بو چمنزار مسیره گاهك تا اورتاسنده بر اولو قیاوار در آنکیچون بر زنك شنلك دیو شهره شهر اولمش بر تماشاگاهدر کیم بوم و عرب و عجمده مثلی یوق بر نظرگاه خدادر کیم اوج آسمانه سر چکمش نیجه بیدعدد بر قاعده و ترتیب دیکلمش درخت منتهالر ایله چنار و قواق و مشه و پلید و سرو و عرعر بیدمشك نکونلر ایله مزین اولمش جا آرامکه کل گلستان و باغ و بوستان حدیقه عالی بر مسیره گاهدر کیم گویا اول مقصوره لر و نشیمن صفه لر و نیجه مصنعتلی حوض و شاذروان فواره لر طوتا آتیق جرمیان ایتده و نیجه مطبخ کیلار و [illegible] و متعدد [illegible] و حجره لر ایله آراسته و کونا کون عمارتلر و دکه لر ایله پیراسته اولمش مرامدر فواره لر و چنارلرك حصیرلرسه ایرر آب حیاتدن نشان ویرر آب شاذروانلر در و نیجه بیدعدد نیجه آقار عینلر جمعا کلدیم و لعل کون کراندوجه املی لر روسار صقلی دلبرانلر ایچون عشاق مشتاقان هزاران بالموافقه ایدوب هزاران هزاره سعمك آتدن فراغت ایدروب هر عشاق عندلیب اسا بو اشجار وجاننده لکلر ایلیه هوش الحان و اصوات حزین ایتکلرنده بلبلان چمنستان دم بسته و حیران اولورلر هر طرفنده کوشه بکوشه جمیع عشاقان معشوقلر ایله جلوه لر ایدوب برهای هوی طرب و عیش و عشرتلر اولورکم گویا روزلری روز نوروز خوارزمشاهی اولوب شبلری [illegible] حسین بیقرا مجلسلری اولور و هر طرفنده کونا کون خواننده و سازنده و مطربان و مداحانلرك سراغاره هنکامه لرندن جمیع هزاران خاموش باش اولوب دم چکمزلر و بو مسیره گاه میداننده اول بر زنك سنك یعنی اولو قیا التندن بر آب حیات مثالی نبعان ایدوب بر آب ایتمه چیقار کم گویا [illegible] کبی [illegible] شعشعه و در جمیع زمانده ایله حیات [illegible] زلالی [illegible] ایتده در ماه تموز روز نوروزنده دکمه عشاق بو عین زلالدن ایچمکه اوچ مصعه [illegible] جرأت ایده من مکر بر عاشق معشوقه لر سوصوده [illegible] ایله دیو قرمان ایده اول زمان صویه کیرمك مقرردر یعنی تا بو مرتبه برودت اوزره [illegible] اولمش [illegible] زلال [illegible] شهره ظهور در و بو مسیره گاهه شهردن و اطراف اکناف قرا و قصبالرندن نیجه بیك اعیان کبار خیمه و خرکاهلر ایله کلوب نیجه بیك عدد کلبه اخوانلر بنا اولنوب یلده برکره بر جمعیت کبرا بر آدم دریاسی بازار برپا اولور کیم بیوك [illegible] صغیر دللال [illegible] گویا [illegible] کبی بازار عظیم قوربو اولور بیع و شرا اولورکم [illegible] مصر [illegible] کیم مال [illegible] اوکونه [illegible] مال اتلاف اولوب اهالی ایلبصان بونده ذوق و صفالر ایدوب [illegible] کام [illegible] قدر روزلری روز عید اضحی اولوب صحبت خاص الخاص اولور آندن مسیره گاه

نیجه تفرجگاهلر وار اما بونلر مشهوردر

در تتمه شهر انکیز گلستان شهر ایلبصان اوّلا بو شهرك جانب اربعه‌سنده کم یوللر ایله گلرکن بو ایلبصان شهرینك اصلا عمارتلری تا شهر ایچنه کیرمینجه بر علامتی کورنمز همان افلاکه سر چکمش درخت منتهالر ایچره طباغ و باغچه لر ایچره پنهان اولمش باغ ارم مثال بر شهر عظیمدر الحاصل بو شهر معموره قدیم مجمع علما و منبع فضلا و مسکن شعرا و اقلیم عجیبه و غریبه در علما و ظرفاری علوم کبیریه و فنون عربیه مالکلردر.

در بیان زیارتگاه مراقد پر انوار کبار اولیاء اللّٰه شهر البیما اولا قلعه خندقی مقابله سنده چلبی افندی مرحوم قبر شریف سنده زائرنده کی جلی خط مذهب ایله تحریر اولنان تاریخ مصنّفدر دور عالمدن اگر سکسکا اکر آه ۞ هیچ شکیمیکی تغییر اولنه حکم اللّٰه ۞ بیحال حال سفر اتمده احبا تاریخی ۞ کوچدی آه کوی فنادن چلبی طابد شراه ۞ سنه ۱۰۲۷ ۞ تاریخ تربهٔ وقتیه زاده دریغ ایلدی تاراج ملک معرفتی ۞ همیشه بویله ستخیز اولور فلک دانا ۞ افندیلر بو دعا ایله دیلم تاریخ ۞ وقتیه زاده یه حق رحمت ایلسون ابدا ۞ سنه ۱۰۷۴ ۞ تاریخ مشهد یحیی بک زاده یحیی بک زاده عبودیت ایله صالح ایدی ۞ روحنه رحمتکی ایله عطایا مسعود ۞ بو دعا ایله الهادی یدی دوموی تاریخ ۞ جنت عدن اوله لطفکله مقام محمود ۞ سنه ۱۰۷۳ ۞ ایت تاریخ طاعون دیدی وقتی بی صفا تاریخ ۞ قلدی ویران شهری طاعون آه ۞ سنه بو تاریخ سنان پاشا جامعی دیوارنده مرقومدر تاریخ مرقد حسن شاه درشعر مستزاد کرادم شمایله ایره سکت قبر شاکلنه ۞ هیچ اوتمه امانی ۞ کم ارعو سماواته کلن انس و ملکدن ۞ هیچ اولمدی فانی کوش ایلیجک دیدی هلالی بو بیتمی ۞ هم اوله بو تاریخ ۞ جام اجلی ایچدی حسن دست فلکدن ۞ صوی بو جهانی ۞ سنه ۱۰۷۲ ۞ دخی بیک بویله مصنع تاریخلر جمیع خان و جامع و مساجد و مدرسه لرده منظورمز اولمشدر اما تحریرنده عجزمز اولوب سیاحتمزه مانع اولور و تطویل کلام اولماسن ایچون بو قدر ایله اکتفا اتدک و مرقد پر انوار امیر سلطان قلعه الجند سنان پاشا تکیه سنده مدفونلردر کم زیارتگاه ارباب دلاندر آندن الشیخ الهمام سلطان زیارتی اندن الشیخ قطب آفاق محبوب علی الاطلاق عاشق حمیر دود یعنی الشیخ ده ده مقصود ملا وجودکشریفلکی ابو الفتح عصرندن برو قبر منورلری اثره بر سجاده حرمه سیله دستشریفنده نسبتله وجود بروتازه در دیو نقل ایدیلر رحمة اللّٰه علیهم اجمعین در بیان اجداد قدیم قوم عمارنا بود ۞ یعنی قبر جبل الهمة نا محمود ۞ البیما شهری خارجنده نام محلده برسیره گاه یرده مدفونلردر کم جمیع عمرناوود قوملری جتفلیامیز ندر دیو زیارتنه ایدرلر قدیما وزیره زمان قدیم اوزره ایری طاشلر قومشلردر نجه برکره مقایسه سیله احوال ترقیم اولنمشدر اما شمدی بو محلده مدفون اولدقلری برشمه سرگوزشت مزار تحریر ایده لم بو جبل الهمة بالذات قومز قرنشدن حضرت رسالت پناهه صحابه کرامدن اولوب تبوک و احد و تا بو سوخت و بدر حنین غزالرنده بیله اولوب نیچه غزالرایدیب حضور رسول کبریایه نیچه کره باسو دللر ایله بر عار سنکشعیع و شوانا میر عرب ایمش بعده حضرت عمر خلافتنده بر شیخ العربک نا خطا آنا قصدا کوزن چیقاروب شیخ العرب دخی بر کوزی چیقمش نوزن الینه آلوب حضور حضرت عمره کلوب یا عمر امر شرع رسول ندر کوزم یرینه جبل الهمة نک کوزن استرم دیدکده جبلی حضرت عمر حضورنه دعوا ایدوب سؤال اولندقده جبل ایدر یا عمر کندو مسلمدن برعره بهله کوزیدیر چیقاردم دیدکده امر ایتدی شرعه تسلیم ویرمیم اولوب سوره و کتبنا علیهم فیها ان النفس بالنفس والعین بالعین سطوقا طمیر لهم ایجنه جبل الهمهنک کوزن چیقارمه فرما اولنجه الهمه الهام ناشرعه ایله رضا ورمیوب عار ناموداید یکی جمله لعلقات اویماغیله فرار ایدوب نوعزی قیصر روم هرقله کلوب انده جبالیه داغلارن عمار اتدیکندن جبالیه درلر انده رحمی حضرت عمر قکسی فتح ایدنجه نوره میوب کهیره سوار اولوب اشپانیه قرالنه دخیل دشوب اشپانیه دخی کت حکمنده اولان آرناوود لقادولان اولمیسه ده لوبجه حالالرنده دعما سعی بودعراد و فرنکس داغلارن جبالی الهمه جبالیلی بوسیار ضمالیه ایکی از زمانده مسکن مأوی ایدوب فرزند ایله حساط ایدر عرب لسانن عربا وودلسانی پیدا ایدوب ساسل موله راف حالا انده اوصل اسنده دلری سره مورد یلسود اعجمیدر لر زیرا موبلرالحلی ماتل عربدر مرسلدر انجیون ارناوود طائفه لری بر اصحاب کزین اولاد لرندن قریشیلر ز دیو تفاخر کسب ایدرلر اکثر جبل الهمه عقبی اسلام اوزره مرحوم اولدقده نصکره وصیتی اوزره بو جیا بانده دفن اولنوب بعده اولاد اولادلری فرنکلر ایدر ایله ایله فرفوروب متز الدقلر تعدت برفرقه کی فرنک اولوب کافر اولماق ایله کمسه و قره داغلر و مورلیش و سور عوریا و بن داغلرینه جمله ارناوودلری کتابسز کفره لر اولوب شمدی و نیه اهره بالرحلاه مسلمان آرناوود ایله ستمبرزنجیل ادرلر

اسد

واسيرا ولدرنا ابو الفتح غازينك كاليچه چوق آرناود دستان قومي مرتد اولدي بعده اسكندريه و لشو و اولكون و بار و لش و درنج و آرناود بلغراد وبو البصان لري و نوينه وز لونينه قلعه لري جمله دست آل عثمانه كروب آرناود دستان جمله اسلام ايله مشرف اولوب الحاق كلمتين و قره داغلر و قوربلش و نيچه داغلرده كفره لري عصيان اوزره چيقنجه جبل الهمه خاقان مرحوم اوزره مرتد اولديلر اما تواريخده اسلام ايله كتديكينه ذاهب اولمشلر نجا كوز چيقار صنعه عار ابدى فرار ايدوب قيصره قبل باننده ايكن اوزره جنكه كلن كافري قيصر كفره لرندن باش كسته نها اتچه احساننر ابدى كتدي قيصره امداد ايتمه يوب جنكه كرمز مش اندن بعده قسطنطينيه كلوب آنكله دخي انطاقيه اوزره عرب جنكنه كيدوب ينه كفره يه امداد ايتمه يوب صواش پرخاش ايتمز ايمش اول اجلدن عار نافورد لر جدي جبل الهمه اصحاب كزيدن اولوب اسلام ايله مرحوم اولمشدرلر خلاصهٔ كلام آرناود قومنك اصلي قوم قريشدن جبل الهمه اولوب حضرت عمر خلافتنده آرناود دستانه عار ايتمش نو پيدا كفره سي بي كتاب مسلمانلري پر صوات پر الاسلامانك مجاهدانها ظاهر صوابي تبليغ فنالردر والسلام

بو شهر منزيننده دخي سير تماشا ايدوب جمله احباب ايله وداعلشوب پرارزقيمله آلوب اوخري سمتنه كيتديكمز تماشالري بيان ايدر اولا بسم الله ايله البصاندن چيقوب جانب شرقه ساعتده بابنيه نام ييلاغن آنغدق اما نه عجايب شاهراه اكلمش مكر مرحوم بالقوپاشا روم ايلي ايالتنه متصرف ايكن قطور و ينديكي كافر اوزره سفره مامور اولدقده بو يوللر ديبال صربو لرده عساكر اسلاملر رها هستلر اوزره عبور اتمسو يلر دنو بو يوللري تطهير ايدوب چمن جنكلستان و خيابان داغلرده نشانلر قوروب جمله ايسماور سبيلياره صار سركه لر دوب تماشاحر اهل ايلمش آنلر ايله چريداو نيايژاق عبور ايدك اصلا عاند وكفره لرنيه برنجكاه يراتماميوب امرايمان اوزره حد خدا اسلام مثله ۲۴ ساعتده منزل قريهٔ بابنيه حالا بودربندها ايدر عمرماب پادشاهيله امر امام ايدو تطهيرينه مامور اولمشلر اسم معبر آرناود دو روم و بلغار كفره سي كويلدر آندن ينه شرق طرفه عظيم درخت منتهالر و كوه بي ستون مثال اوج آسمانه سر چكمش قيالر اوزره جريان ايدن آب حيانلر اچه ركذر تطهير اولنمش يوللر ايله كيدرك ۲۴ ساعت كيدوب قريهٔ چوره بو دخي دربند الحوف مسلم اولمش كفره كوييدر اندن ينه جانب شرقه ۸ ساعت كيدوب البصان صويني بر دخي كچوب آندن دوموزا او واسن دخي عبور ايدوب درحدود سنجاق اوخري هما باتيه داغندن غرب طره في البصان هاكيدر بو شرق طرفي بير كنيزاد اوخري لواسي حدوديدر بعده بو محلده متوجه بيلاسن باش اشغي شرق طرفنه ۵ ساعت ايندوب اوخري كولكن شرق طره نهنزه آلوب اوخري كولي كنارنجه چمنزارلرده فراز ايدوب كيدوب

اوصاف قلعهٔ بندرما هي اوستورقه

زمان قديمده اوخري نام قرالك صيد شكاركاهي اولمق الچون اوستورقه نام بر بري قلعه انشا ايلديكيچون آنكنامي ايله مشتهر اولوب اهو ستورقه دير لر لسان   ده   دمكدر اوخري كولنك بوغازي اوزره كشهرالحنده چار كوشه شداد بنا برقلعهٔ رعنا ايمش غازي اورنوس سنه تاريخنده سوط كرالي اوغلي اللندن فتح ايدوب بو قلعه منهدم الحكم بردخي كفار استيلا اتمكه طمع اتمه سون ديو خراب اتمش بعده مختار غازي اورنوس بو قلعه بوغازندن اوخري كولين قرشو كچوب بو عرادا سن نفهرن و اصطار اووا شهرلرن فتح ايدوب كفارينه عسكر كا اردن الماغچون بو كول كنارنده اهو ستورقه قلعه سنه كلوب كوردي كه قلعه خراب اولوب متحصن اولمق برجاي خاص يوق هما كفار خائف خاسر اوله رود نوبت غازي اورنوس سلامتله ينه اوخري بوغازندن كچوب اهوستورقه قلعه سندن فرار ايدر اما جنباله كول بوغازنده بر قلعهٔ زيبا ايمش اكر عمار اولسه كول بوغازندن قرشو بر عظيم جسر عبور ايده مز بعد بنه برقرداقريه كيمه ايله قيولري قياني بو اوستورقه قصبه سي وقلعه سي اوخري سنجاغي حاكمنده در اما علوميندن صلب سياسه جرم صاسي اوخري كولكي امينن حكمنده اولوب مقصوع قلم ومعزور العذم قرق كول اقچه خاص همايون مال پادشاهيله امانتدر كم كوكبه اوجات ويرده كزن وكولده يوزن جميع مخلوقات موجودات امينك التزامنده اولوب جمله باجقين كوله لرو جميع يوللر

وباج وبازار وعشر و اغنام و اسیجه و سلاخ‌خانه و دونغ و توتون و دلوم حقی و بیت المال و خاص و خراج و خانه عوارض الحاصل جمیع تکالیف عرفیه سایره لر جمله اوخری کولی امیننک حکمنده اولوب اوخری بکینک اصلا علاقه‌سی یوقدر بیوك امانتدر کیم ایکیوز عدد نفرات ایله بو حکومتی فرمان پادشاهیله ضبط و ربط تصرف ایدوب سپاه و یکیچری و کولی امرا عسکریله دولت ابدی عشرینه حفظ و حراست ایدوب کولک اطرافلرنده صید اولنان ماهیلرک عشرین صاحبلرندن آلوب انبارلرینه صیادلر بالق صید ایدرلر اکر امیننک اذنسز بر کمسنه نهان بر بر ماهی صید ایدرسه جرم و تعزیر ایدوب سیاستلر ایدرلر و جمله او بستوروقه قضیه‌سنده رعایالری و یدی پاره کوی رعایالری بو امینک قبضه تصرفنده اولوب معاف و مسلملردرکم میری بالق صیدینه تکه مامورلردر هر کیجه جمله رعایالر اون اون بش دانه قایقلره سوار اولوب قایقلره مشعلار یقوب بالق شبکه‌لری و اغزلری چکوب صید اتدکلری ماهیلری قایق قایق امینه تسلیم ایدرلر اولدخی جمله روم ایلنده اولان بازرکانلره بالقلری فروخت ایدوب آنلر دخی طوز ایله صلامورة ایدوب ولایت ولایت اوخری بالغی کتورلر

در

در وصف اشکال بحیرهٔ اوخری بعضیلر اوهری یازارلر وجه تسمیه‌سی

بو بحیره نک کرداکردی کاملا اون بش میلدر طوله مائل مثلث الشکلدر کیم کاملا یکرمی یدی ساعتده دور اولنور بر آب حیات شیرین کولدر بر کره سهاله لو قایقیله شاناو شاطر باشسنی چیش ایله دور ایتمشدر اما اولدن کله میوب بعد الغروب کوجیله کلوب بر کونده سر تا دور اتمشدر اطرافنده نیجه دیاره تکلفه کنارلری اولا بری بو او بستورقه قلعه‌سیدر بری بوغراداس قلعه‌سیدر جمله کیسوکو کول کنارنده اوچه سرچکمش مسا اوزره اوخری قلعه‌سیدر کیم کولک شمال طرفنده واقع اولمشدر اما کولک جانب اطرافی غایت معمور آبادان چفتلکلر ایله مزین اولمشدر و بو بحیرده اولا کونا کون ماهیلر بردیار بحیرسنده اولمازدر باخصوص یلان بالغی مشک عنبر خام کبی بر رائحه طیبه‌سی واردر غایت سمین و تر و تازه‌سن نعمه‌سی راعاله لیا ساییدقن تناول ایده نک بدننده اولقدر قوت حاصل اولور اولقدر موبدر کیم اهلیله پهلوان اسا کولنش انسه اهلنی بش التی کره یکوب البته آلوب غلبه لرایده تا بو مرتبه صمصمور بر مثال یلان بالقلری اولور و اغری جستلکنه بیوب باسنی طوزلیوب بالقباشی کنده باشنده کتورسه بامر الله اول آدم آغری خسته لکندن خلاص اولور و اوشتوق بالغی و مسازیه بالغی و صازان بالغی و آله بالغی یوبلر دخی لذیذ ماهیلردر اما بیله کونه ماهیلر اولور اما بو مذکور بش عدد بالقلرده با مرحق قدیر اصلا بالق یاغی‌لری یوقدر و بو ماهیلر امین اغا اوشتورقه قصبه‌سنده چاق اورتاسنده بر بو عمارده اون ایکی عدد تور اغاچ جسر یوز الی آدم طویل بر جسر عظیمدر اول مصطبهٔ طویل اوزره امین اغانک سرای عظیمی بیولنمازقدرکلر اوزره بنا اولنمش خاندان عظیمدر بو سرای اورتاسنده جسر اوزره بر اغاچ قپو واردر هر کیجه بو جسر قپوسن باسا موا بانلر منسدد ایدوب اوتدن بریسه و بریدن اوتیه بر آدم عبور ایده مز زیرا هر کیجه بو جسر قپوسی اوزره تا صباحه دك قرق الی عدد پرسلاح دیده بانلر جاسوسلق ایدوب کشیک یعنی نوبت بکلرلر زیرا قاچقون کوله لر و جرامیلر و مالیلر و بالق اوغریلری عبور ایتمسون مصلحتیچون بو جسر اوزره بو سرای قپو بنا اولنمشدر و بو کولک آیاغی تا اون قناق عرنا و ودلیق ایچنده اسکندریه سنجاغنده لس قلعه‌سی دبنده کور فز دریاسنه سجوا لیمانی ایچنده مخلوط اولور بر طرفدن اصلا کچمت درمز اوخری کولی بو ولایت اورتاسنده شذ اولمش بر بحیرهٔ عظیمدر و ایکی یردن دخی ایاغنده جسرلری واردر انده دخی امیننک آدملری بکلیوب ایشده ورونده کانلردن باج و بازار و عشر ماهیلر الور حکومت ایله قوس اوجور بازلر اما مهر بانی شاهراه بو اوستورقه جسر بحیر بو قیتره نک الت یانندنه پنجه یوز عدد بالق دالیانلری وارکم تعبیر اولنماز کورمکه محتاجدر و بو جسرلد التنده کولک آیاغی اول مرتبه اقارکم کوز کورمز یاز و قیش نهر دیرلوا کبی یوز رد قولدن آقار اصلا اکسلمز حکمت اولکم بو کولك ایچنه عظیم نهرلر مخلوط اولماز منبه بویله ایکن صیف و شتاده بو کولك ایاغی نهر جیحون کبی آقار و غرب طرفنده جره یانی ایدوب قصبه اوغراز

[illegible] اوچ ایکی [illegible] اوچ [illegible] [illegible] سلیمان یانغنده [illegible]

منقسم اولور [illegible] لوندرا [illegible] اماسیه [illegible] دوروب [illegible] هوا اتسه بوز

پارکی اولور [illegible] اولدیغی اولزمان بالکلیه زیاده [illegible] اولسون و بو اوشنشور قده قصبه یه

اوچری مصاحبه [illegible] و لوالمارنده [illegible] و چمنزار [illegible] جمله اوچیوز عدد

[illegible] کارکیر بنالی عثمانی و فوقانی باغ و باغچه لی [illegible] هواسی [illegible] قصبه جکدر جمله اوچ محله در

[illegible] جمله [illegible] عدد [illegible] اوکاده جامعی [illegible]

[illegible] جامعی [illegible] جمله اوغرلر اده خیرات

وجمله اوچ عدد مساجدلری [illegible] وجمله [illegible] عدد [illegible] خان [illegible] وجمله

[illegible] عدد دکانلری [illegible] اما [illegible] کفایت مقداری [illegible] کتیلردر [illegible]

[illegible] عمارت و مدرسه [illegible] اولکو عمار [illegible]

[illegible] ایدنلر [illegible] کسب هوا ایدرلر و جمله [illegible] بوشهر [illegible]

صوده قایقلر لیمانه باغلرلر و بو شهر [illegible] ساعت [illegible] فرقیللی بیک آدم جمیع اولکو اوپ

[illegible] هوفی [illegible] جمعیت کبرا اولورکم [illegible] جمله اوچ عدد

[illegible] دکانلری [illegible]

کیدرلر بوندن اعلا [illegible] خان [illegible] صاحبی [illegible] اعا و امام افندی [illegible] صاحبی [illegible]

[illegible] واسطوق

[illegible] اوچ [illegible] بالقولاباجق [illegible]

[illegible] بنوجه ساعت وده

دربیان اوصاف داراماهی یعنی قلعه شهر ارکان اوخری

[illegible] ابتدا روم پادشاهلرنده ملک [illegible]

[illegible]

[illegible]

[illegible]

[illegible]

[illegible]

[illegible]

[illegible] میثاق [illegible]

روم تکوری [illegible] لاتین [illegible]

[illegible] ارنائود و [illegible] [illegible]

[illegible]

[illegible]

[illegible]

[illegible]

[illegible] حکمت خدا

دفعهٔ ثانیه‌ده سنه ... مراد خان ... فتح ایدوب ... مستقل ... پادشاه ... اولدوقده اول ... لعنه الله فیجه
اوجی قلعه‌سی اسلام‌ایدوب ... خان ... ... عصمت ... اوجی قلعه‌سی
جوبه‌سی ... اسلامه ... ان شاء الله ... اسلامده در حالا سلیمان خان تحریری اوزره روم ایلی
ایالتنده سنجاق ... حکومتدر ... اوزره خاصی ۲۹۹۰۰ ... ۳۳ ... ۶۰ ...
تیماری ۳ ... عددی ... ... وارد ... اوزره ... جبه‌لو ... ایله
... عدد ... روم ایلی ... ماموره اولدقلری سفره گیدرلر حالا ...
... قلعه ... ... اما ... ... اوزره قلعه ...
ایله ... روم ... جمیع تکالیفلردن بریلردر و قلعه ... ماموره ...
معاف مسلّملردر اما غیری مسلّملردر و حاکم شرعی شیخ الاسلامی ... اعیان اشرافی و ... الله شریف
مصابی و حاله ... اوج ... ... عدری ...
سپاهی ... ... معمور ... روم ... استانبول ... شکره بوآوخری غایت معمور و مزیّندر
حاکمان عرفیلری ... اغاسی ... اغاسی ... اغاسی ... اغاسی ... اغاسی ... اغاسی
و ... اغاسی ... عدد قلعه ... اغاسی ... اوزره ...
در صفت اشکال کرداکرد قلعهٔ اوخری ... ... اوزره شکل
مخمّس ... ... قلعه ... ... رباط ... ...
... ... اوزره ... قلعه‌سی ... کوشه‌ده قلعه ...
... ادم ... ... وارد ... ... قرق آرشن ... ...
... ... المسلم ... قلعه ... الحاصل ...
... قلعه‌ده ... ایکی عدد قپوسی وار ... قبلیه ناظر ... خنکار جامعنه ناظردر ...
اوزره قلعه ... ... شب و روز ... آنده چالینر ... ...
... از جهان ... ...
... ... قلعه دیوارنک ادنی آرشن یوکسکدر و جمله ...
عدد قلعه ... ...
و جمله اوج عدد قپولری وار ... قلعه آتنده شماله ناظر ... ...
... ... قلعه ... شماله ... ...
... ... قلعه ... ... قلعه ...
... ...
قلعه دیوارلری ... ... اوچه کرچکمش ...
... ... شکللی دیوارلر بنا ایلمشلر اما ... ایام ... منهدم اولمش
و بو سور قلعه ... جمله ... ...
... ...
اما ... ...
... ... قلعه ... ...
او قلعه‌ده جمله ۳ عدد ... ... جوامع سلاطین قلعه‌ده عظیم ... ...
کنارنده

کنارنده آیاصوفیه جامعی غایت اولو جامعدر کم مثلی مکر سلانیکده و بروده کز ساحلنده طرفه امزونده و اسلامبولده کوچوک
آیاصوفیه جامعلری اوله اما بو آیاصوفیه جامعی حضرت سلیمان اوغلی ملک رحبعم عصرنده ناتمامات قرینده اسلوب اوزره نام ملک
بنا ایتدیکی اول بنا اتمامنا ایله آنلر اسمیله مسمی اولدی بو شهرک اسمی اوخریباندر اما لسان رومده اسمی ندر و
ولسان لاتینده فلاندر لسان فرنکده در اما بو اول عصرده کفره کمی عصرنده بلا تشبیه قدسلری ایمش حضرت
خدا شهیدی معبدکاه مسلمیندر لکن بعضی زمان کفره لر بو آبدیه تمامنده برقاچ اتجه دوروب جامعه کروب ... ایلی عیسی
اینکه طشره چیقارلر جمله صغیر و کبیر اون یدی عدد قبه عظیملر در اما جمله قرمزی کرمه ستا ایله وجه سانی کرچ ایله شهر
جامع برنوردر بونده اولان آثار قدیمه لر و عمود منتهالری بر بر تعبیر و توصیف انسم مصنع اوزمات اولور و صفتنده
لسان قاصر و قلملر کاسردر اما غریب جامع ویرانه بوردی تمشدر بجه مصنع بیچ قیولری و صد نکاری بخیره متانکر مابو ملشدر
زیرا اصلا جماعتی یوقدر جمله کفره الیده ما مثمر اکر مسملا کفره النده تا السنه بو جامع لری بهشت ایدرلر دعالجاف حقتده
بر کره جمعه کون قیولری اچیلی حذا ملری سلوب سپوروب بش اون عدد ناساکنلر جمعه نمازن قلدیغینه قیودکرسد
ایندکی کیدرلر وحین فتحده فتحنده جامع بو ایدی خدا عمار ایلیه آندن یوقارو ایچ قلعه اوکنده بر مرتبه یرده جامع اولمق زاد
بونلر حسب نسب خاندان صاحبی قرالی زاده لرایمش هلا بو سعر آنلر احکمنده فرمان بردر بر قبو برشو ملی عظمت قبه اوز توله
و بیکار کیر مناره لی بر معبر جامع بنا ایدرکن الله اعلم سلطان بایزید ولی برغزایه کیدرکن بو جامعی کوروب دوه بارك الله
نه کوزل جامع اولمغه دید کده همان عاقبت اندس ... ملرا و خریسزاده زمین بوس ایدیب خدا قبول ایلیه صوابی و بناسی
پادشاهمه هبه اولسون دیدکده پادشاه حظ ایدوب بر صاغ طرفه بر مناره عالی دخی بنا ایتمکه فرمان ایدکلرنده بنا ایدن
اول اجلدن حالا ایکی مناره لی اولدی منکار جامعی یرلرغایت اولو متین جامع جهان نمادر جمله کول جنوب طرفنده نمایان اولور
جمیعی سلسله ... جمله بالجمع قانقارینده ... نمایاندر و قبلا سی اوکنده روزنلر تیزه بحیره و صحرایی پایایلره
جمله معمار ستان فلاحی و پا هر در وحرمنده که کشتان اسا سایه سز جکمس درخت منتهالر وار هر بریله صلهمانیکسنده کی
چمنزار برلرده جمله احیا و یاران با صفای ارباب معارف اوطوروب ... مباحثه علم شرعیه لر ایدوب بر طرفده
دخی کوندان منقوله سیپاره خوانلر کونا کون لحنده بازلنلر و سلامتی لغات تعلیم اتمده درلر و بو جامع بر انوار ایله
قیوسنده عتبه علیاسی اوزره جلی خط ایله لا اله الا الله محمد رسول الله ... و بو قلعه ده بونلر
بو نعیر ... جمله ایکی عدد محله مساجدلری وار در آنلر دخی جماعتن غریبلردر اما اتتی عدد کفره منصفلر کروار
ایله معمور درکم و ایله مزین ابا داندرکم هر برنده قرقر و اللیشر عدد رهبان بطریق لری وار در حالا ... دیر
لاتین دیری غایت معمور درکم صبح و مسا ... بیوسنده باباسلر ... دخی ...
برل ایدرلر و بو قلعه ده اصلا خان و حمام و چارسو بازار یوقدر ماعدا ارض حالنه ... جمله باغ و باغچه و ... تدلوکم
ارض حالیه ... در زیرا بو کوک قلعه یر در ستایش آشفیه شهر عظیم ارمزات غا ... معمور دیمور ندر کم
لونا سام ... مسام ... در صفتده لسان قاصر در اسمعی ملا ... لورب ... ونوری
مدور وارد در لرا مسا درعدد اسماء محلا اوخری جمله اون یدی عدد محلالردر اونی مسلمان محله سیدر
... روم ... محلالردر اولا جمله محلالری معمور و مزین اوخری راد محله سی
محله سی ... محله سی ... محله سی ... محله سی مدرسه محله سی ... محله سی
حاجی ... محله سی ... محله سی ... محله سی ... محله سی ... محله سی ... محمود
محله سی ... محله سی ... محله لری ... معمور و اباداندرکم ... در
در فصل جوامعهای سلاطین و وزرا و کبار اعیان جمله اون یکی عدد محراب قبله ارباب حاجاتدر اولا
محلدا ... جامعی ... حاجی قاسم جامعی ... صاحب ... اوز توله جار کوشه

تخته قبه اورتولی بر طرفه طرز قدیم منارەلی جامع زیبادر آندن تکیه جامعی سلطان سلیمان خان کبی بر عجب مفرح جامع پرنوردر آندن قتول آغاسی جامعی طرز قدیمدر آندن حیدر پاشا جامعی معبدگاه قدیمدر آندن طلمیه (?) جامعیدر اما منور جامعدر لکن اطرافی ظلم ایله بنا اولنمش اوله آندن حاجی حمزه جامعی آندن بیقلو (?) قلعه ده چفته منارەلی هنکار جامعی آندن قلعه ده ایاصوفیه کبیر جامعی بو مذکور جوامعلر مشهور آفاق معبدگاهلردر

در دفتر مساجدهای مومنان عابدان جمله ۱۷ عدد محلات مسجدلریدر اولا جمله دن اسکندر بک مسجدی و یوسف بک پوادا (?) مسجدی و کوموی بک مسجدی و امیر محمود مسجدی و چارسو مسجدی و چنارلی مسجد و قره حمزه (?) مسجدی الحاصل اون یدی عدد جامع اولمغه مستعد مساجدلر واردر هر بریله اوقاف کثیری اولمدیغندن مسجددر

در وصف سرای اعیان اغوات و غیری بیوت مشیدنان جمله سجل شرعده مرقوم اولدیغی اوزره [illegible] عدد کرمیتلی کارگیر بنالی تحتانی و فوقانی جمله روضه رضوان مثللی باغ جنانلی واسع خاندان شهر عظیمدر کم باغ و باغچه سی اله اوچ موضع (?) اس زینا تنمشدر کوردن بو شهرک اوراوندبش بیک اولردر [illegible] تخته املا قلعه بو قدر هما شمالی و غربی و جنوبی و قبله سی هر [illegible] کوکی اوکی شرق طرفی [illegible] اوطلاق بلا اسم انگاریندوار بجه سرا پا خیابان کلستان ایچره برشهر مرامدر اطرافنه قلعه اولماغله [illegible] زیرا باغچه لری وتشبیک بوستانلری جنان ارزن اتمشدر جملة مکلف ومکمل سرای عظیم اوجری زاده سرای قلعه شمالده منعقد دیوانخانه لری اصحاب الکرو کول کنارنده مقصوره لری و [illegible] سرای دخی عبرتدر بونلر مشهوردر

در قایمه مدارس عالمان مفسران جمله ایکی عدد دار التدریس عالمانلردر اولا کول کنارنده مذکور الحاج قاسم جامعنده صو لنده یول اشرنسنده اسکی سیاوش پاشا مدرسه سی کویا باغ [illegible] اقدم مره منکل [illegible] افندی منعقد حجره لری وار درس عامی و طلبه لری موجود اوکی هر حجره ده طلبه لرینه جا و قعدت لحیه [illegible] معتیندر اندن سلطان [illegible] خان تکیه مدرسه سی بو دخی معمور و ایکیه زاویه مدرسه لریدر [illegible]

در شرح دار الحدیث محدثان جمله بر یرده علم حدیث و علم تجوید تلاوت اولنور اما محدثی و جمله حافظ قرائی مشهوردر کلدر علم تجویده الحاق حفص قراءتی تلاوت اولنور علم حدیثده [illegible]

در تعریف مکتب [illegible] جمله یدی عدد دار التعلیم الجدیدخانه در اولا اوجری زاده مکتبی و آغا مکتبی وار

در شهر انکلیز خان خواجگیان تجاران جمله اوج عدد خاندر زیبا لردر اما صاحب الخیر [illegible] لذت [illegible] قدم

در تعریف حمام غاسلان راحت جان جمله ایکی عدد حمام خاص عاملریدر اولا برسی اوجری زاده حمامی طرز قدیمدر اما هوسی هوادر و بری غازی حسین پاشا حمامیدر هواسی و بناسی لطیف حمام روشندر

در توصیف حمام مخصوص کنیلر اعیان ولایت العمه لرنده نعللری اوزره جمله یمش یدی عدد سرای حماملری واردر ذیو فخر کسب ایدرلر حقیقت الحال واردر اولا اوجری زاده بک [illegible] سراینده ایکی حمامی وار و قرنداشی [illegible] افندی سراینده حمامی وار و

در تحریر عدد چارسوی [illegible] جمله یوز اللی عدد دکانلردر و یدی عدد مکلف و مزین جمیع الفوات قهوه خانه لری واردر اما بوزه خانه و میخانه لری آشکاره ده یوقدر لکن ملمع کفره محله لرنده باده نابی غایت چوقدر لکن بزازستانی یوقدر بینه هر کونه متاعلر فراواندر لکن چارسوسی [illegible] پاره کنده و پریشاندر و شاهراه چارسوسی صوقاقلر ایچره عظیم درخت سایه دار چنار منتهالر له زین اولمشدر اما اکثریا چشمه لری معطلدر وصویه دخی احتیاج یوقدر زیرا کول صوی کبی آب حیاتی وار ایکن چشمه سازلار کلدر انکچون جمله عیونلری معطلدر واکثریا خاندانلر عظیملری کول کنارینه واقع اولمشدر

در تعریف آب و هواء خوب جاودان ابهواسند لطافتدن محبوبه و محبوبه لری غایت چوقدر جمله سیم بر و نازک

اندام اهلنه بندرام محبوب القلوب جوانلری اولورلر حسن جمالری ایله جهان آرا اولمشلردر بنجه خانلر بونده بالمشلردر
در مدح صنایع هدایای گزیده فاکهات ممدوحه‌سی اولدر طعمنده گونه آیواسی طرابا ایواسی و اکمک ایواسی و
باخصوص یکرمی درلو گونه الالال الوسی و یکرمی درلو الوان امرودلری سیجلاتلرده مسطوردر کم بویله
آبدار موش خور امرودلر ملاطیه شهرنده و کماخ بستاننده تفلیس شهرنده و تبریز ولایتنده شهوا وزرده وار شهر
لرنده بویله آبدار امرودلر گورمدم جمله آبدار لما و ردیف اولعتم لوزیز و آبدار درکم گویا بر حلوای شیر بنادر لکن
حالم شهرلری میوه‌لری بر بردن بری هدایا کیده مرزیز اغابت سیر اما الماسی قطعه‌لرله هر دیاره کیدوب
هنوز لطافت حلاوتی باقی فاکوت صولرنمازده تفاحند رنگنده و را الجذ طیبه‌سنه اصلا تغییر کلمز اما غیری میوه
لری درمیسره کمز اما بو حقیر ایوا اسنده نا اصطورد جه شهرنده دلاء بمنه الچنده ایوای سفرجلی کوردم
در وصف نعمت عظمای مأکولات بو شهر اعیاننه مخصوصدرکم قیش گیجه‌لری جمله صغار و کبار بر برلرینه ضیافت
عظیمه ایدوب بر صحبتده ییلن طعام نفیسه بر غیری صحبتلرده یمزلر هر بر ضیافتنده مزرام ممتنک
طعام گونا گونلر ییملر بو شهره مخصوص حلویاتی و گونا گون حوس املری کذالک بر صحبتده کی حوس ایلره و
حلویاتلره اصلا و قطعا مشابهتلری یوقدر حتی امورده ضیافتنده یکرمی التی گونه حوس ایدیلوب حقیر
حوس ایدوب شهود اولمشلردم روم دیارنده اوخری ضیافتی و حوسی ایلر مشهور محمد حدر
در تکتیب عمارت دار الماکل سوخته و آشخانه جمله اوج عدد برده دار الضیافت فقرا انعاملر اولا یوقاری
قلعه اوکنده اوخری زاده پادشاهه احسان ایتدکی جامع دلکشانک عمارتی صبیح و مسا با عام و گدایه و
پیر و جوان ولی رسانه برر صحن چوربه برر بورنان پاره‌سی فقیرانه مبذولدر و یری تکیه جامع عمار تمرآ
در تسطیر مهمانسرای کاربان روان جمله اوج عدد مهمانخانه حبسلردر جمله‌دا کوچوک بازارده چنار
اغاجلری سایه‌سنده قرق اوجاقلی کاربانسرای معموردر و اوخری زاده مهماندار ستانی بنای متیندر
در ترقیم بنای عبرت نمای آبادان جمله‌دا جامع ایاصوفیه کبیره و اجب السیر اینا یوقاری قلعه اوکنده
اوخری زاده پادشاهه هیبه ایتدکی جامع اوکنده بر آب حیات صو قیوسی معمارکم استاد فرهاد بوجاه
مایه ایله فرهاد دیکو لو نکلر اولمیوب بر بینز عبرت نما قارغیب عمیقی کامل سکسن قولاجدر غرائب آنده کم
اسناد لوه لی قیاری لغم ایله دلوب یا اوخری بولننده علم هندسیه ایله صو کیروب آب دللانلر ایله صوبی
چکلوب عمارته و جامع حوض و حنفیه چشمه‌لرینه و غیری یرلرده استعمال اولنور بر تماشاگاه واجب السیردر
در تقریر مسیره گاه مفرحات بو شهرک اطرافنده جمله اون ایکی عدد برده نفرجگاه ارباب مرام اولمدارکم
بر دیاره مخصوص دکلدر الا اوخری بده در اولا قیقلر ایله گول ایچره ایام موافقلر ایله مادرماللری آچوب جفتلکلره
گیدوب گونا گون ماهیلر صید ایدوب دریا اوزره عیش عشرتلر ایتمک بو شهره مخصوصدر بوری رطوبی قلعه‌نک
قبله طرفنده یول آشری بر صازلق بولمعاردر بو عرمن جزینده واردر اما غایت عمیقدر درلر آنده اولا گونا گون
مارو اوردکلر صید شکاری عجائبدر آندن بالق دالیانلری زوقیت آکدن اسطوقیلاسی صنوره‌لری عجایبدرلر
در تنقیل لهجه مخصوصا اهالی بلادد جمله خلقی بلغارجه وارمنیجه تکلم ایدرلر اما ارناودچه بلمزلر زیرا
روم ایلیدر ارناود و بوسنه نکلدر لکن فصیح و بلیغ لسان ترکی بیلرلر غایت شعرا ظریف تکیه‌دان تکیه شناس ارباب
معارف ادملری واردر
در اشکال لباس فتیان شجیعان دلیران جمله یاره بکتکری قرمزی صایه چوقه‌لی نسمورزرده و اطلیاقلر و گونا گون
چوقه دولامالر و قوشچاقی در راجق صیقما جانتنزر کیچی پاپاقلرنده صاری قبادی یا پاپوش کیوب بلرنده یالاچاقلر
طلقو سرینازایدرلر اما اختیارلری باشلرینه گونا گون صالی دستار محمدیلر صاروب و گونا گون چوقه‌دن

سرحدده فوت نیکلرو فراجه‌لر کیسه‌لر امتعه‌لر رتابه‌لری کوناکون بولنکلو فراجه‌لر کیوب یوموق یاغلری اولورلر
دولبند چبیل‌لر باغلیوب چارسو بازارنده بیغیری بسوق سلطانیلرده مانندانه کزرلر
در فصل تتمه شهر انکیت کلیا آشهر اوخریدا لا بونده دخی مانیمولا استیما فنطه بچوق کرد بکمزا مربادشاهی دیوان
پادشاهیده اوخریه بکمعلی بلیحصوریند قلاو اولنوب الامرا مرکم دیوب جمله عساکر اسلام مانیه ولایتده کتمکه
آماده اولدیلر بو حقیره بذا ایلیمیوغرضوش ویر آستیو عاما اربا دوتغلامی ویرتیلم احسان ایدیب خدا امراه دخی اوزرالنوب
احسان ایدرسه نرو فسونخیره مفید اولوب انلر دخی عسکر جمعیته حد اهتمام اتدیلر
در تماشای سکه کاه ضربخانهٔ قدیم بو شهر عظیم ابو الفتح تختگاه قدیمی اولوب بونده جمیع عساکر اسلام ایله بایزید خان ولی برسنه
مسافر اتدیکندن تختگاه آل عثمان اولوب تا سلطان مراد خان رابع عصرینه کلنجه بو شهرده سکه کسیلر دیو حالا ضربخانه‌سی
آشتو قلعه‌ده پاشا سرایی قربنده بر کار خانه عظیمه در کم حالا ایچی مسدود در جمیع آلات بسنا طلری و جمله اسکانی
وسکه‌لری موجود در رحمة حقوق خالص العیار اقچه‌سن کوردکا اولوب سلطان احمد بن محمد خان غز نصره ضرب اوخری
دیو سکه‌سی بیوار ایدی

زیارتگاه اوخریدا کلا مرقد اوخری نادره وسلطان بک یوقارو قلعه خنکار جامعی محرابی اوکنده مدفونلردر و شهید خزینه‌دار پاشا سرایینک
یاننده آیاصوفیه جامعی حاغنده کول کنارنده بر صیا اوزره کبره بتلی برقبه‌ده مدفونلردر
بعده اوخریده دلانه لرایله نیجه بورآدملر اتلر بیره سوار اولوب اسطوق بیلاسی تفرجکاهنه روانه اولدق اولا اوخری
قریهٔ چرچی باشی اوخری صحرا استده بلماز رعایالی معمور باغچه‌لی و ایکیوزخانه لی مزین کویدر آندن باش یوقارو جانب شرقه
۵ ساعتده افلاکه عروج ایدمیب در بستا بیش بیلاق عظیم اوسطوق بو بیلاق عرب و عجمده مشهور آفاق بر ییلاق
یه طاقدرکم هر جانبده بیع قضایلرانداغ وطاغلری جمله نمایاندر حتی بو بیلاقدن جانب غربه اوخری شهری جنوب
جانبنه شمال ۸ ساعتلک ردر بحیره کسیله و جمیع هامونه اسمتا الاقطار مزارعا ملر بله یابهال رمال کبی نمایان
و بو بیلاده ولی نخم اوخری نادره بک جکز افندیند کامل اوجیوز عدد اکرک قیونلری اوطلیوب بیلانلرکم جمله یمشق
بیلمعدد کوسفندی کوناکون دیار روم ده املن بیلاسنده نصکره و ربله و دشت بوطوسرو و طوس ییلا
لرنده نصکره بو اسطوق ییلاسی مشهوردر بونده هیمانلر ایله قیون صابه لرده واکرکلرنده قنوب کوچوب قیماق
و یغورد و تلمه پینرلری اغزدا کزلر و کوله مزلر و هتوشنرمار و بالکی قیماقد و بالکی قیمقنار و تازه پینرلر یوب
وصارییکیلرکنسوروتقه نام جکرتازه لرمادجبن صولرن انجوب و طوقلی قیوزو کبابلری و الابالقلری بیوکونا
کون بوزیار کمی آب حیات صولرن نوش ایدوب نیجه بیک کونه نباتات کیاهاتدن زنبیاسی عاشقی وجلک وبروشنه
لری بیوب کوناکون عسل مصفی شربتکر نوش ایدوب زوق و صفالر اندک بو بیلاده اولان سنبل و مشک نوم ولاله نوبرین
و نرکیس مکر ارض مدیر دیارنده بیک کول بیلاسنده و کوه بیستونده و کوه دماوند و کوه ارجیشده اوله بو بیلاده
بر هفته زوق صفالر ایدوب آندن جانب شرقه کاه یقوش آشخی پیاده و کاه اسب سواره ساعتده قریهٔ پازی کچوب
ینه جانب شرقه ۲ ساعت ایدوب اوصا قصبهٔ معمور زنستا اوخری طوبراغنده نیابتیدر و سربستزعامتدر
قصبه‌یه بروواسع اوزا نجنده دره کجره بان ایدر بروواسع یرده جمله یوز کسن عدد کره متلی
معمور باغچه لی اولاردر جمله ایکی محله در نصفی مسلم و نصفی کفره لردر جمله ایکی محرابدر بری جارسو
الجنده منصور شهرلی رمضان بکث جامعی کره متلی و کارکیر مناره لی وجره منده بر مکتبلی جامع لطیفدر و بری حاجی
مرادجامعیدر وجمله بر مدرسهٔ سوخنکانو جمله بر تکیهٔ درویشات وجمله بر حمامی وار صاورز
ناده خبرا ایدر وجمله بر خانی وار وجمله یکرمی عدد مفید مختصر دکانلری وار اما هفته بر کون جمیع
اطراف

اطراف قرالرنده بجه بك سى ادم هيچ اولوب رحمت الله تعالى يارارغم تدبير لرمالر مربيع وسمالر اولدى حقير
تيمارلرنده مانيه محافظه سنده مامور اولنلر اسدورمه لردوه للالرندا اندروب موسم اعالرنده موجوده
ومربعه بحاسه حاندانصا حملرندر الرهمدع واوجره زاده لره غصم صا لنلر ايدوب ارسه لوه مانيه
سمرينه روانه اولدلر بوقضه رسنانك محمد حاسدر لسانكمه وفسى اروده وداعلرنده مرمرى احرام
تسكمه كوكلرى وحومه سوباسى اراعماب مسعود يماسا سوبالرلدر وحمله حلعدا مار لسعلرى بوبتويا كوكلريدركم
قرباسانه لسوررلرعاسراالحذر حسنعو ولا سلرلسارزمالرى كلوسحه سل توب سوبا لوطرى ماعلوسوكلميت
وكلاسه سوبا لولى لسوررلر بوعملدر سرسسه مصلكه مولهرده عاس بمس ماكو ايعسنه لرويه عمود ايدب ايدو
دفعا منزل ييلاق اوشسطوقى برلوز بوكجه دخى انده روف ايتك ايدوب اندن جانب قبله يه قوش آشنى يلاد اينوب
٥ ساعتده ينه قريه چرى باشى كوپب دفعا منزل شهر عظيم اخرى سوبده برلجه دحمه حمام اوكوار تشوكوب
جمله احباب الله وداغلشوب اوجره بالمى بهره جانه سرعالراو حمله عسكر يله مانيه عامصه سنه روانه اولوب

حقير بر تقصير اوخرين اسلامبوله كتديكم قناقلر عيان وبيان ايدر

اولا اولوبولمرسه اسمعون سلاسم ايلى انده لمموسا اوجره سماعين مانيه عراسه مامور اولكب ارباب زعامت
وارباب تيمارلرى سعروسورمدا الحوب معمور اوقصابالرى دوه راه وعمراب احمد الحوب اوجريدى سه حا
سماله لندوب قصبهٔ اوستورقهٔ عمور ابدوب اوجرى لولى لسارب لدرانده ركب حاسحنويه ٥ ساعتده كيدب
اوصاف قصبهٔ شيرين يوغراداش بودجه اوجره يالسلحا صمو نما دالمى حلميده اسسو اوا
قضاسو نيا بتندور توسهرلوسو لول اسرى معصه اسو بره وملحقهٔ اوجره نما بالدر مانسما لريده ٥ حما
كوكل آزدر بومصمه حمله لدر دعددعر ابدر اولا جار سو الحده
جامولره ملمومار لريماره لى جامع زيبادر و جامع جماعت كثيريه مالكدر حمله الموعدمعمور
محله مساجدلريدر وجمله برعدد مدرسه سوجمالدر وجمله الى عدد ملتب صبيان الحمدخوانلر
وجمله برعدد دار الثة دروبسا عبدالاندر وجمله اوج عدد خانلرى واردر وجمله برعدد حمام
محمد وارددر وجمله السعد عدد باغ وباغچه لى وسرايلره مشاور بولى حاندالرده بالرمى عدد اوجمالرى
دحمودار دور وجمله مورالمى عدد دكانلرى واردر اما كاركير بنالى بنادر سافى معصمر لكمولول لسارنده باك
دباغ دحالرى جوقدر وبوسهر لول لسارنده واقع اولماغيله بعضو حاندار عممرلرنسا هسمن ومعموره كركول
لسارنده اوكو حمله مرورلرى صويه باصردر بعضو يارالمر بحره لرده اوصعدروب لولده مارلسا مالى اولرلر اما هر بحيه نسا
حاسكو اولريده مالو اولوب هربار لوبريالو برلر اب هواسى بعمه اوللدعمدوب باغ وباغچه لرتك كوناكون
انوارهوس حمار سنوه لرنك امرودلرى عالى لريرويدر كسهرى دحومسوكه لسى مسرير وبطلهٔ رسا اولوب بالقه
بر روحم وارددر بومصمه بك حاسه عالمه سلكه سهرلوزجه ٨ ساعتلك بريدر مصدما سه نار يحمده سهر كورجهٔ
دشمر هورنوشته دشمر بلمهسته وشمر كولي كتترى كورمك ايله اوكجانبلره توجه اتميوب بنه اوجره كوللركنا لرنجه
حا سماله ٧ ساعت لدوروامسيح محصولدار مرالرباغ وباغچه وحملحلى برلرده معمعه ومعمره اموايما لرلرى صفا ايله كيدوب
اوصاف قصبهٔ معمور اضطار اووا بوزنطلن يوغراداش قصبه سى غايت نماياندر وبوقصبه دخى
اوجره سماعر حالنده بلسدحاصمر وونيواد ايوحاكمندر مورالمى الحمه بالكسله مصادر باحمه كرحس ياره قرالردر
جمله رعايا وبرايالرى بلعاردر ذميانوب مسلما حاب اوبدره سراى خاصته سعادتلو پادشاه ٥ الجوف لوسهره بكلربكى
اوجاعددر برهو ياصوى دلسرمه اغاسى كلو بويدب بنجه يوز عدد كزيده بلعار وروم اوغلانلرى دلسرمه بالسربنه
قرمزيه شبكلا هلر واكتلرنه قرمزى عبا خلعتلر كيدوروب بر توكلته دكشرمه غلاملرى كتوروب غايت الغايه عجب اوكون

اصلنزاده اولنلری غلمان خاصه ایدوب دخی فنالرینی بوستان اوجاقلرینه ویکیچری اوجاقلرینه ودخی زیر دستکی طوغانه وجبه خانه اوجاقلرینه ویریرلر اما غیری قضالرکبی کثرتده غلامانلری هر اوجاقلره واعیان کبارلره نفرلر ایلمزلر علمی کمال معرفت اولکرندکلرندن عسکره قجمزلر وغلمانی علوفه سنه کچوب اندن یکیچری قپوسنه اندن سپاه قپوسنه چیقارلر اکرکم تقدیر خدا اولورسه نیچه لری وزیر اعظملر ومفتی وعلمالر اولمشلردر بعنی بو اصطلاح اوزره شهرینک جوانانی کثرتده کان ترغیب مبارک ربطه زیبا درکم افندیکولندن بعید دیبک آدم اچمیوب قوپه الارقه لر وجمله نقدر دیوز عدد لره ملی معمور اباداندر بعضیلری قتلرا اولری اوطاق ایله صازاوردر اما هر اوده ناعرو ناعمه ایتمزلر وجمله دورت عدد محلاتدر نصفی مسلم ونصفی عدد مسلم محلاتلردر وجمله دورت عدد جامعدر ایکسی جامع چارسو ایچنده جامع کره تملی وبر مناره لیدر جامع منیفی بیندر وجمله ایکی محله زاویه سی واردر وجمله بر عدد مدرسه سی صکا بو وار وجمله بر عدد ملتب صبیان واردر وجمله بر عدد خانقاه ارباب طریقی وار وجمله بو عدد دکاکیندر اما بزستانی یوقدر لکن مطاعم مجوقدر وسه هر شی موجوددر وجمله اوچ عدد خانلری وار وجمله بر عدد حمامی وار اما بیوتلرنده دخی اوحماملری واردر وباغ وباغچه لری فراواندر الحاصل سرین قصبه باغ حماملردر بونده جامدلر جماهلری عمارتدر اعیانی وعبریلری هر مانادیساهلری ... محاصه سنه ... اندن اوله هر مهتر لر در ... اوجر بسم سنه کچمیوب هان قبله طره ضنه اوجر ... ساعت ... اسوق سلاغی ایلنده ینفقریه چری باشی کچوب بلغار رعایالری ... رعایا ... اسمعوق سلاغی ... ساعت اینجوب قریه سیار صاری بلغار ... ساعت یقوش اشفی کیدوب اوصاف قضاء قریه عظیم پیرپینسه ... جامع ... ... اللی ... قصبه ... اعیان ... فرق ... هر بر ... دروضنی بحیره پرتسپه اوجره ... طغوز میلدر اما ... بر ... قره ... نه ... اوجر ... مصطفی ... اول ... قره صو ... اوبسه ... ساعت ... قریه کوشات ... مصطفی ... ساعت کیدوب ... کنار نده میسوکا ... سهل آرام استراحت ایدوب ... اسماع ... مرام خیابانته تا زنخنده لریر کلکیات ایله ... بو زوغ ... صبیع ... مرام ... روم ... واراسنه بو مصطفی شهری ... اندن منزل اشهر عظیم وبلده قدیم مهنیه منضبط ... ساعت ... کره کلو ملث ... اوصاف ... اولمسدر ... مره منظر اولنه نه ... معمور واباداندر اوصلحی معلوم اولنه ... عمر اغا ... اولوب ... علی الصباح جمله دوستانلر ایله وداعلشوب مصطفی ... ساعت ... قریه بنشلو عمر اغا زعامتیدر رعایاسی صاری بلغارلردر اندن تینه منضبط ... بارکلا ... کین وولایت ... شرقه ۷ ساعتده معمور اباداندر ... شهری ... منزل قریه وارنیه صاری مسلمان قراسیدر ... زعامتیدر اندن ساعتده ... کیدوب منزل قلعه اشتب

PLATES

The Halveti Tekke of Berat

Outer walls of the fortress of Bashtova

Main gate of the fortress of Elbasan with the three quadrangular blocks of white marble

Büzürg Seng or Big Rock Park, now Byshek near Elbasan

Xhamia e Plumbit (the Lead Mosque) in Berat, constructed ca. 1553–1555.

The bathhouse of Sinan Pasha in the fortress of Elbasan.

The mosque of Hasan Bali Zade or Ballia Mosque (*Xhamia e Ballies*) in Elbasan, constructed in 1608 and demolished ca. 1970–1971. Photo 1920.

←

The so-called Red Mosque in the fortress of Berat, perhaps the oldest Islamic construction extant in Albania.

EVLİYA ÇELEBİ'S BOOK OF TRAVELS

Edited by Klaus Kreiser

2. Dankoff, R. (ed.) *Evliya Çelebi in Bitlis.* The Relevant Section of the Seyahatname. 1990. ISBN 90 04 09242 0
3. Buğday, K.M. *Evliyā Çelebi Anatolienreise.* Aus dem Dritten Band des *Seyāḥatnāme.* Edition, Übersetzung und Kommentar. 1996. ISBN 90 04 10445 3
4. Tezcan, N. *Manisa nach Evliyā Çelebi.* Aus dem Neunten Band des *Seyāḥat-nāme.* Übersetzung und Kommentar. 1999. ISBN 90 04 11485 8
5. Dankoff, R. & Elsie, R. *Evliyā Çelebi in Albania and Adjacent Regions (Kosovo, Montenegro, Ohrid)* The Relevant Sections of the Seyahatname. Edited with Translation, Commentary and Introduction. 2000. ISBN 90 04 11624 9